Archaic Words
and the
Authorized Version

Books by Laurence M. Vance

The Other Side of Calvinism
A Brief History of English Bible Translations
The Angel of the Lord
Archaic Words and the Authorized Version

Archaic Words
and the
Authorized Version

by
Laurence M. Vance, Ph.D.

Vance Publications
Pensacola, FL

Archaic Words and the Authorized Version
Copyright © 1996 by Laurence M. Vance
All Rights Reserved

Second Printing 1997

ISBN 0-9628898-4-9
Library of Congress Catalog Card Number: 96-60107

Published and Distributed by: Vance Publications
P.O. Box 11781, Pensacola, FL 32524, 904-474-1626

Printed in the United States of America

Table of Contents

	PREFACE	vii
	INTRODUCTION	ix
1	Abase to Axletrees	1
2	Backbiters to By and By	28
3	Calve to Curious	58
4	Dainty to Dureth	89
5	Ear to Experiment	115
6	Fain to Furniture	134
7	Gaddest to Guile	158
8	Habergeon to Husbandry	172
9	Ignominy to Issue	188
10	Jangling to Jot	200
11	Kerchiefs to Know	203
12	Lade to Lusty	206
13	Magnifical to Murrain	218
14	Napkin to Nurture	233
15	Obeisance to Overcharge	242
16	Palmerworm to Pygarg	258
17	Quarter to Quit	276
18	Rail to Rush	280
19	Sackbut to Swelling	296
20	Tabering to Twined	327
21	Unawares to Utter	347
22	Vagabond to Vocation	352
23	Want to Wrought	370
24	Ye to You-ward	385
	EPILOGUE	389

Appendixes

1	Archaic Words in Contemporary Publications	391
2	AV Archaic Words in Contemporary Publications	395
3	Archaic Words in the NIV	407
4	Archaic Words in the NASB	414
5	Archaic Words in the NKJV	421
6	Archaic Words in the NRSV	426
7	AV Archaic Words Retained in the NIV	435
8	AV Archaic Words Retained in the NASB	437
9	AV Archaic Words Retained in the NKJV	440
10	AV Archaic Words Retained in the NRSV	443
11	Uniformity in Translating from English	446
12	Uniformity in Translating into English	450
13	Archaic Personal Pronouns	452
14	Archaic Verb Inflections	455
	NOTES	457
	BIBLIOGRAPHY	577

Preface

The Authorized Version of the Holy Bible, which originally appeared in 1611, is the best-selling, most read, most loved, and most revered book in history. This is beyond dispute. But doesn't the Authorized Version contain archaic words? Certainly. Should we therefore replace it with something else? Certainly not. This is what is disputed.

Since the publication of the Authorized Version in 1611, a steady stream of new and updated English Bibles have appeared. Although many accusations have been hurled at the Authorized Version down through the years in regards to the merit of its underlying Greek text, its many supposed mistranslations, and the character of its namesake, every new English translation since 1611 has charged the Authorized Version with having archaic words that render it unintelligible, difficult, or misleading. But this charge is starting to wear thin, for every six months a new English translation of the Bible appears on the market with the claim that its modern, up-to-date, contemporary language is needed to make the Bible more understandable. Nevertheless, it is apparent that the Authorized Version does contain some archaic words that need explanation.

This book provides an explicit and comprehensive examination of every word in the Authorized Version of the Bible that has been deemed archaic, obsolete, antiquated, or otherwise outmoded. The result is both a fascinating and encyclopedic study of words—their meaning, derivation, usage, and significance. Two things about the title of the book require explanation. The word *archaic,* as it is employed in this book, is painted with the same broad brush that is used to paint the Authorized Version with the charge of being archaic. And secondly, it is not just the archaic words *in* the Authorized Version that we are interested in, for there are not that many of them, it is archaic words *and* the Authorized Version that we are concerned with.

The thesis of this seminal work is that the Authorized Version is no more archaic than daily newspapers, current magazines, and modern Bible versions. To further supplement the work and to substantiate the underlying thesis, reference will not only be made to various newspapers and magazines, but to contemporary Bible versions like the New King James Version, the New International Version, the New American Standard Bible, and the New Revised Standard Version. Ample evidence as to the inconsistency of modern versions will be presented throughout the text and summarized in appendixes.

It is the contention of this book that the Authorized Version is the Bible for English speaking Christians and the standard by which all other versions should be judged. Just as a certain vocabulary is necessary to understand science, medicine, engineering, or computers, so to learn and understand the Bible one must be familiar with its vocabulary instead of dragging it down to one's own level. And just as no one revises Shakespeare or Milton, but instead learns the vocabulary necessary to understand those particular works, so every man who desires to read and understand the Bible must first become acquainted with the vocabulary of the Authorized Version rather than revise it. Therefore, this book is unique in that it seeks neither to criticize nor to correct the text of the Authorized Version.

Introduction

The Authorized Version of the Bible is often lauded for its place in literature, its majestic style, and its poetic rhythm, but unfortunately, these statements are always qualified by the charge that the language of the Authorized Version is archaic Elizabethan English that renders the Bible unintelligible, difficult, or misleading. The archaic label painted on the Authorized Version concerns both words that are obsolete and therefore hard to understand as well as words that have changed their meaning:

> While a major portion of the KJV is understandable to any person who reads English, because of the choice of words and/or the change of the English speech since 1611, some sentences in the Kings James will not be understood without the help of a commentary.[1]

> Not only are there difficult sentences, but there are words used in the KJV which have passed completely out of use, so that they convey no meaning to the modern reader.[2]

> More subtle, however, is the problem created by those words that are still in use but which now have a different meaning from what they had in 1611.[3]

> The plain truth of the matter is that the version that is so cherished among senior saints who have more or less come to terms with Elizabethan English, is obscure, confusing, and sometimes even incomprehensible to many younger or poorly educated Christians.[4]

> The KJV is no longer completely intelligible to all readers. It is no longer the most accurate and the most

readable English rendering of the Word of God.⁵

Although the Authorized Version is also demeaned in regards to supposed textual and doctrinal problems, they are not the concern of this book. As mentioned previously, the concern of this book is to provide an explicit and comprehensive examination of every word in the Authorized Version of the Bible that has been deemed archaic, obsolete, antiquated, or otherwise outmoded.

The procedure is straightforward. Each word in question is listed in alphabetical order, organized into chapters corresponding to the initial letter of the word. After the listing of each particular word, a verse of Scripture is furnished to put the word in context. The discussion of each word begins with an inventory of what forms of the word appear in the Authorized Version and how many times each form is used. All derivatives of a given word appear under the root form given in the Authorized Version. Thus, not only is the word *satiated* found under *satiate,* but the form *unsatiable* appears there as well. After cataloging the various forms of the word, a brief etymology of the word is given as well as anything peculiar or interesting about the word under discussion. We are primarily concern with how the word came into English, not the origin of the word in antiquity. Following this, a brief definition is furnished that often includes the wide range of meanings that many of these words have. The emphasis is on how words are used in the Authorized Version. After this, reference is then made to how the word in question is translated in four modern Bible versions. And finally, after mention of how other related words are rendered by these modern versions, evidence of the significance and contemporary usage of the supposedly archaic Authorized Version word is presented from various newspapers and magazines. For identification and emphasis, words in the Authorized Version under discussion appear in bold print as well as forms of these words when quoted in contemporary sources.

The modern Bible versions under consideration are four of the most popular: the New Revised Standard Version, the New American Standard Bible, the New International Version, and the New King James Version. The New Revised Standard Version, released in 1989, is a revision of the Revised Standard Version of 1952. It is typically the Bible of those who would be called

Liberals. The New American Standard Bible, issued in 1971, was first published as a New Testament in 1963. It is supposed to be an update of the American Standard Version of 1901. The New American Standard Version is generally used by those who could be termed Conservatives. The New International Version, first released as a New Testament in 1973, was completed in 1979. It is a fresh translation that is both ecumenical and eclectic. The New International Version is commonly used by those who would classify themselves as Evangelical. The New King James Version appeared in 1982, although a New Testament was issued in 1979. It claims to be the fifth revision of the Authorized Version. The New King James Version is normally used by those who could be identified as Fundamentalists. Any reference made to modern versions in general should be taken as a reference to these four versions only. The standard abbreviations for these modern versions as well as *AV* for the Authorized Version will be used throughout the book.

The various newspapers and magazines referred to as containing the same archaic words as found in the Authorized Version are generally less than ten years old. When the archaic words in question are documented, it is always in a complete sentence and is not just a quotation of an older source. The inclusion of any particular newspaper or magazine in this book should not be taken as an endorsement of it. A complete list of the publications appears in an appendix.

The words under consideration in this book all have several things in common. They are usually corrected by most or all of our modern versions and are not just current words with a different spelling. Words like *ancles, plaister, counsellor, publick,* and *shew* are easily recognized as merely having an obsolete spelling; thus, they are not included. Other words like *alway, excellency, intreat, enquire, throughly,* and *ware,* which are equivalent to the modern forms of *always, excellent, entreat, inquire, thoroughly,* and *aware,* are likewise not included. Sometimes the Authorized Version employs a compound word where we would now use two separate words and vice versa. Since this does not make the word archaic, only selected examples will be discussed. The Authorized Version also contains irregular verb forms such as *awaked, holden, girt, shapen, holpen, wringed,* and *bare.* These are only discussed if the base form of the word is itself archaic or does not appear at all. Expressions like *by and by* are discussed only when the phrase in question is used like it is one word.

This book is not intended to be a Bible dictionary or commentary. When it comes to animals, precious stones, weights, measures, and plants, they are only covered when they are corrected by the modern versions because of the perceived use of an archaic word. Thus, the length of a cubit is not pertinent to the purpose of the book since the word *cubit* is used by all of our modern versions. Likewise, the identification of a chalcedony. Theological words like propitiation, regeneration, and reconciliation are also not included.

Following the main body of the work, a series of appendixes both summaries the information given about archaic words in daily newspapers, current magazines, and modern Bible versions, as well as providing further information concerning archaic words and the Authorized Version.

Chapter 1
Abase to Axletrees

Abase

> Now I Nebuchadnezzar praise and extol and honour the King of heaven, all whose works *are* truth, and his ways judgment: and those that walk in pride he is able to **abase**. (Dan 4:37)

The word **abase** occurs in various forms nine times in the AV. **Abase** is found four times,[1] **abasing** appears once,[2] and **abased** occurs four times.[3] The word **abase** comes from the French *abaissier*, "to bring low." To **abase** means to reduce or lower in rank or estimation; to humble or humiliate. Of the nine times a form of the word **abase** is found in the AV, the NRSV retains two[4] but inserts a form of the word in four additional places.[5] The NASB preserves the AV reading just once,[6] but uses a form of "**abase**" on thirteen further occasions.[7] The NKJV uses "**abase**" only one time, and that to follow a familiar reading in the AV.[8] The NIV removes these words each time, substituting "disturbed,"[9] "humble,"[10] "in need,"[11] and forms of "bring low"[12] or "lower,"[13] but utilizing "self-abasement" in another passage.[14] **Abase** is still commonly used today, such as this example from *Sierra* magazine: "The mud that fills them is seen as something that **abases** us and holds us down."[15]

Abated

> And the waters returned from off the earth continually: and after the end of the hundred and fifty days the waters were **abated**. (Gen 8:3)

The word **abated**, found six times in the AV,[16] is the past tense and the only form of the word *abate* that appears in the AV.

The word *abate* comes from the French *abatre*, "to beat down." To be **abated** means to be reduced or diminished in intensity or amount. The word does not appear in the NKJV or NIV. It is changed three times to three different words (decreased, deducted, subsided) in the NASB.[17] The NRSV replaces **abated** by "subsided" three times[18] and "reduced" once,[19] but then alters "decreased continually" to "continued to abate."[20] Yet in the *Philadelphia Inquirer* for November 3, 1994, we read: "Beginning on Jan. 1, 1995, the law requires all lead to be **abated** in all pre-1960 federal housing (including public housing)."[21]

Abjects

But in mine adversity they rejoiced, and gathered themselves together: *yea,* the **abjects** gathered themselves together against me, and I knew *it* not; they did tear *me,* and ceased not: (Psa 35:15)

The word **abjects** appears only once in the AV. It comes from the Latin *abjectus,* a form of *abjicere,* "to cast away." To be an **abject** signifies a castaway, an outcast, or a degraded person. The NRSV changes the word to "ruffians," the NASB to "smiters," and the NIV and NKJV to "attackers." Although not often used substantively as in the AV, the word *abject* is employed as an adjective countless times in the modern liberal cliché "abject poverty." It also commonly appears in other contexts such as this from *The Washington Times:* "The only international accord governing land mines–Protocol II of the 1980 Convention on Conventional Weapons–has by general agreement been an **abject** failure."[22]

Abode

And they two made a covenant before the LORD: and David **abode** in the wood, and Jonathan went to his house. (1 Sam 23:18)

The word **abode** occurs sixty-nine times in the AV, three times as a noun[23] and sixty-six times as a verb.[24] **Abode,** from the Old English *abidan,* "delay, bide," developed as both a noun a verb and is still so used today. The noun **abode** is a residence or a dwelling place, and the verbal form serves as the past tense of *abide* along with the more awkward *abided*. Hence, to have **abode** is to have remained, dwelt, or stayed. All of our modern versions eliminate the verbal form. The NRSV and NASB employ **abode** as a noun in several additional places than the AV, thus demonstrating that they did not consider it an archaic word.[25] However, the NIV and NKJV diminish the use of **abode** to twice[26] and once[27] respectively. The NIV even extricates the plain word "abide" from the text of the Bible, replacing it one time with the more difficult "be enthroned."[28] The word **abode**, however, is very much in use today, even in *Garbage* magazine: "With or without AC, everything you do to make your **abode** energy efficient will lighten the heat load."[29]

Acceptation

> This *is* a faithful saying, and worthy of all **acceptation,** that Christ Jesus came into the world to save sinners; of whom I am chief. (1 Tim 1:15)

Acceptation occurs only twice in the AV.[30] Although it comes to English by way of the French *acceptation,* "acceptance," like the word *accept,* it is ultimately from the Latin *accipere,* "to receive." Consequently, **acceptation** means approval, approbation, or acceptance, as it is unanimously rendered in our modern versions. The sense of this word is obvious to anyone who was familiar with the word *accept* and the suffix *-ation,* denoting action or state. Certainly **acceptation** is easier to understand than why the NIV altered the word "oppressor" in the AV to "tyrannical" when the other modern versions all read as the AV.[31] The NIV also corrected "oppression" to "tyranny" when the AV reading was retained by the new translations.[32]

Adamant

> As an **adamant** harder than flint have I made thy forehead: fear them not, neither be dismayed at their looks, though they *be* a rebellious house. (Ezek 3:9)

The word **adamant** is found twice in the AV.[33] It is from the French *adamaunt,* "the hardest stone." An **adamant** is a rock or mineral of extreme hardness. Although beginning as a noun referring to a hard rock, and then any hard substance, the word is primarily used today as an adjective, hence its omission in our modern versions since the AV uses it substantively. After the seventeenth century, **adamant** was used as a synonym of *diamond*. Indeed, the word *diamond* comes from the same root: *adamaunt, adimant, diamant, diamond*. Of the two times **adamant** appears in the AV, it is rendered by the NASB as "emery" and "like flint."[34] The NIV adopts "hardest stone" and "hard as flint."[35] The NRSV turns it into an adjective once,[36] while the NKJV follows the AV the first time but chooses the NASB reading the second.[37] However, the modification of the AV text was not required since **adamant** is still used today to refer to an extremely hard substance. Cognate forms of the word include *adamellite*, "any quartz monzonite," and *adamantine*, "a crystalline high melting hydrocarbon—$C_{10}H_{16}$." An adamantine drill is what is used for drilling exceptionally hard substances.

Adjure

> But Jesus held his peace. And the high priest answered and said unto him, I **adjure** thee by the living God, that thou tell us whether thou be the Christ, the Son of God. (Mat 26:63)

The word **adjure** appears five times in the AV,[38] plus twice in the form **adjured**.[39] **Adjure** is from the Latin *adjurare*, "to swear to." Thus, **adjure** means to charge or command earnestly or solemnly, often under an oath or threat. The NRSV only retains the AV reading twice,[40] but then uses "**adjure**" six more times in other verses.[41] The NASB preserves the AV reading in four instances,[42] but then uses adjure five additional times in other verses, thereby needlessly correcting the AV again.[43] The NRSV and NASB also superfluously amend another verse with the word "adjuration."[44] The word **adjure** is completely absent in any form in the NIV and NJKV. Not only is **adjure** evaded, in the NIV and NKJV it is changed into five different words or expressions out of the seven times it appears in the AV. The NIV used "pronounced this solemn oath," "bound under an oath," "make swear," "charge under oath," and "command."[45] The NKJV preferred "charged," "placed under oath," "make swear," "implore," and "exorcise."[46] The word **adjured**, however, can still be found in print in the 1990's: "'Stop begging for more aid,' **adjured** an editorial in the Oct. 15, 1992 issue of the magazine

Down to Earth."⁴⁷

Admiration

> And I saw the woman drunken with the blood of the saints, and with the blood of the martyrs of Jesus: and when I saw her, I wondered with great **admiration**. (Rev 17:6)

Found only twice in the AV,⁴⁸ **admiration** is from the French *admiration*, which, like all forms of the word *admire*, ultimately comes from the Latin *admirari*, "to wonder at." **Admiration** is a feeling or contemplation of wonder or astonishment. The word does not appear in our modern versions. Even the elementary word "admired" is removed by all of them, except the NKJV, from the only place it occurs in the AV.⁴⁹ Yet the NIV changes the modest phrase "a good report" to the more difficult "admirable."⁵⁰ That the word **admiration** is not arachic can be seen by its use in the *Los Angeles Times:* "As he works at duplicating the spear points found atop the hill, his **admiration** for the early flint workers grows."⁵¹

Ado

> And when he was come in, he saith unto them, Why make ye this **ado**, and weep? the damsel is not dead, but sleepeth. (Mark 5:39)

The word **ado** is used only one time in the AV. It is a contraction of the Middle English *at do*, "to do." Whereas it is now used as a noun, **ado** was previously just a form of the infinitive "to do." Although **ado** is uniformly rendered "commotion" in our modern versions, it can still be found in newspapers in the 1990's: "Ken Lloyd, director of the Regional Air Quality Council, said the debate over the downtown intersections is much **ado** about nothing."⁵²

Advertise

> And now, behold, I go unto my people: come *therefore, and* I will **advertise** thee what this people shall do to thy people in the latter days. (Num 24:14)

The word **advertise** appears twice in the AV.⁵³ However, all modern uses of the word **advertise** have unfortunately been subverted by the concept of newspaper or television advertisements. But such has not always been the case. **Advertise** is from the French *advertissant*, from *advertir*, "to warn or inform." To **advertise** is to reveal, inform, or advise, often with a warning. This word is not found in our modern versions in any form. It is usually changed to "advise."[54] However, on one occasion the NIV changes the concise "**advertise** thee" of the AV to "bring the matter to your attention."[55] The word **advertise** can nevertheless still be found when not referring to advertising in the newspaper. This example is from *U.S. News & World Report:* "It is also hard to pinpoint the origin of low-frequency sounds, a good characteristic for animals that may not want to **advertise** themselves to predators."[56]

Advisement

And there fell *some* of Manasseh to David, when he came with the Philistines against Saul to battle: but they helped them not: for the lords of the Philistines upon **advisement** sent him away, saying, He will fall to his master Saul to *the jeopardy of* our heads. (1 Chr 12:19)

Found only one time in the AV, **advisement** is from the French *aviser*, from *avis*, "opinion." An **advisement** can be a deliberation, reflection, consultation, or consideration. The NIV and NASB altered the word to "consultation." The NRSV adopted "counsel" and the NKJV employed "agreement." Even the elementary word "advise," found three times in the AV, is corrected on two occasions by all of our modern translations.[57] Nevertheless, the word **advisement** is still in use today. It is a commonly accepted legal term and has been so defined as: "The consultation of a court, after the argument of a cause by counsel, and before delivering their opinion."[58] But the utilization of **advisement** is not limited to the legal profession: "Secretary Byrnes heard argument and received memoranda from me, Colonel McCormack, and the geographic assistant secretaries, taking the issue under **advisement**."[59]

Affinity

Now Jehoshaphat had riches and honour in abundance, and

joined **affinity** with Ahab. (2 Chr 18:1)

The word **affinity** appears three times in the AV.[60] It is from the French word *affinite,* and ultimately from the Latin *affinis,* "bordering on." Thus, **affinity** is a connection, similarity, mutual attraction, or relationship, often by marriage. The word has been replaced in our new versions with some variety of the phrase "marriage alliance,"[61] except for the one time it is changed to "treaty" in the NKJV.[62] Although the word **affinity** was deemed too archaic for use in modern Bible translations, the *Washington Post* did not consider it so: "She had a rich, full-bodied contralto, musical imagination, impeccable taste in music and an **affinity** for fresh treatments of her material."[63]

Affording

> *That* our garners *may be* full, **affording** all manner of store: *that* our sheep may bring forth thousands and ten thousands in our streets: (Psa 144:13)

The word **affording** occurs only once in the AV. It is a form of the strictly English word *afford.* The Middle English form was *aforthen,* "to further." **Affording** means accomplishing, furthering, promoting, or providing. Naturally, **affording** is not used in this sense in any of our modern versions. The NRSV and NIV render **affording** as "with," the NKJV as "supplying," and the NASB as "furnishing." **Affording** does appear, however, in the *Denver Post* in 1994: "No TV request **affording** the league much-needed exposure was too big a favor to ask Kearney."[64]

Affright

> Then they cried with a loud voice in the Jews' speech unto the people of Jerusalem that *were* on the wall, to **affright** them, and to trouble them; that they might take the city. (2 Chr 32:18)

Although the word **affright** occurs only once in the AV, the form **affrighted** is found nine times.[65] **Affright** is another exclusively English word. It goes back, in a variety of spellings, to the Old English *afyrht,* a form of *afyrhtan,* "to frighten." It is at once apparent that the modern word *fright* is a derivative of **affright** and that it would be a simple matter to update the word.

But such was not the case. Of the ten times a form of **affright** is used in the AV, it is rendered five times by a similar form of "fright" in the NKJV,[66] but only twice in the NASB,[67] and once in the NRSV[68] and NIV.[69] This in itself is not so alarming until one examines two other factors. First of all, out of the ten occurrences of **affright** or **affrighted** in the AV, the NRSV uses eight different words to correct the AV readings (dread, frighten, horror, dismayed, appalled, panic, alarmed, terrified),[70] the NASB uses seven (dread, frighten, horror, dismayed, overwhelm, terrified, amazed),[71] and the NIV uses six (terrified, horror, afraid, tremble, alarmed, frightened).[72] Then the NRSV employs a form of *frighten* seventeen additional times,[73] the NIV eighteen,[74] and the NASB a whopping twenty-six times.[75] Although **affright** is somehwat archaic, its meaning can still be readily determined. Not so, however, for the word "tresses," introduced by all of our modern versions to replace the AV reading of "galleries."[76]

Afoot

> And the people saw them departing, and many knew him, and ran **afoot** thither out of all cities, and outwent them, and came together unto him. (Mark 6:33)

The compound word **afoot**, found twice in the AV,[77] is from the Middle English *a fote,* "on foot." To go **afoot** obviously means to go on foot or walk. This is apparent from the parallel passage in Matthew where the same Greek word is translated "on foot."[78] If it be objected that the same Greek word should not be translated two different ways then it should be noticed that the NRSV and NASB both use "by land" in the same passage where the NIV and NKJV each use "on foot."[79] The word **afoot** is so archaic that it was used in the *Christian Science Monitor* in 1994: "A movement is also **afoot** to expand Seattle's convention center, and rumblings are being heard about a new symphony hall."[80]

Afore

> Let them be as the grass upon the housetops, which withereth **afore** it groweth up: (Psa 129:6)

Another compound word from an earlier English form is **afore**. This word appears seven times in the AV[81] but is also found seven times fashioned as **aforetime**[82] and once as **aforehand**.[83] The word **afore** is from the Middle English *aforn*, which was derived from the Old English *onforan*, "in front." Even the modern equivalent *before* is from the same root. Understandably, none of these forms of **afore** appear in our modern versions. Where the AV reads **afore**, it is usually updated to "before."[84] However, in two cases "beforehand" is used in the NASB, NRSV, and NIV.[85] But when the AV utilizes "beforehand," the modern versions routinely change it.[86] On one occasion, the NRSV conjectures the translation "above" where the AV reads **afore** and is followed with similar forms by our modern versions.[87] The NASB even uses the word "aforesaid" that contains the same archaic prefix it corrects in the AV.[88] The NIV is even worse, for it utilizes this supposedly archaic prefix five times in the word "aforethought."[89] In spite of its correction by the modern versions, the word **afore** is still current today: "A chance to eat haggis **afore** Robbie Burns day."[90] Moreover, the extended form **aforetime** can still be found in *National Review:* "Under this theory, lawsuits are not, as was thought **aforetime**, necessary evils; rather, litigation is a positive force in the regulation of society, a means, through aggressive tactics and huge punitive damages, to right the wrongs of the rich and powerful and deter future depredations against common folk."[91] The word **afore** can also still be heard down South and is even officially classified as a Southern expression.[92]

Agone

> And David said unto him, To whom *belongest* thou? and whence *art* thou? And he said, I *am* a young man of Egypt, servant to an Amalekite; and my master left me, because three days **agone** I fell sick. (1 Sam 30:13)

The word **agone** is found only once in the AV and is another example of an old English spelling that was still in vogue during the seventeenth century. The spelling of this word that survived is *ago*. Both forms are from the Middle English verb *agon*, "to pass away." All of our modern versions update the word to "ago." Although **agone** can be genuinely classified as archaic, its meaning can easily be determined from the context. Yet **agone** can be found in the writings of Hawthorne and Twain, which no

Ague

> I also will do this unto you; I will even appoint over you terror, consumption, and the burning **ague**, that shall consume the eyes, and cause sorrow of heart: and ye shall sow your seed in vain, for your enemies shall eat it. (Lev 26:16)

The word **ague** appears only once in the AV. It is from a French word of the same spelling and is actually short for *fievre ague*, "an acute fever." Thus, an **ague** is a fever, and is so rendered by all of our modern versions. But if **ague** obscures the meaning of the text, then how does the altering of "false" in the AV to "malicious" by the NRSV and NASB help to clarify the Bible by putting it into the contemporary English of today?[94]

Albeit

> Have ye not seen a vain vision, and have ye not spoken a lying divination, whereas ye say, The LORD saith *it;* **albeit** I have not spoken? (Ezek 13:7)

Albeit, found only twice in the AV,[95] is a Middle English compound of *al be it,* "all though it be that." Thus, it means although or even though. The *it* was also dropped to form what we now spell *able*. Not only is **albeit** not found in any of our modern versions, in the two places that it occurs in the AV, it is rendered two different ways in each of them. The NRSV preferred "even though" in one passage but left the underlying Greek word untranslated in the other.[96] The NASB uses "but" and "lest,"[97] and the NIV "though" and "not to mention."[98] The NKJV takes the best of two translations, using "but" one time and "not to mention" the next.[99] In their rush to get rid of the word **albeit**, it was overlooked that **albeit** is still in use, this example being from the *San Jose Mercury News:* "What is publicly owned has been built recently and is among the nicest low-cost housing available—**albeit** in very limited supply."[100]

Allow

> For that which I do I **allow** not: for what I would, that do I not; but what I hate, that do I. (Rom 7:15)

This word occurs three times in the AV as **allow**,[101] and once each as **allowed** and **alloweth**.[102] The form **disallow** is used once,[103] while **disallowed** can be found five times.[104] The word **allow** is from the French *alouer*, "to approve of." **Allow** is actually related to the word *laud*, as both are originally derived from the Latin *allaudare*, "to praise." Thus, **allow** originally meant to praise, commend, sanction, or accept. Since they all limited the meaning of **allow** to the current concept of permit or tolerate, our modern versions have corrected every occurrence of **allow** and its derivatives in those passages where the AV contained them. **Alloweth** is unanimously replaced with "approves"[105] and **allowed** is unanimously updated to "approved."[106] The word **allow** is given as "approve" in one verse[107] and "understand" in another,[108] but "accept" and "cherish" in a third.[109] Yet when the AV uses the word "approved," the NRSV alters it to the phrase "to have met the test."[110] Moreover, when the AV says "approvest," the NRSV changes it to "determine" even though the other new translations follow the AV reading.[111]

All to

And a certain woman cast a piece of a millstone upon Abimelech's head, and **all to** brake his skull. (Judg 9:53)

Although the words *all* and *to* appear together in the course of a sentence several times, the expression **all to** is found only once in the AV. It originated from the practice of adding the prefix *to-* on the front of verbs (to-break, to-rend, etc.). In time, the prefix became separated from the verb and linked with the preceding word *all*. To do something **all to** is to do it entirely or wholly. The phrase survives in the similar Southern expressions "all get-out," "all the far," "all the fast," and "all tore up."[112]

Alms

Take heed that ye do not your **alms** before men, to be seen of them: otherwise ye have no reward of your Father which is in heaven. (Mat 6:1)

The word **alms** appears thirteen times in the AV,[113] while the related **almsdeeds** occurs once.[114] Although **alms** is used on many occasions by some modern versions, a study of its usage in these translations reveals the manifest inconsistencies present in them. The word **alms** is singular with a plural ending, like the word *clothes* or *riches*. It was originally a plural but came to be used for both forms. It goes back, in various spellings, to the Old English *aelmysse*. This was in turn borrowed from the Latin *eleemosyna*, "**alms**." It is from this Latin word that we get the English adjective *eleemosynary*, "charitable." **Alms** is charitable relief for the poor. The NRSV follows the AV on every occurrence of **alms** in the Bible. Excepting the textual variant that it follows in one verse,[115] the NASB thrice renders the Greek word for **alms** as "charity"[116] while retaining "**alms**" in ten other passages.[117] Thinking it archaic, the NIV removes the word completely but then translates the underlying Greek word as "gifts to the poor" three times,[118] "to the needy" twice,[119] and "to the poor" twice.[120] Then the NIV alters **alms** once each to "giving," "beg," "money," "begging," and "helping the poor."[121] Finally the phrase "which gave much **alms** to the people" is transformed into "he gave generously to those in need,"[122] completely ignoring the underlying Greek.[123] The NKJV uses **alms** on nine occasions[124] but five times translates the same word as "charitable deeds."[125] Yet when the AV uses "charity," the NKJV removes all trace of the word.[126] Needless to say, the word **alms** is still in use today: "One little old lady would ask for **alms** near a tea shop, while the kids would tease and chase her all over the place."[127]

Ambassage

> Or else, while the other is yet a great way off, he sendeth an **ambassage**, and desireth conditions of peace. (Luke 14:32)

The word **ambassage** only appears once in the AV. **Ambassage** is strictly an English word that is thought to have been influenced by the French *ambasse* or Latin *ambassare*. It has also been spelled in the past as *embassage*. This can be seen in two modern words derived from French: *ambassador*, "a diplomatic official sent by one sovereign or state to another as its resident representative or on a temporary mission," and *embassy*, "the official headquarters of an ambassador." An **ambassage** is a group of men sent out on a mission. It is unanimously rendered as "delegation" in our modern versions. But after correcting **ambassage** because it was archaic, the NKJV altered "pin" in the AV to "batten," even though all the other new, up-to-date translations retained the AV reading.[128]

Ambushment

> But Jeroboam caused an **ambushment** to come about behind them: so they were before Judah, and the **ambushment** *was* behind them. (2 Chr 13:13)

The word **ambushment** occurs twice in the AV in the same verse and one additional time in the plural.[129] It is from the French *embushement*, which is derived from the same word that we get *ambush* from: *embuscher*, "to set in ambush." Following the Latin, this literally means "to set in the bush." An **ambushment** is the act of hiding so as to attack by surprise, the concealed position, or those who do the attacking. Obviously, it is a synonym for *ambush*, which is usually how the word is rendered in our modern versions.[130] But the word **ambushment** is a perfect example of a word that retains the meaning of its shorter cousin even with the addition of a suffix. Other examples include payment—pay and commandment—command. The new translations do not hesitate to use both forms of a word to translate a single Greek word. The NRSV translates the same Greek word as both "command" and "commandment." [131]

Amerce

> And they shall **amerce** him in an hundred *shekels* of silver, and give *them* unto the father of the damsel, because he hath brought up an evil name upon a virgin of Israel: and she shall be his wife; he may not put her away all his days. (Deu 22:19)

Found only once in the AV, **amerce** is from the Anglo-French *amercier*, "to fine." To be amerced was originally to be *estre a merci*, "at someone's mercy." To **amerce** is to punish by imposing a fine. Our modern translations all update the word to "fine." Although deemed archaic, **amerce** and amercement are legal terms in vogue today.[132] But when the AV, followed by all of the other modern versions, mentions the Ethiopians, the NIV alone calls them the "Nubians."[133]

Amiable

How **amiable** *are* thy tabernacles, O LORD of hosts! (Psa 84:1)

The word **amiable** occurs but once in the AV. It is from the French *aimiable*, "friendly." It also gathered the meaning of "lovely" due to its resemblance to *amable*, "lovely." Hence, **amiable** means friendly, agreeable, sociable, or lovely. The word is unanimously altered in our modern versions to "lovely." Yet a major newspaper in 1994 saw fit to use the word: "The parting was less than **amiable**."[134] The Latin root can be found today in the legal term *amicus curiae*, "friend of the court."[135]

Amiss

Ye ask, and receive not, because ye ask **amiss,** that ye may consume *it* upon your lusts. (James 4:3)

The word **amiss** appears four times in the AV.[136] It is a compound of the Middle English *a mis,* from *on mis,* "in error." To be **amiss** is to be incorrect, improper, out of order, or astray. Only the NKJV retains the word, following the AV in two places,[137] and using **amiss** in another passage.[138] The NASB employs four different words or phrases to get rid of the AV reading (iniquity, offensive, wrong, with wrong motives).[139] On three occasions, the NIV consistently substitutes "wrong" or "wrong motives" for **amiss,**[140] but completely refuses to translate *shalah* in another place the AV reads **amiss**.[141] In lieu of the numerous corrections of the word **amiss,** it should be surprising to those who deemed it archaic to find that the word was used in a *Washington Post* article in 1994: "As the day wore on, it became clear that something was **amiss**."[142]

Anathema

If any man love not the Lord Jesus Christ, let him be **Anathema** Maranatha. (1 Cor 16:22)

Anathema only appears one time in the AV, although the Greek word from which it ultimately comes is used in other passages. The English word **anathema** is transliterated from the

Latin which in turn is transliterated directly from the Greek *anathema*, "devoted to evil." To be **anathema** is to be accursed or consigned to destruction. Without fail, our modern versions substitute "accursed." This surrogate is unnecessary, however, for the word **anathema** is still used by the *Chicago Tribune:* "But any talk of raising taxes by Republicans has been **anathema** to Edgar."[143]

Ancient

> With the **ancient** *is* wisdom; and in length of days understanding. (Job 12:12)

Although the words **ancient** and **ancients** appear many times in the Bible, their use in the AV in certain instances has been deemed archaic. **Ancient** is used with an obsolete meaning seven times[144] and **ancients** nine times.[145] The word **ancient** is the substantive form of the adjective *ancient,* from the French *ancien,* "old, former." The commonly used Latin root is *ante,* "before." The mention of **ancients** typical conjures up **ancient** Greeks or Romans, but in the AV these words commonly refer to someone who is old or aged and still alive. **Ancient** and **ancients** are normally corrected by our modern versions to forms of "old,"[146] "aged,"[147] or "elder."[148] But on one occasion, the NIV supplants the AV reading of "elders" to "**ancients.**"[149] Moreover, the NASB one time substituted "**ancient**" for "old" when the other translations followed the AV reading.[150] The word **ancients** is certainly comprehensible, but why the NKJV changed "breach" into "dilapidation" is certainly not.[151]

Angle

> The fishers also shall mourn, and all they that cast **angle** into the brooks shall lament, and they that spread nets upon the waters shall languish. (Isa 19:8)

The noun **angle** is found only twice in the AV.[152] It is formed from the Old English *angul,* "a fishhook." This word and its homonym used in geometry and trigonometry are from the same root meaning "to bend." An **angle** is a fishhook. Excepting "a line," found once in the NASB,[153] the word is consistently altered to "hook" in our modern versions. Yet isn't it strange that up near the end of the twentieth century a fisherman is called an angler and not a hooker?

Anise

> Woe unto you, scribes and Pharisees, hypocrites! for ye pay tithe of mint and **anise** and cummin, and have omitted the weightier *matters* of the law, judgment, mercy, and faith: these ought ye to have done, and not to leave the other undone. (Mat 23:23)

There is only one mention of the herb **anise** in the AV. The word itself is from the French *anis,* which is shortened from the Latin *anisum.* The Greek form in the Bible is similar. Anise is technically *pimpinella anisum,* a plant of the parsley family with flowers that yield aniseed. The NIV, NASB, and NRSV all revise **anise** to "dill" even though one can purchase **anise** at any store that sells herbs. It is also documented in the *Orlando Sentinel* that **anise** is native to Florida.[154]

Anon

> But he that received the seed into stony places, the same is he that heareth the word, and **anon** with joy receiveth it; (Mat 13:20)

Found only twice in the AV,[155] **anon** is a compound of the Old English *on an,* "in one," that signified "in one moment." Hence, **anon** means immediately, at once, or without delay. **Anon** is usually updated to "immediately"[156] or "at once,"[157] but after correcting the AV the first time, the NIV neglected to translate anything the second.[158]

Apace

> And the watchman cried, and told the king. And the king said, If he *be* alone, *there is* tidings in his mouth. And he came **apace,** and drew near. (2 Sam 18:25)

The word **apace** occurs three times in the AV.[159] **Apace** is from the French *a pas,* "at pace." It originally referred to men or horses travelling at not too great a pace; literally, one pace. It now means quickly or swiftly. **Apace** is sometimes altered to "in haste."[160] But more often than not, our modern versions could not decide on what to change it to. The phrase "came **apace,** and drew near" that is found in the AV has been modified to "kept coming, and drew near" in the NRSV, "came nearer and nearer" in the NASB, "closer and closer" in the NIV, and "came rapidly and drew near" in the NKJV.[161] However, the word **apace** is so archaic that it was used by the *Boston Globe* in 1994: "The effort comes amid public demand for greater accountability from colleges and universities that has grown **apace** with the rise in tuition and fees."[162]

Apothecary

> Dead flies cause the ointment of the **apothecary** to send forth a stinking savour: *so doth* a little folly *him* that *is* in reputation for wisdom *and* honour. (Eccl 10:1)

The word **apothecary** is found six times in the AV, five in the singular[163] and once in the plural.[164] It is from the French *apotecaire*, which is from the Latin *apothecarius*, "a storekeeper," from *apotheca*, "a storehouse." In English the word **apothecary** retains both meanings. This word is now relegated to just that of a pharmacist or pharmacy. Without fail, all of our modern versions render **apothecary** as "perfumer." Although the word **apothecary** is very common throughout England and Canada, it can also be found in *The Philadelphia Inquirer:* "Even the countries where the tiger still roams and **apothecaries** stock musk tiger bond plasters and a tiger whisker concoction for toothaches are increasingly worried."[165]

Apparel

> I have coveted no man's silver, or gold, or **apparel.** (Acts 20:33)

The word **apparel** occurs twenty-eight times in the AV in twenty-seven verses.[166] The verb **apparelled** appears twice.[167] **Apparel** has the same root as *apparatus:* the Latin *parare*, "to prepare." This was compounded to *apparare*, "to prepare for," then *apparatus*, "preparation," and finally into the English *apparatus*, "equipment prepared for a particular use." The Latin *parare* also made its way into French as *apareillier*, "to prepare." From this came the noun *apareil*, "a thing prepared." It is from these words that we got **apparelled** and **apparel**. By the sixteenth century, the primary meaning of "clothing" had been established. The NKJV follows the AV with regularity, but the NIV omits the words altogether. The NRSV and NASB were lax in their attempt to modernize **apparel**. The NRSV forgets to update the AV in one instance,[168] and then uses "**apparel**" again three more times.[169] The NASB neglects to modernize **apparel** in five passages,[170] and then alters "garments" to "**apparel**."[171] Both the NASB and NRSV follow the AV in translating *lebuwsh* as "**apparel**" in one place,[172] but when the same word appears again, it is rendered as "robe."[173] The NASB likewise emulates the AV in translating *labash* as "**apparel**,"[174] but then yields the same word in another verse as "robes."[175] In the New Testament, the NASB matches the AV reading of **apparel** one time[176] and then renders the same Greek word as "clothing" on another occasion.[177] However, all the energy expended in attempting to get rid of the word **apparel** was unwarranted, for every department store has a ladies **apparel** department. The word **apparel** is also still very much in vogue: "The dilemma for organized labor is that trade creates losers as well as winners, especially in industries such as **apparel** and consumer electronics, where union contracts have driven wages to uncompetitive levels.[178]

𝔄ppertain

> But if the LORD make a new thing, and the earth open her mouth, and swallow them up, with all that *appertain* unto them, and they go down quick into the pit; then ye shall understand that these men have provoked the LORD. (Num 16:30)

This word is found twice in the AV as **appertain**,[179] twice as **appertaineth**,[180] and three times as **appertained**.[181] It is from the French *apartenir*, "to belong to." Thus, **appertain** means to belong to, pertain to, or relate to. It would have been a simple matter to update the word to *pertain*, but this was only done by one of our modern versions, the NKJV, and only on one occasion.[182] Once again, in the case of a supposedly archaic word, the meaning is quite evident from both the context and the form of the word. And furthermore, the word **appertain** can still be found in use today, even in *Fortune* magazine: "When King

Philip II proclaimed Madrid the capital of Spain in 1561, he said he chose it because of the 'healthy air and brilliant skies,' both of which still **appertain.**"[183]

Aright

> The tongue of the wise useth knowledge **aright:** but the mouth of fools poureth out foolishness. (Prov 15:2)

The word **aright** appears five times in the AV[184] and is strictly of English origin. It is a compound of the Old English *on riht*, "on right," meaning "in the right way." Hence, it is similar in formation to *afoot*. **Aright** means correctly, properly, or rightly. One would think that it would be easy enough to upgrade the word to *rightly* but such is not the case with our modern translations. The NKJV forgets to update the word three times[185] and then uses it again in another verse.[186] Only once does the NKJV revise the word to "rightly."[187] The NRSV omits the word completely; the closest it comes to it is "the right way" found on one occasion.[188] The NASB ignores "**aright**" in one verse, thus inadvertently matching the AV.[189] Then it updates the word to "right" in one passage.[190] The NIV corrects all five of the AV uses of the word **aright** but then introduces the word in another verse.[191] But once again, the context and construction of the word reveal its meaning. And furthermore, **aright** is even still used in the 1990's: "On October 7, Columbus veered his course from west to west-southwest to follow them, certain they would lead him **aright.**"[192]

Armholes

> And Ebedmelech the Ethiopian said unto Jeremiah, Put now *these* old cast clouts and rotten rags under thine **armholes** under the cords. And Jeremiah did so. (Jer 38:12)

Armholes is found only twice in the AV.[193] It is unmistakably a compound of *arm* and *hole*. An **armhole** can be the armpit or the hole in a garment in which the arm is put. Thus, it could include the whole sleeve since the arm goes through the sleeve. The AV uses the word in both ways; the modern versions erase the word completely. The term **armholes** is still used today, albeit not exactly as the AV: "To keep ourselves dry and warm, we put

Art

> She saith unto him, Yea, Lord: I believe that thou **art** the Christ, the Son of God, which should come into the world. (John 11:27)

The word **art** appears 495 times in the AV. Four of these have reference to work or skill like the word **art** is applied today.[195] This leaves 491 occurrences of the word **art** that have been replaced because of an archaic usage. Art, which appeared in Old English as *eart*, is the second person, present indicative form of the being verb. It is frequently coupled with the word *thou*. The NIV, NRSV, and NKJV all completely eliminate the word **art** when used this way. Yet this supposedly archaic word is employed by the NASB 147 times,[196] even in places where the AV did not contain it.[197]

Artificer

> And Zillah, she also bare Tubalcain, an instructor of every **artificer** in brass and iron: and the sister of Tubalcain *was* Naamah. (Gen 4:22)

The word **artificer** is found in the AV twice in the singular[198] and twice in the plural.[199] It is a form of the word *artifice*, which is from the French *artifice*, "skill, craft." **Artificer**, like *artist* and *artisan*, is ultimately from the Latin prefix *ars*, "art." Thus, an **artificer** is one who does or makes something by art or skill. The NIV prefers the word "craftsman."[200] The NKJV uses "craftsman,"[201] but once favors "artisan.[202] Likewise the NASB.[203] The NRSV could not decide which term to utilize so it choose three (artisans, carpenters, magician).[204] But not only was a mechanic in the British Navy formerly called an **artificer**,[205] the word can still be found in such publications as the *New Republic:* "He is an **artificer**, a fabulist whose work, with its gestures toward fantasy and science fiction, has always had the spectacular credibility and the irrevocable logic of dreams."[206] The related form *artifice* is even still used today in the 1990's.[207] But when the AV just utilizes the word "art," the NIV and NASB correct it to "work."[208] Moreover, the NIV even inserts the word "art" where neither the AV nor any of the other modern versions contain it.[209]

Artillery

> And Jonathan gave his **artillery** unto his lad, and said unto him, Go, carry *them* to the city. (1 Sam 20:40)

The word **artillery** appears only once in the AV. It is from the French *artillerie*, from *artiller*, "to equip." The word **artillery** came to be applied to equipment used in war; specifically, ballistic machines to throw projectiles. Because of the modern connotation of **artillery**, this word has harmoniously been corrected by our modern versions to "weapons," since the implements of modern warfare did not exist during the time of the Old Testament. But **artillery** is not limited to modern weapons, at least according to the *Los Angeles Times:* "When elementary school boys on a bus in Eden Prairie, Minn., hurled dirty words at the girls, school officials employed the usual **artillery** of discipline—detention, suspension and transferring a student to another bus."[210]

Assayed

> And when Saul was come to Jerusalem, he **assayed** to join himself to the disciples: but they were all afraid of him, and believed not that he was a disciple. (Acts 9:26)

The term **assayed** occurs four times in the AV,[211] while **assay** and **assaying** each appear once.[212] The AV employs **assay** only in verbal forms, although the word can also be used as a noun. The verb **assay** comes from the French *assaier*, from *assai*, a variation of *essai*, "trial," from which we also get *essay*, "a literary composition." To **assay** can mean to examine, analyze, test, prove, or attempt. Every occurrence of the various forms of **assay** found in the AV is altered in our modern versions to varieties of "attempt" or "try," excepting the NRSV using "ventures" in one verse.[213] Nevertheless, this archaic word was twice thrust into one verse by the NASB, even transforming "try" in the AV to "assay."[214] The NKJV follows the NASB in changing "tower" to "assayer."[215] The term **assay** is still applied to a medical, mineral, or metallurgic test. The word **assayed** can also be found in use as a verb: "David Luban, a scholar of philosophy who divides his time between the University of Maryland School of Law and its Institute for Philosophy and Public Policy, briefly **assayed** teaching professional responsibility as a course in applied philosophy."[216]

Assent

> And the messenger that went to call Micaiah spake to him, saying, Behold, the words of the prophets *declare* good to the king with one **assent**; let thy word therefore, I pray thee, be like one of theirs, and speak thou good. (2 Chr 18:12)

Assent only appears once in the AV, as does the form **assented**.[217] **Assent** is from the French *assentir*, "to agree to." Thus, **assent** means to agree or concur with; to acquiesce or subscribe to. The NKJV alone retains **assented** in one passage.[218] The single word **assented** is converted into a different four-word phrase in each of our other new translations. The NRSV prefers "joined in the charge," the NASB "joined in the attack," and the NIV "joined in the accusation."[219] Although our modern versions considered **assent** to be too archaic to use, the *Los Angeles Times* did not: "With the apparent **assent** of the French government, the European company offered to give away its Viking rocket engine technology to Brazil, something the Americans viewed as a possible violation of international agreements on arms trafficking and the spread of missile technology."[220]

Asswage

> *But* I would strengthen you with my mouth, and the moving of my lips should **asswage** *your grief.* (Job 16:5)

The word **asswage** appears once in the AV, with the form **asswaged** occurring twice.[221] **Asswage** comes from the French *assouagier*, "to sweeten or make agreeable." Thus, the word **asswage** can mean to relieve, lessen, appease, satisfy, or sweeten. **Asswage** is just an old spelling for *assuage,* but not even the modern form appears in the NASB, NIV, or NKJV. The NASB prefers "subsided"[222] and a form of "lessen,"[223] the NIV favors "receded"[224] and forms of "relieve,"[225] while the NKJV utilizes "subsided"[226] with a form of "relieved."[227] Although the NRSV one time alters **asswaged** to "subsided,"[228] it retains this supposedly archaic word on two other occasions.[229] But the word is not that archaic after all, at least according to *The Philadelphia Inquirer:* "**Assuaged** by a quickly drafted letter from Rabin acknowledging that Jericho's borders remained in dispute, Arafat signed the contested documents adding his own reservations."[230]

Astonied

> Then Nebuchadnezzar the king was **astonied,** and rose up in haste, *and* spake, and said unto his counsellors, Did not we cast three men bound into the midst of the fire? They answered and said unto the king, True, O king. (Dan 3:24)

Found ten times in the AV,[231] the word **astonied** is a form of *astony,* from the verb *astone*. *Astone, astonish,* and *astound* are all related and ultimately derived from the French *estoner,* "to stun." To be **astonied** is to be astonished, astounded, amazed, surprised, or startled. The base form *astone* is very descriptive, for it indicates that someone **astonied** would be like a stone. As a genuine archaic word, **astonied** is expectedly absent in our modern versions so as not to astound the reader. However, only the NKJV consistently renders **astonied** as astonished, excepting one passage.[232] Of the ten times **astonied** is found in the AV, the NRSV uses six different words to correct it (appalled, astonished, confused, dismay, distressed, perplexed).[233] The NIV employs five distinct words to replace **astonied** (appalled, surprise, amazement, perplexed, baffled),[234] as does the NASB (appalled, astonished, dismayed, astounded, perplexed).[235] Yet the AV is routinely criticized for rendering the same Greek word by several English words.

Attent

> Now, my God, let, I beseech thee, thine eyes be open, and *let* thine ears *be* **attent** unto the prayer *that is made* in this place. (2 Chr 6:40)

The word **attent** appears twice in the AV[236] and is from the Latin *attentus,* a form of *attendere,* "to attend." To be **attent** is to be intent, attentive, observant, or full of attention. Understandably, this word is uniformly modernized in our modern versions to "attentive." However, the word "attentive" is also found in the AV.[237] But on one occasion, a phrase in the AV, "very attentive to hear him," is altered to "hanging upon His words" in the NASB, "spellbound by what they heard" in the NRSV, and "hung on his words" in the NIV.[238] So even when the AV does not use archaic words, it is still corrected. Moreover, our modern versions often render ordinary words in the AV by words that are noticeably archaic, such as the NRSV replacing "hearth" with "brazier."[239]

Augment

>And, behold, ye are risen up in your fathers' stead, an increase of sinful men, to **augment** yet the fierce anger of the LORD toward Israel. (Num 32:14)

The word **augment** is found only once in the AV. It is from the French *augmenter*, "to increase." To **augment** something is to enlarge, increase, or supplement it. Our modern versions all supplant this word where it is found in the AV, but the NRSV substitutes "**augment**" in another verse where the AV reads "increase"[240] after just correcting the only case of **augment** in the AV to "increase." All the emendations were unnecessary anyway, for the word **augment** is still used on a regular basis: "Sugarloaf trainers eventually will **augment** the dolphins regular diet of dead fish with live fish to help retrain them to catch their meals."[241]

Austere

>And he saith unto him, Out of thine own mouth will I judge thee, *thou* wicked servant. Thou knewest that I was an **austere** man, taking up that I laid not down, and reaping that I did not sow: (Luke 19:22)

Austere is found twice in the AV.[242] It comes from the French *austere*, "harsh." Thus, to be **austere** is to be severe, strict, harsh, or solemn. **Austere** is rendered, in both places in which it appears in the AV, by "harsh" in the NRSV, "exacting" in the NASB, and "hard" in the NIV.[243] The NKJV neglects to change this supposedly archaic word. Perhaps the translators anticipated the word being used in an Oklahoma newspaper in 1994: "In Missouri and Kansas, higher education institutions are facing **austere** times and plenty of questions about how they should be functioning now and in the future."[244]

Averse

> Even of late my people is risen up as an enemy: ye pull off the robe with the garment from them that pass by securely as men **averse** from war. (Micah 2:8)

The word **averse** occurs but once in the AV. It is from the Latin *aversus*, from *avetere*, "to turn away." To be **averse** is to be opposed, unwilling, disinclined, turned back, or opposite. It is rendered "with no thought" in the NRSV, but a form of "returning" in the other new versions. But **averse** is so archaic that it was used in the *Washington Post* in 1994: "The president's fundamental problem, Wilson said, 'is people do not trust him' because he came to Washington as a new kind of fiscally careful Democrat **averse** to big new programs."[245]

Avouched

> Thou hast **avouched** the LORD this day to be thy God, and to walk in his ways, and to keep his statutes, and his commandments, and his judgments, and to hearken unto his voice: (Deu 26:17)

The word **avouched,** past tense of *avouch,* is found only twice in the AV.[246] It is from the French *avochier,* "to call upon as an authority or defender." Thus, **avouched** can mean guaranteed, defended, admitted, affirmed, or vouched for. In both occurrences in the AV, the NRSV substitutes "obtained," the NASB and NIV "declared," and the NKJV "proclaimed."[247] The word **avouched** is the last in a series of words that have been examined in the AV that contain an *a-* prefix. Our modern versions have either removed them completely or severely curtailed their use. Yet many words that contain an *a-* prefix and are not even used by the AV have been introduced into the Bible by some of our new translations. When the AV reads "on fire," it is changed to "ablaze" by the NRSV and NIV.[248] The NRSV renders "burn" in the AV to "be aflame with passion."[249] The

NASB gives "aflame" for the AV phrase "on fire."[250] When all of our modern versions agree with the AV phrase "on fire," the NIV still sees fit to alter it to "afire."[251] When the AV reads "lighting," the NKJV and NRSV join in giving it as "alighting."[252] The NASB and NKJV insert the word "allays" into their text when neither the AV nor the other versions even use the word.[253] Moreover, the NRSV alone employs the word "atop,"[254] the NIV "abutted,"[255] and the NKJV "adjoin."[256]

Away with

> Bring no more vain oblations; incense is an abomination unto me; the new moons and sabbaths, the calling of assemblies, I cannot **away with**; *it is* iniquity, even the solemn meeting. (Isa 1:13)

The expression **away with** is found six times in the AV.[257] The word *away* is itself a compound of the Old English *on weg*, "on the way." **Away with** means tolerate, bear, endure, and also has the meaning of take away. The AV uses **away with** only once as the former, but five times as the latter meaning.[258] Surprisingly, it is only the first type that is usually corrected, the NRSV, NASB, and NKJV using "endure," and the NIV utilizing "bear." Only the NIV alters the remaining occurrences of **away with**, substituting "rid the earth" once[259] and "take him away" twice.[260] In the two other instances of **away with**, the NIV retains the AV reading.[261] Clearly, here is a case where our modern versions have failed to consistently translate the text according to their own intended purposes of clear, modern English.

Axletrees

> And under the borders *were* four wheels; and the **axletrees** of the wheels *were joined* to the base: and the height of a wheel *was* a cubit and half a cubit. (1 Ki 7:32)

The word **axletrees**, the plural of *axletree*, occurs twice in the AV.[262] It is obviously a compound made up of *axle* and *tree*. *Axletree* is from the Old Norse *oxultre*, "axletree," and is akin to *oxull*, "axis." It formerly included the sense of both *axle* and *axis* but gradually came to mean just the shaft on which a wheel rotates. The fact that most axles were made of wood accounts for the original suffix, -*tree,* that is now dropped. The NKJV replaces **axletrees** with "axles" once,[263] but surprisingly uses "axle pins" the other time.[264] Understandably, the other modern versions consonantly render this word as "axle."[265] But what is not understandable is why the NIV altered "sad" to "dejected"[266] and "mad" to "demented."[267]

Chapter 2
Backbiters to By and By

Backbiters

Backbiters, haters of God, despiteful, proud, boasters, inventors of evil things, disobedient to parents, (Rom 1:30)

The word **backbiters** is found only once in the AV, as is the verb **backbiteth.**[1] The form **backbiting** occurs once in the singular[2] and once in the plural.[3] This word is obviously a compound of *back* and *bite*. **Backbiters** are those who backbite. To backbite is to slander, traduce, or otherwise attack the character of someone behind their back, hence the descriptive nature of the term. Only the NKJV retains these words all four times; and only the NIV removes them every time.[4] The NASB and NRSV attempted to eliminate them completely but forgot about "**backbiting.**"[5] The standard replacement for the various forms of **backbiters** is a form of "slander."[6] But the word **backbiters** is certainly not archaic, for even *Sports Illustrated* magazine utilized the word: "That boy was limited, self-centered, frustrated, a pouter, then a bitcher, ultimately a **backbiter** against his coach, Fred Taylor, who once called Knight 'the Brat from Orrville.'"[7]

Badness

And, behold, seven other kine came up after them, poor and very ill favoured and leanfleshed, such as I never saw in all the land of Egypt for **badness:** (Gen 41:19)

Found only once in the AV, **badness** is another example of a common word with a different prefix or suffix than is normally used that is supposed to render the word archaic. **Badness** means inferior or deficient in quality. It is transformed in all of our modern versions to some form of "ugly." But after correcting **badness,** the NASB employed the uncommon word "littleness"[8] and the NRSV, NASB, and NIV each used the word "slowness."[9] The correction of **badness** was unnecessary anyway, for the word is still in use: "Played out from block to block, the results of bad luck, bad health, or just plain **badness** are etched onto brick and concrete, looming as a cautionary backdrop for those who survive another day, an uneasy reminder of how chaotic city life has become."[10]

Banquetings

> For the time past of *our* life may suffice us to have wrought the will of the Gentiles, when we walked in lasciviousness, lusts, excess of wine, revellings, **banquetings,** and abominable idolatries: (1 Pet 4:3)

The word **banquetings** occurs only once in the AV, and although the singular form is also used once,[11] only the plural has been deemed to be archaic. **Banquetings** is a form of the word *banquet,* demonstrating once again that the addition of a suffix is enough to render a word archaic. *Banquet* is a French word meaning "feast" that has been taken into English without a change of form or definition. **Banqueting** is partaking in a ceremonial feast; but it is also overindulgence in luxurious entertainment or gluttony. The word **banqueting** is used in both senses in the AV. The first context is the good one, and is therefore unaltered in our modern versions except for the updating of **banqueting** to "banquet" by the NASB and NIV.[12] The next occurrence of the word is corrected to "carousing" by the NIV and NRSV, but to "drinking parties" in the NASB and NKJV.[13] But upon closer examination, we find that the word rendered "revels" in the NRSV is translated as "carousals" in the NASB.[14] And furthermore, in supplying us with the phrase "drinking parties" where the AV reads **banquetings,** the NASB and NKJV overlooked the warning against "drunkenness" that was already present in the verse.[15] Some may consider the word **banqueting** to be archaic, but not the *Boston Globe:* "The Bible warned them: Be not made a beggar by **banqueting** on borrowing."[16]

Barbarous

> And the **barbarous** people showed us no little kindness: for they kindled a fire, and received us every one, because of the present rain, and because of the cold. (Acts 28:2)

The word **barbarous** is found but once in the AV. It is from the Latin *barbarus,* "foreign." **Barbarous,** like *barbaric* and *barbarian,* is now used exclusively in a bad sense. The word goes back to the Greek *barbaros,* and referred to non-Hellenic language or persons. Then the idea of unpolished speech or uncultured people was attached to the word. It is from *barbaros* that we also get all the forms of the Greek, Latin, French, and English words for *barbarian, barbaric, and barbarism.* **Barbarous** is usually altered in our modern versions to "natives," but the NIV uses "islanders." However, the word **barbarian,** found three times in the AV in the singular[17] and twice in the plural,[18] is translated four different ways in the NIV (islanders, non-Greeks, foreigner, barbarian),[19] three in the NKJV (natives, barbarians, foreigner)[20] and NRSV (natives, barbarians, foreigner),[21] and two in the NASB (natives, barbarians).[22] Yet each one of these occurrences was supposed to be translating the word *barbaros.* The word **barbarous,** however, is presently in use in the 1990's; "For several centuries we insisted that Indians could be 'civilized' and taught English only be removing children from the **'barbarous'** atmosphere of their parents' homes to English-language-only boarding schools where use of Indian languages was absolutely forbidden and punished with physical abuse and humiliation."[23]

Barked

> He hath laid my vine waste, and **barked** my fig tree: he hath made it clean bare, and cast *it* away; the branches thereof are made white. (Joel 1:7)

The word **barked** occurs only once in the AV. There are three distinct words in English formed from *bark.* The first is a dog bark, from the Old English *beorcan.* This can be found as a noun or a verb. The second *bark* word means a small ship, and is from the French *barque.* Although this word is now obsolete as a noun, it is still used as a verb: embark and disembark. However, our word *barge* is actually just a different form of the same word underlying *bark*. The third *bark* word is tree bark, from a common Swedish and Danish word of the same spelling. This word is still utilized as a noun but is archaic when used as a verb like it appears in the AV. To be **barked** is literally to have the bark scraped off. This can also be applied to the skin being rubbed or scraped. Naturally, our modern versions do not employ the word **barked** as a verb. The NRSV and NASB updated **barked** with a form of "splintered," but the NIV and NKJV preferred "ruined." But even though it is not as natural as the connection between *bark* and **barked**, a derivative of a dog bark is a **barker**—a noisy man at the entrance of a show or fair who attempts to entice customers to partake of a particular event.

Bastard

> A **bastard** shall not enter into the congregation of the LORD; even to his tenth generation shall he not enter into the congregation of the LORD. (Deu 23:2)

The word **bastard** appears in the AV twice in the singular and once in the plural.[24] It is from the French word *bastard*, synonymous with *fils de bast*, "child of the packsaddle." Although the word is commonly used today as a term of reproach, a **bastard** is properly an illegitimate child. The term has also been applied to someone of mixed breed. Notwithstanding its frequent use today, our modern versions have all excised it from the Bible. **Bastard** is usually rendered by some form of "illegitimate."[25] However, the NIV utilizes three different phrases,[26] and on one occasion, replaces the single word **bastard** with "born of a forbidden marriage."[27] The word **bastard**, in addition to its common use as a term of censure, is still used today to refer to an illegitimate child.[28]

Battlement

> When thou buildest a new house, then thou shalt make a **battlement** for thy roof, that thou bring not blood upon thine house, if any man fall from thence. (Deu 22:8)

Battlement is found twice in the AV, one of these being in the plural.[29] It is from the French *bastillement*, "fortification," from *bastille*, "fortress," from *bastir*, to build." Our word *bastion* is related to this. A **battlement** is a formation on top of a wall or tower used for defense or protection. Our new translations correspondingly alter **battlement** to "parapet" in one place[30] and "branches" in the other.[31] These alterations were completely unnecessary considering that the word **battlement** remains in vogue today. It is even used when not referring to a castle or fortification, such as this example from *The Seattle Times/Post-Intelligencer:* "The soaring ridges tend to lead the eye and foot on and on, up sweeping grassy swales to lava **battlements**."[32]

Beckoned

> Simon Peter therefore **beckoned** to him, that he should ask who it should be of whom he spake. (John 13:24)

The word **beckoned** appears six times in the AV.[33] The form **beckoning** can be found twice.[34] *Beckon* is strictly an English word and is from the Old English *beacnian,* "to make a sign." This in turn came from *beacen,* "a sign," from which we get the modern word *beacon.* Out of the ten times a form of **beckoned** appears in the AV, the NKJV alone follows the AV text, but only one time.[35] The NASB substitutes five different words or phrases (kept making signs, signaled, gestured, motioning, nodded) in modernizing the AV.[36] The NIV usually alters **beckoned** to "motioned,"[37] but twice it introduces "beckon" where no other version contains the word.[38] The updating of **beckoned** was a little premature, however, for it is still in use today: "Soon American vessels could be found around the world, their captains sailing to wherever profit **beckoned**."[39]

Bedstead

> For only Og king of Bashan remained of the remnant of giants; behold, his **bedstead** *was* a **bedstead** of iron; *is* it not in Rabbath of the children of Ammon? nine cubits *was* the length thereof, and four cubits the breadth of it, after the cubit of a man. (Deu 3:11)

The word **bedstead** appears twice in the AV, but both times in the same verse. It is an English word, a compound of the Old English *bed,* "a bed," and *stede,* "a place." A **bedstead** is literally a place for a bed. It has since come to mean the stand on which a bed is raised. The NASB and NKJV completely forgot to update this archaic word. The NIV and NRSV change **bedstead** to "bed," but this is not entirely accurate. Nevertheless, the word is still being used in the 1990's: "**Bedsteads** were made with sassafras or red buckeye, because it was believed that these woods would not become infested with insects."[40]

Beeves

> *Ye shall offer* at your own will a male without blemish, of the **beeves**, of the sheep, or of the goats. (Lev 22:19)

The word **beeves** occurs seven times in the AV.[41] It is the plural of beef; the singular form *beeve* was derived from the plural. The word originally referred to oxen, but then came to be applied to any fattened beast. Only the NKJV steadily renders the word **beeves** as "cattle."[42] The NASB and NIV prefer cattle, but one time substitute "herd."[43] The NRSV uses "cattle" and "herd" each one time,[44] and "oxen" five times.[45] But if **beeves** made the Bible difficult understand, the alteration of "fear" in the AV to "deference" by the NRSV made it even more so.[46]

Beforetime

> And if the avenger of blood pursue after him, then they shall not deliver the slayer up into his hand; because he smote his neighbour unwittingly, and hated him not **beforetime**. (Josh 20:5)

Beforetime appears eleven times in the AV in ten verses.[47] It is obviously a compound of *before* and *time*. It literally means "the time that was before." We would now say previously or formerly. **Beforetime** is not found in any of our modern versions, although they do not hesitate to use "lifetime," "seedtime," and "mealtime." The word **beforetime** is routinely updated to "formerly."[48] However, the NIV one time uses the archaic "aforethought."[49] On another occasion, the NRSV and NIV upgrade **beforetime** to "beforehand,"[50] but when the AV utilizes "beforehand," they correct it.[51] Our modern versions were very discordant in correcting the word **beforetime**. The NASB uses the word "anytime" although it is not found in any other of our new translations nor the AV.[52] The NKJV three times employs "meantime" when it does not appear in the AV nor any of our modern versions.[53] The NASB uses "noontime" in a verse where the AV and all of our other translations have "noon."[54] The NIV has "daytime" in one passage where all the others including the AV read "day."[55] Notice further the inharmonious contrasts of "daytime" and "night" found in the NASB,[56] "daytime" and "noon" found in the NIV,[57] and "peacetime" and "war" found in the NKJV.[58] Furthermore, the NIV reads "springtime" in one passage where the NASB and NRSV say "spring."[59] After all this, it is incredible that these translations would recast a simple word like **beforetime** used in the AV.

𝕭egat

Abraham **begat** Isaac; and Isaac **begat** Jacob; and Jacob **begat** Judas and his brethren; (Mat 1:2)

The word **begat** occurs 225 times in the AV in 139 verses. **Begat** is the past tense of **beget,** which occurs ten times.[60] Other forms include the past participle **begotten,** occurring twenty-four times,[61] **begettest,** found twice,[62] and **begetteth,** found three times.[63] The compound form **firstbegotten** occurs once as one word and once as two.[64] **Beget** is from the Old English compound *begitan,* "to get." To **beget** is to get additionally, especially in the sense of generating offspring. Forms of this word can scarcely be found in our modern translations. In fact, these forms occur so infrequently that it can be ascertained that the translators of these versions were very careless in their attempt to remove all trace of the words from the text. Only the NKJV retains **begat** on par with the AV, using the alternate form "begot."[65] The NRSV used "begot" in one passage[66] and "beget" in two passages,[67] while the NASB employed "begot" twice[68] and "beget" three times.[69] Both of these versions, however, did make some attempt to continue to use "**begotten.**"[70] The NIV completely excises all constructions of **beget** except for utilizing "begotten" one time.[71] However, the lone "begotten" in the NIV passage applies to just a man, while all references to the Lord Jesus Christ being **begotten** of God have been erased.[72] Although our modern versions considered the word **begat** to be archaic, *Psychology Today* magazine employed the word exactly like the AV uses it: "Celebrity parents may produce celebrity progeny: Janet Leigh **begat** Jamie Lee Curtis, Debbie Reynolds **begat** Carrie Fisher, Kirk Douglas **begat** Michael, Lloyd Bridges **begat** Beau and Jeff, Martin Sheen **begat** Charlie and Emilo, Henry Fonda **begat** Jane and Peter, who **begat** Bridget."[73] The word **begat** is also used by *Psychology Today* when not referring to human births: "The run with the botanical recording **begat** no mood changes, and negligible hormonal changes."[74]

Beggarly

> But now, after that ye have known God, or rather are known of God, how turn ye again to the weak and **beggarly** elements, whereunto ye desire again to be in bondage? (Gal 4:9)

Appearing only once in the AV, the adjective **beggarly** comes from the noun *beggar*, which is from the verb *beg*. **Beggarly** means befitting a beggar, indigent, inadequate, or poverty stricken. Surprisingly, the NRSV and NKJV passed up another opportunity to update a lesser known word: they retain "**beggarly**" in their text. However, the NASB adopts "worthless" and the NIV employs "miserable." Not only is it apparent from the context and the form of the word that **beggarly** does not refer to anything good or worthwhile, the word is still in vogue today: "These things are relative, of course; by the time Witt (who died in 1992 at the age of 83) handed over the reins to Jack in 1957, while retaining his petroleum interests and serving as the presiding genius of the firm, Stephens Inc. was worth a **beggarly** $7.5 million."[75]

Belied

> They have **belied** the LORD, and said, *It is* not he; neither shall evil come upon us; neither shall we see sword nor famine: (Jer 5:12)

Belied, the past tense of *belie,* is also found only one time in the AV. It is of English origin, the Old English form being *beleogan,* formed from the simple word *lie.* **Belie** is a very versatile word signifying to deceive by lying, assert falsely, give a false representation, counterfeit, prove to be false, or contradict.[76]

Naturally, the word is not to be found in any of our modern versions. The usual choice to update the AV is "lied," but the NRSV prefers "spoken falsely." There was no reason to change the word **belied** anyway, for the *Washington Post* did not consider it archaic in 1992: "Though she had shown courage and stoicism that **belied** both her age and her terror, repeated injections of painkillers could not stop her screaming."[77]

Bemoan

> For who shall have pity upon thee, O Jerusalem? or who shall **bemoan** thee? or who shall go aside to ask how thou doest? (Jer 15:5)

The word **bemoan** occurs five times in the AV.[78] The related forms of **bemoaned** and **bemoaning** each appear once.[79] This word appeared in Old English as *bimaenan*, "to lament." To **bemoan** means to bewail, moan over, lament, or express pity for. One would think that the word could be easily updated to *moan*, or even *mourn*, but such is not the case. The NKJV only modernizes the word in one verse.[80] The NRSV retains the word four times,[81] but then uses three other words or expressions (showed sympathy, pleading, mourn) the other three times the word appears in the AV.[82] The word **bemoan** is not found in the NASB. It chooses a form of "console" twice,[83] "grieve" twice,[84] and "mourn" three times.[85] The word of choice for the NIV was "mourn," found four times.[86] The NIV also preferred "comforted," "show sympathy," and "moaning" each one time.[87] The updating was superfluous, however, for **bemoan** can still be found in use today: "We may **bemoan** what we sometimes think of as the 'senseless' violence attendant on the conflicts that arise out of ethnic identity."[88]

Beseech

> I **beseech** you therefore, brethren, by the mercies of God, that ye present your bodies a living sacrifice, holy, acceptable unto God, *which is* your reasonable service. (Rom 12:1)

The word **beseech** appears sixty-seven times in the AV in sixty-four verses,[89] while the form **beseeching** occurs three times.[90] It is an English word formed during the Middle English period from *be* and *seken*, "to seek." Hence, **beseech** can mean to implore, solicit, beg, appeal, or seek. The NIV consistently expurgates this word from the Bible, but our other modern versions were not so dependable. The NKJV retains the word, following the AV reading three times.[91] Likewise the NRSV.[92] The NASB contains a form of the word **beseech** eleven times,[93] but two of these are in verses where the AV does not use the word.[94] And furthermore, the NKJV manifests its inconsistency even more by translating *parakaleo,* usually given in the AV as **beseech,** by five different words (appeal, urge, implore, plead, beg)[95] besides the instances where it renders the word "**beseech.**" The search for alternate words was in vain, for even the *Atlantic Monthly* did not consider the word archaic: "Dasaro's former colleagues are quick to tell of the occasion, after a critical political meeting in 1990, when an embassy official **beseeched** Yeltsin, then the president of the Russian Federation, for information."[96]

Besom

> I will also make it a possession for the bittern, and pools of water: and I will sweep it with the **besom** of destruction, saith the LORD of hosts. (Isa 14:23)

Besom is another word that appears only one time in the AV. It is also another strictly English word. The Old English form was *besma,* "a broom." It was originally an implement for sweeping, then any agent used for cleaning or purifying. **Besom** is expectedly replaced in our modern versions by "broom." But the meaning of the word **besom** is evident from the context since the **besom** is said to be used to "sweep." An interesting sideline to this word is the substitution by our modern versions of "broom tree" for "juniper tree" on several occasions.[97]

Bestead

> And they shall pass through it, hardly **bestead** and hungry: and it shall come to pass, that when they shall be hungry, they shall fret themselves, and curse their king and their God, and look upward. (Isa 8:21)

The word **bestead** is also found only once in the AV. The Middle English form was *bestad,* from *be* and *stad,* "placed."

The word is actually from Old Norse. **Bestead** means placed, beset, or situated unfavorably. The NRSV and NIV each render this as "distressed," but the NASB and NKJV prefer "pressed." Yet when the AV uses a simple word like "dedicated," it replaced in the NRSV by "votive."[98]

Bestir

> And let it be, when thou hearest the sound of a going in the tops of the mulberry trees, that then thou shalt **bestir** thyself: for then shall the LORD go out before thee, to smite the host of the Philistines. (2 Sam 5:24)

Bestir is another word of English origin found only one time in the AV. The Old English form was *bestyrian*, "to heap up." **Bestir** means to stir up or rouse to action, to manifest activity, or to begin to actively move. The meaning is quite apparent from the very form of the word. Our modern versions could not agree on how to render the word. The NRSV reads "be on the alert," the NASB "act promptly," the NIV "move quickly," and the NKJV "advance quickly." The word was so archaic that it was used by *Time* magazine way back in 1988: "Similarly, natural events such as hurricanes can **bestir** pollutants from the sediment."[99]

Bethink

> Yet *if* they **bethink** themselves in the land whither they are carried captive, and turn and pray unto thee in the land of their captivity, saying, We have sinned, we have done amiss, and have dealt wickedly; (2 Chr 6:37)

Occurring twice in the AV,[100] **bethink** is formed from the Old English *bethencan*, "to consider." **Bethink** can mean remember, remind, recall, think, or consider. The connection with the word *think* is obvious. Naturally, **bethink** is updated in our new translations. But once again, they could not decide on how to translate the underlying word. Each time the phrase "**bethink** themselves" occurs in the AV, the NRSV renders it as "come to their senses," the NASB "take thought," the NIV "have a change of heart," and the NKJV "come to themselves." Although **bethink** is not common anymore, the similar form *methinks* is very much in use today: "**Methinks** they live north of the Mason-Dixon line, and should acquire some empathy by going through a winter without heat."[101]

Betimes

> He that spareth his rod hateth his son: but he that loveth him chasteneth him **betimes**. (Prov 13:24)

Betimes appears five times in the AV.[102] It is a compound based on the Old English *tima*, "time." Hence, **betimes** can mean early, in a good time, in due time, early in life, before too late, and while there is yet time. **Betimes** is rendered in a variety of ways in our new versions. Only once is it consistently supplied as "early."[103] Other translations include "persistently,"[104] "diligently,"[105] "earnestly,"[106] and "promptly."[107] One occurrence of **betimes** is simply removed with no replacement.[108] These corrections were unnecessary, for the word **betimes** can even be found in the publication *American Scholar*: "But he promptly attributes the failure of audiences to respond to 'social' themes by saying glibly that 'audiences and reviewers prefer to think of plays wholly in terms of entertainment, or, **betimes**, of art.'"[109]

Bettered

> And had suffered many things of many physicians, and had spent all that she had, and was nothing **bettered,** but rather grew worse, (Mark 5:26)

The word **bettered** appears only once in the AV. The Old English form was *beterian*. This word was obviously formed from the word *better* and means improved, amended, rendered more excellent, or made better. **Bettered** is usually updated in our modern versions to "better," but the NASB prefers "helped." The word was so archaic that it was used by *Health* magazine in 1994: "And no man or woman has ever **bettered** the English Channel record of Penny Dean, an American who in 1978 made her way across the chilly waters in seven hours, 40 minutes."[110]

Betwixt

> For I am in a strait **betwixt** two, having a desire to depart, and to be with Christ; which is far better: (Phil 1:23)

Betwixt appears sixteen times in the AV in fifteen verses.[111]

It is an English word, the Middle English form being *betwix*, and the Old English being *betweohs*. It was formed from *be* and a form of *twa*, "two." **Betwixt** simply means between. Our new translations all modernize **betwixt** to "between," but once again the NASB breaks ranks and substitutes "from both directions" in one passage.[112] The word **betwixt**, however, is still used in the 1990's: "We are **betwixt** and between, trying to find balances where there are none, and everybody gets shorted: our bosses, our husbands and our babies."[113]

Bewail

> And she shall put the raiment of her captivity from off her, and shall remain in thine house, and **bewail** her father and her mother a full month: and after that thou shalt go in unto her, and be her husband, and she shall be thy wife. (Deu 21:13)

The word **bewail** is found six times in the AV.[114] It further appears once under the form of **bewaileth**[115] and three times as **bewailed**.[116] **Bewail** is another strictly English word. Its present form dates back to the Middle English *bewailen*, "to lament." In this case, the *be* functions as an intensive. To **bewail** means to express sorrow, lament, mourn, or bemoan. The NIV completely removes the word, but our other modern versions were not so consistent. The NASB retains this supposedly archaic word once,[117] the NRSV three times,[118] and the NKJV five times.[119] Only twice out of the ten times the AV uses a form of the word do all of our modern versions agree on a modern equivalent.[120] **Bewail** is usually rendered by a form of "weep"[121] or "mourn."[122] Some of the more "up-to-date" renderings include "grasping for breath," found in the NRSV, NIV, and NASB,[123] and "beating their breasts," used once by the NRSV.[124] Moreover, the NRSV inserts the word "bewailed" into a verse where the AV reads "wept."[125] The variety of words and expressions used to correct the AV were all unnecessary, for the word **bewail** was not considered archaic by *The Humanist* magazine: "To hypostatize natural rights and then **bewail** their violation is futile and senseless."[126]

Bewitched

> O foolish Galatians, who hath **bewitched** you, that ye should

not obey the truth, before whose eyes Jesus Christ hath been evidently set forth, crucified among you? (Gal 3:1)

Bewitched, the past tense of *bewitch,* occurs three times in the AV.[127] It is conspicuously a compound of *be* and *witch.* The Old English form was *wiccian,* "to witch," from *wicca* (masculine) and *wicce* (feminine) "a witch." To be **bewitched** means to be affected by witchcraft, enchanted, charmed, or fascinated. The word is altered on two occasions to "amazed" by the NRSV and NIV.[128] However, in these same two passages, the NKJV and NASB preferred a form of "astonish."[129] The interesting thing is that on the third occasion when **bewitched** is used in the AV, all of our modern versions follow suit and forget to update the word.[130] Besides being the name of a television show, the word **bewitched** is also used on a regular basis: "In Virginia the colonists at Jamestown were at first so **bewitched** by the prospect of El Dorado that many of them searched for gold rather than plant crops."[131]

Bewray

Take counsel, execute judgment; make thy shadow as the night in the midst of the noonday; hide the outcasts; **bewray** not him that wandereth. (Isa 16:3)

The word **bewray** appears once in the AV but the form **bewrayeth** can be seen three times.[132] The present form of the word dates back to the Middle English *bewreyen,* "to reveal," formed from the Old English *wregan,* "to accuse." To **bewray** means to reveal, expose, disclose, or simply to betray. Out of the four times a form of the word appears in the AV, it is only updated to "betray" twice by the NRSV[133] and once by the NKJV.[134] Once again, a simple updating of the word was not good enough. And although our modern versions have so much trouble with words in the AV that begin with a *be-* prefix, the NASB, in deference to both the AV and the other new translations, inserted the archaic "benumbed" into the Bible when the AV read "feeble."[135] Moreover, the NIV utilizes the word "befuddled"[136] and the NASB amends "gave" in the AV to "bestowed."[137] The corrections to **bewray** were unnecessary anyway, for unusual words with a *be-* prefix like "bewhiskered"[138] and "bedeviled"[139] are in common use today.

Bier

> And he came and touched the **bier:** and they that bare *him* stood still. And he said, Young man, I say unto thee, Arise. (Luke 7:14)

Bier occurs only twice in the AV.[140] The Old English form, *baer*, is from *beran*, "to carry." The modern spelling is thought to be in imitation of the French *biere*. Hence, a **bier** is a frame or stand on which a corpse or casket is laid on and usually carried. Bier is normally updated to "coffin," but the NRSV forgot to eradicate the word on one occasion.[141] In addition to this, the NIV and NRSV inject "**bier**" into another passage where the word does not appear in the AV.[142] Once again, this archaic word can be found in print in 1994: "The face is covered while the body is being carried on a **bier** but the veil is drawn aside before the chief mourner lights the pyre."[143]

Bishoprick

> For it is written in the book of Psalms, Let his habitation be desolate, and let no man dwell therein: and his **bishoprick** let another take. (Acts 1:20)

Appearing only once in the AV, **bishoprick** is another word of English origin. The Old English construction of the word was *bisceoprice*, formed from *bisceop*, "bishop," and *rice*, "realm." All forms of the word *bishop* ultimately come from the Greek *episkopos*, "overseer." A **bishoprick** is the office of a bishop. Our modern versions unanimously replace this word with something else. The NASB and NKJV use "office," but the NRSV opted for "position of overseer" and the NIV "place of leadership." Not one of our modern versions consistently render this passage as they do the other occurrences of the word "bishop." The same Greek word rendered as **bishoprick** in the AV, and translated as "office of a bishop" in another passage, is rendered "office of an overseer" in the NASB after using just "office" where the AV read "**bishoprick.**"[144] The NIV used "place of leadership" for **bishoprick** but "on being an overseer" for "office of a bishop."[145] The NKJV began with "office" for **bishoprick** but then used "position of a bishop" the next time it translated the same underlying Greek word.[146] And furthermore, the NRSV renders the same Greek word as "bishop" three times,[147] but "guardian" one other,[148] while the NASB favored "overseer" three times[149] and "guardian" once.[150] And finally, the NKJV choose to follow the AV by using "bishop" three times,[151] but then emulated the NIV's "overseer" in the fourth passage where the same Greek word appeared.[152]

Bittern

> But the cormorant and the **bittern** shall possess it; the owl also and the raven shall dwell in it: and he shall stretch out upon it the line of confusion, and the stones of emptiness. (Isa 34:11)

A **bittern** appears on three occasions in the AV.[153] The word is derived from the French *butor*, "a bittor." A **bittern** is a bird similar to a heron. The American **bittern** is classified as *botaurus lentiginosus* and the European **bittern** is classified as *botaurus stellaris*. A small heron like the *ixobrychus exilis* is also called a **bittern**. Our new translations could not decide how to alter the word **bittern**. The NASB consistently preferred "hedgehog."[154] The NRSV liked "hedgehog" twice[155] but selected "screech owl" the third time.[156] The NIV choose "screech owl" twice[157] and just plain "owls" once.[158] The NKJV thought a **bittern** was a "porcupine" on two occasions,[159] but in the end went with the AV reading of "**bittern**."[160] If the translators of these new versions had only subscribed to *Audubon* they would have known that "the [American] **bittern** always lives here in the reeds; here it raises its young."[161]

Blackish

> Which are **blackish** by reason of the ice, *and* wherein the snow is hid: (Job 6:16)

The word **blackish** occurs only once in the AV. This word is another example of a common word with an unusual prefix or suffix added to it, thus making it archaic. **Blackish** is manifestly a compound formed by adding the suffix *-ish* to the substantive *black*. **Blackish** means inclining to black or somewhat black. The NKJV, NIV, and NRSV changed the word to a form of "dark," but the NASB introduced the word "turbid" in case anyone did not understand **blackish**. Moreover, the NASB also corrected plain "black" to "swarthy."[162] The changes to **blackish** were completely unwarranted anyway, for the word **blackish** is still used in the 1990's: "Named for its **blackish** pigmentation, the substantia nigra is the brain's main supplier of dopamine, a neurotransmitter that helps regulate movement."[163]

𝕭lains

> And it shall become small dust in all the land of Egypt, and shall be a boil breaking forth *with* **blains** upon man, and upon beast, throughout all the land of Egypt. (Exo 9:9)

The word **blains,** the plural of *blain,* occurs twice in the AV.[164] The word is of English origin and is from *blegen,* "a boil." A **blain** is an inflammatory swelling or sore; a boil, blister, lesion, or pustule. The word is either found in our modern versions as "sores"[165] or the context is rearranged to give us "festering boils."[166] The context of the AV was said to be "a boil breaking forth" so it is obvious that **blains** could not possibly be anything healthy or pleasant. A **blain** is still listed in medical dictionaries as "a lesion on the skin."[167]

𝕭lasting

> I smote you with **blasting** and with mildew and with hail in all the labours of your hands; yet ye *turned* not to me, saith the LORD. (Hag 2:17)

The word **blasting** is used five times in the AV[168] and is formed by adding the suffix *-ing* to the noun *blast.* The verb is also derived from the noun *blast,* the Old English form being *blaest,* "a blowing." A **blasting** can be the production of blasts of wind or breath, or it can be the withering caused by atmospheric conditions. **Blasting** is normally translated "blight" in our modern versions,[169] but sometimes "scorching"[170] or "scorching wind."[171] The NRSV halfway slips up one time and employs "**blasting** wind."[172] The word **blasting** is often used when referring to sound, wind, or voice travelling through the air. Two examples will suffice: "In February, Cynthia Struzik, an FWS special agent, fired off a letter to the Alameda County Planning Department, **blasting** not only the installation but also the proposed study."[173] "Amid the cacophony of diesel-driven reconstruction and loudspeakers **blasting** street-corner bingo games, Phnom Penh's mood is no longer somber."[174]

Blaze

> But he went out, and began to publish *it* much, and to **blaze** abroad the matter, insomuch that Jesus could no more openly enter into the city, but was without in desert places: and they came to him from every quarter. (Mark 1:45)

Blaze, found only once in the AV, is another English word that comes from the Old English form of *blaesan,* "to blow." The word originally meant to blow a trumpet or sound an alarm. To **blaze** means to make known, proclaim, or publish; to be conspicuous with brilliancy of character. This word also means a flame or fire, and is the only way it is used in our new translations; the verbal form having been banished. **Blaze** is unanimously rendered by a form of "spread." Yet **blaze** is commonly used all the time without referring to a fire. Sometimes it is utilized in the sense of leading in the discovery of a new method, activity, or course: "And robotic spacecraft will **blaze** a path in space for humans once again."[175] The word **blaze** is also found in usage parallel to the AV: "As they arrived in a **blaze** of publicity, an astronomer I know was visiting friends in Argentina."[176]

Blueness

> The **blueness** of a wound cleanseth away evil: so *do* stripes the inward parts of the belly. (Prov 20:30)

Blueness appears in only one instance in the AV. It is visibly formed from the suffix *-ness* added to the word *blue*. **Blueness** is the state or quality of being blue, the mark of a bruise, or a state of depression. This simple compound word has been changed in all of our modern versions. Where the AV has "the **blueness** of a wound," the NRSV reads "blows that wound," the NASB "stripes that wound," and the NKJV "blows that hurt." The maverick NIV renders this "blows and wounds." But is **blueness** archaic? How many times do we hear of someone being beaten "black and blue"? What about someone holding their breath until they turn blue? Blue disease, technically known as cyanosis, is "a condition of **blueness** seen particularly about the face and extremities, accompanying states in which the blood is not properly ogenated."[177] The connotation of blue as pertaining to the human body is always bad: And as I'm sure you know, high fever, difficulty breathing, loss of consciousness, as well as any unusual skin color such as extreme realness, **blueness**, or severe paleness, cold clammy skin, chest pain, or severe burns, injuries, or any other serious symptoms, require professional medical advice as soon as possible."[178]

Bolled

And the flax and the barley was smitten: for the barley *was* in the ear, and the flax *was* **bolled**. (Exo 9:31)

Bolled, occurring one time in the AV, is from the Old Norse *bolginn*, "swollen." The root word also made its way into Old English as *bolla*, "a bowl." To be **bolled** is to be swollen or inflated, as in the bud of a plant. The NKJV, NASB, and NRSV all update this word to "in bud," but once again the renegade NIV prefers "in bloom." Yet as any Southern Farmer knows, a boll is a rounded seed vessel or pod of a plant, as of flax or cotton, and the *anthonomus grandis,* better known as the boll weevil, is a snout beetle that attacks the bolls of cotton. Tomato fruit worms are also known as "cotton boll worms."[179]

Bolster

And Michal took an image, and laid *it* in the bed, and put a pillow of goats' hair for his **bolster,** and covered *it* with a cloth. (1 Sam 19:13)

The word **bolster** appears six times in the AV.[180] It comes up unchanged from the Old English *bolster.* A **bolster** is a pillow or cushion or anything resembling them used as a means of support. All six times the word shows up in the AV, it is rendered "head" in our modern versions.[181] But from this original usage has come the modern sense of **bolster**: to uphold, support, or add to. This modern sense of the word occurs regularly: "There are several steps that African nations must take in order to **bolster** cooperation."[182]

Bondmen

I *am* the LORD your God, which brought you forth out of the land of Egypt, that ye should not be their **bondmen;** and I have broken the bands of your yoke, and made you go upright. (Lev 26:13)

The word **bondmen** occurs seventeen times in the AV,[183] and is the most common form of the compounds formed from the word *bond.* **Bondwoman** appears eight times,[184] **bondman** six times,[185] **bondwomen** three times,[186] and **bondmaid** twice.[187] **Bondservant, bondservice,** and **bondmaids** each appear once respectively.[188] The prefix *bond-* originally referred to a householder, peasant, or serf. Then, someone in slavery or bondage. Thus, the meaning has gone from bond to bound. These words have all but disappeared in our modern versions. It is enlightening, however, to see the inconsistent and discordant way that these words were handled. The word **bondman** is unanimously altered to "slave" by all of our modern versions.[189] So is **bondservant** the one time it appears,[190] **bondwomen** the three times it occurs,[191] and **bondmaids** the two times it is found.[192] But that is where the coinciding stops. The word **bondmen** is usually rendered as "slaves,"[193] but sometimes as "bondage" or "slavery."[194] **Bondservice** is corrected to "slave labor" in the NRSV, "forced laborers" in the NASB, "slave labor force" in the NIV, and "forced labor" in the NKJV.[195] **Bondmaid** is not translated at all in one passage in the NKJV.[196] After altering **bondmen** to "slaves" on fourteen occasions,[197] the NKJV eight times corrects "servant" in the AV to "**bondservant**,"[198] using the term seven more times than it appears in the AV.[199] The NKJV also nine times corrects "servants" to "bondservants,"[200] a word that does not occur in the AV. Then the NKJV alters **bondmaid** to "**bondwoman.**"[201] The NASB forgot to update **bondwoman** in four passages[202] after correcting it four times,[203] and then revised **bondmaid** to "**bondwoman.**"[204] The NASB calls Hagar a "maid" twice[205] but a "**bondwoman**" two other times.[206] The NASB also modifies several different words (handmaid, maiden, servant) to "bondslave."[207] The NIV edits **bondwoman** to "maidservant,"[208] but then turns around and corrects the AV when it reads "maidservant."[209] Then, after disdaining these compound words, the NASB corrects the AV reading of "man that kept the watch" to "watchman,"[210] and the AV reading of "of cunning work" to "the work of a skillful workman."[211]

Bosses

> He runneth upon him, *even* on *his* neck, upon the thick **bosses** of his bucklers: (Job 15:26)

The word **bosses,** the plural of *boss,* occurs only once in the AV. It comes from the French *boce,* "hump." **Bosses** are knobs or projections protruding from a flat surface, usually ornamental or architectural in nature. The familiar word *boss,* as in employer, is a homonym. It is from the Dutch *baas,* "master." The NRSV unnecessarily altered the form of "thick **bosses**" found in the AV to "thick-bossed." Our other modern versions could not get together on a translation. The NASB selected "massive," the NIV "think, strong," and the NKJV "strong, embossed." The term *boss,* however, is still used today in a variety of forms besides working for a boss. *Boss* is used as an expression for cool, nice, great, or first-rate. Ford had a 302 Boss and a 429 Boss engine for their Mustang. *Boss* is still used as a medical term for "a circumscribed rounded swelling."[212] And the word *boss* is still employed as it is in the AV: "Sales chief Michele Scannavini admits he's asked for a new design that reverts to three spokes and a smaller wheel **boss.**"[213]

Botch

> The LORD will smite thee with the **botch** of Egypt, and with the emerods, and with the scab, and with the itch, whereof thou canst not be healed. (Deu 28:27)

Botch can be seen on two occasions in the AV.[214] It is akin to *boss* and is from the French *boche,* "a swelling." A **botch** is a bump, pimple, tumor, boil, swelling, or eruptive disease. Our new translations unanimously update the word to "boils."[215] Yet when the AV uses the term "boils," the NIV and NRSV change it to "sores."[216] Once again, this manifests the tendency of these modern versions to frivolously alter the text of the AV, for the word **botch** is still defined as "an inflammatory sore spot (as a boil or ulcer)."[217]

Bowels

> Now this man purchased a field with the reward of iniquity; and falling headlong, he burst asunder in the midst, and all his **bowels** gushed out. (Acts 1:18)

Bowels appears thirty-nine times in the AV in thirty-seven verses.[218] The word comes from the French *boel*, from a Latin word meaning "a sausage." **Bowels** can be the interior of anything, although the term is commonly applied to internal body organs in general and the intestines in particular. It also has the meaning of compassionate feelings. The NKJV completely removes the word, but our other modern versions slip up and leave it in on several occasions. The word **bowels** is variously rendered in our modern versions as "affections,"[219] "hearts,"[220] "stomach,"[221] "entrails,"[222] "body,"[223] "intestines,"[224] and "womb."[225] In one passage where **bowels** is found, the simple word *belly* is altered by the NASB and NIV to "abdomen,"[226] while converting the phrase "fifth rib" in the AV to "belly."[227] In spite of these manifold corrections, the NRSV neglects to remove **bowels** on six occasions,[228] the NASB forgets five times,[229] and the NIV overlooks this archaic word four times.[230] After leaving **bowels** in the text as it stands, the NASB in one verse gives us "and make your womb discharge, your uterus drop!" in opposition to all other modern versions.[231] Even today, however, the word **bowels** can be found not applied to the intestines: "These cosmic wraths only reveal themselves when the great torrent of other radiation is absent, which is why the enormous cavern has been built in the **bowels** of the earth."[232]

Bray

> Though thou shouldest **bray** a fool in a mortar among wheat with a pestle, *yet* will not his foolishness depart from him. (Prov 27:22)

The word **bray** can be found twice in the AV[233] and the form **brayed** can be seen once.[234] **Bray** has two distinct meanings, each of which is derived from different words. To **bray** as in our text comes from the French *breier*, "to crush." Thus, to **bray** means to beat, bruise, pound, or crush. **Bray** also means to cry out or make a roaring noise. This usage is from the French *braire*, "to cry." Two examples of this type can be found in the AV: one referring to the **bray** of a donkey,[235] and the other to men.[236] The passage mentioning the **bray** of a donkey is left unscathed in our modern versions.[237] The word **brayed** is also retained, except for the NASB.[238] But it is the use of the word in the phrase "**bray** a fool" that brings out the best in our up-to-date translations. The NASV prefers "crush," the NASB "pound," but the NIV and NKJV fancied "grind."[239] **Bray** might be archaic, but the use of "acquisition" by the NASB when the AV said "price" is certainly not updating the AV into modern English.[240]

𝔅𝔯𝔢𝔢𝔠𝔥𝔢𝔰

And thou shalt make them linen **breeches** to cover their nakedness; from the loins even unto the thighs they shall reach: (Exo 28:42)

Found five times in the AV,[241] **breeches** is from the Old English *brec,* plural of *broc,* "garment for loins and thighs." The breech is the lower part of the trunk of the body or anything else for that matter. Thus, **breeches** came to mean the garment to cover this area. The term was then applied to knee-length trousers. Naturally, the word is routinely changed in our modern versions. The NKJV consistently adopts the translation of "trousers."[242] The NRSV and NIV unwaveringly use "undergarments."[243] The NASB altered **breeches** to "undergarments" three times,[244] but forgot to eradicate the word on two occasions.[245] All these emendations notwithstanding, the *New Republic* did not consider the word **breeches** in reference to clothing to be archaic: "'Old Timers Games,' painful exercises in which aged pros of summers long past gather in their knee **breeches** for a less-than-brisk three innings, have been gaining steadily in popularity."[246] The term **breech** is also commonly used to refer to the birth of a baby feet first.[247]

𝔅𝔯𝔦𝔠𝔨𝔨𝔦𝔩𝔫

Take great stones in thine hand, and hide them in the clay in the **brickkiln,** which *is* at the entry of Pharaoh's house in Tahpanhes, in the sight of the men of Judah; (Jer 43:9)

A **brickkiln** is mentioned three times in the AV.[248] It is a combination of *brick* and *kiln,* a kiln being a furnace or oven for burning, baking, or drying something, and especially for firing pottery or baking bricks. The Old English form of *kiln* was *cyln,* borrowed from the Latin *culina,* "a kitchen," hence *culinary,* "pertaining to the kitchen." Although the same Hebrew word is used in all three instances of **brickkiln** in the AV, our new versions use six different phrases to translate the word. Three times there appears a form of "brickworks,"[249] and twice we see "brick mold"[250] and "pavement."[251] "Brickmaking,"[252] "brick terrace,"[253] and "brick courtyard"[254] each appear once. But after making all these corrections, the NASB and the NKJV each neglected to remove the word **brickkiln** from one passage.[255] Then the NASB alters "furnace" in the AV to "kiln" on two occasions,[256] while the NRSV does it three times.[257] If one did not know the meaning of *kiln,* at least the prefix *brick-* would help clarify its meaning. But to substitute "kiln" for "furnace" contradicts any claim to be translating into modern English.

Brigandine

> Against *him that* bendeth let the archer bend his bow, and against *him that* lifteth himself up in his **brigandine:** and spare ye not her young men; destroy ye utterly all her host. (Jer 51:3)

The word **brigandine** appears once in the AV along with the plural **brigandines.**[258] **Brigandine** is from the French *brigantine,* "armor for a brigand." A brigand is an irregular soldier, a robber, bandit, or desperado. Thus, **brigandine** is truly armor for a brigand. Naturally, this word does not appear in our modern versions. Only the NIV and NKJV consistently supply the translation of "armor."[259] The NASB presents us with the arduous "scale-armor."[260] The NRSV further confuses matters by employing "coats of mail,"[261] which is no more understandable than **brigandine.** Actually, **brigandine** is not as archaic as one would think. Our modern words brig, brigade, and brigadier are all ultimately derived, like **brigandine,** from the Italian *brigare,* "to fight."

Brimstone

Then the LORD rained upon Sodom and upon Gomorrah

brimstone and fire from the LORD out of heaven; (Gen 19:24)

Brimstone appears fifteen times in the AV,[262] six of these in the familiar expression "fire and brimstone."[263] Brimstone is an English word, the Old English form being *brynstan*, a compound of *burn* and *stone*. Burn is from *brin*, a stem of *brinnen*, "to burn." This developed into *brim-* due to its association with the adjective *brim*, "fierce."[264] Brimstone is sulphur. Although the NKJV and NASB follow the AV in retaining brimstone, the NIV and NRSV omit the word completely. The preferred translation of the NIV for "fire and brimstone" is "burning sulphur."[265] The NRSV opts for "sulphur" instead of brimstone most of the time.[266] However, the term brimstone is very much in vogue today, both literally and in the expression "fire and brimstone." First is the *Atlanta Journal & Constitution:* "For years, when the United States pressed Japan to spend more in its own defense, the opposition parties, media and intellectuals threatened fire and brimstone if the limit were touched."[267] The word is also used in its true sense: "Ancient mariners used to think that the exhalations of whales were poisonous—a caustic mixture of sulfur and brimstone, which could strip the flesh from any man who chanced too close."[268]

Broided

In like manner also, that women adorn themselves in modest apparel, with shamefacedness and sobriety; not with broided hair, or gold, or pearls, or costly array; (1 Tim 2:9)

Appearing only once in the AV, broided is formed from *broiden*, the past participle of *braid*, meaning to plait or interweave. Expectedly, all of our modern versions update the word to "braided." Yet when the AV uses a simple word like "porch," it is regularly corrected in our modern versions to "portico."[269] The NIV likewise "updates" the AV word "porch" to "colonnade."[270]

Broidered

Thus wast thou decked with gold and silver; and thy raiment was of fine linen, and silk, and broidered work; thou didst eat fine flour, and honey, and oil: and thou wast exceeding beautiful, and thou didst prosper into a kingdom. (Ezek 16:13)

The word **broidered** occurs eight times in the AV.[271] It is the past tense of *broider,* which is from the French *broder,* "to stitch." **Broidered** means embroidered or adorned with needlework. Excepting one passage,[272] this word is updated to "embroidered" or "embroidery" in all of our modern versions.[273] However, when the AV reads "embroider," it is corrected to "weave" in the NASB and NIV, "skillfully weave" in the NKJV, and "make" in the NASB.[274] Moreover, when the AV uses a one-syllable word like "made," it is replaced in the NKJV with "fostered."[275]

Bruit

> *There is* no healing of thy bruise; thy wound is grievous: all that hear the **bruit** of thee shall clap the hands over thee: for upon whom hath not thy wickedness passed continually? (Nahum 3:19)

Bruit, found twice in the AV,[276] is from a French word of the same spelling meaning a rumor. It in turn comes from the noun form, *bruire,* "to make a noise." Thus, a **bruit** can be a rumor, report, sound, or noise; also, renown, reputation, or fame. **Bruit** is remotely related to *bray.* This supposedly archaic word is normally rendered by our modern versions as "news"[277] or "report,"[278] but is still in vogue today: "'The Diniz kidnapping was nothing more than a little **bruit** during the campaign,' said the prominent Brazilian journalist Boris Casoy."[279]

Brutish

> Whoso loveth instruction loveth knowledge: but he that hateth reproof *is* **brutish.** (Prov 12:1)

The word **brutish** occurs eleven times in the AV.[280] It is an adjective formed from *brute,* which is from the French *brut,* "heavy, dull." To be **brutish** is to be stupid, bestial, slow, uncivilized, brutal, crude, cruel, or without understanding. This word is translated a variety of ways in our modern versions. The two preferred renderings are "senseless"[281] and "stupid."[282] Only in one instance do our new translations agree with each other.[283] Besides "senseless" and "stupid," there are seven other ways that **brutish** is updated. The NKJV uses "foolish" and "dull-hearted."[284] The NIV one times employs "ignorant."[285] On one occasion, the NIV, NKJV, and NASB all utilize "brutal."[286] The NRSV tries to get creative with "dolt," "dullard," and "dullest" each used once.[287] But after taking the trouble to alter **brutish** in four different ways, the NASB retained the word in one passage.[288] And not only the NASB, for *Forbes* magazine tendered the word also: "Whether you're innocent or not, tax audits are too often nasty, **brutish** and long."[289]

𝔅𝔲𝔠𝔨𝔩𝔢𝔯

As for God, his way *is* perfect: the word of the LORD is tried: he *is* a **buckler** to all those that trust in him. (Psa 18:30)

The term **buckler** can be found eleven times in the AV in the singular[290] and five times in the plural.[291] It comes into English by way of the French *bocler*, from *boucle*, "a shield." The Latin root of both *buckle* and **buckler** possessed the meanings of both words. A *buccula* was the cheek strap of a helmet or the boss of a shield. Hence, besides the word *buckle*, the word **buckler** is also akin to *botch, boss,* and *bulge*. A **buckler** is a round shield held by a grip. It can also refer to any means of defense; thus, one can be a **buckler** in the sense of a defender. Our modern versions usually correct **buckler** to "shield."[292] Yet when the AV reads "shield and **buckler**," **buckler** is usually left alone.[293] **Buckler** is also rendered in the NKJV as "defense,"[294] the NASB as "bulwark,"[295] and the NIV as "rampart."[296] All told, this archaic word is retained seven times in the NKJV[297] and NRSV.[298] The NASB forgets to be up-to-date five times[299] and the NIV forgets about the word once.[300] Then for good measure, the NRSV alters "shield" in the AV to "**buckler**."[301] The word, **buckler**, however, is still currently in use, for an article that appeared in 1995 in the *Economist* about the president of France was entitled "Swashing His **Buckler**."[302]

𝔅𝔲𝔣𝔣𝔢𝔱

And lest I should be exalted above measure through the abundance of the revelations, there was given to me a thorn in the flesh, the messenger of Satan to **buffet** me, lest I should be exalted above measure. (2 Cor 12:7)

Buffet occurs twice in the AV,[303] while the form **buffeted** appears three times.[304] **Buffet** comes from the French *buffet*, "a blow." To **buffet** is to strike, beat, or contend against. In addition to modernizing the word to a form of "beat,"[305] other translations in our modern versions include "roughly treated,"[306] "brutally treated,"[307] "torment,"[308] "strike,"[309] and forms of "struck."[310] However, in one familiar passage of the AV, the NASB and NKJV preserve the word **buffet**,[311] thereby demonstrating their incomplete updating of the text into modern English. Yet the word did not need to be rendered into modern English in the first place; it was already part of modern English: "Gas pressure behind the advancing shock wave is so much higher than that normally found in the interstellar medium that the shock wave will **buffet** and squeeze the solar wind into a much smaller region around the Sun."[312]

Bulrush

> Is it such a fast that I have chosen? a day for a man to afflict his soul? *is it* to bow down his head as a **bulrush,** and to spread sackcloth and ashes *under him?* wilt thou call this a fast, and an acceptable day to the LORD? (Isa 58:5)

Bulrush can be found in the AV twice in the more commonly known plural[313] and once in the singular.[314] The Old English form was *bulrysche,* the word being a compound of *bul* and *rush,* neither of which seem to have anything to do with its meaning. However, *bul* is a variation of *bole,* "trunk," and *rush* means "a plant." A **bulrush** is a tall aquatic plant or a cattail. It can include any rush of the genus *scirpus, juncus,* or *typha.* **Bulrush** is several times altered to "papyrus"[315] or "reed."[316] The NASB one time used "wicker" to update **bulrush.**[317] But with all these corrections, the NKJV still followed the AV twice,[318] and even the NRSV forgot to expunge **bulrush** on one occasion.[319] The updating to "papyrus" and "reed" notwithstanding, the term **bulrushes** is still in use today: "In such a case, says Euliss, cattails might gain a foothold in waters where salt-tolerant **bulrushes** formerly thrived."[320]

Bunches

The burden of the beasts of the south: into the land of trouble and anguish, from whence *come* the young and old lion, the viper and fiery flying serpent, they will carry their riches upon the shoulders of young asses, and their treasures upon the **bunches** of camels, to a people *that* shall not profit *them*. (Isa 30:6)

The word **bunches** is found three times in the AV.[321] It was originally synonymous with *bulch, bouch, bulge,* and *botch,* and signified a hump, bump, swelling, or tumor. It also came to mean a cluster of things of the same kind, either growing or fastened together. **Bunches** is used in the AV once in the former[322] and twice in the later.[323] It is the first usage that is deemed archaic, for all our modern versions change **bunches** to "hump."[324] Yet in the two other instances where the word **bunches** has the common meaning of the word today, it is altered to "clusters" and "cakes" in the NKJV.[325] The NIV prefers "cakes" both times.[326] The NASB and NRSV could not agree on which word to correct the AV reading so the NRSV retained **bunches** the first time and altered it to "clusters" the second,[327] while the NASB revised **bunches** to "clusters" the first time and left it alone the second.[328] This demonstrates that even when words are used as they are in the twentieth century, they still are not safe from the scalpel of modern scholarship.

𝕭𝖚𝖙𝖑𝖊𝖗𝖘𝖍𝖎𝖕

And he restored the chief butler unto his **butlership** again; and he gave the cup into Pharaoh's hand: (Gen 40:21)

The word **butlership** appears only once in the AV. It is obviously a compound of *butler* and *ship,* signifying the office of a butler. The NKJV follows the AV reading, but the NIV prefers "position" and the NASB "office." These are admissible, but the NRSV rendering of "cupbearing" is obscure, for anyone knows what a butler is; few would understand the duties of a "cupbearer," other than to bear cups. The suffix *-ship* is in common use today and refers to state, condition, quality, office, or rank. Although correcting **butlership,** our modern versions usually retain "apostleship" where the AV contains the word.[329] Likewise, when the AV reads "stewardship," the NKJV and NASB follow it exactly.[330] The NKJV alone injects the word "eldership."[331] What is enigmatic is that after revising the word

butlership, the NRSV alters "kingdom" in the AV to "kingship" nine different times.[332] The NIV follows suit seven times[333] and the NASB once.[334] Although the word does not appear in the AV, the NIV also introduces "leadership" into its text.[335] Yet we are to believe that the AV was updated because it was hard to understand.

By and by

> And she came in straightway with haste unto the king, and asked, saying, I will that thou give me **by and by** in a charger the head of John the Baptist. (Mark 6:25)

The expression **by and by** occurs four times in the AV.[336] **By and by** originally meant immediately or at once, but like the word *anon,* later came to mean before long or soon. The customary translation in our modern versions is "immediately,"[337] but "at once,"[338] "quickly,"[339] "right now,"[340] and "right away"[341] can also be found. But in the twentieth century we still say *by and large,* meaning "without entering into details" or "in a general aspect."

Chapter 3
Calve to Curious

Calve

> Knowest thou the time when the wild goats of the rock bring forth? *or* canst thou mark when the hinds do **calve**? (Job 39:1)

The word **calve** occurs twice in the AV,[1] while the forms **calved** and **calveth** each appear once.[2] **Calve** is from the Old English *cealfian,* from *cealf,* "calf," and refers to an animal giving birth to a calf. Surprisingly, the NKJV both retain a form of the AV reading once,[3] the NRSV twice,[4] and the NASB three times.[5] But after correcting the AV three times, the NIV inserts "**calved**" into a passage where neither the AV nor any other modern version contained the word.[6] No occurrence of any form of **calve** should have been corrected in the first place, for the word is still in vogue today: "The wildebeest that migrate north from the Serengeti plains give birth in January and February, while the wildebeest that migrate west from the Loita Hills **calve** in April."[7]

Canker

> And their word will eat as doth a **canker**: of whom is Hymenaeus and Philetus; (2 Tim 2:17)

The word **canker** appears only once in the AV, as does the form **cankered**.[8] However, a **cankerworm** is mentioned six times.[9] The word **canker,** whether from the Old English *cancer* or the French *cancre,* is ultimately derived from the Latin *cancer.* A **canker** is a sore, ulcer, or malignant growth. It was formerly a doublet of *cancer* but is now limited to just a sore in the mouth. A **canker** can also refer to anything that corrupts or destroys;

hence, a **cankerworm**. The word **canker** was also formerly applied to tarnish, rust, or corrosion. Naturally, our modern versions remove all forms of the word **canker**. The NKJV replaces **canker** with "cancer," the other translations utilizing "gangrene."[10] **Cankered** is corrected to "rusted" by the NRSV and NASB but "corroded" by the NKJV and NIV.[11] Yet when it comes to the **cankerworm**, our modern versions could not decide what to call it. It is usually altered to a form of "locust," described as either "hopping,"[12] "creeping,"[13] "young,"[14] "great,"[15] or "crawling."[16] But when the AV mentions a "locust," it is changed by the NRSV to a "cicada."[17] The correction of the various forms of **canker** was premature, for not only can tomatoes be infected with "bacterial **canker**,"[18] so can trees: "The crew used knives and hatchets to rip off bark around **cankers** to find the **canker** margin, then used a leather punch to put holes in around the margin."[19]

Carbuncle

> Thou hast been in Eden the garden of God; every precious stone was thy covering, the sardius, topaz, and the diamond, the beryl, the onyx, and the jasper, the sapphire, the emerald, and the **carbuncle,** and gold: the workmanship of thy tabrets and of thy pipes was prepared in thee in the day that thou wast created. (Ezek 28:13)

A **carbuncle** is mentioned in the AV three times in the singular[20] and once in the plural.[21] The word comes from the Latin *carbunculus*, "a small coal." A **carbuncle** is a precious stone, supposedly of a glowing red color. Due to the association of a **carbuncle** with its other meaning of an inflammation under the skin, our modern versions have rejected this word. It is usually replaced with "emerald," but the NIV preferred "beryl."[22] Yet when the AV mentions a "sapphire," something available at any jeweler in the twentieth century, the NASB incredibly alters it to a "lapis lazuli."[23] And when the AV mentions the common "topaz," the NRSV transforms it to a "chrysolite" even though all of the other versions read as the AV.[24] Moreover, the NRSV and NIV each refer to the unintelligible "carnelian."[25] And furthermore, the simple mention of "gold" in the AV is revised to "nuggets" by the NIV in spite of the fact that the new translations all read "gold" as the AV.[26]

Care

Casting all your **care** upon him; for he careth for you. (1 Pet 5:7)

The word **care** occurs twenty times in the AV.[27] Also used are **careful**, found seven times,[28] **careless**, found five times,[29] **cared**, found three times,[30] **careth**, found seven times,[31] **carefully**, found four times,[32] **carefulness**, also appearing four times,[33] **carelessly**, found three times,[34] **cares**, also occurring three times,[35] **caring**, found once,[36] and **carest**, found three times.[37] Care, from the Old English *caru*, is employed in a variety of ways in the AV. The two basic meanings are concern, inclination, or protection, and trouble, worry, or anxiety. It is the latter meaning that has been deemed archaic, for in the AV, to be **careful** is to be full of grief or anxiety and to have **care** is to have trouble or anxiety. The archaic forms of **care** are updated in ways that are too numerous to discuss. Yet at least **care** is a word that is easily recognized, unlike "Sheol," used by the NKJV, NRSV, and NASB in place of "hell" in the AV.[38]

Carnal

Because the **carnal** mind *is* enmity against God: for it is not subject to the law of God, neither indeed can be. (Rom 8:7)

The word **carnal** is used eleven times in the AV[39] and the form **carnally** can be found an additional four times.[40] Carnal is from the Latin *carnalis*, "fleshly." It can mean sensual, fleshly, worldly, secular, not spiritual, or pertaining to or characterized by the passions and appetites of the flesh or body. The NKJV is the only modern version that retains any form of these words, except for the NASB neglecting to remove "**carnally**" once.[41] The NKJV kept "**carnal**" seven times[42] and "**carnally**" every time it appeared in the AV.[43] It even added "**carnally**" two more times where the AV did not use the word.[44] Carnal is normally updated by the other translations to "flesh,"[45] "worldly,"[46] and "material."[47] **Carnally** refers to sexual intercourse three times and is usually translated in our modern versions by forms of "intercourse,"[48] or "relations."[49] The word **carnal**, however, besides appearing in the modern expression "**carnal** knowledge," as in "**carnal** knowledge of a child under 12 was considered a capital offense,"[50] can also be found in other contexts: "He highlights what it means to be both spiritual and **carnal.**"[51]

Carriage

> So they turned and departed, and put the little ones and the cattle and the **carriage** before them. (Judg 18:21)

The word **carriage** is found in the AV three times in the singular[52] and three times in the plural.[53] It is from the French *cariage*, from *carier*, "to carry." Thus, **carriage** literally means "that which is carried." We would now say luggage, baggage, or belongings. Since they obviously limited the meaning of **carriage** to a four-wheeled vehicle, our modern versions have updated every occurrence of these words, except for the NKJV, which forgot to remove "**carriages**" in one passage.[54] Although this word was regularly corrected, the new translations could not decide on how to update it. Some of the revisions of **carriage** include "goods,"[55] "valuables,"[56] "baggage,"[57] "possessions,"[58] "things you carry,"[59] "equipment,"[60] and "supplies."[61] Moreover, in one verse where the AV read "chariots," the NIV altered it to "**carriages**" even though the other modern versions followed the AV.[62] But the word **carriage** should not have been a problem in the first place, for as it is formed from the verb *carry*, so luggage is formed from the verb *lug*.

Caul

> And he took all the fat that *was* upon the inwards, and the **caul** *above* the liver, and the two kidneys, and their fat, and Moses burned *it* upon the altar. (Lev 8:16)

The word **caul** occurs eleven times in the AV with a literal meaning,[63] once with a figurative meaning,[64] and once in the plural with an entirely different connotation.[65] **Caul** is from the French *cale*, "a small cap." The **cauls** mentioned once in the AV are close fitting caps or nets worn by women on their head. Our modern versions render **cauls** as "headbands," except for the NKJV, which preferred "scarves."[66] The other meaning of **caul** is a membrane or fatty tissue that surrounds an organ in the body of a man or animal. The term **caul** has also been applied to the membrane enclosing a baby in the womb and sometimes covering the head at birth. Although our modern versions united in their attempt to excise the word **caul** from the Bible, they could not agree on what to replace it with. The NRSV chose "appendage," the NIV "covering," the NKJV "fatty lobe," and the NASB "lobe."[67] But the word **caul** is still in vogue today in both a medical and a scientific sense. From *Natural History* we read: "A child born with a red **caul**, or amniotic membrane, covering its head was regarded as a potential vampire."[68] And from another issue of *Natural History:* "The true face of Venus was finally revealed when radar measurements pierced the obscuring **caul** of carbon dioxide and sulfuric acid vapor."[69]

Ceiled

> And the greater house he **ceiled** with fir tree, which he overlaid with fine gold, and set thereon palm trees and chains. (2 Chr 3:5)

The word **ceiled**, formed from *ceil,* appears four times in the AV.[70] It is from the French verb *ceil,* from a noun of the same form meaning a canopy. The original Latin word that this comes from is *caelum,* meaning the heaven or sky. To ceil is to cover or line the interior of something, hence, our word *ceiling.* Our modern versions unanimously update the word **ceiled**, although they all use the derivative "ceiling."[71] The usual replacement for **ceiled** is a form of "paneled,"[72] but "covered" was also employed.[73] Yet when the AV mentions the cherubims "covering" the mercy seat, the NIV and NRSV change it to "overshadowing" the mercy seat.[74]

Celestial

> *There are* also **celestial** bodies, and bodies terrestrial: but the glory of the **celestial** *is* one, and the *glory* of the terrestrial *is* another. (1 Cor 15:40)

The word **celestial** appears twice in the AV in the same verse. It is from a French word of the same spelling that comes from the Latin *caelestis,* "heavenly," from *caelum,* "sky or heaven." **Celestial** means heavenly or pertaining to the sky or heavens. Only the NKJV retains this word, the other translations changing it to "heavenly." Yet after just correcting the AV, the NIV inserts the word "**celestial**" into two other passages where neither the AV nor any other modern version contained the word.[75] The updating of **celestial** was unnecessary anyway, for it is still in use today: "The violent **celestial** theatrics were the first in the solar system to be witnessed 'live' on Earth, and they were big box office."[76]

Chambering

> Let us walk honestly, as in the day; not in rioting and drunkenness, not in **chambering** and wantonness, not in strife and envying. (Rom 13:13)

The word **chambering** occurs only once in the AV. Although **chambering** is formed from the noun *chamber,* it means sexual indulgence or lewdness. Naturally, this word is updated by our modern versions. However, no two versions utilized the same word to amend **chambering**. The NASB preferred "sexual promiscuity," the NRSV "debauchery," the NIV "sexual immorality," and the NKJV "lewdness." Yet when the AV uses the word "lewdness," it is changed by the NRSV to "shame" even though the other new versions retain "lewdness" as the AV.[77] And when the AV employs the word "chambers" in the literal sense, as in "little chambers," the NIV alters it to the more difficult "alcoves."[78]

Chamois

> The hart, and the roebuck, and the fallow deer, and the wild goat, and the pygarg, and the wild ox, and the **chamois**. (Deu 14:5)

A **chamois** is only mentioned once in the AV. The word itself has been taken directly from French into English. A **chamois** is a small antelope. The new versions unanimously call a **chamois** a "mountain sheep." Leather made from a **chamois** is called **chamois** leather or simply **chamois** for short. The correction of this word was completely unnecessary, for both the animal and the leather produced from it are regularly mentioned today. Speaking of the French Alps, *Earthwatch* magazine described the animals to be found there: "Other species leading the high life here include ibex, **chamois,** red fox, and snow hare."[79] And not only can **chamois** cloth be purchased at many stores in the 1990's, it is also made artificially: "Two hints: I lubricate the artificial **chamois** in my Pearl Izumi Fieldsensor shorts with Assos **chamois** cream."[80]

Champaign

> *Are* they not on the other side Jordan, by the way where the sun goeth down, in the land of the Canaanites, which dwell in the **champaign** over against Gilgal, beside the plains of Moreh? (Deu 11:30)

A **champaign** is mentioned just once in the AV. It is from the French *champaigne,* "a plain." A **champaign** is a plain, a field, or flat, open country. Just as the beverage *champagne* got its name from a place in France where it was originally made, so **champaign** originally referred to a rich and level province in Italy near Naples. These words are both derived from the Latin *campus,* "a field," from which we also get our English word *campus.* But if the identification of a **champaign** was obscure, it was made even more so by the NASB, NRSV, and NIV, for they all corrected **champaign** to the arcane "Arabah." Only the NKJV replaced **campaign** with the word "plain." And although the word **champaign** is archaic, it is still the name of a city in Illinois.

Chapiter

> Also he made before the house two pillars of thirty and five cubits high, and the **chapiter** that *was* on the top of each of them *was* five cubits. (2 Chr 3:15)

A **chapiter** is mentioned in the AV thirteen times in the singular[81] and sixteen times in the plural.[82] It is from the French *chapitre* meaning the capital of a column. The words **chapiter,** *chapter,* and *capital* are all derived from the Latin *caput,* "head." Our modern versions customarily render **chapiter** and **chapiters** as "capital" and "capitals.[83] However, four times in the Old Testament, the NASB and NIV translated **chapiters** as "tops."[84] But if the use of the word **chapiter** made the Bible hard to understand, the correction of "for the **chapiter,**" as used by the AV, NKJV, NASB, and NRSV, to "festooned the capitals," as was done by the NIV, certainly does not make the Bible easier to understand.[85]

Chapmen

> Beside *that which* **chapmen** and merchants brought. And all the kings of Arabia and governors of the country brought gold and silver to Solomon. (2 Chr 9:14)

Chapmen appear only once in the AV. This word, the plural of *chapman,* is from the Old English *ceapman,* from *ceap,* "barter, trade." **Chapmen** are men whose business is buying and selling—a merchant, peddler, or businessman. The NRSV and NASB altered **chapmen** to "traders," but the NKJV and NIV preferred "merchants." But it should be pointed out that the commonly used word *chap* is just short for *chapman.* And if the significance of the occupation of **chapmen** was not clear, then what about the duties of "shipwrights" mentioned by the NIV and not found in any other modern version?[86] And when the AV refers to something common like an "officer," the NASB amends it to a "constable."[87] And furthermore, when the AV mentions "countrymen," the NRSV converts them into "compatriots" even though the other versions read as the AV.[88]

Charger

> And she came in straightway with haste unto the king, and asked, saying, I will that thou give me by and by in a **charger** the head of John the Baptist. (Mark 6:25)

A **charger** surfaces in the AV seventeen times in the singular[89] and three times in the plural.[90] The noun **charger** comes from the verb *charge* that means to load. Hence, a **charger** is something that carries a load. The meaning of the word as it appears in the AV is a platter or large dish, but a horse is also called a **charger** for the same reason. Although our modern versions all eliminated the forms of **charger** from the Bible, only the NKJV consistently rendered them by forms of "platter."[91] **Chargers** can be found as "basins"[92] and "plates"[93] by the NRSV, and "dishes"[94] and "plates"[95] by the NIV. **Charger** is rendered as "plate" in the Old Testament by the NIV and NRSV,[96] but "platter" in the New Testament.[97] Yet when the AV refers to "butter," the NRSV alone transforms it into "curds."[98]

Charity

> Charity suffereth long, *and* is kind; charity envieth not; charity vaunteth not itself, is not puffed up, (1 Cor 13:4)

The word **charity** occurs twenty-eight times in the AV.[99] The form **charitably** is only used once.[100] **Charity** is from the French *charitet*, "dearness." It means love, affection, dearness, kindness, benevolence, or hospitality. Our modern versions unite in always rendering **charity** by "love."[101] The only time the word **charity** surfaces in a new translation is to correct the AV reading of "alms."[102] Yet isn't it strange that people will name their girl **Charity** but not Love. And many cities (including Pensacola, FL) have a Faith, Hope, and a **Charity** Drive but not a Love Drive.

Check

> I have heard the **check** of my reproach, and the spirit of my understanding causeth me to answer. Job 20:3)

The noun **check** is only used once in the AV. It is from the French *eschec*, meaning a sudden stop. The word **check** comes from the game *chess* and not the other way around. In fact, the word *chess* is just a corrupted form of *checks*, from *eschecs*, the plural of *eschec*. The original sense of this word was "king," as it ultimately goes back to the Persian *shah*, "a king." The exclamation *checkmate* is actually from the Persian *shah mat*, literally meaning "the king is dead." From its literal application to a chess game, the word **check** came to mean any sudden stop or repulse. There then developed the meaning of a reproof, reprimand, rebuke, or censure. This is how the AV uses the word. Naturally, our modern versions have all updated **check**. The NKJV and NIV preferred "rebuke," the NASB "reproof," and the NRSV "censure." Yet when the AV mentions something simple like a "flood," the NIV alters it to a "torrent" even though the other versions follow the AV.[103]

Chide

> Wherefore the people did **chide** with Moses, and said, Give us

water that we may drink. And Moses said unto them, Why **chide** ye with me? wherefore do ye tempt the LORD? (Exo 17:2)

The word **chide** appears four times in the AV.[104] The form **chiding** occurs once[105] and the past tense **chode** can be found twice.[106] **Chide** is from the Old English *cidan,* "to quarrel," and means to contend, strive, or argue. Our modern versions have completely eliminated all forms of **chide** from the Bible. The usual replacement is a form of "quarrel."[107] Other translations include "criticized,"[108] "strive,"[109] "upbraided,"[110] and forms of "contended."[111] Yet when the AV reads a form of "upbraid," it is corrected every time by the NIV, NKJV, and NASB.[112] The NRSV, although it corrected **chide** to "upbraided," altered the forms of "upbraid" in the AV three out of the four times they occurred.[113] The word **chide,** however, was not considered archaic by the *Boston Globe:* "Many Democrats **chide** Bush's energy policy for its failure to focus on conservation."[114]

Choler

And I saw him come close unto the ram, and he was moved with **choler** against him, and smote the ram, and brake his two horns: and there was no power in the ram to stand before him, but he cast him down to the ground, and stamped upon him: and there was none that could deliver the ram out of his hand. (Dan 8:7)

The word **choler** occurs twice in the AV.[115] Although it is from the French *colere,* "anger," **choler** goes back to the Latin *cholera,* "bile," from which we also get the disease *cholera.* The ancients thought that the health and temperament of the body was determined by a mix of blood, phlegm, **choler** (yellow bile), and melancholy. Anger was supposed to be due to excess **choler.** Thus, **choler** means anger, wrath, or irascibility. But although our modern versions all update **choler** to a form of "rage,"[116] *National Review* did not consider the word **choler** to be archaic: "If the anti-Nixon brigades wish to **choler** up for the purpose of interpreting such a remark as betraying true, lethal anti-Semitism, they are free to do so, and other are free not to take them seriously; and these would include Mr. Kissinger, who would not have been appointed Secretary of State by a functioning anti-Semite."[117]

Churl

> The instruments also of the **churl** are evil: he deviseth wicked devices to destroy the poor with lying words, even when the needy speaketh right. (Isa 32:7)

The word **churl** appears twice in the AV[118] and the form **churlish** occurs once.[119] **Churl** is from the Old English *ceorl*, originally meaning just a man, then a man without rank, then a serf or peasant, and finally, a rude or coarse man. Although our modern versions all excised the word **churl**, they could not agree on what to replace it with. **Churl** can be found as "villain" in the NRSV, "rouge" in the NASB, and "scoundrel" in the NIV.[120] The NKJV could not decide between correcting the word **churl** to a "miser" or a "schemer."[121] The NASB and NKJV rendered the adjective **churlish** as "harsh" but the NKJV and NRSV preferred "surly."[122] But although our modern versions deemed **churl** and **churlish** to be archaic, both words are still in use today: "Indeed, the very idea that John is so concerned for the health of his tenant adds credence to my reading that John is not a **churl**."[123] And from *The American Spectator:* "I suppose it's **churlish** to suggest that there's something scandalous about the South African elections, when just about everyone down there is delighted with the results."[124]

Circumspect

> And in all *things* that I have said unto you be **circumspect**: and make no mention of the name of other gods, neither let it be heard out of thy mouth. (Exo 23:13)

The word **circumspect** is found once in the AV as is the form **circumspectly**.[125] These words are from the Latin *circumspectus*, derived from *circumspicere*, literally meaning "to look around." To be **circumspect** is to be cautious, wary, considerate, or discreet. The NKJV retains both of these words but the other versions usually update them to forms of "careful."[126] These corrections, however, were completely unnecessary, for the word **circumspect** is still in vogue today: "Anne Kershaw, whose husband was killed in an air accident in Antarctica in 1990, was **circumspect** when I spoke with her a few days after the November crash and rescue."[127]

Cleave

And there shall **cleave** nought of the cursed thing to thine hand: that the LORD may turn from the fierceness of his anger, and show thee mercy, and have compassion upon thee, and multiply thee, as he hath sworn unto thy fathers; (Deu 13:17)

The word **cleave** not only appears in the AV many times under various forms, it also has two distinct meanings. The word **cleave** appears four times in the AV with the meaning of split or divide.[128] The word itself comes from the Old English *cleofan*, "to split." The other word **cleave** occurs twenty-six times in the AV.[129] It is from the Old English *cleofian*, "to stick," and means to cling or adhere to. Other forms of **cleave** include **clave,** found six times with the former meaning[130] and eight times with the latter,[131] **cleaveth,** appearing four times with the meaning of split[132] and nine times with the meaning of cling,[133] **cleaved,** found three times, always used in the sense of cling,[134] and **cloven,** found twice with the meaning of split.[135] The derivative **clovenfooted** can also be seen three times.[136] To be **cloven** is to be divided. **Cleft** appears once as a verb[137] and six times as a noun.[138] Another related word is **clift,** occurring in the AV as a noun once in the singular and once in the plural.[139] **Clift** is just an older form of **cleft.** A **cleft** or **clift** is a space made by cleaving. With the exception of the noun **cleft,** our modern versions have deemed these words to be archaic.[140] However, they were very lax in completely removing all of the various forms of **cleave.** The NRSV employed forms of "**cleft**" as a verb six times.[141] The NKJV utilized forms of "**cloven**" eleven times,[142] even when the AV did not contain a form of the word.[143] The NASB is the most inconsistent of our modern versions, for it uses "cleaves" four times[144] and "**cleave**" seven times.[145] In fact, in two of the passages where the NASB says "**cleave,**" the AV did not even contain the word—it said "stuck" and "joined."[146] The NASB also employs "**cleft**" as a verb one time when the AV simply said "divided."[147] But in spite of all these corrections, the word **cleave** is still used today in the sense of cling or adhere to: "Perhaps as a result, most therapists no longer **cleave** rigidly to the dictates of a single school but, rather, pick and choose according to personal preference, the needs of their clients and the problem at hand."[148]

Clouts

> And Ebedmelech the Ethiopian said unto Jeremiah, Put now *these* old cast **clouts** and rotten rags under thine armholes under the cords. And Jeremiah did so. (Jer 38:12)

The word **clouts** is used twice in the AV,[149] while the form **clouted** is employed once.[150] **Clouts**, the plural of *clout*, is from the Old English *clut*, "a patch." The verb **clouted** is from *clutian*, "to patch." A clout is a piece of cloth or a rag, often used as a patch. Once again, although our modern versions removed every occurrence of the word **clout**, they were not unanimous in their selection of a replacement. The NIV and NRSV rendered **clouts** as "rags," the NASB as "cloths," and the NKJV as "clothes."[151] **Clouted** is jointly given as "patched" by all of our modern versions.[152] Yet forms of the word **clouts** can still be found today: "Presently, the One Who Is Father appeared behind his closed eyelids, looking much like Ramos himself: headband, single-thonged sandals strapped to bare legs, a **breechclout** secured by a tasseled girdle covering his loins."[153]

Coast

> And their **coast** was from Mahanaim, all Bashan, all the kingdom of Og king of Bashan, and all the towns of Jair, which *are* in Bashan, threescore cities: (Josh 13:30)

The word **coast** appears in the AV sixty-two times in the singular[154] and fifty-one times in the plural.[155] It is from the French *coste* and originally referred to the side of the body fortified by the ribs; the Latin root is *costa*, "rib." The word **coast** then came to be applied to the side of anything until finally obtaining the modern designation of the edge of the land by the sea. Thus, a **coast** is a border, region, country, or area that may not be next to a body of water. Our modern versions render **coast** by such things as "country,"[156] "border,"[157] "territory,"[158] "land,"[159] and "boundary."[160] However, when the AV reads "border," the NRSV changes it to "**coast**."[161] And when the AV says "isle," the NRSV does likewise.[162] And when the AV mentions something simple like a "city," the NRSV changes it to "citadel" even though the other versions read as the AV.[163]

Cockatrice

> Rejoice not thou, whole Palestina, because the rod of him that smote thee is broken: for out of the serpent's root shall come forth a **cockatrice,** and his fruit *shall be* a fiery flying serpent. (Isa 14:29)

A **cockatrice** is mentioned in the AV three times in the singular[164] and once in the plural.[165] Although the word itself is from the French *cocatris,* referring to a type of serpent, its etymology is rather curious. A **cockatrice** has been identified as a hybrid serpent and fowl, a crocodile, a weasel-like animal, and a serpent. The French word *cocatris* is actually a corruption of the Latin *calcatrix,* from *calcare,* "to tread." Naturally, a **cockatrice** is nowhere to be found in any of our modern versions. It is always updated to "adder"[166] or "viper,"[167] except for the NASB once rendering **cockatrices** as "serpents."[168] But when the AV mentions the familiar "crane and swallow," the NASB and NIV alter it to the arcane "swift and thrush."[169] Moreover, all of our modern versions make mention of an unidentified animal they term a "gecko."[170]

Cockle

> Let thistles grow instead of wheat, and **cockle** instead of barley. The words of Job are ended. (Job 31:40)

Cockle is only mentioned once in the AV. The word is from the Old English *coccel* and refers to a weed that grows in grain fields. **Cockle** is darnel, weeds, or tares. It is changed to "weeds" by the NKJV and NIV, but "foul weeds" by the NRSV and "stinkweed" by the NASB. Yet when the AV just says "weeds," the NIV alters it to "seaweed" even though the other new translations followed the AV.[171] And when the AV mentions "bramble," the NIV alone corrects it to "thornbush."[172] And furthermore, when the AV mentions a "cypress" tree, the NRSV corrects it to the unknown "holm" tree.[173] Thus, if the AV translators are to be faulted for using the word **cockle,** the translators of our modern versions should not escape unscathed, for they should not be considered horticulturists either.

Coffer

> And take the ark of the LORD, and lay it upon the cart; and put the jewels of gold, which ye return him *for* a trespass offering, in a **coffer** by the side thereof; and send it away, that it may go. (1 Sam 6:8)

The word **coffer** appears three times in the AV.[174] It is from the Old English *cofre*, "a chest." A **coffer** is a chest, box, trunk, or coffin. Every occurrence of **coffer** has been removed by our modern versions. The NKJV and the NIV agreed on "chest" as a replacement and the NRSV and NASB united on "box."[175] But the word **coffer** is still in use today: "Solarz's $1.8 million campaign **coffer**—the biggest in the House—makes it easy for the congressman to buy himself this type of goodwill."[176]

Cogitations

> Hitherto *is* the end of the matter. As for me Daniel, my **cogitations** much troubled me, and my countenance changed in me: but I kept the matter in my heart. (Dan 7:28)

The word **cogitations,** plural of *cogitation,* appears only once in the AV. *Cogitation* is from the Latin *cogitationem,* from *cogitatio,* "thinking," from *cogitare,* "to think." **Cogitations** are thoughts, reflections, considerations, or meditations. Our modern versions unanimously updated **cogitations** to "thoughts." This was entirely superfluous, for the word **cogitations** is still in use today: "When he does talk, he speaks in rapid-fire bursts, often punctuating lines with a littler humming noise or a laugh, as if he's already bored by a listener's effort to catch up with his galloping **cogitations.**"[177]

Collops

> Because he covereth his face with his fatness, and maketh **collops** of fat on *his* flanks. (Job 15:27)

The word **collops** is used only once in the AV and is of rather obscure origin. **Collops** are slices of meat or folds of fat on the body. Naturally, our modern versions have eliminated this word. It is updated to forms of "heavy" by the NKJV and NASB, but "gathered" by the NRSV and "bulges" by the NIV. Yet when the AV uses an unambiguous word like "pen," it is altered by the NASB to a "stylus."[178]

Comely

> Rejoice in the LORD, O ye righteous: *for* praise is **comely** for the upright. (Psa 33:1)

The word **comely** appears sixteen times in the AV,[179] while the form **comeliness** can be seen five times.[180] **Comely** is from the Old English *cymlic* and can mean beautiful, pretty, fair, pleasing, appropriate, fitting, or becoming. Our modern versions completely expurgate the word **comely** except for the NRSV forgetting to remove it twice[181] and the NASB neglecting it once.[182] **Comeliness** was likewise exterminated; however, the NKJV forgot to remove it once.[183] The usual replacement for **comeliness** was "splendor,"[184] while **comely** can be found as "handsome,"[185] "splendid,"[186] "becoming,"[187] "stately,"[188] and "fitting."[189] But after all of these corrections, the NASB altered **comeliness** to the equally as archaic "seemliness."[190] Then the NASB amended the perfectly understandable "goodness" in the AV to the supposedly archaic "**comeliness**."[191] The word **comely**, however, is still in vogue today: "In just this way: when an ideal, however **comely**, fails to accord with deep necessity."[192]

Commodious

> And because the haven was not **commodious** to winter in, the more part advised to depart thence also, if by any means they might attain to Phenice, *and there* to winter; *which is* an haven of Crete, and lieth toward the south west and north west. (Acts 27:12)

The word **commodious** occurs just one time in the AV. It is from the Latin *commodissus*, "useful," from *commodus*, literally meaning "with measure." To be **commodious** is to be profitable, convenient, accommodating, opportune, suitable, beneficial, or useful. Although the word **commodious** is always rendered in our modern versions by forms of "suitable," it is still regularly used today: "Of the species unique to this environment, none finds the ancient forest so **commodious** as the northern spotted owl, which nests almost exclusively in large tracts of old-growth stands."¹⁹³

Communicate

> Let him that is taught in the word **communicate** unto him that teacheth in all good things. (Gal 6:6)

The word **communicate** appears four times in the AV,¹⁹⁴ while the form **communicated** is used twice.¹⁹⁵ Although the form **communication** also occurs six times in the singular¹⁹⁶ and twice in the plural,¹⁹⁷ it is only used in an archaic sense once in the singular¹⁹⁸ and once in the plural.¹⁹⁹ **Communicate** is from the Latin *communicatus*, from *communicare*, "to make common." To **communicate** means to impart, give, confer, or to convey knowledge, information, or something tangible. **Communications** is a word that refers to that which one is common with. Thus, it means companions, company, or associations. The word **communicate** is unanimously updated by our modern versions to a form of "share."²⁰⁰ Surprisingly, the NKJV retains "**communicated**" once.²⁰¹ **Communications** is replaced by "company" in all of the new translations.²⁰² Yet when the AV reads "sanctify," the NRSV alters it to the awkward "**communicate** holiness."²⁰³

Compass

> Woe unto you, scribes and Pharisees, hypocrites! for ye **compass** sea and land to make one proselyte, and when he is made, ye make him twofold more the child of hell than yourselves. (Mat 23:15)

Although the word **compass** is used a variety of ways in the AV, most of them have been deemed archaic. **Compass** is from the French *compasser*, "to measure," and is most frequently utilized as a verb meaning to go or come around, encompass, surround, or encircle. As a verb, the form **compass** is used twenty-eight times,²⁰⁴ **compassed** forty-four times,²⁰⁵ **compassest** once,²⁰⁶ **compasseth** five times,²⁰⁷ and **compassing** three times.²⁰⁸ The expression "fetch a **compass**" or "fetched a **compass**" is employed five times and means to turn about or make a circuit.²⁰⁹ The phrase "set a **compass**" is also used once.²¹⁰ The noun **compass** is also employed four times in reference to a round object.²¹¹ Every one of these occurrences of a form of **compass** has been corrected by our modern versions. The only exception is the one time where the AV does use the word **compass** to refer to a measuring device; however, the NIV corrects this also.[212] Then when the AV says "four winds of heaven," it is changed to "four points of the **compass**" by the NASB even though the other versions read as the AV.[213] One would think that the verb **compass** could easily be updated in the new versions to the more familiar *encompass,* but this was rarely done. Yet the NASB twice inserted forms of "encompass" into passages where the AV did not contain the word **compass** at all.[214] Every correction of the word **compass** was unnecessary, for various forms of the word are still in use today. From *American Scholar* we read: "Rather he saw the nation's sole justification as its provision of circumstances that would enable him to make that selfhood, to **compass** the widest possible view of existence; this was the goal of our species as he conceived it."[215] And neither should the expression "fetch a **compass**" have been corrected: "When Noonan's octant indicated that the Lockheed, heading northeast, had reached a line of position that cut the **compass** at 157 degrees to the southeast and 337 degrees to the northwest, he knew that Howland was either to the left on a course of 337, or to the right on 157."[216]

Concision

> Beware of dogs, beware of evil workers, beware of the **concision**. (Phil 3:2)

The word **concision** is used only once in the AV. It is from the Latin *concisio,* literally meaning "a cutting to pieces." **Concision** is ultimately derived from *concisus,* from which we also get *concise*. **Concision** is the action of cutting or mutilation or a division or schism. The term **concision** is also figuratively applied in the AV to the circumcised Judaizers. The new versions render **concision** by a form of "mutilate," except for the NASB, which preferred "false circumcision." Although the word **concision** is not used today exactly like it appears in the AV, it is still used as a synonym of *conciseness:* "Professor Ingrao has achieved a masterpiece of **concision** and his book can be recommended for use by both sixth-formers and undergraduates."[217]

Concord

> And what **concord** hath Christ with Belial? or what part hath he that believeth with an infidel? (2 Cor 6:15)

The word **concord** occurs just once in the AV. It is from the French *concorde*, "agreement." The Latin root is made up of *con*, "together," and *cor*, "heart." To be in **concord** is to be in agreement, harmony, accord, or unanimity. Although the NASB and NIV updated **concord** to "harmony," the NKJV preferred "accord" and the NRSV "agreement." But even when the AV uses a simple phrase like "of one mind," the NASB corrects it to "harmonious."[218] But although they corrected **concord**, every translator of a modern Bible version regularly used a **concordance**. And furthermore, the word **concord** is still in vogue today: "As in Africa after decolonization, some citizens of the Newly Independent States (NIS) call for the retention of familiar lines if only for the sake of **concord**; any threats to the territorial integrity of the new states, they argue, would produce certain conflict."[219]

Concourse

> She crieth in the chief place of **concourse**, in the openings of the gates: in the city she uttereth her words, *saying*, (Prov 1:21)

The word **concourse** appears twice in the AV.[220] It is from the French *concours*, literally meaning "a running together." A **concourse** is an assembly of people or a crowd. It also later came to mean the place where an assembly or crowd was gathered together. Although they corrected **concourse** every time it occurred, our modern versions never used the same word in both cases. The NKJV extended **concourse** to "concourses" once but "disorderly gathering" the other time.[221] The NASB said "disorderly gathering" and "noisy streets."[222] The NIV also said "noisy streets," but preferred "commotion" the second time."[223] The NRSV liked the word "commotion," but selected "busiest corner" for the other passage.[224] The correction of **concourse**, however, was completely unnecessary, for not only can a **concourse** be found in any airport, the word is still in use today: "It was the **concourse** of the common man—'common people,' as

Concupiscence

> Mortify therefore your members which are upon the earth; fornication, uncleanness, inordinate affection, evil **concupiscence,** and covetousness, which is idolatry: (Col 3:5)

The word **concupiscence** occurs three times in the AV.[226] It is from a French word of the same spelling meaning eager desire. The word is ultimately derived from the Latin *cupere,* "to desire." The name for the Roman god of love (Cupid) is also derived from this Latin root. **Concupiscence** is lust, sexual appetite, or strong desire. Not surprisingly, the word **concupiscence** has been eliminated from the Bible by our modern versions. The first occurrence is changed to a form of "covetous" by the NASB and NRSV, but "covetous desire" by the NIV and "evil desire by the NKJV.[227] The second passage where **concupiscence** occurs is unanimously rendered by a form of "desire."[228] The final occurrence of **concupiscence** is also unanimous in our modern versions, but this time they chose a form of "passion."[229] Yet when the AV utilizes the word "passion," every new translation changes it to "suffering" even though every Easter time a Passion Play is performed.[230] And regarding the word **concupiscence,** it is still in use anyway: "That summer a girl moved in up the road, and she was ready to go anywhere by outboard, a situation that added **concupiscence** to navigation."[231]

Coney

> Nevertheless these ye shall not eat of them that chew the cud, or of them that divide the cloven hoof; *as* the camel, and the hare, and the **coney:** for they chew the cud, but divide not the hoof; *therefore* they *are* unclean unto you. (Deu 14:7)

A **coney** is mentioned in the AV twice in the singular[232] and twice in the plural.[233] Although the origin of the actual word **coney** is disputed, it originally referred to a rabbit. The **coney** of the AV is a small, rabbit-like, nocturnal animal that lives in holes in rocks. Surprisingly, the NIV retains every occurrence of the word "**coney.**"[234] The usual translation for **coney** in the other versions is a form of "rock badger."[235] However, the NKJV twice made a **coney** into an obscure "rock hyrax."[236] And although the NRSV corrected **coney** and **conies** in three passages, it forgot to remove the word from the fourth place it occurred in the AV.[237] Although our modern versions consider the word **coney** to be archaic, even the residents of Jamaica know better, for in their country a **coney** is considered an endangered animal.[238]

Confection

> And thou shalt make it a perfume, a **confection** after the art of the apothecary, tempered together, pure *and* holy: (Exo 30:35)

Although the word **confection** occurs just once in the AV, the form **confectionaries** also appears one time.[239] **Confection** is from the French *confeccion*, literally meaning "something mixed together." The noun **confection** was originally formed from the verb *confect*, meaning prepare, make up together, or mix together. A **confection** is something made or prepared by the mixture of ingredients: a concoction. **Confectionaries** are the ones who make the **confection**. Since this word is limited today to just something sweet that uses **confection**ers sugar, our modern versions have completely eliminated both of these words. **Confectionaries** is unanimously rendered as "perfumers."[240] **Confection** is given as "perfume" by the NRSV, "work" by the NIV, and "compound" by the NKJV.[241] The NASB restructures the sentence and makes **confection** into the verb "blended."[242] But after correcting these words, the NIV inserted the word "confections" into a verse where neither the AV nor any modern version contained the word.[243] The word **confection**, however, is still used today when not referring to something sweet: "Then, as chefs embraced it in the 1980s, goat cheese came to be seen by many diners as an extravagance, a **confection** to be ordered in upscale eateries, where a dainty disk of the stuff might be served warm atop a bed of baby greens."[244]

Confederate

> For they have consulted together with one consent: they are **confederate** against thee: (Psa 83:5)

The word **confederate** appears three times in the AV,[245] while the form **confederacy** is also used three times.²⁴⁶ **Confederate** is from the Latin *confoederatus*, from *confoederare*, "to unite in a league." The Latin root *foedus* means a league or treaty. To be **confederate** is to be united with, allied with, or joined together with. Thus, the eleven states of the old Southern **Confederacy**. Although the NKJV retained a from of these words twice,²⁴⁷ the other versions corrected them every time. The usual replacement is a form of "allies,"²⁴⁸ but **confederacy** was unanimously twice altered to "conspiracy."²⁴⁹ And in the same verse where it just corrected **confederacy**, the NRSV inserted the word "confederates" to further correct the AV.²⁵⁰ The word **confederate**, however, is still used today when not referring to the Civil War: "So, up front, we should propose that the Serbs in Bosnia **confederate** with Serbia and move people so they're living in areas contiguous to Serbia itself."²⁵¹

Constrain

> As many as desire to make a fair show in the flesh, they **constrain** you to be circumcised; only lest they should suffer persecution for the cross of Christ. (Gal 6:12)

Although the word **constrain** appears only once in the AV, the form **constrained** occurs six times,²⁵² while **constraineth** is utilized twice²⁵³ and **constraint** once.²⁵⁴ **Constrain** is from the French *constraindre*, "to bind together." To **constrain** is to compel, force, oblige, or strongly encourage. This word is often confused with *restrain* and has hence been deemed to be archaic. Our modern versions unanimously render **constrain** by forms of "compel,"²⁵⁵ but could not come to an agreement on the other forms of the word. **Constrained** can be found as "urged,"²⁵⁶ "persuaded,"²⁵⁷ "made,"²⁵⁸ "prevailed upon,"²⁵⁹ "forced,"²⁶⁰ and "compelled."²⁶¹ **Constraineth** is normally given as "compels,"²⁶² but the NASB and NRSV revised **constraineth** to the supposedly archaic "constrains."²⁶³ **Constraint** is rendered as "compulsion" in the NKJV, NRSV, and NASB, but the NIV alone selected "must."²⁶⁴ But after all of these corrections, the NRSV and NASB added the word "**constraint**" to a passage where the AV did not contain the word.²⁶⁵ Then the NASB substitutes the word "**constraint**" for "necessity" even though the NKJV and NRSV followed the AV.²⁶⁶ Nevertheless, the word

Contemn

> Wherefore doth the wicked **contemn** God? he hath said in his heart, Thou wilt not require *it*. (Psa 10:13)

The word **contemn** appears in the AV twice as **contemn**,[268] four times as **contemned**,[269] and once as **contemneth**.[270] It comes from the French *contemner,* "to despise." To **contemn** is to slight, scorn, disdain, despise, or treat with contempt. All of the forms of **contemn** are extracted by our modern versions. In its place one can usually find forms of "despise,"[271] but "renounce,"[272] "spurned,"[273] "revile,"[274] "degraded,"[275] "scorned,"[276] and "brought into contempt"[277] can also be found. These corrections were unfortunate, for not only do all of our modern versions use the related word "contempt,"[278] the word **contemn** can still be found today: "The years **contemn** in many way, but one of the most insidious is Parkinson's disease."[279]

Contrariwise

> Not rendering evil for evil, or railing for railing: but **contrariwise** blessing; knowing that ye are thereunto called, that ye should inherit a blessing. (1 Pet 3:9)

The word **contrariwise** occurs three times in the AV.[280] It is obviously a combination of *contrary* and *wise.* **Contrariwise** means on the other hand, on the contrary, or in the opposite way or direction. Although our modern versions usually update this word to "on the contrary,"[281] this was unnecessary, for the word **contrariwise** is still in vogue today: "**Contrariwise,** no flaws of any kind were uncovered in the phantom Denbeigh test car; for what cannot be examined cannot fail the examiner!"[282]

Conversation

> For our rejoicing is this, the testimony of our conscience, that in simplicity and godly sincerity, not with fleshly wisdom, but by the grace of God, we have had our **conversation** in the world, and more abundantly to you-ward. (2 Cor 1:12)

The word **conversation**, from a French word of the same spelling, although used twenty times in the AV, never refers to speaking.[283] Thus, it has been deemed to be archaic and is corrected by all of our modern versions. **Conversation** means behavior, social intercourse, conduct, or engagement with things. Our modern versions update **conversation** to "way,"[284] "behavior,"[285] "way of life,"[286] "life,"[287] or "conduct."[288] Yet when the AV and all of the modern versions said "speech," the NIV alone altered it to "**conversation**."[289] And when the AV just says "voice," the NIV corrects it to "cooing" even though the other new translations follow the AV reading.[290]

Convince

> Holding fast the faithful word as he hath been taught, that he may be able by sound doctrine both to exhort and to **convince** the gainsayers. (Titus 1:9)

The word **convince** appears twice in the AV,[291] while the form **convinced** occurs four times[292] and **convinceth** once.[293] This word is from the Latin *convincere*, "to overcome." It means to prove to be guilty, vanquish, refute, or to demonstrate that a person or thing is possessed of a certain quality. Since they obviously limited the meaning of **convince** to its modern definition of persuade, our modern versions did not approve of the AV use of the various forms of **convince**. The various translations for these words in our modern versions include "confuted,"[294] "refuted,"[295] "convicted,"[296] and "reproved."[297] However, the NKJV forgot to remove this supposedly archaic word on two occasions,[298] while the NIV was negligent once.[299] Yet when the AV employs a simple word like "haste," the NRSV corrects it to the more difficult "consternation."[300]

Cormorant

> But the **cormorant** and the bittern shall possess it; the owl also and the raven shall dwell in it: and he shall stretch out upon it the line of confusion, and the stones of emptiness. (Isa 34:11)

A **cormorant** is mentioned four times in the AV.[301] The word comes from the French *cormoran* and refers to a large, voracious sea bird. Surprisingly, the NIV, NRSV, and NASB all retain **cormorant** in two of the four places it occurs in the AV.[302] In these two passages, the NKJV preferred "fisher owl."[303] In the two other verses a **cormorant** is called a "pelican,"[304] "desert owl,"[305] and a "hawk."[306] But **cormorant** should not have been updated at all, for sightings of cormorants still regularly occur today: "A **cormorant** skimmed over the surface, its wings pelting the water in a volley of tiny splashes like soundless machine-gun fire."[307]

Corn

At that time Jesus went on the sabbath day through the **corn**; and his disciples were an hungred, and began to pluck the ears of **corn**, and to eat. (Mat 12:1)

Corn is mentioned 102 times in the AV.[308] The derivative **cornfloor** occurs once.[309] The word **corn** is from an Old English word of the same spelling that is a doublet of *grain*. In fact, our modern versions always update **corn** to "grain,"[310] except for the NIV, which used "kernel" one time.[311] Yet when the AV says "grain," it is sometimes corrected to "seed."[312] **Cornfloor** in the AV is unanimously given as "threshing floor" by all of the new versions.[313] But it should not seem strange that the AV uses the word **corn** after this fashion, for the word **corn** is used today in a sense that is not even remotely related to its origin. When something is trite, ridiculous, or old-fashioned we say it is **corny**. Moreover, when the AV uses a word that is perfectly modern like "servants," it is revised by the NRSV to "courtiers."[314]

Cornet

With trumpets and sound of **cornet** make a joyful noise before the LORD, the King. (Psa 98:6)

A **cornet** is a wind instrument mentioned seven times in the AV in the singular[315] and twice in the plural.[316] The word **cornet** is from a French word of the same spelling that is a diminutive of *corne*, "horn," since a **cornet** was originally made from a horn. Our modern versions have completely eliminated a **cornet** from the Bible. The usual replacement is "horn,"[317] but "ram's horn"[318] and "trumpet"[319] can also be found. The plural **cornets** is given as a form of "horn,"[320] "castanets,"[321] and "sistrums."[322] But the correction of the word **cornet** was very premature, for even *Rolling Stone* magazine recognized their existence in the 1990's: "This new release, recorded at the Ed Blackwell Project's final concert, just two months before the master drummer's death in the fall of 1992, features his longtime associates Carlos Ward on alto sax and flute and Mark Helias on contrabass and newcomer Graham Haynes on **cornet**."[323]

Cotes

> Storehouses also for the increase of corn, and wine, and oil; and stalls for all manner of beasts, and **cotes** for flocks. (2 Chr 32:28)

Cotes are only mentioned once in the AV, but a **sheepcote** can be found twice in the singular[324] and once in the plural.[325] A cote, which comes unchanged from Old English, is an enclosure or shelter for animals or storage. The word **cote** is actually a variant of *cot*, "cottage." Naturally, these words have been removed by our modern versions. **Cotes** in the AV is changed to "sheepfolds" by the NASB and NRSV, but the NIV preferred "pens" and the NKJV "folds."[326] The NIV, NRSV, and NASB update **sheepcote** to "pasture," but the NKJV chose "sheepfold."[327] **Sheepcote** may be archaic but it is certainly easier to understand than why the NIV altered "porch" to "colonnade."[328]

Couch

> When they **couch** in *their* dens, *and* abide in the covert to lie in wait? (Job 38:40)

The word **couch** occurs only once in the AV but **couched** is used twice,[329] **coucheth** once,[330] **couching** once,[331] and **couching-place** once.[332] **Couch** is from the French *coucher*, "to lay down." This goes back to the Latin *collocare*, "to put in place." The root of this word is *locare*, from which we also get *locate*. To **couch** is to crouch or lie down. Transitively, it means to lay something down. To **couch** can also mean to express in an obscure or veiled way. Since they obviously limited the meaning of **couch** to the modern conception of a piece of furniture, our modern versions have completely eliminated all forms of this word; however, the

NASB carelessly retained a form of it one time.[333] The various forms of **couch** are rendered in our modern versions by forms of "crouch"[334] and "lie."[335] Yet in one passage where the AV said "stooped down," the NASB altered it to "couches."[336] In spite of these corrections, forms of the word **couch** are still in use. Not only is it very common to hear that someone is **couching** his words, in an article about making homemade paper, *Mother Earth News* relates what is called the **couching** technique: "Your other option is to '**couch**' (or lay down) the paper onto wet felt (felt is available at fabric stores).[337]

Coulter

> But all the Israelites went down to the Philistines, to sharpen every man his share, and his **coulter,** and his ax, and his mattock. (1 Sam 13:20)

A **coulter** is mentioned in the AV once in the singular and once in the plural.[338] The word itself appeared in Old English as *culter* and refers to an iron blade in front of a plow that makes a vertical cut in the soil. The Old English word was actually borrowed directly from the Latin word for knife. **Coulter** and **coulters** are unanimously rendered by a form of "mattock" in our modern versions.[339] Yet when the AV uses the word "mattock," it is always corrected.[340] The word **coulter** may be archaic, but that was no excuse for the NRSV to introduce a "handpike" into the Bible when neither it nor the base form *pike* occurs in any other modern version.[341]

Countervail

> For we are sold, I and my people, to be destroyed, to be slain, and to perish. But if we had been sold for bondmen and bondwomen, I had held my tongue, although the enemy could not **countervail** the king's damage. (Est 7:4)

The word **countervail** occurs only once in the AV. It is from the French *contrevaloir*, "to avail against." To **countervail** is to be equivalent to in value, equal to, counterbalance, or to reciprocate. The NKJV and NRSV rendered **countervail** as "compensate," but the NIV chose "justify" and the NASB "commensurate." This correction was quite hasty, for the word

countervail is still in use today: "But I don't think we should be compelled to pay the price of their subsidy. We ought to be able to **countervail** [retaliate]."³⁴²

Covert

> I will abide in thy tabernacle for ever: I will trust in the **covert** of thy wings. Selah. (Psa 61:4)

The word **covert** appears nine times in the AV.³⁴³ It is from the French *covert,* from *covrir,* "to cover." A **covert** is a place of covering, a shelter, or a hiding place. Although our modern versions attempted to completely eliminate this word, the NRSV carelessly retained it on four occasions,³⁴⁴ while the NKJV and NASB each kept it once.³⁴⁵ The replacements for **covert** include "cover,"³⁴⁶ "ravine,"³⁴⁷ "shelter,"³⁴⁸ "refuge,"³⁴⁹ and "hiding place."³⁵⁰ But after correcting **covert** in the AV the majority of the time, the NRSV altered "den" and "secret places" to "**covert**."³⁵¹ Then when the AV said "secret," the NASB amended it to "concealment."³⁵² Nevertheless, we still regularly hear secret activity termed **covert** activity.

Cracknels

> And take with thee ten loaves, and **cracknels**, and a cruse of honey, and go to him: he shall tell thee what shall become of the child. (1 Ki 14:3)

Cracknels are only mentioned once in the AV. The word itself is an alteration of the French *craquelin,* so named for its crispness, and is ultimately related to our word *crack.* **Cracknels** are light, crisp biscuits. Our modern versions unite in replacing this word with "cakes." But when the AV mentions something simple like "great men," the NRSV alters it to "magnates."³⁵³

Crib

> Where no oxen *are,* the **crib** *is* clean: but much increase *is* by the strength of the ox. (Prov 14:4)

A **crib** is mentioned three times in the AV.³⁵⁴ The word is from the Old English *cribb,* "a manger." The modern definition of a baby **crib** can not be found until 1649.³⁵⁵ As expected however, the new versions usually update **crib** to "manger."[356] However, the NRSV, NASB, and NKJV each forgot to change the word **crib** one time.[357] The NKJV also used "trough" one time.[358] Although the word **crib** may be archaic, but this was no excuse for the NIV to inject the arcane word "clerestory" into the Bible.[359]

Crisping pins

> The changeable suits of apparel, and the mantles, and the wimples, and the **crisping pins**, (Isa 3:22)

Crisping pins are mentioned just once in the AV. The word *crisp* comes to us unchanged from Old English. It originally came from the Latin *crispus,* "curled." A crisp was a thin veil or head covering worn by women. As a verb, to crisp means to curl; as an adjective, to be crisp is to be curly. Thus, **crisping pins** would be curling pins for the hair. However, the meaning of the underlying Hebrew word is disputed by our modern versions. Thus, the NIV and NKJV render **crisping pins** as "purses," the NASB "money purses," and the NRSV "handbags." Yet when the AV is perfectly clear, it is still corrected, for the word "silent" is unnecessarily enlarged to "dumbfounded" by the NRSV.[360]

Cruse

> For thus saith the LORD God of Israel, The barrel of meal shall not waste, neither shall the **cruse** of oil fail, until the day *that* the LORD sendeth rain upon the earth. (1 Ki 17:14)

A **cruse** is mentioned nine times in the AV.[361] Although its origin is obscure, it refers to a small vessel for holding liquids. The word **cruse** was deemed to be archaic by our modern versions so it was corrected every time it occurred. The usual translations for **cruse** were "jug"[362] and "jar."[363] However, "bowl" was used once by the NKJV, NIV, and NRSV.[364] But when the AV mentions a simple object like a "storm of wind," the NIV unnecessarily terms it a "squall."[365]

Cumbered

> But Martha was **cumbered** about much serving, and came to him, and said, Lord, dost thou not care that my sister hath left

me to serve alone? bid her therefore that she help me. (Luke 10:40)

Although the word **cumbered** occurs just once in the AV, the forms **cumbereth** and **cumbrance** also each appear once.[366] The base form of these words is *cumber*, from the French *combrer*, "to hinder." To cumber is to overwhelm, trouble, hinder, or burden. The longer form *encumber* appeared later than *cumber* and is the word that survives today. Our modern versions unanimously render **cumbered** as "distracted."[367] **Cumbereth** is replaced by a form of "use up," except for the NRSV, which preferred "wasting."[368] Surprisingly, no form of **cumbered** was updated to a form of *encumbered*. Yet when the AV says "weight," the NASB alters it to "encumbrance."[369] The short form of this word should have been no problem for our modern versions since they use the uncommon "conciliation"[370] and "conciliate"[371] when the familiar forms are *reconciliation* and *reconciliate*. Yet when the AV employs the short form of a word, it is often unnecessarily lengthened. "Planted" in extended by the NIV and NRSV to "transplanted."[372] And when the AV just says "man," the NIV and NASB elongate it to "mankind."[373] Nevertheless, forms of the word **cumbered** can still be found today: "This is quite an interesting circuit with one difficult uphill bend, taken in 2nd gear with the F355's 6-speed box; a treacherous 3rd-gear downhill bend with no **cumber**; two slow hairpins; and a fairly fast 4th-gear bend leading to another, wider 2nd-gear hairpin leading on to the nearly half mile-long main straight."[374]

Curious

> And thou shalt take the garments, and put upon Aaron the coat, and the robe of the ephod, and the ephod, and the breastplate, and gird him with the **curious** girdle of the ephod: (Exo 29:5)

The word **curious** appears ten times in the AV.[375] It is from the French *curios* and is ultimately related to the Latin *cura*, "care." **Curious** means particular, detailed, or carefully, intricately, or skillfully made. The "**curious** arts" mentioned in the New Testament is a reference to divination, sorcery, or astrology.[376] Since the meaning of **curious** is now that of being desirous of seeing or knowing something, our modern versions have updated the word **curious** every time it appeared in the AV. The preferred translation of the NRSV was "decorated,"[377] but the NASB and NIV preferred "skillfully woven"[378] and the NKJV "intricately woven."[379] In one passage, the new versions all united on "artistic" to update **curious**.[380] The "**curious** arts" of the New Testament is given as "magic" by all but the NIV, which chose "sorcery."[381] But if the word **curious** made the Bible difficult to understand, then what about the NASB using a word like "capricious,"[382] and the NIV a word like "surmounted"?[383] And although the word **curious** is not used today like it appears in the AV, the word *curio*, short for *curiosity*, is still applied today to an object of art or something valued. Many people also have a curio cabinet.

Chapter 4
Dainty to Dureth

Dainty

> Eat thou not the bread of *him that hath* an evil eye, neither desire thou his **dainty** meats: (Prov 23:6)

This word appears three times in the AV as **dainty**[1] and three times as **dainties**.[2] It comes from the French *daintie,* "pleasure." **Dainty** is a doublet of *dignity,* and is most commonly used as an adjective meaning delicate, pleasing, delicious, valuable, or anything that is choice. The customary translation found in our modern versions is "delicacies."[3] However, twice the NRSV forgets to update the word.[4] The NKJV and the NASB each retain "**dainties**" in one passage,[5] but the NASB also inserted "**dainty**" into three additional verses,[6] one of which read "delicate" in the AV.[7] When the text of the AV was not altered to "delicacies," our new translations could not decide on which word to use. **Dainty** or **dainties** can also be found as "favorite,"[8] "choicest,"[9] "succulent,"[10] "luxurious,"[11] and "rich."[12] The word **dainty**, however, was not archaic in the first place, at least according to *Audubon* magazine: "The most notable track here was made by the **dainty** step of the coyote, one of which magically appeared on our right."[13]

Dale

> And the king of Sodom went out to meet him after his return from the slaughter of Chedorlaomer, and of the kings that *were* with him, at the valley of Shaveh, which *is* the king's **dale**. (Gen 14:17)

The word **dale** appears twice in the AV.[14] The Old English form was *dael,* meaning a valley. Our modern versions unanimously render **dale** as "valley."[15] Yet when the AV uses the simple word "valley," it is sometimes changed to words that are supposedly archaic or even worse, unintelligible. The NRSV twice transforms "valley" in the AV to the supposedly archaic "vale."[16] But the favored translation in the NRSV for "valley" is "wadi."[17] The NASB even uses this incredible translation one time.[18] So once again we see that often times these modern versions employ words that are more difficult than the supposedly archaic words in the AV. **Dale** can be seen today in geographical names like Scotts**dale**, Arizona.

𝔇𝔞𝔪

> If a bird's nest chance to be before thee in the way in any tree, or on the ground, *whether they be* young ones, or eggs, and the **dam** sitting upon the young, or upon the eggs, thou shalt not take the **dam** with the young: (Deu 22:6)

The word **dam** occurs four times in the AV.[19] **Dam** is a variant of *dame*, from the French *dame*, "a lady." **Dam** is the term usually applied to a mother animal. Our modern versions all update **dam** to "mother."[20] However, before these new translations are congratulated for making the Bible clearer, perhaps it should be explained why the NRSV altered "covetousness" in the AV to "avarice,"[21] and "neck" to "nape."[22]

𝔇𝔞𝔪𝔫𝔢𝔡

> He that believeth and is baptized shall be saved; but he that believeth not shall be **damned**. (Mark 16:16)

The word **damned** appears three times in the AV,[23] while the form **damnation** can be found eleven times.[24] Both of these words are formed from *damn*, from the French *damner*, "to condemn." To damn means to condemn to a particular penalty, to give judicial sentence against, or to pronounce adverse judgment upon. No one is ever **damned** in any of our modern versions—no forms of *damn* appear in any of them. The usual translation is a form of "condemnation"[25] or "judgment."[26] However, in one passage the NRSV and NASB use a form of "sentence,"[27] and in another they are joined by the NIV in employing "sin."[28] The NIV also chooses "punished" in two places.[29] But what happens when the AV already has forms of the word condemn? "Condemnation" in the AV can be found as "sentence" in the NIV,[30] "judgment" in the NASB[31] and NKJV,[32] "verdict" in the NIV,[33] and "found guilty" in the NIV and NKJV.[34] The NRSV even renders "condemnation" as "declared to be in the wrong."[35] "Condemn" and "condemned" in the AV can be found as "judge" and "judged" in the NASB.[36] When the AV reads "judgment," it is even corrected in the NIV to "making decisions."[37] Nevertheless, the word **damned** is so unarchaic as to not call for further comment.

Damsel

> And the **damsel** *was* very fair to look upon, a virgin, neither had any man known her: and she went down to the well, and filled her pitcher, and came up. (Gen 24:16)

Although the word **damsel** occurs forty times in the AV in the singular[38] and three times in the plural,[39] it can not be found in any of our modern versions. **Damsel** comes from the French *damoisele*, "a girl." It is related to *dam* and *dame*, and remotely to *domain*. **Damsel** is customarily rendered as "girl" in our new versions.[40] The NKJV, however, preferred "young woman" most of the time.[41] Sometimes a compromise was reached, as in "young girl," found in the NASB.[42] However, the plural **damsels** was usually changed into "maids" or "maidens,"[43] except for "girl," found once in the NRSV.[44] The expulsion of **damsel** from the text of the Bible was unnecessary, however, for **damsel** can still be found in use today: "As the man aids the **damsel** in distress, muscling tires and jacks with ease, the detectives snap photographic proof of his prowess."[45]

Darling

> Deliver my soul from the sword; my **darling** from the power of the dog. (Psa 22:20)

The word **darling** is found only twice in the AV.[46] The Old English form was *deorling*, from *deor*, "dear." **Darling** is a term of endearment that refers to the one and only, in this case the soul, because it is dear and valuable. The only child is the **darling** of his parents. The NRSV chose to supply this word as "life,"[47] and the NASB as "only life,"[48] but the NIV and NKJV preferred "precious life."[49] The word **darling** is certainly not archaic, for it is used everyday by husbands and wives as a term of endearment. The NIV and NASB even substitute "my **darling**" for "my love," found nine times in the AV.[50] The NRSV replaces the AV phrase "only one" with "**darling**."[51] The NKJV also used **darling** one time, exchanging it for "beloved fruit."[52] If it be objected that the word **darling** in the AV obscures the meaning, then what about "adjudicates" in the NASB?[53]

Daub

> Say unto them which **daub** *it* with untempered *mortar*, that it shall fall: there shall be an overflowing shower; and ye, O great hailstones, shall fall; and a stormy wind shall rend *it*. (Ezek 13:11)

Daub occurs only once in the AV in the singular,[54] but also six times as **daubed**[55] and once as **daubing**.[56] **Daub** is from the French *dauber*, "to plaster." The original Latin root meant to whiten over or whitewash. The word then took on the meaning of to cover, coat, or plaster with any substance. Except for "**daubed**" accidentally being used once in the NKJV,[57] no form of **daub** appears in any of our modern versions. The NRSV embraced "smear" or "smeared" most of the time,[58] but also adopted "whitewash" or "plastered."[59] The NASB preferred a form of "plaster,"[60] but also used "covered it over" once,[61] and "smeared"[62] once. The NIV could not decide among forms of "coated,"[63] "cover,"[64] or "whitewash."[65] The NKJV was the most consistent, employing forms of "plaster" seven times[66] and "mortar" once.[67] All these attempts at revision, however, were totally unnecessary, for the word **daub** is certainly not archaic: "He leaves a fine **daub** of gray-maroon color on the palette of film, though always destined to sit next to that rainbow rash of pigment named Orson Welles."[68]

Daysman

> Neither is there any **daysman** betwixt us, *that* might lay his hand upon us both. (Job 9:33)

The word **daysman** appears only once in the AV and is

formed from the word *day*. A **daysman** is an umpire, mediator, or arbitrator. This is because the word *day* was also formerly used as a verb meaning to decide, appoint, or submit a matter to arbitration. The NRSV and NASB each render **daysman** as "umpire." But as this reminds one too much of a baseball umpire, the NIV preferred "someone to arbitrate," while the NKJV chose "mediator." **Daysman** is admittedly archaic, but what about "alcoves" in the NIV[69] and "antimony" in the NASB?[70]

𝔇𝔞𝔶𝔰𝔭𝔯𝔦𝔫𝔤

> Hast thou commanded the morning since thy days; *and* caused the **dayspring** to know his place; (Job 38:12)

The word **dayspring** occurs only twice in the AV, once in the Old Testament and once in the New Testament.[71] It is obviously a compound made up of *day* and *spring*. The **dayspring** is the daybreak, the early dawn, or the sunrising. The Old Testament reference to **dayspring** is unanimously rendered by our modern versions as "dawn."[72] In the New Testament, where we have a prophetic reference to Jesus Christ, the NKJV retains the AV reading and the NASB has the same general idea,[73] but the NRSV simply uses "dawn" and the NIV "rising sun," destroying the prophetic reference.[74] Many people still say the "spring of the day," meaning the earliest part of the day.

𝔇𝔢𝔞𝔩

> Then shall he that offereth his offering unto the LORD bring a meat offering of a tenth **deal** of flour mingled with the fourth *part* of an hin of oil. (Num 15:4)

The word **deal,** when used as a noun, is found nine times in the AV.[75] It has developed from the Old English *doel,* "a share." Therefore, a **deal** is a portion, share, part, allotment, fraction, or section. The word *dole* is a variant of **deal**. Although the meaning of the word is apparent from the context, our modern versions have rendered the phrase "tenth **deal**" by a number of expressions. "Tenth **deal**" can be found as "one-tenth of a measure,"[76] "a tenth,"[77] or "one-tenth."[78] The more obscure "one-tenth of an ephah"[79] or "a tenth of an ephah"[80] is also

Dearth

> And the seven years of **dearth** began to come, according as Joseph had said: and the **dearth** was in all lands; but in all the land of Egypt there was bread. (Gen 41:54)

The word **dearth** appears eight times in the AV.[81] **Dearth** is from the Middle English *derthe*, "dearness," which was formed from the Old English *deore*, "dear." It originally meant high price, then it gradually came to mean scarcity. Hence, a **dearth** is a lack or scarcity of anything, especially as applied to agriculture or the environment. In all but the one place where **dearth** is rendered "drought,"[82] our modern versions have updated the word to "famine."[83] But after all these corrections, the NASB somehow managed to insert **dearth** into a verse where neither the AV nor any modern version contained the word.[84] And furthermore, **dearth** is still in use today: "It has been a strange campaign, one marked by a **dearth** of activity and much secrecy surrounding the movements and plans of both candidates."[85]

Debase

> And thou wentest to the king with ointment, and didst increase thy perfumes, and didst send thy messengers far off, and didst **debase** *thyself even* unto hell. (Isa 57:9)

The word **debase** occurs just once in the AV. It was formed in the sixteenth century from *de*, meaning down, and *base*. To **debase** is to reduce in value, quality, dignity, rank or position. The NIV and NKJV preferred "descended," while the NRSV used "sent down" and the NASB employed "go down." But after just changing the word in this verse, the NKJV alone inserts "debases" into another passage in the Old Testament.[86] Then in the New Testament, the NRSV and NKJV utilize the word "debased" to further correct the AV.[87] The word **debase**, however, was not considered archaic by the *Los Angeles Times*: "These voices are still few in number, but there is growing circulation to their arguments that pets are a form of slavery and debase both people and animals."[88]

Deceivableness

> And with all **deceivableness** of unrighteousness in them that perish; because they received not the love of the truth, that they might be saved. (2 Th 2:10)

The word **deceivableness** is found only once in the AV. It is formed from the word *deceive,* from the French *deceivre,* "to deceive." **Deceivableness** is deceit, deception, or deceitfulness, all of which are etymologically related to the word *deceive.* The obvious problem with the word **deceivableness** is the double suffix *-ableness.* Our modern versions preferred the word "deception," except for the NIV, which chose "deceives." But if this suffix is so archaic, then why does the NKJV use "unprofitableness" in one passage[89] and the NASB utilize "unchangeableness" in another?[90]

Deck

> They **deck** it with silver and with gold; they fasten it with nails and with hammers, that it move not. (Jer 10:4)

Although the word **deck** can only be found twice in the AV,[91] the form **decked** appears six times,[92] while **deckedst** occurs twice,[93] and **decketh** and **deckest** each appear once.[94] **Deck** is from the Dutch *decken,* "to cover," and is certainly a common, elementary word, but its use as a verb is what is troubling to our modern versions. **Deck,** as found in the AV, means to adorn, cover, or clothe. The usual translation for all of the various forms of **deck** is a form of "adorn."[95] Other translations include the words "glittering,"[96] "spread,"[97] "decorated,"[98] "covered,"[99] "made,"[100] and "put on."[101] The NKJV forgot to update the word on two occasions,[102] while the NIV[103] and NASB[104] each retained the AV reading once. Surprisingly, the NRSV only corrected the various forms of **deck** five times,[105] but then inserted "**decked**" into three passages where neither the AV nor any modern version used the word.[106] Forms of **deck,** however, are still in use today as a verb: "More than 5,000 fans **decked** out in waves of green, yellow, maroon and gold awaited the action."[107]

Decline

> Thou shalt not follow a multitude to do evil; neither shalt thou speak in a cause to **decline** after many to wrest judgment: (Exo 23:2)

The word **decline** can be seen five times in the AV.[108] However, **declined** occurs four times,[109] and **declineth** appears twice.[110] This word is from the French *decliner,* "to decline." To **decline** is to deviate, turn from, diverge, or fall from. Our modern versions correct the AV every time a form of **decline** shows up. The usual up-to-date translation is "turn aside,"[111] but "turn away" is also employed.[112] Some other translations that can be found are "deviated,"[113] "strayed,"[114] "departed,"[115] "swerve,"[116] "turn,"[117] and "lengthens."[118] But after all these corrections, the NRSV and NASB went against not only the AV, but the other modern versions as well, in implanting forms of "**decline**" into their text in several additional verses. When the AV and all others use "afternoon," the NRSV changes it to "the day **declined**."[119] When the AV and all others read "gone down," the NRSV alters it to "**declined**."[120] When the AV employs the phrase "passed away," the NASB amends it to "**declined**," even though the other versions follow the AV.[121] If the AV says "wear away," the NASB has to change it to "**declined**."[122] And finally, when the AV reads "goeth away," both the NRSV and NASB revise it to "**declines**."[123]

Delectable

> They that make a graven image *are* all of them vanity; and their **delectable** things shall not profit; and they *are* their own witnesses; they see not, nor know; that they may be ashamed. (Isa 44:9)

Delectable occurs only once in the AV and is from the French *delectable,* "delightful." **Delectable** means delightful, pleasing, or delicious. This word has been corrected to "precious" in the NKJV and NASB, but "delight" in the NRSV and "treasure" in the NIV. Yet the NRSV introduces the word into another passage where no other modern version uses the word.[124] Moreover, the word **delectable** is not archaic at all: "That process exposes him or her to the mole-rat's natural enemies, long-billed birds and, even more deadly, snakes—sand boas, rufous-beaked snakes and mole snakes—all of which find mole-rats **delectable** cuisine."[125]

Delightsome

> And all nations shall call you blessed: for ye shall be a **delightsome** land, saith the LORD of hosts. (Mal 3:12)

This word appears only once in the AV. It is plainly formed from *delight* and the suffix *-some*. This is another case of a word in the AV that is not archaic but contains a suffix that makes the word suspect. **Delightsome** means delightful, enjoyable, or pleasing. The word is corrected by all of our modern versions to "delight" or "delightful." Yet all these new translations formed words with a *-some* suffix that are not even in the AV. All four of our versions employed both "quarrelsome"[126] and "troublesome."[127] The NKJV uses "gruesome"[128] and the NIV "toilsome."[129] Certainly **delightsome** is not any harder to understand than these words.

Deputed

> And Absalom said unto him, See, thy matters *are* good and right; but *there is* no man **deputed** of the king to hear thee. (2 Sam 15:3)

Found only once in the AV, the word **deputed** is the past tense of the verb *depute*, from the French *deputer*, "to assign." **Depute** can mean to assign, commit, impute, ascribe, attribute, appoint, or authorize. Our common word *deputy* is just someone who has been **deputed**. Since the verbal form is not used today, our modern versions, excepting the NRSV, which mistakenly followed the AV, have concluded that **deputed** must be archaic. The NIV alters **deputed** to "on the part," the NASB to "representative," but the NKJV just makes the word into a noun. Yet when the AV says "deputies," all of the supposedly modern, up-to-date versions altered it to "proconsuls."[130] Moreover, the word **deputed** is still in use, at least according to *U.S. News & World Report:* Eight leading institutes, think tanks and universities have been **deputed** to help the government rebut foreign criticism in more sophisticated fashion."[131]

Deride

And they shall scoff at the kings, and the princes shall be a scorn unto them: they shall **deride** every strong hold; for they shall heap dust, and take it. (Hab 1:10)

Although **deride** occurs only once in the AV, the form **derided** can be found twice[132] and the noun **derision** fifteen times.[133] **Deride** is from the Latin *deridere,* "to laugh down." To **deride** is to laugh or mock in ridicule, scorn, or contempt. Out of the three times **deride** and **derided** appear in the AV, the NKJV retains them twice,[134] while the other modern versions erase them every time. The NRSV, NASB, and NIV all modify **deride** in the AV to "laugh."[135] However, our four new translations could not decide among themselves how to alter **derided**. The NRSV chose "ridiculed" and "scoffed,"[136] and the NASB selected "scoffing" and "sneering,"[137] but the NIV preferred to use forms of *sneer* on both occasions.[138] But in spite of all these corrections, every one of our modern versions introduced a form of "**deride**" into their text in other passages where the AV did not contain the word. The NASB used "**deride**" twice,[139] as did the NKJV,[140] which also employed "**derided**" once.[141] The NASB inserts a form of "**deride**" seven times.[142] The NIV is the worst culprit, for in the very same passage where "**deride**" was altered to "laugh," the word "scoff" in the AV is changed to "**deride**."[143] The NIV also uses "**deride**" in another passage where the AV did not contain the word.[144] Surprisingly, the word **derision** is retained by our new translations part of the time.[145] And even if our modern versions never used the word **deride** in other passages, the word **deride** did not need to be updated, for even the *Fort Worth Star-Telegram* did not consider it to be archaic: "They **deride** her as a career politician, a female 'good ol' boy' who has gone along to get along while taxes, bureaucracy and government regulation increased in Texas."[146]

Describe

Ye shall therefore **describe** the land *into* seven parts, and bring *the description* hither to me, that I may cast lots for you here before the LORD our God. (Josh 18:6)

The word **describe** appears four times as **describe**,[147] once as description,[148] and twice each as **described**[149] and **describeth**.[150] It is from the Latin *describere,* "to write down." This word has gradually come to mean write down, narrate, mark out, and distribute. The modern use of **describe** is basically limited to narrate, relate, report, depict, or disclose. This latter usage cannot be found in the AV, although our modern versions abound with it.[151] The AV reading is retained by the NRSV once,[152] the NKJV once,[153] and the NIV once.[154] However, the NASB keeps it four times.[155] The normal substitution made for forms of the word **describe** is some form of "write a description."[156] The NKJV liked to use the word "survey."[157] It is obvious that **describe** has something to do with writing if one considers the English words *scribe* and *script.* The influence of the AV on the NIV can be seen in the passage where, although the Greek word in question is *grapho,* the NIV follows the AV and renders it "describes,"after translating it by a form of *write* in all the other passages where *grapho* is found.[158]

Descry

> And the house of Joseph sent to **descry** Bethel. (Now the name of the city before *was* Luz.) (Judg 1:23)

The word **descry,** appearing only once in the AV, is actually a variant of *descrive.* Its meaning has been confused because another word **descry** is a variant of *decry,* from the French *descrier,* "to proclaim." *Descrive* has been superseded by *describe.* To **descry** means to write out, map out, write down, describe, or discover. Our modern versions all alter **descry** to a form of "spy." Yet when the AV reads "spy" or "spied," it is sometimes corrected. The NIV updates the modest "spy out the land" to "explore the land."[159] Likewise, when the AV mentions men sent to "spy" out a city, the NIV replaces it with "explore the city."[160] In one passage where the AV read "spy," the NKJV and NASB updated it to "see," the NRSV to "find," and the NIV to "find out."[161] On another occasion when the AV utilizes the elementary word "spied," the NKJV, NIV, and NASB alter it to "saw."[162] **Descry** may be archaic, but the similar form **decry** is still in use today: "In his lecture, Westling **decried** the government and its over-regulation of institutes of higher learning."[163]

Despite

> Of how much sorer punishment, suppose ye, shall he be thought worthy, who hath trodden under foot the Son of God, and hath counted the blood of the covenant, wherewith he was sanctified, an unholy thing, and hath done **despite** unto the Spirit of grace? (Heb 10:29)

Despite, appearing twice in the AV,[164] is joined by **despiteful**[165] and **despitefully**,[166] each found three times. This word is from the French *despit,* "a despising," and means contempt, disdain, scorn, malice, hatred, or spite. *Spite* is merely short for **despite**, which is commonly used today as a preposition meaning "in spite of" or "notwithstanding," and is the only way **despite** is used by our modern versions.[167] The various forms of **despite** in the AV have been rendered in many different ways. It can be found as "malice,"[168] "scorn,"[169] "disdain,"[170] "contempt,"[171] "abuse,"[172] "violent,"[173] "mistreat,"[174] "outraged,"[175] "insulted,"[176] and "spiteful."[177] The NIV, NASB, and NRSV all correct "**despiteful**" in one verse to the more difficult "insolent."[178] So once again, when the AV employs a modern word with a different meaning than is used today, it is corrected, even if a more difficult word has to be put in its place.

Devotions

> For as I passed by, and beheld your **devotions**, I found an altar with this inscription, TO THE UNKNOWN GOD. Whom therefore ye ignorantly worship, him declare I unto you. (Acts 17:23)

The word **devotions**, the plural of *devotion,* from the French *devocion,* occurs only once in the AV. Devotion is dedication, attention, or attachment to a cause, object, or person. **Devotions**, usually found in a religious context, can refer to the act or the object of worship, adoration, or praise. Although our modern versions had no trouble with the verb forms of "devote,"[179] they in unison altered **devotions** to a phrase after the form of "the objects of your worship." Evidently, none of the children of the translators of these new versions ever went to summer camp and had morning and evening **devotions**. Nevertheless, the word is still in use today as it is found in the AV: "Until then, it was famous among Hasidic groups for the intensity of its mystical devotions."[180]

Dignities

> Likewise also these *filthy* dreamers defile the flesh, despise dominion, and speak evil of **dignities.** (Jude 1:8)

Dignities are mentioned twice in the AV.[181] The word is the plural of *dignity,* from the French *dignete,* "worthiness." Dignity is the quality of nobility, worthiness, honor, distinction, or excellence. **Dignities** are persons holding a high position worthy of honor, distinction, or merit. The modern word for **dignities** is *dignitaries.* Although our modern versions utilize the word "dignity,"[182] they avoid applying the word to a person as the AV. However, our new translations could not agree on how to render the replacement for the AV reading. On both occasions the word **dignities** appears in the AV, the NRSV reads "the glorious ones," the NASB "angelic majesties," and the NIV "celestial beings."[183] Only the NKJV employs the similar "dignitaries."[184] Furthermore, when the AV employs a simpler word than "dignitaries," it is often corrected. The more difficult "dignitaries" is substituted in the NRSV for the AV reading of "honourable."[185] The NIV replaces "elders"[186] and "princes"[187] with "dignitaries." But what happens when the AV uses simple, plain, easy-to-understand words? The NRSV alters "chariots" to "charioty," and the NIV, in the same verse, corrects "horsemen" to "charioteers."[188] The AV may contain archaic words, but at least they are real words and not just made up.

Disannul

> For the LORD of hosts hath purposed, and who shall **disannul** *it?* and his hand *is* stretched out, and who shall turn it back? (Isa 14:27)

The word **disannul** appears three times in the AV,[189] but is also found once each as **disannulled, disannulleth,** and **disannulling.**[190] Although the *dis-* prefix usually signifies negation, in this case it is intensive. Thus, **disannul** means to cancel, abolish, annul, abolish, void, or nullify. It would be a simple matter to update this word to *annul,* but our modern versions preferred a variety of translations. "Annul" can be found several times,[191] but the NIV uses "discredit" once,[192] the NASB employs "invalidate" and "canceled" each one time,[193] and the NRSV once utilizes the much harder "abrogation."[194] Other translations include "turn it back,"[195] and forms of "set aside."[196] Yet after correcting **disannul** because the *dis-* prefix makes the word archaic, the NRSV introduced the word "disbelieving,"[197] the NKJV "disfigurement,"[198] the NIV "disillusionment,"[199] and the NASB "dispossessing."[200] None of these "archaic" *dis-* words can be found in the AV.

Discomfited

And Joshua **discomfited** Amalek and his people with the edge of the sword. (Exo 17:13)

The word **discomfited** occurs nine times in the AV,[201] while the form **discomfiture** can be found once.[202] *Discomfit* is from the French *desconfit*, from *desconfire*, "to defeat." To be **discomfited** is to be defeated, destroyed, overthrown, or frustrated. The word *discomfit* also means embarrass or make uncomfortable, due to its association with the similar word *discomfort*. Our modern versions unanimously corrected all forms of these words but could not decide on what to substitute. The NKJV uses six different words or expressions to update the AV (defeated, drove them back, routed, confused, vanquished, forced labor).[203] The NASB also employed six diverse words or expressions to bring the AV up-to-date (overwhelmed, beat them down, confounded, routed, confused, forced laborers).[204] The NRSV uses "defeated" twice,[205] "routed" twice,[206] and "confusion" once,[207] but preferred forms of "threw them into a panic."[208] The NIV also practiced diversity in choosing the proper translation, even incorporating the long phrase "threw them into such a panic" to correct **discomfited**.[209] Yet when the AV contains a simple word like "defeat," it is corrected both times it occurs to the discomfiting "thwart" in the NASB and "frustrate" in the NIV.[210] Although these modern versions considered **discomfited** to be archaic, *The Seattle Times* certainly did not: "The manufactures are **discomfited** by the perilous state of their customers, the airlines, but take heart in the fact that the United States has the industrial world's oldest airplane fleet."[211]

Discover

> Then said Jonathan, Behold, we will pass over unto *these* men, and we will **discover** ourselves unto them. (1 Sam 14:8)

The word **discover** occurs twelve times in the AV.[212] The past tense **discovered** appears twenty-two times,[213] the form **discovereth** twice,[214] and **discovering** once.[215] **Discover** is from the French *descovrir*, "to uncover." Hence, to **discover** is to remove the covering of, to uncover, withdraw, divulge, reveal, disclose, make known, exhibit, display, or to catch sight of. Seeking to limit the meaning of **discover** to finding something, our modern versions correct every occurrence of **discover, discovereth** and **discovering,** and all but two of **discovered**.[216] But in doing so, the modern equivalents *uncover* and *uncovered* were rarely used.[217] Instead, **discover** was rendered as "dishonor,"[218] "show,"[219] "reveal,"[220] "strip off,"[221] and "remove."[222] **Discovered** can be found as "exposed,"[223] "showed,"[224] "revealed,"[225] "laid bare,"[226] "stripped away,"[227] "removed,"[228] and "sighted."[229] Yet when the AV uses **discovered** in the sense of finding something, the NRSV changes it to "located" even though the NIV, NASB, and NKJV follow the AV reading.[230] And furthermore, when the AV employs the word "uncover," it is changed in the NRSV to the arcane "dishevel."[231]

Dispensation

> If ye have heard of the **dispensation** of the grace of God which is given me to you-ward: (Eph 3:2)

The word **dispensation** is found four times in the AV.[232] It comes into English from a French word of the same spelling and is related to the verb *dispense*. A dispensary is a place where things are dispensed. A **dispensation** is a distribution, management, economy, regulation, disbursement, arrangement, or administration. Although the NIV utilized four different words or expressions to update the AV,[233] the NRSV normally used "commission,"[234] and the NASB "stewardship."[235] The NKJV also liked "stewardship,"[236] but twice followed the AV.[237] These corrections were completely unnecessary, for the word dispensation is still used today, even in non-biblical contexts: "The May decision ended what for European farmers was a long period of doubt and uncertainty, giving them a three-year transitional period in which to adjust their operations to the new **dispensation**."[238]

Disputation

> When therefore Paul and Barnabas had no small dissension and **disputation** with them, they determined that Paul and Barnabas, and certain other of them, should go up to Jerusalem unto the apostles and elders about this question. (Acts 15:2)

This word is found in the AV once in the singular and once in the plural.[239] **Disputation** comes from the Latin *disputatio*, "dispute." A **disputation** is an argument, debate, discussion, or controversy. In the first passage where this word appears in the AV, it is unanimously corrected by our modern versions to "debate."[240] In the second, the NRSV and NASB choose "opinions," the NIV "matters," and the NKJV "things."[241] Yet when the AV employs the phrase "mine opinion," the NIV changes it to "what I know" and the NASB to "what I think."[242] The word **disputation**, however, is still current at the end of the twentieth century, whether in the singular: "Anonymous and pseudonymous pieces were the norm for political **disputation** in those days,"[243] or in the plural: "Soon Jews were called upon to defend their faith in public **disputations**."[244]

Disquiet

> Their Redeemer *is* strong; the LORD of hosts *is* his name: he shall thoroughly plead their cause, that he may give rest to the land, and **disquiet** the inhabitants of Babylon. (Jer 50:34)

The word **disquiet** appears once in the AV, as does the form **disquietness**,[245] but **disquieted** can be found six times.[246] **Disquiet** is a compound formed from the negating prefix *dis-* and *quiet*. To **disquiet** is to deprive of quietness, disturb, alarm, trouble, or make restless. The NIV and NASB completely eliminated all forms of these words from the Bible, usually substituting "disturbed,"[247] but also utilizing "agitation,"[248] "anguish,"[249] "make an uproar,"[250] "bustles about,"[251] "quakes,"[252] "trembles,"[253] "turmoil,"[254] and "unrest."[255]

Besides collaborating on the word "disturbed," no other verses were translated alike in the NIV and NASB. The NRSV accidentally followed the AV reading of "**disquieted**" three times,[256] but obviously could not decide on how to correct the other forms of **disquiet**, since five different phrases were used to do so (disturbed, tumult, in turmoil, trembles, unrest).[257] The NKJV followed the AV on four occasions,[258] but also emulated the other modern versions in using four distinct words to alter the other forms of **disquiet** (disturbed, turmoil, busy themselves, perturbed).[259] Our modern versions may have considered **disquiet** to be archaic, but *The Washington Times* undoubtedly did not: "It is very polarizing, but it has also provided a handle, for many people have had a vague **disquiet** they could not articulate."[260]

𝔇𝔦𝔰𝔰𝔢𝔪𝔟𝔩𝔢𝔡

> And the other Jews **dissembled** likewise with him; insomuch that Barnabas also was carried away with their dissimulation. (Gal 2:13)

The word **dissembled** occurs three times in the AV.[261] The form **dissemblers** can be found once,[262] as can **dissembleth**.[263] *Dissemble* is a form of *dissimule,* from the French *dissimuler,* "to disguise." To *dissemble* is to disguise, neglect, ignore, conceal, or otherwise act hypocritically. Our modern versions have removed all forms of this word from the Bible, except for the NRSV, which forgot to remove "dissembles" from one verse.[264] A variety of translations to update these words can be seen in our new translations. The common rendering is a form of "hypocrite."[265] **Dissembleth** is corrected to "disguises."[266] **Dissembled** is often given as "deceived."[267] Other translations include "lied,"[268] "acted deceitfully,"[269] "pretenders,"[270] and "made a fatal mistake."[271] But once again, the effort expended in making all these corrections was in vain, for forms of the word *dissemble* are still in use today: "Joyce Cunha, executive director of Mass. Choice, also said Romney could not be considered a 'prochoice' candidate and accused him of **dissembling** on the issue."[272]

𝔇𝔦𝔰𝔰𝔦𝔪𝔲𝔩𝔞𝔱𝔦𝔬𝔫

> *Let* love be without **dissimulation**. Abhor that which is evil; cleave to that which is good. (Rom 12:9)

The word **dissimulation** appears twice in the AV[273] and is from a French word of the same spelling. It is ultimately derived from the same Latin root as *dissimuler*, which gave us *dissembled*. These words are also remotely related to *similar*, from the Latin *simulare* "to pretend." **Dissimulation** is duplicity, hypocrisy, or deception. Our modern versions ordinarily render **dissimulation** as "hypocrisy."[274] The AV phrase "without **dissimulation**," can be found as "genuine" in the NRSV, and "sincere" in the NIV.[275] But when the AV reads "without hypocrisy," the NIV changes it to "sincere."[276] The meaning of the word **dissimulation**, however, is certainly easier to understand than why the NASB alone altered "grief" to "sickliness."[277]

𝔇istil

> My doctrine shall drop as the rain, my speech shall **distil** as the dew, as the small rain upon the tender herb, and as the showers upon the grass: (Deu 32:2)

The word **distil** (modern American spelling: **distill**) occurs twice in the AV[278] and is from the French *distiller*, "to drip down." The modern American meaning is usually limited to the process of vaporization and condensation used by industry or moonshiners. But **distil** also means to drip or trickle down, to expel in small amounts, and to instil, infuse, or impart. Both occurrences of **distil** in the AV are unanimously corrected by the NIV and NRSV,[279] but the NASB and NKJV were careless in only correcting the AV in one passage.[280] The NRSV one time revises **distil** to "drop,"[281] but when the AV reads "drop," it is corrected to "**distill**."[282] Although the NKJV alters **distil** to "pour" in one verse,[283] it joins our three other translations in correcting the AV reading of "pour down" to "**distill**."[284] These corrections were entirely unnecessary, for the word **distil** is still in use today when not referring to distilling a product: "The skill of the advertiser, the skill of the creative person is to **distil** it down into a form that is communicable."[285]

𝔇ivers

> **Divers** weights, *and* **divers** measures, both of them *are* alike abomination to the LORD. (Prov 20:10)

The word **divers** occurs in the AV thirty-seven times in thirty-four verses.[286] It is from the French *divers,* "different." Thus, **divers** means different, diverse, varied, unlike, distinct, various or several. Both **divers** and *diverse* existed in Middle English but *diverse* became the form that survived. Judging from the **divers** ways that **divers** is rendered, our modern versions agreed on only one thing: it had to be removed from the Bible. There are perhaps more replacements for the word **divers** than any other word in the AV. A brief list would include "varied,"[287] "various,"[288] "diverse,"[289] "different,"[290] "differing,"[291] "many,"[292] "some,"[293] "all kinds,"[294] "many kinds,"[295] "any kind,"[296] "all kinds of,"[297] "two kinds of,"[298] "a second kind of,"[299] and "dyed."[300] Yet after wearing out a thesaurus to correct **divers,** our modern, up-to-date translations introduced words into the Bible like "wafted,"[301] "indolence"[302] and "cordage."[303]

Divorcement

> It hath been said, Whosoever shall put away his wife, let him give her a writing of **divorcement:** (Mat 5:31)

The word **divorcement** occurs six times in the AV.[304] The suffix *-ment* that gives our new translations so much trouble is a suffix of nouns formed from verbs that denotes an action or resulting state. Other examples would include the words *abridgement* and *punishment.* Our modern versions correct **divorcement** to "divorce" every time it occurs in the AV,[305] except for the one time the NRSV said "dismissal."[306] However, where the AV does read "bill of divorce," the NASB changes it to the more difficult "writ of divorce."[307] As for the suffix *-ment,* all of our modern versions did not hesitate to use the words "amazement"[308] and "astonishment."[309] In fact, the NASB even altered "amazed" in the AV to "amazement."[310] The NASB also utilizes the words "confinement"[311] and "bewilderment"[312] even though they are not found in the AV, NKJV, or NRSV. And furthermore, not only did Hollywood make a movie entitled "Bill of **Divorcement,**" the word is still regularly used today: "Before the **divorcement** proceedings that ordered studios to divest themselves of their exhibition monopolies, a film's content could be repetitious, especially with block-booking in effect."[313]

Doctor

> Then stood there up one in the council, a Pharisee, named Gamaliel, a **doctor** of the law, had in reputation among all the people, and commanded to put the apostles forth a little space; (Acts 5:34)

The word **doctor** occurs in the AV once in the singular[314] and twice in the plural.[315] It is from the French *doctour*, "teacher." Contrary to the American Medical Association and our modern Bible versions, a **doctor** is a teacher, an instructor, or a learned man. Every occurrence of **doctor** or **doctors** in the AV has been updated by our modern versions to "teacher" or "teachers."[316] Yet every translator of these modern versions who has earned his Ph.D. calls himself a **doctor** even though none can tell a tibia from a fibula. Desiring to be the most up-to-date, the NIV five times alters "physician" in the AV to "doctor."[317] However, the NIV was highly inconsistent, since it retained the AV reading of "physician" six times.[318] For some reason the NRSV corrected "physician" to "doctor" only one time.[319] Nevertheless, even the Yellow Pages follow the AV: medical **doctors** are listed under physicians.

Doleful

> But wild beasts of the desert shall lie there; and their houses shall be full of **doleful** creatures; and owls shall dwell there, and satyrs shall dance there. (Isa 13:21)

The word **doleful**, found twice in the AV,[320] is a hybrid made up of the French *doel*, "grief," and the English suffix *-ful*. **Doleful** means sorrowful, mournful, dismal, gloomy, or grieved. Our modern versions have eradicated this word from the Bible. "**Doleful** creatures" in the AV has been updated to "howling creatures" in the NRSV,[321] but just a nondescript animal in our other translations. The NASB and the NKJV just say "owls," while the NIV prefers "jackals."[322] Yet when the AV uses the three-letter word "owl," it is still corrected. The "screech owl" in the AV has been converted to a "night monster" in the NASB, a "night creature" in the NIV and NKJV, and a "Lilith" in the NRSV.[323] Then the plain, lowly "owl" in the AV is transformed into an "ostrich" by the NASB, NRSV, and NKJV.[324] The second occurrence of **doleful** in the AV is altered to "bitter" by the NRSV, NASB, and NKJV—the NIV alone used "mournful."[325] The word **doleful**, however, was not archaic to begin with, at least according to *The San Diego Union-Tribune*: "Dennis gyrated and stuck out his tongue as he depicted Tigger, the bouncing forest tiger, explaining that he didn't mean to knock Eeyore, the **doleful** donkey, into the water."[326]

Dote

> A sword *is* upon the liars; and they shall **dote**: a sword *is* upon her mighty men; and they shall be dismayed. (Jer 50:36)

Dote occurs once in the AV,[327] as does **doting**,[328] while **doted** can be found six times.[329] **Dote** appeared in Middle English as *doten*. To **dote** is to say or think foolishly, be foolishly fond of, or to bestow extravagant affection on. All forms of **dote** have been removed by our modern versions. **Doted** is always corrected to "lusted,"[330] and **dote** to a form of "be fools,"[331] yet they could not agree on how to alter **doting**. The NRSV chose "morbid craving," the NASB "morbid interest," the NIV "unhealthy interest," and the NKJV "obsessed."[332] Yet when the AV reads "lusted," the NRSV, NIV, and NASB amend it every time.[333] Although our new versions considered **dote** to be archaic, the *Oregonian* newspaper certainly did not: "As Oregonians—and the rest of the nation—continue to **dote** on their dogs, the technology in treating them also will improve, Merril said."[334]

Doth

> For God **doth** know that in the day ye eat thereof, then your eyes shall be opened, and ye shall be as gods, knowing good and evil. (Gen 3:5)

The word **doth**, the most frequently occurring form of *do* that appears in the AV beside the word *do* itself, occurs 207 times. The conjugate form **doeth** appears ninety-six times. *Do* appeared in Old English as *don*. **Doth** and **doeth**, the third person singular forms of *do*, were superseded by *does* during the sixteenth and seventeenth centuries.[335] The second person, singular forms of *do*, **dost** and **doest**, appear respectively 56 and 122 times in the AV. The plural forms of *do* are always *do*. In the past tense, all of the plural, as well as the forms of the first and third person singular, are handled by *did*. The second person singular form is **didst**, found 122 times in the AV. Obviously, **doth, doeth, dost, doest,** and **didst** are archaic. They are so archaic that, excepting **doeth**, all of them can be found in the NASB. None of our other modern versions use any of these words, but the NASB forgot to remove "**doth**" one time[336] and "**doest**" twice.[337] Judging from the number of times, however, that the NASB contains the words **dost** and **didst**, it is apparent that these supposedly archaic words were intentionally left in the Bible, for "**dost**" appears 187 times[338] in the NASB and "**didst**" is found 176 times.[339] And not only that, these words can still be found in newspapers in the 1990's: "'The aide, Ken Brock, said: 'They **doth** protest too much.'"[340]

Downsitting

Thou knowest my **downsitting** and mine uprising, thou understandest my thought afar off. (Psa 139:2)

The word **downsitting** is found only once in the AV. It is obviously a compound of *down* and *sitting* meaning sitting down. Naturally, our modern versions separate the word. The NRSV and NASB made it "sit down," the NKJV "sitting down" and the NIV just "sit." But stranger compound words than **downsitting** can be found in our new, contemporary translations. The NRSV assembles the compounds "vinestock" and "vinegrower" even though neither the AV nor any modern version employs the words.[341] The NASB even altered the AV expression "many colours" to the fabricated compound "varicolored."[342]

Drams

They gave after their ability unto the treasure of the work threescore and one thousand **drams** of gold, and five thousand pound of silver, and one hundred priests' garments. (Ezra 2:69)

Drams are mentioned six times in the AV.[343] The word *dram* is a doublet of *drachma,* directly from the Greek, which appeared in Latin and French under various forms. The closest form to the word *dram* being the French *drame.* A *dram* was literally a handful, then a weight or a coin, and finally a measure. If **drams**

needed to be updated because its meaning was arcane and obscure, then why was it replaced in our modern versions with equally cryptic words like "darics"[344] and "drachmas"?[345] A *dram* is still an English measurement of weight or fluid, chiefly in compounding and dispensing drugs. A fluid dram is the eighth part of a fluid ounce. And **drams** can also be found in referring to money: "When tenges, **drams,** leus, som-coupons and others were unveiled over the last few months, the republics were cut off from cheap ruble credits as well as from the cheap ruble-priced oil that is still available to Russian consumers."[346]

Draught

> Do not ye yet understand, that whatsoever entereth in at the mouth goeth into the belly, and is cast out into the **draught?** (Mat 15:17)

The word **draught** occurs five times in the AV[347] and appeared in Old English as *dragan*. **Draught** has two basic and distinct meanings. As a synonym of *draft*, **draught** refers to something derived or extracted, the act of drawing, something used in drawing, or a quantity drawn. Thus, **draught** is customarily applied to a catch of fish. This usage can be found twice in the AV, where our modern versions unanimously render it as "catch."[348] The other connotation of **draught** is thought to be short for *withdraught,* a place of retirement or retreat, a private chamber; hence, a privy, sink, bathroom, or sewer. The NKJV translates this once as "refuse" in the same verse where the other versions employ "latrine."[349] The other two occurrences of **draught** are rendered by the NRSV as "sewer," but are not translated at all by the rest.[350] Instead, the phrase "goeth out into the **draught**" is twice shortened to "is eliminated" by the NKJV and NASB,[351] and changed to "then out of [the, his] body" by the NIV.[352] But if these new translations were interested in getting rid of archaic words then why was the word "**draught**" inserted twice by the NRSV where neither the AV nor any other new version contained the word?[353]

Dromedary

> How canst thou say, I am not polluted, I have not gone after Baalim? see thy way in the valley, know what thou hast done:

thou art a swift **dromedary** traversing her ways; (Jer 2:23)

A **dromedary** is mentioned in the AV once in the singular and three times in the plural.[354] **Dromedary** is from the French *dromadaire*, "a camel." A **dromedary** is a one-humped camel. The NKJV retains the AV reading on two occasions,[355] but the other new translations remove the word completely. Our modern versions had a terrible problem in updating the word **dromedary**. In one particular verse, the NRSV made a **dromedary** a plain "camel," the NASB a "young camel," and the NIV a "she-camel."[356] Other translations include "horses"[357] and "steeds."[358] Yet when the AV says "swift beasts," the NRSV alters it to "**dromedaries**."[359] But in spite of these corrections, camels are still called **dromedaries** in the 1990's: "About 20,000 people came to the two-day Selcuk festival this year to watch 120 **dromedaries** scuffle it out in the dust of a 2,000-year-old stadium in the ancient city of Ephesus."[360]

Duke

These *were* **dukes** of the sons of Esau: the sons of Eliphaz the firstborn *son* of Esau; **duke** Teman, **duke** Omar, **duke** Zepho, **duke** Kenaz, (Gen 36:15)

Duke can be seen forty-three times in the AV,[361] while **dukes** appears fifteen.[362] **Duke** is from the French *duc*, "leader." Thus, a **duke** is a chief, commander, leader, sovereign, or nobleman. In England, a **duke** is ranked just below a prince and above a marquis. Our modern versions have unanimously expurgated **duke** and **dukes** from the text of the Bible. The NASB, NIV, and NKJV preferred "chief" and "chiefs."[363] The NRSV independently elected to use "clans" to update the archaic **duke** and **dukes**.[364] The NRSV admired "clans" so much that it also substituted it for "governors,"[365] "families,"[366] and "the house of their fathers."[367] Although these new translations judged **duke** to be archaic, there are some men that this was a surprise to: Philip, **Duke** of Edinburgh, and Andrew, **Duke** of York.

Dulcimer

That at what time ye hear the sound of the cornet, flute, harp, sackbut, psaltery, **dulcimer**, and all kinds of music, ye fall

Dainty to Dureth

down and worship the golden image that Nebuchadnezzar the king hath set up: (Dan 3:5)

A **dulcimer**, mentioned three times in the AV,[368] is from the French *doulcemer*. A **dulcimer** is a stringed instrument but could also refer to any instrument making a pleasant sound, for the Latin root is *dulce melos*, "a sweet sound." *Melos*, it should be recognized, is similar to our modern English word *melody*. Although our modern versions were in agreement that **dulcimer** should be purged from the Bible, they could not concur on a replacement for it. In every place **dulcimer** occurs in the AV, the NRSV has substituted "drum," the NIV "pipes," and the NASB "bagpipes."[369] The NKJV removes the word **dulcimer** by expanding the next phrase, "and all kinds of music," to "in symphony with all kinds of music."[370] But whereas our modern versions deemed **dulcimer** archaic, the *Washington Post* undoubtedly did not: "Hard times in the country run counter to Appalachia's image as a land of folklore and handicrafts, Daniel Boone and **dulcimers**."[371]

𝔇ung

And one shall burn the heifer in his sight; her skin, and her flesh, and her blood, with her **dung**, shall he burn: (Num 19:5)

Dung is mentioned twenty-eight times in the AV,[372] while the related compound **dunghill** occurs seven times in the singular[373] and once in the plural.[374] **Dung** survives from the Old English *dung* and refers to waste matter, manure, excrement, or anything morally filthy. Surprisingly, the NRSV retains the word "**dung**" almost every time it occurs in the AV.[375] The word "**dunghill**," however, did not fare as well, for the NRSV only followed the AV once.[376] The NASB only preserves the word "**dung**" about half the time,[377] but totally rejects the AV reading of **dunghill**. The NKJV very inconsistently maintained the AV reading of "**dung**" and "**dunghill**" each one time.[378] The NIV only followed the AV six times on "**dung**"[379] but not once on **dunghill**. The words and phrases used to update **dung** and **dunghill** are quite numerous. For **dung** one can find "refuse,"[380] "excrement,"[381] "waste,"[382] "rubbish,"[383] "manure,"[384] "offal,"[385] and "seed pods."[386] The translations for **dunghill** include "ash heap,"[387] "refuse heap,"[388] "manure pile,"[389] "rubbish heap,"³⁹⁰ "ash pits,"³⁹¹ "piles of rubble,"³⁹² "manure,"³⁹³ "dung-pit,"³⁹⁴ and "ruins."³⁹⁵ When the AV uses the verb phrase "**dung it**," it is rendered by the NRSV "put manure on it," the NASB "put in fertilizer," and the NIV and NKJV as "fertilize it."³⁹⁶ All of these replacements for **dung** and **dunghill** are given to not only show the number of times they have been corrected, but also to demonstrate the inconsistency and duplicity of these modern versions. Our modern versions very rarely agree on how to update these words, and when they do modernize them, it is never in up-to-date, contemporary English; indeed, sometimes it is a more "archaic" word than **dung** like the translation of "offal" found in the NIV and NKJV.³⁹⁷ But is the word **dung** archaic in the first place? *Wildlife Conservation* magazine in 1994 certainly did not consider it to be: "It is likely the senior male's distinctive signature is written in odor molecules in the **dung** that he scatters on prominent rocks in his territory."³⁹⁸

Dureth

> Yet hath he not root in himself, but **dureth** for a while: for when tribulation or persecution ariseth because of the word, by and by he is offended. (Mat 13:21)

The word **dureth**, the third person singular form of *dure*, occurs only once in the AV. It comes from the French *durer*, "to last." To dure is to last, persist, or continue in existence or state. *Dure* is obsolete and has been superseded by *endure*, although both forms were in existence at the same time. Nevertheless, only the NKJV and NRSV update **dureth** to "endures."³⁹⁹ Yet when the AV reads a form of "endure," it is often corrected. The NIV changes "endure" to "stand the strain" when all of our modern versions follow the AV reading.⁴⁰⁰ The NASB updates "endureth for ever" to "is everlasting" even though the other translations read as the AV.⁴⁰¹ The NRSV and NIV change "endure" to "bear" in contradiction to the NKJV and NASB, which agree with the AV.⁴⁰² On another occasion, our modern versions unite in purging the AV reading of "endureth" from the Bible and substituting "is no more."⁴⁰³ And furthermore, it should be pointed out that when a word in the AV like **dureth** does not contain a prefix, one is added; but when a word like "disannul" includes one, the prefix is removed.⁴⁰⁴

Chapter 5
Ear to Experiment

Ear

And he will appoint him captains over thousands, and captains over fifties; and *will set them* to **ear** his ground, and to reap his harvest, and to make his instruments of war, and instruments of his chariots. (1 Sam 8:12)

The word **ear**, a homonym of the word for the organ of hearing, occurs three times in the AV as a substantive[1] and five times as a verb. The verbal forms appear as **ear** twice,[2] **earing** twice,[3] and **eared** once.[4] The substantive form of **ear** is from the Old English *ear* and refers to a head of corn or the part of a plant which contains its flowers or seeds. The NIV and NKJV consistently render **ear** by a form of "head" every place that it occurs,[5] but the NRSV and NASB left it as "**ear**" on one occasion.[6] The word **ear** as used as a verb comes from the Old English *erian*, "to plow." Thus, to **ear** is to plow, till, or otherwise turn up the ground. Our modern versions unanimously render **earing** and **eared** as "plowing"[7] and "plowed,"[8] but the base form **ear** only shows up as "plow" or "plowing" one time.[9]
The one other instance is rendered as "till" by the NRSV and "work" by the others.[10] This seemingly tedious and unnecessary recounting of how these words are translated in our modern versions is not without a purpose, for as we shall see, when the AV employs the same simple words as the modern versions it is still corrected. When the AV and all the others read "plowed," the NIV alone says "planted."[11] The NASB preferred "labor" in a passage where the AV and all others read "work."[12] And furthermore, when the AV, NRSV, and NKJV use the word "till," the NIV says "work" and the NASB utilizes the more

difficult "cultivate."[13] And finally, every translator of any modern version still eats an ear of corn.

𝔈arnest

> Now he that hath wrought us for the selfsame thing *is* God, who also hath given unto us the **earnest** of the Spirit. (2 Cor 5:5)

Although the word **earnest** is found eight times in the AV, there are two distinct and etymologically unrelated meanings of the word. **Earnest** appears five times as an adjective meaning serious, important, or zealous.[14] This usage is common today; therefore, these cases of the word **earnest** are usually not corrected by our modern versions. The problem is with the other three instances of the word **earnest**.[15] This usage of the word comes from the French *erres*, the plural of *erre*, "pledge." Thus, an **earnest** is a pledge, deposit, installment, or anything securing a contract. The French *erre* was altered in English to *ernesse*, and due to its confusion with the homonym **earnest** because a transaction was supposed to be made in **earnest**, a "t" was added in Middle English. Of the three times **earnest** is used in the sense of a pledge, the NKJV renders it "guarantee,"[16] the NIV "deposit,"[17] and the NASB "pledge."[18] The NRSV could not decide on how to translate the underlying word, so it used three different words (first installment, guarantee, pledge) to do so.[19] And then when the AV and the other modern versions agree on "pledge," the NRSV changes it to "pawn."[20] The updating of **earnest** was certainly unnecessary, for **earnest** money is required at every real estate transaction in the 1990's and is legally defined as: "A sum of money paid by a buyer at the time of entering a contract to indicate the intention and ability of the buyer to carry out the contract."[21]

𝔈ffect

> For Christ sent me not to baptize, but to preach the gospel: not with wisdom of words, lest the cross of Christ should be made of none **effect**. (1 Cor 1:17)

The word **effect** appears fourteen times in the AV.[22] The form **effected** occurs once,[23] while **effectual** is found six times[24] and **effectually** twice.[25] **Effect** is from a French word of the same spelling and as a noun can mean something accomplished, caused or produced; efficacy, power, or authority; operation, execution, or initialization; or purpose, intent or impression. As a verb, to **effect** is to accomplish or produce. Something is **effectual** that produces the intended **effect** or effective result. All forms of the word **effect** are ultimately derived from the Latin *efficere*, "to accomplish." Although our modern versions use the word **effect,** it is usually corrected when it occurs in the AV due to the limited range of meaning put upon it by our modern versions. Only the NKJV follows the AV the majority of the time,[26] for the NIV retains "**effect**" as the AV only once,[27] as does the NRSV.[28] Yet in several places our modern versions use **effect** in a place and in such a way that neither the AV nor the other new translations do. When the AV, NIV, and NKJV say "make a new covenant," the NASB says "**effect** a new covenant,"[29] even though the passage in the Old Testament from which the phrase was quoted reads "make" in the NASB, the AV, and all the others.[30] When the AV reads "deliver him," and our other modern versions say "rescue him," the NRSV changed it to the more difficult "**effect** a rescue."[31] In one passage, the NRSV altered **effect** to "result" but in the same verse changed "work" to "**effect.**"[32] Concerning the word **effectual** and its derivatives, one would think that a simple updating to "effective" would be simple enough, but only the NKJV did it with any consistency.[33] Moreover, the NASB forgot to remove **effectually** from one passage.[34] Archaic words and archaic usage of words are certainly not limited to the AV—they also surface in the *Charlotte Observer:* "What has **effected** this change is not so much what goes on inside the courtroom as the cultural atmosphere outside it."[35]

Effeminate

> Know ye not that the unrighteous shall not inherit the kingdom of God? Be not deceived: neither fornicators, nor idolaters, nor adulterers, nor **effeminate,** nor abusers of themselves with mankind, (1 Cor 6:9)

The word **effeminate** appears only once in the AV and is from the Latin *effeminatus,* from *effeminare,* literally meaning "to make a woman of." **Effeminate** can mean unmanly or unnaturally delicate, soft, or weak. In a general sense, **effeminate** refers to anything characteristic of a woman. Only the NASB retains this word. The NKJV changes it to "homosexuals," but the NRSV and NIV make it "male prostitutes." Yet these translations are certainly incorrect when compared with the three other instances the underlying Greek word *malakos* is used. All of our modern versions render *malakos* as "soft," except for the NIV, which preferred "fine."[36] A man can be **effeminate** without being a homosexual. In fact, the scourge of Christianity today is **effeminate** men and especially preachers. And furthermore, the word **effeminate** is certainly not archaic, at least according to *Kiwanis Magazine:* "Weak, frail, and **effeminate** boys are targets of punches in the arm; heavy girls are frequently reminded that they're fat and find dog biscuits in their desks."[37]

𝕰𝖒𝖇𝖔𝖑𝖉𝖊𝖓𝖊𝖉

> For if any man see thee which hast knowledge sit at meat in the idol's temple, shall not the conscience of him which is weak be **emboldened** to eat those things which are offered to idols; (1 Cor 8:10)

The word **emboldened** is found once in the AV, as is the form **emboldeneth**.[38] To embold or embolden is to make bold, encourage, or incite. Surprisingly, the NIV and NKJV neglected to remove this supposedly archaic word in one passage.[39] However, our modern versions could not decide on how to render these words the rest of the time. "Provokes" is used twice,[40] with "plagues"[41] "ails,"[42] "encouraged,"[43] and "strengthened"[44] employed the other times. The *em-* prefix should not have given our modern versions any difficulty since the NIV uses "embedded,"[45] the NASB employs "emasculated,"[46] the NKJV utilizes "embankment"[47] and "embellished,"[48] and the NRSV includes the word "embarrassment."[49] Additionally, the NASB, NRSV, and NIV all use the word "embittered."[50] The AV contains none of the abovementioned *em-* type words. And furthermore, the word **emboldened** is still used today: "In short, the statistics indicate that, if anything, the Salt Lake City waiting period contributed to an increase, not a decrease, in drive-by shootings (perhaps because some of the thugs involved were **emboldened** by the knowledge that so many law-abiding city residents had to wait to buy a gun)."[51]

Emerods

> The LORD will smite thee with the botch of Egypt, and with the **emerods,** and with the scab, and with the itch, whereof thou canst not be healed. (Deu 28:27)

Emerods are mentioned eight times in the AV.[52] The word was formed from the Latin *haemorrhoides,* from which we get the modern *hemorrhoids.* This word developed from a combination of the Greek words meaning "blood" and "to flow." Our modern versions unanimously render **emerods** as "tumors,"[53] except for the NRSV, which used the word "ulcers" one time.[54] But when it comes to simple medical terms like *sick* and *sickness,* the NRSV still altered them. "Sick" in the AV is replaced by "in the infirmity"[55] and "sickness" is corrected to the more arduous "malady," even though the other versions read as the AV.[56]

Eminent

> *That* thou hast also built unto thee an **eminent** place, and hast made thee an high place in every street. (Ezek 16:24)

The word **eminent** appears four times in the AV.[57] It is from the Latin *eminentem,* from *eminere,* "to project." To be **eminent** is to be prominent, outstanding, projecting, great, or distinguished. The word can be applied to both persons and physical objects. Since **eminent** only applies to physical objects in the AV, our modern versions excise the word whenever it occurs in the AV. An "**eminent** place" in the AV has been changed by the NKJV and NASB to a "shrine,"[58] the NRSV to a "platform,"[59] and the NIV to a "mound."[60] The other occurrence of **eminent** was altered to "prominent" by the NKJV, but to "lofty" by the rest.[61] But if this word was so archaic, then why did the NASB insert it into another passage[62] as well as use the similar form "eminence" in another?[63] Twice the NASB and NKJV even replace "chiefest" in the AV with "**eminent**."[64] Moreover, the NIV, NRSV, and NASB all corrected the simple "form" to the harder "embodiment."[65] The word **eminent,** however, is still in general use: "Among **eminent** scientists, the percentage of firstborns is higher than among scientists in general."[66]

Emulation

If by any means I may provoke to **emulation** *them which are my flesh, and might save some of them.* (Rom 11:14)

The word **emulation** appears once in the AV in the singular and once in the plural.[67] **Emulation** is from the Latin *aemulationem,* from *aemulari,* "to rival." Hence, it is related to *imitari,* "to imitate." **Emulation** is the effort or ambition to equal or surpass, a jealous rivalry for honor or power. Our modern versions all update these words to a form of "jealousy,"[68] save the NIV, which used "envy" one time.[69] Yet when the AV reads "jealously," it is corrected in the NRSV to "passion" and the NIV to "zeal."[70] Moreover, in the same passage where **emulations** was updated to "jealousy," the NASB and NRSV revised the simple "hatred" to the more troublesome "enmities."[71] And furthermore, the word **emulation** is not archaic at all, at least according to *American Heritage* magazine: "Compared with this, the influence of communism and the **emulation** of the Soviet Union were minimal."[72]

Endamage

Be it known now unto the king, that, if this city be builded, and the walls set up *again, then* will they not pay toll, tribute, and custom, and *so* thou shalt **endamage** the revenue of the kings. (Ezra 4:13)

The word **endamage** occurs only once in the AV. It was formed from the *en-* prefix, signifying to bring into a certain condition or state, being added to the verb *damage*. To **endamage** is to inflict damage upon, injure, or discredit. Our modern versions could not decide on how to update this word. The NRSV choose "reduced," the NASB "damage," the NIV "suffer," and the NKJV "diminished." These modern, up-to-date translations should have had no trouble with the word **endamage** or any other word in the AV deemed archaic because of an *en-* prefix. Doesn't the NRSV change "overlaid" to "encrusted"?[73] Doesn't the NIV render "enter" as "encroach"?[74] What about the NASB altering "saw" to "envisioned"?[75] The NKJV likewise replaces "dowry" with "endowment"?[76] These "archaic" words with an *en-* prefix do not even occur in the AV.

Endued

> And now I have sent a cunning man, **endued** with understanding, of Huram my father's, (2 Chr 2:13)

The word **endued** appears five times in the AV.[77] It is from the French *enduire*, "to lead into." To endue is to bring in, introduce, cover, clothe, overlay, to bring to a certain condition, supply, endow, or to invest qualities in. The usual rendering of this word in our modern versions is "endowed."[78] However, the NIV used "presented" one time,[79] the NIV, NASB, and NRSV employed "clothed" once,[80] and the NKJV mistakenly retained the AV reading on one occasion.[81] The AV phrase "**endued** with knowledge" is also unanimously updated to "understanding."[82] But after correcting this word in the AV, the NRSV, NIV, and NASB went on to revise the simple "comfortably" to the more difficult "encouragingly."[83]

Engines

> And he shall set **engines** of war against thy walls, and with his axes he shall break down thy towers. (Ezek 26:9)

Engines are mentioned twice in the AV.[84] The word comes from the French *engin*, "skill." An engine is a mechanical device or machine, formerly applied almost exclusively to weapons of warfare. The word **engines** is connected with skill because it took skill to make **engines**. Our modern versions, excepting the negligence of the NASB in one passage,[85] excised the word **engines** because they associated it only with a modern automobile engine. The NIV and NRSV render **engines** as "machines" in one place, while the NKJV selected "devices."[86] The other occurrence of **engines** was unanimously corrected to "battering rams."[87] But not only does a fire **engine** signify the whole truck and not just the motor, the word **engines** is still commonly applied to things that are not car **engines**: "As computers—the **engines** of modern cryptography—have proliferated, so have ever more powerful encryption algorithms."[88]

Engrafted

> Wherefore lay apart all filthiness and superfluity of naughti-

ness, and receive with meekness the **engrafted** word, which is able to save your souls. (James 1:21)

The word **engrafted** appears only once in the AV. It is another word formed by the addition of the *en-* prefix to a verb, in this case *graft*. *Graft* is a corrupt form of *graff* and is ultimately derived from the Greek word meaning "to write." Thus, it is related to our English words *grammar, diagram, program, graphic,* and *graph*. To graft is to insert the bud or shoot of one plant into another. The shoot or bud was called a graft because it resembled a stylus or instrument with a sharp point used for writing. *Graft* was then applied to anything "grafted" from one thing to another. To be **engrafted** signifies to be grafted in, inserted, implanted, or introduced. When the AV does use the word "grafted" (spelled graffed), all our modern follow suit,[89] so the problem with **engrafted** had to be just the *en-* prefix. But instead of just shortening **engrafted,** it is replaced by "implanted,"[90] or "planted."[91] Yet when the AV reads "number," the NASB replaces it with "enumeration,"[92] and when the simple word "weight" is used, the NASB "updates" it to the more difficult "encumbrance."[93] Nevertheless, forms of *graft* with the *en-* prefix are still in vogue in the twentieth century: "The experiments showed that the transplanted fetal pancreatic tissue would **engraft,** differentiate into insulin-producing islets and survive."[94]

Enjoin

Wherefore, though I might be much bold in Christ to **enjoin** thee that which is convenient, (Phile 1:8)

The word **enjoin** occurs only once in the AV, but **enjoined** can be found three times.[95] **Enjoin** is from the French *enjoindre*, "to impose." This word initially meant "to join to," since it was originally formed from the Latin word for *join* and the addition of an *in-* prefix. However, to **enjoin** now means to prescribe, command, encourage, or to prohibit, proscribe, or discourage. Although the NRSV was negligent is removing "**enjoined**" one time,[96] all four occurrences of these words have been corrected by our modern versions.[97] And although these new translations were in concord in their mission to correct the AV, they never agree completely among themselves as to how to do it. To correct

enjoin and **enjoined** one can find "established,"[98] "decreed,"[99] "prescribed,"[100] "appointed,"[101] "assigned,"[102] "command,"[103] "order,"[104] and "ordained."[105] Evidently the NRSV did not deem these words archaic after all, for "enjoining" is inserted in another passage[106] and "**enjoined**" is used where the AV and all the other modern versions read "commanded."[107] The word **enjoin**, however, is unquestionably not archaic at all anyway: "Where they exist, government investment policies typically **enjoin** managers to maximize the safety of funds and investment returns."[108]

Enlargement

> For if thou altogether holdest thy peace at this time, *then* shall there **enlargement** and deliverance arise to the Jews from another place; but thou and thy father's house shall be destroyed: and who knoweth whether thou art come to the kingdom for *such* a time as this? (Est 4:14)

The word **enlargement** appears once in the AV. It is obviously a combination of the prefix *en-* with the word *large* and the suffix *-ment*. An **enlargement** is the action or state of enlarging, increasing, or being enlarged; an increase in extent, capacity, size, diffusion, or propagation. Our modern versions unanimously amend **enlargement** to "relief." This time, however, the *en-* prefix was not the cause of the trouble with this word, for all of our new translations regularly use the word "enlarge."[109] Evidently the combination of the *en-* prefix with the *-ment* suffix rendered the word archaic. But the new versions were very inconsistent when it came to words ending with the *-ment* suffix. When the AV reads "task," the NRSV replaces it with the harder "assignment."[110] The NASB replaced the word "dwelling" in the AV with "settlement."[111] The NRSV even adds both an *en-* prefix and a *-ment* suffix to a word in the AV, for when the AV reads "light," the NRSV "updates" it to "enlightenment."[112] The word **enlargement** is so archaic that millions of people every year get a photo **enlargement**. And furthermore, the word **enlargement** is even still used when not referring to photography: "On the proposed **enlargement** of the U.N. Security Council, a majority of respondents in the four countries said they think both Germany and Japan should become permanent members."[113]

Ensample

> Brethren, be followers together of me, and mark them which walk so as ye have us for an **ensample**. (Phil 3:17)

Ensample occurs in the AV three times in the singular[114] and three times in the plural.[115] **Ensample** is an altered form of *asaumple*, from the French *assample*, a variation of *essample*. Our word *example* is from the French *example*, a refashioning of *essample*. The English *sample*, both an aphetic form of **ensample** and a derivation of the French *saumple*, is also related to *essample*. All of these forms are ultimately derived from the Latin *exemplum*, signifying "something taken out." An **ensample** is a sample, pattern, model, precedent, or example. Our modern versions update **ensample** to "example" the majority of the time.[116] Likewise, **ensamples** is usually given as "examples."[117] **Ensample** can also be found as "model"[118] and "pattern."[119] The *en-* prefix on **ensample** should have posed no difficulty to our modern versions since they all use various forms of "encamp"[120] and "entreat."[121] In fact, all of our modern, up-to-date versions employed the word "entreaty."[122]

Ensign

> Every man of the children of Israel shall pitch by his own standard, with the **ensign** of their father's house: far off about the tabernacle of the congregation shall they pitch. (Num 2:2)

The singular **ensign** appears eight times in the AV,[123] while the plural is found only once.[124] This word is from the French *enseigne*, "a sign." The Latin for this word is *insignia*, from which we get the English *insignia*. Hence, **ensign** and *insignia* are doublets. An **ensign** is a signal, sign, token, mark, emblem, badge, symbol, standard, or flag. Out of the nine times **ensign** and **ensigns** appear in the AV, every occurrence is corrected by our modern versions,[125] excepting the one occasion when the NRSV inadvertently retains the AV reading.[126] However, as we have seen many times previously, our new translations were not in agreement on the proper choice of words to update the AV. Here we can find "banners" fifteen times,[127] "emblems" twice,[128] "standard" or "standards" eight times,[129] and "signal" seven times.[130] Moreover, the NRSV, which corrected **ensign** in the AV eight times, injected the word into two other passages where neither the AV nor any modern version contained the word.[131] The modern rank of **ensign** in the Navy originated with this word **ensign.**

𝕰𝖓𝖘𝖚𝖊

> Let him eschew evil, and do good; let him seek peace, and **ensue** it. (1 Pet 3:11)

The word **ensue** occurs only once in the AV and is from the French *ensuir,* "to follow after." To **ensue** is to follow in order, come afterward, or follow as a consequence of. Our modern versions unanimously amend this word to the similar "pursue." However, the NRSV demonstrated that it did not consider **ensue** to be archaic when it inserted "ensues" into the Bible six times where neither the AV nor any other translation contained the word.[132] But what should one expect out of a version that altered "word" to "edict"[133] and "taken" to "exacted."[134] Nevertheless, the word **ensue** is still in general use: "Scientists feared that widespread famine would **ensue** unless ways were found to greatly increase rice production."[135]

𝕰𝖓𝖙𝖊𝖗𝖕𝖗𝖎𝖘𝖊

> He disappointeth the devices of the crafty, so that their hands cannot perform *their* **enterprise.** (Job 5:12)

The word **enterprise** occurs only once in the AV. It is from the French *entreprise,* "an undertaking." An **enterprise** is an undertaking, a business, a work, a project, or a design of which the execution is attempted. The phrase "perform their **enterprise**" in the AV is altered by the NRSV, NASB, and NIV to "achieve success," but the NKJV preferred "carry out their plans." There was no reason for our modern versions to correct **enterprise** since even *Harper's* magazine employs the word: "The only **enterprise** that was able to battle on was Georgia's celebrated wine industry."[136] And don't forget the free **enterprise** system.

𝕰𝖓𝖛𝖎𝖗𝖔𝖓

> For the Canaanites and all the inhabitants of the land shall

hear *of it,* and shall **environ** us round, and cut off our name from the earth: and what wilt thou do unto thy great name? (Josh 7:9)

The word **environ** appears only once in the AV. It is from a French word of the same spelling meaning "round about." To **environ** is to surround, be in attendance upon, stationed by, or to envelop. Our modern versions unanimously update the AV phrase "**environ** us round" to "surround us." But when the AV uses the similar word "compassed," it is amended in the NRSV and NASB to "encompassed."[137] And in another passage where the AV also read "compassed," the NRSV revised it to "enveloped."[138] Moreover, up near the end of the twentieth century, one's surroundings are commonly referred to as the **environ**ment.

Epistle

The salutation of Paul with mine own hand, which is the token in every **epistle:** so I write. (2 Th 3:17)

The word **epistle** is used fourteen times in the AV.[139] The plural **epistles** occurs twice.[140] **Epistle** is from a French word of the same spelling meaning "letter." However, the Old English *epistole* was directly adopted from the Latin *epistola*, which was taken directly from the Greek. **Epistle** is the term for a written communication normally applied to letters written in ancient times, especially those classed as literary productions or for public use. The term **epistle** is also applied to a manifesto, a dedication at the beginning of a literary work, or an important letter. The NRSV, NIV, and NASB completely removed **epistle** and **epistles** from the Bible, substituting "letter" and "letters."[141] At least they were consistent, however, for the NKJV followed the AV in all but two places, even though the same underlying Greek word was used every time.[142] Yet if a letter written from jail by Martin Luther King is called an **epistle,** then certainly a letter written by the Apostle Paul can be classed as one: "Using a smuggled pen and paper, King wrote 'Letter from Birmingham Jail,' an **epistle** depicting protestors as defenders of the Constitution."[143]

Ere

And the midwives said unto Pharaoh, Because the Hebrew

women *are* not as the Egyptian women; for they *are* lively, and are delivered **ere** the midwives come in unto them. (Exo 1:19)

The word **ere** appears ten times in the AV.[144] **Ere** developed from the Old English *aer*, "early," and means before or until. The word **ere** does not occur anywhere in our modern versions, the usual translation being "before."[145] But if these new translations were so concerned about removing archaic words from the Bible then why did they replace perfectly understandable words in the AV with words that are much more difficult? "Destroyed" in the AV is replaced in the NASB by "eradicated"[146] and in the NIV by "decimated."[147] The NIV also corrects "greatly desire" to "enthralled," even though the other versions follow the AV.[148]

Eschew

Let him **eschew** evil, and do good; let him seek peace, and ensue it. (1 Pet 3:11)

Although **eschew** is found only once in the AV, **escheweth** appears twice[149] and **eschewed** occurs once.[150] **Eschew** is from the French *eschiver*, "to shun." To **eschew** is to shun, avoid, abstain from, or escape from. Our modern versions have completely excised this word. The two replacements for the various styles of **eschew** are forms of "shun"[151] and "turn away from."[152] These corrections were certainly unnecessary, for even *Omni* magazine did not consider **eschew** to be archaic: "They understood it wasn't enough to forsake punctuation or **eschew** rhyme; the poets had to find the right combination of variables and rules, in enumeration, enjambment, or alliteration, to make the words work as a poem."[153]

Espoused

Now the birth of Jesus Christ was on this wise: When as his mother Mary was **espoused** to Joseph, before they came together, she was found with child of the Holy Ghost. (Mat 1:18)

The word **espoused** occurs five times in the AV[154] and the form **espousals** appears twice.[155] **Espoused** is from the French *espouser*, "to betroth or promise." To be **espoused** is to be promised in marriage, betrothed, or engaged. Outside of the framework of marriage, the word *espouse* can also mean to adopt, embrace, support, pledge, or put forth. **Espousals** refers to a marriage ceremony or engagement celebration. Our modern versions completely remove these words, usually substituting a form of "betrothed,"[156] or "engaged."[157] However, other translations include "promised,"[158] "wedding,"[159] and "pledged to be married."[160] Although not used in the context of marriage, the word **espoused** does appear in the 1990's: "In the 1992 presidential campaign, Bill Clinton effectively attacked the economic policies **espoused** by two successive Republican administrations."[161]

Espy

> Forty years old *was* I when Moses the servant of the LORD sent me from Kadeshbarnea to **espy** out the land; and I brought him word again as *it was* in mine heart. (Josh 14:7)

Espy appears twice in the AV,[162] as does the form **espied**.[163] It is from the French *espier*, "to spy." **Espy** means to watch, spy, inspect, or examine. Our new translations have removed this word in unison. However, they were not in agreement on what to replace it with. **Espy** and **espied** can be found as "spy out,"[164] "explore,"[165] "watch,"[166] "keep watch,"[167] "selected,"[168] "saw,"[169] and "searched out."[170] That **espy** should have been no problem for any modern version is apparent when one considers that the NRSV revised the simple "spoil" in the AV to "despoil," not once but six times.[171] The word **espied** is also still currently in use: "There, while bathing one day, a pharaoh's daughter **espied** a small basket of rushes, snagged in reeds along the water's edge."[172]

Estate

> *Be* of the same mind one toward another. Mind not high things, but condescend to men of low **estate**. Be not wise in your own conceits. (Rom 12:16)

The word **estate** can be found seventeen times in the AV in fifteen verses.[173] It is from the French *estat*, "condition." The words **estate**, *state,* and *status* are all from the same Latin root.

Estate can mean condition, position, status, or state. Due to the modern concept of one's **estate** being one's property or possessions, the word **estate** as used in the AV is ousted by our modern versions. Instead we find "position,"[174] "rank,"[175] "condition,"[176] "place,"[177] "state,"[178] "standard,"[179] "circumstances,"[180] and "domain."[181] However, the NRSV, NASB, and NIV were careless in that they left **estate** in one passage where the AV had it.[182] Although our new translations employ the word **estate** in reference to one's property or inheritance,[183] the NRSV demonstrated that it did not consider the way the AV used **estate** to be archaic when it twice inserted the word **estate** into a verse where the AV did not contain the word.[184] The NASB likewise utilized **estate** as the AV in one passage.[185] Certainly the word **estate** as it is used in the AV is more understandable than "inscrutable," which is what the NASB substituted for the AV word "unsearchable."[186]

Even

> And Moses and Aaron said unto all the children of Israel, At **even**, then ye shall know that the LORD hath brought you out from the land of Egypt: (Exo 16:6)

Although the word **even** can be found hundreds of times in the AV and any modern version, its use as a short synonym for *evening* is what gives our new translations trouble. **Even** is most common in the AV in phrases such as "at **even**," found thirty-one times,[187] and "the **even**," found thirty-six times.[188] Other similar words in the AV are **eventide**, found five times,[189] and **eveningtide**, which appears twice.[190] **Even** appeared in Old English as *aefen* and is a synonym for *evening*. **Eventide** is from *aefen* and the suffix *-tid*, "time." **Eveningtide** is a later form of **eventide**. Naturally, our modern versions usually update **even** to "evening,"[191] but sometimes it is rendered "twilight."[192] However, when the AV reads "twilight," the NIV changes it to "dusk,"[193] the NASB to "dark,"[194] the NKJV to "morning,"[195] and the NRSV to "dawn."[196] **Eventide** is normally given in our modern versions as "evening."[197] Yet the NRSV slips up and inserts the supposedly archaic "**eventide**" into a passage where neither the AV nor any other modern version contained the word.[198] **Eveningtide** is customarily rendered as "evening" in the new translations.[199] On one occasion, however, the NRSV used "afternoon"[200] and the NKJV employed the equally as archaic "eventide."[201] **Even, eventide,** and **eveningtide** may be archaic but certainly not as archaic as "dishevel" used by the NRSV.[202]

Evermore

> I will praise thee, O Lord my God, with all my heart: and I will glorify thy name for **evermore.** (Psa 86:12)

The word **evermore** occurs twenty-six times in the AV.[203] It is an emphatic synonym of *ever* and means always, at all times, continually, constantly, or forever. Our modern versions tried to completely excise this word, usually replacing it with "forever,"[204] although "all time"[205] and "day after day"[206] can also be found. The NIV was successful in removing the word **evermore** but the NASB overlooked one passage,[207] as did the NKJV.[208] Moreover, the NRSV inserted this word in two places where the AV read "continually."[209] The NKJV repeated this in one passage.[210] A similar but even longer word than **evermore** is even used by all of our modern versions. The NASB utilizes the word "forevermore" five times,[211] one of these replacing the AV phrase "for ever and ever,"[212] but three of them revising the simple "for ever."[213] The NIV repeats the use of "forevermore" seven times,[214] three times correcting "for ever."[215] The NRSV slips up and uses "forevermore" a whopping fourteen times.[216] Six of these replace the AV reading of "forever."[217] The worst culprit is the NKJV, employing "forevermore" eighteen times.[218] However, only one of these replaced "for ever" in the AV.[219] The NKJV also corrected "neither" to "nevermore,"[220] while the NRSV extended "never" to "nevermore."[221] Thus, once again we see that archaic words are not limited to the AV. But the word **evermore** is still in vogue anyway: "The series adds fuel to the **evermore** popular fire-consuming social program."[222]

Evilfavouredness

> Thou shalt not sacrifice unto the LORD thy God *any* bullock, or sheep, wherein is blemish, *or* any **evilfavouredness:** for that *is* an abomination unto the LORD thy God. (Deu 17:1)

The word **evilfavouredness** occurs only once in the AV. It is obviously a compound word with a *-ness* suffix. **Evilfavouredness** means in evil favor or having an evil appearance or aspect. The word **evilfavouredness,** no doubt deemed to be archaic by our modern translations due in part to its length, is updated to "defect" by the NASB and NKJV but to "seriously wrong" in the NRSV and to "flaw" in the NIV. With sixteen letters, **evilfavouredness** is definitely one of the longest words in the Bible. But does having sixteen letters automatically make it archaic? The NKJV uses two words that not only have sixteen letters, but also end with a form of a *-ness* suffix: "lovingkindnesses" and "unprofitableness."[223] Yet after using the fifteen-letter "bloodguiltiness,"[224] the NRSV goes on to use the sixteen-letter words "unchangeableness,"[225] "insurrectionists,"[226] and "lovingkindnesses."[227] And in the case of "lovingkindnesses," the AV reading was the simple, five-letter, two syllable "mercy."[228]

Exchangers

> Thou oughtest therefore to have put my money to the **exchangers,** and *then* at my coming I should have received mine own with usury. (Mat 25:27)

The word **exchangers** appears only once in the AV. It is an example of a noun of occupation formed from a verb. An exchanger is one who exchanges. **Exchangers** is updated by our modern versions to "in the bank"[229] or "bankers."[230] Yet when the AV says "creditor," the NIV and NASB alter it to "moneylender."[231] All of these new translations use the word "exchange," so **exchangers** should have presented no difficulty to them, especially since the NASB, NRSV, and NKJV follow the AV in employing the little-used word "buriers."[232] A similar case could be made for the word "exactors," found once in the AV,[233] since all of our modern versions use forms of the verb "exact."[234] Moreover, the NRSV uses the word "employers,"[235] while the NKJV follows the AV reading of "extortioner,"[236] the NKJV, NIV, and NASB follow the AV in using "executioner,"[237] the NRSV, NKJV, and NASB retain the archaic "fuller,"[238] and the NRSV and NKJV keep the unusual "calkers."[239] Yet when the AV mentions a "striker," the NASB revises it to "pugnacious."[240]

Execration

> For thus saith the LORD of hosts, the God of Israel; As mine anger and my fury hath been poured forth upon the inhabitants of Jerusalem; so shall my fury be poured forth upon you, when ye shall enter into Egypt: and ye shall be an **execration**, and an astonishment, and a curse, and a reproach; and ye shall see this place no more. (Jer 42:18)

Found only twice in the AV,[241] the word **execration** is from the Latin *execrationem,* from *excrari,* "to curse." An **execration** is a curse, the act of cursing, the object of cursing, a detestation, abhorrence, or abomination. Our modern versions were consistent in their rendering of this word. The NKJV uses "oath," the NASB "curse," and the NIV "object of cursing."[242] The NRSV was careless, however, in neglecting to remove **execration** both times it occurred.[243] Although the NASB preferred the word "curse," when the AV read "curse," it was replaced by the much more difficult "imprecation."[244] The NIV likewise changed the AV reading of "curse," substituting "condemnation."[245] And furthermore, words that begin with an *ex-* prefix are commonly inserted by our new translations where the AV contains a simple, unadorned word. The NASB, NRSV, and NIV all supplant the simple AV word "rejoice" with "exult."[246] "Exterminate" is used to render the AV reading of "perish" in the NIV,[247] as is "exasperate" used to correct the elementary "provoke."[248] But forms of **execration** are still current today: "In short, PAW, which has demonized the Christian Coalition for its 'extremism,' now **execrates** the organization for seeking a more 'moderate' profile."[249]

Experiment

> Whiles by the **experiment** of this ministration they glorify God for your professed subjection unto the gospel of Christ, and for *your* liberal distribution unto them, and unto all *men;* (2 Cor 9:13)

Appearing only once in the AV, **experiment** is from a French word of the same spelling meaning "a trial." An **experiment** is a test, trial, procedure, method, course of action, or the action of trying anything. This word has been removed by all of our modern versions due to their limiting an **experiment** to a scientific **experiment** performed in a laboratory. The NASB and NKJV substitute "proof," while the NRSV uses "testing" and the NIV employs "service." Yet when the same underlying Greek word is translated in the AV as "proof," it is unanimously corrected to "test."[250] And if the AV use of **experiment** was deemed archaic, then what are we to say about the NRSV changing "covering" to "exoneration,"[251] "purged" to "expiated,"[252] and "atonement to "expiation"?[253] And besides, the word **experiment** is still often used when not referring to a scientific **experiment**: "But the new Russia emerging from the rubble of Soviet rule bears little resemblance to the bulwark of spirituality and tradition that Mr. Solzhenitsyn has often suggested would be Russia's natural destiny if not for the Bolshevik **experiment.**"[254]

Chapter 6
Fain to Furniture

Fain

And he would **fain** have filled his belly with the husks that the swine did eat: and no man gave unto him. (Luke 15:16)

The word **fain**, occurring twice in the AV,[1] can be found in Old English as *faegen*. **Fain** means gladly, willingly, or be content to. Naturally, our modern versions do not contain this word. **Fain** is usually modified to a form of "headlong,"[2] or "gladly."[3] However, in one of the same passages where **fain** occurs, the familiar story of the Prodigal Son, the word "husks" is unanimously altered by all of our modern, contemporary translations to "pods."[4] Yet even *Forbes* magazine did not consider **fain** to be archaic: "And so that it can, so must we, chivvied exit ward with that oh-so-gentle yet unmistakably urgent, snug yet bowel-loosening .410 gun barrel in the small of the back that few hostesses can bring off—or would **fain** even try."[5]

Fairs

Tarshish *was* thy merchant by reason of the multitude of all *kind of* riches; with silver, iron, tin, and lead, they traded in thy **fairs**. (Ezek 27:12)

The word **fairs** appears six times in the AV.[6] It is from the French *feire*, from a Latin word originally meaning a holiday and then a fair or market. A fair is any gathering of buyers and sellers. As used in the AV, **fairs** are anything gotten at a fair. Although it is not current English, this usage makes perfect sense. Our modern word would be *wares*. The new versions almost unanimously update **fairs** to "wares,"[7] but once "goods" was used.[8] The NIV alone preferred to utilize "merchandise."[9] Yet when the AV reads "wares," it is often corrected to "goods"[10] or "cargo."[11] And when the singular "ware" is used, it is corrected to "goods"[12] or "merchandise."[13]

Fallowdeer

> Ten fat oxen, and twenty oxen out of the pastures, and an hundred sheep, beside harts, and roebucks, and **fallowdeer**, and fatted fowl. (1 Ki 4:23)

A **fallowdeer** is mentioned twice in the AV, one time appearing as one word and the other as two separate words.[14] A **fallowdeer** is technically a *cervus dama,* and is called fallow because of its pale brownish or reddish yellow color. *Fallow* can be found in Old English as *fealu.* Another *fallow* word is from the Old English *fealh,* and refers to land that is uncultivated. It is thought that the land got its description due to its fallow-colored soil.[15] Hence, the two words were often confused. Our new translations had no trouble with the word *fallow* by itself, but a **fallowdeer** is extinct in any of our modern versions. The NRSV and NASB consistently render **fallowdeer** as "roebuck."[16] However, if the AV be faulted for making **fallowdeer** alternately one word and then two, it should be pointed out that the NIV and NKJV each use "roe deer" in the first passage but "roebuck" in the second.[17] But it should also be pointed out that the term **fallowdeer** is still used today of a small deer found in mountains and forests across Europe.[18] Furthermore, when the AV describes ground that is "still," the NKJV, NASB, and NRSV change it to the more difficult "fallow."[19]

Familiar

> Regard not them that have **familiar** spirits, neither seek after wizards, to be defiled by them: I *am* the LORD your God. (Lev 19:31)

The word **familiar** occurs eighteen times in the AV,[20] while the plural **familiars** can be found once.[21] Sixteen of these instances are in the expression "familiar spirit" or "familiar spirits."[22] The word **familiar** is from the French *familier,* literally meaning "pertaining to one's family," for the word is ultimately derived from the Latin *familia,* "family." If something is **familiar** then it is intimate, well acquainted, private, in constant or close association, personal, or common. Thus, a **familiar** spirit is a spirit that is in intimate communication with someone. A "**familiar** friend," found twice in the AV,[23] is likewise a close, intimate friend. Obviously, the word **familiar** is still used today exactly like it is found in the AV. Our modern versions, however, had some trouble with the word where it was used in the AV. The usual replacement for one that had a "**familiar** spirit" or "**familiar** spirits" is "medium" or "mediums."[24] However, the NKJV forgot to remove "**familiar** spirits" three times.[25] The NRSV also neglected to remove this phrase twice.[26] When the AV speaks of a "**familiar** friend," it is variously rendered as "close,"[27] "intimate,"[28] and "bosom."[29] The NKJV retains the word "**familiar**" once.[30] Our modern versions could not agree on the proper translation of **familiars.** The NRSV chose "close friends," the NASB "trusted friends," and the NIV just "friends," but the NKJV preferred "acquaintances."[31] Yet when the AV reads "acquaintance," the NASB and NRSV correct it to "**familiar** friend."[32] Although reference to someone having a "**familiar** spirit" could be termed archaic, the words *witch* and *wizard* are certainly in widespread use today, except in modern, up-to-date Bible versions. A witch is not mentioned in any new translation and only the NRSV follows the AV in using the epithet "wizard," except for the NKJV, which employs "wizards" one time where the AV did not contain the word.[33]

𝔉𝔞𝔫

> Whose **fan** *is* in his hand, and he will thoroughly purge his floor, and gather his wheat into the garner; but he will burn up the chaff with unquenchable fire. (Mat 3:12)

The word **fan** occurs four times in the AV as a noun[34] and four times as a verb.[35] The derivative **fanners** appears once.[36] The Old English form was *fann,* from the Latin *vannus,* "a winnowing fan." A **fan** is a fork-like instrument for winnowing—freeing chaff from grain by fanning with wind. Our modern sense of a rotating device to blow air was named after this. Excepting the NKJV, which generally added "winnowing" to the noun **fan,**[37] our modern versions have removed all trace of this word. The

NIV, NRSV, and NASB change the noun **fan** to fork one "time."[38] but "winnowing fork" on the other three occasions.[39] The noun **fanners** is revised to "winnowers," but the NASB strangely uses "foreigners."[40] The verb **fan** is altered to "winnow"[41] in all but one passage where the NKJV follows the AV reading of **fan**.[42] Yet when the AV reads "winnow," followed by the NKJV, NASB, and NRSV, the NIV alone alters it to "spread."[43] Moreover, in this same verse, the NRSV inserts the obscure, arcane word "silage."[44]

Farthing

> Are not two sparrows sold for a **farthing**? and one of them shall not fall on the ground without your Father. (Mat 10:29)

Farthing appears in the AV three times in the singular[45] and once in the plural.[46] **Farthing** occurred in Old English as *feorthing*, meaning "a little fourth." A **farthing** is a fourth part of a penny or a very small piece of anything. The NRSV and NIV unanimously update **farthing** and **farthings** to "penny" and "pennies."[47] The NASB preferred "cent" and "cents."[48] The NKJV, however, altered **farthing** to "penny" one time,[49] "copper coin" or "copper coins" twice,[50] and the arcane "quadrans" the one other time **farthing** occurred.[51] Yet when the AV reads "penny," it is altered in every occurrence by the NASB and NKJV to "denarius."[52] But the word **farthing** is still current anyway: "The drive to exploit every last **farthing** of value in copyrighted material has transformed even such shabby media properties as CBS into rare prizes; it's seldom possible to buy one for a reasonable price."[53]

Fat

> The liberal soul shall be made **fat**: and he that watereth shall be watered also himself. (Prov 11:25)

Although the word **fat** occurs 130 times in the AV, there are several places in the AV where it is used figuratively or in archaic compounds that give modern translations trouble. **Fat** appeared in Old English as *faett*, and although it is usually literally applied in the Bible to animal fat, the word **fat** is also used figuratively to mean good, rich, full, prosperous, or the best.[54] The compound

fatfleshed occurs only once in the AV.[55] It is manifestly a compound of *fat* and *flesh*. **Fatfleshed** is shortened to "**fat**" in all of our new translations.[56] But although the AV is criticized here for using a long, obscure, compound word like **fatfleshed** when a shorter form will do, the NIV and NASB extend "fatted" to "fattened."[57] Moreover, all of our modern versions go even further, using "fattened" or "fatted" where the AV just says "**fat**."[58] And incredibly, in three places where the AV, followed by the NKJV and NIV, reads "**fat**," the NRSV and NASB alter it to the incomprehensible "suet."[59] Another compound in the AV with the word **fat** is **fatling**, occurring once in the singular[60] and five times in the plural.[61] A **fatling** is a calf, lamb, or other young animal fattened for slaughter. Surprisingly however, our modern versions usually retain the AV reading, except for the NIV.[62] In fact, the new versions liked **fatling** and **fatlings** so much that they even used these words to correct the AV.[63]

Fats

> Put ye in the sickle, for the harvest is ripe: come, get you down; for the press is full, the **fats** overflow; for their wickedness *is* great. (Joel 3:13)

The word **fats** occurs twice in the AV,[64] but similar compounds can also be found. **Winefat** appears twice[65] and **pressfat** once.[66] The word *fat* in this case is unrelated to the previous word, for *fat* was the original form of *vat*, "a vessel." Thus, **fats** are vats, a **winefat** is a winevat, and a **pressfat** is a vat for a winepress. Naturally, all forms of **fats** are updated by our modern versions.[67] But when the AV says something plain like "south," the NIV, NRSV, and NASB alter it to the bewildering "Negev" or "Negeb."[68]

Feebleminded

> Now we exhort you, brethren, warn them that are unruly, comfort the **feebleminded**, support the weak, be patient toward all *men*. (1 Th 5:14)

The compound word **feebleminded** only occurs once in the AV. It is obviously a combination of *feeble* and *mind*. The word *feeble* is from the French *feble*, "lamentful." It literally means "to be wept over," as it is derived from the Latin *flere*, "to weep." To be **feebleminded** is to be weak, infirm, frail, or faint, and does not necessarily refer to a state of mind. The NKJV, NRSV, and NASB render this word as "fainthearted," but the NRSV splits it into two words. The NIV selected "timid." But when the AV used "fainthearted," the NASB and NIV changed it to "disheartened,"[69] as did the NRSV,[70] which also used "let your heart be faint."[71] Yet when the AV reads "lest your heart faint," the NRSV changes it to "do not be fainthearted."[72] The word **feebleminded**, however, is still in common use today: "Blanket stereotypes afflicted anyone over 65: sickly, **feebleminded**, confined to nursing homes, a burden on their children, haggard and bitter—or, at best, cute and childlike."[73]

Feign

> And they watched *him*, and sent forth spies, which should **feign** themselves just men, that they might take hold of his words, that so they might deliver him unto the power and authority of the governor. (Luke 20:20)

The word **feign** appears in the AV three times.[74] **Feigned** is used three times,[75] **feignest** twice,[76] **feignedly** once,[77] and **unfeigned** four times.[78] **Feign** is from the French *feindre*, "to form." To **feign** is to invent, forge, make fictitious statements, pretend, act or allege falsely, disguise or conceal. All forms of this word have been removed from our modern versions. The only exceptions are the NKJV forgetting to dislodge "**feigned**" once[79] and the NASB injecting the word "**feigned**" into a passage where neither the AV nor any new translation contained the word.[80] The usual replacement for the various derivatives of **feign** is a form of "pretend."[81] Other translations include "acted,"[82] "inventing,"[83] "deceitful,"[84] "deceptive,"[85] and "in pretense."[86] **Unfeigned** is replaced with either "sincere"[87] or "genuine."[88] All of these corrections were all quite unnecessary, for **feign** is still in use today: "School was boring and an oppression, and she would often **feign** sickness in order to escape."[89]

Felloes

> And the work of the wheels *was* like the work of a chariot wheel: their axletrees, and their naves, and their **felloes**, and

their spokes, *were* all molten. (1 Ki 7:33)

The word **felloes** is found only one time in the AV. It appeared in Old English as *felg* and is a synonym for *felly*, from *feolan*, "to stick to." **Felloes** are parts of a wheel rim. It was so named from the pieces being put together. Naturally, our modern versions unanimously remove this word since it is genuinely archaic. However, when the AV, followed by the NKJV, NASB, and NRSV, uses the simple word "pits," the NIV alone transforms it into "rifts."[90]

Fens

He lieth under the shady trees, in the covert of the reed, and **fens**. (Job 40:21)

The word **fens**, the plural of *fen*, occurs only once in the AV. It appeared in Old English as *fenn* and refers to a marsh or a bog. Our modern versions unanimously update **fens** to "marsh." But when the AV uses a simple word like "beaten," it is altered by the NIV, NASB, and NRSV to "flogged."[91] The word **fens** is not archaic anyway, at least according to *Nature Conservancy* magazine: "The bogs and **fens** where Glaser works are so deserted that he once had to walk 11 miles for help after his research vehicle slipped off a bog road."[92]

Fetch

And Moses and Aaron gathered the congregation together before the rock, and he said unto them, Hear now, ye rebels; must we **fetch** you water out of this rock? (Num 20:10)

The word **fetch** appears in the AV thirty-one times as **fetch**,[93] nineteen times as **fetched**,[94] once as **fetcheth**,[95] and once with the spelling of **fetcht**.[96] Out of these fifty-two occurrences of the various forms of **fetch**, two are in the phrase "**fetch** a compass,"[97] and three appear in "**fetched** a compass."[98] **Fetch** developed from the Old English *feccan*, a variant of *fatian*, "to bring to." To **fetch** means to get and bring back, bring in or receive for, or simply to go and get something. The expression "**fetch** a compass" refers to turning around or making a circuit. Although our modern versions deemed this word archaic and sought to completely eliminate it, the NASB and NKJV carelessly left **fetch** in one passage.[99] The usual updated translation for **fetch** is "bring"[100] or "get."[101] **Fetched** is commonly emended to "brought,"[102] "got,"[103] or "took."[104] But is the word **fetch** archaic? It is certainly used down South in the 1990's. How many boys, whether in the North or South, have thrown a stick and told their dog to **fetch** it? Even *Time* magazine had no trouble with the word: "This summer his marks will **fetch** him discounts and freebies at local pizza parlors and candy stores."[105]

Fillet

> And *concerning* the pillars, the height of one pillar *was* eighteen cubits; and a **fillet** of twelve cubits did compass it; and the thickness thereof *was* four fingers: *it was* hollow. (Jer 52:21)

Although the singular **fillet** is found only once in the AV, the plural **fillets** appears eight times.[106] The verb **filleted** can also be found three times.[107] **Fillet** is from the French *filet*, a diminutive of *fil*, "thread." A **fillet** is an ornamental narrow band that goes around something or a thin strip of any material. **Fillets** is usually updated by our new translations to "bands."[108] The NKJV also used "rings" once,[109] as the NIV once selected "bases."[110] Although the word **fillet** is not too well known today, at least the AV used the word "speaking" instead of the NIV's "fomenting."[111]

Fine

> Surely there is a vein for the silver, and a place for gold where they **fine** *it*. (Job 28:1)

The word **fine**, in the sense that it is used here, occurs only once in the AV. **Finer** also appears once,[112] and **fining** can be found twice.[113] Although **fine** is from the French *fin*, meaning excellent or exquisite, it is ultimately derived from the Latin *finis*, "end." This is because when searching for something that is of **fine** quality, the search is ended once it is found. As used in the AV, **fine** refers to refining, purifying, or removing impurities from metal. A **finer** is one who fines and a **fining** pot is a pot used for **fining**. **Fine** is rendered in our modern versions by "refine" or "refined."[114] A **finer** is changed to a "smith" in the NASB and

NIV, but a "silversmith" in the NIV and NKJV.[115] The **fining** pot that is mentioned in two passages is updated to a "refining" pot in the NASB and NKJV.[116] But incredibly, the NRSV and NIV change the fining pot into a "crucible" pot, making the passage even more obscure.[117]

Firkins

> And there were set there six waterpots of stone, after the manner of the purifying of the Jews, containing two or three **firkins** apiece. (John 2:6)

The word **firkins** appears only once in the AV and is from the Dutch *vierdekijn,* diminutive of *vierde,* "fourth," from *vier,* "four." A firkin was originally a small container for butter or liquids containing half a kilderkin. It was then applied to the measure of the same and represented a quarter of a barrel. "Two or three **firkins**" in the AV is updated by all of our modern versions to "twenty or thirty gallons." But when it comes to other equally archaic measures, our modern, up-to-date translations retain the "cubit,"[118] "shekel,"[119] "talent,"[120] "gerah,"[121] "bekah,"[122] and "omer."[123] The NRSV, NKJV, and NASB also follow the AV measurement of "fathoms" in the New Testament.[124] Consistency is not the forte of modern English versions. And furthermore, no one ever tried to update the title of *Twenty Thousand Leagues Under the Sea,* written by Jules Verne in 1870.

Firmament

> The heavens declare the glory of God; and the **firmament** showeth his handiwork. (Psa 19:1)

The word **firmament** occurs seventeen times in the AV.[125] **Firmament** comes from the Latin *firmamentum,* from *firmare,* "to strengthen." The **firmament** refers to the sky, heavens, outer space, or the sphere of the stars. It is what strengthens or holds up and holds back the stars. The NKJV followed the AV reading every time, but the NIV and NASB preferred "expanse."[126] The NRSV selected "dome" to correct the AV.[127] The NIV uses "skies" and "heavens" each one time.[128] The NRSV overlooked **firmament** in two passages where the word appeared in the AV.[129] But **firmament** was not archaic in the first place, for even

21st Century Science & Technology magazine utilized the word: "But it was not named for Pluto, the god of the underworld or Hades, but for Pluto, the second planet beyond Uranus in the heavenly **firmament**."[130]

Firstling

> And every **firstling** of an ass thou shalt redeem with a lamb; and if thou wilt not redeem it, then thou shalt break his neck: and all the firstborn of man among thy children shalt thou redeem. (Exo 13:13)

The singular **firstling** occurs fourteen times in the AV,[131] while the plural **firstlings** is found six times.[132] **Firstling** is a combination of *first* and the suffix *-ling*, denoting the first of something to be produced, come into being, or appear. The term **firstling** is normally applied to the first offspring of an animal. **Firstling** is ordinarily rendered in our modern versions as "firstborn,"[133] but the NASB preferred "first offspring"[134] or the hyphenated "first-born."[135] **Firstlings** is likewise commonly changed to "firstborn," or "first-born," as it appears in the NASB.[136] However, these supposedly archaic words are retained ten times in the supposedly up-to-date NRSV.[137] The NASB also carelessly leaves **firstlings** in one passage.[138] However, after correcting **firstling** and **firstlings** in the AV, the NASB and NKJV found no problem with using the word "nestlings," a word that does not even appear in the AV.[139] Additionally, the NRSV, NASB, and NIV all inject the archaic "yearling" or "yearlings" into the Bible when the AV and the NKJV do not even contain the words.[140]

Fitches

> When he hath made plain the face thereof, doth he not cast abroad the **fitches,** and scatter the cummin, and cast in the principal wheat and the appointed barley and the rie in their place? (Isa 28:25)

The word **fitches** occurs three times in the AV.[141] *Fitch,* the singular form, is a variation of *vetch,* from the French *veche.* A fitch is the plant *vicia sativa* or *nigella sativa,* or just the seed, which was used as a spice or seasoning. Our modern versions could not decide what **fitches** were. In the first two passages, the

NRSV and NASB altered **fitches** to "dill."[142] However, the NIV thought it should be "caraway" and the NKJV "black cummin."[143] The third verse where the word **fitches** is found has been unanimously revised to the arcane "spelt."[144] **Fitches** may be archaic, but it is not any more difficult than "coriander seed"[145] and "cummin,"[146] retained in new translations just as they appear in the AV.

Flag

> Can the rush grow up without mire? can the **flag** grow without water? (Job 8:11)

The word **flag** occurs in the AV once in the singular and three times in the plural.[147] There are three separate words for **flag** in English, "none of whose origins are known for certain."[148] As it is used in the AV, **flag** is thought to be related to the Danish *flaeg,* "yellow iris." A **flag** is an aquatic plant like an iris, reed, or rush. **Flag** and **flags** are variously rendered by our modern versions as "reeds"[149] or "rushes."[150] However, when the AV says "reeds," it is often changed to "marches"[151] or "bulrushes."[152] But as we have seen, "bulrush" in the AV is several times altered to "papyrus"[153] or "reed."[154]

Flagon

> And he dealt to every one of Israel, both man and woman, to every one a loaf of bread, and a good piece of flesh, and a **flagon** *of wine.* (1 Chr 16:3)

The singular **flagon** appears twice in the AV,[155] while the plural **flagons** is found three times.[156] This word comes from the French *flacon,* "a small vessel," and is related to our word *flask.* A **flagon** is a container for holding liquids or a measure of as much as a **flagon** would hold. In four of the five passages where these words are found, our modern versions correct the AV to "cake of raisins,"[157] or for varieties' sake, "raisin cakes."[158] Once, however, the NIV just says "raisins."[159] Since the Bible mentions "dried grapes," it is possible that it is grapes that is being referred to. A raisin is just a dried grape anyway. The other passage where **flagons** is used is changed to "jars" in the NASB and NIV,[160] but "pitcher" in the NKJV.[161] Surprisingly, the

NRSV retains this supposedly archaic word in this instance.[162] And not only does it keep "**flagon**" in this verse, the NRSV inserts "**flagons**" into four other passages where neither the AV nor any modern version contained the word.[163] Nevertheless, the word **flagons** is still in vogue today: "Dorothy and her gang at the Algonquin Round Table—Robert Benchley, Alexander Woollcott and the rest—supposedly were the sharpest and most cutting minds in Manhattan; writers and critics and drinkers who could skewer an icon at forty paces, if the **flagon** of martinis lasted that long."[164]

Flanks

> And the two kidneys, and the fat that *is* upon them, which *is* by the **flanks,** and the caul above the liver, with the kidneys, it shall he take away. (Lev 3:15)

The word **flanks,** the plural of *flank,* occurs six times in the AV.[165] *Flank* is from the French *flanc,* literally referring to the weak part of the body. The flank is the fleshy or muscular part of the side of an animal. It can also be the side of anything or the extreme left or right side of a fleet or army. Excepting one passage,[166] the NKJV follows the AV. Our other versions remove **flanks** every time it occurs in the AV, usually substituting "loins."[167] Yet when the AV reads "loins," it is sometimes corrected.[168] But in the meat department of any grocery store, one can find flank steak right next to pork loin. And furthermore, **flanks** is even applied by *Audubon* magazine to fish: "Yet somehow Arctic grayling materialized under my bouncing dry flies, slicing the riffles with their golden **flanks.**"[169] It also evident that our modern versions did not consider **flanks** to be archaic anyway, for the NRSV inserted "flank" into two passages where the AV did not contain the word.[170] The NIV did likewise,[171] as did the NASB.[172]

Flay

> And he shall **flay** the burnt offering, and cut it into his pieces. (Lev 1:6)

The word **flay** appears three times in the AV,[173] while **flayed** is found once.[174] **Flay** developed from the Old English *flean,* "to strip." To **flay** literally means to skin or strip off the skin, but it has also been transferred to inflict pain or torture, strip of money or property, and to scold or berate. The usual updating of **flay** is to "skin,"[175] but "strip" can also be found.[176] The NKJV removed **flay** and **flayed** on three occasions but neglected to excise **flay** in one passage.[177] The NRSV was extremely lax, using both "**flayed**" and "**flay**" each one time.[178] But **flayed** can still be found in use today, both literally: "Her sixteen-year-old brother **flayed** and executed with other suspected 'subversives' in the plaza,"[179] and figuratively: "New England preachers **flayed** Jefferson as godless, and the Federalist press called him a French puppet."[180]

Fleshhook

> And the priests' custom with the people *was, that,* when any man offered sacrifice, the priest's servant came, while the flesh was in seething, with a **fleshhook** of three teeth in his hand; (1 Sam 2:13)

The word **fleshhook** occurs in the AV twice in the singular[181] and five times in the plural.[182] A **fleshhook** is another example of an unusual compound word found in the AV that is deemed archaic by our modern translations. A **fleshhook** is obviously a hook for flesh or a large fork. Our modern versions usually render this as "fork"[183] or "meat fork."[184] However, the NASB forgot to replace the word on one occasion.[185] The modern, up-to-date NKJV neglected to remove "**fleshhook**" in two passages.[186] Once again it is apparent that archaic words are not limited to the AV.

Flowers

> And of her that is sick of her **flowers,** and of him that hath an issue, of the man, and of the woman, and of him that lieth with her that is unclean. (Lev 15:33)

The word **flowers,** as it is used here, occurs only twice in the AV.[187] This word is derived from the French *flueurs* and ultimately from the Latin *fluere,* "to flow." **Flowers** refers to the menstrual discharge. It is variously rendered in our modern versions as "impurity,"[188] "menstrual impurity,"[189] "customary impurity,"[190] "period,"[191] "monthly flow,"[192] and "monthly period."[193] Only the NASB consistently translated the passage the same.[194] The word **flowers**, as used here in the AV, is definitely archaic, but what about the NIV's use of "festooned"?[195]

Flux

> And it came to pass, that the father of Publius lay sick of a fever and of a bloody **flux:** to whom Paul entered in, and prayed, and laid his hands on him, and healed him. (Acts 28:8)

Found only once in the AV, this word, although from the French *flux*, is like the previous one, and goes back to the Latin *fluere*, "to flow." A **flux** is a flowing of blood or any liquid discharge from the bowels or other organs. Our modern versions unite in changing **flux** to "dysentery." Indeed, the underlying Greek word is *dusenteria*. Yet when the AV mentions the disease of leprosy, which is still prevalent in some countries today, the NIV alters it to an unnamed "skin disease."[196] **Flux** is so archaic that it is still listed in medical dictionaries as "an excessive discharge from any of the natural openings of the body."[197]

Footmen

> And Saul gathered the people together, and numbered them in Telaim, two hundred thousand **footmen,** and ten thousand men of Judah. (1 Sam 15:4)

The word **footmen** occurs twelve times in the AV.[198] It is manifestly a compound of *foot* and *men*. **Footmen** are men who go on foot such as foot soldiers or attendants. Out of the twelve times **footmen** is found in the AV, our modern versions only unite on an alternate translation seven times, using "foot soldiers."[199] Occasionally, **footmen** was changed to "men on foot" or "on foot."[200] For some unknown reason, though, the NRSV used the hyphenated "foot-soldiers" one time even though it split the word up the seven other times it used it.[201] The NRSV also crafted the hyphenated "foot-runners" once.[202] Although "swordsmen" was retained, **footmen** was deemed archaic by our modern, up-to-date translations—the NASB carelessly forgetting to remove the word twice,[203] and the NRSV and NKJV each once.[204] Moreover, the NASB used the word "policemen"[205] and the NKJV, NIV, and NASB employed the word "woodsmen"[206] when these words do not even occur in the AV. And not only do the NASB and NKJV use the AV word "plowmen,"[207] the NIV even alters "plowers" in the AV to "plowmen" when all of the other versions read as the AV.[208] And furthermore, the word **footmen** is still currently in use: "On this premise do the NRA and its political **footmen** survive and, often, flourish."[209]

𝕱orasmuch

> Therefore, my beloved brethren, be ye stedfast, unmoveable, always abounding in the work of the Lord, **forasmuch** as ye know that your labour is not in vain in the Lord. (1 Cor 15:58)

The word **forasmuch** occurs forty-three times in the AV.[210] It is a combination of the three separate words "for as much." The cognate term **forsomuch,** found only once in the AV,[211] was formed similarly. **Forasmuch** is normally coupled with as: **forasmuch** as. This phrase thus means inasmuch as, in consideration of, seeing that, since, because, or so far as. The phrase "**forasmuch** as" is given in our modern versions as "since,"[212] "inasmuch,"[213] and "because."[214] Yet of the nine times the AV employs the word "inasmuch," the NIV and NRSV correct it every time[215] and the NASB only retains it once.[216] Moreover, not only do the new translations use "inasmuch," the NRSV alone uses the triple compound "insofar."[217] And further regarding **forasmuch,** the NASB indolently left this supposedly archaic word in one passage.[218]

𝕱orbear

> And thou shalt speak my words unto them, whether they will hear, or whether they will **forbear:** for they *are* most rebellious. (Ezek 2:7)

The word **forbear** appears twenty-two times in the AV.[219] The other forms include **forborn,** found once,[220] **forbearing,** found five times,[221] **forbeareth,** found twice,[222] and **forbearance,** appearing twice.[223] The spelling **forbare,** occurring three times,[224] is archaic for *forbore,* the past tense of **forbear.** The word **forbear,** which appeared in Old English as *forberan,* means to bear, endure, submit to, have patience with, tolerate, avoid, abstain, refrain, or restrain. **Forbear** is usually updated to "refrain,"[225] but it can also be found as "hold back,"[226] "abstain,"[227] "stop,"[228] "bear with,"[229] "refuse,"[230] and "endure."[231] **Forbearing, forbeareth, forbare,** and **forborn** are similarly modernized.[232] For some reason, however, our modern versions had no trouble with the word **forbearance:** they all reproduce the AV reading the two times it occurs,[233] except for the NIV using "tolerance" one time.[234] The NKJV and NASB like **forbearance** so much that they substituted it for **forbearing** in the AV once[235] and twice[236] respectively. The NASB then inserted **forbearing** into a passage where neither the AV nor any new translation contained the word.[237] The NRSV, after retaining the archaic **forbear** in one passage,[238] replaced the perfectly understandable "longsuffering" in the AV with "**forbearance.**"[239] The corrections to the various forms of **forbear** were somewhat hasty, since *American Heritage* magazine in 1994 still utilized the word: "Its personal vindictiveness, which Lincoln's partisan neighbors found so effective, is likely to prove somewhat distasteful to modern readers and is certainly out of character with the generous and **forbearing** man who led the nation through the Civil War."[240]

Forepart

> And falling into a place where two seas met, they ran the ship aground; and the **forepart** stuck fast, and remained unmoveable, but the hinder part was broken with the violence of the waves. (Acts 27:41)

The word **forepart** occurs five times in the AV.[241] It is one of the lesser known nouns in the AV containing the *fore-* prefix. The word **forecast,** found twice in the AV,[242] is the only verb with the *fore-* prefix that is not reproduced in modern versions. The *fore-* prefix, when affixed to verbs, gives the additional sense of before, in advance, or beforehand. When conjoined to nouns, *fore-* describes an object occupying a front position or expressing anteriority in time. The **forepart** of something is the front part of it. Although this is quite obvious, our modern versions still corrected **forepart** every time it appeared in the AV.[243] In one instance, when **forepart** referred to the front of a ship, instead of using "bow" like the NRSV and NIV, the NKJV and NASB utilize the more difficult "prow."[244] To **forecast** is to predict or plan ahead of time. Although our up-to-date, contemporary, modern versions likewise replace **forecast,** they regularly insert words with a *fore-* prefix that do not even occur in the AV. The NIV, in contradiction not only to the AV but all of the other new translations as well, twice updates "finger" to "forefinger."[245] The NKJV, NIV, and NASB all use the words "foreman" or "foremen."[246] All of our modern versions use the word "forego."[247] The NASB alone employs the word "forestall."[248] The NRSV is the worst offender, using "foreboding"[249] and "forelocks"[250] when neither the AV nor any other modern version contain the words. The NRSV also uses the archaic "forenoon"[251] and then replaces the simple AV reading of "porch" with "forecourt."[252] And finally, when the AV, followed by all of the other modern versions, reads "fathers," the NRSV replaces it with the archaic "forebears."[253] But the correction of **forepart** was entirely unnecessary, for the word is still used today: "Inside is the full Comfortech insert, which includes a spongy, energy return insert under the entire **forepart** of the foot."[254]

Foreship

> And as the shipmen were about to flee out of the ship, when they had let down the boat into the sea, under colour as though they would have cast anchors out of the **foreship,** (Acts 27:30)

The word **foreship,** found only once in the AV, appeared in Old English as *forscip,* "the forepart of a ship." The **foreship** is the bow of a ship. Like the previous word **forepart,** our modern versions have omitted **foreship** because it was deemed too archaic for twentieth century Americans. Yet the NIV, NASB, and NRSV, saw nothing wrong with calling the sail of a ship the "foresail."[255] Moreover, the forecastle of a ship is still described as such in the 1990's.[256]

Forswear

> Again, ye have heard that it hath been said by them of old time, Thou shalt not **forswear** thyself, but shalt perform unto the Lord thine oaths: (Mat 5:33)

The word **forswear** is found only once in the AV. It is strictly an English word, the Old English form being *forswerian*. To **forswear** is to renounce earnestly, deny or repudiate under oath, abjure, swear falsely or commit perjury. The NKJV and NRSV substitute "swear falsely" for **forswear,** but the NIV preferred "break your oath" and the NASB "make false vows." However, when the AV, followed by our other modern versions, uses the simple word "swear," the NASB revises it to the wordy "make an oath."[257] **Forswear** is still in use as a legal term and has been defined as making "an oath to that which the deponent knows to be untrue."[258] Moreover, forms of the word **forswear** can still be found today when not used in a legal context: "States like Pakistan and Indonesia were willing to make concessions in the military domain deemed important by the West (such as **forswearing** chemical weapons and opening facilities to inspection) in exchange for expectations of enhanced commercial trade."[259]

Forthwith

Some fell upon stony places, where they had not much earth: and **forthwith** they sprung up, because they had no deepness of earth: (Mat 13:5)

The word **forthwith** appears ten times in the AV[260] and is a combination of *forth* and *with,* which developed from *forth mid,* "along with." **Forthwith** means immediately, at once, or without delay or interval. Our modern versions have unanimously removed this word from the AV and instead have substituted "without delay,"[261] "quickly,"[262] "at once,"[263] "as soon as,"[264] "suddenly,"[265] or "immediately."[266] Although **forthwith,** the meaning of which could be determined from the context, was unanimously corrected by our modern versions, it is still used in the 1990's: "The Germans are not going to be inhibited in any way, shape or form by the presence of American troops—any time that we are in the way of their internal policies, we're going to be asked to leave **forthwith.**"[267]

Forward

For indeed he accepted the exhortation; but being more **forward,** of his own accord he went unto you. (2 Cor 8:17)

The word **forward,** as it is used in this passage, occurs three times in the AV.[268] **Forwardness,** used similarly, appears twice.[269] The Old English form was *foreweard.* To be **forward** is to be ardent, eager, zealous, ready, or inclined to do something. Limiting the word to its common meaning of "toward the front" or "into view," our modern versions have replaced **forward** when the AV uses it a different way. The translations used to update forms of **forward** are numerous. Our modern versions agree on a translation only once, all of them using "eager" in one passage.[270] Other translations include forms of "desire,"[271] forms of "earnest,"[272] "enthusiasm,"[273] forms of "diligent,"[274] "readiness,"[275] and "willingness."[276] Yet after correcting **forward** to make the Bible more understandable, the NIV, in one of the same verses where **forward** is found, alters "accord" to "initiative" when all of the other modern versions follow the AV.[277]

Fourscore

Then said he to another, And how much owest thou? And he said, An hundred measures of wheat. And he said unto him, Take thy bill, and write **fourscore.** (Luke 16:7)

The word **fourscore** occurs thirty-six times in the AV.[278] The similar form **threescore** appears ninety-three times,[279] while **sixscore** shows up twice.[280] The suffix added to these words is *-score,* from the Old English *scoru,* "twenty." The value of all these words is given in our new versions: sixty for **threescore,** eighty for **fourscore,** and one hundred and twenty for **sixscore.** Although **fourscore** is archaic, it is endlessly repeated to this day ever since Abraham Lincoln used it in his Gettysburg Address: "Through the goodness of God over **fourscore** years, my father has come to radiate a deep and abiding joy."[281] **Fourscore** may be archaic but it is certainly more readily understood than the NASB and NRSV using "flitting" to correct the AV reading of "wandering."[282]

Foursquare

A cubit *shall be* the length thereof, and a cubit the breadth thereof; **foursquare** shall it be: and two cubits *shall be* the height thereof: the horns thereof *shall be* of the same. (Exo 30:2)

The word **foursquare** appears ten times in the AV.[283] It is manifestly a compound of *four* and *square.* If something is **foursquare** then it has four equal sides. **Foursquare** is obviously another way of saying that something is square. One would think that our modern, up-to-date versions of the Bible would never use such an archaic term as **foursquare,** but such is not the case. The NKJV neglects to remove **foursquare** twice[284] and the NRSV was negligent once.[285] One would also think that any new translation would use the word *square* to update **foursquare,** but again, such is not the case. The NRSV altered **foursquare** to "foursided" in one passage,[286] while the NASB conjectured the reading "perfect square" in another.[287] Yet on one occasion when the AV read "square," the NRSV changed it to the longer "four-sided."[288] Moreover, our modern versions sometimes employ compound words when the simple base form will do, such as the NRSV, NKJV, and NIV lengthening "vine" in the AV to "grapevine" even though they render the same underlying Greek word as "vine" every other time it appears.[289] And similarly, when the AV, followed by all of the other modern versions, reads "waters of the flood," the NIV alone corrects it to the compound "floodwaters."[290] The NIV also changes "on his face" to "facedown" in spite of the fact that all of the other new versions read as the AV.[291] And finally, regarding the word **foursquare,** *American Heritage* magazine did not see any problem with using this word: "**Foursquare** and substantial, the Connecticut chest is instantly recognizable as a product of the seventeenth century."[292]

Fowl

> This *is* the law of the beasts, and of the **fowl,** and of every living creature that moveth in the waters, and of every creature that creepeth upon the earth: (Lev 11:46)

The word **fowl** occurs thirty-one times in the AV in the singular[293] and fifty-five times in the plural.[294] The derivative **fowler** appears three times in the singular[295] and once in the plural.[296] **Fowl** is from the Old English *fugel,* "bird." **Fowler** is from *fugelere,* "one who hunts birds." Although our modern versions all retain the supposedly archaic **fowler** and **fowlers** about half the time,[297] they did not reciprocate for **fowl** and **fowls.** The NASB, NIV, and NKJV all eliminate **fowls** and the NRSV only retains it once.[298] The singular **fowl** is kept only once by the NRSV and NIV,[299] three times by the NASB,[300] and four times by the NKJV.[301] But although they rejected **fowl** as being archaic, our new versions did not hesitate to correct simple words in the AV like "wings" and "feathers." The NIV replaces "wings" with "pinions,"[302] the NKJV and NRSV exchange "feathers" for "pinions,"[303] and the NRSV and NASB trade "feathers" for "plumage."[304] But after all of these corrections, the word **fowl** can still be found in use at the end of the twentieth century: "Acid rain makes once-prime habitat uninhabitable to **fowl**, fish and other lifeforms."[305]

Fray

> And thy carcase shall be meat unto all fowls of the air, and unto the beasts of the earth, and no man shall **fray** *them* away. (Deu 28:26)

The word **fray** occurs three times in the AV.[306] It is an aphetic form of *affray*, from the French *effraier*, "to frighten." Thus, **fray** means to frighten, scare, terrify, or horrify. The modern word *afraid* is actually the past participle of *affrayed*. Our modern versions all unite in rendering **fray** by "frighten,"[307] except for the NRSV employing "terrify" one time.[308] Even though it corrected the AV three times in a row, the NIV evidently did not consider the word **fray** to be archaic since it used it as a noun in another passage where neither the AV nor any other version contained the word.[309]

Frontlets

> And thou shalt bind them for a sign upon thine hand, and they shall be as **frontlets** between thine eyes. (Deu 6:8)

The word **frontlets** appears three times in the AV and is the plural of *frontlet,* from a French word of the same spelling that is a diminutive of *frontal,* from which we get the modern *frontal.* **Frontlets** are things worn on the forehead. Although the NKJV failed to remove this supposedly archaic word every place it occurred in the AV,[310] our other modern translations were not as charitable. The NRSV consistently implemented "emblem" as a replacement for **frontlets**.[311] The NIV used "symbol" one time[312] and didn't translate it as anything the other two.[313] The NASB substituted "frontals" on two occasions,[314] and then used the obscure, archaic "phylacteries" the third occurrence.[315] In fact, in the only place where the AV uses the word "phylacteries," it is surprisingly retained by all of our supposedly modern, clear, up-to-date translations.[316]

Froward

> For the **froward** is abomination to the LORD: but his secret is with the righteous. (Prov 3:32)

The word **froward** occurs twenty-one times in the AV.[317] The form **frowardness** is used three times[318] and **frowardly** appears once.[319] **Froward** is a variation of the Old English *fromweard*, and is the opposite of toward. **Froward** can mean stubborn, perverse, difficult, evil-disposed, turned away from, or disposed to go contrary to what is demanded or reasonable. Although our modern versions could not agree on an updated translation for **froward**, they were in complete harmony in their aspiration to remove all forms of this word from the Bible. The usual choice to replace **froward** was "perverse,"[320] but a variety of other words were also used such as "crooked,"[321] "perverted,"[322] "devious,"[323] "cunning,"[324] "wily,"[325] "shrewd,"[326] "astute,"[327] "deceitful,"[328] "false,"[329] "twisted,"[330] "harsh,"[331] and "unreasonable."[332] **Frowardness** is likewise normally supplanted by forms of "perverse."[333] Yet when the AV says "perverse," it is sometimes corrected by every one of our modern versions.[334]

Fuller

> And his raiment became shining, exceeding white as snow; so as no **fuller** on earth can white them. (Mark 9:3)

The word **fuller** appears five times in the AV,[335] three of these in reference to a "**fuller's** field,"[336] and once as "**fullers'** soap."[337] The word appeared in Old English as *fullere*, "a bleacher," from *fullian*, "to bleach." These are derived from the Latin *fullo*, referring to one whose occupation was to full cloth. Thus, a **fuller** is one who fulls cloth. To full cloth is to clean and make it white, usually by stamping the garments with the feet or rods in water with the aid of various soaps and chemicals. Although **fuller** is supposed to be archaic, the NRSV and NASB retain it four times out of the five it is found in the AV.[338] The NKJV retains it three times[339] but the NIV corrects **fuller** every time.[340] When **fuller** is replaced, it is usually by "launderer"[341] or "washerman's."[342] Yet although the NIV updates **fuller** every time, when the AV, followed by the NKJV, NASB, and NRSV, says "company," the NIV amends it to "horde."[343]

Furbish

> Harness the horses; and get up, ye horsemen, and stand forth with *your* helmets; **furbish** the spears, *and* put on the brigandines. (Jer 46:4)

Although the word **furbish** occurs only once in the AV, the form **furbished** appears five times.[344] **Furbish** is from the French *forbiss*, from *forbir*, "to polish." Thus, to **furbish** is to polish, brighten, brush, or clean up something. Expectedly, this word does not appear in any of our modern versions. The NIV, NKJV, and NASB consistently employ forms of "polish" to update **furbish** and **furbished**.[345] The NRSV used "polished" on three occasions,[346] but could not decide between "whet" or "honed" for the other two.[347] But in the same verse where **furbish** appears in the AV, the NRSV furbishes a "spear" into a "lance" even though the other new translations follow the AV reading.[348] And when the AV does read "polished," the NIV, NKJV, and NRSV alter it to the more difficult "burnished."[349] The word **furbish**, however, is still current English: "Prominent violinists rely on him to minister to ailing instruments, to find and **furbish** old ones."[350]

Furlongs

> Now Bethany was nigh unto Jerusalem, about fifteen **furlongs** off: (John 11:18)

The word **furlongs**, the plural of *furlong*, occurs five times in the AV.[351] *Furlong* appeared in Old English as *furlang*, a combination of *furh*, "furrow," and *lang*, "long." It was originally the length of the furrow in the common field of a square containing ten acres. A furlong was then applied to the eighth part of an English mile. A modern furlong is 220 yards and is equal to the side of a square of ten statute acres.[352] In the NASB and NRSV, **furlongs** are represented by the mile equivalent.[353] The NKJV gives an equivalent three times[354] but then retains the AV reading in the other two instances.[355] The NIV likewise furnishes an equivalent three times,[356] but instead of preserving an archaic word like **furlongs,** the NIV uses the obscure, cryptic "stadia."[357] The are many units of measure that are used in modern physics, manufacturing, and engineering, but a stadia is certainly not one of them. The word *stadia* is nothing but a transliteration of the Greek *stadion.* As for why the NKJV and NIV did not translate this word consistently the five times the AV rendered it as **furlongs,** it has not been revealed by the translators. Moreover, after correcting **furlongs** because it was archaic, the NRSV and NASB replace the perfectly understandable and modern measurement of "acre" with "furrow."[358] Moreover, **furlongs** are still modern measurements, even in India: "This section covers the first few **furlongs** of the barrage structure when it is approached from the barrage office complex."[359]

Furniture

> Now Rachel had taken the images, and put them in the camel's **furniture,** and sat upon them. And Laban searched all the tent, but found *them* not. (Gen 31:34)

The word **furniture** occurs eight times in the AV.[360] Although the word **furniture** is not archaic as everyone has a house full of it, its use in the AV has been deemed archaic. **Furniture** is from the French *fourniture,* from *fournir,* "to furnish." Thus, **furniture** is literally anything that is furnished or provided. It can refer to apparel, personal belongings, necessities, a supply of anything, or equipment for something. Although the NKJV and NASB forgot to remove this word one time,[361] and each of our new translations altered **furniture** to "furnishings" at least once,[362] the usual replacement for **furniture** is "utensils."[363] Twice, however, the NIV furnished the word "accessories."[364] But after correcting the word **furniture,** the NRSV altered the simple word "fear" in the AV to the more difficult "deference."[365]

Chapter 7
Gaddest to Guile

Gaddest

> Why **gaddest** thou about so much to change thy way? thou also shalt be ashamed of Egypt, as thou wast ashamed of Assyria. (Jer 2:36)

Appearing only once in the AV, the word **gaddest** is the second person singular of *gad,* which is of obscure origin. It is thought to have been formed from *gadling,* from the Old English *gaedeling,* "a wanderer." Thus, to gad is to move about restlessly or roam idly. Although the NASB and NIV omit **gaddest** from this passage, changing it to "go,"the NKJV and NRSV neglected to completely update the AV reading—both used the word "gad." In fact, they liked the word so much that the NKJV inserted "gad" into another verse where the AV said "go,"[1] while the NRSV replaced "wandering" in the AV with "gadding."[2] Moreover, the NIV joined with the NRSV in changing "destruction" in the AV to "a gadfly."[3] **Gaddest** should never have been updated in the first place, for forms of this word are still current English: "And Wang himself flat-out refuses to **gad** about playing high-tech visionary as so many New Age CEOs love to do."[4]

Gainsay

> For I will give you a mouth and wisdom, which all your adversaries shall not be able to **gainsay** nor resist. (Luke 21:15)

Although the word **gainsay** occurs only once in the AV, the singular **gainsaying** appears twice,[5] the plural **gainsayings** once,[6] and the noun **gainsayers** once.[7] **Gainsay** is a combination of the

Old English *gegn,* "against" and *say.* Hence, to **gainsay** is to speak against, contradict, oppose, or hinder. Our modern versions remove all forms of this word from the Bible but do not agree on replacements. One can find "rebellion,"[8] "contrary,"[9] "obstinate,"[10] "objection,"[11] "resist,"[12] and forms of "contradict."[13] But all these corrections were unnecessary, for the word **gainsay** is still in vogue today: "Such qualifications do not **gainsay** the point that state sovereignty was the bedrock principle upon which the United Nations was founded."[14]

𝕲allant

> But there the glorious LORD *will be* unto us a place of broad rivers *and* streams; wherein shall go no galley with oars, neither shall **gallant** ship pass thereby. (Isa 33:21)

Gallant is found only once in the AV. It is from the French *galant,* from *galer,* "to rejoice." **Gallant** is remotely related to our word *gala.* To be **gallant** is to be admirable, noble, finely dressed, or beautiful in appearance. Our modern versions did not like the word **gallant** but could not agree on a substitution. The NASB and NIV chose "mighty," the NRSV "stately," and the NKJV "majestic." But **gallant** is still current in the 1990's: "The effect was the opposite of what they intended: the system finally collapsed and the **gallant** defenders of the Motherland landed in jail."[15]

𝕲arner

> Whose fan *is* in his hand, and he will thoroughly purge his floor, and gather his wheat into the **garner;** but he will burn up the chaff with unquenchable fire. (Mat 3:12)

The word **garner** appears twice in the AV in the singular[16] and twice in the plural.[17] It is from the French *gernier,* "storehouse." A **garner** is a storehouse for grain or other farm products. The NASB, NIV, and NKJV in unison adopt "barn" to update **garner,** but the NRSV preferred "granary."[18] The plural **garners** is unanimously rendered in one passage as "storehouses" by all of our new translations,[19] but in the other we find some divergence of opinion. The NKJV, NRSV, and NIV use "barns," but the NASB retained the archaic "**garners.**"[20] Yet when the

AV uses the simple word "barns," the NRSV and NIV alter it to "granaries."[21] And although **garner** is not employed as a verb in the AV, the NRSV and NASB deemed **garner** so archaic that they used it as a verb in a passage where the AV said "gathered."[22] The word **garner**, however, is still utilized in the 1990's by the *Atlantic Monthly:* "Once they do, any respect they might be able to **garner** in the wider system pales in comparison with the respect available in the local system."[23]

𝕲𝖆𝖗𝖓𝖎𝖘𝖍

> Woe unto you, scribes and Pharisees, hypocrites! because ye build the tombs of the prophets, and **garnish** the sepulchres of the righteous, (Mat 23:29)

In addition to appearing once as **garnish,** this word is also found five times as **garnished.**[24] Garnish is from the French *garnir,* "to fortify or furnish." The word **garnish** originally had reference to fortifying and furnishing something for defense. It was then applied to decorating, embellishing, or adorning anything. Our modern versions preferred forms of "adorn" to update forms of **garnish,**[25] but "put in order"[26] and "decorate"[27] can also be found. However, when the AV does use a simple word like "adorned," the NIV changes it to the more difficult "beautifully dressed."[28] But **garnish** is not archaic anyway, at least according to *World Watch* magazine: "Italians snare them, the French catch them in nets, and the Spanish trap them by daubing glue on tree branches—all to **garnish** dinner plates."[29]

𝕲𝖆𝖞

> And ye have respect to him that weareth the **gay** clothing, and say unto him, Sit thou here in a good place; and say to the poor, Stand thou there, or sit here under my footstool: (James 2:3)

The word **gay,** found only once in the AV, is from the French *gai,* "merry." To be **gay** is to be happy, joyful, cheerful, or fine. This good word has been appropriated by Sodomites and is now considered archaic in its original sense. It was not until about 1951 that the slang sense of a homosexual was connected with the word **gay.** This is thought to be short for *gay cat,* "a homosexual boy," a term first used as prison slang in 1935.[30] Naturally, our modern, up-to-date versions all replace **gay** with "fine." Surprisingly however, on two occasions where the AV reads "mirth," the NIV substitutes "gaiety."[31] The NASB likewise updates the AV with terms that are now applied to Sodomites, using "gaiety" four times to correct "joy" and "mirth."[32] But even though homosexuals have appropriated the word **gay**, it nevertheless still means happy or joyful, and forms of it are still so used today: "For being such and for vibrantly and with immense vitality portraying mad **gaiety** and reckless youth, a 'dancing flame on the screen' said one of her directors, she was billed as the Hottest Jazz Baby in Films, the Brooklyn Bonfire."[33]

Gazingstock

> And I will cast abominable filth upon thee, and make thee vile, and will set thee as a **gazingstock**. (Nahum 3:6)

The word **gazingstock** appears twice in the AV.[34] It is a compound of *gazing,* meaning to stare; and *stock,* referring to lineage or family. A **gazingstock** is the object of someone's gaze or stare. The first occurrence of **gazingstock** in the AV is unanimously rendered by our modern versions as "spectacle."[35] The second instance was inharmoniously supplied as "publicly exposed" by the NRSV and NIV, "public spectacle" by the NASB, and just "spectacle" by the NKJV.[36] But if **gazingstock** makes the Bible too hard to understand, then why did a modern English version like the NIV interject "tranquillity" into the Bible when the AV used the elementary word "quietness."[37] And furthermore, the NRSV, NASB, and NIV had no trouble with the word "laughingstock" even though it is not found in the AV.[38]

Gender

> But foolish and unlearned questions avoid, knowing that they do **gender** strifes. (2 Tim 2:23)

The word **gender** occurs twice in the AV,[39] but **gendereth** also appears twice[40] and **gendered** once.[41] **Gender** is from the French *gendrer,* "to beget." Thus, **gender** means to produce, breed, generate, or give rise to. It is only recently that **gender** has acquired the politically correct meaning of sex, whether male or female. Our modern versions variously supplanted the forms of **gender** in the AV by forms of "breed,"[42] "give birth,"[43] "produce,"[44] "generate,"[45] and "bear children."[46] Although the meaning of **gender** could be determined by the context, the alteration by the NRSV of the AV phrase "shall be cut off" to "is gossamer" can not be figured out in the context or out.[47]

Ghost

> While Peter yet spake these words, the Holy **Ghost** fell on all them which heard the word. (Acts 10:44)

The word **ghost** makes an appearance a total of 109 times in the AV. Ninety of these occurrences are in the expression "Holy Ghost."[48] The other nineteen are divided into the phrases "[give, gave, given, giveth] up the **ghost**," found fifteen times,[49] "giving up of the **ghost**," found once,[50] and "yielded up the **ghost**," found three times.[51] **Ghost** appeared in Old English as *gast*, meaning breath or spirit. A **ghost** is the spirit or soul of a dead man, hence "give up the **ghost**" means to die. Our modern versions usually render this phrase as "breathed his last."[52] **Ghost** also referred to a spirit in general and later just an evil spirit or apparition. The expression "Holy **Ghost**" is unanimously rendered by our modern versions as "Holy Spirit."[53] The only time our modern versions use the word **ghost,** excepting the NASB once in the Old Testament,[54] is in translating the Greek word *phantasma*, found twice in the AV and rendered "spirit."[55] It is from this word that we get our English word *phantom*. The common argument against the AV is that the Greek word *pneuma* should always be rendered as "spirit." Yet twice when the AV reads "spirit," the NRSV and NIV translate *pneuma* as "**ghost**."[56] **Ghost** does not always refer to something evil, many famous people have someone **ghost**write their books.

Gier eagle

> And the swan, and the pelican, and the **gier eagle,** (Lev 11:18)

A **gier eagle** is mentioned twice in the AV.[57] The word *gier* is borrowed from the Dutch *gier,* "vulture." A **gier eagle** is obviously a bird of prey. It is thought to be identified with the *neophron percnopterus,* a species of vulture. The NASB, NRSV, and NKJV unanimously render **gier eagle** as "carrion vulture."[58] The NIV, after twice correcting "osprey" to "black vulture,"[59] transforms the **gier eagle** into an "osprey."[60] Obviously the translators of modern Bible versions do not know zoology any better than they think the AV translators did.

Gin

> The **gin** shall take *him* by the heel, *and* the robber shall prevail against him. (Job 18:9)

The singular **gin** appears three times in the AV,[61] while the plural **gins** is found twice.[62] **Gin** is the aphetic form of *engine.* A **gin** then is a mechanical device or machine. A famous example is the cotton **gin**—a machine for separating cotton from its seeds. Due to its confusion with another word meaning "to dupe," **gin** has also come to mean a trap or a snare. All occurrences of **gin** and **gins** have been replaced in our new translations by "trap"[63] or "snare,"[64] excepting "bait," used once by the NASB,[65] and "net," used once by the NKJV.[66] The word **gin,** however, is still applied to mechanical devices in the 1990's: "You can use a crane or a **gin** pole, which is a small crane that attaches to the top of the tower."[67]

Girdle

> And the same John had his raiment of camel's hair, and a leathern **girdle** about his loins; and his meat was locusts and wild honey. (Mat 3:4)

A **girdle** is mentioned thirty-eight times in the AV.[68] The plural **girdles** shows up on six additional occasions.[69] **Girdle** is from the Old English *gyrdel,* a belt worn around the waist. A **girdle** was worn to secure the garments and as a means of carrying light articles. A **girdle** is simply that which girds. Although our modern versions had no trouble with the word *gird,* except the NIV, which attempted to eliminate the word completely but forgot one passage,[70] the modern concept of a woman's **girdle** loomed ominously over the translators. **Girdle** is normally updated by our modern versions to "sash"[71] or "band"[72] or "belt."[73] In four instances, however, the NASB forgot to remove the word and retained the archaic AV reading.[74] In one passage, the NRSV updated **girdle** to a "waistcloth," a word not appearing in any Bible.[75] This updating of **girdle** was unnecessary, for even the *Los Angeles Times* considered the word current: "Presently, the One Who Is Father appeared behind his closed eyelids, looking much like Ramos himself: headband, single-thonged sandals strapped to bare legs, a breechclout secured by a tasseled **girdle** covering his loins."[76]

Glass

> For if any be a hearer of the word, and not a doer, he is like unto a man beholding his natural face in a **glass:** (James 1:23)

Although the word **glass** occurs eight times in the AV, four of these represent **glass** as we know it today and the AV usage is followed by all versions in these passages.[77] The other four times **glass** appears, it is a reference to a mirror, and is so changed in the new translations.[78] The plural **glasses** and the compound **lookingglasses** each appear one time also.[79] **Glass** is from the Old English *glaes,* "shining," and is related to the word *glistering* discussed below. It is argued against the AV that the references to a mirror as a **glass** are incorrect because the ancient mirrors were made of polished metal instead of coated **glass**. But as the original meaning of **glass** had nothing to do with the material used, this criticism is hasty. We call a drinking vessel a **glass** if it is made out of **glass** but we term a window a window and a mirror a mirror even though they are made out of **glass**. In fact, a plastic drinking vessel is still referred to as a **glass**. If something even contains **glass** we call it a **glass**—a telescope and microscope are both designated as a **glass**. Eyeglasses are still referred to as **glasses** even if they have plastic lenses. It should also be remembered that the sequel to *Alice in Wonderland* by Lewis Carroll entitled *Through the Looking Glass* is still read today and the publisher has never received any requests to update the title.

Glede

> And the **glede,** and the kite, and the vulture after his kind, (Deu 14:13)

The **glede** is a bird mentioned only once in the AV. The word itself is from the Old English *glida,* literally meaning "the gliding." Thus it is directly related to the word *glide* that appeared in Old English as *glidan.* A **glede** is a bird of prey like a buzzard or a kite. The NRSV renders **glede** as "buzzard," but the others selected "red kite." Yet when the AV mentions a "kite," the NKJV and NASB call it a "falcon."[80] The simple word "vulture" in the AV is likewise changed into a "buzzard,"[81] a "kite,"[82] a "red kite,"[83] a "falcon,"[84] and a "hawk."[85] So although the new translations do not agree among themselves, they are united in their effort to amend the text of the AV.

Glistering

> And as he prayed, the fashion of his countenance was altered, and his raiment *was* white *and* **glistering.** (Luke 9:29)

The word **glistering,** formed from *glister,* appears twice in the AV.[86] The word *glister* is related to *glitter* and *glisten,* their common origin hidden in the depths of antiquity, as even the Middle and Old English forms differ. To be **glistering** is to be shining, sparkling, or glittering. The **glistering** stones mentioned once in the AV are called "antimony" by the NRSV, "stones of antimony" by the NASB, and "turquoise" by the NIV.[87] The NKJV simply updates **glistering** to "glistening" both times it occurs in the AV.[88] "Dazzling" and "gleaming" are also employed to modernize **glistering** by the NRSV and NASB respectively.[89] There should be no reason to update the AV when it used the modern "glittering," yet it is still sometimes corrected to "flashing" by the NIV, NRSV, and NASB.[90] Moreover, when the AV employed a simple word like "shine," the NASB altered it to "glisten"[91] and the NIV to "glistening."[92] The word "light" in the AV is even changed to "glint" by the NIV.[93] Yet even the supposedly archaic word **glistering** is still in use in the twentieth century: "The island of Moorea presents palm trees, thatched roofs and **glistering** waters from just about every vantage point."[94]

Godhead

> Forasmuch then as we are the offspring of God, we ought not to think that the **Godhead** is like unto gold, or silver, or stone, graven by art and man's device. (Acts 17:29)

The compound word **Godhead** is found three times in the AV.[95] *God* obviously refers to deity, divine personality or nature, the supreme being, or the character and quality of being God. The suffix *-head* is a form of the more common suffix *-hood,* referring to state or condition of being. However, **Godhead** is one of the few words that retains a distinction between **godhead** and *godhood.* The **Godhead** is a good reference to the Trinity as it occurs only three times. This fact is lost in the new translations where **Godhead** is always rendered by two or more words. The NRSV uses "deity" twice[96] and "divine nature" once.[97] The NASB employs "deity" only once,[98] but "Divine Nature" capitalized once[99] and "divine nature" lower case once.[100] The NIV utilizes three different terms (divine being, divine nature, Deity) to update **Godhead.**[101] The NKJV retains the AV reading of **Godhead** twice[102] but changes the third instance to "Divine Nature."[103] Yet the word **Godhead** can even be found in the *Economist* magazine: "The older Kim, who ran the North for nearly 50 years, is being elevated in death to something near **godhead.**"[104]

God-ward

See you-ward.

Goodly

The hills were covered with the shadow of it, and the boughs thereof *were like* the **goodly** cedars. (Psa 80:10)

The word **goodly** occurs thirty-six times in the AV.[105] It is based on the Old English *godlic* meaning of good appearance, well-favored, handsome, fair, notable, or admirable. The meaning of **goodly** is apparent from the context, but up-to-date translations include "fine,"[106] "beautiful,"[107] "stately,"[108] "majestic,"[109] "noble,"[110] "splendid,"[111] "proud,"[112] "royal,"[113] and "precious."[114] Although our modern versions deemed **goodly** to be archaic, two things should be noted. The NRSV completely overlooked **goodly** in four passages[115] and the word is still in common use anyway: "After all, a **goodly** portion of the world's population has already traded in traditional garb for Levi's."[116]

Goodman

> And when they had received *it,* they murmured against the **goodman** of the house, (Mat 20:11)

The word **goodman** appears six times in the AV.[117] It is manifestly a combination of *good* and *man,* but does not refer to a man that is good. A **goodman** is the male head of a household, a host, or a husband. The NKJV preferred "master" to update **goodman,** and the NIV and NRSV "owner,"[118] but the NASB could not decide between "head"[119] and "owner."[120] On one occasion all of our modern versions agreed on "landowner" to amend the AV text.[121] Yet when the AV uses a plain word like "rowers," it is corrected by the NIV and NKJV to "oarsmen."[122] The NRSV and NASB regularly employ the word "layman" even though the idea of a man laying has nothing to do with the word.[123]

Go to

> And they said one to another, **Go to,** let us make brick, and burn them thoroughly. And they had brick for stone, and slime had they for mortar. (Gen 11:3)

The imperative expression **go to** appears nine times in the AV and warrants attention because it is almost as though it is a word all its own.[124] **Go to** is used in the AV as a command or exhortation meaning "come" or "come on." A common "go" expression in modern English is "make a go of it." **Go to** may be archaic but it certainly sounds better than the phrase "nocturnal emission" used by the NRSV, NASB, and NIV.[125]

Grave

> And thou shalt take two onyx stones, and **grave** on them the names of the children of Israel: (Exo 28:9)

The word **grave** appears in the AV with three distinct meanings. Most of the time it has reference to a burying place.[126] This parallels the meaning of a **grave** today and is not a problem. Three times, however, **grave** is used in the sense of sober, serious, important, troublesome, somber, or weighty.[127] The word **gravity,** occurring twice,[128] but not referring to the scientific law of

gravity, is formed from **grave.** In this case the word **grave** is from the French *grave,* "heavy." Our modern versions have united to uproot this usage of the word **grave** from the Bible. The NRSV preferred "serious," the NASB forms of "dignity," the NIV the wordy "worthy of respect," and the NKJV "reverent."[129] However, in one other passage where the AV did not contain the word, the NKJV, NRSV, and NASB inserted it anyway in correction of the AV reading of "grievous."[130] The word **gravity** is similarly corrected,[131] but the NRSV mistakenly left it in one passage.[132] *Time* magazine, however, had no trouble with the word **grave** as found in the AV: "A year ago, after the panel concluded that '**grave** breaches' of international law had been committed, the Security Council created an 11-judge international court to deal with them."[133] The other word **grave** is from the Old English *grafan,* "to carve." This usage appears four times in the AV as **grave,**[134] twice as **graved,**[135] once as **graveth,**[136] three times as **graving,**[137] once as **gravings,**[138] and fifty-five times as **graven.**[139] To **grave** is to engrave, the word *engrave* being formed in imitation of the French *engraver.* The NIV and NRSV completely remove all trace of **grave** with this meaning. The NKJV forgot to remove one instance of "**graven,**" and the NASB neglected "**graving**" once,[140] but twenty-two times the NASB overlooked the supposedly archaic "**graven.**"[141]

Greaves

And *he had* **greaves** of brass upon his legs, and a target of brass between his shoulders. (1 Sam 17:6)

The word **greaves** occurs only once in the AV. It is from the French *greve,* "shin." **Greaves,** usually always found in the plural, refers to armor for the lower leg. It is definitely an archaic word so why the NRSV, NIV, and NASB retained the word as the AV is a mystery. The NKJV alone translates it as "armor." But when the AV employs a simple word like "nations," the NIV, NRSV, and NASB replace it with the arcane "Goiim."[142]

Greyhound

A **greyhound;** an he goat also; and a king, against whom *there is* no rising up. (Prov 30:31)

A **greyhound** is only mentioned once in the AV. The word itself is from the Old English *grighund,* which is from the Old Norse *greyhundr.* The *grey-* has nothing to do with color as *grey* means "dog" and *hundre* means "hound." A **greyhound** is a breed of tall, slender short-haired dogs noted for their swiftness. The NRSV and NIV altered **greyhound** to "strutting rooster" and the NASB to "strutting cock," but the NJKV followed the AV. Nevertheless, **greyhound** racing is still held all over the country in the 1990's.

Grisled

And in the third chariot white horses; and in the fourth chariot **grisled** and bay horses. (Zec 6:3)

The word **grisled,** appearing four times in the AV,[143] is a variation of *grizzled.* The base form *grizzle* is from the French *grisel,* from *gris,* "gray." A **grisled** animal is one that is gray-colored, either whole or spotted. Twice the NIV updates **grisled** to "spotted," and twice the NKJV changes it to "gray-spotted," but NASB and NRSV use the somewhat obscure "mottled."[144] In the other two places where **grisled** is used, our supposedly modern, up-to-date versions replace **grisled** with the arcane "dappled."[145]

Gross

For, behold, the darkness shall cover the earth, and **gross** darkness the people: but the LORD shall arise upon thee, and his glory shall be seen upon thee. (Isa 60:2)

The word **gross** appears four times in the AV.[146] It is from the French *gros,* "thick." **Gross** has nothing to do with quality but rather refers to quantity. **Gross** means large, thick, powerful, or big. Our modern versions could not agree on how to correct the word **gross** in the AV. Twice the NRSV, NASB, and NKJV used "dull" and the NIV employed "calloused."[147] Another time the NRSV and NIV preferred "thick" but the NKJV and NASB settled on "deep."[148] The other instance of the word **gross** was rendered "deep" by the NRSV and NASB, "thick" by the NIV, but "dense" by the NKJV.[149] But after all the trouble to remove the word from those passages where it occurs in the AV, the

NKJV inserted "**gross**" in a verse where no other version contained the word.[150] The NRSV likewise did the same thing.[151] The NASB not only injected "**gross**" into a verse,[152] it used the adjective "grossness" where the AV had "multitude."[153] With all the talk about **gross** weight, **gross** income, and **gross** national product, it is incredible that **gross** was excised from the AV. The word is still very much in use today as it appears in the AV: "One outcome of this situation is a **gross** discrepancy in per-capita water use by Israelis and Palestinians in the occupied territories."[154]

Guile

> Blessed *is* the man unto whom the LORD imputeth not iniquity, and in whose spirit *there is* no **guile**. (Psa 32:2)

Guile appears eleven times in the AV,[155] while the verb **beguile** is found twice,[156] **beguiling** once,[157] and **beguiled** five times.[158] **Guile** is from the French *guile* meaning deceit or trickery. **Guile** is deceit, deception, cunning, craftiness, or trickery. Consequently, to **beguile** is to deceive or trick. Our modern versions sought to completely remove **guile** from the text of the Bible but only the NIV and NKJV were entirely successful. The usual substitution for **guile** in our modern versions is "deceit,"[159] but one can also find "lies,"[160] "fraud,"[161] forms of "trick,"[162] "treachery,"[163] and "craftily."[164] **Beguiled** is likewise normally rendered by forms of "deceived."[165] Yet when the AV reads "deceit," it is corrected by the NIV to "lies,"[166] the NRSV to "cunning" and "treacherous,"[167] and the NKJV to "oppression."[168] But not only does the NASB slip up and forget to remove **guile** from three passages where it appears in the AV,[169] and not only does the NASB insert "**guile**" into a verse where no other version contained the word,[170] the NASB actually altered "deceit" in the AV to "**guile**."[171] The NRSV likewise did the same thing, injecting "**guile**" into a passage where neither the AV nor any other modern version contained the word,[172] and then amending "deceit" to "**guile**."[173] To further correct the AV, the NRSV, after removing **beguiling** from the only place it occurred in the AV,[174] revised "seduce" in another passage to "**beguiling**."[175] All the energy expended in attempting to revise **guile** out of the AV was wasted, for the word **guile** is still common today: "Two years after Kaunda's exit from power, his more notorious counterparts in other countries have used a combination of **guile** and roguishness to hold on to discredited power."[176]

Chapter 8
Habergeon to Husbandry

Habergeon

> And there was an hole in the midst of the robe, as the hole of an **habergeon,** with a band round about the hole, that it should not rend. (Exo 39:23)

The word **habergeon** appears in the AV three times in the singular[1] and twice in the plural.[2] It is from the French *haubergeon*, the diminutive of *hauberc*, from which we get *hauberk*. A **habergeon** is a sleeveless coat, jacket, or poncho of protective armor that is shorter than a hauberk. Although **habergeon** is sometimes replaced by some form of "armor" in our modern versions,[3] it is usually updated to the equally as archaic "coats of mail."[4] But when the AV uses the expression "coats of mail," it is changed by the NASB to "scale-armor" and "armor."[5] The NIV likewise corrected "coats of mail," employing the terms "scale armor" and "coat of armor."[6] But if versions like the NRSV were so concerned about difficult words like **habergeon,** then why was "places" in the AV changed to "localities"?[7]

Haft

> And the **haft** also went in after the blade; and the fat closed upon the blade, so that he could not draw the dagger out of his belly; and the dirt came out. (Judg 3:22)

The word **haft,** found only once in the AV, appeared in Old English as *haeft*, "handle." It literally signifies "that which is held." A **haft** has always referred to a handle. The new translations could not decide between "hilt"[8] and "handle"[9] to update **haft**. But the word **haft** did not have to be updated in the first place, for it is still in use in the 1990's: "It takes only a few seconds to make a scraper from a flint blank, but making the **haft** takes several hours."[10]

Hale

> When thou goest with thine adversary to the magistrate, *as thou art* in the way, give diligence that thou mayest be delivered from him; lest he **hale** thee to the judge, and the judge deliver thee to the officer, and the officer cast thee into prison. (Luke 12:58)

Hale occurs only once in the AV but the form **haling** can also be found.[11] **Hale** is from the French *haler*, "to haul." To **hale** is to draw, fetch, haul, or pull, especially with force or violence. Both **hale** and **haling** are unanimously updated by our modern versions to forms of "drag."[12] Although the meaning of **hale** and **haling** could be determined from the context, the alteration of "drink offerings" in the AV to "libations" by the NRSV and NASB obscures the meaning of the text.[13]

Hallow

> And thou shalt take the anointing oil, and anoint the tabernacle, and all that *is* therein, and shalt **hallow** it, and all the vessels thereof: and it shall be holy. (Exo 40:9)

The word **hallow** appears fifteen times in the AV[14] while **hallowed** is found twenty-two times.[15] **Hallow** comes from the Old English *halgian*, from *halig*, "holy." To **hallow** is to make holy, consecrate, sanctify, devote, purify, or set apart. Although the NKJV had no trouble with these words,[16] the other modern versions substituted words like "consecrate,"[17] "keep,"[18] "dedicate,"[19] "sanctify,"[20] "holy,"[21] and "sacred."[22] Yet in the so-called Lord's Prayer, the NIV, NRSV, and NASB retain **hallowed** even though they considered it archaic.[23] The NRSV even corrected the AV reading of "sanctified" to "hallowed."[24] Moreover, the NRSV also retained the AV reading of **hallow** in three places.[25] Even when not used today in the "Lord's Prayer," the word **hallowed** is still in vogue: "In many rural states such as Chiapas, the **hallowed** values of the Mexican Revolution of 1910—with its suspicion of foreign companies and emphasis on land for peasants—clash with the economic program of President Carlos Salinas de Gortari."[26]

Halt

> And if thy foot offend thee, cut it off: it is better for thee to enter **halt** into life, than having two feet to be cast into hell, into the fire that never shall be quenched: (Mark 9:45)

Halt occurs six times in the AV,[27] while **halteth** is found three times,[28] **halted** once,[29] and **halting** once.[30] **Halt** appeared in Old English as *healt*. As an adjective, like it is used four times in the New Testament,[31] **halt** means lame or crippled. The other seven times **halt** and its derivatives occur in the Old Testament,[32] they are found as intransitive verbs meaning to waver, hesitate, fall, or stumble. The words **halt** and **halteth** are normally replaced in our modern versions with "lame."[33] But when the AV says "lame," the NRSV, NASB, and NIV unite in correcting it to "crippled."[34] Yet on one occasion, the NRSV replaces the AV reading of "delicately" with the supposedly archaic "haltingly."[35]

Handmaid

> And Elisha said unto her, What shall I do for thee? tell me, what hast thou in the house? And she said, Thine **handmaid** hath not any thing in the house, save a pot of oil. (2 Ki 4:2)

The singular **handmaid** occurs forty-five times in the AV,[36] while the plural **handmaids** is found eight times.[37] The similar forms of **handmaiden** and **handmaidens** appear once[38] and three[39] times respectively. Although **handmaid** is a compound of *hand* and *maid*, it is thought to be related to both an Old English word and the Middle English phrase "to serve any one to hand." A **handmaid** or **handmaiden** is a female personal attendant, slave, or servant. Our modern versions have almost completely eliminated all forms of **handmaid** from the Bible. The words used as replacements, however, are quite varied. One can find "maidservant,"[40] "slave-girl,"[41] "maid,"[42] "servant,"[43] and "bondslave."[44] Yet when the AV reads "maidservant," it is often corrected to "female servant" or "female slave."[45] The NASB carelessly left **handmaid** or **handmaids** in three passages.[46] But even though these new translations deemed forms of **handmaid** to be archaic, the *Boston Globe* did not: "It appears that erotic salesmanship will remain a perpetual **handmaiden** to the consumer culture."[47]

𝔥𝔞𝔭

> And she went, and came, and gleaned in the field after the reapers: and her **hap** was to light on a part of the field *belonging* unto Boaz, who *was* of the kindred of Elimelech. (Ruth 2:3)

The word **hap** appears only once in the AV. The similar form **haply** is found six times.[48] **Hap** is from the Old Norse *happ* meaning chance or good luck. For something to occur **haply** is for it to take place by chance, by accident, or with no apparent design or intent. Our modern versions united in removing all trace of these words. **Haply** is often found as "perhaps."[49] The AV phrase "lest **haply**" can be found as "otherwise,"[50] "for,"[51] "or else,"[52] "in that case,"[53] or just simply as "lest."[54] But forms of the word **hap** are commonly used today: "In urban Indian neighborhoods, mazes of **haphazard** cables run from the homes of entrepreneurs with satellite dishes."[55]

𝔥𝔞𝔯𝔡

> And Abimelech came unto the tower, and fought against it, and went **hard** unto the door of the tower to burn it with fire. (Judg 9:52)

The word **hard**, as it is used in this particular sense, is found six times in the AV[56] and is from the Old English adverb *hearde*, "extremely." Thus, **hard** means close, near, or in close proximity to. The word **hardly**, found eight times in the AV,[57] appeared in Old English as *heardlice*. It is used in the AV in the sense of being difficult or harsh rather than in the modern sense of barely, scarcely, or with little likelihood. The aforementioned usage of the word **hard** is rendered in our modern versions by such things as "close,"[58] "near,"[59] and "next."[60] **Hardly** can be found as "hard,"[61] "harshly,"[62] and "with difficulty."[63] The way these words are used in the AV might be archaic, but the NIV changing "displeased" to "galled" certainly does not make the Bible easier to understand, especially since all of the other new translations follow the AV reading of "displeased."[64]

Harrow

> Canst thou bind the unicorn with his band in the furrow? or will he **harrow** the valleys after thee? (Job 39:10)

The verb **harrow** is used only once in the AV but the noun **harrows** appears twice.[65] Harrow is from the Middle English *harwe* and means to break up, rake, crush, or plow. The noun **harrows** refers to instruments used to break up, rake, crush, or plow. Harrows are usually rendered as "picks" in our modern versions, but the NASB instead chose "instruments."[66] Surprisingly, the verb **harrow** is retained in the NRSV and NASB even though the NIV says "till" and the NKJV "plow."[67] In fact, the NRSV and NASB like the archaic word **harrow** so much that twice when the AV said "break the clods," it was changed to "**harrow**."[68] The NIV, after correcting **harrow** and **harrows** three times,[69] injects the word "harrowing" into another verse.[70] But not only is the expression "a **harrowing** experience" very common today, *Horticulture* magazine listed the available attachments for a tractor as an "aerator, bulldozer, cart, cultivator, cutoff saw, generator, **harrow**, leveler (grader), roller, seeder, spreader, sweeper, thatcher, tiller, and wood splitter."[71]

Hart

> My beloved is like a roe or a young **hart**: behold, he standeth behind our wall, he looketh forth at the windows, showing himself through the lattice. (Song 2:9)

A **hart** is mentioned eleven times in the AV, nine in the singular[72] and two in the plural.[73] Hart, which appeared in Old English as *heort,* refers to a male deer. Although our modern versions customarily rendered **hart** as "deer,"[74] on three occasions they unanimously changed **hart** to the arcane "stag,"[75] **Harts** is also revised to "bucks" by the NASB and "stags" by the NRSV.[76] But the hypocrisy of any modern translation correcting **hart** and **harts** should be pointed out, for the NRSV, NASB, and NIV all call a female deer a "doe."[77]

Haunt

> And they shall take up a lamentation for thee, and say to thee, How art thou destroyed, that wast inhabited of seafaring men, the renowned city, which wast strong in the sea, she and her inhabitants, which cause their terror to be on all that **haunt** it! (Ezek 26:17)

The word **haunt** appears three times in the AV.[78] It is from the French *hanter,* "to frequent." A **haunt** is a habit, custom, habitation, or place of frequent abode. To **haunt** means the act of frequenting a particular place. All of the modern, up-to-date translations remove this word from every place it occurs in the AV, except the NASB, which neglected to remove the word in one instance.[79] **Haunt** is rendered in our new versions by such things as "roamed,"[80] "hideout,"[81] "accustomed to go,"[82] and "accustomed to rove."[83] But after correcting the AV when it used the word **haunt,** every one of the modern versions inserts the word in places where the AV does not have it. The NKJV substitutes "haunts" for the AV reading of "habitations."[84] The NRSV does the same thing,[85] and then uses "**haunt**" in six additional places to correct such words as "place," "habitation," "hold," and "cage."[86] The NIV utilizes "haunts" three times,[87] one of which modifies "mountains" in the AV to "mountain haunts" even though the other versions follow the AV reading.[88] The NIV also employs "**haunt**" eight times where it is not found in the AV.[89] The NRSV, in addition to following the AV reading of **haunt** in one verse,[90] injected the word into seven more passages.[91]

Heady

> Traitors, **heady,** highminded, lovers of pleasures more than lovers of God; (2 Tim 3:4)

Heady occurs only once in the AV and is simply formed by the addition of an adjective-forming *-y* suffix signifying to be characterized by. To be **heady** is to be headstrong, domineering, overbearing, or impetuous. The NRSV and NASB unite in rendering **heady** as "reckless," but the NIV and NKJV preferred "rash" and "headstrong" respectively. However, in the same verse that **heady** is found, the NRSV and NASB also join together in correcting the simple word "traitors" to the more difficult "treacherous." The word **heady** is still in common use anyway: "His favorite pastime, reading history books (a passion he picked up as a student in Leningrad during the **heady** liberal atmosphere of the 1960s), only adds to that image."[92]

Heath

> For he shall be like the **heath** in the desert, and shall not see when good cometh; but shall inhabit the parched places in the wilderness, *in* a salt land and not inhabited. (Jer 17:6)

A **heath** is mentioned twice in the AV.[93] This word, appearing in Old English as *haeth,* originally referred to open, uncultivated land—what we would term a wilderness. Since this land was dotted with small shrubs, it was only natural that the most common shrub was later called a **heath.** Our word *heathen* initially meant "one who dwells on the **heath.**" Only the NIV consistently rendered the underlying Hebrew word, using as a replacement the word "bush."[94] The NASB used "bush" once and "juniper" the other time.[95] The NKJV went with "shrub" and "juniper."[96] Incredibly, the NRSV rendered **heath** as both "shrub" and "wild ass."[97] But the word **heath** is not archaic in the first place, for even *National Wildlife* magazine employed the word: "These chickadee-sized birds live on the Australian **heath** in extended family groups."[98]

Helm

> Behold also the ships, which though *they be* so great, and *are* driven of fierce winds, yet are they turned about with a very small **helm,** whithersoever the governor listeth. (James 3:4)

The word **helm,** found only once in the AV, appeared in Old English as *helma.* A **helm** is the wheel in a ship by which the rudder is steered. It can also refer to the rudder itself or the whole steering mechanism. **Helm** is unanimously replaced by "rudder" in all of our modern versions. But after updating the AV, the NKJV regresses and transforms the "owner" of a ship into a "helmsman."[99] The word **helm** is nevertheless still in vogue, at least according to *U.S. News & World Report:* "With Capt. Joe Testaverde at the **helm,** the trawler Nina T slips into it's

Gloucester, Mass., mooring at sunset."[100]

Helve

> As when a man goeth into the wood with his neighbour to hew wood, and his hand fetcheth a stroke with the ax to cut down the tree, and the head slippeth from the **helve**, and lighteth upon his neighbour, that he die; he shall flee unto one of those cities, and live: (Deu 19:5)

The word **helve** is likewise found only once in the AV. It is from the Old English *helfe,* "a handle." It is actually related to the aforementioned word *helm.* The new versions consistently render **helve** as "handle." The word **helve** might not be as easily understood as *handle,* but when the AV employs a simple, modern, up-to-date word like "mad," and it is revised in the NASB to "insanely" even though the other new translations all use a form of the AV reading, the text of the Bible is certainly not made clearer.[101]

Hemlock

> Shall horses run upon the rock? will *one* plow *there* with oxen? for ye have turned judgment into gall, and the fruit of righteousness into **hemlock:** (Amos 6:12)

Hemlock is mentioned twice in the AV.[102] The word is of obscure origin but developed from the Old English *hymlice.* A **hemlock** is a poisonous plant of the genus *cicuta.* It was used for medicinal purposes; thus, **hemlock** is a poisonous substance derived from the **hemlock** plant. The NKJV retains the usage of **hemlock** in one passage and substitutes "wormwood" in the other.[103] The NRSV and NASB also use "wormwood" once, but employed "poisonous weeds" the other time.[104] The NIV preferred "poisonous weeds" and "bitterness."[105] Yet after just correcting **hemlock** to "wormwood," the NRSV altered "wormwood" once in the AV even though it kept all the other occurronces.[106] The NIV changes "wormwood" to "gall" in a passage where all of the other modern versions read as the AV.[107] Moreover, in one of the same verses that **hemlock** appears in, the NRSV alters "judgment" to the more difficult "litigation" when the NKJV and NASB read as the AV.[108] It is interesting that a euthanasia group in the United States founded by Derek Humphry is called the **Hemlock** Society. **Hemlock** is also the name of tree: "Isolated stands of **hemlock** are left uncut to provide snow-shielded winter habitat for deer."[109]

Hence

> Then said Boaz unto Ruth, Hearest thou not, my daughter? Go not to glean in another field, neither go from **hence,** but abide here fast by my maidens: (Ruth 2:8)

The word **hence** occurs thirty times in the AV.[110] The extended form **henceforth** is found thirty-three times[111] and **henceforward** twice.[112] **Hence** is from the Old English *heonan* and is related to *hine,* the masculine accusative of *he.* **Hence** can mean here, from this time, from this place, to this place, or away from here. **Henceforth** and **henceforward** are more emphatic and simply mean from this time forth or forward. **Hence** is given in our modern versions as "this place"[113] or "here."[114] **Henceforth** can be found as "longer,"[115] "again,"[116] or "more."[117] The translations for **henceforward** include "onward,"[118] "thereafter,"[119] "continuing,"[120] or "again."[121] But although our modern versions corrected every occurrence of these words in the AV, except for the NKJV, which forgot "**henceforth**" in one passage,[122] the NASB and NRSV did not hesitate to further correct the AV in other places with forms of the very word **hence.** The NASB uses "**hence**" seven times,[123] two of which update "but" in the AV.[124] The NRSV corrected "for" in the AV to "**hence**" even though the other new versions followed the AV reading.[125] "**Hence**" was also put into four other passages by the NRSV.[126] And finally, when the AV said "before the day was," the NRSV corrected it to "**henceforth**" even though every occurrence of **henceforth** in the AV was removed.[127]

Herein

> **Herein** is love, not that we loved God, but that he loved us, and sent his Son *to be* the propitiation for our sins. (1 John 4:10)

The word **herein,** occurring nine times in the AV,[128] is the first of many *here-* words that appear only in the AV. The word **hereof** appears twice,[129] and the form **heretofore** is found eight times,[130] while **hereunto**[131] and **herewith**[132] each appear twice. **Herein** means in or into this place, in this fact or circumstance, or in view of this. **Hereof** means of this, concerning this, or from this. **Heretofore** means before this time, before now, or formerly. **Hereunto** means unto or to this place, thing, or subject. **Herewith** means with this, along with, or together with. None of these words appear in any modern version, although "hereafter" appears in all but the NIV,[133] and "hereby" can be found in the NRSV[134] and NIV.[135] The word **heretofore** is normally rendered as "before"[136] and the other replacement words are usually found in combinations with "this" such as "of this,"[137] "to this,"[138] or "in this."[139] But in spite of their correction, most these words are still found in current English: "**Herewith** I rest my case for mortality as a blessing."[140] Even the *Times-Picayune* of New Orleans used **heretofore**: "Some black schools are turning to a **heretofore** untapped source for talent—white players."[141] And finally: "'HEREOF FAIL NOT,' the subpoena advised, 'as you will answer your default under the pains and penalties in such cases provided for' in federal law."[142]

Heresy

> But this I confess unto thee, that after the way which they call **heresy**, so worship I the God of my fathers, believing all things which are written in the law and in the prophets: (Acts 24:14)

The word **heresy** appears only once in the AV but the plural **heresies** can be found three times.[143] The similar form **heretick** (modern spelling: **heretic**) can also be found once.[144] **Heresy** is from the French *heresie* and **heretick** is from the French *heretique*. **Heresy** is literally a choice and by implication a sect, faction, or belief that one has chosen that is different from that which is commonly accepted. Thus, **heresy** can be a school of thought, although it is usually taken in the bad sense. A **heretick** is one who maintains **heresy**. According to the NRSV, a **heretick** is one who "causes divisions."[145] The NASB considers a **heretick** a "factious man," the NIV a "divisive person," and the NKJV a "divisive man."[146] **Heresy** is unanimously rendered by our modern versions as "a sect."[147] The plural **heresies** is normally rendered as "factions,"[148] but in one instance the

NASB, NKJV, and NIV all retained the AV reading.[149] The NKJV also followed the AV in one other passage.[150] The five other times the underlying Greek word is used the AV translates it as "sect."[151] The NKJV, NRSV, and NASB follow the AV but the NIV twice uses "party"[152] and three times employs "sect."[153] The word **heresy**, however, is still commonly used today, even in non-religious contexts: "In the last few decades, though, science has advanced so rapidly that today's **heresy** is tomorrow's conventional wisdom."[154] **Heretick** is also still employed to describe someone who deviates from an accepted position: "In 1990, Komhyr inadvertently became a **heretic**."[155]

Highminded

> Charge them that are rich in this world, that they be not **highminded**, nor trust in uncertain riches, but in the living God, who giveth us richly all things to enjoy; (1 Tim 6:17)

The word **highminded** appears three times in the AV.[156] It is obviously a compound of *high* and *mind*. To be **highminded** is to have or be characterized by a haughty, arrogant, or proud spirit. Although our modern versions unanimously excised this word, they could not even agree among themselves on how to translate it. The NASB consistently used "conceited" and the NKJV "haughty,"[157] but the NIV twice employed "arrogant"[158] and once "conceited,"[159] and the NRSV utilized three words or expressions (proud, haughty, swollen with conceit) to correct **highminded**.[160] These alterations were entirely unnecessary, for the word **highminded** is still in use today: "Instead, the use of First Amendment arguments by the press looks like a smokescreen to hide less **highminded**, more selfish motives."[161]

Hind

> Naphtali *is* a **hind** let loose: he giveth goodly words. (Gen 49:21)

A **hind** is mentioned in the AV three times in the singular[162] and seven times in the plural.[163] The word **hind**, which appeared the same way in Old English, refers to a female deer. Although they remove every occurrence of **hind** and **hinds**, the modern versions could not decide between "doe" and "deer" to update

hind.[164] The NASB, however, carelessly left the archaic "**hinds**" in five passages.[165] And in another verse dealing with animals, the AV mentions an animal lowing but the NIV makes the animal "bellow" even though all of the other versions say their animal lowed like the AV.[166]

Hinder

> And he smote his enemies in the **hinder** parts: he put them to a perpetual reproach. (Psa 78:66)

The word **hinder** occurs eight times in the AV.[167] The form **hindermost** can be found twice,[168] while the shorter **hindmost** appears three times.[169] **Hinder** is actually a shortened form of the Middle English *bihinden,* from the Old English *behindan,* but was also influenced by the Old English *hinder,* "rear." **Hindmost** is a corruption of *hindmest,* from the Old English *hindema.* The **hinder** part is that which is behind, at the back, or at the rear. **Hinder** is rendered in several different ways by our modern translations. One can find "butt,"[170] "hindquarters,"[171] "rear,"[172] "blunt,"[173] "back,"[174] and when referring to a ship, "stern."[175] **Hindermost** is usually replaced with "last"[176] and "least."[177] **Hindmost** is now normally "last"[178] or "rear."[179] However, in one verse where the AV read "**hinder** parts," the NASB, NRSV, and NIV used the similar "hindquarters."[180] In the parallel passage, however, where the NIV and NRSV also said "hindquarters," the NASB went with "rear parts."[181] And furthermore, late in the twentieth century, the buttocks are still called the **hiney**.

Hither

> And Saul said, Bring **hither** a burnt offering to me, and peace offerings. And he offered the burnt offering. (1 Sam 13:9)

The word **hither** occurs sixty-seven times in the AV,[182] while the form **hitherto** can be found nineteen times.[183] **Hither,** from the Old English *hider,* is, like *hence,* originally derived from *he.* **Hither** means to or towards this place, up to this point, till now, thus far, to this end, or simply here, as it is usually translated by our modern versions.[184] **Hitherto** denotes up to this time, until now, as yet, or thus far. It normally appears in the new versions as "until now,"[185] "to this very day,"[186] "thus far,"[187] or "this far."[188] But the words **hither** and **hitherto** are still in use today. Even the *Washington Post* had no trouble with **hither:** "At its worst, Appalachian Kentucky is a forlorn caricature of itself, a hardscrabble wilderness with a chancy network of mountain roads leading **hither** and yon among brushy hollows dotted with slapped-together shacks."[189] **Hitherto** is likewise still current: "But it is also possible that due to declining incomes and increasing spare time, a population which has **hitherto** been conditioned to work looks for and finds satisfaction to an increasing degree outside of gainful employment." [190]

Hoar

> Do therefore according to thy wisdom, and let not his **hoar** head go down to the grave in peace. (1 Ki 2:6)

The word **hoar** is found four times in the AV[191] as is the word **hoary.**[192] **Hoar** is from the Old English *har,* "gray," in the sense of old. To be **hoary** is to be old, aged, or gray or white with age. **Hoarfrost,** appearing twice as two separate words (**hoar** frost and **hoary** frost),[193] and once as a compound,[194] is the white deposit formed by the freezing of dew. Our modern versions had trouble determining the color of something **hoary. Hoar** is normally rendered as "gray,"[195] but **hoary** can be found as "gray,"[196] "white,"[197] and "silver,"[198] in addition to "aged."[199] But after updating these words, the NRSV used the word "**hoarfrost**" in one verse where the AV said "**hoar** frost."[200] In spite of all these corrections, the words **hoar** and **hoary** are still in use in the 1990's. The *Canadian Geographic* relates that "during the cold, windless days and nights that followed, a layer of feathery frost crystals, called surface **hoar,** formed on top of the crust."[201] And in America, *Discover* magazine had no trouble with the word **hoary:** "It is a credit to the increased sophistication of the discipline that this **hoary** elder's long-delayed arrival is greeted now not with cries of astonishment but with the solemn, approving nods of expectation fulfilled."[202]

Horseleach

The **horseleach** hath two daughters, *crying,* Give, give. There are three *things that* are never satisfied, *yea,* four *things* say not, *It is* enough: (Prov 30:15)

A **horseleach** is only mentioned once in the AV. The word is manifestly a combination of *horse* and *leach* (now spelled leech). A **horseleach** is a leech or an aquatic sucking worm. By way of application, it can also refer to an extremely insatiable person. Technically, a **horseleach** is a *haemopis marmoratis* that enters the mouth and nasal passages of horses and sucks their blood. Our modern versions shorten **horseleach** to "leech." But often these same new translations add prefixes or suffixes to words that do not result in a change in the meaning of the word. When the AV reads "gate," all of the new versions extend it to "gateway."[203] Regarding the NASB in particular, when the AV, followed by all other versions, says "gate," it is lengthened to "gateway."[204] And as concerning the NKJV, it enlarges "gate" to "gateposts" in a passage where all of the other modern versions follow the AV.[205]

Hosen

> Then these men were bound in their coats, their **hosen,** and their hats, and their *other* garments, and were cast into the midst of the burning fiery furnace. (Dan 3:21)

Hosen is only mentioned once in the AV. The word itself is the plural of *hose*—the singular now being used for both numbers. **Hosen** are articles of clothing to cover the legs. Although our modern versions unanimously update **hosen** to "trousers," it is apparent that articles of clothing to cover the legs are still called hose in the 1990's. And this is not just limited to women. The thick hose that men wear in the winter are called long johns. If **hosen** made this passage more difficult to understand then what about the NIV replacing "gave" with "lavished" when all of the other versions read as the AV.[206] Moreover, the NRSV substitutes "lacerate" for "cut" even though the other new translations follow the AV reading.[207]

Hough

> And the LORD said unto Joshua, Be not afraid because of them: for to morrow about this time will I deliver them up all slain before Israel: thou shalt **hough** their horses, and burn

their chariots with fire. (Josh 11:6)

Although the word **hough** appears only once in the AV, the form **houghed** is found three times.[208] **Hough**, from the Old English *hoh*, "heel," means to disable by cutting the sinew or tendons of the **hough**, the joint in the hind leg of an animal. Thus, the word can equally serve as a noun or a verb. Variations of **hough** include *hock, hox, houx,* and *hoxen*. The new translations all substitute "hamstring" for **hough**[209] and "hamstrung" for **houghed**.[210] Yet when the AV says "diggedst not," and the other modern versions read the synonymous "did not dig," the NRSV changes the text to "did not hew."[211]

Howbeit

Brethren, be not children in understanding: **howbeit** in malice be ye children, but in understanding be men. (1 Cor 14:20)

The word **howbeit** can be found sixty-four times in the AV.[212] Like the similar word *albeit*, **howbeit** was originally three separate words: how be it. **Howbeit** means however, be that as it may, or nevertheless. It can also mean though or although. But like the word *albeit*, none of the modern versions contain this word. The major substitutions for **howbeit** are "but,"[213] "however,"[214] "nevertheless,"[215] and "even though."[216] If it is wrong for the AV to use a compound word like **howbeit**, then it should be pointed out that the NKJV, NASB, NRSV, and NIV all extend "blood" in a passage in the AV to "lifeblood."[217]

Hungerbitten

His strength shall be **hungerbitten**, and destruction *shall be* ready at his side. (Job 18:12)

The word **hungerbitten** appears only once in the AV. It is obviously a compound of *hunger* and *bitten*. Other unusual forms of the word *hunger* include **hungered**, found twice,[218] and **hungred**, found nine times.[219] The word **hungered** is both the aphetic form of *ahungered* and the past participle of *hunger*. **Hungred** is formed from *hungre,* an obsolete form of *hunger,* and is synonymous with **hungered**. To be **hungerbitten** is to be starved, famished, or hungry. The word "hungry" is the usual replacement in our modern versions for **hungerbitten**. Yet when the AV uses the plain word "hungry," it is often replaced with the more difficult "famished."[220] Moreover, the word **hungered** is still common today: "Columbus **hungered** for gold but found little."[221]

Husbandry

> For we are labourers together with God: ye are God's **husbandry,** *ye are* God's building. (1 Cor 3:9)

The word **husbandry** only occurs twice in the AV,[222] but **husbandman** appears seven times in the singular[223] and twenty-one times in the plural.[224] **Husbandry, husbandman,** and **husbandmen** are all formed from the word *husband,* from the Old Norse *husbondi,* originally referring to a landowning peasant or the master of the house. *Hus* is the word for "house." **Husbandry** is the administration and management of a household, including the land. It can also mean land under cultivation. Thus, a **husbandman** can be a man who tills or cultivates the soil: a farmer. Indeed, "farmer" is the usual translation for **husbandman** given in the new versions.[225] Other replacements for **husbandman** and **husbandmen** include "plowman,"[226] "tenants,"[227] "gardener,"[228] "vinegrower,"[229] and "vinedresser."[230] There was no excuse for the removal of the various forms of **husbandry** from the Bible, for the word is still used today to refer to a wide variety of things. The *China Daily* mentions "animal **husbandry,**"[231] *Earthwatch* magazine mentions "reindeer **husbandry,**"[232] and *World Watch* refers to "marine **husbandry**"[233] and "soil **husbandry.**"[234]

Chapter 9
Ignominy to Issue

Ignominy

> When the wicked cometh, *then* cometh also contempt, and with **ignominy** reproach. (Prov 18:3)

The word **ignominy** occurs just once in the AV and is from the French *ignominie,* literally meaning "no name." **Ignominy** is dishonor, disgrace, or shame. The NKJV, NRSV, and NASB preferred the word "dishonor," but the NIV alone used "shame." Yet when the AV utilizes the word "dishonour," the NIV amends it to the cousin of **ignominy:** "ignoble."[1] These corrections were unfortunate, for the word **ignominy** is still current English, at least according to *Skeptic* magazine: "While some of these individuals suffer the **ignominy** of being perceived as 'kooks,' they may receive compensating group support from those who share their beliefs."[2]

Imagery

> Then said he unto me, Son of man, hast thou seen what the ancients of the house of Israel do in the dark, every man in the chambers of his **imagery?** for they say, The LORD seeth us not; the LORD hath forsaken the earth. (Ezek 8:12)

The word **imagery,** also found once in the AV, is from the French *imagerie,* a form of *image.* **Imagery** is images collectively or the visible or mental representation or embodiment of something—as in pictures. Although none of our modern versions had trouble with the word *image,* the NIV changed **imagery** to "idol," the NKJV to "idols," the NASB to "carved images," and the NRSV to just plain "images." But when the AV uses a simple word like "images," it is corrected by the NRSV and NASB to "obelisks."[3] Yet even *Astronomy* magazine did not consider **imagery** to be archaic: "It was the greatest avalanche of astronomical **imagery** since, perhaps, the days of the Voyager flybys."[4]

Immutable

> That by two **immutable** things, in which *it was* impossible for God to lie, we might have a strong consolation, who have fled for refuge to lay hold upon the hope set before us: (Heb 6:18)

The word **immutable** occurs just once in the AV and is from the Latin *immutabilis,* "unchangeable." **Immutable** is the opposite of *mutable,* which means changeable. To be **immutable** is to be unchangeable, not liable to change or variation. The *im-* prefix in this case is equivalent to *in-,* "not," and is used before words beginning with *b, m,* or *p*. The NKJV retains "**immutable**" but the others substitute "unchangeable." However, when the AV, followed closely by the NKJV, NIV, and NASB, says "wicked thing," the NRSV reads "impropriety," a word not found in the AV nor any of the other modern versions.[5] Moreover, the NRSV also corrects the AV reading of "foolish" to "impious," even though all of the other modern versions follow the AV reading.[6] But **immutable** was not archaic to begin with, at least according to *Harper's* magazine: "My encounters with Russian soldiers underscored an **immutable** law of the Caucasus: nobody does anything without first asking the Russians."[7]

Imperious

> How weak is thine heart, saith the Lord GOD, seeing thou doest all these *things,* the work of an **imperious** whorish woman; (Ezek 16:30)

Imperious also appears only once in the AV. It is from the Latin *imperiosus,* "commanding." It is related to our word *imperial.* Thus, to be **imperious** is to be domineering, overbearing, dominant, or commanding. The *im-* prefix here is equivalent to *in-,* "in." Once again, our modern versions considered the word archaic, translating it "brazen," except for the NASB, which preferred "bold-faced." Although the similar word "imperial" is not used in the AV, the NIV inserts it twelve times before "guard" even though the other versions regularly follow the AV.[8] But even the *Washington Post* did not deem the word **imperious** to be archaic: "Subject to constant harassment and banishments by the security forces, she became embittered and **imperious**, developed a drinking problem and turned increasingly militant."[9]

Implacable

> Without understanding, covenantbreakers, without natural affection, **implacable**, unmerciful: (Rom 1:31)

The word **implacable** occurs but once in the AV. It is from a French word of the same spelling and is the opposite of *placable*, meaning appeasable. Therefore, **implacable** means unappeasable, irreconcilable, or that which cannot be mitigated. Due to a textual difference, only the NKJV contains the underlying Greek word. Nevertheless, **implacable** is still changed by the NKJV to "unforgiving." The NRSV, however, does contain the word "**implacable**," but it is a correction for the simple compound AV word "trucebreakers."[10] The word **implacable** is still very much in use in the 1990's, even by such publications as the *Atlantic Monthly:* "But a fascinating and confusing facet of Iranians is their ability to entertain and cajole the enemy if he appears **implacable** and insurmountable."[11]

Implead

> Wherefore if Demetrius, and the craftsmen which are with him, have a matter against any man, the law is open, and there are deputies: let them **implead** one another. (Acts 19:38)

Implead is another word that only appears one time in the AV. It is from the French *emplaidier,* meaning "to sue at law." To **implead** is to sue in a court of justice, accuse, arraign, or raise an action against. This is a case where the *im-* prefix is substituted for the *em-* prefix, which is also equivalent to *in-,* "in." All of our modern versions alter **implead** to "bring charges," except for the NIV, which went with "press charges." Obviously, the new translations considered **implead** to be archaic, yet the NIV, NASB, and NRSV saw no problem with updating "hanged" to "impaled."[12] And furthermore, the NKJV replaced "without number" in the AV with "immeasurable."[13] Notwithstanding its revision, the word **implead** is still a legal term meaning "to sue; to prosecute."[14]

Importunity

> I say unto you, Though he will not rise and give him, because he is his friend, yet because of his **importunity** he will rise and give him as many as he needeth. (Luke 11:8)

The word **importunity**, found only once in the AV, is a form of *importune,* which comes through French from the Latin *importunus,* "unsuitable." *Portus* is a port or harbour; hence, the orignial significance of *importunus* was "without a harbour." Thus, our word *opportune* originally meant the opposite of this, that is, "to the harbour." The nautical meaning of these words gradually faded giving us the modern definitions of *opportune* as timely or suitable and *importune* as untimely or unsuitable. Hence, **importunity** can mean unseasonableness, untimeliness, unsuitableness, or unwanted persistence. The NKJV, NASB, and NRSV unite in replacing **importunity** with "persistence," but the NIV selected "boldness." Although the NASB deemed **importunity** to be archaic, it inserted the word "importune" into a passage where neither the AV nor any other modern version contained the word.[15] Moreover, when the AV used a word like "convenient," the NIV and NRSV altered it to "opportune."[16] The correction of **importunity** was not necessary anyway, for it is still in vogue in the 1990's: "In both cases a variety of nonviolent protest tactics has been effectively employed (for example, the noisy **importunity** of traditional Korean petition-prayer drums beating relentlessly at City Hall eventually got Mayor Bradley's attention)."[17]

Impotent

> And there sat a certain man at Lystra, **impotent** in his feet, being a cripple from his mother's womb, who never had walked: (Acts 14:8)

The word **impotent** occurs four times in the AV.[18] Although it comes into English from an identical French word, most will recognize it as a compound of the Latin *im,* "not," and *potens,* "powerful." To be **impotent** is to be without power, helpless, weak, or ineffective. Due to its appropriation as a term to describe male sexual inability, our modern versions were squeamish in using this word. Impotent has been variously rendered as "sick,"[19] "without strength,"[20] "helpless,"[21] forms of "cripple"[22] or "invalid,"[23] and the politically correct "disabled."[24] Yet after correcting the AV four times, the NASB injects the word "impotent" into a passage where the AV and all other modern versions read "feeble."[25] Although impotent was deemed archaic by our modern versions, the *Orange County Register* did not consider the word to be so: "The CDC grew smallpox, separated its genes, rendered them impotent and cloned them."[26]

Impudent

> So she caught him, and kissed him, *and* with an impudent face said unto him, (Prov 7:13)

The word impudent is found three times in the AV.[27] It comes from the Latin *impudens*, "shameless." To be impudent is to be immodest, disrespectful, or shameless. Surprisingly, the NKJV retains the word in all three occurrences.[28] The NRSV, whether intentionally or not, kept "impudent" twice but altered the third instance to "hard forehead."[29] The NASB used "stubborn" twice[30] and "brazen"[31] once. The NIV could not decide on a word so it chose three of them (brazen, obstinate, hardened) to update impudent.[32] This word should never have been corrected in the first place, for even *Harper's* magazine did not consider it to be archaic: "Now they view the current militancy as just a few more firecrackers: impudent and infuriating but hardly serious."[33]

Incontinent

> Without natural affection, trucebreakers, false accusers, incontinent, fierce, despisers of those that are good, (2 Tim 3:3)

The word incontinent occurs once in the AV, as does the form incontinency.[34] Incontinent is from a French word of the same spelling that is the negation of the word *continent*, which, like the English word *contain*, is originally from the Latin *continere*, "to contain." To be incontinent is to have the inability to contain or restrain oneself. The word incontinency is unanimously rendered in our modern versions by the phrase "lack of self-control."[35] The NASB, NIV, and NKJV likewise updated **incontinent** to "without self-control," but the NRSV chose the more difficult "profligates."[36] But it should be pointed out that the word **incontinent** is not archaic at all, at least according to *U.S. News & World Report:* "It left her **incontinent;** others suffered permanent brain damage, lost their jobs or otherwise deteriorated."[37]

Inditing

> My heart is **inditing** a good matter: I speak of the things which I have made touching the king: my tongue *is* the pen of a ready writer. (Psa 45:1)

The word **inditing** is found only once in the AV. *Indite* is from the French *enditer,* "to dictate or write down." *Indite* is a doublet of *indict,* which in Latin is a combination of *in,* "in," and *dictare,* "to declare." To indite is to declare something that is to be repeated or written down, to enjoin as law, or compose. The translations in our modern versions are all similar to the NASB's "overflows with a good theme." Nevertheless, forms of the word **inditing** can still be found today: "On the campus where I teach, there is a landmark, a large rock on which fraternity and sorority members paint their Greek letters, the political minded announce their slogans, and the whimsical occasionally **indite** their usually unobscene graffiti."[38]

Infamy

> Lest he that heareth *it* put thee to shame, and thine **infamy** turn not away. (Prov 25:10)

The word **infamy,** occurring twice in the AV,[39] is from the French *infamie,* "ill fame." The *in-* prefix simply negates fame. Thus, **infamy** is shame, disgrace, reproach, ill fame, or bad reputation. This word has been eliminated by all of our modern versions. It is usually rendered by a form of "slander"[40] or "bad reputation."[41] Although they ousted **infamy** from the text of the Bible, the new translations retained the similar word "infamous," except for the NASB, which preferred "ill repute."[42] Moreover, the NIV corrected the AV reading of "ashamed" to the supposedly archaic word "**infamy**" that it just twice corrected.[43] But in addition to being popularized by FDR, who uttered the immortal words "a day that will live in **infamy**" in describing the Japanese attack on Pearl Harbor, the word **infamy** is still used today: "The **infamy** of the San Andreas fault has prompted some Californians to move as far away from it as possible."[44]

Infidel

> And what concord hath Christ with Belial? or what part hath he that believeth with an **infidel**? (2 Cor 6:15)

The word **infidel** also appears twice in the AV.[45] **Infidel** is from the French *infidele*, literally meaning "not faithful." An **infidel** is one who is unfaithful or unbelieving toward a belief or duty. Our modern versions faithfully amended **infidel** to "unbeliever."[46] Yet if **infidel** could not stand the scalpel of revision, then why did the NKJV insert "infidelity" into a passage where no other new translation contained the word?[47] The word **infidel** is still commonly used anyway: "So long as Persian Gulf leaders appear to be players on an American **infidel** team, their legitimacy in Moslem eyes will erode."[48]

Infolding

> And I looked, and, behold, a whirlwind came out of the north, a great cloud, and a fire **infolding** itself, and a brightness *was* about it, and out of the midst thereof as the colour of amber, out of the midst of the fire. (Ezek 1:4)

The word **infolding,** formed from *infold,* occurs once in the AV. *Infold* is a variation of *enfold,* meaning to envelop, enclose, contain, or fold inward. The NKJV updates **infolding** to the similar "engulfing," the NRSV and NASB join in describing this fire as "flashing forth continually," and the NIV makes the fire into "flashing lightning." The meaning of **infolding** could certainly be determined by the context, what is not so certain, however, is why modern versions like the NASB and NRSV used the word "inscrutable."[49]

Injurious

> Who was before a blasphemer, and a persecutor, and

injurious: but I obtained mercy, because I did *it* ignorantly in unbelief. (1 Tim 1:13)

The word **injurious** appears one time in the AV. It is from the French *injurieux* meaning "tending to injure." **Injurious** means hurtful, insulting, abusive, injuring, or detrimental. The NRSV, NASB, and NIV unite in rendering **injurious** by a form of "violence." The NKJV, however, replaces **injurious** by an even more difficult word: "insolent." In fact, the NKJV employs the word "insolent" on four other occasions as well.[50] The NASB utilizes "insolent" four times,[51] the NIV three times,[52] and the NRSV even corrects "strangers" in the AV to "insolent" when all of the other new versions read as the AV.[53] The similar word "insolence" is also used by all of our supposedly modern, up-to-date versions.[54] Notwithstanding these corrections, the word **injurious** can still be found in use today: "Despite its social significance, illegal, negligent and **injurious** behaviors of corporations remains a little-studied phenomenon."[55] **Injurious** falsehood is also listed in legal dictionaries as "a defamation which does actual damage."[56]

Inkhorn

And, behold, the man clothed with linen, which *had* the **inkhorn** by his side, reported the matter, saying, I have done as thou hast commanded me. (Ezek 9:11)

An **inkhorn** is mentioned three times in the AV.[57] An **inkhorn** is a small portable vessel for holding ink. It was so called because it was often made of a horn. The NKJV followed the AV all three places where **inkhorn** appeared.[58] The NRSV and NASB united in changing a "writer's **inkhorn**" to a generic "writing case," while the NIV preferred a "writing kit."[59] **Inkhorn** is not an archaic word, it is just an antiquated object, yet the NRSV and NASB had no trouble in making reference to a "washbasin."[60]

Inquisition

When he maketh **inquisition** for blood, he remembereth them: he forgetteth not the cry of the humble. (Psa 9:12)

The word **inquisition** appears three times in the AV.[61] It is from a French word of the same spelling meaning an examination and is etymologically related to the word *inquire*. Thus, an **inquisition** is an investigation, examination, or inquiry. Due to the bad historical connotations of the word **inquisition,** it does not surface in any of our modern versions. The customary translation is a form of "investigate"[62] but the word "inquiry" is also used.[63] Yet the word **inquisition** is still used when not referring to medieval torture: "The audience is laced with sharpshooters and soapboxers who all too often use a guest to draw themselves into the limelight, to engage not in dialogue but in **inquisition.**"[64]

Insomuch

> And, behold, there arose a great tempest in the sea, **insomuch** that the ship was covered with the waves: but he was asleep. (Mat 8:24)

The word **insomuch** occurs twenty times in the AV.[65] It is a combination of the three separate words "in so much." The cognate term **inasmuch,** found nine times in the AV,[6] was formed similarly. **Insomuch** is normally coupled with *that:* "**insomuch** that," and **inasmuch** is usually followed by *as:* "**inasmuch** as." The phrase "**insomuch** that" means to such an extent or seeing that. It has been removed completely from all of the modern versions and usually replaced with "so that."[67] The phrase "**inasmuch** as" means because, since, or according as, and is rendered by our modern versions as "since,"[68] "to the extent that,"[69] and "just as."[70] One time the NASB extends "**inasmuch** as" to "by just so much as."[71] Of the nine times the AV employs the word **inasmuch,** it is retained unanimously by all of the new versions only once.[72] However, the NKJV follows the AV in five other places.[73] The NASB also carelessly retained "**inasmuch**" in one additional verse.[74] But after just correcting **inasmuch** in the AV, the NASB employs the word in twenty-two other passages[75] and the NKJV utilizes it in nineteen.[76] Moreover, the NRSV alone uses the triple compound "insofar," a word that appears in neither the AV nor any other modern version.[77] Although these words were regularly updated by our modern versions, they are still in use today: "**Inasmuch** as there are already more than 40 million refugees and displaced persons worldwide, the primary UN solution has to be repatriation to the refugees' original home country."[78] And from *Newsweek* magazine: "As for me, I'm trying to limit outside projects, to pay attention when he analyzes a race route and to put all of his mail (**insomuch** as is humanly possible) on his dresser."[79]

𝔍𝔫𝔰𝔱𝔞𝔫𝔱

> And they were **instant** with loud voices, requiring that he might be crucified. And the voices of them and of the chief priests prevailed. (Luke 23:23)

The word **instant**, referring to the manner of an action and not the time, occurs three times in the AV.[80] The form **instantly**, with the same connotation, is found twice.[81] **Instant** is from the Latin *instans*, "present." It then came to mean earnest, urgent, insistent, or persistent. The word **instantly** is unanimously updated by our modern versions to "earnestly."[82] However, they could not agree with each other on how to revise **instant**. And not only did they disagree among themselves, no new translation used the same word more than once in upgrading **instant**. One can find "urgently,"[83] forms of "insistent"[84] and "persevere,"[85] "ready,"[86] "faithful,"[87] "steadfastly,"[88] "persistent,"[89] and "prepared."[90] Yet when the AV employs a simple word like "confirmed," the NASB alters it to "interposed."[91]

𝔍𝔫𝔱𝔢𝔩𝔩𝔦𝔤𝔢𝔫𝔠𝔢

> For the ships of Chittim shall come against him: therefore he shall be grieved, and return, and have indignation against the holy covenant: so shall he do; he shall even return, and have **intelligence** with them that forsake the holy covenant. (Dan 11:30)

The word **intelligence** is found only once in the AV. It is from a French word of the same spelling meaning "understanding." The modern conception of **intelligence** is usually limited to how smart a person is. But one can't have **intelligence** unless one has knowledge and understanding of something. **Intelligence,** therefore, can mean knowledge, understanding, information, or the act of acquiring them. The Central **Intelligence** Agency (CIA) is not just a group of men with a high mental capacity. Naturally, our modern versions have updated this word. The NKJV and NASB both selected the phrase "show regard," the NIV chose the similar "show favor," and the NRSV went with "pay heed." Yet when the AV reads "easy to be understood," the NRSV and NIV change it to "intelligible."[92] And when a perfectly understandable word is used in the AV, a word that anyone with average **intelligence** can grasp, it is often made more difficult, as in "directed" being corrected by the NIV to "marshaled."[93]

Intermeddle

> The heart knoweth his own bitterness; and a stranger doth not **intermeddle** with his joy. (Prov 14:10)

The word **intermeddle** appears only once in the AV, as does the form **intermeddleth**.[94] **Intermeddle**, obviously a combination of *inter* and *meddle,* is from the French *entremedler.* To **intermeddle** is to take part, meddle, concern oneself, or interfere. Our new versions unite in correcting **intermeddle** to "share."[95] The AV phrase "**intermeddleth** with" is curiously given as "showing contempt for" by the NRSV, "quarrels against" by the NASB, "defies" by the NIV, and "rages against" by the NKJV.[96] But if it be argued that the AV unnecessarily extended the word *meddle* to **intermeddle,** it should be pointed out that the NIV lengthens "man" to "fellowman,"[97] "nets" to "fishnets,"[98] and "boats" to "lifeboats."[99]

Inward

> All my **inward** friends abhorred me: and they whom I loved are turned against me. (Job 19:19)

The word **inward** occurs once in the AV with this meaning. The word itself appeared in Old English as *innanweard.* The *-ward* suffix signifies direction. **Inward** here has the sense of intimate, close, or personal. When used in the plural, the word **inwards** occurs twenty times in the AV in sixteen verses.[100] It is always a reference to the **inward** parts of the body, commonly called today the innards or guts. The word **inwards** is unanimously corrected by our modern versions. The NKJV, NASB, and NRSV selected "entrails," but the NIV alone chose "inner parts." Directly relating to inner parts, the NRSV replaced "thigh" in the AV with "uterus," even though all of the other modern versions followed the AV reading.[101]

Isle

And when they had gone through the **isle** unto Paphos, they found a certain sorcerer, a false prophet, a Jew, whose name *was* Barjesus: (Acts 13:6)

The singular **isle** appears six times in the AV,[102] while the plural **isles** is found twenty-seven times.[103] **Isle** is from the French *isle*, "an island." The word *island*, which appeared in Old English as *igland*, is a synonym for **isle** but is etymologically unrelated. It was in imitation of **isle** that *igland* acquired its *s*. **Isle** is related to our English words *isolate* and *insulate*, originally developed from the Latin *insula*. Although they are exact synonyms, **isle** was not usually updated by *island* in our modern versions. In addition to "islands,"[104] one can find "coastlands,"[105] "distant shores,'[106] and "coasts."[107] Twice, however, the NRSV forgot to remove "**isles**" from its text,[108] but the NKJV overlooked this supposedly archaic word six times.[109] The word **isle** is certainly not archaic, for it is still employed today as a synonym for *island:* "A butterfly native to the British **Isles** apparently arrived under its own power."[110]

Issue

Command the children of Israel, that they put out of the camp every leper, and every one that hath an **issue,** and whosoever is defiled by the dead: (Num 5:2)

The word **issue** occurs forty times in the AV in the singular[111] and twice in the plural.[112] **Issue** is from the French *eissue*, from *eissir*, "to go out," and ultimately goes back to the Latin *exire*, from which we get *exit*. An **issue** is anything that goes out or comes forth. It could be material or immaterial. Although **issue** and **issues** are abundant in our modern versions, there is a problem with how the AV uses the word the majority of the time, for thirty-seven times an **issue** represents a discharge or flow from the body.[113] Our modern versions customarily render **issue** as "discharge,"[114] but sometimes "flow" is used.[115] However, in one passage the NKJV and NASB retained "**issue**" as the AV had it.[116] Moreover, when the AV clearly specifies a bodily fluid like "piss" in the contemporary language of the people, all the new translations change it to "urine."[117]

Chapter 10
Jangling to Jot

Jangling

> From which some having swerved have turned aside unto vain **jangling**; (1 Tim 1:6)

Jangling, formed from the word *jangle,* is found only once in the AV. It is from the French *jangler,* "to chatter." To jangle is to make a harsh or discordant sound or a noisy altercation. Jangling can be foolish, idle, angry, or meaningless talk. It can also refer to any harsh, unpleasant, jarring, grating, or discordant sound. Predictably, this word does not appear in our new, up-to-date translations. The phrase "vain **jangling**" that appears in the AV is altered in the NIV and NRSV to "meaningless talk." The NKJV chose "idle talk" and the NASB selected "fruitless discussion." These changes were no doubt made because the word **jangling** was thought to be archaic. However, the translators of these new versions were not too well acquainted with contemporary English. *Kiwanis Magazine* obviously did not consider the word to be archaic: "Screaming matches and slamming doors may become a **jangling** daily routine."[1] Even Martin Luther King Jr. used **jangling** in one of his speeches: "We will be able to transform the **jangling** discords of our nation into a beautiful symphony of brotherhood."[2]

Jeopardy

> But as they sailed he fell asleep: and there came down a storm of wind on the lake; and they were filled *with water,* and were in **jeopardy.** (Luke 8:23)

Jeopardy appears six times in the AV,[3] with the form

jeoparded occurring once.[4] **Jeopardy** comes into English from the French *jeu parti,* "an even game." A game in which the chances were equal entailed a risk or a hazard. To be in **jeopardy** is to be exposed to loss, harm, peril, death, or injury. With a television show named **Jeopardy** that some translators of these modern versions probably watch, one would think that this word would be retained in the text of the Bible. Yet only the NKJV consistently follows the AV, excepting one passage.[5] The NRSV omits the word completely, substituting "risk" twice,[6] "danger" twice,[7] and "cost"[8] and "scorned"[9] each one time. The NASB likewise utilizes four words (despised, risk, cost, danger) to correct the text.[10] Notwithstanding these corrections, the NASB maintained the AV reading of **jeopardy** once,[11] and then added the word to another passage.[12] The NIV eliminated **jeopardy** from those places where the AV had it, using four different words to do so (risk, cost, danger, endanger),[13] but inserted the word into two passages where the AV did not use it.[14] Although deemed archaic by modern translations, the word **jeopardy** is certainly still in vogue in the 1990's: "Regard and respect are associated with this concept in large part because of its practical application: if others have little or no regard for a person's manhood, his very life and those of his loved ones could be in **jeopardy.**"[15]

Joinings

> And David prepared iron in abundance for the nails for the doors of the gates, and for the **joinings;** and brass in abundance without weight; (1 Chr 22:3)

The word **joinings** also appears but once in the AV. It was formed by adding a suffix to *join,* which is from the French *joign,* "to join." As we have seen before, this is a case of an ordinary word with a different form that has been thus deemed archaic. The NASB and NRSV update **joinings** to "clamps." The NIV picked "fittings" and the NKJV adopted "joints." Yet when the underlying Hebrew word was translated in the AV by the word "couplings" in another passage, the NIV altered it to the more difficult "joist," a word found in no other new translation.[16] And not only that, the word **joinings** can still be found in modern English: "In addition, mice and termites chew through it, and wind passes easily through its **joinings.**"[17]

Jot

For verily I say unto you, Till heaven and earth pass, one **jot** or one tittle shall in no wise pass from the law, till all be fulfilled. (Mat 5:18)

The word **jot** also occurs just once in the AV. It comes from the Latin *iota,* which in turn is literally derived from the ninth and smallest letter of the Greek alphabet. A **jot** is a little bit or the very least part of something. Hence, to **jot** is to write down something small like a phone number, address, or message. The English letter *j* is a late modification of the letter *i*. No word beginning with *j* is of Old English derivation. The letter *j* first saw use as an initial *i*. According to the English lexicographer Samuel Johnson (1709-1784): "I is in English considered both as a vowel and consonant; though, since the vowel and consonant differ in their form as well as sound, they may be more properly accounted two letters."[18] It was Noah Webster in 1828 who separated the two letters in his dictionary.[19] The letter *j* can not be found in the original 1611 edition of the AV. It was only in the seventeenth century that *i* was used for a vowel, *j* for a consonant, and capital forms of the letters were introduced. This is why there are not very many words with the letter *j* in the middle of the word. The "one **jot**" of the AV is retained in the NKJV, but altered in the NRSV to "one letter," and in the NASB and NIV to "the smallest letter." But when *alpha,* the first letter of the Greek alphabet, occurs in the biblical text, all of our modern versions transliterate the word just as it appears in Greek.[20] Nevertheless, the *San Jose Mercury News* did not consider the word **jot** to be archaic: "Most of us still use pens or pencils to write letters and **jot** down information on note pads and forms."[21]

Chapter 11
Kerchiefs to Know

Kerchiefs

Your **kerchiefs** also will I tear, and deliver my people out of your hand, and they shall be no more in your hand to be hunted; and ye shall know that I *am* the LORD. (Ezek 13:21)

The word **kerchiefs** appears only twice in the AV.[1] A kerchief is literally a coverhead, as it is from the French *covrechief,* a combination of *covrir,* "cover," and *chief,* "head." **Kerchiefs** are cloths used to cover the heads of women. Our modern versions unite in altering **kerchiefs** to "veils." Yet when the AV reads "veils," the NIV corrects it to "shawls" and the NKJV to "robes."[2] Moreover, when the AV uses the word "hoods" to refer to a head covering just like the word is used today, the NIV alters it to the more difficult "tiaras."[3] The word **kerchiefs** should have posed no problem to anyone, for like *handkerchief* and *neckerchief,* it is still used in the 1990's: "Standing today in the village store, wearing a white **kerchief** on her head and a blue-flowered dress, she has a worn, but cheerful face."[4]

Kernels

All the days of his separation shall he eat nothing that is made of the vine tree, from the **kernels** even to the husk. (Num 6:4)

The word **kernels** occurs but once in the AV. The singular Old English form was *cyrnel,* a diminutive of *corn,* "seed or grain." **Kernels** are the seeds contained within any fruit. The kernel is also the soft part enclosed in the hard shell of a nut or the body of a seed within its husk. **Kernels** is unanimously updated to "seed" or "seeds" by the new translations. However, when the AV reads "seed," it is corrected to "grain,"[5] but when the AV says "grain," it is altered to "seed."[6] And furthermore, when the AV and NKJV both read "grain," the NASB updated it with the archaic "kernel."[7] The NIV even inserted "**kernels**" into five passages where neither the AV nor any other modern version contained the word.[8] In fact, in two of these places the other new translations read "grain."[9] The word **kernels**, however, is still in use as it is in the AV: "I try the juicy **kernels** of a Myrianthus arboreus fruit and decide that gorillas know a good taste when they find one."[10]

𝕶𝖎𝖓𝖊

> And, behold, there came up out of the river seven **kine,** fatfleshed and well favoured; and they fed in a meadow: (Gen 41:18)

Kine are mentioned twenty-four times in the AV.[11] The word **kine** is the plural of *cow* but has now been superseded by *cows*. Naturally, our modern versions always render **kine** as "cows."[12] Yet when the AV says "cow," the NASB updates it to the more difficult "heifer."[13] **Kine** may be archaic, but it is not as bad as the NIV, NASB, and NRSV replacing "giants" with the word "Nephilim."[14] But nevertheless, from *Asian Affairs* magazine: "First the **kine,** some thirty head (each milk cow gives about one gallon, twice daily)."[15]

𝕶𝖓𝖔𝖕

> And a **knop** under two branches of the same, and a **knop** under two branches of the same, and a **knop** under two branches of the same, according to the six branches going out of it. (Exo 37:21)

A **knop** can be found in the AV ten times in the singular[16] and nine times in the plural.[17] **Knop** is cognate with *knap,* from the Old English *cnaep,* meaning the top of a hill. Thus, a **knop** can be anything that protrudes. The word is commonly applied to the bud of a flower, a carved representation of the same, or a knob or boss, usually ornamental in nature, on the stem of a candlestick or similar object. Our modern versions each had their own preferred words to update **knop** and **knops**. The NASB chose "bulb" and "bulbs" and the NIV "bud" and "buds."[18] The NKJV used "ornamental knob," "ornamental knobs," or just "knob."[19] However, the NRSV thought **knop** and **knops** were not archaic enough so it replaced them with "calyx" and "calyxes."[20]

Know

> And they called unto Lot, and said unto him, Where *are* the men which came in to thee this night? bring them out unto us, that we may **know** them. (Gen 19:5)

Although forms of the word **know** can be found hundreds of times in the AV, there is a particular use of the word that is considered archaic. In addition to the common meanings of perceive, comprehend, and be aware of, the word **know** also refers to a sexual relationship. This usage occurs seventeen times in the AV.[21] Although professing to be in modern, up-to-date English, the NKJV follows this AV usage of **know** every time.[22] The NRSV retains this archaic usage eleven times.[23] Only the NIV consistently updated forms of **know** that contained this sexual connotation, for even the NASB forgot to change four passages.[24] But when the AV utilizes an unambiguous word like "weak," it is changed by the NRSV to "languishing."[25] And when the AV says "fail," the NASB substitutes "languish."[26]

Chapter 12
Lade to Lusty

Lade

And he said, Woe unto you also, ye lawyers! for ye **lade** men with burdens grievous to be borne, and ye yourselves touch not the burdens with one of your fingers. (Luke 11:46)

Lade occurs three times in the AV,[1] while **laded** appears four times,[2] **laden** is found six times,[3] **ladeth** only once,[4] and **lading** twice.[5] The form **unlade** also appears once.[6] **Lade** appeared in Old English as *hladan*, meaning "to load." The overwhelming replacement in our modern versions for all forms of **lade** is a form of "load."[7] However, "weighed down,"[8] "supplied,"[9] and "provided"[10] can also be found. The NASB and NKJV both forgot to correct one occurrence of **laden** in the New Testament.[11] Then the NKJV inserted "**laden**" into another passage where no other version contained the word.[12] The NASB also did likewise.[13] The NRSV, after amending all forms of **lade** in the AV in every place that they occurred, uses "**laden**" in a passage where the AV and the new translations do not even have the word.[14] The NIV, which also corrected every occurrence in the AV of all forms of **lade,** injected "**laden**" into four verses where no other modern version contained the word.[15] In one particular case, the AV and all other versions read "mountains of spices" but the NIV changed it to "spice-laden" mountains."[16] Nevertheless, forms of **lade** still occur frequently in the 1990's. A "bill of **lading**" is a receipt given by a carrier for goods accepted for transportation. Even *Harper's* magazine had no trouble with the word: "The small meeting room was dark, but there was a table **laden** with copious amounts of Georgian food, including the country's ubiquitous walnut paste."[17]

Lance

> They shall hold the bow and the **lance:** they *are* cruel, and will not show mercy: their voice shall roar like the sea, and they shall ride upon horses, *every one* put in array, like a man to the battle, against thee, O daughter of Babylon. (Jer 50:42)

A **lance,** only mentioned once in the AV, is from a French word of the same spelling meaning a spear. Although the NKJV retained **lance** as the AV, the NASB went with "javelin," the NRSV with "spear," and the NIV with "spears." But after correcting **lance,** the NRSV uses the word in another passage where the AV and all of the other modern versions read "spears."[18] The NIV inserts "**lance**" twice when the other new translations employ the word "javelin."[19] Yet when the AV mentions a "javelin," it is corrected every time by the NRSV, NIV, and NASB, and all but once by the NKJV.[20] The word **lance,** however is still in use today: "Just two days before in the White House, their adult commander had placed **lances** in their hands and instructed them on the art of combat."[21]

Lancets

> And they cried aloud, and cut themselves after their manner with knives and **lancets,** till the blood gushed out upon them. (1 Ki 18:28)

Lancets are also found only once in the AV. The word *lancet* is from the French *lancette,* the diminutive of *lance.* Thus, **lancets** would literally be small spears. A lancet, then, is a small spear, javelin, dart, or other sharp instrument. After previously correcting "lances" in the AV, the NKJV, NASB, and NRSV altered **lancets** to "lances." However, the NIV preferred "spears." Yet in the very same verse as **lancets,** the NIV, NASB, and NRSV amended "knives" to "swords."[22] **Lancets** could certainly not be archaic since they are still used today in medical procedures: "In the wallet, he also packs needles, 'lancets' to prick his fingers, alcohol swabs to cleanse the site he'll be injecting and glucose tablets to take if the level of sugar in his blood gets too low."[23]

Lapwing

And the stork, the heron after her kind, and the **lapwing,** and the bat. (Lev 11:19)

The **lapwing** is only referred to twice in the AV.[24] The word itself appeared in Old English as *hleapewince*. This word was formed from *hleapan*, "to leap," and *wince*, "to turn." The **lapwing** is a bird that was so named because of the irregular manner of its flight. It is understandable that the word **lapwing** would be updated by our modern versions, but why **lapwing** was unanimously rendered as "hoopoe" cannot be fathomed.[25] This is especially perplexing since a **lapwing** can still be found flying in the 1990's: "It was a cold, damp March morning in the Border Country of northern England. Snow lingered along the field walls, making white stripes across the green Northumberland hills. **Lapwings** and curlews tumbled overhead."[26]

Lasciviousness

> Now the works of the flesh are manifest, which are *these;* Adultery, fornication, uncleanness, **lasciviousness,** (Gal 5:19)

The word **lasciviousness** occurs six times in the AV.[27] It was formed from *lascivious,* which is ultimately from the Latin *lascivus,* "sportive." **Lasciviousness** is the quality of being lascivious. To be lascivious is to be lustful, licentious, wanton, or lewd. The NRSV consistently rendered **lasciviousness** as "licentiousness," the NASB as "sensuality," and the NKJV as "lewdness,"[28] but the NIV could not decide on the proper word. "Debauchery" is employed three times,[29] "sensuality" once,[30] "lewdness" once,[31] and "license for immorality" once.[32] These corrections were entirely unnecessary, for not only is "lewd and **lascivious** behavior" a standard charge against perverts, forms of **lasciviousness** are in common use also: "And most waiters today describe dessert trays with the same **lascivious** smirk a sex show barker might use to describe the delights within."[33]

Latchet

> And preached, saying, There cometh one mightier than I after me, the **latchet** of whose shoes I am not worthy to stoop down and unloose. (Mark 1:7)

A **latchet** is mentioned four times in the AV,[34] while the extended form **shoelatchet** occurs only once.[35] **Latchet** is from the French *lacet,* the diminutive of *las,* "lace." Thus, **latchet** is not related to the word *latch.* A **latchet** is a loop or narrow strip of anything to fasten a shoe or sandal. A modern shoelace would be a **latchet.** The usual translation in our modern versions for **latchet** and **shoelatchet** is a form of "thong," except for the NKJV, which preferred "strap."[36] Although the meaning of **latchet** could be determined from the context, the meaning of "impetuous," substituted by the NRSV, NIV, and NASB for "hasty,"[37] is sure to give readers of modern, contemporary English trouble.

Laud

> And again, Praise the Lord, all ye Gentiles; and **laud** him, all ye people. (Rom 15:11)

The word **laud,** occurring only once in the AV, is from the Latin *laudare,* "to praise." To **laud** is to extoll, praise, magnify, worship, or acclaim. Although the NKJV retains the AV reading, the NIV, NASB, and NRSV alter **laud** to "praise." The NKJV liked the word so much that it used it in another passage where the AV did not have it.[38] But although the NASB and NRSV considered **laud** to be archaic and corrected it to "praise," both of these modern versions altered the AV word "praise" to "**laud.**"[39] Moreover, in another passage where the AV employed the word "praise," the NRSV converted it into the more difficult "commendation."[40] The word **laud,** however, is still in modern use: "Many researchers **laud** the Navy for its support of basic research and say the military's use of the animals seems benevolent."[41]

Laver

> And thou shalt set the **laver** between the tent of the congregation and the altar, and shalt put water therein. (Exo 40:7)

The singular **laver** appears fifteen times in the AV,[42] while the plural **lavers** is found five times.[43] **Laver** comes from the French *laveoir,* "a washing vessel." A **laver** is a basin, bowl, or other vessel used for washing. Our word *lavatory* is akin to **laver;** it signifies the place while **laver** specifies the object used.

Surprisingly, the NKJV retains **laver** and **lavers** exactly as the AV.[44] The NRSV and NIV, however, preferred the word "basin."[45] The NASB was undecided as to what to say: **Lavers** is corrected every time,[46] and **laver** is replaced by "basin" six times,[47] but the NASB keeps the AV reading of **laver** nine times.[48] The NRSV got careless only once in retaining **laver** as the AV had it.[49] **Laver** may be somewhat archaic, but the substitution of "Zaphon" for "north" when all of the other new translations read like the AV certainly does not make the Bible clearer.[50]

Leanfleshed

And, behold, seven other kine came up after them out of the river, ill favoured and **leanfleshed;** and stood by the *other* kine upon the brink of the river. (Gen 41:3)

The word **leanfleshed** occurs three times in the AV.[51] It is manifestly a compound of *lean* and *flesh*. Like the similar "fatfleshed," this word is updated in our modern versions. But this time, instead of shortening **leanfleshed** to just "lean" like "fatfleshed" was altered to "fat" in all of the new versions, only the NIV one time corrects **leanfleshed** to "lean."[52] The NRSV replaces **leanfleshed** with "thin" all three times, but the NASB and NKJV both use the word "gaunt."[53] The NIV also employs "gaunt" on two occasions to update **leanfleshed**.[54] But when the AV just says "lean," the NKJV corrects it to "gaunt" as well.[55] The NIV joins in by replacing "leanness" in the AV with "gauntness."[56]

Leasing

Thou shalt destroy them that speak **leasing:** the LORD will abhor the bloody and deceitful man. (Psa 5:6)

The word **leasing** occurs twice in the AV.[57] The Old English form was *leasung,* from *leas,* "false." **Leasing** is an old word for lying, falsehood, or deceit. The NRSV consistently rendered **leasing** as "lies" and the NKJV unfailingly as "falsehood,"[58] but the NIV and NASB together used four different words or phrases to update **leasing**. The NASB choose "deception" and "falsehood," while the NIV selected "false gods" and "lies."[59]

Leasing is definitely archaic, but the correction of "passed over" to "forded" by the NIV is not exactly simple English.[60]

Lees

And in this mountain shall the LORD of hosts make unto all people a feast of fat things, a feast of wines on the **lees,** of fat things full of marrow, of wines on the **lees** well refined. (Isa 25:6)

Lees are mentioned four times in the AV.[61] The word **lees** is from the French *lie* and although in the plural, the singular form is not used. **Lees** are the deposits or dregs that settle from a liquid. It can also refer to the worst part of something. On the other hand, it can also mean the very end or the last drop. **Lees** is usually updated to "dregs" by our modern versions.[62] "Aged" or "well-aged" is another popular choice.[63] But two of the new versions were careless in that they retained the AV reading of **lees** in one passage.[64] Yet when the AV employs the simple word "complainers," it is changed in the NRSV to "malcontents."[65]

Let

Now I would not have you ignorant, brethren, that oftentimes I purposed to come unto you, (but was **let** hitherto,) that I might have some fruit among you also, even as among other Gentiles. (Rom 1:13)

The word **let,** as it is used here, is found three times in the AV.[66] The form **letteth** also appears once.[67] There are two words in English that are both spelled **let**; however, they are entirely unrelated as to their origin. This is also true of many other English words like *lie,* which can mean a falsehood or to lay down. The word **let,** meaning to hinder, prevent, or obstruct, is from the Old English *lettan* meaning to hinder or make late. The corrections employed by our modern versions include "hinder,"[68] "reverse,"[69] "prevented,"[70] and "restrains."[71] Yet in the modern age of the twentieth century, anything that hinders a tennis game—such as the ball hitting the net on a serve—is termed a **let**.

Licence

And when he had given him **licence,** Paul stood on the stairs, and beckoned with the hand unto the people. And when there was made a great silence, he spake unto *them* in the Hebrew tongue, saying, (Acts 21:40)

The word **licence** appears twice in the AV.[72] It comes into English from a French word of the same spelling meaning freedom. To give someone **licence** has nothing do with a fishing or driving **licence** but rather means to give permission, freedom, liberty, opportunity, or authorization. Our modern versions have all removed **licence** and replaced it with "permission" in one passage and "opportunity" in the other.[73] Yet the NRSV saw nothing wrong with using "licentiousness" or "licentious," which are both formed from **licence,** even though they are much more difficult words than **licence.**[74] The NIV and NASB likewise used the word "licentiousness."[75] The word **licence,** however, is still in use when not referring to a government issued document: "The Saudi royal family enforces a fairly strict Islamic regime on its subjects but is notorious for its own moral **licence.**"[76]

Light

And they gave him threescore and ten *pieces* of silver out of the house of Baalberith, wherewith Abimelech hired vain and **light** persons, which followed him. (Judg 9:4)

Although the word **light** appears in various forms over three hundred times in the AV, it is used in a variety of ways, some of which that are considered archaic. **Light** is from the Old English *leoht,* and in addition to meaning something that makes visible or illuminates, whether literally or figuratively, and to be or make less heavy, **light** can also refer to something wanton, reckless, worthless, unstable, frivolous, or not commanding respect. The AV employs this usage for **light** and **lightly** on many occasions.[77] **Lightness** is also used in this manner three times.[78] **Lightly** can also refer to easily or quickly, but it is always in the context of doing something wrong.[79] The other way **light** is used that gives modern translators trouble is in referring to descending, getting off, or going down. The AV utilizes **lighted** after this fashion nine times,[80] **lighteth** once,[81] and **lighting** twice.[82] Our modern versions restricted the various forms of **light** to the basic meanings the words have today. However, four times the word **lightly** is mistakenly left as it appears in the AV,[83] and five times the word **lighted** is replaced with the similar "alighted."[84] Likewise, **lighteth** is replaced with "alighting" once by the NRSV and NKJV,[85] while **lighting** is retained once in the NIV as it is in the AV.[86] The AV word **lightness** is retained by the NASB once,[87] and rendered by the analogous "lightly" three times in the other versions.[88] But when the AV said just plain **light,** the NASB and NKJV change it to "enlighten."[89] And in another passage, the NRSV alters **light** in the AV to "enlightenment."[90] Moreover, when the AV reads "instructed," the NIV replaces it with "englighten."[91] The NRSV further corrects **light** to "luminaries,"[92] the NKJV "lightened" to "illuminated,"[93] and the NASB "enlighten" to "illumines."[94] So even when the AV uses the word **light** like it is employed today, it is still corrected.

Lign aloes

> As the valleys are they spread forth, as gardens by the river's side, as the trees of **lign aloes** which the LORD hath planted, *and* as cedar trees beside the waters. (Num 24:6)

Lign aloes are only mentioned once in the AV. The term is from the Latin *lignum aloes,* "wood of the aloe." **Lign aloes** yield an aromatic wood that is also known as eagle wood. The modern translations all drop the word *lign* from **lign aloes.** But as was mentioned previously, the NIV inserts the word *imperial* twelve times before "guard" even though the other versions regularly follow the AV reading of just "guard."[95] And regarding trees, when the AV mentions a "green bay tree," the NASB alters it to the generic "luxuriant tree."[96]

Ligure

> And the third row a **ligure,** an agate, and an amethyst. (Exo 28:19)

A **ligure** is mentioned twice in the AV.[97] The word is from the Latin *ligurius* referring to a precious stone. A **ligure** is a precious stone like a jacinth. In fact, our modern versions have unanimously updated a **ligure** to a "jacinth."[98] But when the AV reads "jacinth," it is retained by all the new translations in one passage[99] and corrected in another.[100] But in revising "jacinth" in this one instance, our new versions could not agree on the proper translation. The NRSV changed it to "sapphire," the NASB to "hyacinth," the NKJV to "hyacinth blue," and the NIV to "dark blue."[101] Yet when the AV mentions a diamond, a stone that any child is familiar with, the NRSV alters it to a "moonstone."[102]

𝔏𝔦𝔨𝔦𝔫𝔤

> Their young ones are in good **liking,** they grow up with corn; they go forth, and return not unto them. (Job 39:4)

The word **liking** is found twice in the AV[103] and appeared in Old English as *licung*. **Liking,** as it is used in the AV, refers to one's condition, whether good or bad. When the AV mentions "good **liking,**" it is rendered "strong" by the NRSV, NASB, and NIV, but "healthy" by the NKJV.[104] When the AV reads "worse **liking,**" the NRSV changes it to "poorer condition," the NASB to "more haggard," and the NIV and NKJV to "looking worse."[105] But the word **liking** is still used similar to how it is found in the AV: "Even small children test one another, pushing and shoving, and are ready to hit other children over circumstances not to their **liking.**"[106]

𝔏𝔦𝔰𝔱𝔢𝔡

> But I say unto you, That Elias is indeed come, and they have done unto him whatsoever they **listed,** as it is written of him. (Mark 9:13)

The word **listed** occurs twice in the AV,[107] as does the form **listeth.**[108] These words are formed from *list,* from the Old English *lystan,* meaning please, desire, care, want, wish, or like. Our modern versions employed a variety of words to update **listed** and **listeth.** The most common revision was "wished"[109] or "wishes."[110] However, "pleased,"[111] "pleases,"[112] "desires,"[113] "directs,"[114] and "chooses"[115] are also used. **Listed** is definitely archaic, but the alteration of "gained" to "incurred"[116] and "angry" to "indignant"[117] by the NASB is not exactly translating in the modern language of the people.

𝔏𝔦𝔱𝔱𝔢𝔯𝔰

> And they shall bring all your brethren *for* an offering unto the LORD out of all nations upon horses, and in chariots, and in

> litters, and upon mules, and upon swift beasts, to my holy mountain Jerusalem, saith the LORD, as the children of Israel bring an offering in a clean vessel into the house of the LORD. (Isa 66:20)

The word **litters,** occurring only once in the AV, is from the French *litiere,* "bed." A litter was a portable device carried by men or beasts that contained a couch or bed. Surprisingly, the NKJV, NASB, and NRSV retain this archaic word that now is mainly applied to the offspring of animals. The NIV updates **litters** to "wagons." So not only do the new versions correct perfectly clear words in the AV to more difficult ones, often times a genuinely archaic word is left standing as it appears in the AV.

Lively

> Ye also, as **lively** stones, are built up a spiritual house, an holy priesthood, to offer up spiritual sacrifices, acceptable to God by Jesus Christ. (1 Pet 2:5)

Although the word **lively** appears five times in the AV,[118] three of these, all occurring in the New Testament, are used in an archaic sense.[119] **Lively** is from the Old English *liflic,* from *lif,* "life," and means living or animate. The word is now only used in the sense of enthusiastic or spirited. Our modern versions unanimously render **lively** as "living."[120] Yet when the AV uses a word like "dedicated," the NASB and NRSV change it to the more difficult "inaugurated."[121]

Lordly

> He asked water, *and* she gave *him* milk; she brought forth butter in a **lordly** dish. (Judg 5:25)

The word **lordly** occurs only once in the AV. It appeared in Old English as *hlafordlic,* from *hlaford,* "lord." **Lordly** literally means suitable for a lord or noble person; hence, to be **lordly** is to be magnificent, noble, good, or grand. Astoundingly, the NKJV and NASB retain the AV reading of "**lordly**." The NASB revised it to "magnificent" and the NIV updated **lordly** to "fit for nobles." Yet **lordly** should not have been corrected by any version, for it is still in vogue today: "Tiny fungi are the link between even **lordly** Sequoia and the soil."[122]

Lowring

And in the morning, *It will be* foul weather to day: for the sky is red and **lowring**. O *ye* hypocrites, ye can discern the face of the sky; but can ye not *discern* the signs of the times? (Mat 16:3)

The word **lowring** is found only once in the AV. It appeared in Middle English as *louren,* meaning to lurk. Lowring means gloomy, dark, threatening, or menacing. The usual translation in our modern versions is "threatening," but the NIV preferred "overcast." It is understandable that an archaic word such as **lowring** has been updated, but what is not so clear is why plain, ordinary words that the AV uses to refer to storms have been corrected. The NIV extends the simple "storm" in the AV to "windstorm."[123] The NIV also corrects "storm" to "tempest,"[124] while the NRSV and NASB not only do the same, but in the same verse they also amend "tempest" to "storm."[125] Moreover, when the AV, followed by the other modern versions, reads "darkness," the NASB alone changes it to "gloom."[126] Then when the AV mentions "thunder," the NIV alone elongates it to "thundercloud."[127] And finally, "thunderings" in the AV is corrected by the NRSV to "thunderpeals."[128]

Lucre

Not given to wine, no striker, not greedy of filthy **lucre;** but patient, not a brawler, not covetous; (1 Tim 3:3)

The word **lucre** occurs six times in the AV.[129] It is from the Latin *lucrum,* "gain." **Lucre** is illicit, dishonorable, or unlawful gain or advantage. It is commonly applied to gain of money. Our new versions could not agree on the best way to render this word. The NASB was the most consistent, using "dishonest gain"[130] and "sordid gain."[131] The NIV and NKJV preferred "dishonest gain"[132] and just plain "money."[133] The NRSV alternated among "gain,"[134] "money,"[135] and "sordid gain."[136] But in one of the very verses in which **lucre** appears, the NASB inserts the arduous word "pugnacious" when the other new translations all use "violent."[137] Our modern versions may have considered **lucre** to be archaic, but *Sports Illustrated* magazine certainly did not: "Teenage champions turn pro too early and often burn out or become monsters while tennis authorities fail to discipline or educate them, afraid to offend the source of all that **lucre**."[138]

Lunatick

> Lord, have mercy on my son: for he is a **lunatick,** and sore vexed: for ofttimes he falleth into the fire, and oft into the water. (Mat 17:15)

The word **lunatick,** appearing twice in the AV,[139] is from the Latin *lunaticus,* "mad." **Lunatick** literally refers to one affected by the moon. The Latin word for moon was *luna.* It was formerly thought that nervous disorders were in actuality mental disorders and that these were influenced by the moon just like the tides are. A **lunatick** in the Bible is one that has a physical condition like epilepsy. In fact, an "epileptic" is just how the NRSV and NKJV updated **lunatick.**[140] The NASB also used "epileptics"[141] but was careless in leaving the AV reading of **lunatick** in one verse.[142] The NIV did not name a specific disease but instead mentioned "seizures."[143] But when the AV uses a simple word like "wrong," it is changed by the up-to-date, contemporary NIV to "misdemeanor."[144]

Lusty

> And they slew of Moab at that time about ten thousand men, all **lusty,** and all men of valour; and there escaped not a man. (Judg 3:29)

The word **lusty** occurs only once in the AV. It was formed from the Old English *lust,* "pleasure." To be **lusty** is to be vigorous, strong, lively, cheerful, or robust. Although our modern versions all corrected **lusty,** they did not agree among themselves on the proper translation to replace it with. The NRSV went with "strong," the NASB "robust," the NKJV "stout," and the NIV "vigorous." But in another passage where the AV did not even contain the word **lusty,** every one of our modern, up-to-date translations inserted this supposedly archaic word and used it exactly like the AV did.[145] The word **lusty** just so happens to still be in use anyway: "The cavernous tabernacle shook with their **lusty** singing of Luther's hymn 'A mighty fortress is our God.'"[146]

Chapter 13
Magnifical to Murrain

Magnifical

And David said, Solomon my son *is* young and tender, and the house *that is* to be builded for the LORD *must be* exceeding **magnifical,** of fame and of glory throughout all countries: I will *therefore* now make preparation for it. So David prepared abundantly before his death. (1 Chr 22:5)

The word **magnifical** occurs only once in the AV. It is formed from *magnific,* from the French *magnifique.* **Magnifical** is akin to *magnify* and *magnate,* and is a synonym of *magnificent.* Thus, **magnifical** means renowned, glorious, eminent, stately, or splendid. All of these words with the *mag-* prefix are ultimately derived from the Latin *magus,* "great." **Magnifical** is updated in the NKJV, NASB, and NRSV to "magnificent" and in the NIV to "magnificence." But when the AV uses "magnificence," it is altered to "majesty" by the NRSV and NIV.[1] Moreover, when the AV reads "magnify," it is corrected by all of our modern versions to "exalt."[2]

Mail

And Saul armed David with his armour, and he put an helmet of brass upon his head; also he armed him with a coat of **mail.** (1 Sam 17:38)

The word **mail,** appearing twice in the AV,[3] is from the French *maille.* This **mail,** however, has nothing to do with letters and packages delivered by a mailman but rather refers to armor composed of overlapping plates and worn on the body. Surprisingly, the NRSV and NKJV retain this supposedly archaic word in both instances.[4] The NASB renders **mail** one time by "scale-armor" and the other by just "armor."[5] The NIV did the same thing but did not use a hyphen.[6] But after correcting **mail** every time it occurred in the AV, the NASB inserts the word in three additional places where the AV did not contain it.[7] The NKJV liked the word **mail** so much that it employed it on two other occasions where it was not found in the AV.[8] The NRSV used this archaic word in six other verses besides the two places it followed the AV reading.[9]

Maintenance

> And *thou shalt have* goats' milk enough for thy food, for the food of thy household, and *for* the **maintenance** for thy maidens. (Prov 27:27)

The word **maintenance,** found twice in the AV,[10] comes from a French word of the same spelling. The word **maintenance** is now customarily limited to building or automobile repair, but **maintenance** can mean the action of keeping anything in working condition or existence. This would include a person; thus, **maintenance** can refer to that which maintains a persons livelihood or provides him with the necessities of life. In one instance, **maintenance** is altered by our modern versions to a form of "nourish," except for the NASB, which preferred "sustenance."[11] The other occurrence of the word in the AV is in the phrase "have **maintenance.**"[12] This is updated to "share the salt" by the NRSV, "in the service" by the NASB, "under obligation" by the NIV, and "receive support" by the NKJV.[13] Yet after correcting the AV in both passages where **maintenance** appeared, the NASB wields the word the exact same way in another verse.[14] The NRSV does likewise in another place.[15] Furthermore, the corrections of **maintenance** were unnecessary anyway, for even the *Los Angeles Times* used the word as the AV: "Singapore's parliament debated a bill this year allowing elderly parents to sue their children for **maintenance** if they are abandoned financially."[16]

Malefactor

> They answered and said unto him, If he were not a **malefactor,** we would not have delivered him up unto thee. (John 18:30)

The word **malefactor** occurs once in the AV in the singular and three times in the plural.[17] **Malefactor** is from a Latin word of the same spelling meaning a criminal, felon, or one who does evil. The *mal-* prefix that also prefaces words like *malady, malfunction,* and *malcontent* is from the Latin *malus,* "bad, evil." The word **malefactors** is unanimously rendered as "criminals" by all of the new translations. However, the singular **malefactor** is only rendered as "criminal" by the NIV and NRSV,[18] for the NASB and NKJV preferred "evildoer."[19] Yet when the AV uses a simple word like "robber," it is corrected by the NRSV to "bandit" even though the other modern versions embrace the AV reading.[20] The word **malefactor** is still in common use anyway, even by such magazines as *Popular Science:* "The gas that has been indicted as chief **malefactor** in the greenhouse story is carbon dioxide; next to water vapor, it's the most powerful contributor to global warming."[21]

Malignity

Being filled with all unrighteousness, fornication, wickedness, covetousness, maliciousness; full of envy, murder, debate, deceit, **malignity;** whisperers, (Rom 1:29)

The word **malignity,** appearing only once in the AV, is from the French *malignite*. **Malignity** is deep-rooted or wicked ill-will or hatred, wickedness, or malice. Once again, the *mal-* prefix, like that in similar words like *malignant* and *malign,* is from the Latin *malus,* "bad, evil." **Malignity** is replaced with "malice" by the NIV and NASB. However, the NRSV selected "craftiness" and the NKJV "evil-mindedness." Although they corrected **malignity,** the modern versions had no trouble with its cousins. The NASB uses "malignancy,"[22] "malignant,"[23] "malign,"[24] and "maligned."[25] In one case, "malign" is substituted for the simple AV phrase "speak evil of" that also appears in the NKJV and NRSV.[26] The NIV employed the words "malign"[27] and "maligned."[28] The NKJV utilized "malign" once,[29] while the NRSV used it twice,[30] as well as "maligned" twice.[31]

Mammon

No man can serve two masters: for either he will hate the one, and love the other; or else he will hold to the one, and despise the other. Ye cannot serve God and **mammon**. (Mat 6:24)

The word **mammon** appears four times in the AV.[32] It is from the Latin *mamona*, "riches." **Mammon** is a term of reproach for wealth, riches, or money regarded as an evil influence or an idol. Surprisingly, this supposedly archaic word is retained in every instance by the NASB and NKJV.[33] The NRSV consistently substitutes "wealth,"[34] but the NIV proffers "wealth" twice[35] and "money" twice.[36] Yet the word **mammon** is so archaic that it is still in use in the 1990's: "If **mammon** and vainglory were his only objectives, surely Richardson would have dusted the university long, long ago."[37]

𝕸antle

> Then Job arose, and rent his **mantle,** and shaved his head, and fell down upon the ground, and worshipped, (Job 1:20)

The singular **mantle** occurs thirteen times in the AV,[38] while the plural **mantles** is found only once.[39] The word **mantle** is from the French *mantel*, "a cloak." A **mantle** is properly a loose sleeveless cloak of varying lengths but can also refer to anything that enfolds, enwraps, encloses, compasses, or covers. The correction of **mantle** in our modern versions is extensive and critical. The replacements for **mantle** include "rug,"[40] "covering,"[41] "blanket,"[42] "robe,"[43] and "cloak."[44] The NIV, after updating **mantle** every time it appeared in the AV, amended "covered over" in the AV to "mantled."[45] Then the NIV inserts "a **mantle** of" into the middle of the AV expression "with shame," even though all of the other new versions follow the AV reading.[46] The NASB reads as the AV five times,[47] but then changes the AV words "vesture,"[48] "cloak,"[49] and "garment"[50] to "**mantle**." The NRSV replaces "garment,"[51] "veil,"[52] and "cloak"[53] in the AV with "**mantle**." The NKJV only follows the AV about half the time. The word **mantle** is still used today to refer to a covering. Sometimes it is the earth's **mantle**[54] and other times it is a covering of some other kind.[55] The word **mantle** is even used figuratively in imitation of Elisha taking up the **mantle** of Elijah: "With Mandela taking up the presidential **mantle** at a ceremony attended by hundreds of foreign dignitaries, a people long oppressed will lift their voices in praise of a freedom dearly won and deeply cherished."[56]

Maranatha

> If any man love not the Lord Jesus Christ, let him be Anathema **Maranatha**. (1 Cor 16:22)

The word **maranatha** occurs only once in the AV. It is from the Aramaic phrase *maran atha,* "our Lord cometh." The NASB maintains this word as it appears in the AV, but the other translations render it as a longing or prayer. However, when the AV unambiguously translates a Greek word as "hell," it is often unanimously transliterated in the modern versions as "Hades."[57] There was no point in updating **maranatha** in the first place, for most major cities have a **Maranatha** Baptist Church. There are also Bible colleges, Mission organizations, schools, music ministries, and regular businesses with the word **maranatha** in their name.

Marishes

> But the miry places thereof and the **marishes** thereof shall not be healed; they shall be given to salt. (Ezek 47:11)

Marishes, the plural of *marish,* are only mentioned once in the AV. The word *marish* is from the French *marais,* meaning a marsh. Thus, **marishes** are marshes, swamps, bogs, or other wetlands. Our modern versions unite in rendering **marishes** as "marshes." But when the NKJV, NASB, and NRSV unite with the AV in reading "Hebrews," the NIV changes it to "Hebraic Jews."[58]

Matrix

> That thou shalt set apart unto the LORD all that openeth the **matrix,** and every firstling that cometh of a beast which thou hast; the males *shall be* the LORD'S. (Exo 13:12)

A **matrix** is mentioned five times in the AV.[59] This word comes from a Latin word of the same spelling meaning the womb. By application, a **matrix** can also be the point of origin and growth. **Matrix** is unanimously rendered as "womb" by our new versions, excepting the NIV, which neglected to translate the underlying word one time.[60] Moreover, many times when the AV reads "womb," the NIV, showing contempt for the other modern translations, omits the word completely.[61] Moreover, when the AV, followed by the NKJV, NRSV, and NIV says "kiss the Son," the NASB alone corrects it to "do homage to the Son."[62] The word **matrix** can be found in the twentieth century in the terms cartilage **matrix,** bone **matrix,** and mitochondrial **matrix.**

Matter

> Even so the tongue is a little member, and boasteth great things. Behold, how great a **matter** a little fire kindleth! (James 3:5)

The word **matter,** although appearing many times in the AV, is only found one time with this particular meaning. The word itself is from the French *matere,* originally referring to timbers or wood used as building materials, then the substance of which anything is made, and finally, the subject of a discourse or that which is under consideration. The word **matter** is remotely related to the word *mother.* Our new, up-to-date translations unite in rendering **matter** as "forest." But when the AV employs an uncomplicated word like "simple," it is replaced in the NASB to "naive" even though all of the other new translations read as the AV.[63]

Mattock

> But all the Israelites went down to the Philistines, to sharpen every man his share, and his coulter, and his ax, and his **mattock.** (1 Sam 13:20)

A **mattock** is mentioned in the AV twice in the singular[64] and twice in the plural.[65] It is from the Old English *mattuc,* "hoe." A **mattock** is an agricultural tool used for loosening hard ground or cutting roots. Today it might be called a pickax or a hoe. This word is thought to be related to *mace,* a medieval club, often with a spiked head, that was used as a weapon. Our modern versions have called **mattocks** a "hoe,"[66] "sickles,"[67] and "plowshares."[68] However, in two of these passages where the AV also mentions a "coulter," all of the new versions term it the supposedly archaic "**mattock.**"[69] Although it was corrected by modern Bible versions, a **mattock** nevertheless appears on the computer CD-ROM *3D Landscape,* as mentioned by *Forbes* magazine: "It will even tell you when you need a **mattock** and what a **mattock** looks like, in case you don't know. (It's a digging tool, part pick, part adze.)."[70]

Maul

> A man that beareth false witness against his neighbour *is* a **maul,** and a sword, and a sharp arrow. (Prov 25:18)

A **maul** is only mentioned once in the AV. The word is from the French *mail,* "mallet." A **maul** is a heavy hammer, club, or mallet. The word **maul** is unanimously given as "club" by our modern versions. **Maul** may be archaic, but changing "night" into "nocturnal" like the NASB, NIV, and NRSV did certainly can not be considered translating the Bible into up-to-date, modern English.[71]

Maw

> And this shall be the priest's due from the people, from them that offer a sacrifice, whether *it be* ox or sheep; and they shall give unto the priest the shoulder, and the two cheeks, and the **maw.** (Deu 18:3)

The word **maw** is also found only once in the AV. It is from the Old English *maga,* "stomach." The **maw** was originally the stomach, then specifically, the fourth stomach of a ruminant—a cud-chewing animal such as a cow or sheep. It also came to represent the throat, gullet, jaws, or mouth of an animal. The NRSV, NASB, and NKJV all united in replacing **maw** with "stomach." However, the NIV preferred "inner parts." But when the AV, followed by the NRSV, NASB, and NKJV, employed the phrase "inner part," the NIV altered it to the more difficult "sanctuary."[72] The execration of the word **maw** was entirely unnecessary, for it is still in use today both literally and figuratively. *National Wildlife* magazine used it literally: "Waves feed, shelter and transport a myriad of life-forms, often nourishing a rock-bound filter-feeder, then moments later knocking it into the **maw** of a hungry predator lurking below."[73] The word **maw** is also used figuratively: "Wherever you looked in the sky, or maybe under your own feet, it seemed as if the invisible cosmic **maw** was open and waiting."[74]

Mean

> And the **mean** man boweth down, and the great man humbleth himself: therefore forgive them not. (Isa 2:9)

The word **mean,** although found many times in the AV, occurs five times with this particular meaning.[75] The Old English form was *gemaene,* "common." Thus, **mean** denotes that which is common, undistinguished, inferior, unimportant, or of low degree. The word **mean** later developed into the now common definition of bad, malicious, or unkind. Obviously limiting its meaning to the later definition, our modern versions have replaced **mean** by such things as "common,"[76] "obscure,"[77] "unknown,"[78] "ordinary,"[79] and "insignificant."[80] However, the NKJV carelessly forgot to remove the word from one passage.[81]

Meat

> Every moving thing that liveth shall be **meat** for you; even as the green herb have I given you all things. (Gen 9:3)

Although the word **meat** is mentioned nearly 300 times in the AV, it always appears in a supposedly archaic sense. The same goes for the plural **meats,** which can be found eight times,[82] and **bakemeats,** found only once.[83] The word **meat** is from the Old English *mete,* "food." **Meat** was later restricted to just animal flesh, but originally referred to solid food in contrast to liquid drink. **Bakemeats,** although literally baked **meats,** are what we would call baked goods. The modern versions all update **meat** to "food" the vast majority of the time.[84] When the AV says "flesh," it is also usually changed to "**meat.**"[85] The only exception is the "**meat** offering," which is normally rendered as the "meal offering" or "grain offering."[86] Yet when the AV, followed by the NASB and NKJV, uses the plain word "herbs," the NRSV alters it to "herbage."[87]

Meet

> And the LORD God said, *It is* not good that the man should

be alone; I will make him an help **meet** for him. (Gen 2:18)

Although the word **meet** occurs a great number of times in the AV, it is used twenty-seven times with the meaning of proper, fitting, suitable, or becoming.[88] The word itself is from the Old English *gemaete*, "suitable." **Meet** is therefore related to the word *mete*. Our modern versions substituted words like "fitting,"[89] "proper,"[90] "right,"[91] "useful,"[92] "worthy,"[93] and "good"[94] for the supposedly archaic **meet**. The word **meet** may be archaic, but when the AV employs a simple word like "endless" the NIV, NRSV, and NASB remove it and substitute the more difficult "indestructible."[95]

Mess

> And he took *and sent* messes unto them from before him: but Benjamin's **mess** was five times so much as any of theirs. And they drank, and were merry with him. (Gen 43:34)

The word **mess** occurs in the AV twice in the singular[96] and once in the plural.[97] It is from the French *mes*, signifying a dish of food. A **mess** is a portion, share, ration, or allotment of food. Since the word **mess** is now commonly applied to a child's messy room, this word has been removed by our modern versions. The usual translation for **mess** and **messes** is "portion" and "portions."[98] But when the AV reads "portion," it is corrected by the NIV and NASB to "allotment," the NRSV to "allowance," and the NKJV to "rations."[99] The translators of these new versions have forgotten that every Army base in the 1990's has a **mess** hall.

Mete

> For with what judgment ye judge, ye shall be judged: and with what measure ye **mete,** it shall be measured to you again. (Mat 7:2)

The word **mete** appears six times in the AV,[100] while the form **meted** can be found three times.[101] **Mete** is from the Old English *metan*, "to measure." To **mete** is to allot, measure, distribute, or apportion. The usual translation for **mete** in the Old Testament is a form of "measure."[102] Yet when the AV, followed by the NKJV, NRSV, and NASB, reads "measured," the NIV altered it to "poured."[103] In the New Testament, **mete** is unanimously rendered as "use" by the NIV and NKJV, but the NRSV preferred "give."[104] Although it was corrected every time it occurred in the AV, **mete** was still used by two of our modern versions. The NIV inserts "**mete**" into a passage where the AV, NKJV, and NASB said "weigh."[105] The NASB updated the AV reading of "weigheth" to the archaic "**meted**."[106] The word **mete**, however, is definetely still in vogue today: "Unable to **mete** out punishment, rapporteurs can only publicly censure the countries they investigate."[107]

Meteyard

> Ye shall do no unrighteousness in judgment, in **meteyard**, in weight, or in measure. (Lev 19:35)

The word **meteyard** occurs only once in the AV. It was formed from the aforementioned verb *mete*. **Meteyard** is an old word for a measuring rod to measure length or a standard of measurement. Predictably, the NRSV and NIV alter **meteyard** to "measuring length." The NKJV used the slightly different "measurement of length." However, the NASB did not translate this term at all. But the fact that **meteyard** was archaic is no reason for the word "measures" in the AV to be corrected to "cors" by the NIV and NRSV and "kors" by the NKJV and NASB.[108]

Milch

> Thirty **milch** camels with their colts, forty kine, and ten bulls, twenty she asses, and ten foals. (Gen 32:15)

The word **milch** is only found three times in the AV.[109] **Milch** is from the Middle English *milche,* from the Old English *-milce* in *tri-milce,* "May," the month in which cows can be milked three times a day. The word **milch** is also related to the Old English *meolc,* "milk." **Milch** refers to an animal that is "in milk," one that gives milk, or one that is kept for milking. Only the NKJV consistently updates **milch** with "milk."[110] Surprisingly, the NRSV retained this supposedly archaic word in all three passages.[111] The NASB forgot to remove **milch** in two verses.[112] The NIV could not decide how to render **milch** so it employed three different words or phrases.[113]

Mill

> And all the firstborn in the land of Egypt shall die, from the firstborn of Pharaoh that sitteth upon his throne, even unto the firstborn of the maidservant that *is* behind the **mill**; and all the firstborn of beasts. (Exo 11:5)

A **mill** can be found twice in the AV in the singular[114] and once in the plural.[115] The related compound word **millstone** appears nine times in the singular[116] and twice in the plural.[117] **Mill** is from the Old English *myln,* borrowed from the Latin *molina,* "a **mill**," which is an extended form of *mola,* literally signifying "that which grinds." In the Bible, a **mill** was a machine consisting of two stones for grinding grain into meal; hence, a **millstone**. Thus, a **mill** was not a large device or building like it is so deemed today. Our modern versions usually altered **mill** to "handmill,"[118] "hand mill,"[119] or "millstones."[120] However, the NKJV and NASB were lax in updating **mill** in one verse.[121] The NRSV, after correcting **mill** twice,[122] inserted the word into two additional passages.[123] Then the NRSV keeps the AV reading of "**mills**" the only time it occurred.[124] **Mills** is then corrected by the other versions but never to the same thing.[125] But when it comes to the word **millstone** or **millstones,** the AV reading is kept every time with but minor variations.[126] Although a **mill** is commonly thought of today as a factory for manufacturing or processing, the word is still applied to machines that grind or shape various materials.

Minish

> And the officers of the children of Israel did see *that* they *were* in evil *case,* after it was said, Ye shall not **minish** *ought* from your bricks of your daily task. (Exo 5:19)

The word **minish**, found once in the AV, is from the French *menuisier,* "to make small." The form **minished** also occurs once.[127] To **minish** is to depreciate, make fewer in number or less in size, degree, power, or influence. Obviously, **minish** is a short form of *diminish.* Our new translations, excepting the NIV, updated **minish** to "diminish" in one passage.[128] However, in the verse where **minish** occurred, the NIV, NKJV, and NASB all chose "reduce" and the NRSV "lessen."[129] Moreover, when the AV reads "diminish," it is often corrected by the NKJV, NIV, and NASB to "reduce"[130] or "take away."[131]

Mite

> I tell thee, thou shalt not depart thence, till thou hast paid the very last **mite.** (Luke 12:59)

A **mite** is mentioned in the AV once in the singular and twice in the plural.[132] **Mite** is from the Dutch word *mite,* "a small insect," that came to be applied to a Flemish copper coin of very small value. The English also applied this term to an extremely small unit of money. Although the word **mite** is still used to describe a particular type of insect, its use as a unit of money is now archaic. Nevertheless, the NKJV retained **mite** and **mites** as the AV had them.[133] However, the other modern versions were not as consistent. Although the same underlying Greek word is found in all three passages, the NRSV and NASB both employ "small copper coins" twice,[134] but the NRSV preferred "penny" the other time and the NASB selected "cent."[135] The NIV made a **mite** a "very small copper coin" twice[136] and a "penny" once.[137]

Mitre

> And thou shalt put the **mitre** upon his head, and put the holy crown upon the **mitre.** (Exo 29:6)

A **mitre** is mentioned thirteen times in the AV.[138] The word is from the French *mitre,* "a cap." A **mitre** is a cap, headband, turban, headdress, or other type of ceremonial headwear normally part of religious attire. Our modern versions have unanimously altered **mitre** to "turban" in every instance. But when the AV just says "hats," the NKJV and NIV still change it to "turban."[139] **Mitre** cannot be that archaic since one can still see a **mitre** today on the head of every pope in the twentieth century.

Mollified

> From the sole of the foot even unto the head *there is* no soundness in it; *but* wounds, and bruises, and putrifying sores: they have not been closed, neither bound up, neither **mollified**

with ointment. (Isa 1:6)

The word **mollified**, formed from *mollify*, appears only once in the AV. *Mollify* is from the French *mollifier*, "to soften." Thus, to be **mollified** is to be softened, soothed, made tender, appeased, mitigated, or pacified. The NRSV and NASB united in replacing **mollified** with "softened," while the NIV and NKJV preferred "soothed." These corrections were hasty, however, for the word **mollified** is still in vogue: "Neighborhood activists were not **mollified**, but for illegal immigrants, it served notice that local officials were keeping tabs."[140]

Morrow

And the LORD did that thing on the **morrow**, and all the cattle of Egypt died: but of the cattle of the children of Israel died not one. (Exo 9:6)

The word **morrow** occurs in the AV 101 times in 99 verses.[141] **Morrow**, a doublet of *morn*, is from the Middle English *morwe*, a shortened form of *morwen*, "morning." **Morrow** can refer to the next day, the next morning, or the time immediately following a particular event. Fifty-four times in the AV the word **morrow** follows the word "to."[142] Understandably, these are all compounded to "tomorrow" by the new translations.[143] The other occurrences of **morrow** in the AV all take the form of "the morrow."[144] These are variously rendered the majority of the time as "tomorrow,"[145] "morning,"[146] and "the day."[147] But after correcting the AV ninety-eight times, the NASB forgot to remove the archaic "**morrow**" from three passages.[148]

Mortify

For if ye live after the flesh, ye shall die: but if ye through the Spirit do **mortify** the deeds of the body, ye shall live. (Rom 8:13)

The word **mortify**, appearing twice in the AV,[149] is from the French *mortifier*, "to make dead." **Mortify**, like our words *mortal, mortuary*, and *mortician*, is ultimately related to the Latin *mors*, "death," from *mori*, "to die." To **mortify** is to destroy, kill, render insensible, deprive of life, or destroy the vitality, vigour, or activity of. The usual translation found in our modern versions is a form of "put to death."[150] But if the modern versions considered **mortify** to be archaic, the *San Francisco Chronicle* certainly did not: "But this radio is one of those modern techno-things, like digital watches and microwave ovens, that seem to be designed with a secret agenda, which is to **mortify** us and break our spirits."[151]

Mote

> And why beholdest thou the **mote** that is in thy brother's eye, but perceivest not the beam that is in thine own eye? (Luke 6:41)

A **mote** is mentioned in the AV on six occasions.[152] The word is from the Old English *mot* that referred to a small speck. A **mote** was also later designated as a single straw of hay. A **mote** can be a speck of dirt or dust, a splinter or chip of wood, or any particle of foreign matter. Although every occurrence of the word **mote** was based on the same Greek word, the NIV rendered it twice as a "speck of sawdust"[153] and four times as just a "speck."[154] The other versions all changed **mote** to "speck."[155] But although our modern versions considered **mote** to be archaic, the *New York Times* did not: "But even one **mote** of dirt can short circuit a whole chip, so the workers inside clean rooms must wear Gore-Tex jumpsuits that keep foreign objects from escaping from their bodies, plus three pairs of repellant gloves and nonconductive shoes."[156]

Mufflers

> The chains, and the bracelets, and the **mufflers,** (Isa 3:19)

Mufflers are only mentioned once in the AV. A muffler is literally anything that muffles. Although its meaning today is usually limited to a car muffler, a muffler is also a kerchief or scarf worn by women to either conceal part of their face and neck or to protect them from cold or wind. Our modern versions preferred the word "scarfs" to update **mufflers,** except for the NASB, which selected "veils." **Mufflers** may be archaic but the introduction of the word "seine" into the Bible by the NRSV definitely does not make the Bible clearer.[157]

Munition

> He that dasheth in pieces is come up before thy face: keep the **munition,** watch the way, make *thy* loins strong, fortify *thy* power mightily. (Nahum 2:1)

A **munition** is mentioned in the AV twice in the singular[158] and once in the plural.[159] The word comes from the French *munition,* "a fortification." A **munition** is a fortification, defensive structure, or anything that serves as a defense or protection. **Munition** gradually came to mean weapons of war and what we now term ammunition. Since this word is now limited to military supplies, weapons, and ammunition, our modern versions remove all trace of it. However, only the NIV consistently renders it "fortress" every time.[160] The other translations are divided between "fortress,"[161] "stronghold,"[162] and "fort."[163] The NRSV, however, adopts the equally as archaic "ramparts."[164] But when the AV mentions "bulwarks" it is unanimously corrected to "siegeworks."[165] And when the AV says "forts," the NRSV, NKJV, and NIV change it to the harder "siegeworks" as well.[166]

Murrain

> Behold, the hand of the LORD is upon thy cattle which *is* in the field, upon the horses, upon the asses, upon the camels, upon the oxen, and upon the sheep: *there shall be* a very grievous **murrain.** (Exo 9:3)

A **murrain** is only mentioned once in the AV. The word is from the French *morine* and refers to a plague, pestilence, or disease, especially in cattle. The word **murrain,** like the aforementioned *mortify,* is ultimately related to the Latin *mori,* "to die." The NRSV and NASB preferred to render **murrain** as "pestilence," but the NIV and NKJV decided on "plague." Although **murrain** is not found in any of our modern versions, they often contain words that have been invented and appear in no other new translation. The NIV, for example, originates both the terms "highborn" and "lowborn," found in no other modern version.[167]

Chapter 14
Napkin to Nurture

Napkin

> And another came, saying, Lord, behold, *here is* thy pound, which I have kept laid up in a **napkin:** (Luke 19:20)

A **napkin** is mentioned three times in the AV.[1] The word itself is from the French *nape,* "cloth," with the diminutive English suffix *-kin*. Thus, a **napkin** is a small cloth. Throughout history a **napkin** has been any small towel or cloth used as absorbent material. A kerchief, neckerchief, or handkerchief can be a **napkin**. Due to their limiting the meaning of **napkin** to a dinner **napkin,** our modern versions have removed all trace of this word. But although the same Greek word is used in all three passages where **napkin** is found in the AV, the new translations never rendered it the same more than twice. The NRSV used "cloth" twice[2] but "piece of cloth" once.[3] The NKJV went with "handkerchief" twice[4] and "cloth" once.[5] The NIV and NASB both employed three different terms to update **napkin**. The NASB liked "handkerchief," "cloth," and "face-cloth,"[6] while the NIV preferred "piece of cloth," "cloth," and "burial cloth."[7] Yet in the 1960's, British medical dictionaries referred to a diaper as **napkin**.[8] And in the 1990's, the term **napkin** is applied to a woman's sanitary **napkin**.

Nativity

> And Haran died before his father Terah in the land of his **nativity,** in Ur of the Chaldees. (Gen 11:28)

The word **nativity** appears seven times in the AV.[9] This has come into English from the French *nativite,* "birth." **Nativity** refers to ones birth with reference to descent or national identity. This word is usually rendered as "birth" in our modern versions,[10] but sometimes "origin"[11] or "native."[12] After correcting the AV reading of **nativity** twice,[13] the NKJV retains this supposedly archaic word five times.[14] But if **nativity** is so archaic, then why do we still see **nativity** scenes every Christmas in the 1990's?

Naught

> And the men of the city said unto Elisha, Behold, I pray thee, the situation of this city *is* pleasant, as my lord seeth: but the water *is* **naught,** and the ground barren. (2 Ki 2:19)

The word **naught** occurs three times in the AV.[15] It appeared in Old English as *nawiht,* from *na,* "no," and *whit,* "thing." Thus, **naught** literally means "no thing." From **naught** has derived two basic meanings, only one of which is found in the AV. **Naught** can be an alternate form of *nought,* meaning nothing, or it can mean wicked, evil, worthless, wayward, unacceptable, or mischief. This later meaning is also found in the AV in the words **naughty,** appearing three times,[16] and **naughtiness,** also found three times.[17] Thus, **naught, naughty,** and **naughtiness** all denote something bad. These words have all been removed by our modern versions when they appear in the AV. They have been replaced by such things as "bad,"[18] "wickedness,"[19] "evil,"[20] "greed,"[21] "poor,"[22] "malicious,"[23] "scoundrel,"[24] and "spiteful."[25] However, the NRSV inserts **naught** into two passages where the AV did not contain the word.[26] Moreover, when the AV simply reads "nothing," the NIV corrects it to the archaic "**naught.**"[27] And furthermore, in one verse where the word **naughtiness** appears in the AV, the NRSV alters "filthiness" to the more difficult "sordidness."[28] The NKJV considered **naughtiness** so difficult that it replaced it in one place with the not well know word "insolence."[29] All these corrections were frivolous, for the various forms of the word **naught** are still used today. Children are still said to be **naughty** and **naught** can be found used just as the NIV corrected the word "nothing" in the AV: "He was certainly helped by the intelligence we supplied, and his efforts would have been for **naught** without Beria's talent in mobilizing the nation's resources."[30]

Naves

> And the work of the wheels *was* like the work of a chariot wheel: their axletrees, and their **naves,** and their felloes, and their spokes, *were* all molten. (1 Ki 7:33)

Naves are only mentioned once in the AV. The word is from the Old English *nafu* in the feminine and *nafa* in the masculine. **Naves** are the hubs of wheels. Naturally, the new versions have removed the word **naves** since it is archaic. But when the AV uses an easy word like "temple," it is replaced by the NASB and NRSV with "nave."[31]

Nay

> And there was much murmuring among the people concerning him: for some said, He is a good man: others said, **Nay;** but he deceiveth the people. (John 7:12)

The word **nay** occurs fifty-five times in the AV in fifty verses.[32] **Nay** is from the Old English *nei,* "no," a compound of *ne,* "not," and *ei,* "ever." **Nay** is used to express negation, dissent, or denial; hence, it can mean just plain "no." **Nay** can also mean indeed, also, and not only. Like the word *yea,* **nay** was formerly utilized when the preceding statement had no negative word in it; when a negative was communicated, yes or no was the usual answer.[33] Our modern versions have completely eliminated the word **nay,** usually substituting "no,"[34] but also "on the contrary,"[35] "rather,"[36] "yes,"[37] "indeed,"[38] or "instead."[39] But in addition to the word **nay** continually employed in the phrase "**nay**-sayers," and in addition to the word **nay** being uttered every day Congress has a vote, the word **nay** is also very much alive today in other senses: "Surely no one could have foreseen the incredible popularity—**nay,** addictiveness—of electronic mail."[40]

Necromancer

> Or a charmer, or a consulter with familiar spirits, or a wizard, or a **necromancer.** (Deu 18:11)

A **necromancer** is only mentioned once in the AV. A **necromancer** is one who practices necromancy. Necromancy is from the French *nigromancie*. The original form was the Greek *nekromanteia*, a combination of *nekros*, "dead" and *manteia*, "divination." Thus, necromancy is divination by the dead; a **necromancer** foretells the future by communication with the dead. Due to being considered the black art, the *necro-* prefix was altered to *negro-* after the Latin *niger*, "black." Although the Middle English form was *negromancie*, the original *necro-* has been restored in the modern English period. Our modern versions have all united in eliminating **necromancer** from the Bible; however, they could not agree on the proper translation. The NASB preferred "calls up the dead," the NRSV "seeks oracles from the dead," the NIV "consults the dead," and the NKJV "calls up the dead." Although a **necromancer** cannot be found in any modern version, they all had no trouble using the word "enchanter."[41] But four times when the AV uses a form of the word "enchantments," the NRSV replaces it with the obscure, cryptic term "augury."[42] Moreover, when the AV employs the simple words *witch* and *wizard*, they are corrected as well. A "witch" in the AV is a "sorceress," or a "female sorcerer," as the NRSV puts it.[43] A "wizard" in the AV is a "spirtist" in the NASB, NIV, and NKJV.[44] And finally, "witchcraft" in the AV has been changed to "divination" in the NRSV, NIV, and NASB.[45] But not only are these words still in common use, the word **necromancer** is also: "If you put a mage, sorceress, wizard, warlock, witch, or **necromancer** into fantasy, it's more than likely that they will want, sooner or later to work some magic."[46]

Needlework

> And thou shalt make an hanging for the door of the tent, *of* blue, and purple, and scarlet, and fine twined linen, wrought with **needlework**. (Exo 26:36)

Needlework is mentioned nine times in the AV.[47] It is manifestly a compound of *needle* and *work* and simply means work done with a needle such as embroidery, tapestry, crochet, or quilting. Surprisingly, the NASB retains the AV reading in six passages.[48] The NIV consistently rendered **needlework** by forms of "embroider."[49] The NASB was somewhat consistent in that it termed **needlework** the "work of a weaver" most of the time.[50] But the NKJV could not decide among forms of "weaver,"[51] "woven,"[52] "embroider,"[53] and "many colors."[54] Yet the word **needlework** was not archaic in the first place, at least according to the citizens and newspaper of San Jose, California: "At the Tapestry in Talent Festival in San Jose last weekend, we ate Thai food, bought Hmong **needlework** and listened to Peruvian and African music."[55]

Neesings

> By his **neesings** a light doth shine, and his eyes *are* like the eyelids of the morning. (Job 41:18)

The word **neesings,** appearing only once in the AV, is a variant of *neezing,* from *neeze,* originally *fnesen,* from which we derived *snesen* and then *neeze.* Our modern word *sneeze* is the only form that has survived. The new versions quite naturally update **neesings** to forms of "sneeze," but the NIV selected "snorting." **Neesings** is obviously archaic, but what is not so obvious is why the NASB revised "worm" to "grub" when all the other versions followed the AV reading.[56]

Nephew

> He shall neither have son nor **nephew** among his people, nor any remaining in his dwellings. (Job 18:19)

The word **nephew** occurs in the AV twice in the singular[57] and twice in the plural.[58] **Nephew** is from the French *neveu.* This in turn is from the Latin *nepos,* which could refer to a grandson or descendant. Since the modern conception of a **nephew** is only that of a brother or sister's son, our modern versions have omitted **nephew** and **nephews** from the text of the Bible. **Nephews** is unanimously rendered as "grandsons" in one passage[59] and "grandchildren" in another.[60] **Nephew** is replaced with "posterity"[61] or "descendant."[62] But it should be pointed out that nepotism, from the same Latin source, is favoritism shown toward relatives not just **nephews.**

Nether

> And Moses brought forth the people out of the camp to meet with God; and they stood at the **nether** part of the mount. (Exo 19:17)

The word **nether** occurs fifteen times in the AV.[63] The extended form **nethermost** is found only once.[64] **Nether** is from the Old English *neothera*, "lower," and was originally a comparative adjective related to *neothor*, "downward." **Nether** is normally rendered as "lower" in the modern versions,[65] but is also found as "below"[66] and "foot."[67] The NASB neglected to remove the supposedly archaic **nether** from one passage.[68] But even though our new, up-to-date translations considered **nether** to be archaic, *Popular Science* magazine did not: "And by managing to simulate in their laboratories the hellish conditions that exist in the **nether** regions, geophysicists have established that the temperature of the core is probably hotter than the surface of the sun."[69]

Nigh

And he said, Draw not **nigh** hither: put off thy shoes from off thy feet, for the place whereon thou standest *is* holy ground. (Exo 3:5)

The word **nigh** appears 100 times in the AV.[70] The Old English form was *neah*. **Nigh**, which originally had the comparative form *near* and the superlative form *next*, literally signifies "that which reaches to" or "that which suffices." The common meaning of **nigh** is simply near. Thus, **nigh** denotes proximity in place, time, or position. The usual substitution for **nigh** in our modern versions is "near." Occasionally however, one can find "on the verge,"[71] "close,"[72] "at hand,"[73] or forms of "approach."[74] Yet when the AV, followed by all of the other new versions, just says "near," the NIV alters it to "approached."[75] But the word **nigh** was not archaic anyway: "Jamaica has had a two party democracy from 1944. The parliamentary system has survived for **nigh** 50 years."[76]

Nitre

As he that taketh away a garment in cold weather, *and as* vinegar upon **nitre**, so *is* he that singeth songs to an heavy heart. (Prov 25:20)

Nitre, mentioned only twice in the AV,[77] is from a French word of the same spelling. **Nitre** is sodium carbonate, and was taken from salt deposits and used as a cleansing agent. Thinking **nitre** to be an archaic word, our modern versions have expurgated it from the Bible. It is rendered as either "soda"[78] or "lye."[79] The NRSV curiously supplants **nitre** with "a wound" in one passage.[80] Yet even the *Washington Post* recognized the existence of **nitre:** "During the past 15 years, the review has eliminated certain products from the market such as daytime sedatives, oral insect repellents, camphorated oil, spirits of **nitre,** aphrodisiac and baldness tonics, as well as certain cough tablets containing chloroform that in high concentrations is lethal."[81]

Noised

> And again he entered into Capernaum after *some* days; and it was **noised** that he was in the house. (Mark 2:1)

The word **noised,** occurring four times in the AV,[82] is simply the verb form of the word *noise*. To noise can mean to make a noise, spread a rumor, discuss something, or report an event. Since **noised** in its use as a verb has been deemed archaic by all modern translations, the word has been unanimously corrected to "talked about,"[83] "reported,"[84] "spread,"[85] and "discussed."[86] Yet when the AV does use the noun "noise," it is changed to "tumult" by the NRSV and NIV.[87] The word **noised,** however, can still be found in use today: "American society still wrestles with many of the issues **noised** at 23 Fifth Avenue."[88]

Noisome

> And the first went, and poured out his vial upon the earth; and there fell a **noisome** and grievous sore upon the men which had the mark of the beast, and *upon* them which worshipped his image. (Rev 16:2)

The word **noisome** appears four times in the AV.[89] **Noisome** is not at all related to *noise* and its derivatives. It is from *noy,* the aphetic form of *annoy,* and the suffix *-some*. Hence, to be **noisome** is to be annoying or bad. Each of our modern versions uses three different words to update **noisome**. The NRSV choose "deadly," "wild," and "foul," but the NIV preferred "deadly," "wild," and "loathsome."[90] The NKJV selected "perilous," "wild," and "foul," while the NIV settled on "deadly," "wild," and "loathsome."[91] All these corrections were entirely unnecessary, for the word **noisome** is still in current use: "But real connoisseurs of malodorousness, like composting consultant Clark Gregory, a soil scientist who has helped communities compost such **noisome** waste products as chicken manure and scallop guts, will tell you differently."[92]

Noontide

> And let that man be as the cities which the LORD overthrew, and repented not: and let him hear the cry in the morning, and the shouting at **noontide**; (Jer 20:16)

The word **noontide** occurs only once in the AV. It appeared in Old English as *nontid*, "noon time." Thus, **noontide** simply means at noon or noontime. As expected, our modern versions unanimously update **noontide** to just plain "noon." However, the NRSV injected this supposedly archaic word into a verse where neither the AV nor any modern version contained the word.[93] But when the AV simply reads "noon," it is often extended for no reason. The NRSV and NIV both lengthen "noon" to "noonday,"[94] while the NASB extends it to "noontime."[95] The word "night" in the AV is similarly corrected. The NIV extends "night" to both "nightfall" and "nighttime."[96] And furthermore, the NRSV also uses the archaic "forenoon."[97] But the word **noontide** can still be found in use today: "There are plenty of **noontide** demons in this utterly original novel, which tracks the rudderless wanderings of a young couple who break into Florida vacation homes and attempt to assume the lives of the inhabitants."[98]

Nought

> But why dost thou judge thy brother? or why dost thou set at **nought** thy brother? for we shall all stand before the judgment seat of Christ. (Rom 14:10)

The word **nought** occurs thirty-six times in the AV[99] and is a variant of *naught*. **Nought** simply means nothing, and is so translated the majority of times in the modern versions. However, after correcting "naught" every time it appeared, the NRSV substituted "naught" for the AV reading of **nought**.[100] Then when the AV read "nothing," the NIV and NRSV changed it to the archaic "naught."[101] But **nought** is not archaic anyway. The expression "**nought** feet" refers to being very close to the ground.[102] Even the New York *Newsday* did not consider the word **nought** to be archaic: "But all this counts for **nought** in the face of a picture of a stick-thin child silently imploring us for help."[103]

Nurture

And, ye fathers, provoke not your children to wrath: but bring them up in the **nurture** and admonition of the Lord. (Eph 6:4)

The word **nurture** is found only once in the AV. It is from the French *noriture*, "to nourish." **Nurture** means breeding, training, education, discipline, or rearing. The words **nurture**, *nutriment, nourish,* and *nurse* are all ultimately derived from the Latin *nutrire*, "to nourish." **Nurture** is replaced in our modern versions by either "discipline"[104] or "training."[105] But when the AV, followed by the NKJV and NRSV, reads "brought up," the NIV corrects it to "nurtured."[106] The NIV also inserts "well-nurtured" into another passage.[107] On two occasions where the AV reads "nourished," the NASB revised it to the supposedly archaic "nurtured."[108] The word **nurture** is certainly still in vogue, as here witnessed by *Money* magazine: "Most teachers are dying for young, motivated minds to **nurture**."[109]

Chapter 15
Obeisance to Overcharge

Obeisance

And he dreamed yet another dream, and told it his brethren, and said, Behold, I have dreamed a dream more; and, behold, the sun and the moon and the eleven stars made **obeisance** to me. (Gen 37:9)

The word **obeisance** occurs nine times in the AV[1] and is from the French *obeissance*, "obedience." **Obeisance** is an expression of respect or submission, often involving a bowing down of the body. Our modern versions usually alter the word to a form of "bow down"[2] or "prostrated himself."[3] Sometimes **obeisance** was corrected to "homage"[4] or "honor."[5] One time the NIV substituted "knelt."[6] Surprisingly however, the NRSV only altered the word on three occasions.[7] In fact, the NRSV liked this supposedly archaic word so much that it inserted it thirteen additional times.[8] No other new translation utilizes the word **obeisance** anywhere. In seven instances, the NRSV replaced the elementary phrase "bowed himself" found in the AV to "**obeisance**."[9] The NASB likewise corrected the simple "bowed himself" to the more onerous "prostrated himself."[10] The NIV, considered to be in modern, contemporary English, also exchanged "bowed himself" for "prostrated himself."[11] Although the NKJV, NIV, and NASB could not handle the word **obeisance**, the *Washington Post* had not trouble with it: "No longer, in most places, does a nurse's question about treatment have to be hidden in a ritual of **obeisance**."[12]

Oblation

As for the **oblation** of the firstfruits, ye shall offer them unto the LORD: but they shall not be burnt on the altar for a sweet savour. (Lev 2:12)

The word **oblation** appears thirty-five times in the AV in the singular and five in the plural.[13] It comes from the French *oblation*, "offering." An **oblation** is a sacrifice or offering, usually made to God or a god. Our modern versions overwhelmingly rendered **oblation** as "offering."[14] Occasionally, however, **oblations** were made into "contributions"[15] or "sacrifices."[16] In addition to not even being translated,[17] forms of **oblation** were also expressed as "allotment,"[18] or "district."[19] They could also be found as "portion"[20] and "special portion,"[21] or "gifts"[22] and "special gift."[23] Yet when the AV reads "offering," it is sometimes corrected to "contribution."[24] And even worse than this, on two occasions the AV says "sacrifice" and the NRSV emends it to "**oblation**."[25] The word **oblation**, however, was no problem for the magazine *National Review:* "Here, it would seem, is something on the order of an **oblation**—an offering, by the people of the United States, to the emblem of their country."[26]

Occupy

> And he called his ten servants, and delivered them ten pounds, and said unto them, **Occupy** till I come. (Luke 19:13)

The base form **occupy** is found only twice in the AV.[27] Other forms include: **occupiers**-found once,[28] **occupied**-found seven times,[29] and **occupieth**-found once.[30] The word *occupy* is from the French *occuper*, "to seize." It is remotely related to the word *capture*, as both words are derived from the Latin *capere*, meaning to take, hold, or seize. The problem with the various forms of **occupy** in the AV is the manner in which they are used; yet, even the modern uses of the word **occupy** incorporate several shades of meaning. One can **occupy** a position or place. This usage is found once in the AV[31] as well as in our modern versions.[32] One can **occupy** land, as by military invasion. Our new translations likewise contain this meaning of the word.[33] To **occupy** can mean engaging one's attention. The AV employs this sense of the word[34] as does our modern versions.[35] It can also mean to be busy at something. Our new translations also use **occupy** in this fashion.[36] The specific problem is the use of the word in nine other passages in the AV. In two of these, **occupy** appears in the sense of something being used for a particular task.[37] Our modern versions unanimously render these as "used."[38] The seven other occurrences of forms of the word **occupy** broadly concern doing business. Evidently, our new translations could not decide on how to update the various forms of the word. Four times the AV uses the form **occupied**,[39] and four times the NIV renders **occupied** by a different word or phrase.[40] The NKJV twice used "traded"[41] and the NRSV twice employed "exchanged,"[42] but the NASB preferred "paid," using it three times.[43] The AV uses the base form **occupy** twice.[44] This has been rendered six different ways by our four modern versions. The NRSV selected "barter" and "do business," the NASB adopted "deal" and "do business," and the NKJV chose "market" and "do business."[45] The NIV, after using "trade" the first time,[46] employed five words ("put this money to work") to correct one word in the AV.[47] The final form of **occupy** in the AV appears as **occupiers**.[48] This was rendered three different ways: "dealers" in the NASB and NRSV, "merchants" in the NIV, and "merchandisers" in the NKJV.[49] Yet every modern version uses the related word "occupation" in the same sense that the AV employs **occupy, occupiers,** and **occupied**.[50] And furthermore, these new translations consistently update archaic words while leaving intact plain, ordinary words. The NASB corrected "take" in the AV to "**occupy**" when the other modern versions followed the AV.[51] The NIV replaced "possess" in the AV with "**occupy**" in two passages where the other new translations read "possess" as the AV.[52] Obviously, consistency was not the occupation of the translators of our modern versions.

Occurrent

> But now the LORD my God hath given me rest on every side, *so that there is* neither adversary nor evil **occurrent**. (1 Ki 5:4)

The word **occurrent** appears only once in the AV. It is from the French *occurrent,* "an occurrence." An **occurrent** is something that occurs; an event, action, fact, or incident. The modern form of this word is *occurrence.* The older form **occurrent** is nevertheless more etymologically correct, for the Latin root of the base form *occur* was formed by the addition of the prefix *o-* to *currere,* "to run," from which we get our modern word *current.* Many times the Old English is much more descriptive and accurate. One would think that our modern versions could easily update **occurrent** to *occurrence.* However, the NRSV and NASB alter "evil **occurrent**" in the AV to "misfortune," while the NIV chose the word "disaster." If the translators of these modern versions had only looked in the *Journal of the American Medical Association* they would have seen a modern usage of the word **occurrent,** for in 1993 an article appeared entitled: "Periconceptional folic acid exposure and risk of **occurrent** neutral tube defects."[53]

Odd

> And thou shalt give the money, wherewith the **odd** number of them is to be redeemed, unto Aaron and to his sons. (Num 3:48)

The word **odd** appears only once in the AV. The Middle English form was *odde.* **Odd** originally referred to a pointed object; then a triangle, from which it was connected with the number three; and finally, one left over from two. From this developed four distinct meanings: an **odd** number—a number not divisible by two; something extra or left over; peculiar, strange, or bizarre; irregular or approximately. Our modern versions altered the word **odd** to "excess," except for the NIV, which preferred the word "additional." Yet the word **odd** is still commonly used today as it is in the AV: "Japan finished the year as the **odd** man out."[54]

Odious

> For an **odious** *woman* when she is married; and an handmaid that is heir to her mistress. (Prov 30:23)

The word **odious** is found on two occasions in the AV[55] and is from the French *odieus,* "hated." To be **odious** is to be offensive, disgusting, detestable, hateful, or repugnant. This supposedly archaic word was not only left in one verse by the NASB and NRSV,[56] it was also inserted in seven others by the NASB[57] and five others by the NRSV.[58] On two of these occasions, the simple words "stink" and "stank" in the AV were the ones corrected to "**odious**."[59] The NIV, after replacing **odious** with "stench" and "unloved,"[60] injected the word into another passage where neither the AV nor any other modern version used it.[61] Although the NKJV decided to modify **odious** to "repulsive" and "hateful,"[62] The *San Diego Union-Tribune* saw no problem with using the word: "A payroll tax to pay for health care is more **odious** to many employers than premiums and would drive some businesses out of state, they say."[63]

Offend

> But whoso shall **offend** one of these little ones which believe in me, it were better for him that a millstone were hanged about his neck, and *that* he were drowned in the depth of the sea. (Mat 18:6)

The word **offend** occurs twenty-five times in the AV,[64] as does the form **offended**.[65] This word comes from the French *offendre*, "to strike against." The English words *defend, defense,* **offend**, and *offense* are all ultimately derived from the Latin *fendere*, "to strike." To **offend** can mean to irritate, anger, hurt, or cause to stumble. Intransitively, it means to sin or transgress. The main problem with the word **offend** is the way it is used in the AV, for in the AV it usually refers to causing one to stumble. Our modern versions usually correct the AV because of this.[66] The NKJV retains the AV reading in ten instances,[67] but only the AV consistently translates the underlying word in the New Testament, *skandalizo,* from which we get *scandal* and *scandalize,* by a form of **offend**. Our modern versions variously render *skandalizo* as "deserters,"[68] "put a stumbling block,"[69] "stumble,"[70] "led into sin,"[71] "offense,"[72] "fall away,"[73] "offended,"[74] "turn away,"[75] "makes you stumble,"[76] and "causes you to sin."[77] This shows again that it is not just the AV that is inconsistent when translating Greek words.

Offscouring

> Being defamed, we entreat: we are made as the filth of the world, *and are* the **offscouring** of all things unto this day. (1 Cor 4:13)

Offscouring, found twice in the AV,[78] is a compound made up of the prefix *off-* attached to the verb *scour,* from the Dutch *schuren,* "to clean." The original signification was "to take care of," from the Latin *curare,* derived from *cura,* "care." To be the **offscouring** is to be what is scoured off; filth or refuse cleaned off and thrown away. Only the NKJV retains this word in both passages.[79] The NIV updates **offscouring** to "scum" and "refuse,"[80] but when the AV reads "scum," it is corrected to "deposit."[81] The NRSV preferred to modify **offscouring** to "filth" and "dregs,"[82] but when the AV used the word "filth," it was corrected to "rubbish."[83] The NASB forgot to update "**offscouring**" in one passage while using "dregs" in the other.[84] So not only is the somewhat difficult word *dregs* left as it appears in the AV,[85] the NRSV and NASB also replace the simpler **offscouring** with it.[86] But what should one expect out of a version like the NRSV that replaces a simple word in the AV like "softly" with "dejectedly."[87]

Oft

> Then came to him the disciples of John, saying, Why do we and the Pharisees fast **oft,** but thy disciples fast not? (Mat 9:14)

The word **oft** is found thirteen times in the AV.[88] Rather than being a short form of the word *often,* it is the other way around: *often* is an extended form of **oft**. However, the AV also contains the word "often" and the two words are used interchangeably.[89] The AV also includes the form **oftener** one time.[90] **Oft** means frequently, many times, or repeatedly. The word is not found in our modern versions. It is usually rendered as "often,"[91] but sometimes as "whenever,"[92] "again and again,"[93] "repeatedly,"[94] or "many times."[95] One time the NASB and NIV do not even translate the word.[96] The word **oft,** however, is not archaic at all, for it is still used today as a prefix in adjective compounds: "Sanders was so hyped for the game he got into his silly **oft**-replayed fight with Rison the first time they lined up across from each other in the game."[97]

Ofttimes

> Lord, have mercy on my son: for he is a lunatick, and sore vexed: for **ofttimes** he falleth into the fire, and oft into the

water. (Mat 17:15)

Ofttimes occurs three times in the AV.[98] It is plainly a compound made up of *oft* and *times*. **Ofttimes** was originally *oftsithes*, plural of *oftsithe*. *Sithe* was a word for time. The AV also contains the form **oftentimes** in six instances.[99] **Ofttimes** and **oftentimes** are synonyms of *oft* and *often*, and are used interchangeably in the AV.[100] Other than the NASB forgetting to update "**oftentimes**" in one passage,[101] our new versions have expurgated these words from the Bible. The claim is also made that the AV was inconsistent in translating "oft" and **ofttimes** in some passages and "often" and **oftentimes** in others. But how do these new translations handle the underlying Greek words? The word *pollakis,* rendered in the AV as "oft," "often," **ofttimes,** and **oftentimes,**[102] although generally given as "often" in our modern versions,[103] can also be found translated by several other words. The NKJV used "repeatedly,"[104] while the NIV preferred "many times,"[105] "many a time,"[106] and "again and again."[107] The NASB selected "time after time,"[108] while the NRSV chose "again and again"[109] and "repeatedly."[110] So much for the AV being inconsistent. At least it used forms all derived from the same word. And furthermore, if **ofttimes** is so archaic, then it should have never appeared in the *New England Journal of Medicine:* "As many as 10 percent of patients with pulmonary emboli have an associated, **ofttimes** occult, cancer."[111]

𝔒𝔦𝔩𝔢𝔡

And one loaf of bread, and one cake of **oiled** bread, and one wafer out of the basket of the unleavened bread that *is* before the LORD: (Ex 29:23)

The word **oiled** is formed from the word *oil* and occurs twice in the AV.[112] It has been omitted from our up-to-date, contemporary, new versions due to the modern conception of a car or piece of machinery being **oiled,** not a piece of bread. To be **oiled** is to be smeared, lubricated, or moistened with oil—not necessarily motor oil. Our modern translations normally change **oiled** to "made with oil"[113] or "mixed with oil,"[114] but the NKJV one time described bread as being "anointed with oil."[115] The word **oiled,** however, is certainly used today when not referring to a piece of equipment lubricated with machine oil.

Bodybuilders don't put motor oil on their muscles: "Consider the muscle: strings of highly motile tissue, most notable perhaps when developed, **oiled** and pumped in the public displays for which humans are best known."[116] The word **oiled** is also used figuratively: "The automakers say they've been forced to defend themselves against a well-**oiled** onslaught from environmental groups who've organized their massive grassroots memberships to press for higher mileage standards."[117] It is strange that a modern version like the NASB would worry about the word **oiled** when it replaced a simple word in the AV like "sinner" with "culprits."[118]

Omnipotent

> And I heard as it were the voice of a great multitude, and as the voice of many waters, and as the voice of mighty thunderings, saying, Alleluia: for the Lord God **omnipotent** reigneth. (Rev 19:6)

The word **omnipotent** appears only once in the AV. Although it comes into English from an identical French word, most will recognize it as a compound of the Latin *omnis,* "all," and *potens,* "powerful." To be **omnipotent** is to be all-powerful, capable of anything. Only the NKJV retains this word. Although **omnipotent** is still used in most theology books to describe God,[119] the NIV, NASB, and NRSV replaced the word with "Almighty." But the word **omnipotent** can be found in use today—even when it is not referring to God: "But when Orestes Lorenzo can fly in and Alina Fernandez can get out disguised as a tourist, the perception of the **omnipotent,** monolithic state begins to crumble."[120]

Operation

> Because they regard not the works of the LORD, nor the **operation** of his hands, he shall destroy them, and not build them up. (Psa 28:5)

The word **operation** is found in the AV three times in the singular and once in the plural.[121] It comes from the French *operation,* "a work." Hence, an **operation** can refer to a military expedition, a business venture, a manner of functioning, a manufacturing process, or a mathematical procedure. Since the word is commonly applied to a surgical procedure, our modern versions thought it best to alter the word. The NKJV, however, forgot to correct two passages in the Old Testament,[122] while changing the two New Testament occurrences to "activities" and "working."[123] The NASB utilizes four words (deeds, work, effects, working) to correct the AV,[124] as does the NIV.[125] The NRSV altered **operation** to "work" on two occasions,[126] but could not decide between "activities" and "power" the other two times.[127] Yet when the AV uses a simple word like work, it is corrected by the NRSV to "service," the NIV to "thing," and the NASB to "deed."[128] Other times it is rendered as "task."[129] When the AV reads "power," that too is sometimes corrected by the NASB, NRSV, and NIV.[130] But in addition to the word **operation** being used in the 1990's for a military campaign like **Operation** Desert Storm, this term was also used to describe the efficient system of package delivery of Federal Express: "The logistics of coordinating such an **operation** are daunting."[131]

𝔒𝔯𝔞𝔠𝔩𝔢

> And for the entering of the **oracle** he made doors *of* olive tree: the lintel *and* side posts *were* a fifth part *of the wall.* (1 Ki 6:31)

The word **oracle** appears seventeen times in the AV in the singular[132] and four in the plural.[133] It comes into English from the French *oracle,* which was derived from the Latin *orare,* "to pray." An **oracle** is someone or something regarded as an infallible guide. It is also a place where divine revelation is obtained. Although the word **oracle** is found in every one of our modern versions more than it is in the AV, it is ordinarily used in a different sense. The problem is that the AV uses **oracle** to describe a place and not just a divine word or prophecy. This place is usually given as "inner sanctuary" in our new translations.[134] In the Old Testament, the NRSV contains the word **oracle** thirty-five times in the singular[135] and five in the plural.[136] The AV is corrected every time but one,[137] and words like "parable"[138] and "prophecy"[139] and "burden"[140] are changed to "**oracle**." Then the word "**oracle**-priests" is invented to correct "branches" in the AV.[141] The NASB uses **oracle** thirty-two times in the Old Testament in the singular[142] and twice in the plural.[143]

Every occurrence of **oracle** in the AV is changed. Like the NRSV, the NASB also replaces such words in the AV as "prophecy"[144] and "burden"[145] with "**oracle.**" The NASB further needlessly corrects the AV by changing "liars" to "oracle priests."[146] The NIV employs "**oracle**" a whopping forty-four times in the singular[147] and once in the plural.[148] Once again, the AV is corrected every time and the word "**oracle**" is substituted for such elementary words in the AV as "prophecy,"[149] "parable,"[150] and "burden."[151] In the Old Testament, the NKJV contains an "**oracle**" seventeen times[152] and "**oracles**" once.[153] However, the AV is only followed one time.[154] Obviously, our modern versions limited an **oracle** to divine word or prophecy. Yet in the New Testament, when the AV uses the word **oracles** four times to translate *logion,* it is still corrected.[155] Only the NKJV follows the AV in every instance in the New Testament.[156] The NASB preferred "utterances" one time,[157] while the NRSV selected "very words" to revise **oracles** in the AV.[158] The NIV translates *logion* by three different words or phrases (words, truths, very words).[159] So after all the revision in the Old Testament—adding to or subtracting **oracle** from the AV—the NIV still doesn't retain the word in the New Testament even though it is used exactly like the NIV uses it in the Old Testament. Contrary to all of our new translations, the word **oracle** is not always used in the 1990's to refer to something spoken or prophesied or revealed. A man can be an **oracle,** like Thomas Jefferson, "Democracy's greatest **oracle,**"[160] or Barry Goldwater, "the **Oracle** of Paradise Valley."[161] So just as in the Bible, the thing that gives an **oracle** can be referred to as an **oracle.**

Oration

> And upon a set day Herod, arrayed in royal apparel, sat upon his throne, and made an **oration** unto them. (Acts 12:21)

The word **oration** occurs but once in the AV. Although it is based on a French word of the same spelling, it is ultimately derived, like the abovementioned word *oracle,* from the Latin *orare,* "to pray." Thus, an **oration** can be an official prayer, a formal speech, or other form of public discourse. While the NKJV reads as the AV, the NIV and NRSV updated **oration** to "public address," but the NIV preferred just plain "address." Yet in the same verse where **oration** occurs, the NASB replaced the word "throne" in the AV with the more difficult "rostrum." But does anyone still give an **oration** in the twentieth century? The *Associated Press* thinks so: "In his fulsome **oration,** Squicciarini gave a glowing account of Waldheim's tenure as U.N. Secretary-General from 1972-1982."[162]

Osprey

> But these *are they* of which ye shall not eat: the eagle, and the ossifrage, and the **osprey,** (Deu 14:12)

The **osprey** is mentioned twice in the AV.[163] The word is from the French *osfraie,* derived from the Latin *ossifraga,* which has also passed into English as the name of a bird. An **osprey** is a large bird of prey. Its technical name is *pandion haliaetus.* In each instance that this bird is mentioned, the NKJV and NASB call it a "buzzard."[164] Surprisingly, the NRSV forgets to modernize this supposedly archaic word both places in which it occurs.[165] The NIV, after twice correcting **osprey** to "black vulture,"[166] transforms the "gier eagle," found twice in the AV, to an "**osprey.**"[167] But if there is no such thing as an **osprey,** then why is it mentioned in the *Washington Post* in 1994? "Did a parent of the unhatched embryo kill two baby Velociraptors and bring them to the nest for food, much as a modern **osprey** or eagle would do?"[168] The **osprey** is also the name of a Bell helicopter: the V-22.

Ossifrage

> And these *are they which* ye shall have in abomination among the fowls; they shall not be eaten, they *are* an abomination: the eagle, and the **ossifrage,** and the osprey, (Lev 11:13)

The **ossifrage** is also found twice in the AV.[169] This is the name of the bird that comes from the Latin *ossifraga,* which literally means "bone-breaker," since it is formed from *ossis,* "bone," and *frangere,* "to break." To ossify is to turn to bone. An ossicle is a small bone. Osteitis is the inflammation of a bone. Evidently, this large bird of prey had a bone-breaking bite. Our modern versions all termed an **ossifrage** a "vulture."[170] But in one passage where the AV said "vulture," the NRSV changed it to "buzzard," the NIV "red kite," and the NKJV and NASB "kite."[171] The only other time the AV read "vulture" it was altered to "kite," except by the NIV, which preferred "falcon."[172] But when the AV mentions a "kite" in two places, the NASB and NKJV convert it into a "falcon."[173] Although our new translations thought an **ossifrage** did not exist, the *Reuters* news agency knew better: "An **ossifrage** is a bird of prey that crushes the bones of its victims."[174] And furthermore, when three mathematicians devised a secret code in 1977 that was recently cracked, they found a secret message encrypted inside that read "squeamish **ossifrage**."[175]

Ouches

> And the fourth row, a beryl, an onyx, and a jasper: *they were enclosed in* **ouches** *of gold in their enclosings*. (Exo 39:13)

The word **ouches** is the plural of *ouch*—the true form of which is *nouch*—and is found eight times in the AV.[176] It is from the French *nosche,* "a jewel or necklace." An ouch is a brooch or clasp worn as jewelry. It is also a socket or setting for a precious stone. The former meaning was obviously derived from the latter, and it is this latter meaning that is found in the Bible. Our modern versions all updated the word because it was deemed to be archaic. But what did they replace it with? Only the NKJV truly updates **ouches** consistently: seven times it used "settings,"[177] and once it used "mountings."[178] The NRSV replaced **ouches** with "settings" only twice.[179] Incredibly, the other six times the NRSV changes "**ouches** of gold" to "settings of gold filigree."[180] The NIV updated **ouches** to "settings" only three times,[181] using the arcane "gold filigree settings" five other times to modernize "**ouches** of gold."[182] The NASB unanimously inserts "filigree settings" into every passage.[183] There is no denying that **ouches** is an archaic word, but how changing it to "filigree" can be considered updating the Bible into modern, contemporary English is a great mystery.

Outgoings

> And the coast descended unto the river Kanah, southward of

the river: these cities of Ephraim are among the cities of Manasseh: the coast of Manasseh also was on the north side of the river, and the **outgoings** of it were at the sea: (Josh 17:9)

The compound word **outgoings** occurs eight times in the AV.[184] It also occurs eleven times with the same meaning as "goings out."[185] The eight troublesome instances of **outgoings** have reference to the end of a border or boundary. This could easily be determined from the meanings of the two words that make up **outgoings**. Our modern versions usually updated this word with an expression using a form of "ended," as in a boundary ending at a certain place.[186] Sometimes, however, we read of the "farthest limits"[187] or "farthest extent"[188] of a border or boundary. But what happens when the AV employs the word "end" to describe the end of a physical object? The "end of the city" is changed to the "outskirts"[189] or "edge"[190] of it. The "end of the staff" is replaced with "the tip of the staff."[191] When the AV speaks of the "end" of a mountain, it is altered to the "foot"[192] or "border"[193] or "edge"[194] of it. The "end" of a river is now the "mouth" of a river.[195] So once again, it is not just the archaic words in the AV that are corrected.

Outlandish

Did not Solomon king of Israel sin by these things? yet among many nations was there no king like him, who was beloved of his God, and God made him king over all Israel: nevertheless even him did **outlandish** women cause to sin. (Neh 13:26)

The word **outlandish** appears only once in the AV and was formed from *outland*—a foreign land. Thus, **outlandish** means belonging to a foreign land or a foreigner. The Old English form of this word was *utlendisc*. Although **outlandish** originally referred to a foreigner, it is now also used in the sense of wild, strange, crazy, or bizarre. Our modern versions preferred the word "foreign," except for the NKJV, which choose the word "pagan." However, the word **outlandish**, in the context in which it appears, can have the sense of both meanings; thus, it is more accurate than "foreign" or "pagan." And furthermore, the word **outlandish** was not archaic anyway—at least not in 1994: "And his often **outlandish** on-court behavior—the brawl with Michael

Jordan, the head-butt incident with John Starks, the dialogue with Spike Lee—have fostered a rebel image."[196]

Outmost

> Yet gleaning grapes shall be left in it, as the shaking of an olive tree, two *or* three berries in the top of the uppermost bough, four *or* five in the **outmost** fruitful branches thereof, saith the LORD God of Israel. (Isa 17:6)

The word **outmost** appears four times in the AV.[197] It is a compound made up of *out* and *most*. Once again, the meaning is apparent to anyone familiar with the words underlying the compound. Our modern versions all alter the word **outmost**, sometimes simply changing it to the form "outermost."[198] The continued use of a word with a *-most* suffix demonstrates that these up-to-date translations should have had no trouble at all with the word **outmost**. Indeed, all of our modern versions are filled with words that end in *-most*. They even go so far as to insert additional words with a *-most* suffix that are not even found in the AV. The word "topmost" surfaces in all of our modern versions even though it is not found in the AV.[199] The NIV uses the word "southernmost" when it is found neither in the AV nor any other new translation.[200] But what should one expect out of a modern, contemporary version that changes "strong" to "blustering."[201]

Outwent

> And the people saw them departing, and many knew him, and ran afoot thither out of all cities, and **outwent** them, and came together unto him. (Mark 6:33)

The word **outwent** is found only once in the AV and is plainly a compound of *out* and *went*. To **outwent** someone is to go before, go farther than, or go ahead of them. The NRSV choose "arrived ahead" and the NKJV "arrived before," but the NASB and NIV selected the four word phrase "got there ahead of" to update **outwent** in the AV. The word **outwent** should not have been any trouble to our modern versions, for they are filled with words formed with the prefix *out-* that do not occur at all in the AV. The NIV uses the word "outstanding," both in reference to something spectacular and a debt that is due.[202] The NRSV and

NIV each use the word "outweigh"[203] and "outlying,"[204] even though the words are not found in the AV, the NKJV, or the NASB. They also employ the words "outlaw"[205] and "outpoured"[206] when the AV, NKJV, and NASB do not use the words at all. The NRSV and NKJV implement the word "outskirts" when it not only doesn't appear in the AV, it does not occur in the NIV and NASB either.[207] All of our modern versions utilize forms of "outlet,"[208] "outbreak,"[209] "outcome,"[210] "outpost,"[211] "outsider,"[212] and "outskirts."[213] These words do not even appear in the AV. The NIV even uses two words with an *out-* prefix that occur in none of our new translations (outdoor, outline).[214] The NASB does likewise (outdoors, outlines).[215] The NRSV alone introduces the word "outdo" into its text.[216] Yet after all this energy was expended in correcting **outwent,** when the AV uses the simple word "cry," the prefix *out-* is added to it by our modern versions—giving us "outcry."[217]

Overcharge

> But if any have caused grief, he hath not grieved me, but in part: that I may not **overcharge** you all. (2 Cor 2:5)

The word **overcharge,** found once in the AV, is the first of many compound words in the AV that are formed with the prefix *over-*. Several of these forms have been eliminated from our modern versions because they were considered to be archaic. In addition to **overcharge,** other words that have been removed include: **overcharged**–found once,[218] **overdrive**–found once,[219] **overlived**–found once,[220] **overmuch**–found once,[221] but also occurring twice as "**over much,**"[222] **overpass**–found once,[223] **overpast**–appearing twice,[224] **overplus**–found once,[225] **overran**–found once,[226] **overrunning**–found once,[227] and **overspread** and **overspreading**–each occurring once.[228] The prefix *over-* signifies above, higher, across, too much, beyond, upper, or outer. To **overcharge** in the Bible refers to overburdening someone, not to demanding more money from them. The word "charge" is found in all of our modern versions with a variety of meanings.[229] To **overdrive** refers to driving an animal too hard, not to a part of a car's transmission. Once again, this should have been no problem, for all of our new translations employ the word *drive* in referring to animals[230] and nations being expelled from some land.[231] To have **overlived** someone is to have outlived them, not physically lived above them. In the place where this term appears in the AV, three of our new versions have updated **overlived** to "outlived."[232] To be **overmuch** is to be excessive or too great an amount. **Overmuch** is actually a synonym for the Old English *ofermicel,* "overmickle." The word **overmuch** is not even archaic anyway: "We won't worry **overmuch** about who is getting how much money out of our fun once the pitcher starts to throw."[233] To **overpass** is to pass by, to go beyond, to pass through, or to surpass. The *sur-* prefix is just the French *over.* The modern conception of a highway **overpass** has undoubtedly influenced the translators of our modern versions. To be **overpast** is to be over or completed. Of the eight times this word appears in the AV, our new translations have rendered it seven different ways (pass by, passes by, has passed, have passed by, is past, runs its course, has passed by).[234] An **overplus** is a surplus—that which is in addition to the main amount. To be **overran** is to be outrun or surpassed. The NKJV, NIV, and NRSV all use the form "overrun."[235] Extra books that are printed are called overruns. A job that cost more than expected is also said to have overruns. But even the word **overran** is still used today: "As the political culture of the Soviet Union grew more diverse, more complicated, Gorbachev had trouble accommodating ideas that **overran** his own."[236] An **overrunning** is the overflowing of water. To be **overspread** is to be spread over or out. Even the NKJV uses forms of this word.[237] That the AV contains compound words formed with the prefix *over-* that do not occur in new versions should not be a problem, for these new, up-to-date, translations do the same thing. The NRSV contains the word "overheated," although it is found in no other modern version.[238] The NASB includes the word "overlapping," not appearing in the AV or any other new translation.[239] "Overall" and "overwork" are found in the NKJV but not in any other version.[240] The NIV is the worst offender. There are eight compounds in the NIV formed with the prefix *over-* that occur neither in the AV nor any of our other new versions. The NIV uses "overbearing,"[241] "overawed,"[242] "overrighteous,"[243] "overstep,"[244] "overhang,"[245] "overcast,"[246] and "overfed."[247] Then the NIV invents "overweening" and uses it three times.[248] So not only do the new versions use obscure compound words with an *over-* prefix, they do so more than the *AV does.*

Chapter 16
Palmerworm to Pygarg

Palmerworm

> That which the **palmerworm** hath left hath the locust eaten; and that which the locust hath left hath the cankerworm eaten; and that which the cankerworm hath left hath the caterpillar eaten. (Joel 1:4)

A **palmerworm** is mentioned three times in the AV.[1] This word is obviously a compound of *palmer* and *worm*. A worm is self-evident, but a palmer is a pilgrim who had returned from the Holy Land. He was called a palmer because of the palm branch he wore or carried back with him. Thus, a **palmerworm** is a worm or caterpillar that is migratory. Naturally, this word has been omitted by our modern versions. The usual substitution is a form of "locust,"[2] but "caterpillar"[3] and "cutter"[4] are also used. However, when the AV mentions a "locust," it is changed by the NRSV to a "cicada" and the NASB to a "cricket."[5] And furthermore, when the AV employs the simple word "worm," it is changed by the NASB to "grub."[6]

Palsy

> And they come unto him, bringing one sick of the **palsy**, which was borne of four. (Mark 2:3)

The **palsy** is referred to twelve times in the AV.[7] The plural **palsies** occurs just once.[8] The word **palsy** is from the French *paralysie*, which is from the Latin *paralysis*. **Palsy** is just a doublet of *paralysis*, and is a disease of the nervous system characterized by the impairment of muscular activity or sensation. **Palsy** is generally rendered by our modern versions as "paralyzed"[9] or forms of "paralytic."[10] But although the word **palsy** can be found today in such expressions as cerebral **palsy**, the word also appears alone just like it does in the AV: "IBM has a simple device for people with conditions like **palsy** that make it difficult to keep hands centered on the keyboard: a plastic overlay that snaps onto the keyboard, creating depressions into which the fingers can fit."[11]

Pangs

> The king of Babylon hath heard the report of them, and his hands waxed feeble: anguish took hold of him, *and* **pangs** as of a woman in travail. (Jer 50:43)

The word **pangs** is used nine times in the AV.[12] It is from the Middle English *prang,* and is related to, if not identical with, our word *prong,* "a sharp point." Thus, **pangs** are sharp pains. Surprisingly, this word has not been unanimously updated by the new, modern translations to *pains.* The NKJV actually retains the AV reading in every instance.[13] However, the renderings given by the other versions are very inconsistent. The NRSV retains the AV reading six times,[14] but uses "pain"[15] and "labor"[16] the other three. The NIV forgot to remove "**pangs**" twice,[17] and likewise employed "pain" and "labor" to update **pangs.**[18] The NASB only kept "**pangs**" once,[19] and utilized not only "pains"[20] and "labor"[21] to correct **pangs**, but "agony" as well.[22] But even though they regularly corrected the AV, the NRSV and NASB replaced "sorrows" in the AV with the supposedly archaic "**pangs.**"[23] The NRSV also changes "offence" to "**pangs.**"[24] And incredibly, in one place where the AV just said "pains," the NKJV and NRSV alter it to "**pangs.**"[25] None of the passages where **pangs** was used by the AV should have been corrected in the first place, for the word **pangs** is still common today: "He'd been without heroin all day, yet felt no **pangs.**"[26]

Paps

> For, behold, the days are coming, in the which they shall say, Blessed *are* the barren, and the wombs that never bare, and the **paps** which never gave suck. (Luke 23:29)

The **paps** are mentioned four times in the AV.[27] *Pap* is from the Middle English *pappe* and is thought to be of Scandinavian origin. The **paps** are the nipples or the entire breast of a female. When used of a male, **paps** refers to the chest. Our modern versions usually render **paps** as "breasts" when the context is a female.[28] However, when referring to a male, the NKJV, NIV, and NRSV say "chest" but the NASB "breast."[29] But if **paps** was so difficult to understand, then why was "made" in the AV changed by the NASB to "perpetrated"[30] and "raise up" replaced by the NKJV with "perpetuate"?[31]

Paramours

> For she doted upon their **paramours,** whose flesh *is as* the flesh of asses, and whose issue *is like* the issue of horses. (Ezek 23:20)

The word **paramours** occurs only once in the AV. This word was formed from the French expression *par amur,* "by love." A paramour is a mistress, concubine, or illicit lover. Surprisingly, the NKJV, NRSV, and NASB all retain this word as the AV.[32] Only the NIV choose to update **paramours** to "lovers."[33] Yet when the AV employs a simple word like "fear," it is changed to "timidity" by the NASB and NIV.[34] But even the NIV should not have corrected the word **paramours,** for it is still used today: "When Ms. Armes sued her **paramour** for $1.5 million in U.S. District Court in Newnan in November, she joined dozens nationally who have tolerated unwanted publicity to seek retribution against a lover for spreading a sexually transmitted disease (STD)."[35]

Pate

> His mischief shall return upon his own head, and his violent dealing shall come down upon his own **pate.** (Psa 7:16)

The **pate** is mentioned once in the AV. **Pate** is a shortened form of *plate,* referring to the crown of the head. Although it is plainly archaic, **pate** is retained by the NASB.[36] The other versions, however, could not agree on the proper translation. The NKJV selected "crown," the NIV "head," and the NRSV "heads."[37] Yet the word **pate** is still used today in referring to the head: "They laughed harder as defensive end Charles Haley repeatedly encouraged Cowboy owner Jerry Jones to pluck the hairpiece from the **pate** of a team executive standing beneath him."[38]

Patrimony

> They shall have like portions to eat, beside that which cometh of the sale of his **patrimony**. (Deu 18:8)

The word **patrimony** appears only once in the AV. It is from the French *patremoine*, literally meaning an inheritance from one's father. The NKJV alone renders **patrimony** as "inheritance," the NIV and NRSV unite in giving us "family possessions," and the NASB preferred "fathers' estates."[39] It is bizarre that the word **patrimony** would be corrected by our modern versions, for they all follow the AV when it says "patriarch,"[40] except for the NRSV once using the term "ancestor."[41] The NRSV and NIV go even further, utilizing "patriarchs" to correct the AV reading of "fathers."[42] Moreover, the word **patrimony** is still currently in use: "Even before the failed 1991 coup civil war had broken out within the Soviet Union, pitting Armenians against Azerbaijanis for control of Nagorno-Karabakh, a territory populated principally by Armenians but lying within Azerbaijan and claimed by both groups as part of their **patrimony**."[43]

Peculiar

> For the LORD hath chosen Jacob unto himself, *and* Israel for his **peculiar** treasure. (Psa 135:4)

The word **peculiar** occurs seven times in the AV.[44] It is from the French *peculier*, "one's own." The word **peculiar** originally referred to private property, literally "property in cattle." As used in the AV, this word means special, singular, particular, or belonging exclusively to a person. Naturally, our modern versions do not use the word **peculiar** in this sense. The NKJV alone was consistent, changing **peculiar** to "special" in every place it occurred.[45] The other versions used forms of "his own"[46] or "treasured possession"[47] or "own possession."[48] Yet when the AV says something is "strange," the NRSV alone changes it to the more difficult "illicit."[49]

Penny

> And when he had agreed with the labourers for a **penny** a day, he sent them into his vineyard. (Mat 20:2)

A **penny** is mentioned nine times in the AV.[50] The plural **pence** occurs five times[51] and the derivative **pennyworth** is found twice.[52] **Penny** is from the Old English *pening* and referred to a coin of very small value. Thus, it means exactly what it does today. **Pence** is the collective plural of **penny**. **Pennyworth** is the amount that can be bought for a **penny**. The word **penny** has been applied to various pieces of English money for many years, yet the usual replacements for **penny** and **pence** in our modern versions are the arcane "denari"[53] and "denarius."[54] The NIV once renders **pence** as "silver coins"[55] and twice as "a years' wages."[56] **Pennyworth** is given as "denarii" by the NKJV and NASB,[57] but one time the NIV said "eight months' wages" and the NRSV said "six months' wages."[58] These corrections were all entirely unnecessary, for even the word **pence** is still used today: "By contrast, Britain's bilateral aid to Latin America during the same period was worth just under eight **pence** per capita per annum."[59]

Penury

> In all labour there is profit: but the talk of the lips tendeth only to **penury**. (Prov 14:23)

The word **penury** occurs twice in the AV.[60] It is from the French *penurie,* "want, need." **Penury** is the condition of being destitute or in poverty. Our modern versions have united in updating **penury** to "poverty."[61] But in one passage where the AV, followed by the NKJV, NIV, and NRSV, read "impoverished," the NASB alone changes it to "brought very low."[62] Yet forms of **penury** still regularly occur today: "In the early 1960s some 200,000 **penurious** immigrants thronged this stagnant urban community, more than the total black unemployed youths in all America's urban areas at the time."[63]

Perdition

> But they that will be rich fall into temptation and a snare, and

into many foolish and hurtful lusts, which drown men in destruction and **perdition**. (1 Tim 6:9)

The word **perdition** occurs eight times in the AV.[64] It comes from the French *perdicion,* "utter loss." **Perdition** means damnation, utter ruin, destruction, or loss. Although the NKJV retained this word as the AV,[65] the other new versions had trouble with it. The standard translation for **perdition** in the NRSV, NIV, and NASB is a form of "destruction."[66] However, the NASB mistakenly kept "**perdition**" in one passage.[67] Yet when the AV employs a simple one-syllable word like "ruin," it is also changed to "destruction" by the NIV, NRSV, and NASB.[68] Moreover, when the AV simply says "ungodly men," the NRSV alters it to "**perdition**."[69] The word **perdition,** however, is still in vogue today: "In particular, during the Rio Conference it was quite clear that an excessive spirit of conquest might drag the world to its **perdition**."[70]

Pernicious

And many shall follow their **pernicious** ways; by reason of whom the way of truth shall be evil spoken of. (2 Pet 2:2)

The word **pernicious** only appears once in the AV. It is from the French *pernicieux,* "destructive." Thus, **pernicious** means destructive, hurtful, or wicked. Our modern versions could not agree on the proper word to update **pernicious.** The NRSV chose "licentious," the NASB "sensuality," the NIV "shameful," and the NKJV "destructive."[71] But in addition to the medical condition known as **pernicious** anemia, the word **pernicious** is still used today: "Long before 'ethnic cleansing' entered popular parlance, its **pernicious** effects were painfully apparent in Mauritania."[72]

Phylacteries

But all their works they do for to be seen of men: they make broad their **phylacteries,** and enlarge the borders of their garments, (Mat 23:5)

The word **phylacteries** occurs only once in the AV. Although this word came into English from the Latin *phylacterium,* like most words with an initial *ph-,* it is of Greek origin. The Greek roots signify "to guard." **Phylacteries** are small boxes containing texts of Scripture that are worn by Jews during prayer as a reminder to keep the law. Surprisingly, all of our supposedly modern, up-to-date versions have retained this word.[73] And not only that, the NASB has even inserted "**phylacteries**" into a passage where neither the AV nor any other modern version contained the word.[74] Yet when the AV employs a simple word like "pile," it is altered to "pyre" by the NKJV even though all of the other new translations follow the AV reading.[75]

Pilled

> And Jacob took him rods of green poplar, and of the hazel and chestnut tree; and **pilled** white streaks in them, and made the white appear which *was* in the rods. (Gen 30:37)

The word **pilled** occurs twice in the AV.[76] It is from the verb *pill*, which is from the French *piller*, "to plunder." This word was often confused with *peel*, from *peler*. Thus, although to be **pilled** is to be robbed, plundered, pillaged, or ravished, it can also mean to be peeled. Understandably, our modern versions all change **pilled** to forms of "peeled."[77] Yet when the AV says "passed through," the NRSV alone changes it to "traversed."[78] But when the AV says "traversing," the NRSV solitarily alters it to "interlacing."[79]

Pipe

> And even things without life giving sound, whether **pipe** or harp, except they give a distinction in the sounds, how shall it be known what is **piped** or harped? (1 Cor 14:7)

When referring to a musical instrument, a **pipe** is mentioned four times in the AV in the singular[80] and four times in the plural.[81] **Pipers** are also mentioned one time[82] and the verb **piped** occurs four times.[83] **Pipe**, which comes unchanged from Old English, is a musical wind instrument formed from a tube. Obviously, **pipers** play **pipes** and hence it is said that they **piped**. Our modern versions all call a **pipe** a flute,[84] although the NKJV and NRSV each forgot to update "**pipes**" one time.[85] To have **piped** is, according to our modern versions, to have "played"[86] or to have "played the flute."[87] However, the NKJV carelessly retained "**piped**" in one instance.[88] But after correcting **pipe** and **pipes** in the AV, the NASB replaces "organ" and "organs" with "**pipe.**"[89] The NASB also inserts "**pipes**" in three additional places.[90] The NRSV, after likewise correcting "organ" and "organs" to "pipe,"[91] four times altered "flute" in the AV to "**pipe.**"[92] Yet in some of the same verses where a **pipe** is found, the NRSV and NASB mention a "trigon" and the NIV mentions a "zither."[93] And furthermore, at the end of the twentieth century, we still use the expression "pay the **piper.**"

Plaiting

> Whose adorning let it not be that outward *adorning* of **plaiting** the hair, and of wearing of gold, or of putting on of apparel; (1 Pet 3:3)

The word **plaiting** appears just once in the AV. **Plaiting** is formed from *plait,* which is from the French *pleit,* "a fold." To plait is to braid, fold together, or weave. Our word *pleat* is a variant of *plait.* **Plaiting** is changed to "arranging" by the NKJV, but forms of "braiding" by the other new translations. But these changes were unnecessary, for the word **plaiting** is still used today: "Clearly, Clinton had been **plaiting** his political braid for a long time before he announced his candidacy for president, weaving together many differing constituencies into what are now known as Friends of Bill."[94]

Platted

> And the soldiers **platted** a crown of thorns, and put *it* on his head, and they put on him a purple robe, (John 19:2)

The word **platted** occurs three times in the AV.[95] It is formed from *plat,* which is a variant of *plait.* Thus, to be **platted** is to be braided or weaved. The two replacements for **platted** in our new versions are forms of "wove"[96] and forms of "twisted."[97] Yet when the AV mentions things that are "creeping," the NASB, NIV, and NKJV describe them as "teeming."[98]

Poll

> Thou shalt even take five shekels apiece by the **poll,** after the shekel of the sanctuary shalt thou take *them:* (the shekel *is*

twenty gerahs:) (Num 3:47)

The word **poll** can be found in the AV three times in the singular[99] and six times in the plural.[100] The verb **polled** occurs three times.[101] **Poll** is from the Dutch *polle,* meaning the head. Since a **poll** is an individual head, to number by **polls** is to count individually or head by head. When **poll** is used as a verb it means to trim or cut the hair on the head. The translations given in our modern versions for **poll** or **polls** when they are used as a noun are "individually" [102] "head by head,"[103] "one by one,"[104] and forms of "for each one."[105] The verbs **poll** and **polled** are usually rendered by forms of "cut."[106] But in spite of the correction of **poll**, some taxes are still referred to as a **poll** taxes.

Pommels

And four hundred pomegranates on the two wreaths; two rows of pomegranates on each wreath, to cover the two **pommels** of the chapiters which *were* upon the pillars. (2 Chr 4:13)

Pommels are mentioned three times in the AV.[107] The word is from the French *pomel,* the diminutive form of *pom,* "hilt of a sword." This in turn goes back to the Latin *pomum,* "apple." A pommel is a knob, boss, projection, or ornamental ball or similar object. The word has also been applied to protrusions like the horn of a saddle. The NRSV and NASB unite in replacing **pommels** with "bowls."[108] However, the NKJV and NIV join the phrases "the **pommels,** and the chapiters which were on the top of the two pillars" giving us "the two bowl-shaped capitals on top of the pillars."[109] But if the word **pommel** was so archaic, then why is it still applied to a horn of a saddle: "Just before nightfall on Oct. 5, 1877, with snow falling across the high prairies, he rode out across a dry riverbed, wearing a blanket and moccasin leggings, his rifle across the **pommel** of his saddle."[110]

Post

One **post** shall run to meet another, and one messenger to meet another, to show the king of Babylon that his city is taken at *one* end, (Jer 51:31)

Although the word **post** occurs in the AV in reference to the **post** of a door, it is also used twice in what has been deemed an archaic sense.[111] The plural **posts** occurs six times.[112] **Post** is from the French *poste* and originally meant the place where one is stationed; then, a station on a road; then, the person who travelled the road; and finally, the material carried. The singular **post** is updated by our modern versions to either "runner"[113] or "courier."[114] The plural **posts** is always replaced with "couriers,"[115] except for the NKJV using "runners" twice.[116] Yet it is strange that the word **post** was updated in the first place, for every town has a **post** office where one can buy **post**age and a **post**man who delivers the mail. Moreover, the NRSV extends "watch" in the AV to "watchpost."[117] And furthermore, when the AV does use the word **post** in the modern, literal sense, the NRSV corrects it to "pilasters."[118]

Potentate

> Which in his times he shall show, *who is* the blessed and only **Potentate,** the King of kings, and Lord of lords; (1 Tim 6:15)

The word **potentate** appears only once in the AV. It is from the French *potentat*, literally meaning a powerful person. It is obvious that **potentate** is akin to *power* and *potent*. Thus, a **potentate** is a sovereign, a ruler, a king, a dictator, or a supreme ruler. Although the NKJV follows the AV reading, the NRSV and NASB have corrected **potentate** to "sovereign" and the NIV to "ruler." But aside from the fact that the Shriners call their leader the **potentate,** this word is still commonly used today: "More likely, he concocted the fable to reconcile the two points of view—to prod some greedy **potentate** into looking beyond his hoard."[119]

Pottage

> Then Jacob gave Esau bread and **pottage** of lentiles; and he did eat and drink, and rose up, and went his way: thus Esau despised *his* birthright, (Gen 25:34)

The word **pottage** occurs seven times in the AV.[120] This word is from the French *potage*, literally signifying "that which is put in a pot." **Pottage** is stew, broth or thick soup. The word **pottage** is actually another form of *porridge*. Our modern versions normally replace **pottage** with "stew,"[121] but once the NASB uses "cooked food."[122] The NASB and NRSV also employ the word "stuff" in one instance.[123] But even though it was deemed to be archaic by our modern versions, the word **pottage** is still employed like it appears in the AV: "Issuing new paper to cover old paper. Selling birthrights for a mess of **pottage**."[124]

Pound

> Then came the first, saying, Lord, thy **pound** hath gained ten **pounds**. (Luke 19:16)

The word **pound** occurs in the AV ten times in the singular[125] and five times in the plural.[126] **Pound** appeared in Old English as *pund* and is thought to be related to the Latin *pondo*, which literally means "by weight." The words **pound,** *ponder, perpendicular,* and *poise* are all ultimately derived from the Latin *pendere,* "to weigh." A **pound** is a unit of money in Britain that was originally a **pound** weight of silver. The NRSV alone retains forms of **pound** some of the time.[127] However, the other supposedly up-to-date, modern translations usually correct **pound** and **pound** to "mina"[128] and "minas."[129] Even the NRSV uses these abstruse words on four occasions to update forms of **pound**.[130] The difficult "maneh" is made even more arduous by its correction in the NRSV, NIV, and NKJV to "mina."[131] The correction of the various forms of **pound** to "mina" and "minas" is inexcusable, for the **pound** is still a unit of measure in the 1990's: "The **pound** sterling, the Italian lira and the Spanish peseta went spinning out of the Exchange Rate Mechanism (ERM)."[132]

Prating

> He that winketh with the eye causeth sorrow: but a **prating** fool shall fall. (Prov 10:10)

The word **prating** is found three times in the AV.[133] **Prating** is formed from *prate,* from the Dutch *praten,* "to chatter." **Prating** is foolish, idle, boastful, excessive, or vain talk. Although the NKJV retained the AV reading, the other new versions had trouble with **prating**.[134] The usual translation for **prating** is "babbling,"[135] but "chattering,"[136] "spreading false charges,"[137] "unjustly accusing,"[138] and "gossiping maliciously"[139] can also be found. But obviously the word **prating** could not be archaic, for not only does the NKJV retain it where the AV utilizes the word, two additional forms of the word are inserted elsewhere. When the AV reads "prophesy," the NKJV alters it to "prattle."[140] Likewise, when the AV mentions a "prophet," the NKJV corrects it to a "prattler."[141]

Presbytery

> Neglect not the gift that is in thee, which was given thee by prophecy, with the laying on of the hands of the **presbytery**. (1 Tim 4:14)

The word **presbytery** appears just once in the AV. This word came into English by way of Latin from the Greek *presbuteros*, "an elder." Thus, a **presbytery** is an assembly of elders. The NASB alone retains this word as the AV. The NRSV says "eldership," the NIV "body of elders," and the NKJV "eldership." But although not used in the biblical sense, the word **presbytery** is still used today to refer to the place in a church where the clergy sits. A **presbytery** is also part of the denominational church-government of presbyterian churches. The pastor and elders of the church make up the session, followed by the **presbytery**: all the elders from each congregation in a particular area. Then comes the synod. And finally, the general assembly.

Prevent

> For this we say unto you by the word of the Lord, that we which are alive *and* remain unto the coming of the Lord shall not **prevent** them which are asleep. (1 Th 4:15)

The word **prevent** occurs seven times in the AV.[142] The form **preventest** is found once,[143] and the form **prevented** appears nine times.[144] **Prevent** is manifestly not an archaic word, but it is used in the AV in an archaic sense. The word is from the Latin *praeventus*, from *praevenire*, "to come before." Thus, the original meaning of **prevent** was to come or go before, anticipate, meet beforehand, obviate, or precede. Our modern versions correct every occurrence of all forms of **prevent** that appear in the AV. Among the new translations are "precede,"[145] "confronted,"[146] "come,"[147] "rise before,"[148] "receive,"[149] and forms of "anticipate."[150] **Prevent** might be confusing when it is used with its older meaning, but if the AV says something simple like "wonder," it is made obscure by the NIV and NRSV changing it to "portent."[151]

𝔓rincipality

> And ye are complete in him, which is the head of all **principality** and power: (Col 2:10)

The word **principality** occurs in the AV twice in the singular[152] and seven times in the plural.[153] It is from the French *principalite* meaning the government of a prince. Thus, a **principality** is a kingdom, state, country, or realm that is ruled by a prince. The NKJV retained the AV reading most of the time,[154] but the other versions preferred to substitute "rulers" the majority of the time.[155] Once however, the NASB slips up and keeps the AV reading of "**principalities.**"[156] The NIV also rendered **principalities** as "demons" one time[157] and "powers" on another occasion.[158] But these corrections were uncalled for, since the word **principality** is still in use: "His **principality** remains independent of France only as long as there is a male heir."[159] And furthermore, the sister word *municipality* is commonly applied a city or town.

𝔓rivy

> And kept back *part* of the price, his wife also being **privy** *to it,* and brought a certain part, and laid *it,* at the apostles' feet. (Acts 5:2)

The word **privy** occurs four times in the AV,[160] while the form **privily** appears fifteen times.[161] **Privy** is from the French *prive,* "private." To be **privy** to something is to have knowledge of private information. To do something **privily** is to do it in a **privy,** secret, or deceitful manner. **Privy** is normally rendered in our modern versions by forms of "knowledge."[162] In a convoluted attempt at euphemism, the NIV and NKJV alter "**privy** member cut off" to the uncommon word "emasculated."[163] The translations for **privily** include "secretly,"[164] "stealthily,"[165] "deceitfully,"[166] "hidden,"[167] "wantonly,"[168] and "quietly."[169] But when the AV uses the word "secretly," it is changed by the NASB to "stealthily"[170] and the NIV to "privately."[171] The correction of **privy** was entirely unnecessary, for the word is still currently in vogue: "Stickney says that even while he was FEMA's director he was not **privy** to some of the most sensitive plans."[172]

Progenitors

> The blessings of thy father have prevailed above the blessings of my **progenitors** unto the utmost bound of the everlasting hills: they shall be on the head of Joseph, and on the crown of the head of him that was separate from his brethren. (Gen 49:26)

The word **progenitors** appears only once in the AV. It is from the French *progeniteur,* literally meaning to bring forth. Thus, **progenitors** are ancestors or forefathers. Although the NKJV and NASB update **progenitors** to "ancestors," the NRSV says "eternal mountains" and the NIV "ancient mountains." The word **progenitors,** however, still regularly appears today: "The mesonychids, which ranged from the size of a house cat to a grizzly bear, arrived on the scene at just the right time to be the **progenitors** of whales."[173]

Prognosticators

> Thou art wearied in the multitude of thy counsels. Let now the astrologers, the stargazers, the monthly **prognosticators,** stand up, and save thee from *these things* that shall come upon thee. (Isa 47:13)

The word **prognosticators** occurs only once in the AV. A prognosticator is one who prognosticates. To prognosticate is to predict, forecast, or foretell. All of the various forms of these words ultimately go back to the Greek word meaning "to know." Thus, our medical term *prognosis* is related to **prognosticators.** The NKJV retains this word as the AV, but the NRSV and NASB rendered "monthly **prognosticators**" by forms of "predict by the new moon." The NIV has "make predictions month by month." But the word **prognosticators** was never archaic to start with, at least according to *Psychology Today:* "The slight dip in the divorce rate in recent years has caused some **prognosticators** to predict that younger people, particularly those who've experienced the pain of growing up in broken homes, are increasingly committed to making marriage stick."[174]

Proper

> For I would that all men were even as I myself. But every man hath his **proper** gift of God, one after this manner, and another after that. (1 Cor 7:7)

The word **proper** surfaces four times in the AV.[175] It is from the French *propre*, "one's own." Although the word **proper** is now limited in meaning to just suitable or correct, the AV uses this word in the original sense of one's own or particular. **Proper** also appears once in AV with the meaning of fair to look upon. The most common substitution for **proper** in our modern versions is "own."[176] Yet when the AV says someone is "miserable," the NKJV alone invents the designation "pitiable."[177]

Provender

> So he brought him into his house, and gave **provender** unto the asses: and they washed their feet, and did eat and drink. (Judg 19:21)

The word **provender** appears seven times in the AV.[178] It comes into English from the French *provendre*, "provisions." Although **provender** can be food or provisions, it is commonly applied to dry food for animals. Thus, **provender** is feed or fodder. Our modern versions render **provender** as either "fodder"[179] or "feed."[180] However, the NRSV one time amends **provender** to the arcane "silage."[181] The correction of **provender**, however, was not necessary to begin with, for it can be found today in *American Horticulturist:* "Progeny we must have, company, **provender**, friends, and even enemies."[182]

Psaltery

> Praise the LORD with harp: sing unto him with the **psaltery** *and* an instrument of ten strings. (Psa 33:2)

A **psaltery** is mentioned in the AV thirteen times in the singular[183] and fourteen times in the plural.[184] The word is from the French *psalterie* referring to an ancient stringed musical instrument. The Book of Psalms, often called the Psalter, is connected with this word, for a psalm originally meant the twitching of the harp. From this developed the meaning of the song that was played and the harp-like instrument to play it. Thus, a **psaltery** is a type of harp. Although they deemed it to be archaic, the NKJV forgot to remove "**psaltery**" three times[185] and the NASB four.[186] The usual correction for **psaltery** by the NRSV, NIV, and NASB is "harp."[187] Sometimes, however, one can find the equally as archaic "lyre"[188] or "lute."[189] The NKJV regularly used "lute."[190] The plural **psalteries** is similarly corrected. Yet when the AV reads "harp," it is often corrected to the arcane "lyre."[191] The NIV even corrects a "harp" to a "zither."[192]

Publican

> And after these things he went forth, and saw a **publican,** named Levi, sitting at the receipt of custom: and he said unto him, Follow me. (Luke 5:27)

A **publican** is mentioned in the AV six times in the singular[193] and seventeen times in the plural.[194] This word is from the French *publicain,* from a Latin adjective which signified "pertaining to the public revenue." A **publican** is not to be confused with a republican, although they are both from the same Latin root. A **publican** was originally a tax collector for the Roman Empire. The word **publican** was also later used to describe the owner or manager of a tavern or inn. In updating these words, our modern versions were at least consistent. The NKJV, NIV, and NRSV always update **publican** and **publicans** to "tax collector" and "tax collectors."[195] The NASB preferred the words "tax-gatherer" and "tax-gatherers."[196] But in spite of these corrections, even *Sports Illustrated* magazine did not consider the word **publican** to be archaic: "The photo session done, I give Donnelly's Arm back to the **publican** and return to my Murphy's stout and my Mornay."[197]

Pulse

> Prove thy servants, I beseech thee, ten days; and let them give us **pulse** to eat, and water to drink. (Dan 1:12)

Pulse is mentioned three times in the AV.[198] **Pulse** is from the French *pols,* which is from a Latin word meaning porridge. **Pulse** is grain or seed of beans, peas, or lentils used as food. Naturally, the new versions excise this word. In two passages they unite in rendering it as "vegetables."[199] The one other occurrence of **pulse** is given as "grain" by the NIV and NRSV, but "seeds" by the NKJV and NASB.[200] But when the AV mentions "remembrances," they are altered to "platitudes" by the NKJV and "maxims" by the NIV and NRSV.[201]

Purloining

Not **purloining,** but showing all good fidelity; that they may adorn the doctrine of God our Saviour in all things. (Titus 2:10)

The word **purloining,** from *purloin,* likewise appears only once in the AV. *Purloin* comes from the French *purloigner,* meaning to prolong, retard or delay. It then came to mean conceal, detain, or steal. Although the NIV altered **purloining** to the phrase "to steal from them," the other versions used a form of "pilfer." But when the AV uses a simple word like "rob," it is changed by the NASB and NRSV to "bereave."[202] But these corrections notwithstanding, the word **purloining** is still in vogue today: "No one else on the Democratic ticket can be accused of **purloining** it."[203]

Purtenance

Eat not of it raw, nor sodden at all with water, but roast *with* fire; his head with his legs, and with the **purtenance** thereof. (Exo 12:9)

The word **purtenance** only appears once in the AV. It is actually a short form of *appurtenance,* from the French *apurtenaunce,* "that which belongs to." Thus, **purtenance** is related to our word pertain. **Purtenance** is now usually always applied to the organs of an animal. We would say the guts or intestines. The NKJV and NASB united on the substitution of "entrails," but the NRSV said "inner organs" and the NIV "inner parts." But when the AV mentions a "mixed multitude," the NIV, NRSV, and NASB call them to a "rabble."[204]

Putrifying

> From the sole of the foot even unto the head *there is* no soundness in it; *but* wounds, and bruises, and **putrifying** sores: they have not been closed, neither bound up, neither mollified with ointment. (Isa 1:6)

The word **putrifying** also occurs just once in the AV. It was extended from *putrefy*, which is from the French *putride*, "rotten." If something is putrid it is rotten, corrupt, decaying, stinking, or all of the above. Our four modern versions could not agree among themselves as to the proper replacement for **putrifying**. The NKJV follows the AV reading, while the NASB says "raw," the NIV "open," and the NRSV "bleeding." But not only does the NKJV add the word "putrefy" where the AV did not contain the word,[205] the simple phrase "to stink" is changed by the NKJV to "obnoxious."[206] The NASB even corrected "stink" in the AV to "putrefaction."[207] But the correction of **putrifying** was superfluous anyway, for forms of **putrifying** still appear in *U.S. News & World Report:* "Residents wear surgical masks and peasants cover their faces with rags to ward off the **putrid** stench of decomposition that smothers the city."[208]

Pygarg

> The hart, and the roebuck, and the fallow deer, and the wild goat, and the **pygarg,** and the wild ox, and the chamois. (Deu 14:5)

A **pygarg** surfaces only once in the AV. It has a very descriptive name in that it is from the Latin *pygargus,* meaning "white rump." A **pygarg** is obviously an antelope with a white rump. The NKJV alone calls a **pygarg** a "mountain goat," but incredibly, the supposedly up-to-date, modern NIV, NRSV, and NASB term a **pygarg** an "ibex."

Chapter 17
Quarter to Quit

Quarter

But he went out, and began to publish *it* much, and to blaze abroad the matter, insomuch that Jesus could no more openly enter into the city, but was without in desert places: and they came to him from every **quarter**. (Mark 1:45)

The word **quarter** appears seventeen times in the AV, eight in the singular[1] and nine in the plural.[2] It comes into English from a French word of the same spelling, which in turn is from the Latin *quartus*, "forth." Although commonly used today to indicate a measurement, the word **quarter** has several other meanings. A **quarter** can be a region, district, place, locality, or section, especially that occupied by a particular class of people. New Orleans has the French **Quarter**, while most large cities have a Jewish **quarter** or Black **quarter**. A quarter is also the region of any of the four principal points of the compass. **Quarters** are the place where one lodges or resides, chiefly military accommodations such as the BOQ. **Quarter** can also refer to good or fair treatment, given or not given. Obviously, **quarter** is not an archaic word, but apparently it was thought to be so judging from its correction in the AV. The use of **quarter** in the AV as a measure is not found. Four times the AV reads "four **quarters**."[3] The NIV retains this expression only once,[4] changing **quarters** to "corners" on two occasions.[5] But when the AV says "four corners," the NIV corrects it to "four **quarters**."[6] The NASB maintains the AV reading only one time out of seventeen,[7] but then inserts a form of "**quarter**" into five additional passages, none of which refer to a measurement.[8] The NRSV amends "every **quarter**" in the AV one time,[9] retains it once,[10] and then injects the phrase into two extra passages.[11] The NKJV corrects "south **quarter**" to "south border" one time but "south side" the next.[12] Then the NKJV retains "north **quarter**" once, but updates it to "far north" in another verse.[13] The NKJV also preferred "region," "territory," "direction," and "parts of the country" instead of **quarter** or **quarters**,[14] but saw no problem with introducing these words into seven additional passages.[15] The NIV corrected **quarter** with almost a different word every time (part, borders, side, corners, boundary, error, far north, everywhere, country, area, nearby),[16] after just adding a form of the word in five places where the AV read differently.[17] The NKJV, NASB, and NRSV also add the word "quartermaster" to their text where the AV has "quiet prince."[18] Although certain uses of the word **quarter** have been stricken from our new translations, the word is still used by *Time* magazine as it is in the AV: "The taste was especially sweet in the White House, which had persisted in its plan despite opposition from almost every **quarter**."[19]

Quaternions

> And when he had apprehended him, he put *him* in prison, and delivered *him* to four **quaternions** of soldiers to keep him; intending after Easter to bring him forth to the people. (Acts 12:4)

The word **quaternions** occurs only one time in the AV. From the prefix, it is apparent that **quaternions** is related to the previous word *quarter*. **Quaternions** is from the Latin *quaternion*, from *quaterni*, "a set of four things." Four **quaternions** of soldiers would be a total of sixteen soldiers. Our modern versions unanimously update this word to "squads." But how many men are in a squad? **Quaternions** is a much more accurate and descriptive word, but evidently our modern versions deemed it to be archaic. Yet the NKJV inserts the Latin word "quadrans" into a passage where the AV reads "farthling."[20] Then in the other verse where the same underlying Greek word appears, the NKJV translates it as "penny."[21] But when the AV reads "penny," it is changed in every occurrence to "denarius."[22] And finally, when the AV says "common hall," the NKJV, NIV, and NASB inject the Latin word "praetorium."[23] Thus, it is not just the AV that uses archaic words.

𝕼𝖚𝖎𝖈𝖐

> I charge *thee* therefore before God, and the Lord Jesus Christ, who shall judge the **quick** and the dead at his appearing and his kingdom; (2 Tim 4:1)

The word **quick** appears ten times in the AV.[24] Other forms of **quick** include **quicken,** occurring thirteen times,[25] **quickened,** found seven times,[26] **quickeneth,** appearing five times,[27] and **quickening,** found once.[28] All of these are derived from the Old English *cwic,* "living." The original meaning was "characterized by the presence of life,"[29] and it is from this sense that developed the meaning of fast or prompt. This latter usage is not found in the AV. **Quick** also means tender, sensitive flesh; vivid, or the most vital part. The primary connotation of the various forms of **quick** in the AV is to have life, give life, restore life, or revive life; however, on two occasions **quick** signifies flesh.[30] The NKJV and NIV update every single occurrence of every form of **quick.** The NASB and NRSV attempted to do the same but forgot to upgrade one passage.[31] The usual translation of **quick** in our modern versions is "alive"[32] or "living."[33] For **quicken,** the NKJV and NASB consistently employ "revive,"[34] but the NIV prefers "preserve."[35] **Quickening** is always rendered "life-giving,"[36] while **quickeneth** is unremittingly "gives life."[37] **Quickened** is variously given as "revived,"[38] "preserved,"[39] "made alive,"[40] or "given life."[41] After all these corrections, one would think that all forms of the word **quick,** except in reference to being fast or prompt, were archaic. If so, then why does the NASB use the expression "cut to the **quick**" in two passages?[42] Yet when the AV uses a compound of **quick** exactly like it is found today, these modern versions correct it. "Quicksands" in the AV has been altered to "Syrtis" in the NRSV, "shallows of Syrtis" in the NASB, "sandbars of Syrtis" in the NIV, and "Syrtis sands" in the NKJV.[43] In addition to the computer program **Quicken,** forms of the word **quick** are still in use today. To be "**quick** with child" is to be pregnant. **Quickening** is still defined in medical dictionaries as: "The signs of life felt by the mother as a result of the fetal movements."[44] Moreover, the *Christian Science Monitor* did not appraise **quicken** to be archaic:

"Meanwhile, urban planners, municipal officials, community organizers, and others are seeing historic preservation as a tool to enhance the livability and **quicken** the economies of cities and towns."[45] And neither did *Time* magazine regard **quick** archaic: "Never before have the creations of laboratories come so close to crossing the threshold that separates living from nonliving, the **quick** from the dead."[46]

Quit

Watch ye, stand fast in the faith, **quit** you like men, be strong. (1 Cor 16:13)

Quit appears six times in the AV.[47] It comes from the French *quite*, "released." The French word is from the Latin *quietus*, "at rest, free," from which we get the English words *quiet* and *quite*. **Quit** is short for *quite*. The word **quit** means to cease or relinquish, but since it is not used in this sense in the AV, it has been deemed archaic and a candidate for alteration. **Quit** is used in two ways in the AV: to do ones part or behave,[48] and to release from an obligation.[49] The former meaning is usually updated to "be men,"[50] while the latter, instead of being replaced by "acquitted," like it is in the NKJV,[51] is diversely rendered as "free of liability,"[52] "unpunished,"[53] "not be held responsible,"[54] "released,"[55] or "free."[56] **Quit** is not as archaic as one would think—sk anyone who has ever signed a **quit**claim or a **quit**claim deed. The issue is not archaic words, for when the AV is perfectly clear, it is still amended. Why was energy expended by the NRSV in correcting the AV reading of "borders of Dor" to "Naphoth-dor"?[57] Why did the NASB waste time in changing "seasons" to "epochs," not once, but three times?[58] What is so much clearer about "convulsed" in the NKJV when the AV reads "torn"?[59] And why did the NIV use the word "commemorate" when the AV and all of the other versions read "remember."[60]

Chapter 18
Rail to Rush

Rail

He wrote also letters to **rail** on the LORD God of Israel, and to speak against him, saying, As the gods of the nations of *other* lands have not delivered their people out of mine hand, so shall not the God of Hezekiah deliver his people out of mine hand. (2 Chr 32:17)

Although the word **rail** appears only once in the AV, the form **railed** is found three times,[1] **railer** occurs once,[2] **railing** surfaces three times,[3] and **railings** appears once.[4] **Rail** is from the French *railler*, "to jeer at." To **rail** is to upbraid, denounce, scorn, slander, revile, or deride. A **railer** is one who practices these things. **Railing** is maliciousness, an insult, a denunciation, or slander. Our modern versions have completely removed all forms of these words, excepting the NASB, NRSV, and NIV each utilizing a form of "**rail**" one time.[5] The usual replacement for these words is a form of "revile"[6] or "insult."[7] Other translations include forms of "slander,"[8] "derided,"[9] and "blasphemed."[10] Only the NKJV was consistent, employing forms of "revile" most of the time.[11] But when the AV reads "slander," it is corrected by the NRSV to "whispering" even though all of the other new translations follow the AV reading.[12] The NRSV also altered "blasphemed" in the AV to "reviled" in spite of the other versions following the AV.[13] Moreover, when the AV says "reviled," the NIV changes it to "hurled insults" even though the other modern versions read as the AV.[14] And finally, after updating **railed** with forms of "derided,"[15] the NRSV corrected "derided" in the AV every time it occurred.[16] The elimination of **rail** and its derivatives from the Bible was unnecessary, for they are still commonly used today: "However, as they entered each new region, they met strong opposition from citizens, who **railed** against what they referred to as 'toxic terrorism' and 'toxic colonialism,' and from governments which quickly passed legislation prohibiting waste imports."[17]

Raiment

> And having food and **raiment** let us be therewith content. (1 Tim 6:8)

The word **raiment** occurs fifty-seven times in the AV.[18] **Raiment**, the aphetic form of *arrayment*, from the French *araiement*, "clothing," is clothes, clothing, attire, dress, or apparel. This word has been expurgated from all of our modern versions; however, the NASB carelessly left this archaic word in one passage.[19] The customary renderings for **raiment** in the new versions are "clothing,"[20] "garment,"[21] and "clothes."[22] Other translations for **raiment** include "cloak,"[23] "garb,"[24] "covering,"[25] "robes,"[26] and "coats."[27] However, the publication *American History Illustrated* did not consider **raiment** to be archaic: "No longer would man be utterly dependent on 'animals, plants, and the crust of the earth for food, **raiment,** and structural material.'"[28]

Rampart

> Art thou better than populous No, that was situate among the rivers, *that had* the waters round about it, whose **rampart** *was* the sea, *and* her wall *was* from the sea? (Nahum 3:8)

A **rampart** is mentioned twice in the AV.[29] It is from the French *rempart*, from *remparer*, "to fortify." A **rampart** is a bank of earth raised around a fort for defense or anything serving as a bulwark or defense. Although a **rampart** is mentioned in the Star-Spangled Banner (Whose broad stripes and bright stars, thru the perilous fight, O'er the ramparts we watched, were so gallantly streaming), not many Americans know what a **rampart** is. Yet in spite of this, our modern versions retained the word **rampart** every time it appeared in the AV, except the NIV, which used "defense" once.[30] And not only did they retain **rampart,** the NASB used it two additional times in the singular[31] and two in the plural.[32] The NRSV employed **rampart** three times in the singular[33] and three in the plural.[34] The NIV, after correcting **rampart** once in the AV,[35] inserted it into another passage where none of the other modern versions followed suit.[36] Then the NIV used the plural "ramparts" three times.[37] The NKJV injected "**rampart**" into only two additional places.[38] But when the AV utilizes a simple, uncomplicated word like "defence," it is altered to the arcane "mantelet" by the NRSV and NASB.[39]

Range

> The **range** of the mountains *is* his pasture, and he searcheth after every green thing. (Job 40:8)

The word **range** appears in the AV under several forms with distinct meanings. While **range** appears once, **ranges** can be found four times[40] and **ranging** once.[41] **Range** is from the French *ranger*, from *rangier*, "to put in rank." To **range** originally meant to lay out or put in order or rank; the sense of roam, rove, traverse, or wander about developed later based on the trooping about of ranks of armed men. The substantive **range** is from the French *range*, from *rangier*, and refers to a row, place, distance, or area. The "**range** of the mountains" in the AV is the area over which an animal would roam. Although the word **ranges** is used once in the AV in the modern sense of a cooking device,[42] the **ranges** referred to the other three times are ranks of soldiers.[43] "Ranks" is what is usually substituted by our modern versions for **ranges** in these passages.[44] The "**ranging** bear" mentioned once in the AV is termed by our modern versions as "charging" or "rushing."[45] But this use of **ranging** should have been no problem, for the NIV, NRSV, and NASB all employed "**range**" as a verb.[46]

Rank

> And he slept and dreamed the second time: and, behold, seven ears of corn came up upon one stalk, **rank** and good. (Gen 41:5)

Although the word **rank** appears six times in the AV,[47] in two of these occurrences **rank** has a meaning that is completely opposite what the word means today.[48] **Rank** is from the Old English *ranc*, "strong." *Ranc* is related to similar words in other ancient languages that meant upright, slender, or straight. To be **rank** is to be full-grown, upright, robust, ripe, healthy, or strong. **Rank** gradually came to mean rancid or disgusting due to its being confused with the French *rance,* "musty." Our modern versions all unite in correcting **rank** to "plump," except the NIV, which preferred "healthy."[49] Yet when the AV says something is "pleasant," the NIV changes it to "melodious," a word not found in any modern version.[50]

𝕽𝖆𝖛𝖊𝖓𝖎𝖓𝖌

> And the Lord said unto him, Now do ye Pharisees make clean the outside of the cup and the platter; but your inward part is full of **ravening** and wickedness. (Luke 11:39)

The word **ravening** is found five times in the AV,[51] while the similar and better known form **ravenous** appears three times.[52] **Ravening** and **ravenous** are formed from *raven,* which is from the French *raviner,* "to ravage." This was derived from *ravine,* "to rob or rapine." **Ravening,** used in the AV as a noun, verb, and an adjective, means plundering, tearing, seizing, pillaging, ravishing, ferocious, or otherwise full of greed or viciousness. **Ravenous** can mean starving, ferocious, predatory, voracious, or covetous. The NRSV and NASB each retained "**ravening**" only one time.[53] Once, however, they corrected **ravening** with "**ravenous.**"[54] But when the AV said **ravenous,** it was then corrected.[55] The NRSV also inserted "**ravenous**" into two more passages where the AV did not contain the word.[56] The NRSV even replaced "destroying" in the AV with "**ravening**" when the NASB read as the AV.[57] The NASB only added "**ravenous**" to one additional verse where it was not found in the AV.[58] **Ravening** is updated every time it appears by the NIV and NKJV.[59] On one of these occasions, the NKJV altered **ravening** to "**ravenous,**"[60] but when the AV said **ravenous,** it was twice corrected.[61] The NIV revised **ravening** to "tearing,"[62] "ferocious,"[63] and "greed."[64] Then after correcting **ravenous** in the AV every time it appeared,[65] the NIV inserted the word into two other passages where it was not found in the AV.[66] Moreover, even though it corrected every occurrence of **ravening** in the AV, the NIV also managed to use the word to emend the AV reading of "destroying."[67] But in spite of these corrections of **ravening,** the word can still be found in *Time* magazine: "Meanwhile, the **ravening** tabloids were already squaring off for the November confrontation between two royal tell-all books."⁶⁸

Ravin

> Benjamin shall **ravin** as a wolf: in the morning he shall devour the prey, and at night he shall divide the spoil. (Gen 49:27)

The word **ravin** occurs twice in the AV.⁶⁹ It is from the French *ravine*, "to rob or rapine." Thus, like our words *ravish*, *ravine*, and *ravage*, **ravin** is related to the previous word, as all are ultimately derived from the Latin *rapere*, "to seize." To **ravin** is to plunder, seize, rob, ravage, or pillage; **ravin** is prey, meat, flesh, or the result of one's plunder. Naturally, our modern versions have all removed this word. Once, however, it is unanimously replaced by "ravenous."⁷⁰ But as mentioned previously, when the AV says "ravenous," it is often corrected.⁷¹ Although the word **ravin** is not exactly current English, it certainly is not archaic: "'They fear nothing [and are] the enemies of every creature they can master, living almost entirely by **ravin** and slaughter,' wrote the great ornithologist Robert Cushman Murphy, who came to know skuas intimately from his investigations on the subantarctic island of South Georgia in 1912-13."⁷²

Rear

> And thou shalt **rear** up the tabernacle according to the fashion thereof which was showed thee in the mount. (Exo 26:30)

The word **rear** occurs four times in the AV.⁷³ Never a reference to the back of something, the word **rear** is from the Old English *raeran*, "to raise." Thus, to **rear** is to raise, build, erect, take care of, elevate, or to rise up. Although the NKJV mistakenly retains "**rear**" in one passage,⁷⁴ all of the modern versions unite in replacing **rear** with "erect,"⁷⁵ "set up,"⁷⁶ "build,"⁷⁷ or "raise."⁷⁸ Besides their use of **rear** to designate the back part of something, our modern versions do employ forms of the word **rear** to describe the raising of children.⁷⁹ But when the AV just says "bring up," the NIV replaces it with "**rear**" even though the other new translations follow the AV reading.⁸⁰

Record

> Moreover I call God for a **record** upon my soul, that to spare you I came not as yet unto Corinth. (2 Cor 1:23)

The word **record** is found under various forms forty-three times in the AV. The vast majority of cases, however, have been deemed an archaic usage. The word **record** is from the French noun *record,* from the verb *recorder,* but one must go back to the Latin to see the true significance of the word. The original Latin form was *recordari,* a combination of *re,* "again," and *cor,* "heart," meaning to recall to mind, think over, ponder, or remember. In the AV, **record** appears twice as a verb[81] and once as a noun[82] with the modern meaning of to write down or something written down. The forms **recorded**[83] and **records**[84] are similarly used. Nine times the word **recorder** is used to describe one who actually did the writing.[85] This parallels modern usage and is consequently left intact in the new versions.[86] The other twenty-seven occurrences of the word **record** are with the older meaning of a witness or testimony, or to bear witness or testify. Our modern versions consistently update **record** with these terms.[87] But when the AV uses the word **record** in the modern sense, the NIV and NASB alter it to "memorandum."[88]

Redound

> For all things *are* for your sakes, that the abundant grace might through the thanksgiving of many **redound** to the glory of God. (2 Cor 4:15)

The word **redound**, occurring only once in the AV, is from the French *redonder,* "to overflow." To **redound** is to abound, contribute, come back as a result of, or to reflect on. It is related to our words *redundant, abound,* and *abundance.* **Redound** is given as "abound" and "overflow" in our modern versions. Although our modern versions had trouble with **redound,** they regularly corrected plain, commonly known words in the AV to forms of "resound." "Sound" is extended to "resound" by the NKJV,[89] while the NRSV changes "declared" to "resound."[90] The NASB and NRSV unite in altering "rang again" to "resounded."[91] The NIV even amends "roar" to "resounded" in a verse where all of the other modern versions follow the AV.[92]

Nevertheless, the word **redound** is still in use today: "'School districts were quiet in the past because they hoped that the development activity would spill over and **redound** to their benefit,' says Michael Pagano, who follows local government finances at Miami University in Ohio."[93]

𝕽𝖊𝖍𝖊𝖆𝖗𝖘𝖊

> And the LORD said unto Moses, Write this *for* a memorial in a book, and **rehearse** *it* in the ears of Joshua: for I will utterly put out the remembrance of Amalek from under heaven. (Exo 17:14)

The word **rehearse** appears twice in the AV,[94] but the form **rehearsed** can be found four times.[95] **Rehearse** is from the French *rehercier*, "to harrow again." To harrow is to plow. Thus, to **rehearse** is literally to plow again. By way of application, **rehearse** can mean to recite, say over, repeat, speak, give an account of, relate, narrate, or mention. Due to their limiting **rehearse** to a Hollywood actor rehearsing for a part, our modern versions have removed both forms of this word from the Bible. The replacements are "recite,"[96] "recount,"[97] and forms of "repeat,"[98] "explain,"[99] and "report."[100] However, the word **rehearse** is still used today without referring to an actor rehearsing his lines: "I believe that the constraints placed on morality by language and concepts prevent such a slide into relativism, but this is not the place to **rehearse** that debate."[101]

𝕽𝖊𝖎𝖓𝖘

> Whom I shall see for myself, and mine eyes shall behold, and not another; *though* my **reins** be consumed within me. (Job 19:27)

The **reins** are mentioned fifteen times in the AV.[102] The word comes directly into English from the French. It was derived from a Latin word that referred to the kidneys. But like the word *heart*, **reins** in the Bible is never a reference to a bodily organ. The **reins** are the seat of emotions, feelings, or affections. **Reins** is completely removed from the Bible by all of our modern versions. The replacements are exceedingly numerous. One can find "kidneys,"[103] "heart,"[104] "hearts,"[105] "minds,"[106] "mind,"[107] "soul,"[108] "within,"[109] "inward parts,"[110] "waist,"[111] "feelings,"[112] "vitals,"[113] "loins,"[114] "spirit,"[115] and "inmost being."[116] But in the twentieth century, the artery that goes to the kidneys is called the **renal** artery, not the kidney artery. And the veins that return the blood from the kidneys are termed the **renal** veins, not the kidney veins.

Remit

> Whose soever sins ye **remit,** they are **remitted** unto them; *and* whose soever *sins* ye retain, they are retained. (John 20:23)

The word **remit** is found only once in the AV, as is the word **remitted,** which occurs in the same verse.[117] The form **remission** appears ten times.[118] **Remit** comes from the Latin *remittere,* "to send back." To **remit** is to abate, relax, slacken, forgive, pardon, put off, or send back. **Remission** is the act of remitting, forgiveness, pardon, or the relinquishment of an obligation. Although the NKJV retains "**remission**" nine out of ten times,[119] the other versions substitute "forgiveness" equally as many times.[120] **Remit** and **remitted** are changed in all the modern versions to "forgive" and "forgiven."[121] But then the NRSV and NASB united in inserting the supposedly archaic "**remission**" into four passages where neither the AV nor the NKJV or NIV contained the word.[122] And furthermore, the NRSV employed the similar form "**remiss**" on one occasion.[123] The correction of **remit** and **remission** was entirely unnecessary, for a notice about an overdue bill usually says to please **remit,** while a disease is often said to be in **remission.**

Rend

> Give not that which is holy unto the dogs, neither cast ye your pearls before swine, lest they trample them under their feet, and turn again and **rend** you. (Mat 7:6)

The word **rend** occurs nineteen times in the AV[124] and the form **rending** appears once.[125] The related word **rent** is found sixty times,[126] while **rented** occurs once.[127] **Rend** is from the Old English *rendan,* "to tear." Hence, to **rend** is to tear, pull apart, or break. **Rent** can be three things. As a noun, it refers to a tear, crack, or torn place. The word **rent** is also the past tense and past participle of **rend**. And finally, **rent** is often just a variant of **rend**. The word **rend** is usually given in our modern versions as "tear."[128] **Rent** is either rendered as "tore,"[129] "torn,"[130] or "tear."[131] But after judging these words to be archaic, the NKJV retained "**rending**" as it appeared in the AV[132] and the NASB altered **rent** to "was rending."[133] The NASB then forgot to remove "**rend**" three times,[134] the NIV and NKJV two times,[135] and the NRSV once.[136] The word **rend**, however, is current English: "There are real issues, tough issues—from immigration policy to the inevitable competition among different groups for resources and jobs—that **rend** fissures in a society struggling toward some undefined new equilibrium."[137] The word **rent** can also be found in use when not referring to paying **rent**: "There's a sense that the entire social fabric is increasingly **rent** by violence, and schools cannot be immune."[138]

Reprobate

> And even as they did not like to retain God in *their* knowledge, God gave them over to a **reprobate** mind, to do those things which are not convenient; (Rom 1:28)

The word **reprobate** appears four times in the AV in the singular[139] and three times in the plural.[140] It is from the Latin *reprobatus*, from *reprobare*, "to reject." This was a compound verb based on *probare*, "to test." To be **reprobate** is to fail a test, to be rejected, condemned, or unapproved. In the Bible, a **reprobate** is someone or something that is unapproved and therefore rejected. The word **reprobate** later came to be applied to anyone who was depraved, worthless, or otherwise worthy of condemnation. Although our modern versions reprobated every occurrence of **reprobate** when it appeared in the AV, they could only agree on the proper translation one time. Besides uniting on "rejected,"[141] the new versions utilized "debased,"[142] "depraved,"[143] "failed,"[144] "disapproved,"[145] "unapproved,"[146] "disqualified,"[147] "worthless,"[148] "unfit,"[149] and forms of "fail the test."[150] But after correcting the AV because it was deemed archaic, the NASB changes a "vile person" in the AV to a "**reprobate**."[151] The word **reprobate**, however, is still in common use today: "Perhaps it's time that those people—whether they be Hollywood stars or blue collar workers—who casually bring children into the world without a long-term commitment to assume child care and economic obligations should be scorned as selfish, irresponsible **reprobates**."[152]

Requite

> But if any widow have children or nephews, let them learn first to show piety at home, and to **requite** their parents: for that is good and acceptable before God. (1 Tim 5:4)

The word **requite** appears nine times in the AV.[153] The form **requited** is found twice[154] and the form **requiting** occurs once.[155] **Requite** is a combination of *re*, "back," and *quite*, "released." To **requite** is to pay back, make return for, reward, avenge, or retaliate. The usual substitution in our modern versions is a form of "repay."[156] Other translations include "deal with,"[157] "show,"[158] and return."[159] Yet after correcting **requite** because it was deemed archaic, the NRSV inserted "requital" twice into one verse where neither the AV nor any modern version contained any form of the word.[160] Moreover, the NASB used "**requited**" twice[161] and "**requite**" twice[162] in places where no other versions included the words. Although is was excised where it appeared in the AV, forms of **requite** are still popular today: "You sort of collected and showed off to your friends the number of people you could interest without **requiting** it."[163]

Rereward

> And the armed men went before the priests that blew with the trumpets, and the **rereward** came after the ark, *the priests going on, and blowing with the trumpets.* (Josh 6:9)

The word **rereward,** a variant of *rearward,* occurs six times in the AV.[164] **Rereward** appeared in Middle English as *rerewarde,* short for *arere-warde,* "guard in the rear." The *-ward* in this word is not the suffix *-ward* indicating direction but rather the word *ward* meaning a guard, watch, or defense. Thus, we say ward off an intruder or ward of the court. The **rereward** is the "rear guard," as it is customarily rendered by our modern versions.[165] Yet when the AV mentions a "troop," the NRSV corrects it to "marauder."[166] And when the AV simply says "robbers," it is changed to "marauders" by the NIV.[167]

Respite

> But when Pharaoh saw that there was **respite**, he hardened his heart, and hearkened not unto them; as the LORD had said. (Exo 8:15)

The word **respite** occurs only twice in the AV.[168] It is from the French *respit*, "delay." **Respite** was originally a doublet of *respect*, but now means a delay, an interval of rest, a reprieve, postponement, or extension of time. Surprisingly, the NRSV retains this word on both occasions.[169] The usual new rendering, however, is "relief."[170] Not only did the NRSV keep this word where the AV had it, it also inserted it into three additional passages,[171] one of which simply said "rest.[172] Moreover, after correcting the AV both times, the NIV injects "**respite**" into another verse where all of the other modern versions closely followed the AV reading of "quietness."[173] The word **respite**, however, can still be found in use today: "For his part, Clinton wins a **respite** from his effort to round up support for U.N. sanctions against North Korea—a campaign that was not going well."[174]

Revellings

> For the time past of *our* life may suffice us to have wrought the will of the Gentiles, when we walked in lasciviousness, lusts, excess of wine, **revellings,** banquetings, and abominable idolatries: (1 Pet 4:3)

The word **revellings**, mentioned twice in the AV,[175] is formed from the verb *revel*, originally a doublet of *rebel*. **Revellings** are noisy feasts, loud merry-making, or any kind of disorderly or immoral festivity. The NKJV alters **revellings** to the similar "revelries," the NIV to "orgies," and the NASB to forms of "carousal."[176] The NRSV, however, could not decide between "carousing" or shortening **revellings** to "revels," even though the underlying Greek word was the same.[177] But after correcting the AV every time, the NASB employed forms of "reveled" five times.[178] The NKJV uses forms of "revelry" an additional three times,[179] while the NRSV does so on eight occasions.[180] The NIV utilizes forms of "revelry" thirteen times,[181] including the substitution of "revelry" for "gladness" when the NASB and

NKJV followed the AV reading.[182] The NIV also corrected the simple word "play" found in the AV and the other modern versions to "indulge in pagan revelry."[183]

Rid

> Send thine hand from above; **rid** me, and deliver me out of great waters, from the hand of strange children; (Psa 144:7)

The word **rid** occurs six times in the AV,[184] while the form **riddance** is found twice.[185] **Rid** is from the Old Norse *rythja*, "to clear." **Riddance** was formed much later from the English **rid**. The usage of the word **rid** in the AV has been deemed troublesome since it does not parallel that of the word **rid** today. In the AV, **rid** has the sense of rescue, deliver, or set free; hence, it is no surprise that our modern versions have unanimously updated **rid** to "deliver,"[186] "rescue,"[187] and "free."[188] The NKJV, however, did retain "**rid**" in one instance where it carried the meaning of removing something.[189] Although not quite as the AV, the NIV does employ the word "**rid**" in an unconventional manner on two occasions.[190] **Riddance** is also corrected by our modern versions,[191] except for the NKJV retaining it in one passage.[192] But the word **riddance** is still used as part of a popular expression up near the end of the twentieth century: "And all I can say is a resounding 'Thank God! Good **riddance!** And thanks to everyone who supported me in this ordeal!'"[193]

Rifled

> For I will gather all nations against Jerusalem to battle; and the city shall be taken, and the houses **rifled,** and the women ravished; and half of the city shall go forth into captivity, and the residue of the people shall not be cut off from the city. (Zec 14:2)

The word **rifled** appears only once in the AV. It is from the French *rifler*, "to scratch or plunder." To be **rifled** is to be plundered, robbed, pillaged, searched, ransacked, or examined thoroughly. Thus, this word has nothing to do with a rifle. Although the NKJV retained this word, the other versions could not decide on a replacement for it. The NRSV chose "looted," the NIV "ransacked," and the NASB "plundered." But even

Time magazine did not consider **rifled** to be archaic: The desks had been **rifled;** none of the telephones worked; records were so disorganized that by last week the mayor still had no idea how many employees were on the city payroll."[194]

𝕽𝖎𝖔𝖙

> If any be blameless, the husband of one wife, having faithful children not accused of **riot** or unruly. (Titus 1:6)

The word **riot** occurs three times in the AV,[195] while the form **riotous** can be found four times.[196] **Riot** is from the French *riote*, "dispute." **Riot** is wanton, loose, or wasteful living, intense disputing, debauchery, or extravagance. **Riotous** is just the adjective form of **riot**. Due to their limiting of the word **riot** to the modern meaning of a violent public disturbance, our modern versions have corrected **riot** and **riotous** every time they appear in the AV.[197] **Riot** can be found as "debauchery,"[198] "revel,"[199] and the more difficult "dissipation."[200] **Riotous** appears most of the time as "gluttons" or "gluttonous."[201] Other translations include "dissolute,"[202] "loose,"[203] "wild,"[204] "prodigal,"[205] "carousing,"[206] and "orgies."[207] Yet when the AV uses a simple word like "full," the NIV and NASB change it to "glutted."[208] Although the word "revellings" is corrected in the AV, the NKJV and NRSV use forms of the word to update **riotous** one time.[209] The NASB, after removing **riot** and **riotous** every time, uses both "**riot**" and "**riotous**" as the AV each one time to amend the AV in other passages.[210] The correction of these words was unnecessary, for forms of them are still in use as they appear in the AV: "A particular theme is that she enjoyed a life of **riotous** excess, receiving priceless gifts, buying, with her husband, 14 luxury cars, and having golden sand imported for the private beach outside their holiday home in Vilm."[211]

𝕽𝖎𝖘𝖎𝖓𝖌

> When a man shall have in the skin of his flesh a **rising,** a scab, or bright spot, and it be in the skin of his flesh *like* the plague of leprosy; then he shall be brought unto Aaron the priest, or unto one of his sons the priests: (Lev 13:2)

A **rising** is mentioned seven times in the AV.[212] This word is obviously formed from the common verb *rise,* but its use in the AV as a noun is what is suspect. A **rising** is a swelling, an abscess, a tumor, or a boil. Our modern versions have unanimously rendered **rising** as "swelling" in every instance,[213] except for the NIV, which employed "swollen sore" one time.[214] Yet when the AV says something is "**swelling,**" the NIV and NRSV alter it to "bulging."[215] The word **rising,** however, is not that out of date. Truman Capote stated in 1949: "I had me a **rising** on my butt big as a baseball."[216] And a more recent home remedy stated that after scraping the white of an Irish potato and binding the scrapings on a boil with a clean cloth, "this will draw the **risin'** (boil) to a head."[217]

Road

> And Achish said, Whither have ye made a **road** to day? And David said, Against the south of Judah, and against the south of the Jerahmeelites, and against the south of the Kenites. (1 Sam 27:10)

A **road** is only mentioned once in the AV. What the modern versions call a **road** the AV terms a way. The word **road** is from the Old English *rad.* It originally signified a journey, a hostile incursion, or a raid. In fact, our modern versions unanimously update **road** to forms of "raid." But if this usage of the word **road** makes the Bible hard to understand, then what about "irresolute," used by the supposedly up-to-date NRSV.[218]

Roe

> Deliver thyself as a **roe** from the hand *of the hunter,* and as a bird from the hand of the fowler. (Prov 6:5)

A **roe** is mentioned seven times in the AV in the singular[219] and five in the plural.[220] The longer form **roebuck** is found four times in the singular[221] and once in the plural.[222] **Roe,** which appeared in Old English as *raha,* is a small species of deer. A **roebuck** is a male **roe** deer. **Roes** and **roebucks** are all changed into "gazelles" by our modern versions.[223] However, there are some exceptions. A **roe** is once termed a "doe" by the NKJV, NRSV, and NASB, and a "deer" by the NIV.[224] Twice when the AV mentions "young **roes,**" they are called "fawns" by all of the new translations.²²⁵ But obviously the modern versions did not consider **roe** and **roebuck** to be archaic, for the NRSV and NASB consistently render "fallowdeer" in the AV as "roebuck."²²⁶ The NIV and NKJV say "**roe** deer" in one passage and "**roebuck**" in the other.²²⁷ But **roe** is not archaic in the first place: "**Roe** rings, well-trodden runs in the shape of a circle or a figure-of-eight, are evidence of **roe** residence if they have been recently used."²²⁸

Rude

But though *I be* **rude** in speech, yet not in knowledge; but we have been thoroughly made manifest among you in all things. (2 Cor 11:6)

The word **rude,** occurring only once in the AV, is from a French word of the same spelling derived from the Latin *rudis,* "raw, rough." **Rude** originally meant unformed, inexperienced, unlearned, uneducated, unskilled, or otherwise unrefined. Due to their limiting the word **rude** to the modern concept of being impolite, **rude** is rendered by forms of "untrained" in the NKJV, NIV, and NRSV, but "unskilled" in the NASB. However, when the AV refers to simple things like "wise men," the NIV and NASB alter them to "magi."²²⁹

Rudiments

Wherefore if ye be dead with Christ from the **rudiments** of the world, why, as though living in the world, are ye subject to ordinances, (Col 2:20)

The word **rudiments** appears twice in the AV.²³⁰ It came into English from the Latin *rudimentum,* "beginning." This word is also ultimately derived from the Latin *rudis* and literally signifies a thing in the first rough state. Hence, **rudiments** are first attempts or principles, the elements of a subject, foundation or fundamental principles, or an initial or imperfect form, stage, or appearance. Although our modern versions united in extracting **rudiments** from the Bible, they could not agree on what to replace it with. The NIV and NKJV joined together in updating **rudiments** to "basic principles," but the NRSV selected "elemental spirits" and the NASB "elementary principles."²³¹

The word **rudiments,** however, is still in vogue today: "The **rudiments** of a solution are thus apparent: An overarching Euro-Atlantic authority that provides collective security and economic incentives to destroy weapons and dismantle the capacity to produce them must go hand in hand."[232]

𝕽𝖚𝖘𝖍

> Can the **rush** grow up without mire? can the flag grow without water? (Job 8:11)

A **rush** is mentioned in the AV three times in the singular[233] and once in the plural.[234] The word comes from the Old English *risc* and refers to a grasslike aquatic plant with hollow stems found on the banks of rivers or ponds or in marshy ground. The plural **rushes** is retained by the NKJV, NRSV, and NASB, but the NIV preferred "papyrus."[235] The singular **rush,** however, was unanimously altered to "papyrus" in one verse,[236] while the NIV and NRSV corrected the other two occurrences to "reed" and the NKJV and NASB extended them to "bulrush."[237] But when the AV reads "bulrush" or "bulrushes," it is several times altered to "papyrus"[238] or "reed."[239] And when the AV mentions "reeds," it is often changed to "marches" or "bulrushes."[240] Yet when the AV says "flags," the new versions regularly update them to "**rushes.**"[241]

Chapter 19
Sackbut to Swelling

Sackbut

> *That* at what time ye hear the sound of the cornet, flute, harp, **sackbut,** psaltery, dulcimer, and all kinds of music, ye fall down and worship the golden image that Nebuchadnezzar the king hath set up: (Dan 3:5)

A **sackbut** is mentioned four times in the AV[1] and is from the French *saquebute*. A **sackbut** is a medieval wind instrument. The word was first used by the Geneva Bible for the obscure instrument in Nebuchadnezzar's band due to its resemblance in sound to the underlying Aramaic word. But if **sackbut** was hard to understand, the new translations given by our modern versions are even worse. The NASB and NRSV call a **sackbut** a "trigon" and the NIV and NKJV call it a "lyre."[2] But obviously a **sackbut** is an instrument still in existence, or else there would not be a magazine called *Cornett and Sackbut*.[3]

Sacrilege

> Thou that sayest a man should not commit adultery, dost thou commit adultery? thou that abhorrest idols, dost thou commit **sacrilege?** (Rom 2:22)

The word **sacrilege** occurs only once in the AV. It comes from a French word of the same spelling meaning the stealing of sacred things. Thus, **sacrilege** means stealing or misappropriating what is consecrated to God's service or profaning anything held sacred. Our modern versions have unanimously updated **sacrilege** to "rob temples." Yet in two other passages where the other versions read as the AV, the NRSV inserts the word "**sacrilege**" that it just corrected.[4] Nevertheless, this word is still used today:

"Although even klansmen refer to the ceremony as a cross-burning, Klan purists call it a cross-lighting to avoid any appearance of **sacrilege**."[5]

Satiate

> And I will **satiate** the soul of the priests with fatness, and my people shall be satisfied with my goodness, saith the LORD. (Jer 31:14)

The word **satiate** appears twice in the AV,[6] while the forms **satiated**[7] and **unsatiable**[8] each occur once. Satiate is from the Latin *satiatus,* from *satiare,* "to fill." To **satiate** is fill to repletion, glut, saturate, or satisfy. Surprisingly, the NKJV retains a form of the AV reading every time.[9] The NIV and NRSV both correct **satiate** and **satiated** the three times they occur, but with a different word each time.[10] Then they leave in the word **unsatiable** in the form of "insatiable."[11] The NASB corrected **satiate** once,[12] altered **satiate** to "satiated" once,[13] but then changed **satiated** to "satisfy"[14] and **unsatiable** to "not satisfied."[15] The NRSV, after correcting the AV three out of four times, amended "cannot cease" in the AV to "insatiable."[16] Moreover, when the AV simply says "filled," the NRSV and NASB amend it to the arcane "sated."[17] But every correction of **satiate** was unnecessary, for the word still appears today, even in *Time* magazine: "Furthermore, those hungering for Columbus T shirts, watches or other memorabilia should not have to search far to **satiate** themselves."[18]

Save

> And that no man might buy or sell, **save** he that had the mark, or the name of the beast, or the number of his name. (Rev 13:17)

Although the word **save** occurs over 200 times in the AV, it is used in an archaic sense on fifty-nine of these occasions.[19] The word **save,** when used as a preposition or conjunction meaning except or but, is from the French *sauf.* Our modern versions almost unanimously update **save** to "except."[20] But when the AV is completely unambiguous, like when it uses the word "covered," the NIV alone amends it to "sheathed."[21]

Scall

> Then the priest shall look on him: and, behold, if the **scall** be spread in the skin, the priest shall not seek for yellow hair; he *is* unclean. (Lev 13:36)

A **scall** is mentioned fourteen times in the AV.[22] This word comes from the Old Norse *skalli,* "a bald head." A **scall** is sore or scab, usually on the head. Today we might say eczema, psoriasis, or impetigo. The NRSV and NIV normally correct **scall** to "itch" and the NKJV and NASB to "scale."[23] But when the AV mentions something simple like a "scab," the NRSV alone makes it into the more difficult "eruption."[24] The word **scall,** however, is still defined in medical dictionaries as "any crusted or pustular scaly eruption or lesion of the skin or scalp."[25]

Scrabbled

> And he changed his behaviour before them, and feigned himself mad in their hands, and **scrabbled** on the doors of the gate, and let his spittle fall down upon his beard. (1 Sam 21:13)

The word **scrabbled,** from scrabble, occurs only once in the AV. Scrabble is from the Dutch *schrabbelen,* "to scratch." To scrabble is to rake, scrape, or scratch hurriedly with the claws, paws, hands, or feet, or to struggle in a disorderly fashion. The NKJV and NRSV have united in changing **scrabbled** to "scratched," but the NIV chose "making marks," and the NASB "scribbled." But these corrections were unfortunate, for the word **scrabbled** is still used today: "Meanwhile, a thousand interest groups **scrabbled** to protect themselves."[26]

Scrip

> And commanded them that they should take nothing for *their* journey, save a staff only; no **scrip,** no bread, no money in *their* purse: (Mark 6:8)

A **scrip** shows up seven times in the AV.[27] The word is thought to come from either the French *escreppe* or the Old Norse *skreppa,* both meaning a small bag. A **scrip** is a small bag, satchel, or purse. Naturally, our modern versions have eliminated this word. In the only time it appears in the Old Testament, **scrip** is unanimously changed to "pouch."[28] In the New Testament, **scrip** is always replaced with "bag," except for the NKJV using "knapsack" three times."[29] But if the use of **scrip** made the Bible hard to understand, then it should be noted that when the AV mentions a "bundle," the NIV corrects it to a "sachet."[30]

Seatward

See you-ward.

Seemly

> As snow in summer, and as rain in harvest, so honour is not **seemly** for a fool. (Prov 26:1)

The word **seemly** is used twice in the AV,[31] as is the form **unseemly**.[32] **Seemly** is from the Old Norse *soemiligr*, from *soemr*, "becoming." If something is **seemly** then it is fitting, becoming, pleasing, proper, or appropriate. Although our modern versions have removed every trace of these words when they are used by the AV, the NASB adds "**seemly**" to two passages where the AV did not contain the word,[33] "**unseemly**" to another,[34] and "**seemliness**" to yet another.[35] **Seemly** is always updated by our modern versions to "fitting,"[36] but the corrections for **unseemly** are varied. One can find "unbecomingly,"[37] "rude,"[38] "shameless,"[39] "indecent,"[40] and "shameful."[41] But in spite of all these emendations, the word **seemly** was considered **seemly** by the *Washington Monthly*: "Fortunately, most of the promotion was very **seemly**."[42]

Seethe

> The first of the firstfruits of thy land thou shalt bring into the house of the LORD thy God. Thou shalt not **seethe** a kid in his mother's milk. (Exo 23:19)

The word **seethe** appears nine times in the AV.[43] Other forms include **seething**, found three times,[44] the past tense **sod**, found twice,[45] and **sodden**, found six times.[46] **Seethe** is from the Old English *seothan*, "to boil." To **seeth** means to boil or cook food by boiling. Naturally, the AV is corrected every time it uses one of these words, except for the NRSV and NASB forgetting to remove "**seeth**" on one occasion.⁴⁷ **Seething** is always updated to "boiling,"⁴⁸ but **seeth** sometimes appears as "make,"⁴⁹ "cook,"⁵⁰ or "simmer."⁵¹ **Sod** is unanimously given as "boiled" one time⁵² and forms of "cooked" the next.⁵³ **Sodden** is usually replaced by "boiled,"⁵⁴ but "cooked" was also utilized.⁵⁵ Yet when the AV read "boiled," the NASB one time corrected it to "**seething**."⁵⁶ But just as the word boil is used figuratively today, so is the word **seethe**, even by *Time* magazine: "The prisons **seethe** with the conflict."⁵⁷

Selfsame

> In the **selfsame** day was Abraham circumcised, and Ishmael his son. (Gen 17:26)

The compound word **selfsame** is used fifteen times in the AV.⁵⁸ Like many compound words, it was originally written as two words. **Selfsame** means the very same, identical, or one and the same. This word does not appear in any of our modern versions but is instead replaced with "very same,"⁵⁹ "same,"⁶⁰ or "very."⁶¹ This was unfortunate, for the word **selfsame** is still current today: "With its flawless uniformity and **selfsame** appearance at all degrees of magnification, the Sierpinski gasket, Linderberg knows, is not an ideal model for a structure that occurs in nature."⁶²

Selvedge

> And thou shalt make loops of blue upon the edge of the one curtain from the **selvedge** in the coupling; and likewise shalt thou make in the uttermost edge of *another* curtain, in the coupling of the second. (Exo 26:4)

The word **selvedge** occurs only twice in the AV.⁶³ It is from the Dutch *selfegge*, literally meaning "self-edge." The **selvedge** is the edge of woven fabric finished to prevent unraveling. Surprisingly, the NKJV retains this supposedly archaic word. The NRSV and NASB reword these sentences to refer to the "outermost curtain."⁶⁴ The NIV does the same but preferred "end curtain."⁶⁵ But when the AV employs a simple word like "strong," the NASB alone alters it to "stalwart."⁶⁶

Sepulchre

> There laid they Jesus therefore because of the Jews' preparation *day;* for the **sepulchre** was nigh at hand. (John 19:42)

A **sepulchre** is mentioned in the AV fifty-four times in the singular[67] and sixteen times in the plural.[68] This word comes into English from the French *sepulcre,* "tomb." Thus, a **sepulchre** is a tomb, grave, or burial-place. Our modern versions have completely excised both of these words. The usual replacement is "tomb,"[69] but "grave"[70] and "burial place"[71] also appear. The plural **sepulchres** is similarly updated.[72] Nevertheless, the word **sepulchre** can still be found today as a substitute for tomb: "For Christians, it is The Church of the Holy **Sepulchre** and for Muslims The Dome of the Rock and Al Aqsa Mosque."[73]

Servile

> And on the fifteenth day of the seventh month ye shall have an holy convocation; ye shall do no **servile** work, and ye shall keep a feast unto the LORD seven days: (Num 29:12)

The word **servile** appears twelve times in the AV.[74] It is from the Latin *servilis,* "belonging to a slave." If something is **servile** it is befitting a slave, such as doing physical work. Although our modern versions all updated the word **servile,** they could not agree on what to replace it with. The NASB chose "laborious," the NIV "regular," and the NKJV "customary."[75] "**Servile** work" in the AV is "work at your occupations" in the NRSV.[76] These corrections were entirely unnecessary, for the word **servile** is still in vogue: "Education, entrepreneurship, women's political participation, the widespread rejection of **servile** status, the mutual knowledge through mass media, and many other more powerful realities than the recent coup—these show Peruvian society is moving ahead."[77]

Servitor

> And his **servitor** said, What, should I set this before an hundred men? He said again, Give the people, that they may eat: for thus saith the LORD, They shall eat, and shall leave *thereof.* (2 Ki 4:43)

A **servitor** is mentioned only once in the AV. Coming into English from the French *servitour*, a **servitor** is a servant, slave, attendant, or anyone who provides a service. This word was too archaic for our modern versions. The translation of choice was "servant," but the NASB went with "attendant." Yet although **servitor** it was deemed to be archaic by the new versions, *Forbes* magazine had no trouble with the word: "SALLIE MAE—Student Loan Marketing Association—is a quasi-private company that is the country's largest holder and **servitor** of student loans, with assets of $54 billion."[78]

Settle

And the settle *shall be* fourteen *cubits* long and fourteen broad in the four squares thereof; and the border about it *shall be* half a cubit; and the bottom thereof *shall be* a cubit about; and his stairs shall look toward the east. (Ezek 43:17)

The word **settle** occurs six times in the AV with this particular meaning.[79] **Settle** is from the Old English *setl*, "a seat." A **settle** is a sitting place, a ledge, or a raised platform. This was the original meaning of the word; the modern concept of settling a quarrel came later. Nevertheless, the word **settle** is updated anyway. The standard replacement for **settle** is "ledge,"[80] but the NIV three times said "upper ledge."[81] Yet when the AV employed the word **settle** in the modern sense, it was still corrected by the NIV, NRSV, and NASB.[82] Moreover, although they corrected **settle,** all of our modern versions use the derivative "settlements."[83]

Sever

So shall it be at the end of the world: the angels shall come forth, and **sever** the wicked from among the just, (Mat 13:49)

The word **sever** occurs four times in the AV but never with the modern definition of cut.[84] The form **severed** likewise appears three times.[85] The similar word **several** is used twelve times in the AV but never in the modern sense of "a few" or "three or more."[86] **Severally** is also employed once.[87] **Sever** is from the French *sevrer*, "to separate," while **several** comes from a French word of the same spelling meaning a thing set apart. They are both ultimately derived from the Latin *separare*, "to separate." To **sever** is to set apart, separate, or make a distinction. If something is **several** then it is apart, separate, or distinct. **Sever** is given in our modern versions by such things as "set apart"[88] and "make a distinction."[89] The new translations altered **several** to "own,"[90] "separate,"[91] "isolated,"[92] or "single."[93] But when the AV utilized a simple word like "went," the NKJV made it unnecessarily more difficult by changing it to "wend."[94]

𝔖𝔥𝔞𝔪𝔟𝔩𝔢𝔰

> Whatsoever is sold in the **shambles**, *that* eat, asking no question for conscience sake: (1 Cor 10:25)

The word **shambles**, plural of *shamble*, appears only once in the AV. *Shamble* is from the Old English *scamel*, "a stool." **Shambles** were tables or counters for exposing goods offered for sale. Since they often held meat, the word **shambles** began to be associated with just a meatmarket. In fact, our modern versions all replace **shambles** with "meatmarket." But unfortunately some of them also replace "purge" with "smelt."[95]

𝔖𝔥𝔞𝔪𝔢𝔣𝔞𝔠𝔢𝔡𝔫𝔢𝔰𝔰

> In like manner also, that women adorn themselves in modest apparel, with **shamefacedness** and sobriety; not with broided hair, or gold, or pearls, or costly array; (1 Tim 2:9)

The word **shamefacedness** occurs only once in the AV. The base *shamefaced-* was derived from the word *shamefast*, from the Old English *scamfaest*, literally meaning "fast in shame." **Shamefacedness** means the state or quality of being shamefaced; in other words: modest, virtuous, or sober. The NASB and NRSV have altered this word to "modestly," the NIV to "decency," and the NKJV to "propriety." But then the NKJV inserts the word "shamefaced" into another passage.[96] Moreover, when the AV just says "shame," the NASB alone changes it to "reproach"[97] Nevertheless, the word **shamefacedness**, is in fact still in use today: "'I think there may be a closet Toryism, a kind of Conservative **shamefacedness** about voting one's self-interest,' said Martin Ceadel, a political scientist at New College, Oxford."[98]

Share

> But all the Israelites went down to the Philistines, to sharpen every man his **share**, and his coulter, and his ax, and his mattock. (1 Sam 13:20)

A **share** only surfaces once in the AV. The extended plural **plowshares** occurs three times.[99] **Share** is from the Old English *scear* meaning "that which cuts."A **share** is a farm implement that got its name from a verb meaning to shear. Our modern versions have extended a **share** to a "plowshare."[100] They have also retained the AV usage of "**plowshares**."[101] This in spite of the fact that most people do not even know what a **plowshare** is. The influence of the AV even extends to the United Nations, for a verse from the AV that mentions **plowshares** appears on the UN building.

Sherd

> And he shall break it as the breaking of the potters' vessel that is broken in pieces; he shall not spare: so that there shall not be found in the bursting of it a **sherd** to take fire from the hearth, or to take water *withal* out of the pit. (Isa 30:14)

Although a **sherd** is only mentioned once in the AV, the plural **sherds** also appears once,[102] while the extended form **potsherd** occurs four times in the singular[103] and once in the plural.[104] **Sherd** is a variant of *shard*, from the Old English *sceard*, "fragment." Thus, **sherd** it is related to the previous word *share*. A **sherd** is a fragment, remnant, or piece of something. A **potsherd** limits the **sherd** to a piece of pottery. Our modern versions could not decide whether to retain the AV words or not. The NRSV keeps the forms of "**sherd**" both times[105] but "**potsherd**" only twice.[106] The NASB likewise retains "**potsherd**" twice[107] but rejects **sherd** one time.[108] The NIV liked "**potsherd**" three times[109] but not **sherd** at all.[110] The NKJV only corrected **potsherd** once.[111] But after correcting **potsherd** in at least one verse in the AV, every one of our modern versions inserted "**potsherds**" into two verses where the AV did not contain the word.[112] The terms **sherd** and **potsherd** are still very common today and should never have been updated in the first place.

Shivers

And he shall rule them with a rod of iron; as the vessels of a potter shall they be broken to **shivers:** even as I received of my Father. (Rev 2:27)

The word **shivers** is used only once in the AV. It is the plural of *shiver,* the diminutive of *shive,* thought to be of Scandinavian origin. **Shivers** are fragments, chips, splinters, or slivers. When it is directly replaced by our modern versions, the substitution is "pieces." But in paper manufacturing, "a dark particle in finished paper resulting from incomplete digestion of impurities in the raw material" is termed a **shive.**[113] And a homemade prison knife is called a **shiv.**

Shod

And your feet **shod** with the preparation of the gospel of peace; (Eph 6:15)

The word **shod** appears four times in the AV,[114] while the forms **unshod** and **dryshod** each occur one time.[115] **Shod** is properly the past participle of the verb *shoe.* To be **shod** is to be wearing shoes or furnished with shoes. To **shod** someone is to provide them with shoes. The NIV and NRSV correct **dryshod** but the NASB and NKJV hyphenate it to "dry-shod."[116] And surprisingly, the NKJV, NASB, and NRSV retain "**unshod.**"[117] But when the AV just says **shod,** the NKJV and NASB only retain it in once.[118] Naturally, the NASB and NIV amend **shod** every time it occurs.[119] But in addition to the word *shoe* still being used as a verb (shoe a horse), forms of the word **shod** still regularly appear: "Keeping American yuppies well-**shod** has been good for South Korea."[120]

Silverlings

And it shall come to pass in that day, *that* every place shall be, where there were a thousand vines at a thousand **silverlings,** it shall *even* be for briers and thorns. (Isa 7:23)

The word **silverlings** is used only once in the AV. It is thought to be from the German *silberling.* A **silverling** is a piece of money, obviously made of silver. The customary replacement for **silverlings** in our modern versions is "shekels of silver," but the NIV preferred "silver shekels." Yet the NIV is the only modern version to use the word "inkling."[121] Moreover, the NKJV and NASB had no trouble with using the word "hireling" as it appeared in the AV.[122] But after correcting "hireling" in the AV to "hired man," the NKJV, NASB, and NIV alter "hired men" in the AV to "mercenaries."[123] And furthermore, the NKJV utilizes the word "seedlings," a word that occurs in no other modern version.[124] And finally, when the AV, followed by all of the other modern versions, says "sound," the NASB alone alters it to "tinkling."[125]

Single

> The light of the body is the eye: if therefore thine eye be **single,** thy whole body shall be full of light. (Mat 6:22)

Although the word **single** appears many times in our modern versions, it only occurs twice in the AV and has an entirely different meaning.[126] The form **singular** is also used once,[127] while **singleness** appears three times.[128] **Single,** which comes from the French *sengle,* means having a single aim or purpose, honest, sincere, or free from deceit. Thus, having a **single** eye does not mean having only one physical eye. The NIV and NKJV replace **single** with "good," but the NASB chose "clear" and the NRSV "healthy."[129] **Singleness** is usually corrected to "sincerity,"[130] but one time the NRSV forgot to remove the word.[131] The word **single** may have been somewhat difficult to understand, but this was no reason for the NASB and NRSV to add the word "palatial" to the Bible[132] or the NIV to change "palace" to "palatial structure."[133]

Sith

> Therefore, *as* I live, saith the Lord GOD, I will prepare thee unto blood, and blood shall pursue thee: **sith** thou hast not hated blood, even blood shall pursue thee. (Ezek 35:6)

The word **sith** occurs only once in the AV. It is short for the Middle English *sithen,* from the Old English *siththan,* "after that," from which we also get the word *since.* As it is used in the AV, **sith** is equivalent to *since,* and is so translated by our modern versions. But although the NASB corrected **sith** because it was archaic, it forgot to remove other words equally as archaic like "shalt,"[134] "shouldst,"[135] and "shouldest."[136]

Situate

> The forefront of the one *was* **situate** northward over against Michmash, and the other southward over against Gibeah. (1 Sam 14:5)

The word **situate** appears three times in the AV[137] and the form **situation** occurs twice.[138] **Situate** is from the Latin *situatus*, from *situare*, "to place." The Latin prefix was derived from *situs*, "a place," from which we get the English word *site*. Thus, to be **situate** is to be placed or located and a **situation** is a place or location where something is **situate**. The modern sense of a **situation** being a condition, case, or circumstance, although found in the NASB and NIV,[139] does not appear in the AV. The NRSV removes all forms of these words, but surprisingly, the NASB and NKJV followed the AV meaning of "**situation**" one time.[140] Moreover, the NASB, NIV, and NKJV all update **situate** to the more familiar modern form of "situated."[141] But when the AV simply says "placed," the NKJV alone also alters it to "situated."[142] The word **situate**, however, did not have to be amended in the first place, for it is still in use today: "Precolonial African historians at least tried to **situate** man in time, even if they did not always succeed in doing so."[143]

Sixscore

See fourscore.

Skill

> Send me also cedar trees, fir trees, and algum trees, out of Lebanon: for I know that thy servants can **skill** to cut timber in Lebanon; and, behold, my servants *shall be* with thy servants, (2 Chr 2:8)

The word **skill**, although appearing three times in the AV as a noun, and several more times as an adjective with the same meaning that it has today,[144] is also used four times as a verb.[145] When employed as a verb, **skill** is from the Old Norse *skilja*, meaning to distinguish or divide. The phrase "**can skill**" in the AV means to have knowledge or **skill** about something, but since the word **skill** is not used as a noun, it is deemed to be archaic by our modern versions. The NKJV transforms the phrase in question to forms of **skill** that are not used as a verb.[146] The NIV did this three times but settled on "experienced" the next.[147] The NRSV only retained a form of **skill** twice[148] and the NASB once.[149] Yet when the AV utilizes the word **skill** as a noun, the NASB and NIV correct it every time.[150] But the AV is not alone in using words as verbs that are normally found as nouns, for the word *office* is now being utilized as a verb in America.[151]

Sleight

> That we *henceforth* be no more children, tossed to and fro, and carried about with every wind of doctrine, by the **sleight** of men, *and* cunning craftiness, whereby they lie in wait to deceive; (Eph 4:14)

The word **sleight** occurs only once in the AV. It is from the Old Norse *slaegth*, "slyness," from *slaegr*, "sly." Thus, **sleight** is related to our word *sly* and means craft, cunning, or skill. The usual replacement for **sleight** in our modern versions is "trickery," except for the NIV, which chose "cunning." But not only is the expression "**sleight** of hand" very common today, the word **sleight** is still employed in other ways: "By some **sleight** of mind, we not only come to accept these images, we come to except them as truths."[152]

Slime

> And they said one to another, Go to, let us make brick, and burn them thoroughly. And they had brick for stone, and **slime** had they for mortar. (Gen 11:3)

Slime is mentioned twice in the AV[153] while **slimepits** appear once.[154] **Slime,** from the Old English *slim*, is soft mud or any viscous matter. The AV applies the word **slime** to what is now termed tar. In fact, the NIV and NASB both update **slime** to "tar."[155] The NRSV and NKJV, however, were not so modest. The NRSV replaces **slime** with the arduous "bitumen."[156] The NKJV calls **slime** "asphalt," a substance usually only associated with paved roads.[157] But if the AV be faulted for calling tar **slime**, then what about the NKJV and NRSV calling a "chariot" a "palanquin."[158]

Slothful

> The way of the **slothful** *man is* as an hedge of thorns: but the way of the righteous *is* made plain. (Prov 15:19)

The word **slothful** is used fifteen times in the AV.[159] The extended form **slothfulness** occurs twice.[160] **Slothful** is from *sloth,* from the Middle English *slowthe* or an older English form meaning slowness, from *slaw,* "slow." **Slothful** means sluggish, idle, slow, lazy, or inactive. Excepting the two passages where the NASB and NKJV slothfully forgot to remove this word, **slothful** is completely excised by our modern versions.[161] It is usually rendered as "lazy,"[162] but "slow,"[163] "sluggard,"[164] "slack,"[165] "lagging,"[166] and "sluggish"[167] can also be found. **Slothfulness** is unanimously corrected to "laziness" in one verse,[168] but in the other place it occurs the NRSV substitutes the base form "sloth" and the NASB employs the harder word "indolence."[169] But when the AV uses the word "sluggard," it is sometimes corrected by the NRSV, NASB, and NKJV even though the NIV keeps it every time.[170] On two occasions when the NKJV, NASB, and NIV all follow the AV reading of "sluggard," the NRSV alone alters it to "lazybones."[171] The word **slothful,** however, did not need to be corrected in the first place, for it is still common today, even in *Time* magazine: "And yet the selfish, **slothful** heroines of the hit British TV show Absolutely Fabulous have attracted a cult of admirers worldwide."[172]

Sluices

> And they shall be broken in the purposes thereof, all that make **sluices** *and* ponds for fish. (Isa 19:10)

The word **sluices** is used only once in the AV. A sluice, from the French *escluse,* is a barrier by which water is held back or water that is artificially held back. The French word is from the Latin *exclusa,* thought to be short for *aqua exclusa,* "water shut out." Naturally, our modern versions deemed the word **sluices** to be archaic. Not so however, for *Life* magazine: "These days, the

Everglades' water flow is regulated by the computer-controlled concrete **sluices** of the South Florida Water Management District."[173]

Smith

> Behold, I have created the **smith** that bloweth the coals in the fire, and that bringeth forth an instrument for his work; and I have created the waster to destroy. (Isa 54:16)

The word **smith** occurs in the AV three times in the singular[174] and four times in the plural.[175] The derivative **goldsmith** occurs twice in the plural[176] and three times in the singular.[177] **Silversmith** also occurs once,[178] as does **coppersmith**.[179] **Smith**, which comes unchanged from Old English, refers to a craftsman or skilled worker. Although the most commonly known type of **smith** is a blacksmith, few really know how the name came to be. A **smith** who works in black metal (iron) is a blacksmith; a **smith** who works in white metal (tin) is a whitesmith. Although only certain derivatives of **smith** are still used today (gunsmith, etc.), the NRSV retained the base "**smith**" six times,[180] the NASB five times,[181] and the NKJV four times.[182] The NRSV and NASB even inserted "**smith**" into an additional verse where the AV did not contain it.[183] The NIV usually replaced **smith** with "artisans."[184] The derivatives of **smith** that are used in the AV are retained in all cases except for the NIV updating **coppersmith** to "metalworker."[185] Clearly, the word **smith** is an example of the profound influence of the AV on new versions that profess to use modern, contemporary language.

Snuffed

> And the wild asses did stand in the high places, they **snuffed** up the wind like dragons; their eyes did fail, because *there was* no grass. (Jer 14:6)

The word **snuffed** appears twice in the AV[186] and the form **snuffeth** can be seen once.[187] The word *snuff* represents two entirely different verbs in English. The commonly used one today means to put something out like a candle flame. The other *snuff* word is from the Dutch *snuffen*, "to sniff." This means to inhale, draw up, smell, or sniff. The AV only uses forms of the later *snuff* word. Naturally, our modern versions correct **snuffed** and **snuffeth** to forms of "sniff."[188] However, "pant"[189] and "sneer"[190] are also used. Yet when the AV simply says "put out," the NIV alters it to the more difficult "**snuffed** out" even though the other versions read as the AV.[191] And although **snuffed** and **snuffeth** were corrected by the new translations, tobacco that is taken orally and inhaled is still called **snuff.**

Soever

> And he said unto them, In what place **soever** ye enter into an house, there abide till ye depart from that place. (Mark 6:10)

Although the word **soever** occurs sixteen times in the AV,[192] there are numerous other forms that are also used. **Whatsoever** can found 152 times,[193] **whosoever** 183 times,[194] **whensoever** 3 times,[195] **whomsoever** 20 times,[196] **howsoever** 4 times,[197] **wheresoever** 12 times,[198] **whithersoever** 29 times,[199] and **whereinsoever** once.[200] Soever, a combination of the adverbs *so* and *ever*, gives emphatic force to the word preceding it. By itself it usually means whenever. Although our modern versions have completely extricated all forms of **soever** from the Bible, many of them are still in use today:

> Most voters now feel, deeply and instinctively, that their congressman does not represent them in any way **whatsoever.**[201]

> But I hope in the future the award-givers bestow their favors on **whosoever** writes a short biography.[202]

> Japan has taken measures, **howsoever** half-hearted, to blunt this criticism but it seems with only a limited success, as Ensign's study tends to conclude.[203]

Solace

> Come, let us take our fill of love until the morning: let us **solace** ourselves with loves. (Prov 7:18)

The word **solace** occurs only once in the AV. It comes from the French *solaz,* "comfort." To **solace** is to comfort, sooth, console, cheer, or relieve. **Solace** is replaced by "delight" in the NKJV, NRSV, and NASB, but the NIV preferred "enjoy." Yet after correcting the AV, the NRSV and NASB inserted the word "solace" into a verse where the AV did not contain the word.²⁰⁴ But the word **solace** is still in use anyway, even by *Fortune* magazine: "Stokes would escape to the Sonoma County wine country, finding **solace** with friends."²⁰⁵

Soothsayer

> Balaam also the son of Beor, the **soothsayer**, did the children of Israel slay with the sword among them that were slain by them. (Josh 13:22)

Although **soothsayer** appears only once in the AV, the plural **soothsayers** can be found six times²⁰⁶ and the form **soothsaying** once.²⁰⁷ This word is a compound of the Old English *soth*, "true," and *sayer*, "to say," literally meaning "one who says the truth." A **soothsayer** is one who claims or pretends to have the power of foretelling future events. Although the NKJV follows the AV every time in retaining the singular and plural forms of "**soothsayer**,"²⁰⁸ the other versions tried to completely eliminate the word. Only the NIV, however, was wholly successful,²⁰⁹ for the NRSV forgot two places²¹⁰ and the NASB one.²¹¹ The usual replacement for **soothsayers** is "diviners."²¹² **Soothsaying** is unanimously given in our modern versions by forms of "fortune-tellers."²¹³ Excepting this one instance, the NKJV liked these words so much that it used forms of them eight more times.²¹⁴ Moreover, after correcting the AV six times, the NRSV inserted all three of these words into five passages where the AV did not use them.²¹⁵ The NASB, after amending the AV text all but once, used two of these words where the AV did not.²¹⁶ And furthermore, the NIV employed forms of "**soothsayer**" twice after correcting the same words in the AV every time.²¹⁷ but when the AV utilized the word "enchanter" that is common to all modern versions, it was changed into the more difficult "augur" by the NRSV.²¹⁸ In spite of all the corrections of the AV, the word **soothsayer** is still in vogue today: "The hurricane **soothsayer** himself sits in an office jammed with stacks of paper and old aerial photos of hurricanes, pondering the big picture."²¹⁹

Sop

> And after the **sop** Satan entered into him. Then said Jesus unto him, That thou doest, do quickly. John 13:27)

The word **sop** is used four times in the AV.[220] It is from the Old English *sopp* and refers to a piece of bread dipped in water, wine, etc. before being eaten or cooked. **Sop** is unanimously corrected by our modern versions. "A piece of bread" or simply "bread" is the replacement in the NKJV, NRSV, and NIV, but the NASB preferred "morsel."[221] But three things about the word **sop** should be noticed. First, a weak or effeminate man is called a milk **sop**. Second, a thorough soaking is termed being **sopping** wet. And third, The word **sop** by itself is still used today: "As a **sop** to frustrated House conservatives, Newt Gingrich has agreed to call a vote next April 15 on a constitutional amendment that would mandate a three-fifths congressional majority to raise federal tax rates."[222]

Sore

> Therefore Abimelech rose early in the morning, and called all his servants, and told all these things in their ears: and the men were **sore** afraid. (Gen 20:8)

Although the word **sore** appears nine times in the AV with the meaning of an injury, to injure, or to be injured,[223] the word **sore** is also used eighty-nine times as an adjective or adverb with the meaning of grievous, severe, painful, great, serious, or intense.[224] The form **sorely** is used twice,[225] while **sorer** is found only once.[226] **Sore** is from the Old English *sar*, "painful." Except for the NASB neglecting to twice remove "**sore**" when it is used as the AV,[227] our modern versions only use the word "**sore**" to apply to an injury.[228] The replacements for **sore** include "painful,"[229] "grievous,"[230] "very much,"[231] "severe,"[232] "very,"[233] and "greatly."[234] Yet one time when the AV says "grievous," the NASB changes it to the supposedly archaic "**sorely**."[235]

Sottish

> For my people *is* foolish, they have not known me; they *are* **sottish** children, and they have none understanding: they *are* wise to do evil, but to do good they have no knowledge. (Jer 4:22)

The word **sottish** occurs only once in the AV. It is formed from *sot*, from a French word of the same spelling meaning a fool. To be **sottish** is to be foolish or stupid. The meaning of this word gradually came to embody just that of a drunkard. The NRSV and NASB unite in altering **sottish** to "stupid," but the NIV preferred "senseless" and the NKJV "silly." This was unfortunate, for not only is a drunk still termed a drunken sot, the word **sottish** is still used today: "Rose must get free of her **sottish** novelist husband (Broadbent) and Lotty of hers, an ambitious mean-spirited lawyer (Molina)."[236]

Speed

> If there come any unto you, and bring not this doctrine, receive him not into *your* house, neither bid him God **speed**: (2 John 1:10)

Although the word **speed** is used many times in the AV, it only appears three times in this sense.[237] **Speed** is from the Old English *sped*, "success." Thus, **speed** means abundance, success, prosperity, or good fortune. The expression "good **speed**," found once in the Old Testament, is unanimously corrected by our modern versions to "success."[238] In the New Testament, to bid someone "God **speed**" is now to "welcome" in the NRSV and NIV, and to "greet" in the NKJV and NASB.[239] Yet the expression "God **speed**" is still current today: "But when a hare jumped up, I merely wished him God-**speed**."[240]

Spoil

> And Saul said, Let us go down after the Philistines by night, and **spoil** them until the morning light, and let us not leave a man of them. And they said, Do whatsoever seemeth good unto thee. Then said the priest, Let us draw near hither unto God. (1 Sam 14:36)

Although the word **spoil** can be found in the AV as a noun just like it is used in our modern versions, the AV also employs it as a verb thirty-one times.[241] **Spoiling** is also similarly used five times,[242] **spoileth** four times,[243] **spoiled** fifty-five times,[244] and **spoilest** once.[245] The nouns that describe one who spoils, **spoiler** and **spoilers**, are used nine[246] and seven[247] times respectively. **Spoil** is from the French *espoillier*, "to strip." To **spoil** is to strip of skin, goods, or possessions; to rob, plunder, or pillage; or to damage, ruin, or affect detrimentally. Like the word "skill," the verbal forms of **spoil** have been deemed to be archaic because they are not used as nouns like the word **spoil** is today. The usual replacement for the forms of **spoil** in our modern versions is a form of "plunder."[248] However, the NIV one time employs "**spoil**" as a verb in a verse where the AV did not contain the word **spoil** in any form.[249] The NKJV does likewise,[250] but also follows the AV reading one time.[251] The NRSV retains "**spoilers**" as the AV one time[252] just as the NKJV keeps "**spoiler**" once.[253] The NKJV also inserts the word "**spoiler**" into a passage where the AV did not use it.[254] When the AV does utilize the word **spoil** as a noun, the NRSV and NASB both transform it into the word "**spoiler**" that they corrected elsewhere.[255] The NRSV and NASB even change "marred" in the AV to "**spoiled**."[256] But although they corrected the verbal forms of **spoil** the vast majority of the time, our modern versions did use the extended forms "despoil" or "despoiled" on a number of occasions, both as replacements for **spoil** and **spoiled**,[257] and where the AV did not contain either form of these words.[258] All the corrections of the various verbal forms of **spoil** were unnecessary anyway, for not only do we say that food has **spoiled**, the word **spoil** is still used as a verb in other contexts: "The boycotting parties could not even agree on whether opponents to Fujimori should abstain (potentially subjecting themselves to a fine in the $15 range), **spoil** their ballots, or vote for collegial parties."[259]

Stanched

> Came behind *him*, and touched the border of his garment: and immediately her issue of blood **stanched**. (Luke 8:44)

The word **stanched**, formed from *stanch*, occurs only once in the AV. *Stanch* is from the French *estanchier*, meaning to stop the flow of. **Stanched** is related to our word *stagnate*. To be **stanched** is to simply be stopped. In fact, our modern versions all replace **stanched** with "stopped." But the word **stanched** was not deemed archaic by *U.S. News & World Report:* "The tesobonos would become blue-chip securities paying premium interest rates attractive to investors, and Mexico's credit squeeze would be temporarily **stanched**."[260]

Stay

> They prevented me in the day of my calamity: but the LORD was my **stay**. (2 Sam 22:19)

The word **stay** is used in the AV with three basic meanings, two of which have been deemed archaic. One of these words is from the French *estayer*, "to support," from *estaie*, "a support." Thus, a **stay** is something that supports a thing or an object of reliance. As a verb, to **stay** means to support or uphold. The AV employs this usage ten times as a noun, six in the singular[261] and four in the plural.[262] As a verb, it can be found eight times as **stay**[263] and five times as **stayed**.[264] The other word **stay** is from the French *ester*, meaning to stand or stop. From this has derived two basic connotations, that of abiding or remaining and that of stopping or restraining. Only the former meaning is in common use today. The AV contains the latter meaning twice in the noun **stay**,[265] eight times in the verb **stay**,[266] and seventeen times in the verb **stayed**.[267] The form **stayeth** is utilized by the AV only once.[268] Our modern versions only utilize forms of the word **stay** to mean abiding or remaining, except for the NASB and NRSV each retaining "**stay**" when it is used in the AV in the sense of a support.[269] But although they regularly corrected **stay,** our modern versions inconsistently used the extended form "mainstay" on several occasions.[270]

Stomacher

> And it shall come to pass, *that* instead of sweet smell there shall be stink; and instead of a girdle a rent; and instead of well set hair baldness; and instead of a **stomacher** a girding of sackcloth; *and* burning instead of beauty. (Isa 3:24)

A **stomacher** is only mentioned once in the AV. The word itself is thought to be from the French *estomachier*, a waistcoat or an ornamental covering for the chest or the stomach. A **stomacher** is termed a "rich robe" by the NKJV and NRSV, "fine clothes" by the NASB, and "fine clothing" by the NIV. Although the word **stomacher** is archaic, from the context it is obvious that the word has something to do with a garment for the stomach, what is not so obvious, however, is why the NRSV altered the word "peace" in the AV to "weal."[271]

Straightway

And **straightway** one of them ran, and took a sponge, and filled *it* with vinegar, and put *it* on a reed, and gave him to drink. (Mat 27:48)

The word **straightway** occurs forty-two times in the AV.[272] It is obviously a compound word literally meaning "straight to or from a place." **Straightway** means immediately or right away. The usual replacement in our modern versions is "immediately,"[273] but "without delay,"[274] "at once,"[275] and "suddenly"[276] also appear. Yet not only is a section of every racetrack called a straightaway, the word **straightway** is still in use today: "Some people are timid, other bold—often **straightway** from birth."[277]

Strait

Strive to enter in at the **strait** gate: for many, I say unto you, will seek to enter in, and shall not be able. (Luke 13:24)

The word **strait** occurs ten times in the AV.[278] Many other forms of **strait** also appear. **Straits** is found twice,[279] **straitly** eleven times,[280] **straiten** once,[281] **straitened** eight times,[282] **straitest** once,[283] **straiteneth** once,[284] and **straitness** five times.[285] **Strait** is from the French *estreit,* "narrow." The French word is derived from the Latin *strictus,* from which we get the English word *strict.* To be **strait** is to be narrow, tight, strict, or close. A **strait** is a narrow, tight, or confined place. To **straithen** is to render more rigorous, restrict, deprive, or put in a **strait** condition. Some of the replacements in our modern versions for the various forms of **strait** include "strictly,"[286] "distress,"[287] "sternly,"[288] "narrow,"[289] and "hampered."[290] But although they corrected the various forms of **strait** the majority of time they appeared, our modern versions were careless in completely excising all of these words. The NASB forgot to remove "**strait**" one time[291] and the NKJV neglected "**straits**" once.[292] The NRSV and NKJV altered **strait** to "**straits**" on three occasions.[293] Nevertheless, not only are narrow bodies of water still called **straits,** and not only are people referred to as being **strait**-laced, men are still put in **strait** jackets and other forms of the word **strait** can still be seen today: "Wright, bound no less **straitly** by the truths of death and arranged language, sees the immediate sensuous life (when offered in language) as no less a mythological fiction than the gods on Parnassus."[294]

Strakes

> And Jacob took him rods of green poplar, and of the hazel and chestnut tree; and pilled white **strakes** in them, and made the white appear which *was* in the rods. (Gen 30:37)

The word **strakes** is used twice in the AV,[295] while the derivative **ringstraked** is found six times.[296] This word is related to the Old English *streccan*, "to stretch." A strake is a streak or stripe of a different color than the rest of an object. It can also refer to a section of the rim of a cart wheel or the wooden planks in a ship that run from stem to stern. Understandably, the usual replacement for **strakes** and **ringstraked** is a formed of "streaked"[297] or "striped."[298] However, the word **strakes** can still be found today: "While the horizontal **strakes** over each wheel recall the 1963-1967 Sting Ray, the low, oval grille is so European in flavor that the car's parentage is thoroughly obscured."[299]

Strawed

> And a very great multitude spread their garments in the way; others cut down branches from the trees, and **strawed** *them* in the way. (Mat 21:8)

The word **strawed** occurs five times in the AV,[300] while the spelling **strowed** appears once.[301] These words are both archaic variations of the verb *strew*. The literal meaning of **strawed** is to scatter straw, as it goes back to the Old English *streaw*, "straw." Surprisingly, none of our modern versions replace **strawed** or **strowed** with *strewed*; the usual translation is "scattered."[302] However, the NIV inserts the word "strewn" into two passages where neither the AV nor any other modern version utilized any form of the words.[303] The NRSV employs the words "strewn" and "strew" each one time under the same circumstances.[304] But if **strawed** and **strowed** were so archaic then what about the NASB retaining the plainly archaic forms of "seest"[305] and "speakest"?[306]

Stripling

>And the king said, Inquire thou whose son the **stripling** *is*. (1 Sam 17:56)

The word **stripling** occurs only once in the AV. It is a diminutive formed from the noun *strip*, "narrow piece." Thus, a **stripling** is literally someone thin as a strip. In practice, however, a **stripling** is a youth or young person. The NKJV and NIV altered **stripling** to "young man" and the NASB to "youth," but the NRSV forgot to remove the word. Yet when the AV says a man is "weak," the NRSV and NIV change it to "weakling."[307] And when the AV mentions a "pricking brier," the NASB amends it to a "prickling brier."[308] The NIV even corrects the word "servant" to "underlings" when all of the other versions follow the AV.[309] The word **stripling** should never have been corrected in the first place, for it is still in use today: "Put another way, Hubble is seeing galaxies as they were when the universe was a 2-billion-year-old **stripling**."[310]

Suborned

>Then they **suborned** men, which said, We have heard him speak blasphemous words against Moses, and *against* God. (Acts 6:11)

The word **suborned** is used just once in the AV. It is formed from *suborn*, from the French *suborner*, and is related to our word *adorn*. To suborn means to procure secretly, bribe, induce to do wrong, or obtain by corrupt or counterfeit means. Although the NKJV and NASB replaced **suborned** with "secretly induced," the NRSV chose "secretly instigated" and the NIV "secretly persuaded." These corrections are unfortunate, for the word **suborned** is still in use today: "If Nowak knew about the invoices, then the government had **suborned** perjury by presenting evidence that the accounting firm was unaware of the tax fraud."[311]

Succour

>And when the Syrians of Damascus came to **succour** Hadadezer king of Zobah, David slew of the Syrians two and twenty thousand men. (2 Sam 8:5)

The word **succour** appears three times in the AV.[312] The form **succoured** can be found twice[313] and the form **succourer** once.[314] **Succour** is from the French *succurre,* "to help." The original Latin root literally signified "to run under." To **succour** someone is to help, aid, assist, or relieve them. Our modern versions usually render the forms of **succour** by forms of "help,"[315] but the NRSV calls a **succourer** a "benefactor,"[316] the NIV once terms **succour** "support,"[317] and forms of the phrase "came to his aid" are substituted for **succoured**.[318] But even though all of our modern versions removed every form of **succour,** it can still be found today: "Almost always, imposing trade sanctions gives **succour** to your own protectionists, of whom there are dispiritingly many in the new Congress."[319]

Such like

> Making the word of God of none effect through your tradition, which ye have delivered: and many **such like** things do ye. (Mark 7:13)

The phrase **such like,** which also appears in English as one word, occurs four times in the AV but only as two words.[320] **Such like** means something of that kind, of such a kind, of the like, or similar. Naturally, this phrase is removed by our modern versions.[321] Besides the NKJV twice using just "such,"[322] and the NIV once employing "such things,"[323] almost every replacement for **such like** contains a form of the word "like."[324] But this phrase did not have to be corrected in the first place, for it can still be found today: "I know that he was in a regiment, or a battalion, or **suchlike,** called the Timber Wolves, and that it was a 'spearhead' unit sent furiously forward through France and Belgium and into the Reich itself."[325]

Suckling

> Now go and smite Amalek, and utterly destroy all that they have, and spare them not; but slay both man and woman, infant and **suckling,** ox and sheep, camel and ass. (1 Sam 15:3)

The word **suckling** occurs in the AV three times in the singular[326] and four times in the plural.[327] It appeared in Old

English as *suklynge* and refers to a young child before it is weaned. Every occurrence of **suckling** and **sucklings** in the AV has been removed by our modern versions; however, only the NIV consistently renders these words as "infants."[328] The NRSV uses "nursing child,"[329] "nursing babies,"[330] "babes,"[331] and forms of "infant."[332] The NKJV could not decide among "nursing child,"[333] "nursing infants,"[334] and forms of "infant."[335] The NASB utilized "nursing babes,"[336] "nursing babies,"[337] forms of "infant,"[338] and then the similar word "nursling."[339] But after correcting the AV every time, the NASB, NIV, and NKJV transformed "sucking" in the AV to "**suckling**."[340] The NASB also amended "young" in the AV to "**suckling** lambs."[341] And when the AV simply mentioned "young," the NRSV alone transformed them into "fledglings."[342] But the word **suckling** did not need to be updated in the first place, for it is still common today: "Roast **suckling** pig is a delicacy in many parts of the world, including Rome."[343]

Suffer

> But Jesus said, **Suffer** little children, and forbid them not, to come unto me: for of such is the kingdom of heaven. (Mat 19:14)

Although the word **suffer** and its derivatives occur many times in the AV, they are employed in two distinct senses. The word **suffer** is from the French *sufrir*, which comes from the Latin *sufferre*, literally meaning to bear under. Although **suffer** means to feel pain or great distress, it also means to allow, permit, tolerate, or let. With this latter meaning, the word **suffer** appears fifty-one times,[344] while **suffered** occurs twenty-nine times,[345] **suffereth** four times,[346] and **suffering** and **sufferest** each once.[347] These words are usually updated by our modern versions to forms of "permit,"[348] "allow,"[349] or "let."[350] But when the AV uses an unambiguous word like "sad," the NASB and NIV correct it to "sullen."[351]

Sunder

> I will go before thee, and make the crooked places straight: I will break in pieces the gates of brass, and cut in **sunder** the bars of iron: (Isa 45:2)

The word **sunder** appears seven times in the AV,[352] while the form **sundered** is used once,[353] and **asunder** can be found twenty-one times.[354] **Sunder** is from the Old English *sundrian,* from *sundor,* "separate." To **sunder** is to separate, divide, dissolve, split, or sever. **Asunder** is a compound of the Old English *on sundrian,* "to separate into parts." Thus, **asunder** means to separate, reposition, or divide; either widely, into parts, or just apart. Our modern versions completely eliminated **sunder** and **sundered** but were careless when it came to excising the word **asunder**. The NRSV forgot to eliminate **asunder** in one verse,[355] but then joins the NASB one time in extending **sunder** to "**asunder**."[356] In one instance, the NRSV, NASB, and NIV all use "**asunder**" in the same verse where the term does not appear in the AV.[357] Then the NIV and NASB alter the clear, up-to-date English of "into parts" to "**asunder**."[358] The word **asunder** is rendered in our modern versions by things like "apart,"[359] "in two,"[360] and "separate."[361] However, the deposing of the word **asunder** was premature, for it is still used in the 1990's by the *Christian Science Monitor:* "But the past few decades have been particularly brutal: Political chaos, civil war, drought, and poverty have torn the region **asunder**."[362] And furthermore, every translator who corrected **asunder** in the AV heard at his wedding: "let not man put **asunder**." The word **sunder** is variously translated as "two,"[363] "apart,"[364] "away,"[365] or "pieces."[366] **Sundered** is usually replaced with "separated."[367] But the removal of the word **sunder** was also hasty, for it is still in use today: "The present federal leader of the opposition, the federalist turncoat Lucien Bouchard, heads a bloc of Quebec separatists in the parliament of the very country he wishes to **sunder**."[368]

Sundry

> God, who at **sundry** times and in divers manners spake in time past unto the fathers by the prophets, (Heb 1:1)

The word **sundry** is used only once in the AV. It is from the Old English *syndrig,* from *sundor,* "separate." Thus, **sundry** is related to the previous word *sunder.* **Sundry** means separate, special, private, various, or diverse. The standard translation for **sundry** in our modern versions is "many," but the NKJV preferred "various." But not only are small, miscellaneous items of little value still called **sundries**, the word **sundry** can even be found in *Time* magazine: "Is this not the very thing that all the Republican presidential candidates, and **sundry** moral scolds upholding the alleged 'true meaning' of civil rights, have been clamoring to denounce?"[369]

Sup

> And will not rather say unto him, Make ready wherewith I may **sup,** and gird thyself, and serve me, till I have eaten and drunken; and afterward thou shalt eat and drink? (Luke 17:8)

This word appears in the AV three times as **sup**[370] and once as **supped.**[371] The word **sup,** as it is used in the AV, is thought to be a combination of the French verb *super,* meaning to take something to eat, and the Middle English *supen,* "to drink," from the Old English *supan,* meaning to sip or suck. **Sup** and **supped** are unanimously extracted by our modern versions. In one passage, however, the NKJV, NIV, and NRSV change the sentence and transform the verb **sup** into the noun "supper."[372] Yet in the other place in the New Testament where **sup** is used, the NRSV and NIV substitute "eat" and the NKJV and NASB "dine."[373] The AV phrase "when he had **supped**" is unanimously amended to "after supper."[374] But the word **sup** did not have to be corrected in the first place, for it is still in vogue today: "Is Africa really that bottomless bucket, into which so much aid disappears before the needy are given the chance to **sup** from it?"[375]

Superfluity

> Wherefore lay apart all filthiness and **superfluity** of naughtiness, and receive with meekness the engrafted word, which is able to save your souls. (James 1:21)

The word **superfluity,** appearing just once in the AV, is from the French *superfluite,* a derivative of the word **superfluous,** found three times in the AV,[376] and from the Latin *superfluus,* literally meaning "superflowing." To be **superfluous** is to be excessive, overflowing, or unnecessary. **Superfluity** is the state of being, or something that is **superfluous.** Although the NKJV and

NASB each retained "**superfluous**" one time,[377] the word **superfluity** is unanimously removed by our modern versions. Yet not only is the word **superfluous** very common today, the form **superfluity** can still be found also: "The flowers—almost a **superfluity**—are the usual blue, but they gain in elegance against the background of ghostly foliage."[378]

Supple

> And *as for* thy nativity, in the day thou wast born thy navel was not cut, neither wast thou washed in water to **supple** *thee;* thou wast not salted at all, nor swaddled at all. (Ezek 16:4)

The word **supple** occurs only once in the AV. It is from the French *souple,* from the Latin *supplex* literally meaning flexible or bending under. The word **supple,** although it means pliant, limber, and yielding, can also mean to soften or reduce the harshness of. Although all of our modern versions replace **supple** with a form of "cleanse," the word can even be found today in *National Review:* "This requires smarter, more **supple** and sophisticated diplomacy, and more forward-looking concepts."[379] The word **supple** also still refers to something done to the body: "Although nothing can turn back the clock, keeping the skin as moist and **supple** as possible will help prevent fragility."[380]

Suppliants

> From beyond the rivers of Ethiopia my **suppliants,** *even* the daughter of my dispersed, shall bring mine offering. (Zep 3:10)

The word **suppliants** occurs only once in the AV. **Suppliants** is the plural of *suppliant,* from a French word of the same spelling meaning one who supplicates. To supplicate is to petition, beg, pray, entreat humbly, or beseech. Surprisingly, the NRSV forgot to remove this word; expectedly, the other versions did not: they change it to "worshipers." Yet the word **suppliants** is still in use today: "The two greatest Sienese painters of the age, Duccio and Simone Martini, both painted representations of the Virgin in Majesty in which these four martyrs were depicted as **suppliants** kneeling on either side of the Virgin's throne, conveying to her the wishes and prayers of the Sienese people."[381]

Surfeiting

> And take heed to yourselves, lest at any time your hearts be overcharged with **surfeiting,** and drunkenness, and cares of this life, and *so* that day come upon you unawares. (Luke 21:34)

The word **surfeiting,** appearing once in the AV, is from the verb *surfeit,* from the noun, which is from the French *surfait,* "excess." **Surfeiting** is gluttony, overindulgence, or excess. The usual rendering for **surfeiting** in our modern versions is "dissipation," but the NKJV says "carousing." But after correcting the AV, the NRSV replaced "abundance" in the AV with "surfeit" even though the NKJV and NIV read as the AV.[382] Nevertheless, forms of the word **surfeiting** still occur today: "But you're surely **surfeited** on info about him, right?"[383]

Surmisings

> He is proud, knowing nothing, but doting about questions and strifes of words, whereof cometh envy, strife, railings, evil **surmisings,** (1 Tim 6:4)

The word **surmisings,** from *surmise,* is used just once in the AV. Although the noun *surmise* is from a French word of the same spelling, the verb is from the French *surmettre,* "to accuse." The word **surmisings** is actually related to our word *missile,* as both are ultimately derived from the Latin *mittere,* "to throw." **Surmisings** are allegations, imaginations, charges, conjectures, or suppositions. Naturally, the verb means to allege or accuse. The new versions have unanimously rendered **surmisings** as "suspicions." However, the NASB inserted the word "surmise" into a passage where no other new translation contained the word.[384] And in the same verse where **surmisings** occurs, the NRSV alone alters "evil" to "base."[385] Nevertheless, forms of the word **surmisings** still appear today: "My initial **surmising**—that it would be intriguing to study how a plant can alter genetically in response to the environment—has proved all too true."[386]

Swaddling

> And she brought forth her firstborn son, and wrapped him in **swaddling** clothes, and laid him in a manger; because there

was no room for them in the inn. (Luke 2:7)

The word **swaddling** appears twice in the AV,[387] while the form **swaddled** is also found twice[388] and a **swaddlingband** is mentioned once.[389] The verb *swaddle* was formed from the Old English noun *swaethel,* a derivative of *swathu,* "band," that literally signifies "that which swathes." Thus, to swaddle is to swathe, bind, or wrap with strips of cloth. **Swaddling** clothes and a **swaddlingband** are used to swaddle. These words are usually applied to infants; thus, for an infant to be **swaddled** implies that care is given to it. The NKJV is the only modern version to retain a form of these words most of the time.[390] However, the NRSV and NASB retain **swaddlingband,** they just split it up into two separate words.[391] The NIV, NRSV, and NASB employed "wrapped in cloths" for **swaddled** one time,[392] and twice used forms of "cloth" for "**swaddling** clothes."[393] These corrections were unneeded, for not only do ladies speak of a swatch of cloth, forms of **swaddled** still appear today, even in magazines like *Popular Mechanics:* "And because of the climate, concrete must **swaddle** everything, even the cables."[394]

Swelling

These are murmurers, complainers, walking after their own lusts; and their mouth speaketh great **swelling** words, having men's persons in admiration because of advantage. (Jude 1:16)

Although the word *swell* and its derivatives occur in both the AV and the new versions, **swelling** is used by the AV five times in the singular[395] and once in the plural[396] with the figurative sense of inflation by pride, arrogance, or conceit. The "**swelling** of Jordan" mentioned three times in the AV refers to the thick, lush banks of Jordan and is usually translated as "thickets."[397] The **swellings** warned against in the Bible are not cautions against getting fat and bloated, but pride and haughtiness. **Swellings** has been rendered as either "arrogance" or a form of "conceit."[398] The phrase "great **swelling** words" that is used twice in the AV is retained by the NKJV but corrected to forms of "arrogant" in the NASB and "boast" in the NIV.[399] However, the NRSV altered this phrase to a form of the more difficult "bombastic."[400] The word **swelling** should have been no problem, for we still speak figuratively of a conceited person having a big head.

Chapter 20
Tabering to Twined

Tabering

> And Huzzab shall be led away captive, she shall be brought up, and her maids shall lead *her* as with the voice of doves, **tabering** upon their breasts. (Nahum 2:7)

The word **tabering,** occurring only once in the AV, is formed from *taber,* a variant of *tabor,* from the French *tabour,* "a drum." Thus, **tabering** is technically the beating of a drum. It can also refer to the beating or striking of anything. Our modern versions have unanimously updated **tabering** to forms of "beat." But this is to be expected after a "cup" in the AV was changed by the NASB to a "chalice" and the NIV to a "goblet."[1]

Tablets

> The bonnets, and the ornaments of the legs, and the headbands, and the **tablets,** and the earrings, (Isa 3:20)

Tablets are mentioned three times in the AV.[2] The word itself is from the French *tablete,* the diminutive of *table.* However, **tablets** in the Bible are not small, flat things to write on, but rather, small, flat things to wear as an ornament, necklace, jewelry, or pendant. Although our modern versions updated **tablets** every time it appeared, they were rather inconsistent in their selection of replacement words. The NASB uses three different words to update **tablets** (bracelets, necklaces, perfume boxes).[3] The NIV does likewise, but introduces two additional translations (ornaments, necklaces, perfume bottles).[4] The NRSV was not satisfied with these renderings so it used "pendants" in the first two instances.[5] But when the AV refers to a simple thing like "bracelets," the NIV, NASB, and NRSV alter it to the more difficult "brooches."[6] Moreover, the NASB and NRSV also replace "earrings" with the more difficult "amulets."[7] And finally, the NKJV corrects "earrings" in the AV to "nose rings" even though the other new translations follow the AV reading.[8]

Tabret

> And the harp, and the viol, the **tabret,** and pipe, and wine, are in their feasts: but they regard not the work of the LORD, neither consider the operation of his hands. (Isa 5:12)

A **tabret** is mentioned in the AV four times in the singular[9] and five times in the plural.[10] **Tabret** is the diminutive form of *taber*. Thus, a **tabret** is properly a small drum. It could also be applied to any small musical instrument that is beat on. Our modern versions normally correct **tabret** and **tabrets** to "tambourine" and "tambourines."[11] Occasionally however, they alter these words to the more obscure "timbrel" and "timbrels."[12] But in one instance, the NRSV, NASB, and NIV alter **tabrets** to "settings," even though the underlying Hebrew word is the same as all the other verses where **tabret** and **tabrets** are found.[13] Moreover, when the AV does say "timbrel" or "timbrels," it is often corrected by the NKJV, NASB, and NRSV to "tambourine" or "tambourines."[14] But when the AV refers to something simple like a "harp," it is corrected by the NIV, NRSV, and NASB to the archaic "lyre" or "lyres."[15]

Taches

> The tabernacle, his tent, and his covering, his **taches,** and his boards, his bars, his pillars, and his sockets, (Exo 35:11)

Taches are mentioned ten times in the AV.[16] *Tache* is from a French word of the same spelling meaning a clasp, and was originally a doublet of *tack*. **Taches** are devices for fastening two parts together. This could be a clasp, buckle, hook, band, tack, or strap. **Taches** is consistently rendered by our modern versions as "clasps,"[17] except for the NRSV and NASB, which each used "hooks" once.[18] **Taches** may be archaic but the correction of "fruit" in the AV to "fruitage" by the NIV does not make the Bible any easier to understand.[19]

Tale

> Go therefore now, *and* work; for there shall no straw be given you, yet shall ye deliver the **tale** of bricks. (Exo 5:18)

The word **tale** occurs four times in the AV with an archaic meaning.[20] **Tale** appeared in Old English as *talu,* and referred to either a narrative or a number. Only the former meaning of **tale** has survived. Thus, in these four passages, a **tale** is a list, number, enumeration, or quantity. The usual translation given in our modern versions is "quota,"[21] but "quantity,"[22] "number,"[23] and forms of "count"[24] are also employed. The AV does use **tale** in the modern sense of a story—once in the singular[25] and twice in the plural.[26] However, "idle tales" in the AV is altered to "nonsense" by the NIV and NASB.[27] A **talebearer,** mentioned six times in the AV,[28] is obviously one who bears tales. Thus, the AV does employ the modern sense of *tale* more times than it is commonly thought. Yet only the NKJV retains **talebearer** as it appears in the AV.[29] The other modern versions change **talebearer** to "slanderer,"[30] "gossip,"[31] or "whisperer."[32] However, the NASB carelessly retained **"talebearer"** in one passage.[33] And when the AV read "slanders," the NASB replaced it with **"talebearer."**[34] And furthermore, when the AV said "whisperer," the NASB corrects it to "slanderer" and the NIV to "gossip."[35] **Talebearer** should never have been corrected, for other words with a *-bearer* suffix are commonly used by our modern versions. All of the new translations retain "cupbearer" the only place it occurs in the AV.[36] And when the AV says "butler," it is even changed to "cupbearer" by the NASB, NRSV, and NIV.[37] The AV word "amourbearer" is always kept by the new versions.[38] The compound "shield-bearer" is even used when it does not appear in the AV.[39]

Tares

> But while men slept, his enemy came and sowed **tares** among the wheat, and went his way. (Mat 13:25)

Tares surface eight times in the AV.[40] The origin of this word is somewhat obscure. **Tares** can be vetch, darnel, or weeds in general. The **tares** in the wheat fields blended in with the wheat, making it difficult to tell them apart. The NIV and NRSV consistently update **tares** to "weeds."⁴¹ Surprisingly, however, the NKJV and NASB retain this supposedly archaic word every time.⁴² But when the AV uses a simple word like "plain," it is altered to "tableland" by the NASB and NRSV.⁴³

Targets

> And king Solomon made two hundred **targets** *of* beaten gold: six hundred *shekels* of beaten gold went to one **target**. (2 Chr 9:15)

A **target** appears in the AV three times in the singular⁴⁴ and three times in the plural.⁴⁵ **Target** is from the French *targete*, the diminutive of *targe*, "shield." Thus, a **target** is literally a small targe; hence, a shield or buckler. Limiting the meaning of **target** to something one shoots at, the new versions expectedly remove all trace of this word when it refers to a shield. **Target** and **targets** are usually updated to "large shield" and "large shields."⁴⁶ Yet when the AV reads "strength," it is changed by the NASB to the more arduous "virility" even though the NRSV and NKJV follow the AV reading.⁴⁷

Teats

> Thus thou calledst to remembrance the lewdness of thy youth, in bruising thy **teats** by the Egyptians for the paps of thy youth. (Ezek 23:21)

Teats are mentioned three times in the AV.⁴⁸ *Teat* appeared in Old English under the form of what is now the modern slang *tit*. The teat is properly the nipple on the breast or udder of female mammals, but can also refer to the breast or mammary glands themselves. Our modern versions all update **teats** to "breast" in the first two passages⁴⁹ and "bosom" in the other.⁵⁰ But the word **teats** is still used today: "The **teats** of the female ape would have become soft and flexible breasts in order for the infant to be able to direct the milk to its mouth now that it had no body hair to cling to."⁵¹

Teil

> But yet in it *shall be* a tenth, and *it* shall return, and shall be

eaten: as a **teil** tree, and as an oak, whose substance *is* in them, when they cast *their leaves: so* the holy seed *shall be* the substance thereof. (Isa 6:13)

A **teil** tree is mentioned only once in the AV. **Teil** comes from a French word of the same spelling that referred to the linden or lime tree. Although the proper identification of the **teil** tree is somewhat obscure, our modern versions unanimously changed the word **teil** to the arcane "terebinth," a tree that most horticulturists can't even identify. But when the AV mentions trees that are commonly known, the new versions alter them so as to render them unrecognizable. "Elms" are turned into "terebinth" trees by every one of the new translations.[52] On two occasions, the NKJV turns an "oak" tree into a "terebinth" tree even though all of the other modern versions retain the AV reading of "oak."[53] When the AV mentions a "grove," our modern versions unite in terming it a "tamarisk tree."[54] Another common objection to **teil** is that the underlying Hebrew word *elah* is translated eleven other times in the AV as "oak"[55] and once as "elms."[56] But our modern versions did likewise. The NRSV and NASB render *elah* as "oak" eleven times[57] and "terebinth" twice.[58] The NIV uses "oak" ten times,[59] "terebinth" twice,"[60] and "great" once.[61] The NKJV only employed "oak" twice,[62] substituting the perplexing "tamarisk" once[63] and "terebinth" the rest of the time.[64] Moreover, when the AV makes reference to "branches," the NASB calls them "tendrils."[65] And when the AV, followed by all of the other versions, says "trees," the NRSV alone substitutes "trellis."[66]

Tell

And he brought him forth abroad, and said, Look now toward heaven, and **tell** the stars, if thou be able to number them: and he said unto him, So shall thy seed be. (Gen 15:5)

The word **tell** occurs three times in the AV with this particular meaning.[67] The past tense **told** appears five times.[68] **Tell** is from the Old English *tellan*, "to narrate or count." The verb *tellan* was formed from the noun *talu*, meaning a narrative or number. Thus, **tell** and **told** are ultimately related to *tale*. To **tell** is to count, reckon, or name numerically. **Tell** is unanimously given by our modern versions as "count."[69] However, **told** can be found as "counted,"[70] "weighed out,"[71] "recorded,"[72] "apportioned,"[73] "determined,"[74] "conscripted,"[75] "assigned,"[76] and "numbered."[77] But if **tell** and **told** were updated because they were archaic, then why did the NKJV, NRSV, and NASB correct "company" in the AV to the arcane "retinue."[78] But actually, the word **tell** when used in this manner by the AV is not archaic at all. A **teller** would be one who counts—a bank **teller**.

Temper

And thou shalt prepare a meat offering for it every morning, the sixth part of an ephah, and the third part of an hin of oil, to **temper** with the fine flour; a meat offering continually by a perpetual ordinance unto the LORD. (Ezek 46:14)

The word **temper** appears in the AV only once as **temper** but three times as **tempered**[79] and five times as **untempered**.[80] The form **temperance** occurs three times,[81] as does the similar form **temperate**.[82] **Temper** is from the Latin *temperare*, which meant to mix, regulate, or apportion. Thus, as it is used in the AV, **temper** means to mix, season, or apportion. The modern meaning of toning down something or tempering steel by heating and cooling is not found in the AV. **Temperance** is from the Latin *temperantia*, "moderation," while **temperate** is from the Latin *temperatus*, "regulated." Both of these words are ultimately derived, like **temper**, from the Latin *temperare*. In the Old Testament, our modern versions correct **tempered** to "mixed"[83] and forms of "salted,"[84] while **temper** appears as "moisten."[85] In the New Testament, **tempered** is changed to "arranged" by the NRSV and "combined" by the NIV.[86] The NKJV and NASB preferred the word "composed."[87] Yet when the AV says something is **untempered**, the NKJV neglects to erase the word.[88] "Untempered mortar" in the AV is altered to a form of "whitewash" by the NIV, NRSV, and NASB.[89] Although **temper** appears in the AV in an unusual sense, when the AV utilizes the word "spices," the NASB alters it to "aromatic gum," a substance that could easily be misconstrued.[90] **Temperance** is unanimously rendered by our modern versions as "self-control" every time it appears.[91] **Temperate** is also usually given as forms of "self-control,"[92] but one can also find "prudent,"[93] "sensible,"[94] and "disciplined."[95] The NKJV retains **"temperate"** on two occasions.[96] But even though **temperate** was corrected in the AV, the translators of our modern versions obviously could not have deemed **temperate** to be archaic because "vigilant" in the AV is changed to **"temperate"** by the all of them.[97] The word "sober" in the AV is also altered to **"temperate"** by every modern translation.[98] And in one of the very passages that **temperate** appears in the AV, the NRSV, NIV, and NASB correct "sober" to **"temperate"** after just correcting **temperate**.[99] The words **temperance** and **temperate** should not have been updated in the first place, for both of them are still current: "And **temperance** involves much more than moderation in drink."[100] "Parizeau and Bouchard will abandon their current **temperate** tenor and hunt for new pretexts, like the notorious Quebec flag-stomping incident in Brockvill, Ont., to whip up anti-Canada sentiment."[101]

Tenons

> One board had two **tenons,** equally distant one from another: thus did he make for all the boards of the tabernacle. (Exo 36:22)

The word **tenons,** the plural of *tenon,* occurs six times in the AV.[102] It is from a French word of the same spelling which in turn is from *tenir,* "to hold." **Tenons** are projections on the end or side of wood or some other material that fit into a corresponding hole or cavity in another piece—thus joining them together. Surprisingly, the NKJV and NASB retain the AV reading of **tenons** in every instance.[103] The NRSV selected "pegs" and the NIV "projection" or "projections."[104] Yet the singular form of **tenons** can still be found in current English: "The double-story, gable-roofed gate tower was rebuilt in the traditional **tenon** manner, completely without nails."[105]

Teraphim

> And these went into Micah's house, and fetched the carved image, the ephod, and the **teraphim,** and the molten image. Then said the priest unto them, What do ye? (Judg 18:18)

Teraphim are mentioned six times in the AV.[106] Although this word comes into English from the Latin *theraphim,* it is actually a Hebrew word plural in form but with a singular use. **Teraphim** are idols, images, or gods. The NKJV retains **teraphim** once[107] and uses "household idols" the other five times.[108] The NIV consistently updates **teraphim** to "idols" or "idol."[109] Although the NASB substitutes "household idols" every time,[110] it twice changes the simple "images" in the AV to "**teraphim**."[111] The NRSV liked the word **teraphim** so much that it not only kept the AV reading every time,[112] it inserted it in three other passages where the AV read "images."[113] **Teraphim** did not have to be updated by any version, however, for all of them retain the Hebrew word "behemoth" as it appears in the AV.[114]

Terrestrial

> *There are* also celestial bodies, and bodies **terrestrial**: but the glory of the celestial *is* one, and the *glory* of the **terrestrial** *is* another. (1 Cor 15:40)

The word **terrestrial** occurs twice in the AV in the same verse. It is from the Latin *terrestris*, "earthly." *Terra* is the Latin word for *earth*. Thus, **terrestrial** means earthly, worldly, or pertaining to land. Although the NKJV retains this word both times, the other versions unite in replacing it with "earthly." But there was no need to correct **terrestrial** in the first place, for related words are used every day in modern English (terrain, terrarium, subterranean, terrace, territory). And who can forget ET the extra**terrestrial**. The word **terrestrial** itself is even still used today: "This impact would have sent much of the colliding object, along with a much larger amount of **terrestrial** debris, into the earth's atmosphere."[115]

Tetrarch

> Now Herod the **tetrarch** heard of all that was done by him: and he was perplexed, because that it was said of some, that John was risen from the dead; (Luke 9:7)

The word **tetrarch** appears seven times in the AV.[116] It is from the Latin *tetraarcha*, literally meaning the ruler of a fourth part. A **tetrarch** can also refer to one of four rulers of a country or province. The prefix *tetra-* (*tetr-* before a vowel) comes from the Greek *tetra*, "four." There are several English words with this *tetra-* prefix but most of them are quite obscure. Although the governors, chamberlains, porters, butlers, lieutenants, and chancellors mentioned in the Bible may encompass a slightly different connotation than they do today, at least the words are recognizable. It is therefore surprising that the NKJV, NIV, and NASB retain this supposedly archaic word, for only the NRSV consistently updated it to "ruler." But when the AV uses a Latin word like "Calvary," it is corrected in the NIV, NASB, and NRSV to "the skull."[117] Moreover, not only is **tetrarch** retained, the NKJV and NASB join the NRSV in correcting "princes" to "satraps."[118] And in the same verse, the word "governors" in the AV is amended to "prefects" by the NASB, NRSV, and NIV.[119]

Thankworthy

> For this *is* **thankworthy,** if a man for conscience toward God endure grief, suffering wrongfully. (1 Pet 2:19)

The word **thankworthy** occurs only once in the AV. It is manifestly a compound of *thank* and *worthy,* signifying acceptable, commendable, worthy of thanks, gratitude, or credit. **Thankworthy** is corrected in the NRSV to "a credit to you," the NASB to "finds favor," and in the NKJV and NIV to "commendable." Yet a look at how the modern versions use words with a *-worthy* suffix that do not even appear in the AV shows that **thankworthy** should never have been corrected. All of the new translations utilize "trustworthy."[120] The NKJV, NIV, and NRSV employ "praiseworthy,"[121] the NASB and NKJV "untrustworthy,"[122] and the NASB alone uses "noteworthy."[123]

Thee

> While Peter thought on the vision, the Spirit said unto him, Behold, three men seek **thee.** (Acts 10:19)

The word **thee** occurs almost 4000 times in the AV. The form **thee-ward** appears just once.[124] **Thee** is usually one of the first words cited by those who consider the AV to use archaic language. It appeared in Old English as *the* and represented the dative and accusative case of the second person, singular personal pronoun *thu,* "thou." **Thee** is properly the objective case of the second person, singular pronoun and is now normally replaced by *you*. Although the NIV, NKJV, and NRSV remove all trace of this word, the NASB employs it 472 times in 392 verses.[125] In every case, the NASB has capitalized the word and used it strictly to refer to God as if it was somehow more holy to address God this way. But **thee** does nothing more than indicate the second person singular, and is therefore more accurate than the word *you* when referring to the second person. The word **thee** is in fact still used in some instances that are not related to the Bible: "'By virtue of the authority vested in me, I dub **thee** Klansmen, the most honored title among men.'"[126]

Thence

So they, being sent forth by the Holy Ghost, departed unto Seleucia; and from **thence** they sailed to Cyprus. (Acts 13:4)

The word **thence** occurs 145 times in the AV[127] and the form **thenceforth** appears four times.[128] **Thence** is from the Old English *thanan* and means from that time, date, or place; from there, at a distant place, or away from there. **Thence** is normally given in our modern versions as "there"[129] or "from there."[130] **Thenceforth** is variously rendered "that time onward,"[131] "thereafter,"[132] "then on,"[133] "any more,"[134] and "no longer."[135] But these corrections notwithstanding, the word **thence** as well as its derivatives can still be found today: "From Baghdad, the mercantile route extended across the deserts to the Jordan River and **thence** to the ports of Haifa and Ashqelon."[136] And from the *Earth Island Journal:* "The Great law articulated the manner in which the confederated nations would **thenceforth** relate to one another as a single body."[137]

Thereabout

And it came to pass, as they were much perplexed **thereabout**, behold, two men stood by them in shining garments: (Luke 24:4)

The word **thereabout**, which occurs only once in the AV, is the first in a series of uncommon compound words in the AV that are all formed with a *there-* prefix. Others include **thereat**, found 3 times,[138] **therefrom**, also found 3 times,[139] **therein**, appearing 230 times,[140] **thereinto**, found once,[141] **thereof**, occurring 908 times,[142] **thereon**, found 66 times,[143] **thereout**, found twice,[144] **thereto**, appearing 20 times,[145] **thereunto**, occurring 9 times,[146] **thereupon**, found 5 times,[147] and **therewith**, found 36 times.[148] **Therefore** and **thereby** are also quite common, but are retained by all of our modern versions, except the NIV, which does not use **thereby**. The word *there* appeared in Old English as *thaer* and was compounded with various prepositions to give us the above words. Some of these words were originally two words like *thaer abutan*, "about that," but most can be found in Old English as a single word. Although they deemed these *there-* words to be archaic, our modern versions were lax in expurgating them from the Bible. The NKJV uses "**therein**" twice,[149] the NASB employs "**thereon**" once,[150] the NRSV and NASB utilize "**thereupon**" once,[151] and the NRSV, NKJV, and NASB unite in using "thereafter" three times—a word that does not appear in the AV.[152] But in spite of their removal by modern Bible translations, most of these *there-* words are still current English:

> Thus NASA was in a race against the clock to complete Freedom, or some substantial fraction **thereof,** prior to the next shuttle accident.[153]
>
> And **thereon** hangs the curious story of CP symmetry violation—a story that may hold an important key to why the universe is the way it is.[154]
>
> The simple truth of our finiteness is that we could, by whatever means, go on interminably only at the price of either losing the past and **therewith** our real identity, or living only in the past and therefore without a real present.[155]
>
> It is a positive feedback effect: the medium determines the wave's speed, but then the amplitude of the wave alters the medium, which **thereupon** has a further influence on the wave speed.[156]
>
> Survival as such would be the end, consciousness an incremental means **thereto**.[157]
>
> An important aspect of this form of care has been the targeting of patients who require this specialist approach and will benefit **therefrom**.[158]
>
> My daughter, visiting an American Online gathering called Teen Chat, is regularly invited by the teenaged boys who predominate **therein** to enter a private "room."[159]

Thine

> Then saith he to the man, Stretch forth **thine** hand. And he stretched *it* forth; and it was restored whole, like as the other. (Mat 12:13)

The word **thine** appears almost 1000 times in the AV. Like the word "thee," it is often cited by those who consider the AV to contain archaic language. Thine appeared in Old English as *thin* and represented the genitive case of the second person, singular personal pronoun *thu,* "thou." Thine is properly the possessive case of the second person, singular pronoun. It is now normally replaced by *your.* Once again, the NASB alone utilizes this supposedly archaic word, for 164 times "**thine**" is capitalized and used to refer to God.[160] But as mentioned previously, **thine** does nothing more than indicate the second person singular, and is therefore more accurate than the word *your* when referring to the second person. The word **thine** can even be found in use today in a non-biblical context: "And he offers this advice to gay teens: 'To **thine** own self be true.'"[161]

Thither

> And Judas also, which betrayed him, knew the place: for Jesus ofttimes resorted **thither** with his disciples. (John 18:2)

The word **thither** appears ninety-five times in the AV.[162] The extended form **thitherward** can be seen three times.[163] **Thither** appeared in Old English as *thider* and means there, to that place, or towards that place. Our modern versions almost unanimously update **thither** to "there."[164] The word **thitherward** can be found as "toward it,"[165] "in that direction,"[166] or simply "there."[167] But although the new, up-to-date translations considered **thither** to be archaic, *Astronomy* magazine did not: "This motion of the Local Group means different masses in the universe pull us **thither** and yon."[168]

Thou

> For he testifieth, **Thou** *art* a priest for ever after the order of Melchisedec. (Heb 7:17)

The word **thou** occurs over 5000 times in the AV. Like its cousins "thee," "thine," and "thy," **thou** is usually one of the first words cited by those who consider the AV to use archaic language. **Thou** appeared in Old English as *thu*. It was and still is the nominative personal pronoun of the second person singular. Although it is now normally replaced by *you,* **thou** is more accurate than the word *you* when referring to the second person—the person or thing spoken to. Once again, the NASB has retained this supposedly archaic word when referring to God, capitalizing it as well.[169] But one time the NASB slips up and uses "**thou**" to refer to a pagan god.[170] Nevertheless, the word **thou** is still sometimes used today: "In his office in the Old Post Office Building, the mild-mannered Hackney has two warning signs: '**Thou** Shalt Not Whine' and 'No Snivelling.'"[171]

Threescore

See fourscore.

Thrice

Jesus answered him, Wilt thou lay down thy life for my sake? Verily, verily, I say unto thee, The cock shall not crow, till thou hast denied me **thrice.** (John 13:38)

The word **thrice** appears fifteen times in the AV.[172] It is derived from the Middle English *thries,* from the Old English *thriwa,* "three times," from *thri,* "three." **Thrice** means three times in succession or three successive occasions, manners, or respects. Our modern versions unanimously render **thrice** as "three times."[173] However, once when the AV read "the third time," the NRSV replaced it with the supposedly archaic "**thrice.**"[174] And furthermore, the word **thrice** is still in vogue at the end of the twentieth century: "Administered **thrice** weekly from an infant's first month, Bactrim has proved to be an effective prophylactic against PCP."[175]

Thy

Jesus saith unto him, Rise, take up **thy** bed, and walk. (John 5:8)

The word **thy** occurs over 4500 times in the AV. Like

"thee," "thine," and "thou," it is usually one of the first words cited by those who consider the AV to use archaic language. **Thy** appeared in Old English as *thin* and represented the genitive case of the second person, singular personal pronoun *thu,* "thou." Thus, **thy** is equal to *thine,* the genitive case of the second person pronoun. It too is now normally replaced by *your.* **Thy** is actually just a shortened form of *thine,* originally used before consonants except the letter *h.* But once again, the NASB alone utilizes this supposedly archaic word; it can be found over 1000 times.[176] And as it did with "thee," "thine," and "thou," **thy** is capitalized and used to refer to God. But also as mentioned previously, **thy** does nothing more than indicate the second person singular, and is therefore more accurate than the word *your* when referring to the second person. The word **thy** can also be found in use today in a decidedly non-biblical context: "But in an unpoliced, beggar-**thy**-neighbor commons, these animals will either be very expensive or downright impossible to keep in private possession."[177]

Thyine

The merchandise of gold, and silver, and precious stones, and of pearls, and fine linen, and purple, and silk, and scarlet, and all **thyine** wood, and all manner vessels of ivory, and all manner vessels of most precious wood, and of brass, and iron, and marble, (Rev 18:12)

Thyine wood is mentioned only once in the AV. The word **thyine** comes into English from the Latin *thyinus.* This in turn was borrowed directly from the Greek. **Thyine** wood is thought to be wood from the North African thya tree that is known for being both strong and aromatic. The NRSV changes **thyine** wood to "scented wood," but the NIV, NKJV, and NASB exchange **thyine** for the equally as obscure "citron." But on one occasion where the AV simply mentions a "tree," the NRSV conjectures that it is "mulberry wood" even though the other versions say just plain "wood" or read as the AV.[178]

Tillage

Much food *is in* the **tillage** of the poor: but there is *that is* destroyed for want of judgment. (Prov 13:23)

Tillage is mentioned three times in the AV.[179] It was formed from the verb *till* with the addition of an *-age* suffix signifying act, process, function, or condition. **Tillage** is the work of tilling or plowing land or the land itself after this was done. It can also mean land under crops as opposed to land used for pasture, or the crops growing on tilled land. When the sense of the AV is maintained, our modern versions either render **tillage** by forms of "till"[180] and "farmed"[181] or by "field"[182] and "fallow ground."[183] But when the AV employs the plain verb "till," the NASB alone corrects it to "cultivate."[184] These corrections of **tillage** were entirely unnecessary, for "conservation **tillage**" was recently stated to be "the soil-safest farming system in history,"[185] and it was reported by the *Los Angeles Times* that "the state government of Queensland, which borders the reef, has urged local cattle and sugar-cane farmers to sue less fertilizer and to cut erosion by planting trees along riverbanks and leaving **tillage** on fields."[186]

Timbrel

> Praise him with the **timbrel** and dance: praise him with stringed instruments and organs. (Psa 150:4)

A **timbrel** is mentioned in the AV five times in the singular[187] and five times in the plural.[188] The word **timbrel** is the diminutive of *timbre,* from a French word of the same spelling meaning a drum. Thus, like a tabret, a **timbrel** is properly a small drum but can also refer to any small musical instrument that is beat on. A study of how **timbrel** and **timbrel** are updated by our modern versions is a study in inconsistency. Only the NIV consistently updates **timbrel** and **timbrels** to "tambourine" and "tambourines."[189] The NKJV retains the AV reading in all but three places.[190] The NRSV only keeps the AV reading once,[191] using a form of "tambourine" the other nine times.[192] The NASB retains the AV reading six times.[193] But after correcting **timbrel** and **timbrels** in the AV, our modern versions, excepting the NIV, utilize these words to update the equally as archaic "tabret" and "tabrets."[194] And as we have seen under our study of *tabret,* when the AV refers to something simple like a "harp," it is corrected by the NIV, NRSV, and NASB to the archaic "lyre" or "lyres."[195]

Tire

> Forbear to cry, make no mourning for the dead, bind the **tire** of thine head upon thee, and put on thy shoes upon thy feet, and cover not *thy* lips, and eat not the bread of men. (Ezek 24:17)

The word **tire** appears once in the AV but the plural **tires** can be found twice[196] and the verb **tired** once.[197] The word **tire**, which appeared in Middle English as *tir*, is the aphetic form of *atir*, "attire." Thus, **tire** does not mean a Firestone or Goodyear but the same thing as *attire*, both as a noun or a verb. It can denote apparel, clothing, a headdress, a covering in general, or the act of putting these things on. Our modern versions call a **tire** a "turban"[198] and **tires** "turbans."[199] However, in the other place where **tires** occurs—the phrase "round **tires** like the moon"—the NRSV and NKJV say "crescents," the NASB "crescent ornaments," and the NIV "crescent necklaces."[200] But in this very verse, the supposedly up-to-date NIV introduces the cryptic word "bangles."[201] **Tired** is changed to "adorned," except for the NIV, which preferred "arranged."[202] Yet when the AV uses a simple word like "strong," it is corrected by the NIV to "rawboned," even though all of the other new translations read as the AV.[203]

Tittle

> And it is easier for heaven and earth to pass, than one **tittle** of the law to fail. (Luke 16:17)

A **tittle** is mentioned twice in the AV.[204] The word came into English by way of the French *title*, from the Latin *titulus*, meaning an inscription or title on a tomb. Thus, **tittle** and *title* were originally synonymous. The word *title* was even applied to an inscribed monument or tomb and was used this way once in the AV.[205] The word **tittle** later came to mean a small stroke or point in writing or printing; then the smallest point of that which was written such as the little horns or projections by which Hebrew letters that are similar can be distinguished. **Tittle** was also applied to the marks over certain vowels that indicate accent or pronunciation. The word *tilde* (~) also developed from *titulus*. By way of application, **tittle** also came to be applied to the apex or smallest part of a thing. Only the NKJV retained the AV reading of "**tittle.**"[206] The other versions use "stroke,"[207] "stroke of a letter,"[208] or "stroke of a pen."[209] Yet the word **tittle** is still used today: "'Encouraging **tittle**-tattles is destructive,' declares Charles Barber, former chairman and CEO of Asarco, Inc., a FORTUNE 500 company that produces nonferrous metals."[210] And don't forget the expression "to a T," which is actually short for "to a **tittle.**"

Tow

> Now *there were* men lying in wait, abiding with her in the chamber. And she said unto him, The Philistines *be* upon thee, Samson. And he brake the withs, as a thread of **tow** is broken when it toucheth the fire. So his strength was not known. (Judg 16:9)

The word **tow** occurs three times in the AV.[211] **Tow** is unchanged from the Old English where it appeared in compounds and literally meant "a spinning or weaving." It originally referred to the operation not the material used. **Tow** is the fiber of flax or hemp used for spinning or the resulting yarn made from this. **Tow** is unanimously given by our modern versions as "a wick" in one passage,[212] but in another, they unite in changing **tow** to the just as archaic "tinder."[213] In the third case where **tow** is found in the AV, the new versions could not decide how to render it. The NRSV said "fiber," the NIV "string," the NKJV "yarn," and the NASB retained the archaic AV reading.[214] Yet when the AV says something simple like "glorious," it is changed by the NIV and NASB to "resplendent."[215]

Traffick

> By thy great wisdom *and* by thy **traffick** hast thou increased thy riches, and thine heart is lifted up because of thy riches: (Ezek 28:5)

The word **traffick** appears five times in the AV[216] while the form **traffickers** is found once.[217] The origin of the word **traffick** is somewhat obscure. It is thought to be from the French *trafique*, from the Italian *traffico*. To **traffick** is to trade, conduct business, or otherwise engage in commerce. Although our modern versions customarily render **traffick** by forms of "trade,"[218] "merchants"[219] "business,"[220] "wares,"[221] "revenues,"[222] and "income"[223] can also be found. Yet in one passage where the AV did not contain the word, the NIV, NRSV, and NASB employ "trafficked" in the same sense as they earlier corrected in the AV.[224] And furthermore, the word **traffick** can still be found today as it is used by the AV: "In early 1993, Serbia began to complain that Tirana was knowingly helping Kosovar Albanians to **traffic** in arms, and making a profit by shipping weapons to the Bosnian Muslims."[225] And how often do we hear of the evils of the drug **traffic**?

𝔗ranslate

> To **translate** the kingdom from the house of Saul, and to set up the throne of David over Israel and over Judah, from Dan even to Beersheba. (2 Sam 3:10)

The word **translate** only occurs once in the AV,[226] but the form **translation** can also be found once[227] and the form **translated** three times.[228] The word **translate**, although it may have passed through the French *translater,* is from *translatus,* the past participle of the Latin *transferre,* from which we derive our modern *transfer.* To **translate** is to transfer, bear, convey, transport, or otherwise remove from one person, place, or condition to another. Since they obviously limited the meaning of **translate** to the modern concept of translating from one language to another,[229] our modern versions have rejected all forms of this word as they appear in the AV. The various forms of **translate** are usually rendered by forms of "transfer"[230] or "taken,"[231] but "brought"[232] and "conveyed"[233] can also be found. Yet forms of the word **translate** often appear today without referring to translating from one language to another: "However, less strategic dependence has not **translated** into a loss of United States leverage over China on other policy issues."[234]

𝔗ravail

> And it came to pass in the time of her **travail,** that, behold, twins *were* in her womb. (Gen 38:27)

The word **travail** is found in the AV thirty-one times,[235] while **travailed** occurs five times,[236] **travaileth** seven times,[237] travailing three times,[238] and travailest once.[239] The noun **travail** is from a French word of the same spelling meaning "suffering." This word, as well as the verb, developed from the French *travaillier,* "to torment." The modern English word *travel* was originally identical with **travail** and denoted a toilsome journey. All of these words go back to the Latin *tripalium, tri* denoting three and *palus* a stake. Thus, an instrument of torture. The various forms of the word **travail** are rendered in a multitude of ways by our modern versions. When **travail** refers to giving birth, it is corrected to forms of "give birth"[240] or "labor."[241] Other translations include "writhes,"[242] "work,"[243] "business,"[244] "task,"[245] "burden,"[246] "toil,"[247] "anguish,"[248] "suffering,"[249] and "hardship."[250] But after all these corrections, the NASB inserted forms of **travail** into six verses.[251] No version should have updated **travail** in the first place, for it can still be found in the *Atlantic Monthly:* "It seems more likely that the extra money they earn compensates them for the immediate **travail,** the darkness and the dirt and the backaches, of work in the mine."[252]

Trow

> Doth he thank that servant because he did the things that were commanded him? I **trow** not. (Luke 17:9)

The word **trow,** found only once in the AV, is from the Old English *treowian,* from *treowa,* "trust, belief." Thus, the word **trow** is related to *true.* **Trow** means trust, belief, think, give credence to, accept, suppose, or imagine. Due to a textual variant, the NRSV, NIV, and NASB do not contain the phrase from which "I **trow** not" is translated from. The NKJV, however, alters **trow** to "think." But if the AV says something plain like "short," the NIV alters it to "fleeting."[253] And when the AV reads "frail," it is changed to "transient" by the NASB.[254]

Twain

> And the veil of the temple was rent in **twain** from the top to the bottom. (Mark 15:38)

The word **twain** occurs seventeen times in the AV.[255] **Twain** appeared in Old English as *twegen,* the masculine form of *two.* The feminine and neuter form was *twa,* which developed into our word *two*. Thus, **twain** is synonymous with *two*. The word "two" is what is normally put for **twain** by our modern versions.[256] However, "both"[257] and "of them"[258] can also be found. Yet **twain** is so archaic that it was utilized by the internationally distributed *Economist* magazine: "Never, it seemed, were the **twain** to meet."[259]

Twined

And they shall make the ephod *of* gold, *of* blue, and *of* purple, *of* scarlet, and fine **twined** linen, with cunning work. (Exo 28:6)

The word **twined** appears twenty-one times in the AV.[260] It is formed from *twine,* which derives from the Old English *twin,* "a double thread." Twine is certainly a common substance today, but the use of this word to describe "fine **twined** linen" has been deemed archaic by modern Bible versions who limited the word *twine* to the modern concept of a piece of twine to tie something together. To be **twined** is to be twisted, wrapped, coiled, or plaited together with two or more strands. Our modern versions selected "twisted" to update **twined**,[261] except the NKJV, which preferred "woven" every time.[262] These corrections notwithstanding, the word **twined** can still be found today: "During the heart of winter, musk oxen started crossing the frozen tidal flats of Baird Inlet and disappearing into the expanse of lake-**twined** tundra of the Yukon-Kuskokwim Delta."[263]

Chapter 21
Unawares to Utter

Unawares

> Be not forgetful to entertain strangers: for thereby some have entertained angels **unawares**. (Heb 13:2)

The word **unawares** appears twelve times in the AV.[1] It was formed by the addition of the prefix *un-* to the word *aware*. **Unawares** means unknowingly, unexpectedly, or inadvertently. This word has been updated by our modern versions to "unintentionally,"[2] "unknown,"[3] "accidentally,"[4] "by surprise,"[5] "secretly,"[6] "unexpectedly,"[7] "unwittingly,"[8] and "unnoticed."[9] On one occasion, the NASB and NRSV forgot to revise **unawares** and read as the AV.[10] It is also apparent that the NRSV and NASB did not think **unawares** to be archaic anyway since they inserted it into another passage where neither the AV nor any other new translation contained the word.[11] Moreover, the NRSV often substitutes a word with an *un-* prefix where the AV did not utilize one. When the AV reads "draw out," the NRSV changes it to "unsheathe."[12] When the AV says "fornication," it is replaced with "unchastity."[13] If the AV mentions "whole stones," they are termed "unhewn stones."[14] Furthermore, when the AV simply says "loose," the NASB and NRSV alter it to "unbind."[15] And when the AV uses the one-syllable, plain word "new," it is unanimously corrected by our modern versions to "unshrunk."[16] On the other hand, if the AV employs common words with an *un-* prefix, they are still corrected. "Unrighteous" is replaced with the more difficult "iniquitous" by the NRSV.[17] The NRSV also changes "unjust" to "rogues."[18] And finally, the NIV amends "unstable" to "turbulent."[19] In any case, the word **unawares** is still common anyway in the twentieth century: "The nature of disasters is to strike us **unawares**."20

Unction

> But ye have an **unction** from the Holy One, and ye know all things. (1 John 2:20)

The word **unction** is found only once in the AV and is from the French *onction*, "anointing." An **unction** is simply an anointing. The word **unction** is directly related to both *anoint* and *ointment* as well as *unguent*, an old word for ointment. All of these words are originally derived from the Latin *ungere*, "to anoint." Our modern versions change **unction** to forms of "anoint." Yet when one is told to do something earnestly, the expression sometimes used is "do it with **unction**." The word **unction** is also still used as a synonym for anointing: "Pilgrims enter from the side of the building to the Stone of **Unction** that commemorates the anointing of Jesus before burial."21

Undersetters

> And *there were* four **undersetters** to the four corners of one base: *and* the **undersetters** *were* of the very base itself. (1 Ki 7:34)

The word **undersetters** occurs four times in the AV.22 It is derived from the old verb *underset*, meaning to support by means of something placed beneath. **Undersetters** are supports—they set under something to hold it up. As expected, the usual translation in the modern versions is "supports."23 **Undersetters** may be archaic and therefore somewhat difficult, but the NRSV changed the perfectly understandable "earth" in the AV to "underworld."24

Unto

> For thy mercy *is* great **unto** the heavens, and thy truth **unto** the clouds. (Psa 57:10)

The word **unto** appears over 9000 times in the AV. The *un-* originally signified "up to" or "until," but the word **unto** is now simply written as *to*. Only the NRSV was successful in completely removing **unto** from the text of the Bible. **Unto** is normally updated by our modern versions to just "to." However, the NIV neglected to upgrade **unto** on two occasions,[25] the NASB once,[26] and the NKJV a whopping twenty-three times.[27] But is **unto** really archaic? The *San Francisco Examiner* evidently did not think so: "With skill and flexibility he brewed it as medicine to revive a patient, China, that was felt to be sick **unto** death."[28]

𝕌ntoward

> And with many other words did he testify and exhort, saying, Save yourselves from this **untoward** generation. (Acts 2:40)

The word **untoward** occurs only once in the AV and literally signifies "not toward." To be **untoward** is to be corrupt, unfavorable, unfortunate, improper, or perverse. The NRSV and NIV preferred "corrupt" but the NKJV and NASB opted for "perverse." Although our modern versions deemed **untoward** to be archaic, the *Atlantic Monthly* certainly did not: "To the many parents in the trenches concerned about their offspring's shyness, brashness, or other **untoward** tendencies, Kagan offers a few pragmatic insights."[29]

𝕌pbraid

> Then began he to **upbraid** the cities wherein most of his mighty works were done, because they repented not: (Mat 11:20)

The word **upbraid** is found twice in the AV,[30] with the form **upbraided** also appearing twice.[31] **Upbraid** is from the Old English word *upbregdan,* formed from *up* and *bregdan,* meaning to braid but also to lay hold of. So although the *-braid* in **upbraid** contains the usual verb *braid,* it is used in a special sense. To **upbraid** is to rebuke, denounce, condemn, censure, or scold. The translations in the modern versions include "taunted,"[32] "ridiculed,"[33] "reproach,"[34] "rebuke,"[35] "denounce,"[36] and "finding fault."[37] The NRSV, after the correcting the AV three times,[38] retained "**upbraided**" in one passage.[39] In fact, the NRSV thought so much of the word that it also inserted it into two other passages where neither the AV nor any other modern version contained the word.[40] The word **upbraid** is still in common use even though it was not recognized as such by the translators of modern versions: "Farrakhan was equally wrong to **upbraid** those Black leaders in the FINAL CALL, his group's newspaper."[41]

𝔘𝔰𝔲𝔯𝔶

> Thou oughtest therefore to have put my money to the exchangers, and *then* at my coming I should have received mine own with **usury**. (Mat 25:27)

The word **usury** occurs twenty-four times in the AV in seventeen verses.[42] **Usury** is from the French *usure* meaning the use of a thing. **Usury** and words like *utensil, utility,* and *utilize,* as well as *use,* are all originally derived from the Latin *uti,* "to use." **Usury** is always applied to money and hence means interest. The modern sense of exorbitant interest is an extended use of the word. Our modern versions customarily render **usury** as "interest," but such is always not the case, for only the NRSV completely dislodges the word. The other three new translations retain **usury** in a haphazard manner. The NASB kept it in three passages,[43] the NKJV in ten,[44] and the NIV in eight,[45] one of which where **usury** did not appear in the AV.[46] The word **usury** can still be found in the 1990's as a substitute for interest: "During he past two years, class action lawsuits have been brought against a Fleet Finance mortgage subsidiary in Georgia, accusing it of racial discrimination, loan-sharking, fraud, violation of **usury** limits, and breaking the truth-in-lending law."[47]

𝔘𝔰-𝔴𝔞𝔯𝔡

See you-ward.

𝔘𝔱𝔱𝔢𝔯

> And the posts thereof *were* toward the **utter** court; and palm trees *were* upon the posts thereof, on this side, and on that side: and the going up to it *had* eight steps. (Ezek 48:37)

The word **utter** occurs in the AV with three shades of meaning. The first, that of "to **utter** speech," is found in all modern versions and is also so used today. **Utter** is also found in the AV in the sense of "complete or highest action." This usage also appears in our new translations, although the NASB, NRSV, and NIV correct the AV every place it occurs in it.[40] The problem with the word **utter** as it is used in the AV is that it often means "outer." Indeed, the word **utter** originated as a comparative adjective formed from the Old English *ut,* "out." Of the thirteen times **utter** is so used in the AV, it is normally rendered as "outer."[49] The superlatives **uttermost** and **utmost** are also found in the AV with the meaning of "outer." **Utmost** always appears in the sense of "outermost," eleven times in all.[50] Although our modern versions contain the word **utmost,** it is rarely used as it is in the AV.[51] The word **uttermost** appears twenty-eight times in the AV.[52] Like **utter,** it too has several shades of meaning. It is used once in the sense of "know thoroughly,"[53] twice with the function of "the end or the last,"[54] and once to express the idea of "completely."[55] The typical employment of **uttermost,** however, is with the meaning of "outermost." When **uttermost** so appears, it is usually rendered "outermost,"[56] "outer,"[57] or "outskirts."[58] The NKJV follows the AV reading of **uttermost** three times.[59] The other translations remove all trace of the word, except for the NRSV, which injected it once where neither the AV nor any of the other modern versions contained the word.[60] Although the word **utter** is used in the AV in what some consider to be an archaic sense, when the AV mentions "galleries," every one of our modern versions changes it to the unintelligible "tresses."[61]

Chapter 22
Vagabond to Vocation

Vagabond

> When thou tillest the ground, it shall not henceforth yield unto thee her strength; a fugitive and a **vagabond** shalt thou be in the earth. (Gen 4:12)

Vagabond appears three times in the AV,[1] while the plural **vagabonds** can be found once.[2] **Vagabond** is from the French adjective *vagabond,* "wandering." To **vagabond** is to wander from place to place. A **vagabond** is a tramp, vagrant, transient, nomad, or bum. All occurrences of these words are removed from the AV by our modern versions except the NKJV, which retains the word three times.[3] The usual translation in the other modern versions is a form of "wanderer."[4] But after expelling the word completely from its text, the NASB inserts "**vagabond**" in another passage where the AV did not have it.[5] The *Washington Post,* however, certainly did not judge **vagabond** to be archaic: "But he never bothered to resurrect his futuristic novel about the heroic poet Michel, who becomes a homeless **vagabond** after a fruitless odyssey in search of an enlightened society."[6]

Vainglory

> Let nothing be done through strife or **vainglory**; but in lowliness of mind let each esteem other better than themselves. (Phil 2:3)

The word vainglory occurs once in the AV but also appears as two words in another passage.[7] **Vainglory** is a compound of *vain* and *glory,* from the Latin phrase *vana gloria.* **Vainglory** is glory that is empty or worthless, unwarranted pride, self-exaltation, or idle boasting. **Vainglory** is unanimously corrected in our modern versions. It is normally rendered by a form of "conceit."[8] Yet all five occurrences of "conceit" in the AV have been amended. In four passages "conceit" is analogously rendered "eyes,"[9] except two verses in the NRSV where it is furnished as "self-esteem."[10] In the other instance, the NRSV and NASB preferred "imagination," while the NKJV selected "esteem."[11] Once again, the *Washington Post* appears to have a much wider vocabulary than the translators of modern Bible versions: "If mammon and **vainglory** were his only objectives, surely Richardson would have dusted the university long, long ago."[12]

Vale

> And the **vale** of Siddim *was full of* slimepits; and the kings of Sodom and Gomorrah fled, and fell there; and they that remained fled to the mountain. (Gen 14:10)

A **vale** is mentioned nine times in the AV.[13] This word comes into English from the French *val,* valley." Thus, a **vale** is literally a valley. It can also be used figuratively to represent a place of trouble of misery. One would think that **vale** could simply be updated to *valley,* but this would be too easy for our new translations. **Vale** is upgraded to "valley" several times,[14] but "lowland" is also a regular fixture in some instances.[15] The NIV prefers "foothills" in most cases.[16] Incredibly, the NRSV changes **vale** on three occasions to the obscure "Shephelah."[17] However, an examination of when the AV uses the word *valley* is really indicative of the inconsistency of the NRSV. Although the NRSV changes "valley" to "ravine," "lowland," and "plain,"[18] twice it transforms "valley" into "**vale**."[19] But even worse than this, the favorite translation of the NRSV for "valley" is "wadi."[20] The NRSV was not consistent, however, for one time we read of the "Wadi Eshcol"[21] and in another passage the "Valley of Eshcol."[22] The NASB even utilizes "wadi" one time for "valley."[23] And furthermore, **vale** was not archaic in the first place, for it is used both literally and figuratively in the same sentence by the *Los Angeles Times* in the 1990's: "Long famous for its luxurious Victorian houseboats under majestic Himalayan peaks, its handwoven carpets and ancient Mogul gardens, the lush

Vale of Kashmir has turned into a **vale** of suffering and death for many of its 4 million residents."[24]

Valour

> So Joshua ascended from Gilgal, he, and all the people of war with him, and all the mighty men of **valour.** (Josh 10:7)

The word **valour** (modern American spelling: **valor**) appears thirty-seven times in the AV.[25] It is from the French *valour,* "value or worth." **Valour** signifies importance or worthiness; boldness or determination. It goes back to the same Latin root, *ualere,* "to be strong," as the word *valiant.* It is the word **valour,** however, that gives our modern versions trouble. Only the NKJV retains the word in a majority of places like the AV.[26] The NIV omits the word entirely. The NRSV uses the word "**valor**" three times, but never in a verse that the AV does.[27] The NASB employs the term eighteen times, but corrects the AV in six of these.[28] **Valour** is sometimes updated to "valiant,"[29] but when the AV employs "valiant," it is usually corrected to "able,"[30] "brave,"[31] or "mighty."[32] Sometimes "valiant" in the AV is even revised back to "valor."[33] But when the AV reads "able men" instead of "men of **valour,**" the text is still corrected.[34] When the AV mentions "men of might," the NASB further amends it to "men of **valor.**"[35] A concerted effort was obviously made by some of our modern versions to never line up with the AV. This was unnecessary, for the word **valour** is currently used by *USA Today Magazine:* "Their stories of courage, dedication, sacrifice, and **valor** are a part of the fabric of the nation's history."[36]

Variableness

> Every good gift and every perfect gift is from above, and cometh down from the Father of lights, with whom is no **variableness,** neither shadow of turning. (James 1:17)

The word **variableness** is only found once in the AV. It is plainly a compound formed from *variable,* which, although from the French *variable,* "changeable," is akin to *various, vary, variant, variation, varied, variance, and variety*—all derived from the Latin *varius,* meaning varied, different, or changing. **Variable-**

ness is the quality of being variable or changeable. Our modern versions usually pare the word down to "variation." However, this aversion for long or otherwise unfamiliar words that end in a -*ness* suffix is spurious. The NIV and NRSV both insert the word "saltiness" into three passages.[37] All of our new translations conspire in one passage to expand "faith" in the AV to "faithfulness."[38] The NASB regularly replaces "iniquity" with "lawlessness"[39] and the NKJV and NRSV sometimes follow suit.[40] The up-to-date NIV fourteen times uses "unfaithfulness,"[41] a word not found in the AV, while the NRSV wields the jaw-breaker "licentiousness" eight times[42] when it does not appear in any Bible except in one passage in the NASB.[43] The NRSV also coins the word "faithlessness,"[44] arising only one other time in any of our modern versions.[45] Meanwhile, the NASB had trouble with "little," extending it to "littleness."[46] Other words that end in -*ness* are treated likewise, howbeit, inconsistently. The NRSV alters "lowliness" in the AV,[47] but then inserts the word where it did not appear in the AV.[48] "Readiness" is corrected in the AV to "eagerness" by the NASB,[49] but then the word is implanted in other passages where the AV did not have it.[50] These corrections and additions demonstrate once again that "archaic" words are not limited to the AV.

Variance

> For I am come to set a man at **variance** against his father, and the daughter against her mother, and the daughter in law against her mother in law. (Mat 10:35)

The word **variance,** found twice in the AV,[51] is from the French *variance,* "to vary." **Variance** is a variation, difference, alteration, disagreement, or discrepancy; a state of disagreement. Both instances of the word **variance** in the AV are corrected by all of our modern versions.[52] Yet these same translations continuously alter perfectly understandable words in the AV. The NASB and NRSV change the simple word "fear" to "alarm,"[53] while the NKJV, supposedly updated into modern English, amends "fatherless" to "waifs,"[54] a word not found in any modern version. The word **variance,** however, was not archaic to begin with: "Patients also are deprived of important consumer information because of a wide **variance** in regulations from state to state, and between agreement states and NRC-regulated states."[55]

Vaunt

> And the LORD said unto Gideon, The people that *are* with thee *are* too many for me to give the Midianites into their hands, lest Israel **vaunt** themselves against me, saying, Mine own hand hath saved me. (Judg 7:2)

Vaunt, found only once in the AV, also appears one time as **vaunteth**.[56] Used transitively, **vaunt** is from the French *vanter*, "to praise," but the intransitive form comes from *se vanter*, "to boast." The Latin root is the same as that of *vain* and *vanity*: *vanus*, "empty." To **vaunt** is to brag, boast, gloat over, strut, put forth, or flaunt oneself, someone or something else. Both forms of **vaunt** are unanimously corrected by our modern versions. The NASB and NIV both updated **vaunt** to "boast" in one passage,[57] but then the NASB revised "boast" to "**vaunt**" in another.[58] The NRSV replaces **vaunteth** with "boastful"[59] and then corrects "boast" in the AV to "**vaunt**" just like the NASB.[60] The up-to-date, contemporary NIV sticks the supposedly archaic "**vaunt**" into a passage where the AV reads otherwise.[61] The NASB also inserts "**vaunt**" into another passage where the AV said "magnify."[62] These improvements of the AV text were totally unnecessary, however, for the word **vaunt** is still used today as in this example from the *Atlantic Monthly:* "The collapse of the revolution at home could encourage even moderate Islamic revolutionaries—who still, after all, define themselves and hold power by virtue of their Islamic identities—to **vaunt** an 'Islamic' foreign policy."[63]

Vehement

> And it came to pass, when the sun did arise, that God prepared a **vehement** east wind; and the sun beat upon the head of Jonah, that he fainted, and wished in himself to die, and said, *It is* better for me to die than to live. (Jonah 4:8)

The word **vehement** occurs three times in the AV,[64] while the form **vehemently** is found five times.[65] It comes to us from the French *vehement*, "violent." **Vehement** was originally akin to *vehicle* as both terms are ultimately derived from the Latin *vehere*, "to carry." To be **vehement** is to be ardent, vigorous, violent, or intense. Only the NKJV among our modern versions retains the word as the AV.[66] The other translations use a great variety of words or phrases in updating the word. **Vehement** is corrected by four different words (raging, sultry, scorching, mighty) in the NASB, NIV, and NRSV,[67] in addition to a phrase in the NASB that deviates substantially from all other versions.[68] **Vehemently** is updated to words like "emphatically,"[69] "insistently,"[70] and "fiercely,"[71] in the NASB and NIV. The NRSV forgot to remove the word out of two passages,[72] while the NIV and NASB maintained the AV reading on one occasion.[73] The *Christian Sceience Monitor*, however, made no attempt to restrict usage of the word: "Some farmers and ranchers still **vehemently** object to government ownership of even the 180 acres envisioned by the bill."[74]

Vein

> Surely there is a **vein** for the silver, and a place for gold *where* they fine *it*. (Job 28:1)

The word **vein** can only be found once in the AV. It is from the French *veine*, originally meaning a blood vessel because it was a conveyer of the blood. It is thought to be ultimately derived from the Latin *vehere*, "to carry." In addition to being a blood vessel, a **vein** can be a watercourse, an ability, aspect, tendency, or interest, a strand of vascular tissue, a mineral deposit, or an irregular streak in an object. It is a very versatile word that is also used figuratively. Our modern versions are united in correcting **vein** to "mine." Yet the word **vein** is used in the 1990's in all of its meanings. It is used literally to describe a blood vessel: "He probed her thighs with a needle, searching for a **vein** and muttering about all the fat in an animal getting ready to hibernate."[75] **Vein** is also used figuratively: "College Prospects is among a half-dozen businesses in the process of 'reverse-recruiting,' each trying to tap into a rich **vein** of more than 20,000 high schools, each of those schools buzzing with dozens of athletes."[76] The word is also used in the sense of aspect: "In that **vein,** Ellis has tried to turn the stadium question over to the community."[77] And finally, **vein** is still employed just as it is in the AV text: "That's why we find pale green crystals in one **vein** valued at $500 per carat right next to vivid blue-green crystals valued at $20,000 a carat."[78] The same people who object to the word **vein** in the AV have no trouble calling a highway an artery.

Venison

> And Isaac loved Esau, because he did eat of *his* **venison:** but Rebekah loved Jacob. (Gen 25:28)

Venison is mentioned eight times in the AV.[79] It comes into English from the French *veneison*, meaning the flesh of beasts of prey. **Venison** has come to mean exclusively the flesh of deer. Thinking the word archaic, all of our modern versions have altered the word. The standard translation is "game,"[80] but the NIV prefers "wild game" in two verses.[81] Evidently, the *The Washington Times* has more hunters on its staff than the committees that translated these modern versions, for the word **venison** was not considered by them to be archaic at all: "Fear not, **venison** will be on the menu in thousands of area homes come hunting season."[82]

Venture

> And a *certain* man drew a bow at a **venture,** and smote the king of Israel between the joints of the harness: wherefore he said unto the driver of his chariot, Turn thine hand, and carry me out of the host; for I am wounded. (1 Ki 22:34)

The word **venture** occurs twice in the AV.[83] The form **adventure** is used as a verb twice in the AV,[84] plus once in the past tense form of **adventured**.[85] The extended form **peradventure** appears thirty-two times.[86] **Venture** is the aphetic form of **adventure,** from the French *aventure,* "a happening or event." The verbal forms of these words came to mean "to commit to chance or risk." A **venture** is an undertaking involving uncertainty; a risk or hazard. "At a **venture**" means according to chance or at random. The word **adventure** itself is certainly not archaic, but its use as a verb is what is alleged to be troublesome. It was never used in the relatively modern sense of "the adventures of Superman." Hence, to **adventure** means to undertake or embark on a **venture,** often involving risk.

Peradventure is an English compound of the French *par aventure*, "by chance" and means by chance, by accident, perhaps, or as it chanced or happened. When the AV uses the word **adventure** as a verb our modern versions corrected it to "**venture,**" but when the AV employs **venture** it is corrected because it is not used in the verbal sense. The new versions update **venture** in both passages to "random,"[87] except the NRSV, which preferred "unknowingly."[88] Yet three times when the AV and all other modern versions used a form of "dare," the NASB altered it to a more difficult form of "**venture.**"[89] The NRSV also utilizes **venture** as a noun one time.[90] But is the word **venture** archaic when it is not used verbally? Have any of these new versions ever been published with **venture** capital? **Peradventure** is usually given by our modern versions as "perhaps."[91] The word **adventure** is unanimously rendered by our modern versions as "**venture,**" "risked," and "**venture**" in the three places that it occurs in the AV.[92] This was totally unnecessary, for the word is still used today in the sense of a **venture**: "Wilma Roberts has **adventured** across the world to take photos of rare wildlife and exotic landscapes,"[93] and in the sense of a risk: "With its continuing warfare and economic disarray, Angola was more of an **adventure** than either Moscow or Havana could afford."[94]

Verily

> **Verily, verily,** I say unto you, He that heareth my word, and believeth on him that sent me, hath everlasting life, and shall not come into condemnation; but is passed from death unto life. (John 5:24)

The familiar word **verily** occurs in the AV 140 times in 113 verses. **Verily,** formed from *very,* appeared as *verraily* in Middle English. *Very* comes from the French *verai,* "true." **Verily** is an adverb meaning truly, really, or indeed. No trace of this word can be found in our modern versions, excepting the one instance that the NASB forgot to change.[95] Sometimes **verily** was not even translated by our new versions.[96] Although they are agreed against the AV in expelling the word, our modern versions could not agree on how to translate the word when they did. In the Old Testament, it can be found as "truly,"[97] "alas,"[98] "surely,"[99] "certainly,"[100] "really,"[101] "well,"[102] "completely,"[103] "wholly,"[104] or "really."[105] In the New Testament, the expression "**verily** I say unto you" is typically rendered by the NASB as "truly I say to you," the NIV as "I tell you the truth," the NRSV as "truly I tell you," and the NKJV as "assuredly I say to you."[106] The double form **verily, verily** is similarly rendered.[107] But when the Greek word in the Gospels that underlies **verily** shows up later in the middle of another sentence, it is very inconsistently transliterated into English as the familar word "amen."[108] The other instances of **verily** in the New Testament are variously rendered as "indeed,"[109] "certainly,"[110] "so then,"[111] "too,"[112] "on my part,"[113] "though,"[114] "just,"[115] "then,"[116] "in fact,"[117] "it is clear,"[118] "surely,"[119] or "assuredly."[120] Consistency was never the hallmark of modern Bible versions. **Verily** might be archaic, but is certainly much easier to understand than why the NRSV substituted "remonstrated" for "contended."[121]

Verity

> Whereunto I am ordained a preacher, and an apostle, (I speak the truth in Christ, and lie not;) a teacher of the Gentiles in faith and **verity**. (1 Tim 2:7)

The word **verity,** found twice in the AV,[122] is from the French *verite,* "true." Both **verity** and *verily* are ultimately derived from the Latin *verus,* "true," from which we also get the English *very.* **Verity** is truth, an established fact; a true statement, doctrine, or opinion. The word **verity** is removed from our modern versions in both occurrences,[123] but the NKJV overlooked **verity** one time.[124] **Verity** is rendered once by the NIV and NRSV as "faithful,"[125] but in the next passage where the AV reads "faith and **verity**," it is respectively furnished as "true faith" and "truth."[126] The NKJV and NASB also express the word as "truth" in this passage.[127] Yet the underlying Greek word for **verity** is translated in the NIV elsewhere as "certainly,"[128] "indeed,"[129] and "assure."[130] However, **verity** was not archaic to begin with: "The results, they say, are unnecessarily destroying families, damaging the reputation of the mental health community, and undermining the **verity** of real sexual abuse cases."[131]

Vermilion

> And *that* she increased her whoredoms: for when she saw men portrayed upon the wall, the images of the Chaldeans portrayed with **vermilion,** (Ezek 23:14)

The word **vermilion** appears only twice in the AV.[132] It is from the French *vermeillon,* a derivative of *vermeil,* "bright red." The Latin root, however, is from *vermis,* "worm," from which we not only get the English word *worm,* but also the word *vermin.* The word **vermilion** was initially connected with a red-colored worm. **Vermilion** is a brilliant scarlet red color. It was formerly a pigment of mercuric sulfide obtained from cinnabar. Surprisingly, the NKJV and NRSV do not alter the word.[133] The NIV changes it to "red" both times, but the NASB uses "bright red" the first time and retains "**vermilion**" the second.[134] Yet when the AV mentions "rams' skins dyed red," the NRSV converts them into "tanned rams' skins" when all the other new translations follow the AV reading.[135] And when the AV mentions a "pavement of red," the NIV, NRSV, and NASB revise it to a "pavement of porphyry."[136] Nevertheless, the word **vermilion** is still applied today to a shade of red: "And red (Clark's favorite color) is everywhere, from the crimson 19th-century high-back chair in the den to the **vermilion** walls of her third-floor study."[137]

Vestments

> And he said unto him that *was* over the vestry, Bring forth **vestments** for all the worshippers of Baal. And he brought them forth **vestments.** (2 Ki 10:22)

Vestments, the plural of *vestment,* occurs twice in the AV in the same verse. It is from the French *vestement,* "clothing." **Vestments** are garments, attire, clothes, or robes, especially those used ceremonially or in some official capacity. Surprisingly, the NKJV and NRSV retain the word; expectedly, the NASB and NIV alter it. The NASB revised **vestments** to "garments" but then corrected "garments" in the AV to "apparel."[138] The NIV updated **vestments** in this passage to "robes," but in one place where the AV read "apparel," the NIV inserted the archaic word it just corrected: "**vestments.**"[139] Although the NRSV liked the word **vestments,** it was at the expense of forty-five other words in the AV, for the NRSV made Episcopalians out of Aaron and the Levitical priests even though the AV connected **vestments** with Baal worshippers.[140] In the 1990's, **vestments** still carry a bad connotation: "Even Aristide, a Catholic priest who was ousted by a military coup in 1991, used to have voodoo gods sewn into his religious **vestments** as a way to show solidarity with the masses."[141]

Vestry

> And he said unto him that *was* over the **vestry,** Bring forth vestments for all the worshippers of Baal. And he brought them forth vestments. (2 Ki 10:22)

The word **vestry** appears only once in the AV. It is akin to *vestments* and comes from the French *vestiarie*, "a wardrobe." Both *vestments* and **vestry** are ultimately derived from the Latin *vestis*, "clothing." A **vestry** is a room for vestments, especially a room that is in or attached to a church. Hence, a room in a church used for prayer or religious service also came to be called a **vestry**. All of our modern versions change **vestry** to "wardrobe." But what happens when the AV already uses a modern, up-to-date word? The NRSV, NKJV, and NASB replace "speckled" in the AV with "sorrel."[142] The NKJV, NIV, and NRSV correct "servant" to "vassal."[143] Nevertheless, the word **vestry** is still used today to mean a committee in the Episcopal Church.

Vesture

> They said therefore among themselves, Let us not rend it, but cast lots for it, whose it shall be: that the scripture might be fulfilled, which saith, They parted my raiment among them, and for my **vesture** they did cast lots. These things therefore the soldiers did. (John 19:24)

A **vesture** surfaces eight times in the AV.[144] It comes into English from the French *vesture*, "clothing." Like the related words *vestments* and *vestry*, **vesture** goes back to the Latin *vestis*, "clothing," from which we also get the common English word *vest*. **Vesture** is clothing or something that covers. All eight occurrences of **vesture** are unanimously corrected in our modern versions. The NASB couldn't decide how to update the word so it substituted four different ones (garments, clothing, mantle, robe).¹⁴⁵ Yet when the AV employs the word *mantle,* it is corrected by the NASB to "rug" or "robe."¹⁴⁶ And furthermore, in one verse where the AV reads "garment," the NASB changes it to "**vesture**" after just eliminating the word from every place it was found in the AV.¹⁴⁷ The NRSV only utilized three words to replace **vesture** (cloak, clothing, robe),¹⁴⁸ but when the AV said "cloak" it was changed to "mantle."¹⁴⁹ "Cloak" in the AV was also transformed into "coat" by the NRSV,¹⁵⁰ but when coat was used in the AV, it was altered to "shirt."¹⁵¹ The NIV and NKJV also substituted "cloak" for **vesture**.¹⁵²

Vex

> Now about that time Herod the king stretched forth *his* hands to **vex** certain of the church. (Acts 12:1)

Vex, appearing fifteen times in the AV,¹⁵³ is from the French *vexer,* "to agitate." The form **vexed** occurs twenty-two times.¹⁵⁴ The noun **vexation** occurs fourteen times in the singular¹⁵⁵ and once in the plural.¹⁵⁶ It comes from the French *vexation,* "an agitation." Both are ultimately derived from the Latin *vexus.* To **vex** is to trouble, afflict, harass, distress, provoke, or agitate. The word **vex** can not be found anywhere in our modern versions. In fact, they went all out in their search for words to correct **vex** in the AV. Only three times do our new translations agree on a word to correct the AV (rival, torment, trouble).¹⁵⁷ On two occasions, none of our modern versions could agree with each other on the selection of a word to revise the AV.¹⁵⁸ When three modern versions agreed against the AV they said "terrify."¹⁵⁹ The word **vexed** was corrected every time it appeared in the AV, except for one verse in the NKJV.¹⁶⁰ But then the NKJV updated "pricked" to "**vexed**,"¹⁶¹ the NIV altered "limited" and "grieved" to "**vexed**,"¹⁶² and the NASB inserted "**vexed**" three times where the AV did not contain the word.¹⁶³ The word **vexation** is replaced all fourteen times it occurs in the AV, but never by the same word in all four of our modern versions. Three times we can find it as "confusion,"¹⁶⁴ and three times we can find it as "sheer terror."¹⁶⁵ The NKJV used six different words to bring the AV up-to-date (confusion, grasping, striving, distressed, terror, grief).¹⁶⁶ Likewise the NIV (confusion, chasing, anxious striving, distress, sheer terror, brokenness).¹⁶⁷ The NRSV, after correcting the AV fourteen times in a row, inserted the word **vexation** into seven additional passages where the AV had such "archaic" words as "grief," "wrath," "indignation," and "sorrow."[168] The NASB likewise employed the word "**vexation**" after just correcting it in the AV fourteen times. The NASB used "**vexation**" six times to update "wrath" twice,[169] "grief" once,[170] "spite" once,[171] "and sorrow" twice.[172] The word **vexation vexed** the translators of our modern versions, but not the editors of the *Los Angeles Times:* "And Santos gives voice to a universal community **vexation**: 'One of the problems we have here in Oakwood is longtime residents have a small-town mentality.'"[173] Nevertheless, after all this effort to correct the text of the AV, we find that the word **vex** is not archaic after all: it is still used by the *Christian Science Monitor* in the 1990's: "The low prices help rein in inflation and benefit consumers. But they **vex** many farmers."[174]

Vial

> Then Samuel took a **vial** of oil, and poured *it* upon his head, and kissed him, and said, *Is it* not because the LORD hath anointed thee *to be* captain over his inheritance? (1 Sam 10:1)

A **vial** can be found eight times in the AV.[175] **Vial** is from *viole,* a variation of the Middle English *fiole.* This came into English from the French *fiole,* "a small vessel." The word *phial* also developed from this French source. A **vial** is a small container for holding liquids. This word is jointly changed by our modern versions on seven occasions to "bowl."[176] The only other occurrence of **vial** is replaced by "flask," except in the NRSV, which retained the AV reading only here.[177] However, when the AV read "bottle," the NKJV also changed it to "flask."[178] Although the translators of the NKJV drink out of a bottle and not a skin, they corrected "bottle" in another passage to "skin."[179] If it be argued that "skin" is more accurate, then why was the same Hebrew word, *nebel,* rendered as "bottle" in another place just like the AV?[180] After correcting the AV eight times, the NASB went ahead and inserted the word "**vial**" into four passages where neither the AV nor any other of our modern versions used the word.[181] But the word **vial** was not archaic in the first place: "Pushing his sunglasses into his black hair, the first one kneels to scoop up some sand in a little **vial**, while the other one records an identifying number in his notebook."[182]

Victuals

> And when it was evening, his disciples came to him, saying, This is a desert place, and the time is now past; send the multitude away, that they may go into the villages, and buy themselves **victuals**. (Mat 14:15)check singular

The singular **victual** and the plural **victuals** occur in the AV respectively five[183] and seventeen[184] times. The word **victual** is from the French *vitaille*, "food." The Latin root is derived from *vivere*, "to live." **Victual** is found most often in the plural and is still pronounced *vit'l*, after the Middle English form of the word. **Victuals** are food, supplies, sustenance, or provisions. Our modern versions had no use for the word but could not decide how to update it. Sometimes the word "food" was used.[185] Other times it was "provisions."[186] Occasionally though, "food supply"[187] or "sustenance"[188] or "grain"[189] or "maintenance"[190] was utilized to update the AV. The NASB also employs "something to eat" and "ration" each one time.[191] Although they all disagreed among themselves, our modern versions were unanimous in their mission to update the word **victuals** because it was supposedly archaic. But the word **victuals** is still used down South, and although classified as a Southern expression,[192] this word is still in use by the *Christian Science Monitor:* "Atop a pile of **victuals**, ranging in weight from six pounds to 35 pounds, depending on the time of year, Prairie Crossing sets a bouquet of zinnias, sea lavender, delphiniums, yarrow, and other flowers."[193]

Villany

> For the vile person will speak **villany**, and his heart will work iniquity, to practice hypocrisy, and to utter error against the LORD, to make empty the soul of the hungry, and he will cause the drink of the thirsty to fail. (Isa 32:6)

The word **villany** (modern spelling: **villainy**), occurring only twice in the AV,[194] is from the French *vileinie*, from *vilain*, from which we have also acquired the English word *villain*. **Villany** is conduct characteristic of a villain: evil, wicked, sinful. The modern spelling of **villainy** gradually replaced **villany** after the eighteenth century.[195] Our modern versions employed a variety of words to update **villany**. The NIV and NRSV each use "folly" one time,[196] but this is the only time two of our versions were in agreement with each other or themselves. The NIV chose "outrageous things" in one passage while the NKJV selected "disgraceful things."[197] The NASB decided on "nonsense" and "foolishly."[198] The labor expended in correcting **villany** in the AV was all in vain, however, for the NRSV introduced the word into two passages in the New Testament.[199] And not only that, but the Old Testament as well, for a "wicked man" in the AV has been corrected by the NRSV to a "villain,"[200] and the doubly archaic phrase "villainies of villains" has also been implanted.[201] The NIV likewise changes "wicked man" to "villain."[202] And besides the NRSV, the *Atlantic Monthly* thought **villany** worthy of use in the 1990's: "Iran is no longer at the gates of Baghdad, Saddam Hasten's **villainy** and the Gulf War have made Iranian Shi'ism seem less menacing, and Khomeini is dead."[203]

Virtue

> And Jesus said, Somebody hath touched me: for I perceive that **virtue** is gone out of me. (Luke 8:46)

The word **virtue** is used seven times in the AV.[204] It comes from the French *vertu*, "worth, bravery." Etymologically, **virtue** is literally "manliness," being formed initially from the Latin *virtus*, from *vir*, "man." **Virtue** can mean chastity, unusual ability, merit, valor, worth, moral excellence or the power inherent in a supernatural being. The adjective **virtuous** appears three times in the AV,[205] with the form **virtuously** occurring once.[206] It came into English from the French *vertueus*, but is also ultimately related to the Latin *virtus*. **Virtuous** means moral, excellent, upright, or ethical. Except for three passages in the NKJV,[207] **virtue** is corrected by our modern versions all seven times it appears in the AV. In four passages, the NIV, NASB, and NRSV could not decide between "goodness"[208] or forms of "excellence"[209] even though they translated the same Greek word every time. The other three occurrences of **virtue** have been unanimously altered to "power."[210] But when the AV translates *dunamis* as "mighty works," it is altered to "miracles" by the NIV.[211] And when the AV renders *dunamis* as "miracles," the

NIV changes it to "powers."[212] Furthermore, after correcting **virtue** in the AV seven times, the NRSV inserts the word into another passage.[213] Regarding the word **virtuous,** only the NIV was consistent in its correcting of the AV.[214] The NASB preferred a form of "excellent" three times,[215] but settled for "nobly" the fourth.[216] The NKJV slipped even further, only using the same word twice—the word "**virtuous,**" just as the AV.[217] The NRSV was confused on how to update the word, using "worthy," "good," "capable," and "excellently" to modernize the AV text.[218] The word **virtue,** however, was not deemed archaic by *Newsweek* magazine: "Witness virgin goddess Tori Spelling, whose 'Beverly Hills 90210 character clings to her **virtue** even when she feels like the last virgin on Rodeo Drive.'"[219] And although the NIV, NASB, and NRSV don't contain the word **virtuous,** the *Washington Post* had no trouble with the word: "Other parents preach to their teenagers or insist that their kids are too **virtuous** to be sexually active."[220]

Viol

That chant to the sound of the **viol,** *and* invent to themselves instruments of music, like David; (Amos 6:5)

A **viol** is mentioned twice in the AV in the singular[221] and twice in the plural.[222] It is from the French *viole*, "a stringed instrument." A **viol** is an instrument similar to a violin. Although the names for the violin, viola, violone, and violoncello all come to English from Italian, they are all ultimately derived, like the word **viol**, from the Latin *vitula*. The word *fiddle* is also remotely connected with the Latin *vitula*. Naturally, a **viol** cannot be found in our modern versions. Although the meaning of the word could be ascertained due to its similarity to *violin*, the NIV changed it to the obscure "lyres" in one passage but "harps" in another.[223] Surprisingly, none of our new translations update the word **viol** to violin. The NRSV and NASB use "harp" or "harps" every time,[224] but when the AV says "harp" or "harps" it is altered to the cryptic "lyre" or "lyres."[225]

Visage

As many were astonied at thee; his **visage** was so marred

more than any man, and his form more than the sons of men: (Isa 52:14)

Visage occurs three times in the AV.[226] It is from the French *visage,* from *vis,* "face." The **visage** can be the countenance, aspect, face, expression, or appearance. Of the three times the word is used in the AV, it is rendered by three different words in the NKJV, NIV, and NRSV.[227] The NKJV retained the word in the first passage while using "appearance" in the next.[228] The NRSV does just the opposite, correcting the first occurrence to "appearance" but leaving "**visage**" in the second.[229] Only the NASB employed the same word in more than one verse: it used "appearance" twice.[230] When the others use "face"[231] or "facial expression"[232] to update the AV, the NIV brandishes the word "attitude."[233] These botched attempts at amending the AV text were all unnecessary, for the word **visage** was not considered archaic by the *Sacramento Bee* in 1994: "His bottle glasses give him a learned if watery **visage.**"[234]

𝔙𝔦𝔰𝔦𝔱𝔞𝔱𝔦𝔬𝔫

> Having your conversation honest among the Gentiles: that, whereas they speak against you as evildoers, they may by *your* good works, which they shall behold, glorify God in the day of **visitation.** (1 Pet 2:12)

The word **visitation** can be found fifteen times in the AV.[235] It comes into English unchanged from the French *visitation,* "the act of visiting." A **visitation** is a visiting to administer aid or affliction, especially in reference to a supernatural visit. It can be an official visit, a periodic visit, an inspection, or a religious visit; hence, church visitation. Our modern versions have only retained **visitation** a total of five times between them out of the fifteen times the word appears in the AV.[236] Apparently all were by accident, for a concerted effort was made to extract the word from the AV text. The usual revision in the Old Testament was a form of "punishment,"[237] but the NIV preferred "judgment" on two occasions.[238] Daring not to read as the AV, the NIV nevertheless came halfway in its rendering of "day of **visitation**" to "day he visits us"[239] and "thy **visitation** cometh" to "the day God visits you."[240] All the corrections of **visitation** were superfluous, however, for the word is still commonly used in the 1990's:

"Moreover, as our society's consumption of materials increases and park **visitation** soars, the waste issues confronting the parks and the communities along their borders are escalating."[241]

Vocation

> I therefore, the prisoner of the Lord, beseech you that ye walk worthy of the **vocation** wherewith ye are called, (Eph 4:1)

The word **vocation** occurs only one time in the AV. It comes into English through the French *vocation* from the Latin *vocationem*, "a calling." A **vocation** is an occupation, profession, business, function or calling. Since the word **vocation** is now commonly applied only to one's profession, our modern versions unanimously update the word to "calling." However, we know the NRSV did not deem the word **vocation** to be archaic because it introduces the word into another verse where neither the AV nor any other modern version contained it.[242] This is nothing new for the NRSV, for in one passage where the AV read "stranger" it was changed to "alien."[243] But in the very same verse, when the AV said "alien," the NRSV altered it to "foreigner."[244] The word **vocation,** however, is still commonly used today, even when not referring to one's employment: "He wore his political **vocation** on his sleeve."[245]

Chapter 23
Want to Wrought

Want

>Much food *is in* the tillage of the poor: but there is *that is* destroyed for **want** of judgment. (Prov 13:23)

The word **want** occurs thirty-one times in the AV.[1] Other forms include **wanteth**, appearing seven times,[2] **wanted**, found three times,[3] **wants**, found twice,[4] and **wanting**, occurring eight times.[5] **Want** is from the Old Norse *vant,* "lack." The word **want** in the AV is never used in the sense of desire but rather with the older meaning of lacking or deficient in. The usual replacement for **want** in our modern versions is "lack,"[6] but "poverty"[7] and "needs"[8] can also be found. The other forms of **want** are similarly corrected.[9] Surprisingly however, all of the new translations were lax in removing from several passages the word **want** as it is used in the AV.[10]

Wanton

>Ye have lived in pleasure on the earth, and been **wanton**; ye have nourished your hearts, as in a day of slaughter. (James 5:5)

The word **wanton** appears three times in the AV,[11] while the form **wantonness** is found twice.[12] The word **wanton** is from the Middle English *wantowen,* literally meaning untrained, as it is from *wan,* "lacking," and *towen,* "to train." Thus, **wanton** originally meant undisciplined, untrained, uneducated, or unruly. It later came to mean malicious, reckless, merciless, or unprovoked; extravagant or excessive; and also lewd or lascivious. Both **wanton** and **wantonness** are corrected in every place by our modern versions,[13] except for the NKJV retaining **wanton** twice,[14] the NASB once,[15] and the NRSV extending **wanton** to "wantonly" once.[16] **Wanton** is not usually replaced by a single word, but **wantonness** can be found as "licentiousness,"[17] "sensuality,"[18] "debauchery,"[19] "lust,"[20] and "lewdness."[21] But after correcting these words the majority of the time, the NRSV inserted forms of "**wanton**" into seven additional passages[22] and the NIV into two.[23] In one of these passages, the NRSV even alters "lewd" in the AV to "**wanton**" even though all the other versions follow the AV reading.[24] The NASB also adds the word "**wanton**" before the AV word "pleasure," even though the other new translations follow the AV.[25] The correction of the word **wanton** in the AV was uncalled for anyway, for even *Newsweek* magazine utilized the word: "For that, I'd nominate the **wanton** predication of superhigh investment gains."[26]

Ward

> And they put him in **ward,** because it was not declared what should be done to him. (Num 15:34)

The word **ward** can be seen twenty-two times in the AV.[27] The plural **wards,** however, only appears three times.[28] **Ward** is from the Old English *weard,* "a guarding." A **ward** is a place for guarding, the action of a watchman or guard, or the one who guards. Every occurrence of **ward** and **wards** has been eliminated by our modern versions. **Ward** can be found as "custody,"[29] "prison,"[30] "under guard,"[31] "confinement,"[32] "guard,"[33] and "post."[34] But in the 1990's, a division or large room of a hospital for a particular class of patients is termed a **ward** and the head of a prison is still called a **warden.**

Warp

> And if the priest shall look, and, behold, the plague be not spread in the garment, either in the **warp,** or in the woof, or in any thing of skin; (Lev 13:53)

The word **warp** occurs nine times in the AV, always with the word "woof."[35] **Warp** comes from the Old English *wearp* and refers to the threads sewn lengthwise in a fabric. These threads were twisted harder than those sewn perpendicular to them (the woof). We still say something is warped if it is twisted out of shape. Surprisingly, the supposedly modern English NASB, NRSV, and NKJV retain this archaic word. They also keep "woof" as well.³⁶

Wax

> But evil men and seducers shall **wax** worse and worse, deceiving, and being deceived. (2 Tim 3:13)

Although the word **wax** occurs four times in the AV referring to physical **wax,** it appears twenty times as a verb with an archaic usage.³⁷ The form **waxed** occurs thirty-seven times,³⁸ while **waxen** is found twelve times,³⁹ **waxeth** twice,⁴⁰ and **waxing** once.⁴¹ **Wax** is from the Old English *weaxan,* "to grow." Thus, to **wax** means to grow or become. The modern versions all omit the various forms of the word **wax** when it does not refer to physical **wax.** Their usual translation for **wax** is "grow."⁴² **Waxed** is normally given as "grew"⁴³ or "became."⁴⁴ The other forms of **wax** are similarly corrected.⁴⁵ The word **wax,** however, is still used today: "Spots on the Sun **wax** and wane in roughly 11 year cycles, too short of a time to create any significant temperature changes on Earth."⁴⁶ And although **wax** is not used in the new versions as it appears in the AV, the NKJV does employ the word "wane" when the AV simply says "be made thin."⁴⁷

Wayfaring

> The highways lie waste, the **wayfaring** man ceaseth: he hath broken the covenant, he hath despised the cities, he regardeth no man. (Isa 33:8)

The word **wayfaring** appears six times in the AV.⁴⁸ It is from the Old English *weg farende,* literally meaning journeying by road. A **wayfaring** man is a traveler or wanderer. The NKJV forgot to remove "**wayfaring**"one time,⁴⁹ the NRSV twice changed the "**wayfaring** man" into a "wayfarer,"⁵⁰ and the NASB once altered "**wayfaring** men" to "wayfarers'."⁵¹ The majority of the time, however, our modern versions correct "**wayfaring** man" to forms of "traveler."⁵² This is unfortunate, for the word **wayfaring** is still in vogue today: "Strung out, carpentered, predictable, the story is basically the old **wayfaring stud** idea, the wanderer out of Tennessee Williams and William Inge who passes through, or intends to, after messing up some lives, particularly women's."[53] And furthermore, the NRSV and NIV saw no problem with using the word "seafarer."[54]

Waymarks

Set thee up **waymarks,** make thee high heaps: set thine heart toward the highway, *even* the way *which* thou wentest: turn again, O virgin of Israel, turn again to these thy cities. (Jer 31:21)

Waymarks are only mentioned once in the AV. This compound word literally means something that marks the way. Our modern versions all corrected **waymarks** but never used the same word. The NRSV chose "road markers," the NASB "roadmarks," the NKJV "landmarks," and the NIV "guideposts." Yet when the AV says "the way," the NRSV alone alters it to "midcourse."[55] And when the AV mentions a "beacon," the NRSV and NIV correct it to the obscure compound "flagstaff."[56] The NIV also employs the words "waylaid"[57] and "waylay"[58] when they are not found in any modern version. The NRSV corrects "stubborn" in the AV to "wayward."[59] The word "waywardness" is also utilized by the NASB, NRSV, and NIV to correct "turning away" in the AV.[60]

Wealth

Let no man seek his own, but every man another's *wealth.* (1 Cor 10:24)

Although the word **wealth** occurs many times in the AV, it is used in an archaic sense on five occasions.[61] The word **wealth** is from the Middle English *wele,* which comes from the Old English *wela,* "prosperity." **Wealth** originally meant prosperity, plenty, abundance, welfare, or well being. It later developed into the modern sense of having a lot of money. **Wealth** is corrected in our modern versions to such things as "prosperity,"[62] "well-being,"[63] and "good."[64] Yet when the AV mentions something simple like "fear," the NIV alters it to "qualm" even though the other new translations follow the AV.[65]

Wen

> Blind, or broken, or maimed, or having a **wen**, or scurvy, or scabbed, ye shall not offer these unto the LORD, nor make an offering by fire of them upon the altar unto the LORD. (Lev 22:22)

The word **wen** only appears once in the AV. A **wen**, from the Old English *wenn*, is a lump, tumor, wart, cyst, or other protuberance on the body. Although our modern versions were unanimous in excising the word **wen**, they could not agree on a replacement. The NRSV said "discharge," the NKJV "ulcer," the NIV "warts," and the NASB "running sore." Yet a **wen** is still listed in medical dictionaries as a "sebaceous cyst."[66] Moreover, when the AV mentions a "lump of figs," the supposedly up-to-date NIV alters it to the obscure "poultice of figs."[67] The NKJV also substitutes the word "poultice" for "plaister in the AV."[68]

Wench

> Now Jonathan and Ahimaaz stayed by Enrogel; for they might not be seen to come into the city: and a **wench** went and told them; and they went and told king David. (2 Sam 17:17)

A **wench** is only mentioned once in the AV. It is a shortened form of the Middle English *wenchel*. A wench was originally a young girl, a maid, or a young woman. Next came the meanings of a mistress, an unchaste woman, or a female servant. The NIV and NRSV both used "servant girl" to update **wench**, but the NASB preferred "maidservant" and the NKJV "female servant." But the word **wench** did not need to be corrected, for it is still used today: "Yet, like Cinderella, the story of Prince Mikhail and Buzhenina the serving **wench** had a happy ending."[69]

Whence

> And thence sailed to Antioch, from **whence** they had been recommended to the grace of God for the work which they fulfilled. (Acts 14:26)

The word **whence**, which occurs seventy-two times in the AV,[70] appeared in Old English as *hwanone*. **Whence** means from what place or from which place. The overwhelming replacement for **whence** in our modern versions is "where."[71] However, the NKJV and NASB carelessly left this word in one passage.[72] Yet even *National Review* still uses the word **whence** in the 1990's: "The Mariner is never explained: we don't know **whence** he sprang or whether there are others like him."[73]

Whereabout

> And David said unto Ahimelech the priest, The king hath commanded me a business, and hath said unto me, Let no man know any thing of the business **whereabout** I send thee, and what I have commanded thee: and I have appointed *my* servants to such and such a place. (1 Sam 21:2)

The word **whereabout**, which occurs only once in the AV, is the first in a series of uncommon compound words in the AV that are all formed with a *where-* prefix. Others include **whereas**, found 33 times,[74] **whereby**, found 39 times,[75] **wherefore**, found 348 times,[76] **wherein**, appearing 167 times,[77] **whereinsoever**, used only once,[78] **whereinto**, used only 3 times,[79] **whereof**, found 71 times,[80] **whereon**, found 27 times,[81] **whereto**, utilized 3 times,[82] **whereunto**, appearing 27 times,[83] **whereupon**, found 17 times,[84] **wherewith**, found 110 times,[85] and **wherewithal**, used just twice.[86] Only the word **whereas** is retained on a regular basis by our modern versions, except for the NIV, which did not use the word at all.[87] But although they deemed these *where-* words to be archaic, our modern versions were negligent in completely removing them from the Bible, for only the NIV omits all of them. The NASB and NKJV each use "**whereby**"[88] and "**wherein**"[89] one time. The NKJV alone keeps "**whereupon**" once.[90] The NASB likewise retains "**wherewith**" one time.[91] And finally, the word "**wherefore**" is used once in the NRSV[92] and five times in the NASB.[93] But in spite of their removal by modern Bible translations, most of these *where-* words are still current English:

> Through Project Uturn, a program run by the city of South El Monte, he counsels homies in youth detention centers and in high schools, and does it with the authority of an Original Gangster, who has seen it from street level and knows **whereof** he speaks.[94]
>
> When they had finished eating, Kenny appeared, **whereupon**

Shirley instructed him to reheat the pot and, as he was the last one for dinner, to wash the dishes.[95]

Without these subject faculties that emerged in animals, there would be much less to preserve, and this less of what is to be preserved is the same as the less **wherewith** it is preserved.[96]

One technique gaining in popularity is "offtake," **whereby** companies promise in advance to buy a fixed amount of a project's production.[97]

We begin with Treasury Form 942, **whereon** you report total wages paid to household employees, along with Social Security and Medicare taxes paid and federal income tax withheld.[98]

A lot of our top atomic energy scientists do feel that Pakistan really does not have the **wherewithal** to make nuclear bombs.[99]

Whet

If he turn not, he will **whet** his sword; he hath bent his bow, and made it ready. (Psa 7:12)

The word **whet** appears four times in the AV.[100] It is from the Old English *hwettan,* "to sharpen." Thus, to **whet** simply means to sharpen. Although the NRSV follows the AV reading every time,[101] and the NKJV retains "**whet**" once,[102] this word is unanimously updated to forms of "sharpen."[103] The NRSV even inserted "**whet**" into a passage where the AV did not contain the word.[104] Yet when the AV says "sharpen," the NIV changes it to "repointing."[105] Nevertheless, the word **whet** is still used today: "Accommodation with Russia's aggressive foreign policy will only **whet** the appetite of the extremists."[106]

Whether

For **whether** is easier, to say, *Thy* sins be forgiven thee; or to say, Arise, and walk? (Mat 9:5)

Although the word **whether** occurs over 100 times in the AV, it appears nine times in the archaic sense of an interrogative pronoun.[107] **Whether,** which appeared in Old English as *hwaether,* means which of the two. Obviously limiting **whether** to a conjunction meaning "if," our modern versions have eliminated the nine occurrences of **whether** in the older sense.[108] But then the supposedly contemporary, up-to-date, easy-to-understand NRSV introduces a word into the Bible like "perennial,"[109] while the NASB injects "perennially,"[110] and the NKJV "primeval."[111]

𝔚𝔥𝔦𝔩𝔰𝔱

> Behold, I waited for your words; I gave ear to your reasons, **whilst** ye searched out what to say. (Job 32:11)

The word **whilst** occurs ten times in the AV.[112] It is an obsolete form of the conjunction *while*. Another variation of *while* is **whiles,** also found ten times in the AV.[113] Naturally, our modern versions remove all trace of these words. Yet the supposedly up-to-date NASB saw no problem with using the archaic words "wouldst,"[114] "wast,"[115] "wilt,"[116] "hast,"[117] and "hadst."[118]

𝔚𝔥𝔦𝔱

> For I suppose I was not a **whit** behind the very chiefest apostles. (2 Cor 11:5)

The word **whit** surfaces five times in the AV.[119] It is from the Old English *wiht,* "thing." A **whit** is a very small amount. No **whit** means none or not at all, any **whit** means to the least amount, and every **whit** means to the full amount. Naturally, our modern versions omit this word. For "every **whit**" they substitute "entirely"[120] or "completely."[121] For "a **whit**" one can find "in the least"[122] or "at all."[123] But these corrections were unnecessary, for even *American Heritage* magazine employed the word **whit:** "And while the early frigate battles against the British were thrilling victories that owed much to superior American ship design, they affected the balance of power not one **whit.**"[124]

𝔚𝔥𝔦𝔱𝔥𝔢𝔯

> Thomas saith unto him, Lord, we know not **whither** thou goest; and how can we know the way? (John 14:5)

The word **whither** occurs 124 times in the AV.[125] The extended form **whithersoever** is found 29 times.[126] **Whither** appeared in Old English as *hwider* and means to what place, to which place, to what result, condition, subject, or extent. As expected, our modern versions have completely excised this word. **Whither** is normally replaced by "where" in our modern versions,[127] while **whithersoever** is customarily updated to "wherever."[128] But although it could not be found in an up-to-date Bible version, the word **whither** managed to make it into *Fortune* magazine: "Whither Mexico now?"[129]

Whore

For a **whore** *is* a deep ditch; and a strange woman *is* a narrow pit. (Prov 23:27)

The word **whore** appears fifteen times in the AV in the singular[130] and twice in the plural.[131] The singular **whoredom** can be found twenty-two times,[132] while the plural **whoredoms** is used thirty-two times.[133] Other forms include **whoremonger**, found once,[134] **whoremongers**, found four times,[135] **whoring**, found nineteen times,[136] and **whorish**, appearing three times.[137] The word **whore** is from the Old Norse *hora*, "an adulteress." A **whore** is a prostitute, a harlot, a slut, or an adulteress. The word **whore** is not really archaic in itself, it is the various derivatives that usually give people trouble. **Whoredom** is the practice of acting like a **whore**. A **whoremonger** is one who practices **whoredom**. Yet no form of the word **whore** occurs in the NKJV, NIV, or NASB. The NRSV omits only **whorish** and the singular and plural of **whoremonger**. The usual replacements for the various forms of **whore** are forms of "harlot" or "prostitute."[138] Yet when the AV reads "harlot," it is changed to "temple prostitute" by the NASB and "shrine prostitute" by the NIV.[139] The supposedly easy-to-understand NIV also replaced **whoredoms** with the word "promiscuity."[140] But derivatives of the word **whore** can still be found today: "Oh, those women! Those women encourage **whoredom** in Kimmage."[141]

Whoso

And **whoso** shall swear by the temple, sweareth by it, and by him that dwelleth therein. (Mat 23:21)

The word **whoso**, short for *whosoever*, occurs fifty-four times in the AV.[142] It appeared in Old English as *swa hwa swa* because the pronoun was preceded and followed by the word *so.* **Whoso** is customarily replaced with "whoever" by our modern versions,[143] but "he who" is also sometimes used.[144] But after correcting **whoso** because it made the Bible difficult to understand, the NIV altered "questioned" to "plied" even though the other new translations followed the AV.[145]

Wiles

> Put on the whole armour of God, that ye may be able to stand against the **wiles** of the devil. (Eph 6:11)

The word **wiles,** the plural of *wile,* is found only twice in the AV.[146] The adverb **wilily** is used once.[147] *Wile* is from the Old English *wil,* "trick." **Wiles** are tricks, deceits, deceptions, or crafty schemes. To do something **wilily** is to do it craftily, deceitfully, or cunningly. The NKJV and NRSV have retained **wiles** in one passage,[148] but other than that, **wiles** and **wilily** are always corrected. Some of the translations for **wiles** are "tricks"[149] and "schemes."[150] **Wilily** is changed to "craftily" by the NKJV and NASB, but the NRSV preferred "cunning" and the NIV "ruse."[151] Yet when the AV says "craftiness," the NIV changes it to "duplicity."[152] And when the AV reads "subtle," the NRSV corrects it to "wily."[153] But the corrections to **wiles** were not needed, for the word is still current in the 1990's: "But I never discovered a key to the greater complexity elsewhere—and I now attribute such a hope to the **wiles** of Scheherazade, rather than the messages of nature."[154]

Wimples

> The changeable suits of apparel, and the mantles, and the **wimples,** and the crisping pins, (Isa 3:22)

Wimples are mentioned only once in the AV. A wimple, from the Old English *winpel,* is a folded garment worn by women to cover the head and neck. "Cloaks" is the updated replacement given by the NRSV, NIV, and NASB. The NKJV preferred "outer garments." But Roman Catholic nuns still wear **wimples** today: "You may hate yourself for laughing, but there is something irresistible about the sight of these gals in **wimples** knocking out ecclesiastically retooled '60s hits like 'I Will Follow Him' and

'My Guy' (now 'My God')."155

Winebibber

> The Son of man is come eating and drinking; and ye say, Behold a gluttonous man, and a **winebibber,** a friend of publicans and sinners! (Luke 7:34)

A **winebibber** is mentioned twice in the AV in the singular[156] and once in the plural.[157] To bib is to drink, so a **winebibber** is literally one who drinks wine. A **winebibber** is more commonly known as a drunkard. Although the NKJV follows the AV reading every time,[158] the NRSV alone keeps **winebibber** once.[159] The usual replacement for **winebibber** is "drunkard."[160] But after correcting **winebibber** every time it appeared in the AV, the NASB altered the simple command in the AV to "drink" to the supposedly archaic "imbibe."[161] The word winebibber, however, is still used today: "The Cork Examiner (which is not, as you might imagine, a journal for **wine-bibbers**) headlined its story topless bar manager shrugs off the criticism."[162]

Wise

> All that the Father giveth me shall come to me; and him that cometh to me I will in no **wise** cast out. (John 6:37)

Although the word **wise** occurs many times in both the AV and all modern versions, there are actually two words in English that have the form **wise,** one of them which is archaic. The AV uses the word **wise** in this archaic sense thirty-one times.[163] **Wise,** which appeared the same in Old English, is a doublet of *guise* and means way or manner. Naturally, our modern versions do not use the word **wise** in this fashion. When it is replaced by one word, **wise** is usually updated to "way"[164] or "manner."[165] Yet when the AV employs the word **wise** after the modern meaning, it is still corrected, for the NRSV altered "**wise** men" in the AV to "sages" even though the other versions followed the AV.[166]

Wit

> Moreover, brethren, we do you to **wit** of the grace of God bestowed on the churches of Macedonia; (2 Cor 8:1)

The verb **wit** occurs twenty-one times in the AV.[167] The present tense **wot** appears ten times,[168] the third person singular **wotteth** is found once,[169] and the past tense **wist** occurs thirteen times.[170] **Wit** is from the Old English *witan*, "to know." None of our modern versions contain any form of these words. The word **wit** is used in the AV three times as an infinitive meaning to know.[171] In these passages, **wit** is corrected to "find out,"[172] "learn,"[173] "see,"[174] and forms of "know."[175] **Wit** also appears seventeen times in the expression "to wit" that means indeed, that is to say, namely, or that is. When this expression is retained, it is corrected to "that is"[176] and "namely."[177] **Wot** and **wist** are usually altered to forms of "know."[178] The phrase "to wit," however, is still very common today: "To **wit**: Managing some $750 million of blue-chip institutional money, she earned 17.7% a year over the past three years, vs. the S&P 500's 13.3% annual gains."[179]

Withal

But the manifestation of the Spirit is given to every man to profit **withal**. (1 Cor 12:7)

The word **withal**, which was originally two words in Old English, appears thirty-three times in the AV.[180] The form **wherewithal** occurs only once.[181] **Withal** is used in the AV both as a preposition and an adverb. It can mean with it all, as well, besides, in addition, along with, with that, therewith, or it can simply mean with. Our modern versions naturally correct every occurrence of **withal**, but as it can rarely be replaced by a single word without rearranging the sentence, it would not be feasible to attempt a list of replacements for it. The word **withal** is still in use anyway: "My relation with Monteux was much closer and, **withal**, much less gentle."[182]

Withs

And Samson said unto her, If they bind me with seven green **withs** that were never dried, then shall I be weak, and be as another man. (Judg 16:7)

Withs, the plural of *withe*, are mentioned three times in the AV.[183] A withe, from the Old English *withthe*, is a band or tie used for binding or tying originally made out of a slender, flexible twig. The NRSV and NKJV united on using "bowstring" to update **withs,** but the NASB chose "cords," and the NIV "thongs."[184] But when the AV mentions something simple like a "decree," the NRSV alters it to "interdict," a word that does not appear in any other modern version.[185]

Wont

> And he came out, and went, as he was **wont,** to the mount of Olives; and his disciples also followed him. (Luke 22:39)

The word **wont** can be found nine times in the AV.[186] It is from the Old English *wunian,* "to dwell or be used to." **Wont** means accustomed to, used to, or in the habit of. The word does not appear in any new translation, having been changed to "disposed,"[187] "accustomed,"[188] "usually,"[189] or "custom."[190] But these changes were unnecessary, for the word **wont** was even utilized by *Newsweek* magazine: "One hapless bureaucrat at the Small Business Administration Office of Advocacy recently made the mistake of laying it out in writing, as bureaucrats are **wont** to do."[191]

Woof

> And if it appear still in the garment, either in the warp, or in the **woof,** or in any thing of skin; it *is* a spreading *plague:* thou shalt burn that wherein the plague *is* with fire. (Lev 13:57)

The word **woof** occurs nine times in the AV, always with the word "warp."[192] **Woof** comes from the Old English *owef* and refers to the threads sewn perpendicular to the warp. The *w* was added to this word in the Middle English period due to the influence of the initial *w* in *warp* or *weave.* Surprisingly, the supposedly modern English NASB, NRSV, and NKJV retain this archaic word. They also keep "warp" as well.[193]

Wreathen

> And the other two ends of the two **wreathen** chains thou shalt fasten in the two ouches, and put them on the shoulder pieces of the ephod before it. (Exo 28:25)

The word **wreathen** occurs ten times in the AV.[194] It is from the Middle English *wrethen,* a variation of *writhen,* meaning to twist. Thus, **wreathen** is related to the previous word *wrest.* If something is **wreathen** then it is formed or arranged by weaving or entwining. This word has been removed by all of our modern versions. When the AV says "**wreathen** chains," it is changed to "cords"[195] or "chains."[196] "**Wreathen** work" is termed "network,"[197] "latticework,"[198] forms of "cords,"[199] and the arcane "twisted cordage work."[200] The NKJV does sometimes use "braided" to update **wreathen.**[201] Yet when the AV mentions something easy to understand like "pavement," the NRSV alters it to the obscure "pediment."[202]

Wrest

> Every day they **wrest** my words: all their thoughts *are* against me for evil. (Psa 56:5)

The word **wrest** is used five times in the AV.[203] It is from the Old English *wraestan,* "to twist." To **wrest** means to pull, detach, twist, wrench, or turn from the proper course. Although they had no problem with the word "wrestled,"[204] our modern versions removed all trace of the word **wrest** from the Bible. In its place they substituted "pervert,"[205] "distort,"[206] or "twist."[207] But after correcting the AV five times in a row, the NKJV twice wrested the word "plucked" from the AV and inserted "wrested."[208] And although the NRSV corrected **wrest,** it did not hesitate to amend "plucked" in the AV to "wrenched."[209] But the correction of **wrest** was premature to begin with, for the word is still current today: "In Kenya, where the opposition had perhaps the best chance of any in Africa to **wrest** power from a strongman (Daniel arap Moi), it splintered along ethnic lines in the December 1992 elections."[210]

Wroth

> But when the king heard *thereof,* he was **wroth**: and he sent forth his armies, and destroyed those murderers, and burned up their city. (Mat 22:7)

The word **wroth** occurs forty-nine times in the AV.[211] It is from the Old English *wrath,* "angry." To be **wroth** is to be angry, indignant, or incensed. Our modern versions have completely removed this word, substituting in its place "angry,"[212] "enraged,"[213] "furious,"[214] and "infuriated."[215] Yet when the AV says someone is "grieved," the NRSV instead makes them "indignant."[216] And when the AV uses the word "displeased," the NKJV, NIV, and NASB amend it to the harder "indignant."[217]

Wrought

> When Jesus understood *it*, he said unto them, Why trouble ye the woman? for she hath **wrought** a good work upon me. (Mat 26:10)

The word **wrought** appears 101 times in the AV.[218] The form **wroughtest** is used only once.[219] **Wrought** is from the Old English *worhte*, the past tense of *wyrcan*, "to work." To have **wrought** is to have fashioned, formed, worked, or made something. Although they tried to completely remove all trace of the word **wrought,** two of our modern versions were careless in their attempt. The NKJV left "**wrought**" in one time[220] and the NASB four times.[221] The replacements for **wrought** include "were doing,"[222] "done,"[223] "crafted,"[224] and "worked."[225] Yet when the AV reads "done," the NRSV and NASB change it to the supposedly archaic "**wrought**."[226] Moreover, when the AV says "did," the NASB alters it to "**wrought**."[227] And when the AV reads "made," the NASB again inserts the word "**wrought**."[228] All of our new versions also correct "bright iron" to "**wrought** iron."[229] But in spite of all these corrections, the word **wrought** can still be found in use today: "Nature on the Rampage describes in lucid and graceful prose the cataclysms **wrought** by powerful natural phenomena, such as volcanoes, earthquakes, droughts, fires, and floods, throughout the world."[230]

Chapter 24
Ye to You-ward

Ye

Now therefore there is utterly a fault among you, because **ye** go to law one with another. Why do **ye** not rather take wrong? why do **ye** not rather *suffer yourselves to* be defrauded? (1 Cor 6:7)

The word **ye** can be found 3983 times in the AV. It is always updated to "you" by all of our modern versions because it is deemed to be archaic. **Ye** developed from the Old English *ge,* the second person, nominative, plural personal pronoun. In the thirteenth century, **ye** also began to be used for the second person, nominative, singular pronoun *thou.* The word *you* was originally the objective and possessive plural of the second person pronoun. When *you* began to take the place of **ye** in the nominative case, **ye** also came to be used as an objective singular and plural for *thee* and *you.* Between the seventeenth and eighteenth centuries, *you* appropriated the use of the nominative form **ye,** and is now the general pronoun of the second person, whether singular or plural, nominative or objective.[1] In the Authorized Version, **ye** is generally the translation of the second person, nominative, plural pronoun. **Ye** is also the customary translation of various inflections of the second person, plural verb.[2] Although **ye** does not appear in our modern versions, it does still surface in various publications in the 1990's: "But lose not **ye** hope with the electorate."[3] "**Ye** who demonize the great god North American Free Trade Agreement, relax."[4]

Yea

Now the serpent was more subtle than any beast of the field

which the LORD God had made. And he said unto the woman, **Yea,** hath God said, Ye shall not eat of every tree of the garden? (Gen 3:1)

The word **yea** appears 340 times in the AV in 320 verses. **Yea** is an affirmative particle. The Old English form was *gea*. As a substantive, **yea** can be an assenting reply, an affirmative vote, or a positive statement. As an adverb, **yea** is used to express affirmation or assent, and as a synonym for *even, truly,* or *verily.* It is also used to introduce an emphatic statement. **Yea** also serves to express vague assent or opposition much like *indeed* or *well then.* **Yea** in the AV is typically altered to "yes."[5] But *yes* was formerly used in distinction from **yea** in answer to a question involving a negative.[6] Thus, "yes" occurs four times in the AV after this fashion.[7] Since the seventeenth century, however, *yes* has been the normal affirmative particle used in reply to a positive or negative question. Only the NIV and NRSV completely remove **yea** from their vocabularies. The NASB forgot to remove the word on one occasion[8] and the NKJV was remiss three times.[9] But is **yea** archaic? Every session of Congress has literally hundreds of votes where congressmen vote either **yea** or nay. The word is also used in reporting on legislators: "Many legislators are reluctant to vote **yea** on lien laws."[10] **Yea** is also utilized in the indefinite sense: "Greathouse says his investigation—which included studying 'a complete FDA file on Prozac about **yea**-deep'—convinced him that there was no proved link between use of the drug and violent behavior."[11]

Yesternight

It is in the power of my hand to do you hurt: but the God of your father spake unto me **yesternight,** saying, Take thou heed that thou speak not to Jacob either good or bad. (Gen 31:29)

The word **yesternight** occurs three times in the AV.[12] It is an English word compounded from the Old English *geostran niht,* "yester night." The related term *yesterday* is from *geostran daeg.* **Yesternight** obviously means last night, and is so translated in our modern versions.[13] Although **yesternight** is archaic, it is apparent that the similar form *yesterday* is used everyday. The similar archaic form *yesteryear* is still in vogue in the 1990's:

"Remember those tales of **yesteryear** detailing the schoolteacher literally wrestling control of the classroom from the bullies?"[14] Why the usage of **yesternight** declined is a mystery, but its meaning is nevertheless still clear. What is not clear, however, is why the NKJV converted "little rivers" in the AV to the cryptic "rivulets."[15]

Yokefellow

> And I entreat thee also, true **yokefellow,** help those women which laboured with me in the gospel, with Clement also, and *with* other my fellowlabourers, whose names *are* in the book of life. (Phil 4:3)

The word **yokefellow** occurs but once in the AV. It is unmistakably a compound of *yoke* and *fellow*. A yoke is a device to couple animals together. Hence, a **yokefellow** is a person yoked or associated with another, especially in some work or occupation; a partner, associate, or fellowworker. Surprisingly, the NIV retains the AV reading, although when the AV read "workfellow," the NIV changed it to "fellow worker."[16] The NRSV and NKJV preferred "companion," to update **yokefellow** while the NASB selected "comrade." Yet when the AV reads "broken in heart," all of our modern versions make the expression into the compound word "brokenhearted."[17]

Yonder

> Then cometh Jesus with them unto a place called Gethsemane, and saith unto the disciples, Sit ye here, while I go and pray **yonder.** (Mat 26:36)

The word **yonder** occurs seven times in the AV.[18] It is from the Old English *geond*, "beyond." **Yonder** can mean over there, away there, in that place, farther along, beyond, or something beyond. Our modern versions were lax in expelling this supposedly archaic word from the Bible. Only the NIV removes it completely. **Yonder** is ordinarily rendered by our new translations as "over there"[19] or "the other."[20] The phrase "to **yonder** place" in the AV is unanimously altered to "from here to there."[21] Other translations include "far and wide,"[22] "some distance away,"[23] and "there."[24] The NASB retains **yonder** three times,[25] but on one occasion revises it to "abroad,"[26] after correcting "abroad" in the AV seventy times.[27] When the AV reads "the other," the NASB changes it to "yonder."[28] The NKJV, which altered **yonder** in the AV six times,[29] likewise inserts "**yonder**" into a passage where the AV did not have it.[30] Although our new versions had trouble with the word **yonder,** *The Tampa Tribune* did not: "Flying in the wild blue **yonder** was a privilege reserved only for white soldiers until 1941."[31]

𝔜ou-ward

> If ye have heard of the dispensation of the grace of God which is given me to **you-ward**: (Eph 3:2)

The phrase **you-ward** appears three times in the AV.[32] The AV also contains several other expressions similar to this. **Us-ward** occurs three times,[33] as does **God-ward**,[34] while **seatward** only appears once.[35] **Thee-ward** also occurs once,[36] while **thitherward** can be seen three times.[37] The suffix *-ward* signifies a turning in the direction denoted by the preceding element. Thus, **you-ward** means toward you, **us-ward** means toward us, **God-ward** means toward God, **thee-ward** means toward thee, **thitherward** means toward thither, and **seatward** means toward the seat. Naturally, these words have been expelled by our modern versions. But the English language is abundant with words similar to **us-ward** and **you-ward:** backward, afterward, forward, etc. In amending these words, our new up-to-date translations reveal their inconsistency. The NASB corrects the AV reading of "within" to "inward."[38] The NIV updates the AV reading of "strange" to "wayward."[39] The NKJV changed the elementary word "above" in the AV to "upward."[40] And even more disingenuous is the NRSV inserting "outward" into a passage where there is no corresponding word in the AV or any other modern version.[41] The NIV even invents the word "heavenward."[42] And then to further correct the AV, the NASB and NRSV fabricate the word "midheaven."[43] *Forbes* magazine, however, still uses *-ward* words: "And so that it can, so must we, chivvied **exit ward** with that oh-so-gentle yet unmistakably urgent, snug yet bowel-loosening .410 gun barrel in the small of the back that few hostesses can bring off—or would fain even try."[44]

Epilogue

Does the AV contain archaic words? Certainly. But perhaps a better question would be: Do contemporary publications like *Time, U.S. News & World Report*, the *Chicago Tribune, Forbes*, and the *New Republic* contain archaic words? As we have seen throughout the main body of this work, they unquestionably do. Also without dispute is the striking revelation that modern, up-to-date Bible versions like the NRSV, NASB, NIV, and NKJV likewise contain archaic words. We have seen these facts demonstrated in a number of ways.

1. An archaic word in the AV is corrected and then the same word is inserted elsewhere.

2. An archaic word in the AV is retained exactly as it appears in the AV.

3. An archaic word in the AV is retained but in a different form.

4. An archaic word in the AV is corrected and a different form of the word is inserted elsewhere.

5. A simple word in the AV is replaced by a form of an archaic word.

6. A simple word in the AV is replaced by a more difficult word or phrase.

7. The base or root form of a word in the AV is unnecessarily lengthened.

8. An archaic word in the AV is replaced by an even more difficult word.

9. A somewhat difficult word in the AV is replaced by a more arduous word.

So that fact that the AV contains archaic words is just that, a fact that should be accepted. For just as no one revises Shakespeare or Milton, but instead learns the vocabulary necessary to understand those particular works; and just as a certain vocabulary is necessary to understand science, medicine, engineering, or computers; and just as no one ever cancels their subscription or writes a letter to the editor of a contemporary publication to complain that it uses archaic words; and just as no one ever complains about archaic words surfacing in modern Bible versions; so to read and understand the Bible one must be familiar with the vocabulary of the AV instead of dragging it down to one's own level by revising it. Does the AV contain archaic words? Certainly. Should we therefore replace it with something else? Certainly not.

Appendix 1
Archaic Words in Contemporary Publications

The examples given in this book of archaic words found in the AV that also appear in contemporary publications proves that the AV is no more archaic than daily newspapers and current magazines. Another example of this fact is the common occurrence of difficult, perplexing, and obscure words that regularly appear in contemporary publications. This appendix provides a representative sample of some of these words along with the name and date of the publication in which they are found and the page number on which they appear. Most of these publications are available at any major library, bookstore, or newsstand, and all are available by subscription. The majority of these words are unintelligible to the average reader, yet they are either ignored, guessed at, or looked up in a dictionary—no one ever cancels their subscription or writes a letter to the editor of the respective publication to complain that it uses archaic words.

abattoir	*Human Events*	Dec. 8, 1995	p.1
abstemious	*The Economist*	Nov. 4, 1995	p.51
accretions	*Chronicles*	July 1995	p.33
acrimonious	*The New American*	July 10, 1995	p.10
adulation	*The Free Market*	Nov. 1995	p.1
altruism	*Chronicles*	July 1995	p.29
amalgam	*Human Events*	May 26, 1995	p.20
amanuensis	*Byte*	April 1995	p.33
anglophilo	*Chronicles*	June 1995	p.17
anthropocentrism	*The New American*	July 10, 1995	p.12
antithetical	*Chronicles*	July 1995	p.39
aperitif	*Human Events*	Feb. 24, 1995	p.1
aphorism	*The Freeman*	Sept. 1995	p.599
apparatchik	*The New American*	Sept. 18, 1995	p.43

392 Archaic Words and the Authorized Version

arbitrage	*The Free Market*	Nov. 1995	p.7
avariciously	*Chronicles*	July 1995	p.35
bellicose	*U.S. News & World Report*	June 13, 1994	p.76
blithe	*Reason*	Aug./Sept. 1995	p.46
caveat	*Byte*	April 1995	p.48
chortle	*Chronicles*	July 1995	p.48
comeuppance	*The Weekly Standard*	Oct. 2, 1995	p.41
contagion	*The Free Market*	Nov. 1995	p.2
curmudgeonly	*The Freeman*	Sept. 1995	p.600
demimonde	*The Weekly Standard*	Oct. 2, 1995	p.41
demurely	*The Weekly Standard*	Oct. 2, 1995	p.42
demurrers	*Chronicles*	July 1995	p.46
devolutionist	*National Review*	Oct. 23, 1995	p.8
Diogenean	*National Review*	Oct. 23, 1995	p.68
disingenuousness	*Reason*	Aug./Sept. 1995	p.66
doffing	*The Cincinnati Enquirer*	July 24, 1994	p.HO1
ecdysiasts	*The Weekly Standard*	Oct. 23, 1995	p.46
efflorescence	*The Weekly Standard*	Nov. 6, 1995	p.17
egalitarian	*Reason*	Aug./Sept. 1995	p.65
eldritch	*Chronicles*	July 1995	p.35
empirically	*Human Events*	Nov. 10, 1995	p.10
eschatological	*National Review*	Oct. 23, 1995	p.16
excoriated	*Human Events*	Nov. 10, 1995	p.10
exogenous	*Human Events*	Nov. 10, 1995	p.10
expatriate	*National Review*	Oct. 23, 1995	p.61
expropriation	*The New American*	Sept. 18, 1995	p.17
felicities	*The Weekly Standard*	Oct. 9, 1995	p.40
feted	*The New American*	July 10, 1995	p.21
florid	*Chronicles*	June 1995	p.18
frump	*Chronicles*	July 1995	p.35
hagiographic	*The Free Market*	Nov. 1995	p.1
hegemony	*Chronicles*	July 1995	p.29
homogeneity	*Chronicles*	July 1995	p.37
homogenous	*The Weekly Standard*	Nov. 6, 1995	p.23
homonymic	*Chronicles*	July 1995	p.35
hubris	*Forbes ASAP*	April 10, 1995	p.100
iconoclast	*National Review*	Oct. 23, 1995	p.67
iconographers	*The Weekly Standard*	Oct. 30, 1995	p.41
imbue	*The New American*	July 10, 1995	p.12
impunity	*The Free Market*	June 1995	p.7
incendiary	*Chronicles*	June 1995	p.18
ineffable	*Chronicles*	July 1995	p.47
innocuous	*The Weekly Standard*	Oct. 30, 1995	p.10

jejune	*The Weekly Standard*	Oct. 9, 1995	p.41
jeremiad	*The New American*	Oct. 16, 1995	p.23
kibosh	*Forbes*	Feb. 27, 1995	p.28
kleptocracies	*The New American*	July 24, 1995	p.12
klieg	*Reason*	Aug./Sept. 1995	p.28
kvetching	*The Free Market*	Jan. 1996	p.6
lachrymose	*The New American*	Aug. 7, 1995	p.11
latitudinarian	*Human Events*	July 21, 1995	p.14
maelstrom	*The Weekly Standard*	Oct. 23, 1995	p.22
malaise	*Forbes*	March 27, 1995	p.110
malevolently	*USA Today Magazine*	Nov. 1991	p.80
mellifluous	*Destination Discovery*	July 1993	p.12
minions	*The Free Market*	Sept. 1995	p.4
misanthrope's	*National Review*	Oct. 23, 1995	p.68
miscegenation	*Utne Reader*	Nov./Dec. 1994	p.82
mitochondrial	*Science*	Jan. 25, 1991	p.378
modicum	*The New American*	Aug. 7, 1995	p.13
monoglot	*Chronicles*	July 1995	p.19
nascent	*The Free Market*	April 1995	p.7
nefarious	*Reason*	Aug./Sept. 1995	p.55
neologisms	*Forbes ASAP*	April 10, 1995	p.100
obsequious	*Human Events*	Nov. 10, 1995	p.16
opacity	*The Weekly Standard*	Nov. 13, 1995	p.39
oxymoronic	*The Weekly Standard*	Nov. 13, 1995	p.4
pachyderm	*PC Computing*	April 1995	p.159
paean	*Reason*	Aug./Sept. 1995	p.46
pariahs	*Human Events*	Feb. 24, 1995	p.9
patriarchalism	*Chronicles*	July 1995	p.33
pedantry	*Chronicles*	July 1995	p.48
perfunctory	*Chronicles*	June 1995	p.18
petulance	*National Review*	Oct. 23, 1995	p.67
pilloried	*The Weekly Standard*	Oct. 2, 1995	p.33
pomaded	*Chronicles*	June 1995	p.18
propinquity	*The New American*	July 10, 1995	p.41
protuberances	*The Weekly Standard*	Oct. 2, 1995	p.42
prurient	*The Weekly Standard*	Oct. 2, 1995	p.42
pugnacious	*Reason*	Aug./Sept. 1995	p.30
pusillanimous	*The New American*	July 10, 1995	p.19
quadrennially	*Human Events*	Feb. 24, 1995	p.10
quixotic	*The Economist*	Nov. 4, 1995	p.23
recalcitrance	*Reason*	Aug./Sept. 1995	p.28
recidivist	*Chronicles*	March 1995	p.18
recidivists	*Policy Review*	Spring 1995	p.6

scrupulously	*National Review*	Oct. 23, 1995	p.56
self-aggrandizement	*Chronicles*	June 1995	p.30
sequestration	*The Weekly Standard*	Dec. 4, 1995	p.39
serendipitous	*Forbes ASAP*	April 10, 1995	p.92
sigopfutuck	*The Weekly Standard*	Nov. 13, 1995	p.46
snafus	*Chronicles*	June 1995	p.46
statutorily	*The Free Market*	Sept. 1995	p.4
supernumeraries	*Chronicles*	July 1995	p.36
surreptitiously	*Saturday Night*	April 1994	p.40
sycophantic	*Human Events*	Oct. 20, 1995	p.24
tropism	*The New American*	Nov. 13, 1995	p.38
trundled	*The Cincinnati Enquirer*	July 24, 1994	p.HO1
ubiquitous	*Harper's*	March 1994	p.45
unostentatious	*American Heritage*	April 1995	p.72
zeitgeist	*Human Events*	Feb. 24, 1995	p.11

Appendix 2
AV Archaic Words in Contemporary Publications

The examples given in this book of archaic words found in the AV that also appear in contemporary publications proves that the AV is no more archaic than daily newspapers and current magazines. This appendix gives a complete list of the various publications referred to in this book that contain archaic words that appear in the AV. The archaic word in question is also given in the form that it occurs. All of the newspapers listed are available by subscription and most of the other publications are available at any major library, bookstore, or newsstand.

Publication	Word
21st Century Science & Technology	firmament
Across The Board	tittle
Ad Astra	thereof
Africa Events	sup
Africa Report	pernicious
African World	bolster
African World	guile
Air & Space	heretic
Alberta Report	lusty
Alberta Report	temperate
Alberta Report	sottish
American Forests	canker
American Health	blackish
American Health	eminent
American Heritage	disputation
American Heritage	bewitched
American Heritage	foursquare
American Heritage	beckoned
American Heritage	forbearing

American Heritage	emulation
American Heritage	whit
American Heritage	gaiety
American History Illustrated	infamy
American History Illustrated	raiment
American History Illustrated	concourse
American Horticulturist	lordly
American Horticulturist	provender
American Horticulturist	bedsteads
American Libraries	noontide
American Scholar	comely
American Scholar	compass
American Scholar	betimes
American Scholar	indite
American Scholar	withal
American Scientist	thereupon
American Scientist	blaze
Anchorage Daily News	twined
Animals' Agenda	speed
Asian Affairs	kine
Asian Affairs	howsoever
Associated Press News Service	oration
Astronomy	wax
Astronomy	buffet
Astronomy	thither
Astronomy	imagery
Atlanta Journal & Constitution	paramour
Atlantic	scrabbled
Atlantic Monthly	beseeched
Atlantic Monthly	jeopardy
Atlantic Monthly	garner
Atlantic Monthly	travail
Atlantic Monthly	untoward
Atlantic Monthly	liking
Atlantic Monthly	vaunt
Atlantic Monthly	inasmuch
Atlantic Monthly	implacable
Atlantic Monthly	villainy
Audubon	bittern
Audubon	circumspect

Audubon	flanks
Audubon	calve
Audubon	cormorant
Audubon	dainty
Austin American-Statesman	decked
Baltimore Sun	kerchief
BBC Worldwide	bier
Boston Globe	pottage
Boston Globe	dissembling
Boston Globe	banqueting
Boston Globe	apace
Boston Globe	vestments
Boston Globe	chide
Boston Globe	handmaiden
Bulletin of the Atomic Scientists	traffic
Bulletin of the Atomic Scientists	rudiments
Bulletin on Ageing	perdition
Canadian Geographic	bowels
Canadian Geographic	hoar
Canadian Geographic	hemlock
Car & Driver	boss
Car & Driver	contrariwise
Car & Driver	strakes
Ceres	dispensation
Charlotte Observer	effected
Chicago Tribune	anathema
Chicago Tribune	requiting
Chicago Tribune	dearth
China Reconstructs	tenon
Christian Science Monitor	victuals
Christian Science Monitor	vex
Christian Science Monitor	quicken
Christian Science Monitor	vehemently
Christian Science Monitor	haphazard
Christian Science Monitor	afoot
Christianity Today	fourscore
Columbia Journalism Review	highminded
Commentary	bemoan
Commercial Appeal	epistle
Courier-Journal	lancets

CQ Researcher	ensue
CQ Researcher	engrafted
CQ Researcher	countervail
Current	sunder
Current	patrimony
Current	wrest
Current	straightway
Current	forswearing
Current History	translated
Current History	constrain
Current History	spoil
CWRU Magazine	surmising
Daily Oklahoman	austere
Daily Oklahoman	ye
Denver Post	affording
Denver Post	riddance
Detroit News	betwixt
Detroit News	doth
Discover	barbarous
Discover	hoary
Discover	vial
Earth	wrought
Earth	bulrushes
Earth Island Journal	thenceforth
Earthwatch	chamois
Earthwatch	concord
Economist	twain
Economist	contemn
Economist	succour
Economist	buckler
Economist	whereby
Emerge	upbraid
Environment	gross
European	riotous
Everybody's	nigh
Family Life	rent
Far Eastern Economic Review	odd
Far Eastern Economic Review	shod
Forbes	concupiscence
Forbes	brutish

AV Archaic Words in Contemporary Publications

Forbes	mattock
Forbes	servitor
Forbes FYI	fain
Fort Worth Star-Telegram	deride
Fortune	solace
Fortune	appertain
Fortune	whither
Fortune	farthing
Fortune	whereon
Fortune	wit
Forum	thine
Freedom Review	mete
Futurist	plaiting
Garbage	abode
Garbage	potentate
Garden	commodious
Globe and Mail	pangs
Governing	enjoin
Governing	mollified
Governing	redound
Governing	yea
Griffith Observer	terrestrial
Harper's	impudent
Harper's	enterprise
Harper's	laden
Harper's	immutable
Harvard Magazine	feign
Hastings Center Report	therewith
Hastings Center Report	herewith
Hastings Center Report	rehearse
Hastings Center Report	wherewith
Hastings Center Report	thereto
Health	whereof
Health	bettered
Health	carnal
Health	heresy
Health Magazine	confection
Herald	furlongs
History Today	whosoever
History Today	suppliants

History Today	concision
Horticulture	harrow
Horticulture	superfluity
Humanist	bewail
In These Times	pence
India Today	wherewithal
Indianapolis News	outlandish
International Business	goodly
International Wildlife	ravin
Jama	occurrent
Jerusalem Report	devotions
Johns Hopkins Magazine	nay
Journal of Democracy	gainsay
Journal of Popular Film & Television	divorcement
Kiplinger's Personal Finance Magazine	unawares
Kiwanis Magazine	effeminate
Kiwanis Magazine	suckling
Kiwanis Magazine	jangling
Lancet	evermore
LBL Research Review	thereon
Life	sluices
Los Angeles Times	girdle
Los Angeles Times	vale
Los Angeles Times	debase
Los Angeles Times	admiration
Los Angeles Times	breechclout
Los Angeles Times	artillery
Los Angeles Times	vexation
Los Angeles Times	maintenance
Los Angeles Times	assent
Los Angeles Times	tillage
Maclean's	feebleminded
Maclean's	flagon
Maclean's	footmen
Maclean's	suchlike
Maclean's	afore
Maclean's	blasting
Midwest Today	reprobates
Money	nurture
Montreal Gazette	vein

Mosaic	haft
Mosaic	selfsame
Mother Jones	heady
Mother Jones	privy
Mother Earth News	gin
Mother Earth News	couch
Mother Earth News	blueness
Mothering	whereupon
Multinational Monitor	railed
Multinational Monitor	injurious
National Parks	visitation
National Review	suborned
National Review	oblation
National Review	purloining
National Review	choler
National Review	supple
National Review	whatsoever
National Review	aforetime
National Review	whet
National Wildlife	maw
National Wildlife	oiled
National Wildlife	heath
Nation's Business	palsy
Natural History	wiles
Natural History	caul
Nature Conservancy	fens
New England Journal of Medicine	ofttimes
New Internationalist	hungered
New Internationalist	licence
New Perspectives Quarterly	pound
New Republic	wayfaring
New Republic	breeches
New Republic	surfeited
New Republic	beggarly
New Republic	thou
New Republic	wine-bibbers
New Republic	artificer
New Republic	furbish
New Republic	straitly
New York	thrice

New York Times Magazine	mote
News	infidel
News Journal	damsel
Newsday	nought
Newsweek	virtue
Newsweek	stripling
Newsweek	wanton
Newsweek	wont
Newsweek	temperance
Newsweek	insomuch
Newsweek	shamefacedness
Newsweek	wimples
Ocean Realm	brimstone
Ocean Realm	teats
Ocean Realm	armholes
Omni	eschew
Orange County Register	impotent
Orange County Register	enlargement
Orange County Register	laud
Oregonian	dote
Oregonian	amiable
Oregonian	adventured
Oregonian	delectable
Orlando Sentinel	anise
Palm Beach Post	unction
Palm Beach Post	sepulchre
Panoscope	coney
Patriot Ledger	helm
Pharos	therefrom
Philadelphia Inquirer	abated
Philadelphia Inquirer	lances
Philadelphia Inquirer	apothecaries
Philadelphia Inquirer	assuaged
Philadelphia Inquirer	sacrilege
Philadelphia Inquirer	thee
Plain Dealer	variance
Policy Review	bastard
Popular Mechanics	swaddle
Popular Science	malefactor
Popular Science	nether

AV Archaic Words in Contemporary Publications 403

Popular Science	soothsayer
Prevention	forepart
Progressive	flayed
Psychology Today	sleight
Psychology Today	inquisition
Psychology Today	prognosticators
Psychology Today	begat
Public Citizen	usury
Public Citizen	coffer
Reason	thy
Record	vermilion
Reuters	dromedaries
Reuters	ossifrage
Road & Track	cumber
Rocky Mountain News	ado
Rolling Stone	cornet
Runner's World	glistering
Sacramento Bee	visage
San Diego Union-Tribune	augment
San Diego Union-Tribune	daub
San Diego Union-Tribune	doleful
San Diego Union-Tribune	odious
San Francisco Examiner	unto
San Francisco Chronicle	mortify
San Jose Mercury News	needlework
San Jose Mercury News	jot
San Jose Mercury News	operation
San Jose Mercury News	rend
San Jose Mercury News	albeit
Saturday Night	bruit
Sea Frontiers	aright
Sea Frontiers	progenitors
Seattle Times	discomfited
Seattle Times/Post-Intelligencer	battlements
Sierra	abase
Skeptic	ignominy
Smithsonian	lapwings
Smithsonian	espied
Smithsonian	noised
Sojourners	importunity

Southern Exposure	overmuch
Sports Illustrated	pate
Sports Illustrated	cogitations
Sports Illustrated	backbiter
Sports Illustrated	lucre
Sports Illustrated	publican
Student Lawyer	assayed
Sun	experiment
Sun	hallowed
Sun-Sentinel	omnipotent
Swiss Review of World Affairs	mantle
Swiss Review of World Affairs	adjured
Swiss Review of World Affairs	alms
Tampa Tribune	yonder
The American Spectator	churlish
The Financial Post	vocation
The Freeman	penurious
The New American	execrates
The New American	emboldened
The New American	hereof
The News	gallant
The News	hitherto
Time	confederate
Time	quarter
Time	whoredom
Time	engines
Time	quick
Time	ravening
Time	bestir
Time	naught
Time	respite
Time	rifled
Time	satiate
Time	fetch
Time	sundry
Time	kernels
Time	slothful
Time	grave
Time	sop
Time	seethe

AV Archaic Words in Contemporary Publications 405

Times-Picayune	heretofore
U.S. News & World Report	advertise
U.S. News & World Report	apparel
U.S. News & World Report	cleave
U.S. News & World Report	deputed
U.S. News & World Report	incontinent
U.S. News & World Report	oracle
U.S. News & World Report	putrid
U.S. News & World Report	stanched
UNESCO Courier	situate
USA Today Magazine	valor
USA Today Magazine	espoused
Utne Reader	lascivious
Vibe	badness
Washington Monthly	seemly
Washington Post	imperious
Washington Post	vagabond
Washington Post	mammon
Washington Post	vainglory
Washington Post	therein
Washington Post	virtuous
Washington Post	belied
Washington Post	obeisance
Washington Post	drams
Washington Post	affinity
Washington Post	celestial
Washington Post	amiss
Washington Post	oft
Washington Post	osprey
Washington Post	averse
Washington Post Health	nitre
Washington Post National Weekly Edition	dulcimers
Washington Post National Weekly Edition	hither
Washington Post National Weekly Edition	overran
Washington Times	abject
Washington Times	disquiet
Washington Times	venison
Weatherwise	wench
Wichita Eagle	pommel
Wildlife Conservation	dung

Wildlife Conservation	isles
Winchester Star	verity
World & I	joinings
World Link	distil
World Monitor	asunder
World Monitor	principality
World Monitor	servile
World Press Review	thence
World Watch	fowl
World Watch	garnish
World Watch	husbandry
World Watch	noisome
Writer	necromancer

Appendix 3
Archaic Words in the NIV

As we have seen throughout the main body of this work, archaic words are not limited to the AV. Not only do modern versions often retain the supposedly archaic words found in the AV, but many times a more formidable word is used to correct a perfectly understandable word or phrase in the AV. This appendix gives those places in the NIV where a simple word or phrase in the AV is replaced by a more difficult word, the base or root form of a word is unnecessarily extended, and those instances where an archaic or somewhat arduous word in the AV is replaced by an equally archaic or even more onerous word. In two respects, however, this list is not intended to be exhaustive. Not listed are those cases where a word or phrase in the AV is replaced by two or more words in the NIV; however, singular words in the NIV that update a small phrase in the AV are included. And secondly, due to the tremendous size of the Bible itself, an exhaustive list would not be suitable for inclusion as an appendix.

abasement	Ezra 9:5	heaviness
abashed	Is 24:23	confounded
abutted	Ezek 40:18	over against
acclamation	2 Chr 15:14	voice
aghast	Is 13:8	amazed
alcove	Ezek 40:13	little chamber
annotations	2 Chr 13:22	story
armlets	Num 31:50	chains
bewilderment	Acts 2:6	confounded
blunted	Ps 58:7	cut in pieces
blustering	Job 8:2	strong
breakers	Ps 93:4	waves

brooches	Ex 35:22	bracelets
brood	Is 57:4	children
burnished	Dan 10:6	polished
carnelian	Rev 4:3	sardine
charioteers	1 Sam 13:5	horsemen
citron	Rev 18:12	thyine
colonnade	1 Ki 7:6	porch
commemorate	Ex 13:3	remember
cooing	Song 2:12	voice
cors	1 Ki 4:22	measures
curds	Gen 18:8	butter
dappled	Zec 6:6	gristled
debauchery	Gal 5:19	lasciviousness
decimated	2 Sam 21:5	destroyed
dejected	Gen 40:6	sad
deluded	Is 44:20	deceived
denarii	Matt 18:28	pence
denarius	Matt 20:2	penny
desecrate	Lev 21:12	profane
despoil	Jer 30:16	give for a prey
detachment	John 18:3	band
disheartened	Ezek 13:22	sad
disillusionment	Ps 7:14	falsehood
dissipation	1 Pet 4:4	riot
drachmas	Ezra 2:69	drams
dragnet	Hab 1:15	drag
duplicity	Lk 20:23	craftiness
elation	Pro 28:12	glory
embedded	Ecc 12:11	fastened
embitter	Ps 73:21	grieved
embodiment	Rom 2:20	form
emphatically	Mk 14:31	vehemently
encouragingly	2 Chr 30:22	comfortably
encrouch	Pro 23:10	enter
engulf	Ps 69:2	overflow
enrollment	2 Chr 17:14	numbers
enthralled	Ps 45:11	greatly desire
enveloped	Lk 9:34	overshadowed
exasperate	Eph 6:4	provoke
exterminate	Ezek 25:7	perish

exult	Is 14:8	rejoice
factions	1 Ki 16:21	parts
famished	Is 8:21	hungry
fattened	1 Sam 28:24	fat
faultfinders	Jude 16	complainers
fawns	Song 4:5	roes
fellowman	Micah 2:2	man
festival	Ex 5:1	feast
festive	1 Sam 25:8	good
fieldstones	Deut 27:6	whole stones
figurehead	Acts 28:11	sign
filigree	Ex 28:20	enclosings
fishnets	Ezek 26:5	nets
flagstaff	Is 30:17	beacon
flank	Ezek 34:21	side
fleeting	Ps 89:47	short
flinging	Acts 22:23	threw
flogged	Acts 5:40	beaten
floodgates	Gen 7:11	windows
fluttering	Is 16:2	wandering
fomenting	Is 59:13	speaking
forded	Josh 2:23	passed over
forevermore	Jude 25	for ever
frolic	Ps 104:26	play
fruitage	Is 27:9	fruit
gadfly	Jer 46:20	destruction
gaiety	Is 24:8	mirth
galled	1 Sam 18:8	displeased
gateway	Gen 19:1	gate
gaunt	Gen 41:3	leanfleshed
gauntness	Job 16:8	leanness
gecko	Lev 11:30	ferret
glancing	Ex 2:12	looked
glint	Hab 3:11	light
glistening	Job 41:32	shine
gloat	Ps 30:1	rejoice
gloom	Job 10:21	darkness
glutted	Ezek 39:19	full
goblet	Is 51:17	cup
goiim	Gen 14:1	nations

grapevine	James 3:12	vine
Hades	Rev 20:14	hell
harrowing	Is 28:24	break the clods
haunt	Ps 44:19	place
headwaters	Gen 2:10	heads
hoopoe	Lev 11:19	lapwing
horde	Ezek 17:17	army
ibex	Deut 14:5	pygarg
ignoble	2 Tim 2:20	dishonour
impaled	Ezra 6:11	hanged
imperishable	1 Cor 15:50	incorruption
impetuous	Hab 1:6	hasty
improvise	Amos 6:5	invent
incited	1 Chr 21:1	provoked
incurs	Pro 9:7	getteth
indestructible	Heb 7:16	endless
indignant	Mk 10:41	displeased
indispensable	1 Cor 12:22	necessary
infamy	Is 44:11	ashamed
innumerable	2 Chr 12:3	without number
insolence	Jer 48:30	wrath
insolent	Rom 1:30	despiteful
jeered	2 Ki 2:23	mocked
joists	2 Chr 34:11	couplings
jowls	Deut 18:3	cheeks
kingship	1 Sam 10:16	kingdom
lifeboat	Acts 27:30	boat
magi	Matt 2:1	wise men
mainstay	Jer 49:25	chief
marauders	Job 12:6	robbers
marshaled	Job 32:14	directed
mattocks	1 Sam 13:20	coulter
maxiums	Job 13:12	remembrances
melodious	Ps 81:2	pleasant
memorandum	Ezra 6:2	record
mina	Lk 19:16	pound
misdemeanor	Acts 18:14	wrong
naive	Rom 16:18	simple
nationality	Est 2:10	people
naught	Is 40:23	nothing

Archaic Words in the NIV 411

Negev	Gen 12:9	south
Nephilim	Gen 6:4	giants
nightfall	2 Sam 19:7	night
noonday	2 Sam 4:5	noon
Nubians	Dan 11:43	Ethiopians
nuggets	Job 22:24	gold
nurtured	Lam 4:5	brought
oarsmen	Ezek 27:26	rowers
oblivion	Ps 88:12	forgetfulness
obscenity	Eph 5:4	filthiness
offal	Ex 29:14	dung
officiate	2 Ki 17:32	sacrificed
opportune	Mk 6:1	convenient
ore	Job 28:2	stone
overawed	Ps 49:16	afraid
overweening	Is 16:6	very
parapet	Deut 22:8	battlement
piled	Lk 23:9	questioned
pinions	Deut 32:11	wings
porphyry	Est 1:6	red
portent	Is 20:3	wonder
portico	1 Ki 6:3	porch
poultice	2 Ki 20:7	lump
Praetorium	Matt 27:27	common hall
prefects	Dan 3:3	governors
proconsul	Acts 13:8	deputy
profligate	Deut 21:20	glutton
promiscuity	Ezek 16:26	whoredoms
qualm	Jude 12	fear
rabble	Num 11:4	mixed multitude
ramparts	Hab 2:11	tower
rawboned	Gen 49:14	strong
reeked	Ex 8:14	stank
repointing	1 Sam 13:21	sharpen
reposes	Pro 14:33	resteth
reputed	Gal 2:9	seemed
resound	1 Chr 16:32	roar
resplendent	Ps 76:4	glorious
reveled	Neh 9:25	delighted themselves
revelry	Is 22:13	gladness

revening	Jer 2:30	destroying
rifts	Jer 2:6	pits
sachet	Song 1:13	bundle
satraps	Est 3:12	lieutenants
sheathed	Ps 68:13	covered
siegeworks	Ecc 9:14	bulwarks
simplehearted	Ps 116:6	simple
sistrums	2 Sam 6:5	cornets
squall	Mk 4:37	storm of wind
stadia	Rev 14:20	furlongs
stag	Song 2:9	hart
stipulations	Deut 4:45	testimonies
suckling	1 Sam 7:9	sucking
sullen	1 Ki 21:5	sad
temperate	1 Tim 3:11	sober
tempest	Ps 55:8	storm
terebinth	Hos 4:13	elms
tethered	2 Ki 7:10	tied
thong	Lk 3:16	latchet
thornbush	Is 55:13	thorn
thundercloud	Ps 81:7	thunder
timidity	2 Tim 1:7	fear
tinder	Is 1:31	tow
torrent	Rev 12:15	flood
tranquillity	Ecc 4:6	quietness
transcends	Phil 4:7	passeth
transplanted	Ezek 17:10	planted
tresses	Song 7:5	galleries
tumult	1 Sam 14:19	noise
turbulent	Gen 49:4	unstable
tyrannical	Pro 28:16	oppressor
tyranny	Is 54:14	oppression
underlings	2 Ki 19:6	servants
vassal	2 Ki 24:1	servant
vaunts	Job 15:25	strengtheneth
vent	Job 20:23	cast
verdant	Song 1:16	green
vestments	Ezra 3:10	apparel
vexed	Ps 112:10	grieved
wadi	Num 34:5	river

waylaid	1 Sam 15:2	laid wait for
waywardness	Hosea 14:4	backsliding
weakling	Joel	weak
wily	Job 5:13	froward
windstorm	Is 29:6	storm
wrenched	Gen 32:25	out of joint
wretches	Matt 21:41	wicked men
yearling	Is 11:6	fatling

Appendix 4
Archaic Words in the NASB

As we have seen throughout the main body of this work, archaic words are not limited to the AV. Not only do modern versions often retain the supposedly archaic words found in the AV, but many times a more formidable word is used to correct a perfectly understandable word or phrase in the AV. This appendix gives those places in the NASB where a simple word or phrase in the AV is replaced by a more difficult word, the base or root form of a word is unnecessarily extended, and those instances where an archaic or somewhat arduous word in the AV is replaced by an equally archaic or even more onerous word. In two respects, however, this list is not intended to be exhaustive. Not listed are those cases where a word or phrase in the AV is replaced by two or more words in the NASB; however, singular words in the NASB that update a small phrase in the AV are included. And secondly, due to the tremendous size of the Bible itself, an exhaustive list would not be suitable for inclusion as an appendix.

abashed	Is 24:23	confounded
acquisition	Job 28:18	price
adjudicates	Is 29:21	reproveth
adjuration	Lev 5:1	swearing
aforesaid	Lev 14:11	things
allays	Ecc 10:4	pacifeth
amulets	Is 3:20	earrings
antimony	1 Chr 29:2	glistering
appropriate	Ecc 10:17	due
armlets	Num 31:50	chains
arrogantly	Neh 9:10	proudly
befits	Ps 93:5	becometh

Archaic Words in the NASB

begone	Matt 8:32	go
benumbed	Ps 38:8	feeble
bereave	Lev 26:22	rob
bereft	Jer 6:19	without
bewildered	Acts 2:6	confounded
boisterous	Pro 7:1	loud
brazier	Jer 36:22	hearth
breakers	Ps 93:4	waves
bristly	Jer 51:27	rough
brooches	Ex 35:22	bracelets
chalice	Is 51:22	cup
charioteers	Ezek 39:20	chariots
citadel	1 Ki 16:18	palace
citron	Rev 18:12	thyine
comeliness	Zec 9:17	goodness
commemorate	Jud 11:40	lament
concealment	Ps 64:4	secret
conciliate	1 Cor 4:13	entreat
constable	Lk 12:58	officer
corded	Ex 28:14	wreathen
curds	Gen 18:8	butter
dappled	Zec 6:6	grisled
dearth	Pro 14:28	want
deities	Acts 17:18	gods
dejected	Gen 40:6	sad
deliberating	Jn 16:19	inquire
demented	Hosea 9:7	mad
denarii	Matt 18:28	pence
denarius	Matt 20:2	penny
depopulated	Ezek 14:15	spoil
deportation	Matt 1:17	carrying away
depose	Is 22:19	drive
despicable	Dan 11:21	vile
despoil	Ps 17:9	oppress
despondent	Ps 109:16	broken
devastators	Nahum 2:2	emptiers
devoid	Jude 19	having not
disheartened	Dan 11:30	grieved
dissipation	Eph 5:18	excess
domineered	Neh 5:15	bare rule

drachma	Ezra 2:69	dram
dragnet	Matt 13:47	net
dusky	Jer 13:16	dark
earthenware	Lev 6:8	earthen
eczema	Lev 22:22	scurvy
edict	Est 8:13	writing
embittered	1 Sam 30:6	grieved
embodiment	Rom 2:20	form
encompassed	2 Sam 22:5	compassed
encouragingly	2 Chr 30:22	comfortably
encumbrance	Heb 12:1	weight
enigmas	Dan 5:12	hard sentences
enmity	Ezek 35:5	hatred
enumeration	1 Chr 27:1	number
envisioined	Amos 1:1	saw
epochs	Dan 2:21	seasons
eradicated	2 Ki 10:28	destroyed
exasperate	Col 3:21	provoke
excellencies	1 Pet 2:9	praises
expanse	Job 38:18	breadth
expropriations	Ezek 45:9	exactions
exult	1 Chr 16:32	rejoice
famished	Pro 27:7	hungry
fattened	1 Sam 28:24	fat
fawns	Song 4:5	roes
festive	1 Sam 25:8	good
figurehead	Acts 28:11	sign
filigree	Ex 28:20	enclosings
flitting	Pro 26:2	wandering
flogged	Acts 5:40	beaten
forevermore	Ps 9:7	forever
forlorn	Is 27:10	forsaken
frontals	Deut 6:8	frontlets
furrow	1 Sam 14:14	acre
gaiety	Is 22:13	joy
garner	Is 62:9	gathered
gashing	Mk 5:5	cutting
gateway	Deut 21:19	gate
gaunt	Gen 41:3	leanfleshed
gecko	Lev 11:30	ferret

Archaic Words in the NASB

glisten	Ps 104:15	shine
gloat	Job 31:25	rejoiced
gloom	Deut 5:22	darkness
glutted	Ezek 39:19	full
goiim	Gen 14:1	nations
grandeur	Dan 5:19	majesty
grub	Is 51:8	worm
hades	Rev 20:14	hell
harmonious	1 Pet 3:8	of one mind
harrow	Is 28:24	break the clods
haunt	Jer 9:11	den
hedgehog	Is 14:23	bittern
hoopoe	Lev 11:19	lapwing
ibex	Deut 14:5	pygarg
illumines	Ps 18:28	enlighten
imbibe	Song 5:1	drink
impaled	Ezra 6:11	hanged
imperishable	1 Cor 9:25	incorruptible
impetuous	Hab 1:6	hasty
importune	Pro 6:3	make sure
impotent	Is 16:14	feeble
imprecation	Jer 42:18	curse
improvise	Amos 6:5	chant
inaccessible	Job 39:28	strong
inaugurated	Heb 9:18	dedicated
incessantly	Acts 6:13	ceaseth not
incurred	Acts 27:21	gained
indescribable	2 Cor 9:15	unspeakable
indestructible	Heb 7:16	endless
indictment	Micah 6:2	controversy
indignant	Dan 2:12	angry
indolence	Ecc 10:18	much slothfulness
injunction	Dan 6:8	decree
innumerable	Jud 6:5	without number
insanely	1 Sam 21:13	mad
insolence	1 Sam 17:28	pride
insubordination	1 Sam 15:23	stubbornness
interposed	Heb 6:17	confirmed
inundate	Job 12:15	overturn
jettison	Acts 27:18	lightened

jurisdiction	Rom 7:1	dominion
keener	Hab 1:8	more fierce
kiln	Ex 9:8	furnace
kingship	Dan 11:21	kingdom
kors	1 Ki 4:22	measures
lair	Job 37:8	dens
languish	Job 17:5	fail
lapis lazuli	Lam 4:7	sapphire
libations	1 Chr 29:21	drink offerings
licentioiusness	Jude 4	lasciviousness
lifeblood	Gen 9:5	blood
loath	Gal 4:14	rejected
lovingkindnesses	Ps 119:41	mercies
luncheon	Lk 14:12	dinner
luxuriant	1 Ki 14:23	green
magi	Matt 2:1	wise men
mantelet	Nah 2:5	defence
mattock	1 Sam 13:20	coulter
mercenaries	Jer 46:21	hired men
meted	Job 28:25	weighed
mina	Lk 19:16	pound
moneylender	Lk 7:41	creditor
mottled	Gen 31:10	grisled
naive	Pro 1:4	simple
nave	1 Ki 6:3	temple
Negev	Gen 12:9	south
Nephilim	Gen 6:4	giants
noontime	Acts 22:6	noon
nursling	Deut 32:25	suckling
obelisks	Jer 43:13	images
obiliterate	Deut 12:3	destroy
odious	Gen 34:30	stink
officiated	Heb 7:13	attendance
opportune	John 7:6	ready
pangs	Jer 49:24	sorrows
parapet	Deut 22:8	battlement
peasantry	Jud 5:7	inhabitants of the villages
perpetrated	Ezra 4:19	made
phylacteries	Ex 13:16	frontlets
pinions	Ps 91:4	feathers

porphyry	Est 1:6	red
portico	Acts 5:12	porch
Praetorium	Jn 18:28	hall of judgment
prefects	Dan 3:3	governors
prickling	Ezek 28:24	pricking
proconsul	Acts 13:8	deputy
prow	Acts 27:41	forepart
pugnacious	1 Tim 3:3	striker
putrefaction	Is 3:24	stink
pyre	Is 30:33	pile
quartermaster	Jer 51:59	quiet prince
rabble	Num 11:4	mixed multitude
rampart	Hab 2:1	tower
repose	Is 28:12	the refreshing
requite	Ps 28:4	give
requited	Ezra 9:13	punished
resounded	1 Sam 4:5	rang again
resplendent	Ps 76:4	glorious
retinue	2 Chr 9:1	company
reveled	Neh 9:25	delighted themselves
revelers	Is 24:8	them that rejoice
rostrum	Acts 12:21	throne
ruffians	Job 16:11	the ungodly
sage	Jer 18:18	wise
satiated	Pro 1:31	filled
satraps	Dan 3:2	princes
seemly	1 Cor 12:24	comely
Sheol	Is 14:9	hell
sickliness	Is 17:11	grief
siegeworks	Is 29:3	forts
smelt	Is 1:25	purge
sordid	1 Tim 3:8	filthy
sorely	Jer 14:17	grievous
sorrel	Zech 1:8	speckled
stalwart	Amos 2:14	strong
stealthily	Job 4:12	secretly
stylus	Job 19:24	pen
suckling	1 Sam 7:9	sucking
sullen	1 Ki 21:5	sad
swarthy	Song 1:6	black

tableland	Deut 3:10	plain
teeming	Lev 22:5	creeping
temperate	1 Tim 3:2	vigilant
tempest	Is 28:2	storm
tendrils	Is 16:8	branches
teraphim	2 Ki 23:24	images
terebinth	Hos 4:13	elms
throng	Ps 35:18	people
thrush	Jer 8:7	swallow
timbrel	Gen 31:27	tabret
timidity	2 Tim 1:7	fear
tinder	Is 1:31	tow
tinkling	Ex 28:35	sound
torrent	Jud 5:21	river
transient	Ps 39:4	frail
tresses	Song 7:5	galleries
trigon	Dan 3:5	sackbut
tumult	Jer 10:13	multitude
turbid	Job 6:16	blackish
twitter	Is 38:14	chatter
tyrannical	Zep 3:1	oppressing
vanguard	Joel 2:20	face
varicolored	Gen 37:2	many colours
vaunt	Ps 94:4	boast
vestibule	Jud 3:23	porch
vesture	Dan 7:9	garment
vexation	Job 6:2	grief
vexed	1 Ki 21:4	displeased
vexing	Pro 21:19	angry
virility	Ps 78:51	strength
vitality	Ps 32:4	moisture
votive	Lev 23:38	vow
Wadi	Num 21:12	valley
wadis	Num 21:14	brooks
waywardness	Pro 1:32	turning away
wield	Deut 23:25	move
woodland	Micah 7:14	wood
wrangle	2 Tim 2:14	strive
wretches	Matt 21:41	wicked men
yearling	Micah 6:6	of a year old

Appendix 5
Archaic Words in the NKJV

As we have seen throughout the main body of this work, archaic words are not limited to the AV. Not only do modern versions often retain the supposedly archaic words found in the AV, but many times a more formidable word is used to correct a perfectly understandable word or phrase in the AV. This appendix gives those places in the NKJV where a simple word or phrase in the AV is replaced by a more difficult word, the base or root form of a word is unnecessarily extended, and those instances where an archaic or somewhat arduous word in the AV is replaced by an equally archaic or even more onerous word. In two respects, however, this list is not intended to be exhaustive. Not listed are those cases where a word or phrase in the AV is replaced by two or more words in the NKJV; however, singular words in the NKJV that update a small phrase in the AV are included. And secondly, due to the tremendous size of the Bible itself, an exhaustive list would not be suitable for inclusion as an appendix.

abashed	Micah 3:7	confounded
allays	Pro 15:18	appeaseth
antitype	1 Pet 3:21	figure
armlets	Num 31:50	chains
artistically	Ex 28:6	cunning
ascertain	Acts 21:34	know
befitting	Acts 26:20	meet
beveled	Ezek 41:26	narrow
bewildered	Ex 14:3	entangled
boastfully	Ps 75:4	foolishly
bristling	Jer 51:27	rough
brood	Is 14:20	seed

burnished	1 Ki 7:45	bright
bygone	Acts 14:16	past
citadel	Est 2:5	palace
citron	Rev 18:12	thyine
conciliation	Ecc 10:4	yielding
constituency	2 Ki 12:5	acquaintance
convulsed	Mk 1:26	torn
curds	Deut 32:14	butter
dappled	Zec 6:6	grisled
demented	Jer 29:26	mad
demonic	James 3:15	devilish
denarii	Matt 18:28	pence
denarius	Matt 20:2	penny
deranged	Jer 51:7	mad
desisted	Jer 41:8	forbare
despoiled	Jud 2:14	spoiled
devoid	Pro 7:7	void
dilapidation	2 Ki 12:5	breach
disdain	Pro 8:33	refuse
disfigurement	Lev 24:19	a blemish
dissipation	Titus 1:6	riot
drachmas	Neh 7:70	drams
eczema	Lev 21:20	scurvy
edict	Ezra 6:11	word
eldership	1 Tim 4:14	presbytery
embellished	Hosea 10:1	made
emitted	Gen 38:9	spilled
encompass	Jer 31:22	compass
endowment	Gen 30:20	dowry
enigmas	Dan 5:16	doubts
enmity	Hosea 9:7	hatred
enraptured	Pro 5:20	ravished
envisioned	Lam 2:14	seen
envoy	Ps 68:31	princes
evermore	1 Chr 16:11	continually
exorcise	Acts 19:13	adjure
expiration	Acts 21:26	accomplishment
exterminate	1 Ki 13:34	cut it off
faction	Ps 106:17	company
fallow	Ex 23:11	still

fancies	Pro 1:31	devices
fatted	1 Sam 28:24	fat
fattened	1 Ki 1:9	fat
fawns	Song 4:5	roes
figurehead	Acts 28:11	sign
flitting	Pro 26:2	wandering
fluttering	Num 11:31	fall
forefathers	Acts 7:19	fathers
forevermore	Ezek 37:26	evermore
fostered	Ezra 4:19	made
gad	Jer 31:22	go
gateposts	Jud 16:3	posts
gateway	Ezek 40:3	gate
gaunt	Gen 41:20	lean
gecko	Lev 11:30	ferret
goatherds	Zec 10:3	goats
graze	Ex 22:5	eaten
Hades	Lk 10:15	hell
harmonious	Ps 92:3	solemn
haunts	Ps 74:20	habitations
hearth	Ezek 43:15	altar
Hellenists	Acts 11:20	Grecians
hoopoe	Lev 11:19	lapwing
horde	Ezek 23:24	assembly
illuminated	Rev 18:1	lightened
immeasurable	Gen 41:49	without number
imperishable	1 Cor 9:25	incorruptible
incited	Ezra 4:15	moved
indignant	Matt 21:15	displeased
insolence	1 Sam 17:28	naughtiness
insolent	Ps 31:18	grievous
insubordinate	1 Tim 1:9	disobedient
itinerant	Acts 19:13	vagabond
jeering	2 Chr 29:8	hissing
kors	1 Ki 4:22	measures
mainstay	Is 19:13	stay
mankind	Acts 15:17	men
mattock	1 Sam 13:20	coulter
medium	Lev 20:27	wizard
mercenaries	Jer 46:21	hired men

mina	Lk 19:16	pound
moorings	Jonah 2:6	bottoms
nevermore	Ecc 9:6	neither
oarsmen	Ezek 27:26	rowers
obnoxious	Gen 34:30	stink
offal	Lev 8:17	dung
officiated	Heb 7:13	attendance
opportune	Mk 6:21	convenient
ore	Job 28:2	stone
pangs	Ps 116:3	pains
parapet	Deut 22:8	battlement
penitents	Is 1:27	converts
perpetuate	Ruth 4:5	raise up
pinions	Job 39:13	feathers
pitiable	1 Cor 15:19	miserable
platitudes	Job 13:12	remembrances
portico	1 Ki 7:6	porch
poultice	Is 38:21	plaister
Praetorium	John 18:28	hall of judgment
prattle	Micah 2:6	prophesy
proconsul	Acts 13:7	deputy
prodigal	Lk 15:13	riotous
prow	Acts 27:30	foreship
pulverized	2 Ki 23:12	brake
pyre	Ezek 24:9	pile
quadrans	Mk 12:42	farthing
quartermaster	Jer 51:59	quiet prince
rampart	Hab 2:1	tower
reprisal	Oba 1:15	reward
resound	Is 16:11	sound
retinue	2 Chr 9:1	company
rivulets	Ezek 31:4	little rivers
satraps	Dan 3:3	princes
scruples	Rom 15:1	infirmities
seductress	Pro 6:24	strange woman
shards	Ezek 23:24	sherds
Sheol	2 Sam 22:6	hell
siegeworks	Is 29:3	forts
sistrums	2 Sam 6:5	cornets
skiff	Acts 27:32	boat

steeds	Micah 1:13	beast
suckling	1 Sam 7:9	sucking
teeming	Ps 104:25	creeping
temperate	1 Tim 3:11	sober
terebinth	Is 1:30	oak
thornbushes	Matt 7:16	thorns
timbrel	Gen 31:27	tabret
tinder	Is 1:31	tow
torrent	Jud 5:21	river
tresses	Song 7:5	galleries
valuation	Lev 5:18	estimation
vassal	2 Ki 17:3	servant
verdant	Is 28:4	fat
verdure	Song 6:11	fruits
vestibule	1 Ki 6:3	porch
vexed	Ps 73:21	pricked
vice	1 Pet 2:16	maliciousness
vitality	Ps 32:4	moisture
waifs	Lam 5:3	fatherless
wane	Is 17:4	be made thin
wend	Zech 10:2	went
wield	Is 10:15	shake
woodland	Micah 7:14	wood

Appendix 6
Archaic Words in the NRSV

As we have seen throughout the main body of this work, archaic words are not limited to the AV. Not only do modern versions often retain the supposedly archaic words found in the AV, but many times a more formidable word is used to correct a perfectly understandable word or phrase in the AV. This appendix gives those places in the NRSV where a simple word or phrase in the AV is replaced by a more difficult word, the base or root form of a word is unnecessarily extended, and those instances where an archaic or somewhat arduous word in the AV is replaced by an equally archaic or even more onerous word. In two respects, however, this list is not intended to be exhaustive. Not listed are those cases where a word or phrase in the AV is replaced by two or more words in the NRSV; however, singular words in the NRSV that update a small phrase in the AV are included. And secondly, due to the tremendous size of the Bible itself, an exhaustive list would not be suitable for inclusion as an appendix.

abashed	Is 24:23	confounded
abated	Gen 8:8	subsided
abrogation	Heb 7:18	disannulling
adjuration	Lev 5:1	swearing
affront	Pro 17:9	transgression
aghast	Is 13:8	amazed
antimony	1 Chr 29:2	glistering
apportioned	Num 33:54	divide
armlet	2 Sam 1:10	bracelet
armlets	Num 31:50	chains
augments	Pro 28:8	increaseth

Archaic Words in the NRSV

augury	2 Ki 21:6	enchantments
avarice	Mk 7:22	covetousness
avert	Est 8:3	put away
befits	Ps 93:5	becometh
bereave	Lev 26:22	rob
bereft	1 Tim 6:5	destitute
bespattered	Lev 6:27	sprinkled
binders	2 Chr 34:11	couplings
bitumen	Gen 11:3	slime
bombastic	2 Pet 2:18	great swelling words
borderlands	Num 24:17	corners
brackish	Jam 3:11	bitter
brazier	Jer 36:22	hearth
brooches	Ex 35:22	bracelets
bulwark	Ps 8:2	strength
bungler	Ecc 9:18	sinner
bygone	Job 8:8	former
calyx	Ex 25:25	knop
carnelian	Rev 21:20	sardius
charioteer	Jer 51:21	rider
chariotry	1 Ki 9:22	chariots
cicada	Deut 28:42	locust
citadel	Deut 3:4	city
compatriots	1 Thes 2:14	countrymen
consternation	Ps 116:11	haste
convulsed	Mk 9:20	tare
corded	Ex 28:14	wreathen
cors	1 Ki 4:22	measures
courtiers	1 Sam 8:14	servants
covert	Ps 10:9	den
cowardice	2 Tim 1:7	fear
crescents	Jud 8:21	ornaments
curds	Pro 30:33	butter
dappled	Zech 6:6	grisled
debaucheries	Nahum 3:4	whoredoms
decanters	Jer 48:12	wanderers
deference	1 Pet 2:18	fear
defilement	2 Cor 7:1	filthiness
dejectedly	1 Ki 21:27	softly
dejection	James 4:9	heaviness

denarius	Matt 22:19	penny
dennarii	Matt 18:28	pence
denounce	Num 28:7	defy
desecrated	Ps 74:7	defiled
desist	Jud 20:28	cease
despicable	Titus 3:3	hateful
despoil	1 Sam 14:36	spoil
detachment	Jn 18:23	band
devoid	Jude 19	having not
dirge	Jer 9:20	wailing
disciplinarian	Gal 3:24	schoolmaster
dishevel	Lev 21:10	uncover
dissipation	1 Pet 4:4	riot
dissolute	Lk 15:13	riotous
divinities	Acts 17:18	gods
dogged	Lam 4:18	hunt
dolt	Ps 49:10	brutish
dullard	Ps 92:6	brutish
dumbfounded	Ps 31:17	silent
earthenware	Jer 32:14	earthen
ebbing	Jer 49:4	flowing
edict	Ezra 6:11	word
embittered	Ps 73:21	grieved
embodiment	Rom 2:20	form
encompassed	2 Sam 22:5	compassed
encouragingly	2 Chr 30:22	comfortably
encroach	Pro 23:10	enter
encrusted	Song 5:14	overlaid
enlightenment	Dan 5:14	light
enmity	Deut 19:6	hatred
enveloped	Lam 3:5	compassed
envisioned	Ezek 13:6	see
estranged	Col 1:21	alienated
evermore	Ps 35:27	continually
exacted	Job 22:6	taken
exoneration	Gen 20:16	covering
expiated	1 Sam 3:14	purged
expiation	2 Sam 21:3	atonement
exterminated	1 Chr 4:41	destroyed
exult	1 Sam 16:32	rejoice

Archaic Words in the NRSV

fatling	Is 5:17	fat
fatted	1 Sam 28:24	fat
fawns	Song 4:5	roes
festal	Ps 89:15	joyful
festivity	Is 22:13	gladness
figurehead	Acts 28:11	sign
filigree	Ex 28:20	enclosings
flagons	Est 1:8	according to law
flagstaff	Is 30:17	beacon
flailing	Ezek 16:22	polluted
fledglings	Deut 22:6	young
flitting	Pro 26:2	wandering
flogged	Acts 5:4	beaten
fluttering	Is 16:2	wandering
forebears	Ps 39:12	fathers
forecourt	Mk 14:68	porch
furrow	1 Sam 14:14	acre
gadding	1 Tim 5:13	wandering
gadfly	Jer 46:20	destruction
gait	Pro 30:29	going
garner	Is 62:9	gathered
gashing	Jer 16:6	cut
gateway	Gen 19:1	gate
gecko	Lev 11:30	ferret
gloat	Rev 11:10	rejoice
glutted	Pro 30:22	filled
goiim	Jos 12:23	nations
gorged	Rev 19:21	filled
gossamer	Job 8:14	cut off
granaries	Joel 1:17	barns
grapevine	James 3:12	vine
graze	Ex 22:5	feed
gum	Gen 43:11	spicies
hades	Rev 20:14	hell
hallowed	Gen 2:3	sanctified
haltingly	1 Sam 15:32	delicately
handmill	Ex 11:5	mill
handpikes	Ezek 39:9	handstaves
harrow	Is 28:24	break the clods
haunt	Ps 44:19	place

hedgehog	Is 34:11	bittern
Hellenists	Acts 9:29	Grecians
high-handedly	Num 15:30	presumptuously
holm	Is 44:14	cypress
homicide	Deut 19:4	slayer
hoopoe	Lev 11:19	lapwing
horde	2 Chr 32:7	multitude
humankind	Gen 1:26	man
ibex	Deut 14:5	pygarg
idlers	1 Th 5:14	unruly
illicit	Num 3:4	strange
impaled	2 Sam 21:9	hanged
imperishability	1 Cor 15:53	incorruption
impetuous	Hab 1:6	hasty
impiety	2 Tim 2:16	ungodliness
impious	Ps 74:18	foolish
impoverished	Lev 25:39	poor
impropriety	Deut 23:9	wicked thing
improvise	Amos 6:5	invent
inaugurated	Heb 9:18	dedicated
indestructible	Heb 7:16	endless
indignant	Gen 34:7	grieved
indispensable	1 Cor 12:22	necessary
indistinct	1 Cor 14:8	uncertain
indolence	Ecc 10:18	idleness
iniquitous	Is 10:1	unrighteous
insatiable	2 Pet 2:14	cannot cease
insolence	Is 16:6	pride
insolent	Ps 86:14	proud
instinctively	Rom 2:14	by nature
interdict	Dan 6:7	decree
interlacing	Jer 2:23	traversing
intoned	2 Sam 1:17	lamented
irresolute	2 Chr 13:7	tenderhearted
itinerant	Acts 19:13	vagabond
jowls	Deut 18:3	cheeks
kiln	Ex 19:18	furnace
kingship	1 Sam 11:14	kingdom
lacerate	Deut 14:1	cut
lair	Jer 9:11	den

languishing	Ps 6:2	weak
laud	Ps 145:4	praise
lavish	Hab 1:16	fat
legitimately	1 Tim 1:8	lawfully
libations	2 Chr 29:21	drink offerings
licentiousness	Mk 7:22	lasciviousness
lifeblood	Jer 2:34	blood
litigation	Hosea 10:4	judgment
loathing	2 Sam 13:15	hatred
localities	Gen 36:40	places
lovingkindness	Gen 19:19	mercy
luminaries	Ps 74:16	light
luncheon	Lk 14:12	dinner
luxuriant	Hosea 10:1	empty
magnates	Rev 6:15	great men
mainstay	Jer 49:35	chief
malcontents	Jude 16	complainers
manacles	2 Chr 33:11	fetters
mantelet	Nahum 2:5	defence
marauder	Jer 18:22	troop
mattocks	1 Sam 13:20	coulter
maxiums	Job 13:12	remembrances
midcourse	Ps 102:23	way
moonstone	Ex 28:18	diamond
mottled	Gen 31:10	grisled
nape	Lev 5:8	neck
naught	Is 40:23	nothing
nave	1 Ki 6:3	temple
Negeb	Gen 12:9	south
Nephilim	Gen 6:4	giants
nevermore	Is 14:20	never
noonday	2 Sam 4:5	noon
obelisks	Jer 43:13	images
oblation	1 Ki 18:29	evening sacrifice
odious	Gen 34:30	stink
officiate	Heb 13:10	serve
ore	Job 28:3	stones
palanquin	Song 3:9	chariot
pangs	Ps 116:3	pains
parapet	Deut 22:8	battlement

peasantry	Jud 5:7	inhabitants of the villages
pediment	2 Ki 16:17	pavement
penitent	2 Chr 34:27	tender
pilaster	Ezek 40:14	post
pinions	Ps 91:4	feathers
plumage	Ezek 17:3	feathers
porphyry	Est 1:6	red
portico	Acts 5:12	porch
prefects	Dan 3:3	governors
proconsul	Acts 13:8	deputy
profligates	2 Tim 3:3	incontinent
pyre	Is 30:33	pile
quartermaster	Jer 51:59	quiet prince
queenly	Song 7:1	prince's
rabble	Num 11:4	mixed multitude
rampart	Hab 2:1	tower
ravening	Jer 2:30	destroying
remonstrated	Neh 13:11	contended
repose	Is 28:12	the refreshing
repudiated	2 Chr 29:19	cast away
repugnant	Job 22:18	far from
requital	Is 59:18	recompense
resound	Ex 9:16	declared
retinue	2 Chr 9:1	company
rouges	Lk 18:11	unjust
ruffians	Ps 86:14	violent men
sacrilege	Matt 24:15	abomination
sages	Job 15:18	wise men
sated	Pro 1:31	filled
satraps	Ezra 8:36	lieutenants
seine	Hab 1:15	drag
Sheol	2 Sam 22:6	hell
siegeworks	Jer 52:4	forts
silage	Is 30:24	provender
smelt	Is 1:25	purge
sordid	1 Pet 5:2	filthy
sordidness	James 1:21	filthiness
sorrel	Zech 1:8	speckled
stag	Song 8:4	hart
steeds	Micah 1:13	swift beast

stylus	Is 44:13	line
suet	Lev 1:12	fat
sultry	Jonah 4:8	vehement
surfeit	Ecc 5:12	abundance
surly	1 Sam 25:3	churlish
syrtis	Acts 27:17	quicksands
tableland	Deut 3:10	plain
temperate	1 Tim 3:2	vigilant
tempest	Is 28:2	storm
teraphim	Ezek 21:21	images
terebinth	Hos 4:13	elms
throng	Ps 35:18	people
thunderpeals	Rev 19:6	thunderings
timbrels	Is 24:8	tabrets
torrent	Jud 5:21	river
traversed	Jos 18:9	passed through
trellis	Ps 74:5	trees
trifle	2 Ki 3:18	light thing
tumult	1 Sam 14:19	noise
unawares	Gen 34:25	boldly
unbind	John 11:44	loose
unchastity	Matt 19:9	fornication
underworld	Deut 27:6	whole
unsheathe	Lev 26:33	draw out
unshrunk	Matt 9:16	new
uterus	Num 5:21	thigh
valets	1 Ki 10:5	cupbearer
vassal	2 Ki 17:3	servant
vestibule	Jud 3:23	porch
vexation	Job 6:2	grief
villainy	Acts 13:10	mischief
vinestock	Deut 32:32	vine
virility	Deut 21:17	strength
votive	2 Chr 15:18	dedicated
wadi	Num 13:23	brook
wadis	Job 30:6	valleys
waistcloth	Job 12:18	girdle
wanton	Ezek 23:44	lewd
watchpost	Hab 2:1	watch
waywardness	Pro 1:32	turning away

weakling	Joel 3:10	weak
weal	Is 45:7	peace
wheelwork	Ezek 10:2	wheels
wield	Ezek 30:21	hold
wrenched	Matt 5:4	plucked
wretches	Matt 21:41	wicked men
wrought	2 Sam 7:21	done
yearling	Lev 9:3	of the first year
Zaphon	Job 26:7	north

Appendix 7
AV Archaic Words Retained in the NIV

As we have seen throughout the main body of this work, archaic words are not limited to the AV. Not only do modern versions often insert a more formidable word in correction of a perfectly understandable word or phrase in the AV, many times the supposedly archaic words found in the AV are retained. This appendix gives a listing of words found in the NIV that are usually cited as being archaic when they occur in the AV. This would include words retained exactly, whether in the same passage or another verse, and words that are similar in form no matter where they appear. To be equitable, words are only listed when they are employed in the same archaic sense that is usually corrected in the AV. As the previous appendixes, this list is not intended to be exhaustive, for the NIV will often utilize several different forms of a word that is supposedly archaic, obsolete, or otherwise employed in an unacceptable sense by the AV. A full discussion of the words included in this representative sample can be found in the main body of this work under the base form of the word in question.

abode	celestial
ancients	coney
aright	confections
asunder	convince
away with	cormorant
beckon	decked
begotten	deride
bier	distill
bewitched	dung
bowels	effect
calved	estate

forevermore
fowl
girdle
hallowed
haunt
heresies
infamy
inasmuch
insatiable
jeopardy
kernels
laden
lance
lusty
mantle
mattock
naught
nurtured
odious
osprey

pangs
phylacteries
plowshare
rend
respite
rushes
soothsayer
spoil
suckling
temperate
tetrarch
trafficked
unto
usury
vaunt
vestments
vex
wanton
yokefellow

Appendix 8
AV Archaic Words Retained in the NASB

As we have seen throughout the main body of this work, archaic words are not limited to the AV. Not only do modern versions often insert a more formidable word in correction of a perfectly understandable word or phrase in the AV, many times the supposedly archaic words found in the AV are retained. This appendix gives a listing of words found in the NASB that are usually cited as being archaic when they occur in the AV. This would include words retained exactly, whether in the same passage or another verse, and words that are similar in form no matter where they appear. To be equitable, words are only listed when they are employed in the same archaic sense that is usually corrected in the AV. As the previous appendixes, this list is not intended to be exhaustive, for the NASB will often utilize several different forms of a word that is supposedly archaic, obsolete, or otherwise employed in an unacceptable sense by the AV. A full discussion of the words included in this representative sample can be found in the main body of this work under the base form of the word in question.

abase
abated
abode
adjure
alms
ancient
apparel
aright
art
asunder
away with

backbiting
beget
beseech
bewail
bewitched
bondwomen
bowels
breeches
brimstone
calves
canst

cleave
comely
constrains
cormorant
couches
covert
crib
dainty
dearth
deck
deride
didst
distill
doest
dost
doth
dung
effect
eminent
engines
estate
evermore
familiar
feigned
fetch
firstlings
fleshhook
footmen
forbearance
fowl
fuller
gaiety
garners
gavest
girdle
graven
gross
guile
handmaid
harrow

hast
haunt
heresies
hinds
importune
impotent
inasmuch
issue
issue
jeopardy
know
laden
laud
layer
lightness
litters
lordly
lunatic
lusty
mail
maintenance
mammon
mantle
maranatha
mattock
milch
mill
nether
nurtured
odious
offscouring
pangs
paramours
perdition
phylacteries
pipes
plowshare
presbytery
principalities
putrefaction

raiment	teraphim
rampart	tetrarch
ravening	thee
remission	thereon
rend	thine
reprobate	thou
requite	thy
riot	timbrel
rushes	trafficked
seemly	travail
seest	unto
seethe	usury
shalt	vagabond
sherd	valor
shod	vaunt
shouldst	venture
shouldst	verily
smith	vermilion
solace	vex
soothsayer	virtue
sore	wanton
speakest	warp
stay	wayfarers
strait	whence
suckling	wherewith
swaddling	woof
tares	wrought
temperate	yea
tenons	yonder

Appendix 9
AV Archaic Words Retained in the NKJV

As we have seen throughout the main body of this work, archaic words are not limited to the AV. Not only do modern versions often insert a more formidable word in correction of a perfectly understandable word or phrase in the AV, many times the supposedly archaic words found in the AV are retained. This appendix gives a listing of words found in the NKJV that are usually cited as being archaic when they occur in the AV. This would include words retained exactly, whether in the same passage or another verse, and words that are similar in form no matter where they appear. To be equitable, words are only listed when they are employed in the same archaic sense that is usually corrected in the AV. As the previous appendixes, this list is not intended to be exhaustive, for the NKJV will often utilize several different forms of a word that is supposedly archaic, obsolete, or otherwise employed in an unacceptable sense by the AV. A full discussion of the words included in this representative sample can be found in the main body of this work under the base form of the word in question.

abase
abode
alms
amiss
anise
apparel
aright
austere
away with
backbiters
beckoned

beggarly
begot
bemoan
beseech
bewail
bewitched
bittern
bondwomen
brimstone
calves
carnal

AV Archaic Words Retained in the NKJV

celestial
circumspect
cloven
comeliness
concourses
confederacy
convince
covert
crib
dainties
daubed
dayspring
debased
decks
deride
dispensation
disquiet
distill
dung
effect
epistle
eventide
evermore
familiar
fan
feigned
fetch
flanks
flay
footmen
forbearance
foursquare
fowl
fuller
gad
godhead
graven
greyhound
gross
hallowed

haunts
hemlock
henceforth
heresies
immutable
impudent
inasmuch
issue
jeopardy
jot
know
laden
laud
laver
litters
lordly
lusty
mail
mammon
mantle
mattock
mill
mite
nativity
offend
offscouring
omnipotent
pangs
paramours
phylacteries
pipes
plowshare
potentate
principality
prognosticators
psaltery
quarter
rampart
rear
rend

rid	usury
rifled	vagabond
riotous	valor
rushes	vehement
satiate	verity
shamefaced	vermilion
shod	vestments
smith	vex
soothsayer	virtue
spoil	visage
straits	wanton
suckling	warp
tares	wayfaring
temperate	whence
tenons	whereupon
terrestrial	whet
tetrarch	winebibber
therein	woof
timbrel	wrought
tittle	yea
unto	yonder

Appendix 10
AV Archaic Words Retained in the NRSV

As we have seen throughout the main body of this work, archaic words are not limited to the AV. Not only do modern versions often insert a more formidable word in correction of a perfectly understandable word or phrase in the AV, many times the supposedly archaic words found in the AV are retained. This appendix gives a listing of words found in the NRSV that are usually cited as being archaic when they occur in the AV. This would include words retained exactly, whether in the same passage or another verse, and words that are similar in form no matter where they appear. To be equitable, words are only listed when they are employed in the same archaic sense that is usually corrected in the AV. As the previous appendixes, this list is not intended to be exhaustive, for the NRSV will often utilize several different forms of a word that is supposedly archaic, obsolete, or otherwise employed in an unacceptable sense by the AV. A full discussion of the words included in this representative sample can be found in the main body of this work under the base form of the word in question.

abase	beget
abate	beggarly
abode	bemoan
adjuration	beseech
alms	bewail
apparel	bewitched
assuaged	bier
asunder	bowels
augment	calving
away with	cleft
backbiting	comely

coneys
constrains
cormorant
covert
crib
dainty
debased
decked
delectable
disquieted
dissembles
distill
dromedaries
dung
effect
enjoined
ensign
ensues
estate
eventide
evermore
execration
familiar
firmament
firstling
flagon
flay
footmen
forbear
foursquare
fowl
fuller
gad
garner
goodly
gross
guile
hallowed
haltingly
harrow

haunt
henceforth
hoarfrost
impudent
inasmuch
isles
know
laden
lance
laud
laver
litters
lusty
mail
maintenance
mantle
mattock
milch
mill
naught
noontide
obeisance
oblation
odious
pangs
paramours
perdition
phylacteries
pipes
plowshare
pound
rampart
ravening
remission
rend
riotous
rushes
sacrilege
satiate
seethe

sherd	vale
sloth	valor
smith	vaunt
solace	venture
soothsayer	vermilion
stay	vestments
straits	vexation
stripling	vial
suppliants	villainy
surfeit	visage
swaddling	vocation
temperate	wanton
teraphim	warp
thereupon	wayfarer
thrice	whet
timbrel	whoredom
trafficked	winebibber
unshod	woof
upbraided	wrought

Appendix 11
Uniformity in Translating from English

In addition to the charge of containing archaic words, the AV is also regularly faulted for the lack of uniformity in its translation of Hebrew and Greek words. Using English as an example, this appendix demonstrates the folly of insisting upon strict uniformity in the translation of multiple occurrences of the same word into other languages. This would not only include words that have different meanings due to a dissimilar origin, but also words with a common origin that have several completely different shades of meaning.

Bear

The word **bear** can refer to an animal or a rude person. A stock market that declines is said to be a **bear** market. To move rapidly toward something is to **bear** down on it, but to be patient with someone is to **bear** with them. To drive to the left is to **bear** left. If something is worthy of being repeated then it **bears** repeating. To bring someone a gift is to **bear** it, while to give someone bad news is also called to **bear** it. A tree **bears** fruit but a woman **bears** children. To harbor bitterness against someone is to **bear** malice, but to support a load is to **bear** the weight.

Blow

Besides referring to the wind **blowing**, the word **blow** can also refer to expelling a current of air as when one **blows** up a balloon or plays an instrument. Someone who is shot and killed is said to have been **blown** away as is someone who is overwhelmed or defeated. When a photograph is enlarged it is said to be **blown** up, but when a building is cut down with explosives it is also said to be **blown** up. When a storm subsides or someone's anger abates, the storm and the anger are said to **blow** over. To expose something is to **blow** the lid off of it. To be discovered is to **blow** one's cover. A **blow** can also refer to a punch thrown in a fight. To waste money on something is to **blow** the money. To make a mistake is to **blow** it. When a fuse melts or bursts it is also said to **blow**. To depart a town in a hurry is to **blow** it.

Card

A **card** can refer to a piece of paper with information on it such as a credit **card,** playing **card,** or greeting **card.** It can also mean a brush or machine for combing cotton fibers prior to spinning. A **card** can be a device used to raise the nap on a fabric or it can refer to the program of a sporting event. To brush or dress fabric is to **card** it, but to check someone's identification is to **card** them. An amusing person is often called a character or a **card.**

Fair

One can go to a **fair** with a girl of **fair** complexion if the weather is **fair** and the rides at the **fair** are at least **fair.** It would not be **fair,** however, to say that something was **fair** game just because it was at the book **fair.** And the opposite of a foul ball in baseball is **fair** one.

Fan

A **fan** is a device to move air for cooling. It is also someone devoted to a rock star. A winnowing **fan** is used to winnow grain. To fire a gun rapidly is to **fan** it. And to strike out a batter in baseball is to **fan** him.

Ground

In addition to referring to the soil or earth, the word **ground** also means a cause, a basis, or a subject. To be disciplined is to be **grounded.** One throws away coffee **grounds** but never on the school **grounds.** A **grounder** is a baseball that stays on the

ground. The connection between an electric current or equipment and the earth is called a **ground.** At Burger King one can order a hamburger made from **ground** beef. To instruct someone in the basics is to **ground** them. An airplane is usually **grounded** in a bad storm. To be innovative is to break new **ground.** To make progress is to gain **ground.** In painting, the **ground** is the prep coat of paint on which a picture is to be painted.

Gum

Gum is something one chews in the mouth but also refers to foreign matter that clogs up a carburetor or some type of machinery. A man can sit under a **gum** tree and rest. This is especially true if his **gums** hurt. A sticky, adhesive substance from a plant is also called **gum.**

Race

Besides referring to whether or not one is black or white, the word **race** can mean a running event in which someone physically runs or a political contest between men who never set foot on a track. A **race** is also a circular piece of metal that a bearing rides on or an artificial water channel. To speed up a car engine is to **race** it and to do something fast is to **race** through it.

Run

A woman can get a **run** in her hose while a man can **run** a race. To associate with someone is to **run** with them. To resort to someone is to **run** to him. To operate a computer program is to **run** it. When different colors in a garment mix they are said to **run** just like letters written together are said to **run** together. When machinery is operating it is said to be **running.** An unbroken series is also said to be a **run.** To use up something is to **run** short of it. A **run** on a bank has nothing to do with a marathon. A range of variations is often called a **run.** If a building is dilapidated it is said to be **run** down just like if someone's character is attacked then he has been **run** down. But a pedestrian hit by a car is also said to be **run** down.

Spring

Not only can a **spring** can be found in the front end of a car, it is also a season between winter and summer. A pipe can **spring** a leak. One can also swim in a **spring**. To jump over something is to **spring** over it, but to leap into action is to **spring** into action. A door can **spring** shut. And the **spring** of the day is the first part of the day.

Trunk

A **trunk** can refer to luggage, the **trunk** of a tree, or the body of a person. The nose of an elephant is also called a **trunk**. The main artery of a railroad as well as the compartment in the back of a car is also termed a **trunk**. Short pants worn for swimming are likewise called **trunks.**

Appendix 12
Uniformity in Translating into English

In addition to the charge of containing archaic words, the AV is also regularly faulted for the lack of uniformity in its translation of Hebrew and Greek words. For example, a certain Hebrew word may appear in the Hebrew Old Testament thirty times and be rendered in the AV by five different words or phrases. The same is true for words in the Greek New Testament.

This charge is spurious on two accounts. First of all, the English language so rich and versatile that often times the use of a different word better conveys the proper meaning. Consider the various ways in English that one can say something is big:

big	huge
hefty	immense
major	mammoth
sizable	vast
hulking	monstrous
spacious	monumental
prodigious	fat
great	stupendous
voluminous	husky
oversize	enormous
gigantic	large

The second problem with this accusation is that every modern translation of the Bible violates the very standard that the AV is held to. Using Greek as an example, this appendix demonstrates the folly of insisting upon strict uniformity in the translation of multiple occurrences of the same Greek word into English when modern versions of the Bible do not even do so. The example given in this appendix is that of the Greek word *barbaros*, found five times in the Greek New Testament. The translations of the various forms of this word in the AV are given below in bold print immediately followed by the translation found in our four modern versions.

> And the **barbarous people** showed us no little kindness: for they kindled a fire, and received us every one, because of the present rain, and because of the cold. (Acts 28:2)
>
> And when the **barbarians** saw the *venomous* beast hang on his hand, they said among themselves, No doubt this man is a murderer, whom, though he hath escaped the sea, yet vengeance suffereth not to live. (Acts 28:4)
>
> I am debtor both to the Greeks, and to the **Barbarians;** both to the wise, and to the unwise. (Rom 1:14)
>
> Therefore if I know not the meaning of the voice, I shall be unto him that speaketh a **barbarian,** and he that speaketh *shall be* a **barbarian** unto me. (1 Cor 14:11)
>
> Where there is neither Greek nor Jew, circumcision nor uncircumcision, **Barbarian,** Scythian, bond *nor* free: but Christ *is* all, and in all. (Col 3:11)

	NRSV	NASB	NIV	NKJV
Acts 28:2	natives	natives	islanders	natives
Acts 28:4	natives	natives	islanders	natives
Rom 1:14	barbarians	barbarians	non-Greeks	barbarians
1 Cor 14:11	foreigner	barbarian	foreigner	foreigner
Col 3:11	barbarian	barbarian	barbarian	barbarian

Appendix 13
Archaic Personal Pronouns

The archaic personal pronouns *thou, thy, thine, thee,* and *ye* are particularly troublesome to critics of the AV and are normally replaced by forms of the word *you*. These words are usually the first to be cited by those who consider the AV to use archaic language. But although they have been deemed to be archaic, these words are grammatically more accurate. The word *ye,* as discussed in the main body of this work, technically expresses the nominative case of the second person, plural personal pronoun. The other forms are more precise because they indicate the second person singular.

Personal pronouns are those pronouns that change form in the different persons. No other part of speech has so many inflections as the personal pronoun. *Person* is a grammatical term applying to pronouns and verbs that indicates the roles of people and things. It is used to distinguish between the speaker (or writer), the one spoken to, and the one spoken about. *Number* is a grammatical term applying to nouns and pronouns that indicates whether one or more than one person or thing is being referred to. A word that refers to one person or thing is singular in number; a word that refers to more than one is plural in number. *Case* is a grammatical term applying to nouns and pronouns that indicates the relationship of these words to other words in a sentence. The subject of a sentence is always in the nominative case, the object referred to is in the objective case, and any being or thing indicated as possessing is in the possessive case. Thus, a personal pronoun has person, number, and case.

The first person indicates who is speaking:

I am writing this book.
This book is being written by me.

In this sentence, the pronouns *I* and *me* indicate that the author is the speaker. This is said to be the first person. The possessive pronouns in the singular are *my* and *mine*. If this book had more than one author then the first person plural would be used:

> We are writing this book.
> This book is being written by us.

In this sentence, the pronouns *we* and *us* indicate the first person. The possessive pronoun in the plural is *our*.

The second person indicates who is being spoken to:

> Thou art reading this book.
> This book is being read by thee.

In this sentence, the pronouns *thou* and *thee* indicate who is being spoken to. This is said to be the second person. The possessive pronouns in the singular are *thy* and *thine*. If this book was being read by more than one person then the second person plural would be used:

> Ye are reading this book.
> This book is being read by you.

In this sentence, the pronouns *ye* and *you* indicate the second person. The possessive pronoun in the plural is *your*.

The third person indicates who or what is being spoken about:

> He is reading this book.
> This book is being read by him.

In this sentence, the pronouns *he* and *him* indicate neither the author nor the one spoken to. This is said to be the third person. The possessive pronoun in the singular is *his*. If this book was being read by more than one person then the third person plural would be used:

> They are reading this book.
> This book is being read by them.

In this sentence, the pronouns *they* and *them* indicate the third person. The possessive pronoun in the plural is *their*.

Thus, when a Hebrew or Greek word is in the second person singular, a form of the word *thou* is the more accurate translation. And when a Hebrew or Greek word is in the second person plural, a form of the word ye is the more accurate translation. Reverence to God has nothing to do with using the words *thou, thy, thine, thee,* and *ye.* Good grammar, however, does.

Appendix 14
Archaic Verb Inflections

Many words in the AV that are dismissed as being archaic are not archaic at all—they merely have obsolete verb inflections. Inflection refers to changes made in the form of words to show their grammatical relationships. For nouns and pronouns this is called declension; for adjectives and adverbs, comparison; for verbs, conjugation. Typically deemed to be archaic due to obsolete verb inflections are words in the AV like the following:

couldest	eatest
shouldest	gavest
goest	lovedst
hast	durst
creepeth	sheddeth
liveth	pleaseth
seeth	aileth
hath	thinketh
believeth	cometh
judgest	knowest

Although languages like Latin and Greek are highly inflected, English has relatively few inflections. English verbs are inflected for tense, voice, mood, number, and person. Tense denotes action in relation to time—past, present, or future. Voice shows whether the verb's subject is acting or being acted upon. Thus, active or passive voice. Mood indicates the manner in which an action is expressed. The indicative mood states a fact. The subjunctive mood expresses a suggestion or contingency. The imperative mood gives a command or direction. These inflections are generally indicated by using other verbs called auxiliary verbs.

This would include words like *shall, will,* and forms of *have, do,* and *be.* With the exception of the irregular verb *be,* verbs are only inflected for number and person in the third person, singular present indicative. Hence, I *write* the book, you *read* it, they *read* it, but he *reads* it.

Older verb forms, however, like those of the aforementioned words, had special inflections in both the second and third person singular. The suffix *-est* denoted the second person singular and the suffix *-eth* denoted the third person singular. Sometimes the initial *e* in these forms was replaced by an apostrophe or dropped altogether. Some words had both forms: *doeth* and *doth; doest* and *dost.*

Thus, any verb in the AV with an *-est* or *-st* suffix, not just form, is in the second person singular. Likewise, any verb in the AV with an *-eth* or *-th* suffix, not just form, is in the third person singular. Both Hebrew and Greek inflect verbs in number and person. So, since the capability exists in the English second and third person singular, it should not be a problem when the AV does likewise.

Notes

Introduction

1. Jack P. Lewis, *The English Bible From KJV to NIV,* 2nd. ed. (Grand Rapids, Baker Book House, 1991), p.53.
2. Ibid., p.55.
3. Ibid.
4. D.A. Carson, *The King James Version Debate* (Grand Rapids: Baker Book House, 1979), p.101-102.
5. Lewis, p.40.

Chapter 1

1. Job 40:11; Is 31:4; Ezek 21:26; Dan 4:37.
2. 2 Cor 11:7.
3. Matt 23:12; Lk 14:11, 18:14; Phil 4:12.
4. Job 40:11; Ezek 21:26.
5. 2 Sam 6:22; Ps 44:9; Mal 2:9; Col 2:18.
6. Ezek 21:26.
7. 2 Sam 22:28; Ps 18:27; Is 2:9,11,12,17, 5:15, 10:33, 13:11; Mal 2:9; Col 2:18,23.
8. Phil 4:12.
9. Ezek 21:26.
10. Dan 4:37.
11. Phil 4:12.
12. Job 40:11.
13. Ezek 21:26.
14. Ezra 9:5.
15. Peter Steinhart, "Mud Wrestling," *Sierra,* Jan./Feb. 1993, p.54.
16. Gen 8:3,8,11; Lev 27:18; Deut 34:7; Jud 8:3.
17. Gen 8:3; Lev 27:18; Jud 8:3.
18. Gen 8:8,11; Jud 8:3.
19. Lev 27:18.
20. Gen 8:5.
21. Alan J. Heavens, "New Federal Law Renews Concern About Lead in

Homes, Paint, and Pipes," *Philadelphia Inquirer,* Nov. 3, 1994.
22. Ron Miller, "Seeds of Terror: World's 85 Million Land Mines Await Victims," *Washington Times,* Aug. 28, 1994.
23. 2 Ki 19:27; Is 37:28; Jn 14:23.
24. E.g., Gen 29:14; 2 Tim 4:20.
25. NASB: Job 5:3,24; Ps 68:16, 94:17; Is 34:13; Jer 31:23, Jude 6; NRSV: Ex 15:13; Deut 33:28; Ps 68:16, 76:2; Pro 3:33; Is 34:13; Jer 31:23.
26. Job 38:19; Is 33:20.
27. Jude 6.
28. Ps 61:7.
29. Amy Martin, "Why We Need Air Conditioning," *Garbage,* July/Aug. 1992, p.22-28.
30. 1 Tim 1:15, 4:9.
31. Pro 28:16.
32. Is 54:14.
33. Ezek 3:9; Zech 7:12.
34. Ibid.
35. Ibid.
36. Zech 7:12.
37. Ibid.
38. 1 Ki 22:16; 2 Chr 18:15; Matt 26:63; Mk 5:7; Acts 19:13.
39. Josh 6:26; 1 Sam 14:24.
40. Mk 5:7; Acts 19:13.
41. 1 Ki 2:42; Song 2:7, 3:5, 5:8,9, 8:4.
42. 1 Ki 22:16; 2 Chr 18:15; Matt 26:63; Acts 19:13.
43. Song 2:7, 3:5, 5:8,9; 1 Thes 5:27.
44. Lev 5:1.
45. Jos 6:26; 1 Sam 14:24; 1 Ki 22:16; 2 Chr 18:15; Matt 26:63; Acts 19:13.
46. Jos 6:26; 1 Sam 14:24; 1 Ki 22:16; Mk 5:7; Acts 19:13.
47. Bernard Imhasly, "Turmoil in India--Politics, Human Rights, Environment," *Swiss Review of World Affairs,* Aug. 1993, p.6-9.
48. Jude 16; Rev 17:6.
49. 2 Thes 1:10.
50. Phil 4:8.
51. Lee Dye, "In Search of the First Americans," *Los Angeles Times,* Dec. 5, 1993, sec. Magazine, p.34.
52. Katie Kerwin, "State Hedges on Pollution," *Rocky Mountain News,* Aug. 21, 1994, p.5A.
53. Num 24:14; Ruth 4:4.
54. Num 24:14.
55. Ruth 4:4.
56. William F. Allman, "The Dinosaur Hunter," *U.S. News & World Report,* June 7, 1993, p.62.
57. 2 Sam 24:13; 1 Chr 21:12.
58. *Black's Law Dictionary,* 1990 ed., s.v., "advisement."
59. *The Oxford English Dictionary,* 1989 edition, s.v., "advisement."

60. 1 Ki 3:1; 2 Chr 18:1; Ezra 9:14.
61. Ibid.
62. 1 Ki 3:1.
63. Claudia Levy, "Jazz Stylist, Scat Singer Carmen McRae Dies at 74," *Washington Post,* Nov. 12, 1994, p.D7.
64. Natalie Meisler, "Kearney Rides into WAC Sunset," *Denver Post,* June 26, 1994, p.B-11.
65. Deut 7:21; Job 18:20, 39:22; Is 21:4; Jer 51:32; Mk 16:5,6; Lk 24:37; Rev 11:13.
66. 2 Chr 32:18; Job 18:20, 39:22; Is 21:4; Lk 24:37.
67. NASB: 2 Chr 32:18; Lk 24:37.
68. NRSV: 2 Chr 32:18; Lk 24:37.
69. NIV: Lk 24:37.
70. Deut 7:21; 2 Chr 32:18; Job 18:20, 39:22; Is 21:14; Jer 51:32; Mk 16:5; Lk 24:37.
71. Deut 7:21; 2 Chr 32:18; Job 18:20, 39:22; Is 21:14; Jer 51:32; Mk 16:5.
72. Deut 7:21; Job 18:20, 39:22; Is 21:14; Mk 16:5; Lk 24:37.
73. E.g., Deut 18:22; Job 18:11.
74. E.g., Gen 42:35; Job 7:14.
75. E.g., Gen 20:8; Deut 28:26.
76. Song 7:5.
77. Mk 6:33; Acts 20:13.
78. Matt 14:13.
79. Acts 20:13.
80. Mark Trumbull, "Seattle Stands Ready to Reinvent Itself with Wealth of Ambitious Urban Projects," *Christian Science Monitor,* Nov. 17, 1994, sec. The U.S., p.3.
81. 2 Ki 20:4; Ps 129:6; Is 18:5; Ezek 33:22; Rom 1:2, 9:23; Eph 3:3.
82. Neh 13:5; Job 17:6; Is 52:4; Jer 30:20; Dan 6:10; Jn 9:13; Rom 15:4.
83. Mk 14:8.
84. 2 Ki 20:4; Ps 129:6; Is 18:5; Ezek 33:22.
85. Rom 1:2, 9:23.
86. 1 Tim 5:24,25; 1 Pet 1:11.
87. Eph 3:3.
88. Lev 14:11.
89. Deut 4:42, 19:4,6; Jos 20:5.
90. *MacLean's,* July 25, 1994, sec. Calendar, p.50.
91. J. Andrews, "Objection Sustained," *National Review,* June 10, 1991, p.42.
92. Robert Hendrickson, *Whistlin' Dixie: A Dictionary of Southern Expressions,* (New York: Facts on File, 1993), s.v., "afore."
93. O.E.D., s.v., "agone."
94. Deut 19:16.
95. Ezek 13:7; Phil 1:19.
96. Ibid.
97. Ibid.
98. Ibid.

99. Ibid.
100. Mary Anne Ostrom, "U.S. Plan to Aid Poor is Already Working Well in South Bay," *San Jose Mercury News*, Dec. 23, 1994.
101. Lk 11:48; Acts 24:15; Rom 7:15.
102. 1 Thes 2:4; Rom 14:22.
103. Num 30:5.
104. Num 30:5,8,11; 1 Pet 2:4,7.
105. Rom 14:22.
106. 1 Thes 2:4.
107. Lk 11:48.
108. Rom 7:15.
109. Accept—NKJV, NRSV: Acts 24:15; cherish—NASB: Acts 24:15.
110. 2 Cor 13:7.
111. Rom 2:18.
112. Whistlin' Dixie, p.9.
113. Matt 6:1,2,3,4; Lk 11:41, 12:33; Acts 3:2,3,10, 10:2,4,31, 24:17.
114. Acts 9:36.
115. Matt 6:1.
116. Lk 11:41, 12:33.
117. Matt 6:2,3,4; Acts 3:2,3,10, 10:2,4,31, 24:17.
118. Acts 10:4,31, 24:17.
119. Matt 6:2,3.
120. Lk 11:41, 12:33.
121. Matt 6:4; Acts 3:2,3,10, 9:36.
122. Acts 10:2.
123. Ibid.
124. Lk 11:41, 12:33; Acts 3:2,3,10, 10:2,4,32, 24:17.
125. Matt 6:1,2,3,4; Acts 9:36.
126. 1 Cor 13:1; Col 3:14.
127. Oswald Iten, "Friendly Contact," *Swiss Review of World Affairs*, July 1993, p.15-20.
128. Jud 16:14.
129. 2 Chr 20:22.
130. NRSV, NKJV, NASB: 2 Chr 13:13.
131. Jn 10:18, 12:49.
132. *Black's Law Dictionary*, s.v., "amerce," "amercement."
133. Dan 11:43.
134. Mark O'Keefe, "Founding Father," *Oregonian*, Nov. 1, 1994, p.A01.
135. *Black's Law Dictionary*, s.v., "amicus curiae."
136. 2 Chr 6:37; Dan 3:29; Lk 23:41; James 4:3.
137. Dan 3:29; James :3.
138. Job 5:24.
139. 2 Chr 6:37; Dan 3:29; Lk 23:41; James 4:3.
140. 2 Chr 6:37; Lk 23:41; James 4:3.
141. Dan 3:29.
142. Jane E. Stevens, "From Giant Ice Pack, a Loop That May Help Cool Earth," *Washington Post*, Oct. 17, 1994, p.A3.

143. Rick Pearson, "Edgar's Budget Gets a Jolt From U.S. Regulators," *Chicago Tribune*, Oct. 1, 1994, sec. News, p.1.
144. Ezra 3:12; Job 12:12; Is 3:2,5, 9:15, 47:6; Ezek 9:6.
145. 1 Sam 24:13; Ps 119:100, Is 3:14, 24:33; Jer 19:1; Ezek 7:26, 8:11,12, 27:9.
146. Ezra 3:12.
147. Job 12:12.
148. Is 3:2.
149. Heb 11:2.
150. Job 22:15.
151. 2 Ki 12:5.
152. Is 19:8; Hab 1:15.
153. Is 19:8.
154. Kevin Spear, "Exotic Plants Spread Like Disease," *Orlando Sentinel*, March 17, 1994, p.C1.
155. Matt 13:20; Mk 1:30.
156. NASB, NRSV, NKJV: Matt 13:20; NASB: Mk 1:30.
157. NIV: Matt 13:20; NRSV, NKJV: Mk 1:30.
158. Mk 1:30.
159. 2 Sam 18:25; Ps 68:12; Jer 46:5.
160. NIV: Ps 68:12; NRSV, NIV: Jer 46:5.
161. 2 Sam 18:25.
162. Alice Dembner, "Council Aims to Upgrade, Coordinate State Colleges Plan Targets Standards, Aid and Accountability," *Boston Globe*, Sept. 21, 1994.
163. Ex 30:25,35, 37:29; 2 Chr 16:14; Ecc 10:1.
164. Neh 3:8.
165. Mark Jaffe, "Tigers, Rhinoceri Threatened by Medical Trade," *Philadelphia Inquirer*, Nov. 13, 1994.
166. E.g., Jud 17:10; Acts 1:10.
167. 2 Sam 13:18; Lk 7:25.
168. 2 Sam 1:24.
169. Deut 22:5; Zec 3:4,5.
170. 2 Sam 1:24; Ezra 3:10; Is 63:1,2; Acts 12:21.
171. Lk 24:4.
172. 2 Sam 1:24.
173. Est 6:8.
174. Ezra 3:10.
175. Est 5:1.
176. Acts 12:21.
177. Acts 1:10.
178. David Hage, "Unions Feel the Heat," *U.S. News & World Report*, Jan. 24, 1994, p.57.
179. Num 16:30; Jer 10:7.
180. Lev 6:5; 2 Chr 26:18.
181. Num 16:32,33; Neh 2:8.
182. Neh 2:8.

183. Justin Martin, "The Rest of the Major Cities," *Fortune*, Nov. 14, 1994, p.124.
184. Ps 50:23, 78:8; Pro 15:2, 23:31; Jer 8:6.
185. Ps 50:23, 78:8; Jer 8:6.
186. Pro 11:5.
187. Pro 15:2.
188. Ps 50:23.
189. Ibid.
190. Jer 8:6.
191. Ps 90:12.
192. Virginia C. Holmgren, "The Unheralded Story of Columbus," *Sea Frontiers*, Feb. 1992, p.34-41.
193. Jer 38:12; Ezek 13:18.
194. Diane Ackerman, "Whales," *Ocean Realm*, Sept. 1993, p.60-75.
195. Ex 30:25, 35; 2 Chr 16:14; Acts 17:29.
196. E.g., Gen 16:13; Rev 16:5.
197. Gen 16:13; Num 11:15.
198. Gen 4:22; Is 3:3.
199. 1 Chr 29:5; 2 Chr 34:11.
200. 1 Chr 29:5; 2 Chr 34:11; Is 3:3.
201. Gen 4:22; 1 Chr 29:5; 2 Chr 34:11.
202. Is 3:3.
203. Ibid.
204. 1 Chr 29:5; 2 Chr 34:11; Is 3:3.
205. O.E.D., s.v., "artificer."
206. Michael Heyward, "Parallel Universes," *New Republic*, April 10, 1995, p.38.
207. David Zurawik and Christina Stoehr, "Money Changes Everything," *American Journalism Review*, April 1993, p.26-30.
208. Ex 30:25,35.
209. 2 Chr 2:7.
210. Nina J. Easton, "The Law of the School Yard," *Los Angeles Times*, Oct. 2, 1994, sec. Magazine, p.16.
211. Deut 4:34; 1 Sam 17:39; Acts 9:26, 16:7.
212. Job 4:2; Heb 11:29.
213. Job 4:2.
214. Jer 6:27.
215. Ibid.
216. Dale C. Moss, "Out of Balance," *Student Lawyer*, Oct. 1991, p.19-23.
217. Acts 24:9.
218. Ibid.
219. Ibid.
220. Robert W. Stewart, "Lost in Space," *Los Angeles Times*, May 13, 1990, p.D1.
221. Gen 8:1; Job 16:6.
222. Gen 8:1.
223. Job 16:5,6.

224. Gen 8:1.
225. Job 16:5.
226. Gen 8:1.
227. Job 16:5,6.
228. Gen 8:1.
229. Job 15:5,6.
230. Alan Sipress, "Despite Last-minute Dispute, Rabin, Arafat Sign Palestinian Accord," *Philadelphia Inquirer,* May 4, 1994.
231. E.g., Job 17:8; Dan 4:19.
232. Ezek 4:17.
233. Ezra 9:3; Is 52:14; Jer 14:9; Ezek 4:17; Dan 4:19,5:9.
234. Job 17:8; Jer 14:9; Dan 3:24, 4:19, 5:9.
235. Is 52:14; Jer 14:9; Dan 3:24, 5:9.
236. 2 Chr 6:40, 7:15.
237. Neh 1:6,11, 8:3; Ps 130:2; Lk 19:48.
238. Lk 19:48.
239. Jer 36:22.
240. Pro 28:8.
241. Karen Kucher, "Hurdles Reportedly Cleared for Transfer of Dolphins to Florida," *San Diego Union-Tribune,* Nov. 13, 1994, p.B-3.
242. Lk 19:21,22.
243. Ibid.
244. Jim Killackey, "College Woes Widespread," *Daily Oklahoman,* Nov. 13, 1994, sec. News, p.27.
245. Ann Devroy, "President Plots a Course Toward the Political Mainstream," *Washington Post,* Nov. 20, 1994, p.A12.
246. Deut 26:17,18.
247. Ibid.
248. Ps 83:14.
249. 1 Cor 7:9.
250. Is 42:25.
251. Deut 32:22.
252. Matt 3:16.
253. Pro 15:18.
254. Deut 32:13.
255. Ezek 40:18.
256. Gen 49:3.
257. Is 1:13; Jn 19:15; Acts 21:36, 22:22; Lk 23:18.
258. Jn 19:15; Acts 21:36, 22:22; Lk 23:18.
259. Acts 22:22.
260. Jn 19:15.
261. Lk 23:18; Acts 21:36.
262. 1 Ki 7:32,33.
263. 1 Ki 7:32.
264. 1 Ki 7:33.
265. 1 Ki 7:32,33.
266. Gen 40:6.

267. Hos 9:7.

Chapter 2

1. Ps 15:3; Rom 1:30.
2. Pro 25:23.
3. 2 Cor 12:20.
4. Ps 15:3; Pro 25:23; Rom 1:30; 2 Cor 12:20.
5. Pro 25:23.
6. Pro 15:3; Rom 1:30.
7. Frank Deford, "The Rabbit Hunter," *Sports Illustrated,* Jan. 10, 1994, p.68.
8. Matt 17:20.
9. 2 Pet 3:9.
10. David Gonzalez, "Death Row," *Vibe,* May 1994, p.66-71.
11. Song 2:4.
12. Ibid.
13. 1 Pet 4:3.
14. Ibid.
15. Ibid.
16. John Powers, "Feeling the Pinch," *Boston Globe,* Oct. 14, 1990, sec. Magazine, p.17.
17. 1 Cor 14:11; Col 3:11.
18. Acts 28:4; Rom 1:14.
19. Acts 28:4; Rom 1:14; 1 Cor 14:11; Col 3:11.
20. Acts 28:4; Rom 1:14; 1 Cor 14:11.
21. Acts 28:4; Rom 1:14; 1 Cor 14:11.
22. Acts 28:4; Rom 1:14.
23. Jared Diamond, "Speaking with a Single Tongue," *Discover,* Feb. 1993, p.78-85.
24. Deut 23:2; Zec 9:6; Heb 12:8.
25. Heb 12:8; NRSV, NKJV, NASB: Deut 23:2.
26. Deut 23:2; Zec 9:6; Heb 12:8.
27. Deut 23:2.
28. David W. Murray, "Poor Suffering Bastards," *Policy Review,* Spring 1994, p.9.
29. Deut 22:8; Jer 5:10.
30. Deut 22:8.
31. Jer 5:10.
32. Bill Dietrich, "Deep Divide," *Seattle Times/Post-Intelligencer,* July 14, 1991, sec. Magazine, p.10.
33. Lk 1:22, 5:7; Jn 13:24; Acts 19:33, 21:40, 24:10.
34. Acts 12:17, 13:16.
35. Lk 1:22.
36. Lk 1:22, 24:10; Jn 13:24; Acts 12:17.
37. Jn 13:24; Acts 19:33, 21:40, 24:10.
38. Is 13:2, 49:22.

39. John Steele Gordon, "Land of the Free Trade," *American Heritage*, July/Aug. 1993, p.50-61.
40. Liz Dolinar, "Ethnobotany: How People Use Plants," *American Horticulturist*, March 1991, p.8-11.
41. Lev 22:19; Num 31:28,30,33,38,44; Deut 3:11.
42. Ibid.
43. Lev 22:21.
44. Lev 22:19; Lev 22:21.
45. Num 31:28,30,33,38,44.
46. 1 Pet 2:18.
47. E.g., Deut 2:12; Acts 8:9.
48. NASB, NRSV: 1 Sam 9:9; 2 Sam 7:10.
49. Josh 20:5.
50. Is 41:26.
51. 1 Tim 5:25.
52. Is 28:19.
53. 1 Ki 18:45; Lk 12:1; Jn 4:31.
54. Acts 22:6.
55. Ezek 12:4.
56. Num 9:21.
57. Job 5:14.
58. 1 Ki 2:5.
59. Zech 10:1.
60. E.g., Gen 17:20; Ezek 47:22.
61. E.g., Gen 5:4; Rev 1:5.
62. Gen 48:6; Is 45:10.
63. Pro 17:21, 23:24; Ecc 5:14.
64. Heb 1:6; Rev 1:5.
65. Gen 4:18; 1 Jn 5:1.
66. Pro 23:22.
67. Ecc 6:3; Jer 16:3.
68. Deut 32:18; Ps 23:22.
69. 2 Ki 20:18; Is 39:7; Jer 16:3.
70. Job 38:28; Heb 5:5.
71. Is 45:10.
72. Jn 1:14,18, 3:16,18; Acts 13:33; Heb 1:5, 5:5; 1 Jn 4:9.
73. Mary Loftus, "The Other Side of Fame," *Psychology Today*, May/June 1995, p.48.
74. "Fit—But Foul," *Psychology Today*, May/June 1995, p.18.
75. L.J. Davis, "The Name of Rose," *New Republic*, April 4, 1994, p.14.
76. O.E.D., s.v., "belie."
77. Mary Ann French, "The Open Wound," *Washington Post*, Nov. 22, 1992, p.F1.
78. Jer 15:5, 16:5, 22:10; Jer 48:17; Nah 3:7.
79. Job 42:11.
80. Jer 31:18.
81. Job 42:11.

82. Jer 15:5, 16:5, 22:10; Nah 3:7.
83. Job 42:11; Jer 16:5.
84. Jer 31:18; Nah 3:7.
85. Jer 15:5, 22:10, 48:17.
86. Jer 15:5, 22:10, 48:17; Nah 3:7.
87. Job 42:11; Jer 16:5, 31:8.
88. James Q. Wilson, "What Is Moral, and How Do We Know It?" *Commentary*, June 1993, p.37-43.
89. E.g., Ps 116:4; Rom 12:1.
90. Matt 8:5; Mk 1:40; Lk 7:3.
91. Ps 80:14; Rom 12:1.
92. 1 Sam 23:11; Ps 118:25.
93. E.g., 2 Ki 20:3; Neh 1:5,11; Ps 80:14, 110:14, 118:25; Is 38:3; Matt 9:38; Mk 1:40; Lk 10:2.
94. Matt 9:38; Lk 10:2.
95. Phil 1:10, 1 Thes 4:10; Phil 4:2; 2 Cor 6:1; Rom 15:30.
96. Seymour M. Hersh, "The Wild West," *Atlantic Monthly*, June 1994, p.61.
97. NKJV, NIV, NRSV: 1 Ki 19:4.
98. 2 Chr 15:18.
99. Anastasia Toufexis, "The Dirty Seas," *Time*, Aug. 1, 1988, p.44-50.
100. 1 Ki 8:47; 2 Chr 6:37.
101. Amy Martin, "Why We Need Air Conditioning," *Garbage*, July/Aug. 1992, p.22-28.
102. Gen 26:31; 2 Chr 36:15; Job 8:5, 24:5; Pro 13:24.
103. Gen 26:31.
104. NRSV: 2 Chr 36:15.
105. NASB: Pro 13:24.
106. NKJV: Job 8:5.
107. NKJV: Pro 13:24.
108. Job 8:5.
109. Morris Freedman, "Harold Agonistes," *American Scholar*, Summer 1995, p.444.
110. Laura Hilgers, "Catch Me If You Can," *Health*, Jan./Feb. 1994, p.30.
111. E.g., Gen 30:36; Phil 1:23.
112. Phil 1:23.
113. Marney Rich Keenan, "Mother's Nature: There Isn't Any Harder Job Than Leaving Baby Behind," *Detroit News*, May 12, 1990, p.C1.
114. Lev 10:6; Deut 21:13; Jud 11:37; Is 16:9; 2 Cor 12:21; Rev 18:9.
115. Jer 4:31.
116. Jud 11:38; Lk 8:52, 23:27.
117. Lev 10:6.
118. Jud 11:37,38; Gen 37:35.
119. Lev 10:6; Jud 11:37,38; Is 16:9; Jer 4:31.
120. Deut 21:13; Rev 18:9.
121. NASB, NIV: Jud 11:37; NIV, NASB: Jud 11:38; NRSV, NASB, NIV: Is 16:9.

122. Deut 21:13; NRSV, NASB, NKJV: 2 Cor 12:1; NIV, NKJV: Lk 8:52.
123. Jer 4:31.
124. Lk 23:27.
125. Gen 37:35.
126. Delos B. McKown, "Demythologizing Natural Human Rights," *Humanist*, May/June 1989, p.21.
127. Acts 8:9,10; Gal 3:1.
128. Acts 8:9,10.
129. Ibid.
130. Gal 3:1.
131. John Steele Gordon, "Land of the Free Trade," *American Heritage*, July/Aug. 1993, p.50-61.
132. Pro 27:16;, 29:24; Matt 26:73.
133. Is 16:3; Matt 26:73.
134. Matt 26:73.
135. Ps 38:8.
136. Is 28:7.
137. Dan 5:19.
138. Thomas A. Bailey and David M. Kennedy, *The American Pageant*, 10th ed., (Lexington: D.C. Heath and Company, 1994), p.532.
139. Ibid, p.624.
140. 2 Sam 3:31; Lk 7:14.
141. Lk 7:14.
142. NIV, NRSV: 2 Chr 16:14.
143. Malcolm Brabant, "Worldwide Report: Death," *BBC Worldwide*, Sept. 1994, p.20.
144. Acts 1:20; 1 Tim 3:1.
145. Ibid.
146. Phil 1:1; 1 Tim 3:2; Titus 1:7.
147. 1 Pet 2:25.
148. Phil 1:1; 1 Tim 3:2; Titus 1:7.
149. 1 Pet 2:25.
150. Phil 1:1; 1 Tim 3:2; Titus 1:7.
151. 1 Pet 2:25.
152. Ibid.
153. Is 14:23, 34:11; Zep 2:14.
154. Ibid.
155. Is 14:23, 34:11.
156. Zep 2:14.
157. Is 34:11; Zep 2:14.
158. Is 14:23.
159. Is 14:23, 34:11.
160. Zep 2:14.
161. Ella D. Sorensen and Charles E. Dibble, "An Aztec Bestiary," *Audubon*, Jan./Feb. 1993, p.50-55.
162. Song 1:6.
163. Roger Field, "Dr. Parkinson's Disease," *American Health*, Sept.

1991, p.54-58.
164. Ex 9:9,10.
165. NASB, NKJV: Ex 9:9,10.
166. NRSV, NIV: Ex 9:9,10.
167. *Stedman's Medical Dictionary,* 24th ed., s.v., "blain."
168. Deut 28:22; 1 Ki 8:37; 2 Chr 6:28; Amos 4:9; Hag 2:17.
169. 1 Ki 8:37; 2 Chr 6:28.
170. NKJV: Deut 28:22.
171. NASB: Amos 4:9.
172. NRSV: Hag 2:17.
173. Jonathan Weisman, "Tilting at Windmills," *Wildlife Conservation,* Jan./Feb. 1994, p.52-57.
174. Bruce Wallace, "Death Returns to the Killing Fields," *Maclean's,* March 1, 1993, p.32.
175. Bruce C. Murray, "Exploring the Limits: Humanity's Future in Space," *Planetary Report,* Sept./Oct. 1992, p.12-15.
176. William Hively, "How Bleak Is the Outlook for Ozone?" *American Scientist,* May/June 1989, p.219-224.
177. *Black's Medical Dictionary,* 33rd ed., s.v., "blue disease," "cyanosis."
178. "Medicines as Close as Your Door," *Mother Earth News,* June/July 1995, p.46.
179. Joel Garbus, "The Life Story of a Tomato," *EPA Journal,* May/June 1990, p.23-27.
180. 1 Sam 19:13,16, 26:7,11,12,16.
181. Ibid.
182. Okey Ndibe, "Can African Americans Save Africa," *African World,* Nov./Dec. 1993, p.4-19.
183. E.g., Gen 43:18; Jer 34:13.
184. Gen 21:10,12,13; Gal 4:23,30,31.
185. Gen 44:33; Deut 15:15, 16:12, 24:18,22; Rev 6:15.
186. Deut 28:68; 2 Chr 28:10; Est 7:4.
187. Lev 19:20; Gal 4:22.
188. Lev 25:39; 1 Ki 9:21; Lev 25:44.
189. Deut 24:18; Rev 6:15.
190. Lev 25:39.
191. Deut 28:68; 2 Chr 28:10; Est 7:4.
192. Lev 25:44.
193. Gen 43:18; 2 Ki 4:1.
194. Jer 34:13; Deut 7:8.
195. 1 Ki 9:21.
196. Lev 19:20.
197. E.g., Jos 9:23; Ezra 9:9.
198. Rom 1:1; Gal 1:10; Phil 2:7; Col 4:12; Titus 1:1; James 1:1; 2 Pet 1:1; Jude 1.
199. Lev 25:39.
200. 2 Cor 4:5; Eph 6:5,6; Phil 1:1; Col 3:22, 4:1; 1 Tim 6:1; Titus 2:9; 1

Pet 2:16.
- 201. Gal 4:22.
- 202. Gal 4:23,30,31.
- 203. Gen 21:10,12,13.
- 204. Gal 4:22.
- 205. Gen 21:10.
- 206. Gal 4:30.
- 207. Lk 1:38,48; Col 4:12.
- 208. Gen 21:12.
- 209. Ex 11:5; Jud 9:18.
- 210. 2 Sam 13:34.
- 211. Ex 26:1.
- 212. *Stedman's Medical Dictionary,* s.v., "boss."
- 213. Peter Robinson, "Ferrari P355 Spider," *Car & Driver,* Sept. 1995, p.83.
- 214. Deut 28:27, 28:35.
- 215. Ibid.
- 216. Job 2:7.
- 217. *Webster's Third New International Dictionary,* 1986 ed., s.v., "botch."
- 218. E.g., 2 Chr 21:18,19; Phil 1:8.
- 219. 2 Cor 6:12.
- 220. Phile 7,12,20.
- 221. Job 20:14.
- 222. NRSV, NKJV: 2 Sam 20:10.
- 223. NIV, NRSV, NKJV: Gen 15:4.
- 224. NIV: 2 Sam 20:10; NKJV: 2 Chr 11:15.
- 225. Ps 71:6.
- 226. Num 5:22.
- 227. 2 Sam 20:10.
- 228. NRSV: Num 5:22; 2 Chr 21:15,18,19; Acts 1:18.
- 229. NASB: 2 Chr 21:15,18,19; Acts 1:18.
- 230. NIV: 2 Chr 21:15,18,19.
- 231. Num 5:22.
- 232. Wayne Campbell, "Probing the Neutrino Universe," *Canadian Geographic,* March/April 1994, p.46-54.
- 233. Job 6:5; Pro 27:22.
- 234. Job 30:7.
- 235. Job 6:5.
- 236. Job 30:7.
- 237. Job 6:5.
- 238. Job 30:7.
- 239. Pro 27:22.
- 240. Job 28:18.
- 241. Ex 28:42, 39:28; Lev 6:10, 16:4; Ezek 44:18.
- 242. Ibid.
- 243. Ibid.

244. Ex 28:22, 39:28.
245. Lev 6:10, 16:4; Ezek 44:18.
246. Nicholas Dawidoff, "Field of Kitsch: Is Nostalgia Wrecking Baseball?" *New Republic,* Aug. 17 & 24, 1992, p.22-24.
247. *Stedman's Medical Dictionary,* s.v., "labour."
248. 2 Sam 12:31; Jer 43:9; Nah 3:14.
249. NRSV, NKJV: 2 Sam 12:31; NIV: Nah 3:14.
250. NRSV, NASB: Nah 3:14.
251. NRSV, NIV: Jer 43:9.
252. NIV: 2 Sam 12:31.
253. Jer 43:9.
254. NKJV: Jer 43:9.
255. NASB: 2 Sam 12:31; NKJV: Nah 3:14.
256. Ex 9:8,10.
257. Ex 9:8,10, 19:18.
258. Jer 46:4.
259. Jer 46:4, 51:3.
260. Ibid.
261. Ibid.
262. E.g., Gen 19:24; Rev 21:8.
263. Ps 11:6; Ezek 38:22; Lk 17:29; Rev 14:10, 19:20, 20:10, 21:8.
264. O.E.D., s.v., "brimstone."
265. Gen 19:24; Ezek 38:22; Rev 14:10, 19:20, 20:10, 21:8.
266. Is 30:33; Ezek 38:22; Lk 17:9; Rev 14:10, 19:20, 20:10, 21:8.
267. Richard Mathews, "Japanese Happy to have Leaders Picked for Them," *Atlanta Journal & Constitution,* Nov. 1, 1987, p.19.
268. Diane Ackerman, "Whales," *Ocean Realm,* Sept. 1993, p.60-75.
269. NRSV, NASB: Acts 5:12; NIV: 1 Ki 6:3; NKJV: 1 Ki 7:6.
270. 1 Ki 7:6.
271. Ex 28:4; Ezek 16:10,13,18, 26:16, 27:7,16, 27:24.
272. Ex 28:4.
273. Ezek 16:10,13,18, 26:16, 27:7,16, 27:24.
274. Ex 28:39.
275. Ezra 4:19.
276. Jer 10:22; Nah 3:19.
277. NRSV, NIV, NKJV: Nah 3:19.
278. NASB, NIV, NKJV: Jer 10:22.
279. Lev 25:39.
280. E.g., Ps 92:6; Ezek 21:31.
281. NKJV, NIV, NASB: Ps 49:10, 92:6, 94:8.
282. Jer 51:17; NRSV, NASB: Is 19:11; Jer 10:8,14,21; Pro 12:1.
283. Pro 12:1.
284. Is 19:11; Jer 10:8.
285. Pro 30:2.
286. Ezek 21:31.
287. Ps 49:10, 92:6, 94:8.
288. Ezek 21:31.

Notes 471

289. Laura Saunders, "Yellow Lights and Red Lights," *Forbes,* March 27, 1995, p.92.
290. E.g., Ps 91:4; Pro 2:7.
291. 2 Chr 23:9; Job 15:26; Song 4:4; Ezek 38:4, 39:9.
292. 2 Sam 22:31; 1 Chr 5:18; Job 15:26; Ps 18:2,30; Pro 2:7.
293. Ps 35:2; NASB, NKJV, NRSV: Jer 46:3; NASB, NKJV, NRSV: Ezek 23:24; NRSV, NKJV: Ps 91:4.
294. Ezek 23:24.
295. Ps 91:4.
296. Ibid.
297. Ps 35:2, 91:4; Song 4:4; Jer 46:3; Ezek 23:24, 38:4, 39:9.
298. Ps 35:2, 91:4; Song 4:4; Jer 46:3; Ezek 23:24, 38:4, 39:9.
299. Ps 35:2; Jer 46:3; Ezek 23:24, 38:4, 39:9.
300. Ps 35:2.
301. Ezek 38:5.
302. "Swashing His Buckler," *Economist,* July 1, 1995, p.38.
303. Mk 14:65; 2 Cor 12:7.
304. Matt 26:27; 1 Cor 4:11; 1 Pet 2:20.
305. NKJV, NASB: Matt 26:27; NKJV, NASB: Mk 14:65; NRSV, NKJV: 1 Cor 4:11; NRSV, NIV, NKJV: 1 Pet 2:20.
306. NASB: 1 Cor 4:11.
307. NIV: 1 Cor 4:11.
308. NIV, NRSV: 2 Cor 12:7.
309. NRSV: Mk 14:65.
310. NRSV, NIV: Matt 26:27; NIV: Mk 14:65.
311. NKJV, NASB: 2 Cor 12:7.
312. Richard G. Teske, "The Star That Blew a Hole in Space--Geninga: The Gamma-Ray Pulsar," *Astronomy,* Dec. 1993, p.31-37.
313. Ex 2:3; Is 18:2.
314. Is 58:5.
315. NRSV, NIV: Ex 2:3.
316. NASB, NIV: Is 58:5; NKJV: Is 18:2.
317. Ex 2:3.
318. Ex 2:3; Is 58:5.
319. Is 58:5.
320. Bjorn Sletto, "Prairie Potholes," *Earth,* May 1994, p.40-44.
321. 2 Sam 16:1; 1 Chr 12:40; Is 30:6.
322. Is 30:6.
323. 2 Sam 16:1; 1 Chr 12:40.
324. Is 30:6.
325. 2 Sam 16:1; 1 Chr 12:40.
326. Ibid
327. Ibid.
328. Ibid.
329. NASB, NRSV, NKJV: Acts 1:25; NASB, NKJV: Gal 2:8; Rom 1:5; 1 Cor 9:2.
330. NKJV, NASB: Lk 16:2,3,4.

331. 1 Tim 4:14.
332. 1 Sam 10:16,25, 11:14, 14:47; 2 Chr 13:5; Dan 5:18, 7:14,27.
333. 1 Sam 10:16,25, 11:14; 2 Chr 13:5.
334. Dan 11:12.
335. Num 33:1; Ps 109:8; Acts 1:20; Rom 12:8.
336. Matt 13:21; Mk 1:25; Lk 17:7, 21:9.
337. NASB, NKJV, NRSV: Matt 13:21, Mk 6:25.
338. NKJV, NRSV: Mk 6:25.
339. NIV: Matt 13:21.
340. NIV: Mk 6:25.
341. NASB: Mk 6:25.

Chapter 3

1. Job 39:1; Ps 29:9.
2. Jer 14:5; Job 21:10.
3. Job 21:10.
4. Job 21:10, 39:1.
5. Job 21:10, 39:1; Ps 29:9.
6. 1 Sam 6:7.
7. Peter Steinhart, "In the Blood of Cheetahs," Audubon, March/April 1992, p.40.
8. James 5:3.
9. Joel 1:4, 2:25; Nah 3:15,16.
10. 2 Tim 2:17.
11. James 5:3.
12. NRSV: Joel 1:4.
13. NASB: Joel 2:25.
14. NIV: Joel 1:14.
15. NIV: Joel 1:14.
16. NKJV: Joel 1:14.
17. Deut 28:42.
18. Joel Garbus, "The Life Story of a Tomato," *EPA Journal,* May/June 1990, p.23.
19. Ellen Mason Exum, "Healing Earth: Tree in a Coma," *American Forests,* Nov./Dec. 1992, p.20.
20. Ex 28:17, 39:10; Ezek 28:13.
21. Is 54:12.
22. Ex 28:17, 39:10.
23. Ezek 1:26, 28:13.
24. Ex 39:10.
25. Rev 4:3.
26. Job 22:24.
27. E.g., 1 Sam 10:2; 1 Pet 5:7.
28. E.g., 2 Ki 4:13; Titus 3:8.
29. Jud 18:7; Is 32:9,10,11; Ezek 30:9.

30. Ps 142:4; Jn 12:6; Acts 18:17.
31. E.g., Deut 11:12; 1 Pet 5:7.
32. Deut 15:5; Micah 1:12; Phil 2:28; Heb 12:17.
33. Ezek 12:18,19; 1 Cor 7:32; 2 Cor 7:11.
34. Is 47:8; Ezek 39:6; Zep 2:15.
35. Mk 4:19; Lk 8:14, 21:34.
36. 1 Sam 9:5.
37. Matt 22:16; Mk 4:38, 12:14.
38. 2 Sam 22:6.
39. E.g., Rom 7:14; Heb 9:10.
40. Lev 18:20, 19:20; Num 5:13; Rom 8:6.
41. Lev 19:20.
42. E.g., Rom 7:14; 2 Cor 10:4.
43. Lev 18:20, 19:20; Num 5:13; Rom 8:6.
44. Gen 19:5; Jud 19:22.
45. NRSV, NASB: 1 Cor 3:1.
46. NIV: 1 Cor 3:1.
47. Rom 15:27.
48. NASB, NRSV: Num 5:13.
49. NIV, NRSV: Lev 18:20.
50. Charles Ward, "The Ultimate in Rock 'n' Roll," *Houston Chronicle,* May 20, 1989, p.1E.
51. Russ Rymer, "The Life," *Health,* Nov./Dec. 1992, p.58.
52. Jud 18:21; 1 Sam 17:22.
53. Is 10:28, 46:1; Acts 21:15.
54. Is 46:1.
55. NRSV: Jud 18:21.
56. NASB: Jud 18:21.
57. NASB: 1 Sam 17:22.
58. NIV: Jud 18:21.
59. NRSV: Is 46:1.
60. NKJV: Is 10:28.
61. NIV: Is 10:28.
62. Rev 18:13.
63. E.g., Ex 29:13; Lev 9:19.
64. Hos 13:8.
65. Is 3:18.
66. Ibid.
67. Ex 29:13; Lev 9:19.
68. P. Barber, "The Real Vampire," *Natural History,* Oct. 1990, p.74.
69. Harry Y. McSween, Jr., "A Goddess Unveiled," *Natural History,* Nov. 1993, p.60.
70. 2 Chr 3:5; Jer 22:14; Ezek 41:16, Hag 1:4.
71. 1 Ki 6:15.
72. Jer 22:14; Hag 1:4.
73. NRSV: 2 Chr 3:5; NIV: Ezek 41:16.
74. Ex 25:20.

75. 2 Pet 2:10; Jude 8.
76. Kathy Sawyer, "Comet Leaves a Trail of Data in Its Wake," *Washington Post,* July 24, 1994, p.A4.
77. Hos 2:10.
78. Ezek 40:29.
79. Michael LeBerre and Raymond Ramousse, "Marmots of the French Alps," *Earthwatch,* Jan./Feb. 1995, p.48.
80. David L. Matheny, "Fitness Q & A," *Bicycling,* July 1994, p.34.
81. E.g., 1 Ki 7:16; Jer 52:22.
82. E.g., Ex 36:38; Jer 52:22.
83. 1 Ki 7:16; Jer 52:22.
84. Ex 36:38, 38:17,19,28.
85. 1 Ki 7:17.
86. Ezek 27:9,27.
87. Lk 12:58.
88. 1 Thes 2:14.
89. E.g., Num 7:13; Mk 6:28.
90. Num 7:84; Ezra 1:9.
91. Num 7:84; Mk 6:28.
92. Ezra 1:9.
93. Num 7:84.
94. Ezra 1:9.
95. Num 7:84.
96. Num 7:13.
97. Mk 6:28.
98. Pro 30:33.
99. E.g., 1 Cor 8:1; Rev 2:19.
100. Rom 14:15.
101. 1 Cor 8:1; Rev 2:19.
102. NKJV: Matt 6:1; NASB: Lk 11:41.
103. Rev 12:15.
104. Ex 17:2; Jud 8:1; Ps 103:9.
105. Ex 17:7.
106. Gen 31:36; Num 20:3.
107. NASB, NIV, NRSV: Ex 17:2.
108. NIV: Jud 8:1.
109. NASB: Ps 103:9.
110. NRSV: Jud 8:1.
111. NKJV: Ex 17:2.
112. Jud 8:15, Matt 11:20; Mk 16:14; James 1:5.
113. Jud 8:15; Matt 11:20; James 1:5.
114. Michael Kranish, "After the War--At Home, An Unconquered Recession," *Boston Globe,* March 6, 1991, p.1.
115. Dan 8:7, 11:11.
116. Ibid.
117. William F. Buckley, Jr., "Nixon and the Haldeman Diaries," *National Review,* June 27, 1994, p.70.

118. Is 32:5,7.
119. 1 Sam 25:3.
120. Is 32:5,7.
121. Ibid.
122. 1 Sam 25:3.
123. R.T. Lambdin, "Chaucer's The Miller's Tale," *Explicator*, Fall 1993, p.6.
124. Michael Ledeen, "Africa Goes South," *The American Spectator*, April 1995, p.32.
125. Eph 5:15.
126. NRSV, NASB, NIV: Eph 5:15; NIV: Ex 23:13.
127. Jon Bowermaster, "Antarctica: Tourism's Last Frontier," *Audubon*, July/Aug. 1994, p.90.
128. Lev 1:17; Ps 74:15; Hab 3:9; Zech 14:4.
129. E.g., Gen 2:24; Rom 12:9.
130. E.g., Gen 22:3; Is 48:21.
131. E.g., Gen 34:3; Acts 17:34.
132. E.g., Deut 14:6; Job 16:13; Ps 141:7; Ecc 10:9.
133. E.g., Job 19:20; Lk 10:11.
134. 2 Ki 3:3; Job 29:10, 311:7.
135. Deut 14:7; Act 2:3.
136. Lev 11:3,7,26.
137. Micah 1:4.
138. E.g., Deut 14:6; Song 2:14; Is 2:21; Jer 49:16; Amos 56:11; Oba 1:3.
139. Ex 33:22; Is 57:5.
140. Ex 33:22.
141. Lev 11:3,7,26; Deut 14:6,7; Song 2:17.
142. E.g., Lev 11:3; Deut 14:8.
143. Lev 11:4,5,6,7, 14:7,8.
144. Ps 22:15, 44:25, 119:25; Lam 4:4.
145. E.g., Gen 2:24; Eph 5:31.
146. Ps 119:321; Eph 5:31.
147. Job 38:25.
148. Erica E. Goode, "Does Psychotherapy Work?" *U.S. News & World Report*, May 24, 1993, p.56.
149. Jer 38:11,12.
150. Josh 9:5.
151. Jer 38:11,12.
152. Josh 9:5.
153. Alan Weisman, "The Drug Lords vs. the Tarahumara," *Los Angeles Times*, Jan. 9, 1994, sec. Magazine, p.10.
154. E.g., Ex 10:4; Lk 6:17.
155. E.g., Ex 10:14; Acts 27:2.
156. NRSV: Ex 10:4.
157. Num 20:23.
158. NKJV: Deut 16:4.
159. NIV: Deut 16:4.

160. NRSV: Num 22:36.
161. Josh 15:47.
162. Is 23:2.
163. Deut 3:4.
164. Is 11:8, 14:29, 59:5.
165. Jer 8:17.
166. NRSV, NASB: Is 59:5.
167. NASB, NIV, NKJV: Is 11:8.
168. Jer 8:17.
169. Jer 8:7.
170. Lev 11:30.
171. Jonah 2:5.
172. Jud 9:15.
173. Is 44:14.
174. 1 Sam 6:8,11,15.
175. Ibid.
176. Ana Radelat, "An Embarrassment of Riches," *Public Citizen*, July/Aug. 1991, p.9.
177. Ronald Katz, "Triumph of the Swoosh," *Sports Illustrated*, Aug. 16, 1993, p.54.
178. Job 19:24.
179. E.g., 1 Sam 16:18; 1 Cor 12:24.
180. Is 53:2; Ezek 16:14, 27:10; Dan 10:8; 1 Cor 12:23.
181. Song 1:10, 6:4.
182. Jer 6:2.
183. Is 53:2.
184. Ezek 16:14, 27:10.
185. NASB: 1 Sam 16:18.
186. NRSV: Job 41:12.
187. NASB: Ps 33:1.
188. NIV: Pro 30:29.
189. NKJV: Ecc 5:18.
190. 1 Cor 12:33.
191. Zech 9:17.
192. Cynthia Ozick, "Public and Private Intellectuals," *American Scholar*, Summer 1995, p.353.
193. "Whose Forest Is It, Anyway?" *Garden*, July/Aug. 1989, p.12.
194. Gal 6:6; Phil 4:14; 1 Tim 6:18; Heb 13:16.
195. Gal 2:2; Phil 4:15.
196. 2 Sam 3:17; 2 Ki 9:11; Matt 5:37; Eph 4:29; Col 3:8; Phile 6.
197. Lk 24:17; 1 Cor 15:33.
198. Phile 6.
199. 1 Cor 15:33.
200. Gal 6:6; Heb 13:16.
201. Gal 2:2.
202. 1 Cor 15:33.
203. Ezek 44:19.

204. E.g., Num 21:4; Lk 19:43.
205. E.g., Gen 19:4; Rev 20:9.
206. Ps 139:3.
207. Gen 2: 11,13; Jos 19:14; Ps 73:6; Hos 11:12.
208. 1 Ki 7:24; 2 Chr 4:3.
209. Num 34:5; Josh 15:3; 2 Sam 5:23; 2 Ki 3:9; Acts 28:13.
210. Pro 8:27.
211. Ex 27:5, 38:4; 1 Ki 7:35; 2 Ki 4:2.
212. Is 44:13.
213. Dan 11:4.
214. 1 Ki 6:5; Ps 22:16.
215. Quentin Anderson, "A Culture of One's Own," *American Scholar,* Fall 1992, p.533.
216. Stephan Wilkinson, "Amelia Earhart: Is the Search Over?" Air & Space, Aug./Sept. 1992, p.26.
217. John Childs, "Danubia," *History Today,* Aug. 1995, p.59.
218. 1 Pet 3:8.
219. Gail Fondahl, "Mending Cultural Fences," *Earthwatch,* Jan./Feb. 1993, p.14.
220. Pro 1:21; Acts 19:40.
221. Ibid.
222. Acts 19:10; Pro 1:21.
223. Pro 1:21; Acts 19:40.
224. Acts 19:40; Pro 1:21.
225. Edward Oxford, "Hope, Tears, and Remembrance," *American History Illustrated,* Sept./Oct. 1990, p.28.
226. Rom 7:8; Col 3:5; 1 Thes 4:5.
227. Rom 7:8.
228. Col 3:5.
229. 1 Thes 4:5.
230. Acts 1:3.
231. David Taylor, "My Life as an Outboard," *Forbes,* May 8, 1995, p.97.
232. Lev 11:5; Deut 14:7.
233. Ps 104:18; Pro 30:26.
234. Lev 11:5; Deut 14:7; Ps 104:18; Pro 30:26.
235. NRSV, NASB: Lev 11:5; Deut 14:7; NKJV: Ps 104:18; Pro 30:26.
236. Lev 11:5; Deut 14:7.
237. Ps 104:18.
238. Xiong Lei, "Environment: Spreading the Message," *Panoscope,* Jan. 1993, p.16.
239. 1 Sam 8:13.
240. Ibid.
241. Ex 30:35.
242. Ibid.
243. Ezek 27:17.
244. Susan V. Seligson, "Goat Cheese: Take it to Heart," *Health Magazine,* Oct. 1994, p.32.

245. Gen 14:13; Ps 83:5; Is 7:2.
246. Is 8:12; Oba 1:7.
247. Ps 83:5; Oba 1:7.
248. Gen 14:13.
249. Is 8:12.
250. Oba 1:7.
251. Michael Kramer, "A Solution in Three Parts," *Time*, June 12, 1995, p.55.
252. 2 Ki 4:8; Matt 14:22; Mk 6:45; Lk 24:29; Acts 16:15; Acts 28:19.
253. Job 32:18; 2 Cor 5:14.
254. 1 Pet 5:2.
255. Gal 6:12.
256. NRSV, NIV: 2 Ki 4:8.
257. NASB, NKJV: 2 Ki 4:8.
258. Matt 14:22.
259. NRSV, NASB: Acts 16:15.
260. NASB: Acts 28:19.
261. NKJV, NIV, NRSV: Acts 28:19.
262. NIV, NKJV: 2 Cor 5:14.
263. Job 32:18.
264. 1 Pet 5:2.
265. Job 36:16.
266. 1 Cor 7:37.
267. Stephen Viederman, "Sustainable Development: What Is it and How Do We Get There?" *Current History*, April 1993, p.180.
268. Ps 10:13; Ezek 21:13.
269. Ps 15:4, 107:11; Ecc 8:7; Is 16:14.
270. Ezek 21:10.
271. Ps 15:4.
272. NRSV: Ps 10:13.
273. NASB: Ps 10:13.
274. NIV: Ps 10:13.
275. NASB: Is 16:14.
276. NRSV: Ecc 8:7.
277. NRSV: Ecc 16:14.
278. Job 12:21.
279. "New Lives for Old," *Economist*, Feb. 13, 1993, p.83.
280. Cor 2:7; Gal 2:7; 1 Pet 3:9.
281. Gal 2:7; NASB, NKJV: 2 Cor 2:7.
282. Bruce McCall, "Automotorcar Comparison Test," *Car & Driver*, April 1993, p.97.
283. E.g., Ps 37:2 Pet 3:11.
284. NASB: Ps 50:23.
285. 1 Pet 3:16.
286. NRSV: Heb 13:7.
287. NASB: 1 Pet 1:18.
288. NKJV: Ps 37:14.

289. Col 4:6.
290. Song 2:12.
291. Titus 1:9; Jude 15.
292. Job 32:12; Acts 18:28; 1 Cor 14:24; James 2:9.
293. Jn 8:46.
294. NRSV: Job 32:12.
295. Acts 18:28.
296. James 2:9.
297. NRSV: 1 Cor 1r 14:24.
298. Job 32:12; 1 Cor 14:24.
299. 1 Cor 14:24.
300. Ps 116:11.
301. Lev 11:17; Deut 14:17; Is 34:11; Zep 2:14.
302. Lev 11:17; Deut 14:17.
303. Ibid.
304. NASB, NKJV: Is 34:11; Zep 2:14.
305. NIV: Is 34:11; Zep 2:14.
306. NRSV: Is 34:11.
307. Donald Dale Jackson, "Saving the Last Best River," *Audubon,* May/June 1994, p.76.
308. E.g., Gen 27:28; 1 Tim 5:18.
309. Hos 9:1.
310. Gen 27:28; 1 Tim 5:18.
311. 1 Cor 15:37.
312. Hos 9:1.
313. 1 Tim 5:18.
314. 1 Sam 8:14.
315. 1 Chr 15:28; Ps 98:6; Dan 3:5,7,10,15: Hosea 5:8.
316. 2 Sam 6:5: 2 Chr 15:14.
317. Dan 3:5,7,10,15.
318. NIV: Hos 5:8.
319. 2 Chr 15:14.
320. NRSV, NASB: 2 Sam 6:5.
321. NKJV, NIV: 2 Sam 6:5.
322. 2 Chr 15:14.
323. Rodd McLeod, "Recordings," *Rolling Stone,* April 7, 1994, p.74.
324. 2 Sam 7:8; 1 Chr 17:7.
325. 1 Sam 24:3.
326. 2 Chr 32:28.
327. 2 Sam 7:8; 1 Chr 17:7.
328. 1 Ki 7:6.
329. Gen 49:9; Num 24:9.
330. Deut 33:13.
331. Gen 49:14.
332. Ezek 25:5.
333. Num 24:9.
334. Job 38:40.

335. Gen 49:19.
336. Gen 49:9.
337. Marrianne Saddington, "How to Make Homemade Paper," *Mother Earth News*, Dec. 1993/Jan. 1994, p.30.
338. 1 Sam 13:21.
339. 1 Sam 13:20,21.
340. Ibid.
341. Ezek 39:9.
342. Patrick G. Marshall, "U.S. Trade Policy," *CQ Researcher*, Jan. 29, 1993, p.75.
343. E.g., 1 Sam 25:20; Jer 25:38.
344. Job 38:40, 40:21; Is 32:2; Jer 25:38.
345. Job 40:21.
346. NRSV: 1 Sam 25:20.
347. NIV: 1 Sam 25:20.
348. Ps 61:4.
349. NRSV: Is 16:4.
350. NIV: Is 4:6.
351. Ps 10:9; Song 2:14.
352. Ps 64:4.
353. Rev 6:15.
354. Job 39:9; Pro 14:4; Is 1:3.
355. *The Barnhart Dictionary of Etymology*, 1988 ed., s.v., "crib."
356. NASB, NIV, NKJV: Job 39:9.
357. Job 39:9; Is 1:3.
358. Pro 14:4.
359. 1 Ki 6:4.
360. Ps 31:7.
361. E.g., 1 Sam 26:11; 1 Ki 20:20.
362. NASB, NIV, NKJV: 1 Sam 26:11.
363. 1 Ki 19:6.
364. 1 Ki 20:20.
365. Mk 4:37.
366. Lk 13:7; Deut 1:12.
367. Lk 10:40.
368. Lk 13:7.
369. Heb 12:1.
370. NKJV: Ecc 10:4.
371. NASB: 1 Cor 4:13.
372. Ezek 17:10.
373. Gen 7:21.
374. Richard Homan, "Sneak Preview '95," *Road & Track*, Sept. 1994, p.64.
375. E.g., Ex 28:8; Acts 19:19.
376. Acts 19:19.
377. Ex 28:8.
378. NASB: Ex 28:8; NIV: Ex 39:5.

379. Ex 28:27.
380. Ex 35:32.
381. Acts 19:19.
382. Is 3:4.
383. Ezek 40:16.

Chapter 4

1. Job 33:20; Pro 23:6; Rev 18:14.
2. Gen 49:20; Ps 141:4; Pro 23:3.
3. Ps 141:4; Pro 23:3,6.
4. Job 33:20; Rev 18:14.
5. Gen 49:20.
6. Pro 18:18, 26:22; Jer 6:2.
7. Jer 6:2.
8. Job 33:20.
9. Ibid.
10. Ibid.
11. Rev 18:14.
12. Ibid.
13. Jessica Maxwell, "The Moose in the Willows," *Audubon,* May/June 1994, p.112.
14. Gen 14:17; 2 Sam 18:18.
15. Ibid.
16. Ps 60:6, 108:7.
17. Num 21:12; Deut 21:4,6.
18. Num 21:12.
19. Ex 22:30; Lev 22:27; Deut 22:6,7.
20. Ibid.
21. Mk 7:22.
22. Lev 5:8.
23. Mk 16:16; Rom 14:23; 2 Thes 2:12.
24. E.g., Matt 23:14; 2 Pet 2:3.
25. Mk 16:16; Rom 3:8.
26. NIV, NRSV: Rom 13:2; 1 Cor 11:29.
27. Matt 23:23.
28. Mk 3:29.
29. Mk 12:40; Lk 20:47.
30. Lk 23:40.
31. Jn 3:19.
32. Jn 5:24.
33. Jn 3:19.
34. Ps 109:7.
35. Job 32:3.
36. Jn 3:17,18.
37. Ex 28:15.

38. E.g., Gen 24:14; 1 Ki 1:3.
39. Gen 24:61; 1 Sam 25:42; Ps 68:25.
40. Gen 24:14; 1 Ki 1:3.
41. Ibid.
42. Gen 34:4.
43. Gen 24:61; 1 Sam 25:42.
44. Ps 68:25.
45. Eric Ruth, "Eye Spied," *News Journal*, Feb. 21, 1993, p.G1.
46. Ps 22:20, 35:17.
47. Ibid.
48. Ibid.
49. Ibid.
50. Song 1:9,15, 2:2,10,13, 4:1,7, 5:2, 6:4.
51. Song 6:9.
52. Hos 9:16.
53. Is 29:21.
54. Ezek 13:11.
55. Ex 2:3; Ezek 13:12,14,15, 22:28.
56. Ezek 13:12.
57. Ex 2:3.
58. Ezek 13:10,11,12,14,15, 22:28.
59. Ex 2:3; Ezek 13:12.
60. Ezek 13:10,11,12,14,15.
61. Ex 2:3.
62. Ezek 22:28.
63. Ex 2:3.
64. Ezek 13:10,11,12,14,15.
65. Ezek 13:12,15, 22:28.
66. Ezek 13:10,11,12,14,15, 22:28.
67. Ezek 13:12.
68. David Elliott, "Courtly Cotten Always the Craftsman," *San Diego Union-Tribune*, Feb. 9, 1994, p.E-8.
69. Ezek 40:29.
70. 1 Chr 29:2.
71. Job 38:12; Lk 1:78.
72. Job 38:12.
73. Lk 1:78.
74. Ibid.
75. E.g., Ex 29:40; Num 29:15.
76. NRSV: Ex 29:40.
77. NASB: Num 28:29.
78. NRSV: Num 28:13.
79. NRSV: Lev 14:21.
80. NIV: Ex 29:40.
81. Gen 41:54; 2 Ki 4:38; 2 Chr 6:28; Neh 5:3; Jer 14:1; Acts 7:11, 11:28.
82. Jer 14:1.
83. Gen 41:54; 2 Ki 4:38; 2 Chr 6:28; Neh 5:3; Acts 7:11, 11:28.

84. Pro 14:28.
85. Hanke Gratteau, "Machine Gears up for Rostenkowski," *Chicago Tribune*, Nov. 6, 1994, sec. News, p.1.
86. Ecc 7:7.
87. Rom 1:28.
88. John Balzar, "Creatures Great and--Equal?" *Los Angeles Times*, Dec. 25, 1993, p.A-1.
89. Heb 7:18.
90. Heb 6:17.
91. Job 40:10, Jer 10:4.
92. Pro 7:16; Ezek 16:11, 13; Hos 2:13; Rev 17:14, 18:16.
93. Ezek 16:16, 23:40.
94. Is 61:10; Jer 4:30.
95. Job 40:10; NASB, NIV, NKJV: Ezek 16:11.
96. NIV: Rev 17:14, 18:16.
97. NASB, NKJV: Pro 7:16.
98. NASB, NKJV: Jer 10:4.
99. NIV: Pro 7:16.
100. NASB, NIV, NRSV: Ezek 16:16.
101. NIV: Jer 4:30.
102. Is 61:10; Hos 2:13.
103. Hos 2:13.
104. Is 61:10.
105. Ezek 16:11,13,16; Rev 17:14, 18:16.
106. Ps 45:13, 65:13; Pro 7:10.
107. Stuart Exkenazi, Suzanne Gamboa, and David Elliot, "Candidates for Governor a Cut Above," *Austin American-Statesman*, Nov. 6, 1994, p.A1.
108. Ex 23:2; Deut 17:11; Ps 119:157; Pro 4:5, 7:25.
109. 2 Chr 34:2; Job 23:11; Ps 44:18, 119:51.
110. Ps 102:11, 109:23.
111. Deut 17:11; 2 Chr 34:2.
112. NASB, NRSV, NKJV: Pro 4:5.
113. NASB: Ps 44:18.
114. NIV: Ps 44:18.
115. NRSV, NKJV: Ps 44:18.
116. NASB: Ps 119:157; NIV: Pro 4:5.
117. NIV: Ps 119:51; NKJV: Ps 119:157.
118. NASB, NKJV: Ps 109:23.
119. Jud 19:8.
120. 2 Ki 20:11; Is 38:8.
121. Ps 90:9.
122. Lk 9:12.
123. Jer 6:4.
124. Song 7:6.
125. John Painter Jr., "Queen Rat," *Oregonian*, June 1, 1994, p.D01.
126. NRSV: Pro 26:21; NASB: 2 Tim 2:4; NIV: Pro 19:13; NKJV: 1 Tim 3:3.

127. NRSV: Phil 3:1; NASB: 1 Pet 4:15; NIV: Ezra 4:15; NKJV: Deut 28:25.
128. Jer 16:4.
129. Ecc 2:20.
130. Acts 19:38.
131. E. MacFarquhar, "On the Defensive," *U.S. News & World Report*, May 27, 1991, p.37.
132. Lk 16:14, 23:35.
133. E.g., Job 30:1; Hos 7:16.
134. Hab 1:10; Lk 16:14.
135. Hab 1:10.
136. Lk 16:14, 23:35.
137. Ibid.
138. Ibid.
139. Ps 102:8, 119:51.
140. Ps 102:8; Hab 1:10.
141. Lk 16:14.
142. 1 Sam 2:1; Ps 79:4, 102:8, 119:51; Ezek 23:32; Matt 27:39.
143. Hab 1:10.
144. Pro 11:12.
145. Ps 44:13, 79:4.
146. John Gonzalez, "Undefeated Richards Braves Possible Career Turning Point," *Fort Worth Star-Telegram*, Oct. 21, 1994, sec. News, p.1.
147. Josh 18:4,6,8.
148. Jos 18:6.
149. Josh 18:9; Jud 8:14.
150. Rom 4:6, 10:5.
151. Ezek 43:10; NASB, NKJV: Acts 15:3.
152. Jos 18:6.
153. Rom 4:6.
154. Rom 10:5.
155. Jos 18:6,8,9.
156. NIV, NASB, NRSV: Jos 18:4; NRSV, NIV: Jos 18:8.
157. Jos 18:4,6,8,9.
158. Rom 10:5.
159. Num 13:16.
160. 2 Sam 10:3.
161. 2 Ki 6:13.
162. 2 Ki 9:17.
163. "Failed Disability Law Ripe Target for Budget Cutters," *Human Events*, May 19, 1995, p.4.
164. Ezek 25:6; Heb 10:29.
165. Ezek 25:15, 36:5; Rom 1:30.
166. Matt 5:44; Lk 6:28; Acts 14:5.
167. NIV, NASB, NRSV: Lev 26:27; NASB, NIV, NRSV: Num 14:11; NIV, NKJV: Ezek 32:29.
168. NRSV: Ezek 25:6.

169. NASB: Ezek 25:15.
170. NKJV: Ezek 25:6.
171. NRSV: Ezek 36:5.
172. NRSV: Lk 6:28.
173. NKJV: Rom 1:30.
174. NASB: Lk 6:28.
175. NRSV: Heb 10:29.
176. NIV: Heb 10:29.
177. NKJV: Ezek 36:5.
178. Rom 1:30.
179. Lev 27:28; Num 18:14.
180. Micha Odenheimer, "What Made the 'Messiah' Tick," *Jerusalem Report,* July 14, 1994, p.32-33.
181. 2 Pet 2:10; Jude 8.
182. NKJV, NASB: Gen 49:3; NKJV, NRSV: Hab 1:7.
183. 2 Pet 2:10; Jude 8.
184. Ibid.
185. Is 9:15.
186. Gen 50:7.
187. Is 43:28.
188. 1 Ki 9:22.
189. Job 40:8; Is 14:27, Gal 3:17.
190. Is 28:18; Gal 3:15; Heb 7:18.
191. NASB, NKJV: Job 40:8; NRSV, NASB, NKJV: Is 14:27.
192. Job 40:2.
193. Is 28:18; Heb 7:18.
194. Gal 3:17.
195. NASB, NKJV, NIV: Is 14:27.
196. NASB, NIV: Gal 3:15; Heb 7:18.
197. Lk 24:41.
198. Lev 24:19.
199. Ps 7:14.
200. Acts 7:45.
201. E.g., Ex 17:13; Is 31:8.
202. 1 Sam 14:20.
203. Ex 17:13; Num 14:45; Jos 10:10; 1 Sam 7:10; 2 Sam 22:15; Is 31:8.
204. Ex 17:13; Num 14:45; Jos 10:10; Jud 4:15; 1 Sam 7:10; Is 31:8.
205. Ex 17:13; Num 14:45.
206. 2 Sam 22:15; Ps 18:14.
207. 1 Sam 14:20.
208. Josh 10:10; Jud 4:15, 8:12.
209. Josh 10:10.
210. 2 Sam 15:34, 17:14.
211. "Airlines," *Seattle Times,* April 25, 1994, p.A1.
212. E.g., Deut 22:30; Nah 3:5.
213. E.g., Ex 20:26; Acts 27:39.
214. Job 12:22; Ps 29:9.

215. Hab 3:13.
216. 2 Sam 22:16; Ps 18:15.
217. NKJV, NASB: Deut 22:30; Is 57:8.
218. NIV: Deut 22:30.
219. NRSV: 1 Sam 14:18.
220. NASB: 1 Sam 14:18.
221. NIV: Job 41:13.
222. NKJV: Job 41:13.
223. Ex 20:26.
224. NIV, NRSV, NKJV: 1 Sam 14:11.
225. NASB: 1 Sam 14:11.
226. NIV, NASB, NRSV: Ps 18:15.
227. NIV: Is 22:8.
228. NASB: Jer 13:22.
229. NKJV: Acts 21:3.
230. 1 Sam 22:6.
231. Lev 21:10.
232. 1 Cor 9:17; Eph 1:10, 3:2; Col 1:25.
233. Ibid.
234. 1 Cor 9:17; Eph 3:2; Col 1:25.
235. Ibid.
236. 1 Cor 9:17; Col 1:25.
237. Eph 1:10, 3:2.
238. Michael Griffin, "Controlling the Cuckoo," *Ceres*, May/June 1993, p.32-35.
239. Acts 15:2; Rom 14:1.
240. Acts 15:2.
241. Rom 14:1.
242. Job 32:6.
243. Douglas L. Wilson, "A Most Abandoned Hypocrite," *American Heritage*, Feb./March 1994, p.36.
244. Jane S. Gerber, "Sephardic Jewry & 1492," *Humanities*, March/April 1992, p.30-33.
245. Ps 38:8.
246. 1 Sam 28:15; Ps 39:6, 42:5,11, 43:5; Pro 30:21.
247. 1 Sam 28:15; Ps 42:5,11, 43:5.
248. NASB: Ps 38:8.
249. NIV: Ps 38:8.
250. NASB: Ps 39:6.
251. NIV: Ps 39:6.
252. NASB: pro 3:21.
253. NIV: Pro 3:21.
254. NASB: Jer 50:34.
255. NIV: Jer 50:34.
256. Ps 42:5,11, 43:5.
257. 1 Sam 28:15; Ps 38:3, 39:6; Pro 30:21; Jer 50:34.
258. Ps 42:5,11, 43:5; Jer 50:34.

259. 1 Sam 28:15; Ps 38:3, 39:6, Pro 30:21.
260. Larry Witham, "Church in an Uproar Over Worship of 'Sophia,'" *Washington Times,* June 4, 1994, p.A1.
261. Jos 7:11; Jer 42:20; Gal 2:13.
262. Ps 26:4.
263. Pro 26:24.
264. Ibid.
265. NKJV, NIV, NRSV: Ps 26:4; Gal 2:13; NKJV: Jer 42:20.
266. NIV, NASB, NKJV: Pro 26:24.
267. NASB, NKJV: Jos 7:11; NASB: Jer 42:20.
268. NIV: Jos 7:11.
269. NRSV: Jos 7:11.
270. NASB: Ps 26:4.
271. NRSV, NIV: Jer 42:20.
272. Scot Lehigh, "Romney Takes More Heat on Abortion," *Boston Globe,* Sept. 10, 1994, sec. Metro, p.24.
273. Rom 12:9; Gal 2:13.
274. NASB, NKJV: Rom 12:9; Gal 2:13.
275. Gal 2:13.
276. James 3:17.
277. Is 17:11.
278. Deut 32:2; Job 36:28.
279. Ibid.
280. Job 36:28.
281. Job 36:28.
282. Song 4:11.
283. Job 36:28.
284. Job 36:27.
285. Fiona Jebb, "Crossing the Border," *World Link,* July/Aug. 1994, p.24-28.
286. E.g., Deut 22:9; James 1:2.
287. NASB: Heb 13:9.
288. Heb 9:10.
289. NKJV: Pro 20:23.
290. NKJV: Deut 22:9.
291. NIV, NRSV, NASB: Pro 20:23.
292. NASB, NRSV: Ezek 17:3.
293. NASB, NKJV, NIV: 2 Chr 30:11.
294. NIV, NRSV: Heb 13:9.
295. NIV: James 1:2.
296. NRSV: James 1:2.
297. NIV: Titus 3:3.
298. NIV, NASB: Deut 22:9.
299. NRSV: Deut 22:9.
300. NKJV, NASB, NRSV: Jud 5:30.
301. NASB, NRSV: Song 4:16.
302. NRSV: Ecc 10:18.

303. NASB: Ex 28:14.
304. Deut 24:1,3; Is 50:1; Matt 5:31, 19:7; Mk 10:4.
305. Deut 24:1,3; Is 50:1; Matt 5:31, 19:7.
306. Mk 10:4.
307. Jer 3:8.
308. Acts 3:10.
309. Lk 5:26.
310. Lk 4:36; Acts 2:12.
311. Gen 40:3,4,7, 41:10.
312. Deut 28:28; Zec 12:4.
313. Michael T. Marsden and John G. Nachbar, "Annotated Index to Volumes 1-20," *Journal of Popular Film & Television,* Winter 1993, p.93.
314. Acts 5:34.
315. Lk 2:46, 5:17.
316. Lk 2:46, 5:17; Acts 5:34.
317. Matt 9:12; Mk 2:17, 5:26; Lk 5:31; Col 4:14.
318. Gen 50:2; 2 Chr 16:12; Job 13:4; Jer 8:22; Lk 4:23.
319. Lk 4:23.
320. Is 13:21; Micah 2:4.
321. Is 13:21.
322. Ibid.
323. Is 34:14.
324. Lev 11:16.
325. Micah 2:4.
326. Maria C. Hunt, "Actor Pooh-Poohs Idea of Winnie Just For Kinds," *San Diego Union-Tribune,* Oct. 17, 1994, p.B-1.
327. Jer 50:36.
328. 1 Tim 6:4.
329. Ezek 23:5,7,9,12,16,20.
330. Ibid.
331. Jer 50:36.
332. 1 Tim 6:4.
333. Num 11:34; Ps 106:14; 1 Cor 10:6; Rev 18:14.
334. Michelle Trappen, "Doggy Donors," *Oregonian,* May 5, 1994, p.D01.
335. O.E.D., s.v., "doth."
336. Ex 32:11.
337. Ps 86:10, 119:68.
338. Gen 28:22; Acts 4:30.
339. Gen 32:9; Rev 16:5.
340. Mark Hornbeck, "Gender Gap Concerns Engler's Campaign," *Detroit News,* Sept. 13, 1994, p.B1.
341. Deut 32:32; Jn 15:1.
342. Gen 37:3,23,32.
343. 1 Chr 29:7; Ezra 2:69, 8:27; Neh 7:70,71,72.
344. 1 Chr 29:7; NRSV: Ezra 2:69; NRSV, NASB, NIV: Ezra 8:27; NRSV: Neh 7:70,71,72.

345. NKJV, NIV, NASB: Ezra 2:69; NKJV: Ezra 8:27; NIV, NASB, NKJV: Neh 7:70,71,72.

346. Margaret Shapiro, "Winter Lashes Fuel-Short Former Soviets Schools," *Washington Post,* Dec. 7, 1993, p.A1.

347. 2 Ki 10:27; Matt 15:17; Mk 7:19; Lk 5:4,9.

348. Lk 5:4,9.

349. 2 Ki 10:27; Matt 15:17; Mk 7:19.

350. 2 Ki 10:27.

351. Matt 15:17; Mk 7:19.

352. Ibid.

353. Ps 75:8; Rev 18:6.

354. Jer 2:23.

355. 1 Ki 4:28; Est 8:10; Is 60:16.

356. Jer 2:23.

357. NIV: 1 Ki 4:28; NKJV, NIV: Est 8:10.

358. NASB, NRSV: 1 Ki 4:28; NRSV, NASB: Est 8:10.

359. Is 66:20.

360. Suna Erdem, "Jealous Camels Lock Humps in Turkey," *Reuters,* Jan. 25, 1994.

361. E.g., Gen 36:15; 1 Chr 1:54.

362. E.g., Ex 15:15; Josh 13:21.

363. Gen 36:15; 1 Chr 1:54.

364. Gen 36:15; 1 Chr 1:51.

365. Zec 12:6.

366. 1 Chr 6:19.

367. 1 Chr 5:24.

368. Dan 3:5,10,15.

369. Ibid.

370. Ibid.

371. Guy Gugliotta, "The Persistence of Poverty," *Washington Post National Weekly Edition,* Jan. 3-9, 1994, p.6-7.

372. E.g., Ex 29:14; Phil 3:8.

373. 1 Sam 2:8; Ezra 6:11; Ps 113:7; Is 25:10; Dan 2:5, 3:9; Lk 14:35.

374. Lam 4:5.

375. Jer 16:4; Mal 2:3.

376. Ezra 6:11.

377. 2 Ki 18:27; Jer 16:4.

378. Ezek 4:15; Lk 14:35.

379. 1 Ki 14:10; Neh 2:13, 3:13,14, 12:31; Job 20:7.

380. NRSV: Ex 29:14; NKJV, NASB: Job 20:7.

381. NASB: Ezek 4:12; NIV: Ezek 4:15.

382. NKJV: 2 Ki 18:27; Is 36:12.

383. Phil 3:8.

384. NIV: 2 Ki 18:27; NIV: Zep 1:17.

385. NIV: Ezek 4:15.

386. NIV, NKJV: Ex 29:14.

387. NIV: 2 Ki 6:25.

388. 1 Sam 2:8; Ps 113:7.
389. NASB, NKJV: Ezra 6:11.
390. NASB: Is 25:10; NASB, NIV, NRSV: Lk 14:35.
391. NASB, Dan 2:5.
392. NASB: Lam 4:5.
393. NIV: Dan 2:5; NIV: Dan 3:29.
394. NRSV: Is 25:10.
395. NRSV: Dan 2:5, 3:39.
396. Lk 13:8.
397. Ex 29:14; Lev 4:11, 8:17, 16:27; Num 19:5.
398. William Barklow, "Big Talkers," *Wildlife Conservation*, Jan./Feb. 1994, p.20.
399. Matt 13:21.
400. Ex 18:23.
401. Ps 118:3,4.
402. Est 8:6.
403. Ps 72:7.
404. Job 40:8; Is 14:27; Gal 3:17.

Chapter 5

1. Ex 9:31.
2. 1 Sam 8:12; Is 30:24.
3. Gen 45:6; Ex 34:21.
4. Deut 21:4.
5. Ex 9:31; Mk 4:28.
6. Ex 9:31.
7. Gen 45:6; Ex 34:21.
8. Deut 21:4.
9. 1 Sam 8:12.
10. Is 30:24.
11. Hos 10:13.
12. Ex 5:9.
13. Gen 2:5, 3:23.
14. Rom 8:19; 2 Cor 7:7, 8:16; Phil 1:20; Heb 2:1.
15. 2 Cor 1:22, 5:5; Eph 1:14.
16. Ibid.
17. Ibid.
18. Ibid.
19. Ibid.
20. Ex 22:26.
21. *Black's Law Dictionary*, s.v., "earnest money."
22. E.g., Num 30:8; Gal 5:4.
23. 2 Chr 7:11.
24. 1 Cor 16:9; 2 Cor 1:6; Eph 3:7, 4:16; Phile 6; James 5:16.
25. Gal 2:8; 1 Thes 2:13.

26. Matt 15:6; Mk 7:13; Rom 3:3, 4:14, 9:6; 1 Cor 1:17; Gal 3:17.
27. Is 32:17.
28. 2 Chr 34:22.
29. Heb 8:8.
30. Jer 31:31.
31. Pro 19:19.
32. Is 32:17.
33. 2 Cor 1:6; Eph 3:7; Phile 6; Gal 2:8; 1 Thes 2:13.
34. Gal 2:8.
35. Neal Gabler, "Trial by Jury," *Charlotte Observer*," June 12, 1994, p.1C.
36. Matt 11:8; Lk 7:25.
37. Jay Stuller, "The Unpopular Child," *Kiwanis Magazine*, Sept. 1991, p.20-23.
38. Job 16:3.
39. 1 Cor 8:10.
40. NKJV, NRSV: Job 16:3.
41. NASB: Job 16:3.
42. NIV: Job 16:3.
43. NRSV: 1 Cor 8:10.
44. NASB: 1 Cor 8:10.
45. Ecc 12:11.
46. Deut 23:1.
47. Lk 19:43.
48. Hos 10:1.
49. Jud 3:25.
50. Ps 73:21.
51. Robert W. Lee, "Gun Report," *The New American*, June 12, 1995, p.34-35.
52. Deut 28:27; 1 Sam 5:6,9,12, 6:4,5,11,17.
53. Ibid.
54. Deut 28:27.
55. Lev 15:23.
56. Deut 28:61.
57. Ezek 16:24,31,39, 17:22.
58. Ezek 16:24,31,39.
59. Ibid.
60. Ibid.
61. Ezek 17:22.
62. Ezek 17:11.
63. Job 40:10.
64. 2 Cor 11:5, 12:11.
65. Rom 2:20.
66. Robert Ornstein, "Mom Always Liked You Best": Unraveling the Riddles of Birth Order," *American Health*, Jan./Feb. 1994, p.58-59.
67. Gal 5:20.
68. Rom 11:14; Gal 5:20.

69. Rom 11:14.
70. Deut 29:20.
71. Gal 5:20.
72. John Lukacs, "1918," *American Heritage,* Nov. 1993, p.46.
73. Song 5:14.
74. Pro 23:10.
75. Amos 1:1.
76. Gen 30:20.
77. Gen 30:20; 2 Chr 2:12,13; Lk 24:49; James 3:13.
78. 2 Chr 2:12,13.
79. Gen 30:20.
80. Lk 24:49.
81. Ibid.
82. James 3:13.
83. 2 Chr 30:22.
84. 2 Chr 26:15; Ezek 26:9.
85. 2 Chr 26:15.
86. Ibid.
87. Ezek 26:9.
88. Philip Elmer-Dewitt, "Who Should Keep the Keys," *Time,* March 14, 1994, p.90-91.
89. Rom 11:23.
90. NRSV, NASB: James 1:21.
91. NIV, NKJV: James 1:21.
92. 1 Chr 27:1.
93. Heb 12:1.
94. Keneth Jost, "Fetal Tissue Research," *CQ Researcher,* Aug. 16, 1991, p.563-566.
95. Est 9:31; Job 36:23; Heb 9:20.
96. Est 9:31.
97. Est 9:31; Job 36:23; Phile 8; Heb 9:20.
98. NASB: Est 9:31.
99. NIV: Est 9:31.
100. NKJV: Est 9:31.
101. NASB: Job 36:23.
102. NKJV: Job 36:23.
103. NRSV: Phile 8.
104. NASB: Phile 8.
105. NRSV: Heb 9:20.
106. Est 9:21.
107. Jos 23:16.
108. John E. Petersen, "Managing Public Money," *Governing,* June 1991, p.46.
109. Ex 34:24; 1 Chr 4:10.
110. Ex 5:13.
111. Gen 10:30.
112. Dan 5:14.

113. "A Fragile World: What Lies Ahead?" *Orange County Register,* April 3, 1994, p.24-25.
114. Phil 3:17; 2 Thes 3:9; 2 Pet 2:6.
115. 1 Cor 10:11; 1 Thes 1:7; 1 Pet 5:3.
116. 2 Pet 2:6.
117. 1 Pet 5:3.
118. NIV: 2 Thes 3:9.
119. NASB, NIV, NKJV: Phil 3:17.
120. NASB, NRSV, NKJV: Ps 27:3; Ps 34:7; NKJV, NRSV, NASB: Ezek 25:4.
121. NRSV, NASB: Jud 13:8; NRSV, NASB, NKJV: 1 Ki 13:6.
122. NASB: 2 Cor 8:4; NRSV, NIV, NKJV: 2 Chr 33:19.
123. Num 2:2; Is 5:26, 11:10,12, 18:3, 30:17, 31:9; Zec 9:16.
124. Ps 74:4.
125. Num 2:2; Ps 74:4; Is 5:26, 11:10,12, 18:3, 30:17, 31:9; Zec 9:16.
126. Num 2:2.
127. E.g., NIV, NKJV: Is 11:10; NASB, NIV: Num 2:2.
128. NKJV: Num 2:2; NRSV: Ps 74:4.
129. E.g., NASB, NIV: Ps 74:4; NRSV, NASB, NIV: Is 31:9.
130. E.g., NRSV, NASB: Is 11:10; NRSV: Is 18:3.
131. Is 66:10; Ezek 27:7.
132. Num 35:16,17,18,20,21,23.
133. Ezra 6:11.
134. Job 22:6.
135. Mary H. Cooper, "World Hunger," *CQ Researcher,* Oct. 25, 1991, p.803.
136. Misha Glenny, "The Bear in the Caucasus," *Harper's,* March 1994, p.45-53.
137. 2 Sam 22:5.
138. Lam 3:5.
139. E.g., Acts 15:30; 2 Pet 3:1.
140. 2 Cor 3:1; 2 Pet 3:16.
141. Acts 15:30; 2 Pet 3:16.
142. Acts 15:30, 23:33.
143. Anna Byrd Davis, "Many Traveled Paths Different from King's to Change Society," *Commercial Appeal,* Jan. 17, 1993, p.J17.
144. E.g., Ex 1:19; Jn 4:49.
145. Ex 1:19; Num 11:33; Jn 4:49.
146. 2 Ki 10:28.
147. 2 Sam 21:5.
148. Ps 45:11.
149. Job 1:8, 2:3.
150. Job 1:1.
151. NIV, NKJV: Job 1:1,8, 2:3.
152. NRSV, NASB: Job 1:1,8, 2:3, 1 Pet 3:11.
153. Janet Stites, "Complexity," *Omni,* May 1994, p.42.
154. 2 Sam 3:14; Matt 1:18; Lk 1:27, 2:5; 2 Cor 11:2.

155. Song 3:11; Jer 2:2.
156. NASB, NIV, NKJV: 2 Sam 3:14; NASB, NKJV: 2 Cor 11:2.
157. NRSV, NASB: Matt 1:18; Lk 1:27.
158. NRSV, NIV: 2 Cor 11:2.
159. Song 3:11.
160. NIV: Matt 1:18; Lk 1:27, 2:5.
161. Jeremy Rifkin, "Dangers in Pinning Our Hopes on Trickle Down Technology," *USA Today Magazine*, May 1994, p.74-76.
162. Jos 14:7; Jer 48:19.
163. Gen 42:27; Ezek 20:6.
164. NRSV, NASB, NKJV: Jos 14:7.
165. NIV: Jos 14:7.
166. NIV: Jer 48:19.
167. NASB: Jer 48:19.
168. NASB: Ezek 20:6.
169. Gen 42:27.
170. NRSV, NIV, NKJV: Ezek 20:6.
171. 1 Sam 14:36; Ps 35:10; Pro 22:23; Is 17:14; Ezek 29:19, 39:10.
172. Jay Stuller, "Cleanliness Has Only Recently Become a Virtue," *Smithsonian*, Feb. 1991, p.126.
173. E.g., 1 Chr 17:17; Jude 6.
174. Est 1:19.
175. NKJV: 1 Chr 17:17.
176. NKJV: Ecc 3:18.
177. Dan 11:7.
178. NKJV, NIV, NASB: Lk 1:48.
179. NASB: 1 Chr 17:17.
180. NIV, NASB, NKJV: Col 4:8.
181. NASB, NKJV: Jude 6.
182. Ps 136:23.
183. NIV: Ruth 4:6; NKJV: Acts 28:7; NRSV: 1 Ki 2:26.
184. Ps 62:9.
185. Job 8:6.
186. Is 40:28.
187. E.g., Gen 19:1; Mk 13:35.
188. E.g., Lev 11:24; Mk 15:42.
189. Gen 24:63; Jos 7:6, 8:29; Mk 11:11; Acts 4:3.
190. 2 Sam 11:2; Is 17:14.
191. Deut 28:67; Mk 1:32.
192. NRSV, NASB, NIV: Num 28:8; NKJV: Deut 16:6.
193. 2 Ki 7:7.
194. Ezek 12:6.
195. Job 3:9.
196. Ibid.
197. Gen 24:63; Jos 7:6, 8:29; Acts 4:3.
198. Is 24:11.
199. NASB, NIV, NKJV: 2 Sam 11:2; NASB, NRSV, NIV: Is 17:14.

200. 2 Sam 11:2.
201. Is 17:14.
202. Lev 21:10.
203. E.g., Deut 28:29; Rev 1:18.
204. 1 Chr 17:14; Ps 89:28.
205. Ps 77:8.
206. Deut 28:29.
207. Jn 6:34.
208. Ps 105:4.
209. Ps 35:27, 70:4.
210. 1 Chr 16:11.
211. Ps 92:7, 93:5; Is 9:7; Gal 1:5; Rev 1:18.
212. Gal 1:5.
213. Ps 92:7, 93:5; Is 9:7.
214. Ps 113:2, 115:18, 121:8, 125:2, 131:3, 133:3; Jude 25.
215. Ps 125:2, 131:3; Jude 25.
216. NRSV: E.g., 1 Ki 2:33; Micah 4:7.
217. 1 Ki 2:33; Ps 93:5, 125:2, 131:3; Is 9:7; Micah 4:7.
218. NKJV: E.g., 2 Sam 22:51; Rev 1:18.
219. Is 59:21.
220. Is 14:20.
221. Ecc 9:6.
222. David Frankel, "New York's Obstetric Mess," *Lancet,* March 18, 1995, p.716.
223. Ps 25:6; Heb 7:18.
224. Ex 22:3.
225. Heb 6:17.
226. Mk 15:7.
227. Lam 3:22.
228. Ibid.
229. NASB: Matt 25:27.
230. NIV, NRSV, NKJV: Matt 25:27.
231. Lk 7:41.
232. Ezek 39:15.
233. Is 60:17.
234. NRSV, NASB: Deut 15:3; NASB, NIV, NKJV: Neh 5:7.
235. Pro 10:26.
236. 1 Cor 5:11.
237. Mk 6:27.
238. Is 36:2.
239. Ezek 27:27.
240. 1 Tim 3:3.
241. Jer 42:18, 44:12.
242. Ibid.
243. Ibid.
244. Jer 42:18.
245. Ibid.

246. NASB: 1 Chr 16:32; NRSV: 1 Sam 16:32; NIV: Is 14:8.
247. Ezek 25:7.
248. Eph 6:4.
249. "Christian Coalition/PAW: A Peculiar Non-Aggression Pact," *The New American*, June 26, 1995, p.9.
250. 2 Cor 2:9.
251. Gen 20:16.
252. 1 Sam 3:14.
253. 2 Sam 21:3.
254. Scott Shane, "A Real Information Revolution," *Sun*, May 29, 1994, p.1E.

Chapter 6

1. Job 27:22; Lk 15:16.
2. NRSV, NIV: Job 27:22.
3. NRSV, NKJV: Lk 15:16.
4. Lk 15:16.
5. Bruce McCall, "An Impregnable—Yet Cozy—Casa Blanca," *Forbes FYI*, March 13, 1995, p.78.
6. Ezek 27:12,14,16,19,22,27.
7. NRSV, NASB, NKJV: Ezek 27:14,16,19,22,27.
8. NKJV: Ezek 27:12.
9. Ezek 27:12,14,16,19,22,27.
10. NKJV, NRSV, NASB: Ezek 27:16,18.
11. Jonah 1:5.
12. NKJV: Neh 13:16; NIV: Neh 13:20.
13. NRSV, NASB, NIV: Neh 13:16; NRSV, NASB: Neh 13:20.
14. Deut 14:5.
15. O.E.D., s.v., "fallow."
16. Deut 14:5; 1 Ki 4:23.
17. Ibid.
18. *The Zondervan Pictoral Bible Dictionary*, (Grand Rapids: Zondervan Publishing House, 1967), s.v., "Animals of the Bible."
19. Ex 23:11.
20. E.g., Lev 19:31; Is 29:4.
21. Jer 20:10.
22. E.g., Lev 19:31; Is 29:4.
23. Ps 41:9; Job 19:14.
24. 1 Sam 28:3; 2 Ki 23:24.
25. Lev 19:31, 20:6,27.
26. Is 8:19, 19:3.
27. NRSV, NKJV: Job 19:14; NIV, NASB: Ps 41:9.
28. NASB: Job 19:14.
29. NRSV: Ps 41:9.
30. Ps 41:9.

Notes 497

31. Jer 20:10.
32. Ps 55:13.
33. Is 8:19.
34. Is 30:24; Jer 15:7; Matt 3:12; Lk 3:17.
35. Is 41:16; Jer 4:11, 15:7, 51:2.
36. Jer 51:2.
37. Jer 15:7; Matt 3:12; Lk 3:17.
38. Is 30:24.
39. Jer 15:7; Matt 3:12; Lk 3:17.
40. Jer 51:2.
41. Is 41:16; Jer 15:7, 51:2.
42. Jer 4:11.
43. Is 30:24.
44. Ibid.
45. Matt 5:26, 10:29; Mk 12:42.
46. Lk 12:6.
47. Matt 5:26, 10:29; Mk 12:42; Lk 12:6.
48. Ibid.
49. Matt 5:26.
50. Matt 10:29, Lk 12:6.
51. Mk 12:42.
52. Matt 20:2,9,10,13,19; Mk 12:5; Lk 20:24; Rev 6:6.
53. Stratford Sherman, "Who Will Buy CBS?" *Fortune*, Aug. 7, 1995, p.101.
54. Neh 8:10; Pro 11:25; Is 28:1.
55. Gen 41:2.
56. Ibid.
57. Jer 46:21.
58. 1 Sam 28:24.
59. Lev 1:8,12, 8:20.
60. Is 11:6.
61. 1 Sam 15:9; 2 Sam 6:13; Ps 66:15; Ezek 39:18; Matt 22:4.
62. 1 Sam 15:9; Ezek 39:18.
63. NKJV, NRSV: Ezek 34:3; NASB: Amos 5:22.
64. Joel 2:24, 3:13.
65. Is 63:2; Mk 12:1.
66. Hag 2:16.
67. Is 63:2; Joes 2:24, 3:13; Hag 2:16; Mk 12:1.
68. Gen 12:9.
69. Jer 49:23.
70. Deut 20:8.
71. Is 7:4.
72. Jer 51:46.
73. Mary Nemeth, "Amazing Greys," *Maclean's*, Jan. 10, 1994, p.26-29.
74. 2 Sam 14:2; 1 Ki 14:5; Lk 20:20.
75. 1 Sam 21:13; Ps 17:1; 2 Pet 2:3.
76. 1 Ki 14:6; Neh 6:8.

77. Jer 3:10.
78. 2 Cor 6:6; 1 Tim 1:5; 2 Tim 1:5; 1 Pet 1:22.
79. 1 Sam 21:13.
80. Ps 66:3.
81. 2 Sam 14:2; 1 Ki 14:5.
82. NASB: 1 Sam 21:13.
83. NRSV, NASB: Neh 6:8.
84. Ps 17:1.
85. NRSV, NKJV: 2 Pet 2:3.
86. NIV, NRSV: Jer 3:10.
87. NIV, NKJV: 2 Cor 6:6; 1 Tim 1:5; NASB, NIV, NRSV: 2 Tim 1:5; NIV, NKJV, NASB: 1 Pet 1:22.
88. NRSV, NASB: 2 Cor 6:6.
89. George Greenstein, "Our Address in the Universe," *Harvard Magazine*, Jan./Feb. 1994, p.38-47.
90. Jer 2:6.
91. Acts 5:40.
92. Greg Breining, "Rising from the Bogs," *Nature Conservancy*, July/Aug. 1992, p.24-29.
93. E.g., Gen 18:5; Acts 16:37.
94. E.g., Gen 18:4; Acts 28:13.
95. Deut 19:5.
96. Gen 18:7.
97. Num 34:5; 2 Sam 5:23.
98. Jos 15:3; 2 Ki 3:9; Acts 28:13.
99. Job 36:3.
100. Num 20:10; 2 Chr 18:8.
101. Gen 27:13; NIV, NASB, NRSV: Jer 36:21.
102. Gen 18:4.
103. Gen 27:14.
104. Jud 18:18.
105. Christine Gorman, "Dollars for Deeds," *Time*, May 16, 1994, p.51.
106. Ex 27:10,11, 36:38, 38:10,11,12,17,19.
107. Ex 27:17, 38:17,28.
108. Ex 27:11, 38:10,11,12,17,19.
109. Ex 36:38.
110. Ibid.
111. Is 59:13.
112. Pro 25:4.
113. Pro 17:3, 27:21.
114. Job 28:1.
115. Pro 25:4.
116. Pro 17:3, 27:21.
117. Ibid.
118. Ex 25:17.
119. Gen 24:22.
120. Ex 25:39.

121. Ex 30:13.
122. Ex 38:26.
123. Ex 16:16.
124. Acts 27:28.
125. E.g., Gen 1:6; Dan 12:3.
126. Gen 1:6,20.
127. Ibid.
128. Ps 19:1, 150:1.
129. Ibid.
130. Dixy Lee Ray, "Plutonium as a Resource Now and in the Future," *21st Century Science & Technology*, Summer 1994, p.36-43.
131. E.g., Ex 13:12; Deut 33:17.
132. Gen 4:4; Num 3:41; Deut 12:6,17, 14:23; Neh 10:36.
133. Ex 13:12, 34:19,20.
134. Ibid.
135. Num 18:15,17.
136. NRSV, NIV, NKJV: Num 3:41; Neh 10:36; NIV, NKJV: Deut 12:6,17, 14:23.
137. E.g., Gen 4:4; Neh 10:36.
138. Gen 4:4.
139. Is 16:2.
140. NRSV: Lev 9:3; Ezek 46:13; NIV: Is 11.6; NASB: Lev 14:10; Micah 6:6.
141. Is 28:25,27; Ezek 4:9.
142. Is 28:25,27.
143. Ibid.
144. Ezek 4:9.
145. Ex 16:31.
146. Matt 23:23.
147. John Ayto, *Dictionary of Word Origins*, (New York: Arcade Publishing, 1990), s.v., "flag."
148. Ex 2:3,5; Is 19:6.
149. Ex 2:3,5.
150. Is 19:6.
151. NIV, NASB, NRSV: Jer 51:32.
152. NASB: Is 19:7.
153. NRSV, NIV: Ex 2:3.
154. NASB, NIV: Is 58:5; NKJV: Is 18:2.
155. 2 Sam 6:19; 1 Chr 16:3.
156. Song 2:5; Is 22:24; Hos 3:1.
157. 2 Sam 6:19.
158. Hos 3:1.
159. Song 2:5.
160. Is 22:24.
161. Ibid.
162. Ibid.
163. Ex 25:29, 37:16; Num 4:7; Est 1:8.

164. Allan Fotheringham, "In the Lap of Controversy," *Maclean's* Sept. 26, 1994, p.64.
165. Lev 3:4,10,15, 4:9, 7:4; Job 15:27.
166. Nah 2:1.
167. Lev 3:4,10,15.
168. Gen 35:11, 46:26.
169. Ted Williams, "Alaska's Rush for the Gold," *Audubon,* Nov./Dec. 1993, p.50-54.
170. Ezek 25:9, 34:21.
171. Ibid.
172. Gen 49:13; Ezek 25:9.
173. Lev 1:6; 2 Chr 29:34; Micah 3:3.
174. 2 Chr 35:11.
175. 2 Chr 29:34.
176. NASB, NIV: Micah 3:3.
177. Micah 3:3.
178. Lev 1:6; Micah 3:3.
179. Mary Jo McConahay, "Rigoberta Menchu," *Progressive,* Jan. 1993, p.28-31.
180. Gerald Parshall, "The Feuding Fathers," *U.S. News & World Report,* Feb. 1, 1993, p.52-57.
181. 1 Sam 2:13,14.
182. Ex 27:3, 38:3; Num 4:14; 1 Chr 28:17; 2 Chr 4:16.
183. Num 4:14; 1 Chr 28:17.
184. NASB, NIV, NKJV: Ex 27:3.
185. Ex 38:3.
186. 1 Sam 2:13,14.
187. Lev 15:24,33.
188. NRSV, NKJV: Lev 15:24.
189. NASB: Lev 15:24,33.
190. NKJV: Lev 15:33.
191. NRSV: Lev 15:33.
192. NIV: Lev 15:24.
193. NIV: Lev 15:33.
194. Lev 15:24,33.
195. Lev 13:3.
196. Lev 13:2,3,9.
197. *Black's Medical Dictionary,* s.v., "flux."
198. E.g., Num 11:21; Jer 12:5.
199. 1 Sam 14:10, 15:4; 2 Sam 8:4, 10:6; 1 Ki 20:29; 1 Chr 18:4, 19:18.
200. Num 11:21; NIV: Jer 12:5.
201. Jud 20:2.
202. Jer 12:5.
203. 2 Ki 13:7; Jer 12:5.
204. NRSV: 2 Ki 13:7; NKJV: Jer 12:5.
205. Acts 16:35.
206. 2 Chr 2:10.

207. NASB: Jer 52:16; NKJV: Is 61:5.
208. Ps 129:3.
209. Fred Bruning, "Decency, Honor and the Gun Lobby," *Maclean's*, June 12, 1995, p.9.
210. E.g., Gen 41:39; 1 Pet 4:1.
211. Lk 19:9.
212. 1 Cor 11:7; NIV, NRSV, NASB: Gen 41:39.
213. NKJV: Gen 41:39; 2 Sam 19:30; NASB: 1 Sam 20:42.
214. NKJV, NASB: 1 Ki 11:11.
215. E.g., Deut 19:6; 1 Pet 4:13.
216. Heb 7:20.
217. 1 Pet 4:13.
218. Ezra 7:14.
219. E.g., Ex 23:5; 1 Thes 3:5.
220. Jer 51:30.
221. Pro 25:15; Jer 20:9; Eph 4:2, 6:9; Col 3:13.
222. Num 9:13; Ezek 3:27.
223. Rom 2:4, 3:25.
224. 1 Sam 23:13; 2 Chr 25:16; Jer 41:8.
225. 1 Ki 22:6,15.
226. NASB: Ex 23:5.
227. NKJV: Deut 23:22.
228. NIV, NASB: 2 Chr 35:21.
229. NASB: Neh 9:30.
230. Ezek 3:27.
231. NKJV, NASB: 1 Thes 3:1.
232. Jer 20:9, 51:30; Num 9:13; 1 Sam 23:13.
233. Rom 2:4, 3:23.
234. Rom 2:4.
235. Pro 25:15.
236. Pro 25:15; Eph 4:2.
237. Phil 4:5.
238. Job 16:16.
239. Jer 15:15.
240. Douglas L. Wilson, "A Most Abandoned Hypocrite," *American Heritage*, Feb./March 1994, p.36.
241. Ex 28:27, 39:20; 1 Ki 6:20; Ezek 42:7; Acts 27:41.
242. Dan 11:24,25.
243. Ex 28:27, 39:20; 1 Ki 6:20; Ezek 42:7; Acts 27:41.
244. Acts 27:41.
245. Lev 14:16,27.
246. NASB, NIV: Ex 5:6; Matt 20:8; NKJV: 2 Chr 34:10.
247. Neh 10:31.
248. Jonah 4:2.
249. Lk 21:26.
250. Deut 14:1.
251. 2 Sam 2:29.

252. Mk 14:68.
253. Ps 39:12.
254. Maggie Spilner, "Commuter Shoes!" *Prevention*, May 1993, p.94.
255. Acts 27:40.
256. Don A. Schanche, "Where Did Columbus Land?" *Houston Chronicle*, April 8, 1990, p.72EE.
257. Matt 5:36.
258. *Black's Law Dictionary*, s.v., "forswear."
259. Brad Roberts, "Rising Powers," *Current*, March/April 1995, p.20.
260. E.g., Ezra 6:8; Acts 21:30.
261. NRSV: Ezra 6:8.
262. NRSV, NIV: Matt 13:5.
263. NRSV, NIV: Matt 26:49.
264. Mk 1:29.
265. NIV, NRSV: Acts 12:10.
266. Acts 21:30.
267. Mary H. Cooper, "NATO's Changing Role," *CQ Researcher*, Aug. 21, 1992, p.715.
268. 2 Cor 8:10,17; Gal 2:10.
269. 2 Cor 8:8, 9:2.
270. Gal 2:10.
271. 2 Cor 8:10.
272. NIV, NASB, NRSV: 2 Cor 8:8.
273. NIV: 2 Cor 8:17.
274. NKJV: 2 Cor 8:8,17.
275. NASB: 2 Cor 9:2.
276. NKJV: 2 Cor 9:2.
277. 2 Cor 8:17.
278. E.g., Gen 16:16; Lk 16:7.
279. E.g., Gen 25:7; Rev 13:18.
280. 1 Ki 9:14; Jonah 4:11.
281. Nathan Hatch, "The Gift of Brokenness," *Christianity Today*, Nov. 14, 1994, p.34.
282. Pro 26:2.
283. E.g., Ex 27:1; Rev 21:16.
284. Ezek 40:47,48.
285. Rev 21:16.
286. 1 Ki 7:31.
287. Ezek 40:47.
288. 1 Ki 7:5.
289. James 3:12.
290. Gen 7:10.
291. Gen 17:3.
292. Jody Erickson, "The Nutting Chest," *American Heritage*, July/Aug. 1995, p.32.
293. E.g., Gen 1:20; Dan 7:6.
294. E.g., Gen 6:7; Rev 19:21.

295. Ps 91:3; Pro 6:5; Hos 9:8.
296. Ps 124:7.
297. Ps 124:7.
298. Neh 5:18.
299. 1 Ki 4:23.
300. 1 Ki 4:23; Ps 78:27, 148:10.
301. 1 Ki 4:23; Neh 5:18; Ps 78:27, 148:10.
302. Deut 32:11.
303. NKJV: Job 39:13; NRSV: Ps 91:4.
304. NASB, NRSV: Ezek 17:3.
305. Howard Youth, "Flying into Trouble," *World Watch*, Jan./Feb. 1994, p.10-19.
306. Deut 28:26; Jer 7:23; Zech 1:21.
307. Ibid.
308. Zec 1:21.
309. Job 39:21.
310. Ex 13:16; Deut 6:8, 11:18.
311. Ibid.
312. Ex 13:16.
313. Deut 6:8, 11:18.
314. Ibid.
315. Ex 13:16.
316. Matt 23:5.
317. E.g., Deut 32:20; 1 Pet 2:18.
318. Pro 2:14, 6:14, 10:32.
319. Is 57:17.
320. Deut 32:20; Pro 16:28.
321. NRSV, NIV: 2 Sam 22:27.
322. NASB: 2 Sam 22:27.
323. Pro 2:15.
324. NKJV, NASB: Job 5:13.
325. NIV, NRSV: Job 5:13.
326. NIV, NKJV: Ps 18:26.
327. NASB: Ps 18:26.
328. NKJV, NASB: Pro 4:24.
329. NASB: Pro 6:12.
330. NRSV: Pro 8:8.
331. NKJV, NRSV, NIV: 1 Pet 2:18.
332. NASB: 1 Pet 2:18.
333. Pro 2:14; NRSV, NIV, NKJV: Pro 10:32.
334. Job 6:30; 1 Tim 6:5.
335. 1 Ki 18:17; Is 7:3, 36:2; Mal 3:2; Mk 9:3.
336. 1 Ki 18:17; Is 7:3, 36:2.
337. Mal 3:2.
338. 1 Ki 18:17; Is 7:3, 36:2; Mal 3:2.
339. 1 Ki 18:17; Is 7:3, 36:2.
340. 1 Ki 18:17; Is 7:3, 36:2; Mal 3:2; Mk 9:3.

341. NKJV, NIV: Mal 3:2; NASB, NKJV: Mk 9:3.
342. NIV: 1 Ki 18:17; Is 7:3, 36:2.
343. Ezek 38:4.
344. Ezek 21:9,10,11,28.
345. Jer 46:4; Ezek 21:9,10,11,28.
346. Ezek 21:10,11,28.
347. Jer 46:4; Ezek 21:9.
348. Jer 46:4.
349. Dan 10:6.
350. Stanley Kauffman, "Season's Difference," *New Republic*, June 7, 1993, p.26.
351. Lk 24:13; Jn 6:19, 11:18; Rev 14:20, 21:16.
352. O.E.D., s.v., "furlong."
353. Lk 24:13; Jn 6:19, 11:18; Rev 14:20, 21:16.
354. Lk 24:13; Jn 6:19, 11:18.
355. Rev 14:20, 21:16.
356. Lk 24:13; Jn 6:19, 11:18.
357. Rev 14:20, 21:16.
358. 1 Sam 14:14.
359. Hasan M. Jafri, "The Floodgates to Disaster," *Herald*, Oct. 1992, p.20-36.
360. E.g., Gen 31:34; Nah 2:9.
361. Ex 31:7.
362. NIV, NKJV, NASB: Ex 39:33; NRSV: Ex 31:7.
363. Ex 31:9.
364. Ex 31:8, 35:14.
365. 1 Pet 2:18.

Chapter 7

1. Jer 31:22.
2. 1 Tim 5:13.
3. Jer 46:20.
4. Michael Meyer, "No Sex, Just Sales," *Newsweek*, July 17, 1995, p.39.
5. Acts 10:29; Rom 10:21.
6. Jude 11.
7. Titus 1:9.
8. Jude 11.
9. NRSV, NKJV: Rom 10:21.
10. NASB, NIV: Rom 10:21.
11. NKJV, NIV, NRSV: Acts 10:29.
12. NASB, NIV: Lk 21:15.
13. NRSV, NASB, NKJV: Titus 1:9.
14. Carl Gershman, "The United Nations and the New World Order," *Journal of Democracy*, July 1993, p.5-16.
15. Arpad Simenfalvy, "In Search of the Enemy," *The News*, Aug. 1993,

p.1-8.
    16. Matt 3:12; Lk 3:17.
    17. Ps 144:13; Joel 1:17.
    18. Matt 3:12; Lk 3:17.
    19. Joel 1:17.
    20. Ps 144:13.
    21. Joel 1:17.
    22. Is 62:9.
    23. Elijah Anderson, "The Code of the Streets," *Atlantic Monthly,* May 1994, p.81.
    24. 2 Chr 3:6; Job 26:13; Matt 12:44; Lk 11:25; Rev 21:19.
    25. 2 Chr 3:6; NKJV, NASB, NRSV: Rev 21:19.
    26. Matt 12:44; Lk 11:25.
    27. NRSV, NIV: Matt 23:29.
    28. Rev 21:19.
    29. Howard Youth, "Flying into Trouble," *World Watch,* Jan./Feb. 1994, p.10-19.
    30. *The Barnhart Dictionary of Etymology,* s.v., "gay."
    31. Is 24:8,11.
    32. Is 23:13, 24:8,11; Hos 2:11.
    33. Gene Smith, "The it Girl," *American Heritage,* July/Aug. 1995, p.102.
    34. Nah 3:6; Heb 10:33.
    35. Nah 3:6.
    36. Heb10:33.
    37. Ecc 4:6.
    38. Lam 3:14.
    39. Lev 19:19; 2 Tim 2:23.
    40. Job 21:10; Gal 4:24.
    41. Job 38:29.
    42. NRSV, NASB, NKJV: Lev 19:19.
    43. Job 38:29.
    44. NASB, NIV: 2 Tim 2:23.
    45. NKJV: 2 Tim 2:23.
    46. NRSV, NASB, NIV: Gal 4:24.
    47. Job 8:14.
    48. E.g., Matt 1:18; Jude 20.
    49. E.g., Gen 25:8; Acts 12:23.
    50. Job 11:20.
    51. Gen 49:33; Matt 27:50; Acts 5:10.
    52. E.g., Gen 25:8, 49:33.
    53. Matt 1:18; Jude 20.
    54. Is 29.4.
    55. Matt 14:26; Mk 6:49.
    56. Lk 24:37,39.
    57. Lev 11:18; Deut 14:17.
    58. Ibid.
    59. Lev 11:13; Deut 14:12.

60. Lev 11:18; Deut 14:17.
61. Job 18:9; Is 8:14; Amos 3:5.
62. Ps 140:5, 141:9.
63. NIV, NKJV: Ps 140:5, 141:9.
64. NRSV, NASB: Ps 140:5, 141:9.
65. Amos 3:5.
66. Job 18:9.
67. Laurie Stone, "Living Off the Grid: Catching the Wind," *Mother Earth News*, Oct./Nov. 1994, p.70.
68. E.g., Ex 28:4; Rev 1:13.
69. Ex 28:40, 29:9; Lev 8:13; Pro 31:24; Ezek 23:15; Rev 15:6.
70. Ps 45:3.
71. Ex 28:39.
72. Ex 39:21.
73. 2 Sam 18:11.
74. 2 Ki 1:8; Job 12:18; Rev 1:13, 15:6.
75. Job 12:18.
76. Alan Weisman, "The Drug Lords vs. the Tarahumara," *Los Angeles Times*, Jan. 9, 1994, sec. Magazine, p.10.
77. Rev 4:6, 15:2, 21:18,21.
78. Job 37:18; 1 Cor 13:12; 2 Cor 3:18; James 1:23.
79. Is 3:23; Ex 38:8.
80. Lev 11:14; Deut 14:13.
81. NRSV: Lev 11:14.
82. NASB, NKJV: Lev 11:14.
83. NIV: Lev 11:14.
84. Job 28:7.
85. NKJV, NASB: Is 34:15.
86. 1 Chr 29:2; Lk 9:29.
87. 1 Chr 29:2.
88. 1 Chr 29:2; Lk 9:29.
89. Lk 9:29.
90. Job 39:23; Deut 32:11.
91. Ps 104:15.
92. Job 41:32.
93. Hab 3:11.
94. Claire Kowalchik, "Stranger in Paradise," *Runner's World*, Sept. 1994, p.72.
95. Acts 17:29; Rom 1:20; Col 2:9.
96. Acts 17:29; Col 2:9.
97. Rom 1:20.
98. Acts 17:29.
99. Rom 1:20.
100. Col 2:9.
101. Acts 17:29; Rom 1:20; Col 2:9.
102. Rom 1:20; Col 2:9.
103. Acts 17:29.

104. "Slim Kim," *Economist*, Sept. 17, 1994, p.37.
105. E.g., Gen 27:15; Rev 18:14.
106. James 2:2.
107. Lk 21:5.
108. NASB: Ezek 17:23.
109. NKJV: Ezek 17:23.
110. NRSV: Ezek 17:23.
111. NIV: Ezek 17:23.
112. NRSV, NIV: Zec 10:3.
113. NKJV: Zec 10:3.
114. NRSV, NKJV: 2 Chr 26:19.
115. Ps 16:6, 45:1; Pro 28:10; Jer 11:16.
116. Patricia M. Carey, "Population and World Growth: Which Industries Benefit," *International Business*, Oct. 1994, p.50.
117. Pro 7:19; Matt 20:11, 24:43; Mk 14:14; Lk 12:39, 22:11.
118. Matt 24:43; Mk 14:14; Lk 12:39, 22:11.
119. Matt 24:43; Lk 12:39.
120. Mk 14:14; Lk 22:11.
121. Matt 20:11.
122. Ezek 27:26.
123. Lev 22:12.
124. Gen 11:3,4,7, 38:16; Jud 7:3; 2 Ki 5:5; Ecc 2:1; James 4:13, 5:1.
125. Deut 23:10.
126. Gen 35:20; 1 Cor 15:55.
127. 1 Tim 3:8,11; Titus 2:2.
128. 1 Tim 3:4; Titus 2:7.
129. Ibid.
130. Gen 18:20.
131. 1 Tim 3:4; Titus 2:7.
132. Titus 2:7.
133. James O. Jackson, "The Balkans: No Rush to Judgment," *Time*, June 27, 1994, p.48-51.
134. Ex 28:9,36; 2 Chr 2:7,14.
135. 1 Ki 7:36; 2 Chr 3:7.
136. Is 22:16.
137. Ex 32:4; 2 Chr 2:14; Zec 3:9.
138. 1 Ki 7:31.
139. E.g., Ex 20:4; Acts 17:29.
140. NKJV: Is 30:22; NASB: Ex 32:4.
141. Deut 4:16; Jer 8:19.
142. Gen 14:1.
143. Gen 31:10,12; Zec 6:3,6.
144. Gen 3:10,12.
145. Zec 6:3,6.
146. Is 60:2; Jer 13:16; Matt 13:15; Acts 28:27.
147. Matt 13:15; Acts 28:27.
148. Is 60:2.

149. Jer 13:16.
150. 2 Ki 8:13.
151. Ps 119:70.
152. Jude 7.
153. Hos 9:7.
154. Peter H. Gleick, "Water, War & Peace in the Middle East," *Environment*, April 1994, p.6.
155. E.g., Ex 21:14; Rev 14:5.
156. Col 2:4,18.
157. 2 Pet 2:14.
158. Gen 3:13, 29:25; Num 25:18; Josh 9:22; 2 Cor 11:3.
159. Ps 32:2.
160. NIV: Ps 55:11.
161. NRSV: Ps 55:11.
162. NRSV, NIV, NASB: 1 Thes 2:3.
163. NRSV: Ex 21:14.
164. NASB: EX 21:14.
165. Gen 29:25; Jos 9:22; 2 Cor 11:3.
166. Ps 10:7.
167. Ps 119:118; Pro 12:5.
168. Ps 55:11.
169. Jn 1:47; 1 Pet 2:1, 3:10.
170. Is 30:12.
171. Pro 26:26.
172. Ps 119:78.
173. Pro 26:26.
174. 2 Pet 2:14.
175. Rev 2:20.
176. Okey Ndibe, "Can African Americans Save Africa?" *African World*, Nov./Dec. 1993, p.4-19.

Chapter 8

1. Ex 28:32, 39:23; Job 41:26.
2. 2 Chr 26:14; Neh 4:16.
3. NKJV, NIV, NRSV: Neh 4:16; NASB, NIV, NKJV: 2 Chr 26:14.
4. NRSV, NASB, NKJV: Ex 28:32, 39:23.
5. 1 Sam 17:5,38.
6. Ibid.
7. Gen 36:40.
8. NRSV, NKJV: Jud 3:22.
9. NASB, NIV: Jud 3:22.
10. John Pfeiffer, "The Emergence of Modern Humans," *Mosaic*, Spring 1990, p.14-23.
11. Acts 8:3.
12. Lk 12:48; Acts 8:3.

13. NRSV, NASB: 2 Chr 29:21.
14. Ex 28:38; Ezek 44:24.
15. Ex 20:11; Lk 11:2.
16. Ex 28:38; Lk 11:2.
17. NRSV, NASB, NIV: Ex 29:1, 40:9.
18. NRSV, NIV: Ezek 44:24.
19. NASB, NRSV: Lev 22:2.
20. NRSV, NASB: Lev 22:32.
21. NIV, NRSV, NASB: Lev 19:8.
22. NIV, NRSV: Num 5:10.
23. Matt 6:9; Lk 11:2.
24. Gen 2:3.
25. Lev 16:19, 25:10; Ezek 20:20.
26. John M. McClintock, "Chiapas Uprising Attacks Myth of Mexican Stability," *Sun,* Jan. 9, 1994, p.1F.
27. 1 Ki 18:21; Ps 38:17; Matt 18:8; Mk 9:45; Lk 14:21; Jn 5:3.
28. Micah 4:6,7; Zep 3:19.
29. Gen 32:31.
30. Jer 20:10.
31. Matt 18:8; Mk 9:45; Lk 14:21; Jn 5:3.
32. Gen 32:31; 1 Ki 18:21; Ps 38:17; Jer 20:10; Micah 4:6,7; Zep 3:19.
33. Matt 18:8; Mk 9:45; Lk 14:21; Jn 5:3.
34. 2 Sam 9:3.
35. 1 Sam 15:32.
36. E.g., Gen 16:1; Lk 1:38.
37. Gen 33:1,2; 2 Sam 6:20; Is 14:2; Jer 34:11,16; Joel 2:29.
38. Lk 1:48.
39. Gen 33:6; Ruth 2:13; Acts 2:18.
40. NKJV, NIV: Gen 16:1.
41. NRSV: Gen 16:1.
42. NASB: Gen 16:1.
43. NIV: Gen 30:4.
44. NASB: Lk 1:48.
45. NASB, NRSV, NKJV: Ex 20:10,17.
46. Ps 86:16, 116:16; Nah 2:7.
47. Mark Muro, "A New Era of Eros in Advertising," *Boston Globe,* April 16, 1989, p.77.
48. 1 Sam 14:30; Mk 11:13; Lk 14:29; Acts 5:39, 17:27; 2 Cor 9:4.
49. NRSV, NASB, NKJV: Mk 11:13; NRSV, NIV, NASB: Acts 17:27.
50. NRSV, NASB: Lk 14:29; NRSV: 2 Cor 9:4.
51. NIV: 2 Cor 9:4.
52. NASB: Acts 5:39.
53. NRSV: Acts 5:39.
54. NKJV: 2 Cor 9:4; Acts 5:39.
55. David Rohde, "SatelliteTV Leaves Mark on the Developing World," *Christian Science Monitor,* July 13, 1994, p.4.
56. Lev 3:9; Jud 9:52; 1 Ki 21:1; 1 Chr 19:4; Ps 63:8; Acts 18:7.

57. E.g., Gen 16:6; Acts 27:8.
58. Lev 3:9.
59. NKJV, NRSV, NASB: Jud 9:52.
60. Acts 18:7.
61. Mk 10:23.
62. NKJV, NRSV, NASB: Gen 16:6.
63. Acts 27:8.
64. 1 Sam 18:8.
65. 2 Sam 12:31; 1 Chr 20:3.
66. Ibid.
67. Job 39:10.
68. Is 28:24.
69. 2 Sam 12:31; 1 Chr 20:3; Job 39:10.
70. Is 28:24.
71. Steve Ettlinger, "Lawn and Garden Tractors," *Horticulture,* April 1994, p.70.
72. E.g., Deut 12:15; Is 35:6.
73. 1 Ki 4:23; Lam 1:6.
74. Deut 12:5; 1 Ki 4:23.
75. Song 2:9,17, 8:14.
76. Lam 1:6.
77. Gen 49:21; Pro 5:19; Jer 14:5.
78. 1 Sam 23:22, 30:31; Ezek 26:17.
79. 1 Sam 23:22.
80. NRSV, NIV: 1 Sam 30:31.
81. NKJV: 1 Sam 23:22.
82. NASB: 1 Sam 30:31.
83. NKJV: 1 Sam 30:31.
84. Ps 74:20.
85. Ibid.
86. Ps 44:19; Is 34:13, 35:7; Rev 18:2.
87. Ps 74:20; Song 4:8; Is 35:7.
88. Song 4:8.
89. Ps 44:19; Is 34:13; Jer 9:11, 10:22, 49:33, 51:37; Rev 18:2.
90. 1 Sam 23:22.
91. Is 34:13, 35:7; Jer 9:11, 10:22, 49:33, 51:37.
92. Vladimir Klimenko, "A Tale of Two Countries," *Mother Jones,* July/Aug. 1993, p.54-57.
93. Jer 17:6, 48:6.
94. Ibid.
95. Ibid.
96. Ibid.
97. Ibid.
98. John Carey, "The Secret Lives of Birds," *National Wildlife,* June/July 1993, p.38-45.
99. Acts 27:11.
100. Robert Berner, "An Update for Resumes: Software Lets Computer Do

the Choosing," *Patriot Ledger,* Aug. 6-7, 1994, p.23.
101. 1 Sam 21:13.
102. Hos 10:4; Amos 6:12.
103. Ibid.
104. Amos 6:12; Hos 10:4.
105. Hos 10:4; Amos 6:12.
106. Deut 29:18.
107. Pro 5:4.
108. Hos 10:4.
109. Michael Clugston, "Algonquin Park: A Beloved National Treasure Enters Its Second Century," *Canadian Geographic,* Nov./Dec. 1993, p.20-34.
110. E.g., Gen 37:17; James 4:1.
111. E.g., Gen 4:12; Rev 14:13.
112. Num 15:23; Matt 21:19.
113. Gen 42:15.
114. Ex 1:11.
115. Jud 2:21.
116. NIV: 2 Ki 5:17.
117. NASB: 2 Ki 5:17.
118. NKJV, NASB: Num 15:23.
119. NRSV: Num 15.23.
120. NIV: Num 15:23.
121. Matt 21:19.
122. Lk 1:48.
123. Ex 13:18; Lev 20:24; 2 Chr 26:15; Zech 11:7; Heb 7:25, 8:3, 13:13.
124. Ex 13:18; Lev 20:24.
125. Lk 7:47.
126. Rom 1:15; 1 Cor 8:4; Heb 8:3, 9:18.
127. Is 43:13.
128. E.g., Gen 34:22; 1 Jn 4:17.
129. Matt 9:26; Heb 5:3.
130. Ex 4:10, 5:7,8,14; Jos 3:4; Ruth 2:11; 1 Sam 4:7; 2 Cor 13:2.
131. Ecc 2:25; 1 Pet 2:21.
132. Ezek 16:29; Mal 3:10.
133. NASB: Jn 13:7; NKJV, NRSV: Is 41:23.
134. Num 3:12.
135. Gen 41:41.
136. Jos 3:4; 1 Sam 4:7.
137. NRSV, NIV, NKJV: Matt 9:26.
138. NRSV, NIV, NKJV: 1 Pet 2:21.
139. NASB, NIV, NKJV: Mal 3:10; Jn 4:37.
140. Hans Jonas, "The Burden and Blessing of Mortality," *Hastings Center Report,* Jan./Feb. 1992, p.34-40.
141. Charles Bennett, "Baseball & Race: The Final Frontier--Black College Baseball Players," *Times-Picayune,* May 23, 1994, p.D1.
142. Greg Kaye, "Florida Fights the Alien Invasion," *The New American,* Nov. 13, 1995, p.5.

143. 1 Cor 11:19; Gal 5:20; 2 Pet 2:1.
144. Titus 3:10.
145. Ibid.
146. Ibid.
147. Acts 24:14.
148. NRSV, NASB, NKJV: 1 Cor 11:19; NRSV, NASB, NIV: Gal 5:20.
149. 2 Pet 2:1.
150. Gal 5:20.
151. Acts 5:17, 15:5, 24:5, 26:5, 28:22.
152. Acts 5:17, 15:5.
153. Acts 24:5, 26:5, 28:22.
154. Michael Mason, "Trial and Error," *Health*, Jan./Feb. 1994, p.76.
155. Carl A. Posey, "Ozone Forecast: Partly Cloudy," *Air & Space*, Oct./Nov. 1994, p.28-38.
156. Rom 11:20; 1 Tim 6:17; 2 Tim 3:4.
157. Ibid.
158. Rom 11:20; 1 Tim 6:17.
159. 2 Tim 3:4.
160. Rom 11:20; 1 Tim 6:17; 2 Tim 3:4.
161. Suzanne Garment, "Freedom of the Press: Pleading the First," *Columbia Journalism Review*, Nov./Dec. 1991, p.41-55.
162. Gen 49:21; Pro 5:19; Jer 14:5.
163. 2 Sam 22:34; Job 39:1; Ps 18:33, 29:9; Song 2:7, 3:5; Hab 3:19.
164. Gen 49:21; Job 39:1.
165. 2 Sam 22:34; Ps 18:33; Song 2:7, 3:5; Hab 3:19.
166. Job 6:5.
167. E.g., 2 Sam 2:23; Acts 27:41.
168. Gen 33:2; Jer 50:12.
169. Num 2:31; Deut 25:18; Josh 10:19.
170. NRSV, NIV, NASB: 2 Sam 2:23.
171. NRSV, NIV, NASB: 2 Chr 4:4.
172. NRSV, NIV, NASB: Joel 2:20.
173. NKJV: 2 Sam 2:23.
174. NKJV: 1 Ki 7:25.
175. Mk 4:38; Acts 27:41.
176. NRSV: Jer 50:12; NKJV: Gen 33:2.
177. NIV, NKJV,. NASB: Jer 50:12.
178. Num 2:31.
179. Josh 10:19.
180. 2 Chr 4:4.
181. 1 Ki 7:25.
182. E.g., Gen 15:16; Rev 21:9.
183. E.g., Ex 7:16; 1 Cor 3:2.
184. Gen 42:15; Pro 25:7.
185. Ex 7:16; Jud 16:13.
186. NIV: Jn 5:17.
187. NASB, NRSV: Job 38:11.

188. NIV, NKJV: Job 38:11.
189. Guy Gugliotta, "The Persistence of Poverty," *Washington Post National Weekly Edition*, Jan. 3-9, 1994, p.6-7.
190. Meinhard Miegel, "Shorter Hours, Shrinking Paychecks," *The News*, Feb. 1994, p.1-5.
191. Ex 16:14; 1 Ki 2:6,9; Is 46:4.
192. Lev 19:32; Job 38:29, 41:32; Pro 16:31.
193. Ex 16:14; Job 38:29.
194. Ps 147:16.
195. 1 Ki 2:6,9; Is 46:4.
196. NKJV, NASB: Lev 19:32.
197. NRSV, NKJV, NIV: Job 41:32.
198. NKJV: Pro 16:31.
199. NRSV, NIV: Lev 19:32.
200. Job 38:29.
201. Vivien Bowers, "Avalanche! Starting a Slide for Safety's Sake," *Canadian Geographic*, March/April 1994, p.22-31.
202. James Shreeve, "As the Old World Turns," *Discover*, Jan. 1993, p.24.
203. Ezek 40:3.
204. Deut 21:19.
205. Jud 16:3.
206. Dan 2:48.
207. Deut 14:1.
208. Jos 11:9; 2 Sam 8:4; 1 Chr 18:4.
209. Jos 11:6.
210. Jos 11:9; 2 Sam 8:4; 1 Chr 18:4.
211. Deut 6:11.
212. E.g., Jud 4:17; Heb 3:16.
213. NRSV, NIV: Jud 16:22; 2 Sam 2:23.
214. NASB, NKJV: Jud 16:22; 1 Sam 8:9.
215. NRSV: 2 Sam 12:14; NIV: Acts 27:26.
216. NIV: 2 Sam 23:19.
217. Gen 9:5.
218. Matt 21:18; Lk 4:2.
219. Matt 4:2, 12:1,3, 25:35,37,42,44; Mk 2:25; Lk 6:3.
220. NASB: Pro 27:7; NIV: Is 8:21.
221. Wayne Ellwood, "Hidden History: Columbus & the Colonial Legacy," *New Internationalist*, Dec. 1991, p.4.
222. 2 Chr 26:10; 1 Cor 3:9.
223. Gen 9:20; Jer 51:33; Amos 5:16; Zech 13:5; Jn 15:1; 2 Tim 2:6; James 5:7.
224. E.g., 2 Ki 25:12; Lk 20:16.
225. 2 Tim 2:6; James 5:7.
226. NIV: 2 Ki 25:12; NASB: 2 Chr 26:10.
227. NRSV, NIV: Matt 21:34.
228. NIV: Jn 15:1.

229. NRSV: Jn 15:1; NASB: Matt 21:38.
230. NKJV: Matt 21:38; Jn 15:1.
231. Xi Mi, "Farmers Need Growing Income," *China Daily*, Feb. 2, 1994, p.4.
232. Gail Fondahl, "Mending Cultural Fences," *Earthwatch*, Jan./Feb. 1993, p.14-18.
233. Hal Kane, "Growing Fish in Fields," *World Watch*, Sept./Oct. 1993, p.20-27.
234. Holly B. Brough, "A New Lay of the Land," *World Watch*, Jan./Feb. 1991, p.12-19.

Chapter 9

1. 2 Tim 2:20.
2. John Hochman, "Recovered Memory Therapy and False Memory Syndrome," *Skeptic*, Spring 1994, p.58-61.
3. Jer 43:13.
4. David J. Eicher, "Death of a Comet," *Astronomy*, Oct. 1994, p.40-45.
5. Deut 23:9.
6. Ps 74:18.
7. Misha Glenny, "The Bear in the Caucasus," *Harper's*, March 1994, p.45-53.
8. E.g., 2 Ki 25:8; Jer 52:30.
9. Paul Taylor, "Father of His Country," *Washington Post*, Feb. 13, 1994, sec. Magazine, p.10.
10. 2 Tim 3:3.
11. Edward G. Shirley, "Not Fanatics, and Not Friends," *Atlantic Monthly*, Dec. 1993, p.104.
12. Ezra 6:11.
13. Gen 41:49.
14. *Black's Law Dictionary*, s.v., "implead."
15. Pro 6:3.
16. Mk 6:1.
17. Ched Myers, "Looking for Justice, Holding the Peace," *Sojourners*, Nov. 1992, p.30.
18. Jn 5:3,7; Acts 4:9, 14:8.
19. NASB, NKJV: Jn 5:3,7.
20. NASB, NKJV: Acts 14:8.
21. NKJV: Acts 4:9.
22. NIV: Acts 4:9, 14:8.
23. NRSV: Jn 5:3; NIV: Acts 4:9.
24. NIV: Jn 5:3.
25. Is 16:14.
26. Lauran Neergaard, "Scientists Debate Whether to Kill Last Remaining Smallpox," *Orange County Register*, June 20, 1993, p.24.
27. Pro 7:13; Ezek 2:4, 3:7.

28. Ibid.
29. Ezek 3:7.
30. Ezek 2:4, 3:7.
31. Pro 7:13.
32. Pro 7:13; Ezek 2:4, 3:7.
33. Anthony Spaeth, "No Peace in the Valley," *Harper's,* April 1993, p.81-88.
34. 1 Cor 7:5.
35. Ibid.
36. 2 Tim 3:3.
37. Stephen Budiansky, "The Cold War Experiments," *U.S. News & World Report,* Jan. 24, 1994, p.32.
38. Aristides, "Toys in My Attic," *American Scholar,* Winter 1992, p.7.
39. Pro 25:10; Ezek 36:3.
40. NRSV, NIV, NKJV: Ezek 36:3.
41. NIV, NKJV: Pro 25:10.
42. Ezek 22:5.
43. Is 44:11.
44. Brian McGinty, "A Shaky Past," *American History Illustrated,* March/April 1990, p.16.
45. 2 Cor 6:15; 1 Tim 5:8.
46. Ibid.
47. Num 14:33.
48. Frank Greve and Susan Bennett, "A Threatening Trade: Arms for Allies--New World Order: Buy American," *News,* June 9, 1991, p.4A.
49. NRSV: Rom 11:33; NASB: Is 40:28.
50. Ps 31:18, 94:4; Is 3:5; Zep 3:4.
51. Ps 75:5; Pro 21:24; Dan 8:23; Rom 1:30.
52. Num 16:1; Hos 7:16; Rom 1:30.
53. Ps 54:3.
54. NKJV, NASB: 1 Sam 17:28; NIV, NRSV: Is 16:6.
55. Jim Donahue, "The Missing Rap Sheet: Government Records on Corporate Abuses," *MultinationalMonitor,* Dec. 1992, p.17-19.
56. *Black's Law Dictionary,* s.v., "injurious."
57. Ezek 9:2,3,11.
58. Ibid.
59. Ibid.
60. Ps 108:9.
61. Deut 19:18; Est 2:23; Ps 9:12.
62. NASB, NIV: Deut 19:18; NRSV, NASB, NIV: Est 2:23.
63. NKJV, NRSV: Deut 19:18; NKJV: Est 2:23.
64. Stuart Fischoff, "Confession of a TV Talk Show Shrink," Psychology Today, Sept./Oct. 1995, p 38.
65. E.g., Ps 106:40; Gal 2:13.
66. E.g., Deut 19:6; 1 Pet 4:13.
67. Matt 12:22; NIV, NKJV, NRSV: Lk 12:1.
68. Deut 19:6.

69. NRSV: Matt 25:40,45; Heb 3:3; NIV: Heb 3:3.
70. NASB: Matt 25:40,45.
71. Heb 3:3.
72. Rom 11:13.
73. Matt 25:40,45; Phil 1:7; Heb 3:3, 7:20.
74. Heb 7:20.
75. E.g., Gen 19:8; Heb 9:27.
76. E.g., Gen 18:5; Heb 8:6.
77. 1 Pet 4:13.
78. Roy Beck, "The Ordeal of Immigration in Wausau," *Atlantic Monthly*, April 1994, p.84.
79. Maggie McLinney, "Return to the Future," *Newsweek*, March 6, 1995, p.21.
80. Lk 23:23; Rom 12:12; 2 Tim 4:2.
81. Lk 7:4; Acts 26:7.
82. Ibid.
83. NRSV: Lk 23:23.
84. NKJV, NIV, NASB: Lk 23:23.
85. NRSV, NASB: Rom 12:12.
86. NKJV, NASB: 2 Tim 4:2.
87. NIV: Rom 12:12.
88. NKJV: Rom 12:12.
89. NRSV: 2 Tim 4:2.
90. NIV: 2 Tim 4:2.
91. Heb 6:17.
92. 1 Cor 14:9.
93. Job 32:14.
94. Pro 18:1.
95. Pro 14:10.
96. Pro 18:10.
97. Micah 2:2.
98. Ezek 26:56.
99. Acts 27:30.
100. E.g., Ex 29:13; Lev 9:19.
101. Num 5:21,22.
102. Is 20:6, 23:2,6; Acts 13:6, 28:11; Rev 1:9.
103. E.g., Gen 10:5; Zep 2:11.
104. NIV, NASB: Is 42:10.
105. NKJV, NASB, NRSV: Is 24:15.
106. NIV: Ps 97:1.
107. NKJV, NIV: Jer 2:10.
108. Ps 72:10; Is 40:15.
109. Ps 72:10, 97:1; Is 40:15; Jer 31:10; Ezek 27:15,35.
110. Jerry Dennis, "Born of Fire and Stone," *Wildlife Conservation*, Sept./Oct. 1993, p.44.
111. E.g., Gen 48:6; Lk 8:44.
112. Ps 68:20; Pro 4:23.

113. E.g., Lev 12:7; Lk 8:44.
114. Lev 15:2,3.
115. Lev 12:7.
116. Ezek 23:20.
117. 2 Ki 18:27; Is 36:12.

Chapter 10

1. Ted J. Rakstis, "The Kid Market: Pint-Size Consumers," *Kiwanis Magazine,* May 1990, p.29.
2. Archie C. Epps, "He Urged Blacks to Alter the System," *Boston Globe,* Jan. 19, 1986, sec. Focus, p.89.
3. 2 Sam 23:17; 1 Chr 11:19, 12:19; Lk 8:23; 1 Cor 15:30.
4. Jud 5:18.
5. 1 Chr 12:19.
6. 2 Sam 23:17; 1 Chr 11:19.
7. Lk 8:23; 1 Cor 15:30.
8. 1 Chr 12:19.
9. Jud 5:18.
10. Jud 5:18; 1 Chr 11:19, 12:19; Lk 8:23.
11. 2 Sam 23:17.
12. Ruth 4:6.
13. 2 Sm 23:17; 1 Chr 12:19; Lk 8:23; 1 Cor 15:30.
14. Job 3:14; 2 Sam 18:13.
15. Elijah Anderson, "The Code of the Streets," *Atlantic Monthly,* May 1994, p.81.
16. 2 Chr 34:11.
17. Roger L. Welsch, "A Home on the Range," *World & I,* Sept. 1990, p.618-629.
18. O.E.D., s.v., "j."
19. Ibid.
20. Rev 1:8, 21:6, 22:13.
21. Pete Carey, "What'll It Be?" *San Jose Mercury News,* sec. Magazine, p.16.

Chapter 11

1. Ezek 13:18,21.
2. Is 3:23.
3. Ibid.
4. Kathy Lally, "The Wild Amur," *Baltimore Sun,* Sept. 13, 1992, p.1A.
5. Num 20:5.
6. 1 Cor 15:37.
7. Amos 9:9.

8. Deut 23:25, 32:14; Mk 4:28; Lk 6:1; Jn 12:24.
9. Mk 4:28; Jn 12:24.
10. Eugene Linden, "The Last Eden," *Time,* July 13, 1992, p.62-68.
11. E.g., Gen 32:15; Amos 4:1.
12. Ibid.
13. Is 7:21.
14. Gen 6:4.
15. Hugh Leach, "From the Himalayas to the Hindu Raj," *Asian Affairs,* June 1993, p.145.
16. Ex 25:33,35, 37:19,21.
17. E.g., Ex 25:31; 1 Ki 7:24.
18. Ex 25:31, 37:21.
19. Ex 37:17,20,21.
20. Ex 25:31, 37:21.
21. E.g., Gen 4:1; Matt 1:25.
22. Ibid.
23. E.g., Gen 4:1; 1 Ki 1:4.
24. Num 31:17,18,35; Jud 21:12.
25. Ps 6:2.
26. Job 17:5.

Chapter 12

1. Gen 45:17; 1 Ki 12:11; Lk 11:46.
2. Gen 42:26, 44:13; Neh 4:17; Acts 28:10.
3. Gen 45:23; 1 Sam 16:2; Is 1:4; Matt 11:28; 2 Tim 3:6.
4. Hab 2:6.
5. Neh 13:15; Acts 27:10.
6. Acts 21:3.
7. Gen 44:13; 1 Sam 16:2.
8. NASB: Is 1:4.
9. NASB: Acts 28:10.
10. NKJV: Acts 28:10.
11. Matt 11:28.
12. Ps 144:14.
13. Pro 28:17.
14. Ezek 27:25.
15. Job 36:16,17; Ps 105:37; Song 8:14.
16. Song 8:14.
17. Misha Glenny, "The Bear in the Caucasus," *Harper's,* March 1994, p.45-53.
18. Jer 46:4.
19. Job 39:23, 41:29.
20. Num 25:7; 1 Sam 18:10,11, 19:9,10, 20:33; NKJV omits 1 Sam 18:10.
21. Fen Montaigne and Stephen Seplow, "Inside the Revolution," *Philadelphia Inquirer,* Oct. 10, 1993, p.D1.

22. 1 Ki 18:28.
23. Dick Kaukas, "Living with Diabetes," *Courier-Journal,* July 11, 1993, p.H1.
24. Lev 11:19; Deut 14:18.
25. Ibid.
26. Richard Conniff, "The Mole Has a Way of Undermining Our Assumptions," *Smithsonian,* March 1994, p.52.
27. Mk 7:22; 2 Cor 12:21; Gal 5:19; Eph 4:19; 1 Pet 4:3; Jude 4.
28. Ibid.
29. 2 Cor 12:21; Gal 5:19; 1 Pet 4:3.
30. Eph 4:19.
31. Mk 7:22.
32. Jude 4.
33. Jeremy Iggers, "Food Guilt: Innocence Lost," *Utne Reader,* Nov./Dec. 1993, p.53-60.
34. Is 5:27; Mk 1:7; Lk 3:16; Jn 1:27.
35. Gen 14:23.
36. Mk 1:7; Lk 3:16.
37. Hab 1:6.
38. Ps 117:1.
39. NRSV: Ps 145:4; NASB: Ps 117:1.
40. 1 Cor 4:5.
41. Edward Humes, "Deep-Sea Duty," *Orange County Register,* Aug. 7, 1988, p.K1.
42. E.g., Ex 30:18; 2 Ki 16:17.
43. 1 Ki 7:38,40,43; 2 Chr 4:6,14.
44. Ex 30:18; 1 Ki 7:38.
45. Ibid.
46. 1 Ki 7:38,40,43; 2 Chr 4:6,14.
47. Ex 30:18,28, 31:9, 38:8, 39:39, 40:7,11,30; 2 Ki 16:17.
48. E.g., Ex 30:18; 2 Ki 16:17.
49. 2 Ki 16:17.
50. Job 26:7.
51. Gen 41:3,4, 19.
52. Gen 41:9.
53. Gen 41:3,4,19.
54. Gen 41:3,4.
55. Gen 41:20.
56. Job 16:8.
57. Ps 4:2, 5:6.
58. Ibid.
59. Ibid.
60. Jos 2:23
61. Is 25:6; Jer 48:11; Zep 1:12.
62. NRSV, NKJV, NIV: Jer 48:11; NIV, NRSV: Zep 1:12.
63. NRSV, NIV, NASB: Is 25:6.
64. NKJV: Is 25:6; NASB: Jer 48:11.

65. Jude 16.
66. Is 43:13; Rom 1:13; 2 Thes 2:7.
67. 2 Thes 2:7.
68. NRSV: Is 43:13.
69. NIV, NASB, NKJV: Is 43:13.
70. NRSV, NIV, NASB: Rom 1:13.
71. NRSV, NKJV, NASB: 2 Thes 2:7.
72. Acts 21:40, 25:16.
73. Ibid.
74. Mk 7:22; 1 Pet 4:3.
75. Jude 4.
76. Richard Swift, "Fundamentalism: Reaching for Certainty," *New Internationalist*, Aug. 1990, p.4.
77. E.g., Deut 27:16, 32:15; Jud 9:4; 1 Sam 2:30, 18:23, 30.
78. Jer 3:9, 23:32; 2 Cor 1:17.
79. Gen 26:10; Mk 9:39.
80. E.g., Gen 24:64; Is 9:8.
81. Deut 19:5.
82. Is 9:8; Matt 3:16.
83. NASB, NKJV: 1 Sam 2:30, 18:30.
84. NASB: Josh 15:18; Jud 1:14; NASB, NKJV: Jud 4:15; NRSV: 1 Sam 25:23.
85. Matt 3:16.
86. Ibid.
87. Jer 3:9.
88. NRSV: Jer 3:9; NIV, NKJV: 2 Cor 1:17.
89. Ps 13:3.
90. Dan 5:11.
91. Is 40:14.
92. Ps 74:16.
93. Rev 18:1.
94. Ps 18:28.
95. E.g., 2 Ki 25:8; Jer 52:30.
96. Ps 37:35.
97. Ex 28:19, 39:12.
98. Ibid.
99. Rev 21:20.
100. Rev 9:17.
101. Ibid.
102. Ex 28:18.
103. Job 39:4; Dan 1:10.
104. Job 39:4.
105. Dan 1:10.
106. Elijah Anderson, "The Code of the Streets," *Atlantic Monthly*, May 1994, p.81.
107. Matt 17:12; Mk 9:13.
108. Jn 3:8; James 3:4.

109. NASB, NIV, NKJV: Matt 17:12; Mk 9:13.
110. NKJV, NASB: Jn 3:8.
111. NRSV: Matt 17:12; Mk 9:13.
112. NIV: Jn 3:8.
113. NASB, NKJV: James 3:4.
114. NRSV: James 3:4.
115. NRSV: Jn 3:8.
116. Acts 27:21.
117. Dan 2:12.
118. Ex 1:9; Ps 38:19; Acts 7:38; 1 Pet 1:3, 2:5.
119. Acts 7:38; 1 Pet 1:3, 2:5.
120. Ex 1:9; Ps 38:19; Acts 7:38; 1 Pet 1:3, 2:5.
121. Heb 9:18.
122. Donald Culross Peattie, "The Web of Life," *American Horticulturist,* Oct. 1991, p.30-36.
123. Is 29:6.
124. Ps 55:8.
125. Is 28:2.
126. Deut 5:22.
127. Ps 81:7.
128. Rev 19:6.
129. 1 Sam 8:3; 1 Tim 3:3,8; Titus 1:7,11; 1 Pet 5:2.
130. 1 Sam 8:3.
131. 1 Tim 3:8.
132. Ibid.
133. Titus 1:11.
134. 1 Sam 8:3.
135. 1 Tim 3:8.
136. Titus 1:11.
137. 1 Tim 3:3.
138. Sally Jenkins, "The Sorry State of Tennis," *Sports Illustrated,* May 9, 1994, p.78-86.
139. Matt 4:24, 17:15.
140. Ibid.
141. Matt 4:24.
142. Matt 17:15.
143. Matt 4:24, 17:15.
144. Acts 18:14.
145. Jer 5:8.
146. Peter Verburg, "The Devil's in the Fine Print," *Alberta Report,* Nov. 14, 1994, p.34-35.

Chapter 13

1. Acts 19:27.
2. Jos 3:7.

3. 1 Sam 17:5,38.
4. Ibid.
5. Ibid.
6. Ibid.
7. Ex 28:32, 39:23; Job 41:13.
8. Ex 28:32, 39:23.
9. Ex 28:32, 39:23; 2 Chr 26:14; Job 41:13; Jer 46:4, 51:3.
10. Ezra 4:14; Pro 27:27.
11. Pro 27:27.
12. Ezra 4:14.
13. Ibid.
14. Jud 17:10.
15. 1 Chr 26:27.
16. Robin Wright, "The Fuse Still Sizzles on World Population Bomb," *Los Angeles Times*, Aug. 23, 1994, p.H1.
17. Lk 23:32,33, 23:39.
18. Jn 18:30.
19. Ibid.
20. Jn 10:1.
21. Arthur Fisher, "Global Warming: Inside the Greenhouse," *Popular Science*, Sept. 1989, p.63-70.
22. Lev 1:51.
23. Lev 14:44.
24. Titus 3:2.
25. 2 Pet 2:2.
26. Titus 2:2.
27. Ps 12:5.
28. Ezek 28:26.
29. Pro 30:10.
30. Matt 10:25; 1 Pet 2:12.
31. 1 Pet 3:16.
32. Matt 6:24; Lk 16:9,11,13.
33. Ibid.
34. Ibid.
35. Lk 16:9,11.
36. Matt 6:24; Lk 16:13.
37. Charles Trueheart, "Publish and Perish?" *Washington Post*, July 13, 1994, p.B1.
38. E.g., Jud 4:18; Ps 109:29.
39. Is 3:22.
40. Ps 65:13.
41. Ps 89:45.
42. NRSV, NASB: Jud 4:18.
43. NIV: Jud 4:18.
44. NKJV: Jud 4:18.
45. 1 Sam 15:27; Job 1:20.
46. NIV: 2 Ki 2:14.

47. 1 Ki 19:13,19; 2 Ki 2:8,13,14.
48. Heb 1:12.
49. Is 59:17.
50. Jos 7:21.
51. Gen 25:25.
52. Song 5:7.
53. Is 59:17.
54. Andrew Bilski, "The Road Ahead," *Maclean's,* May 16, 1994, p.22-23.
55. Harry Y. McSween, Jr., "A Goddess Unveiled," *Natural History,* Nov. 1993, p.60-65.
56. Kurt Gloor, "Mongolia: The Forgotten Land," *Swiss Review of World Affairs,* Nov. 1993, p.14-19.
57. Matt 16:18.
58. Acts 6:1.
59. Ex 13:12,15, 34:19; Num 3:12, 18:15.
60. Num 3:12.
61. Lk 1:42, 11:27.
62. Ps 2:12.
63. Pro 1:4.
64. 1 Sam 13:20; Is 7:25.
65. 1 Sam 13:21; 2 Chr 34:6.
66. Is 7:25.
67. NRSV, NIV, NKJV: 1 Sam 13:20.
68. 1 Sam 13:21.
69. 1 Sam 13:20,21.
70. Damon Darlin and William G. Flanagan, "Shovelware," *Forbes,* April 10, 1995, p.108.
71. Deut 23:10.
72. 2 Chr 29:16.
73. Michael Rogers, "Simply Awesome!" *National Wildlife,* Aug./Sept. 1992, p.44-49.
74. Dennis Overbye, "God's Turnstile: The Work of John Wheeler and Stephen Hawking," *Mercury,* July/Aug. 1991, p.98-108.
75. Pro 22:29; Is 2:9, 5:15, 31:8; Acts 21:39.
76. NRSV: Pro 22:29.
77. NASB, NIV: pro 22:29.
78. NKJV: Pro 22:29.
79. NIV: Acts 21:39.
80. NASB: Acts 21:39.
81. Acts 21:39.
82. Pro 23:6; Mk 7:19; Acts 15:29; 1 Cor 6:13; 1 Tim 4:3; Heb 9:10, 13:9.
83. Gen 40:17.
84. E.g., Gen 1:29; Heb 12:16.
85. Ex 16:12; Num 11:4.
86. Ex 40:29; Lev 2:6.
87. Pro 27:25.

88. Gen 2:18; 2 Pet 1:13.
89. NRSV, NASB: Ezra 4:14.
90. NIV, NKJV: Ezra 4:14.
91. Ex 8:26.
92. Ezek 15:4.
93. NKJV, NRSV: Matt 3:8.
94. NKJV, NASB: Matt 15:26.
95. Heb 7:16.
96. Gen 43:34; 2 Sam 11:8.
97. Gen 43:34.
98. Ibid.
99. Gen 47:22.
100. Ex 16:18; Ps 60:6, 108:7; Matt 7:2; Mk 4:24; Lk 6:38.
101. Is 18:2,7, 40:12.
102. Ex 16:18; Ps 60:6.
103. Ruth 3:15.
104. Matt 7:2; Mk 4:24; Lk 6:38.
105. Ps 58:2.
106. Job 28:25.
107. Charles J. Brown, "The U.N.'s Own Rushdie," *Freedom Review*, May/June 1994, p.41-44.
108. 1 Ki 4:22.
109. Gen 32:15; 1 Sam 6:7,10.
110. Ibid.
111. Ibid.
112. 1 Sam 6:7,10.
113. Gen 32:15; 1 Sam 6:7,10.
114. Ex 11:5; Matt 24:41.
115. Num 11:8.
116. E.g., Deut 24:6; Rev 18:22.
117. Is 47:2; Jer 25:10.
118. NRSV, NKJV: Ex 11:5.
119. NIV: Ex 11:5; Matt 24:41.
120. NASB: Ex 11:5.
121. Matt 24:41.
122. Deut 24:6; Jud 16:2.
123. Ex 11:5; Matt 24:41.
124. Num 11:8.
125. Ibid.
126. Deut 24:6; Jer 25:10; Lk 17:2.
127. Ps 107:39.
128. Ibid.
129. Ex 5:19.
130. Ex 5:8.
131. Deut 12:32.
132. Mk 12:42; Lk 21:2.
133. Mk 12:42; Lk 12:59, 21:2.

134. Mk 12:42; Lk 21:2.
135. Lk 12:59.
136. Mk 12:42; Lk 21:2.
137. Lk 12:59.
138. E.g., Ex 28:4; Zec 3:5.
139. Dan 3:21.
140. Charles Mahtesian, "Immigration: The Symbolic Crackdown," *Governing,* May 1994, p.52.
141. E.g., Gen 19:34; James 4:14.
142. E.g., Ex 8:10; James 4:13.
143. Ibid.
144. E.g., Gen 19:34; James 4:14.
145. James 4:14.
146. Lev 22:30.
147. Lev 23:11.
148. Gen 19:34; Ex 9:6; 2 Ki 8:15.
149. Rom 8:13; Col 3:5.
150. Ibid.
151. Richard Wolkomir, "Techno-Angst," *San Francisco Chronicle,* Dec. 8, 1991, sec. Magazine, p.7.
152. Matt 7:3,4,5; Lk 6:41,42.
153. Matt 7:3; Lk 6:41.
154. Matt 7:4,5; lk 6:42.
155. Matt 7:3,4,5; Lk 6:41,42.
156. Donovan Webster, "Chips Are a Thief's Best Friend," *New York Times Magazine,* Sept. 18, 1994, p.54-59.
157. Hab 1:16.
158. Is 29:7; Nah 2:1.
159. Is 33:16.
160. Is 29:7, 33:16; Nah 2:1.
161. NKJV, NIV: Is 29:7.
162. NRSV, NASB: Is 29:7.
163. NKJV: Nah 2:1.
164. NRSV: Nah 2:1.
165. Deut 20:20.
166. Is 29:3.
167. Ps 62:9.

Chapter 14

1. Lk 19:20; Jn 11:44, 20:7.
2. Jn 11:44, 20:7.
3. Lk 19:20.
4. Lk 19:20; Jn 20:7.
5. Jn 11:44.
6. Lk 19:20; Jn 11:44, 20:7.

7. Ibid.
8. O.E.D., s.v., "napkin."
9. Gen 11:28; Ruth 2:11; Jer 46:16; Ezek 16:3,4, 21:30, 23:15.
10. NASB, NIV, NRSV: Gen 11:28.
11. NRSV, NASB: Ezek 21:30.
12. NIV, NASB: Jer 46:16.
13. Gen 11:28; Ruth 2:11.
14. Jer 46:16; Ezek 16:3,4, 21:30, 23:15.
15. 2 Ki 2:19; Pro 20:14.
16. Pro 6:12, 7:4; Jer 24:2.
17. 1 Sam 17:28; Pro 11:6; James 1:21.
18. 2 Ki 2:19.
19. NASB: 1 Sam 17:28.
20. NIV: James 1:21.
21. NASB: Pro 11:6.
22. NIV: Jer 24:2.
23. NIV: Pro 17:4.
24. NRSV: Pro 6:12.
25. NKJV: Pro 17:4.
26. Is 8:10, 40:23.
27. Is 40:23.
28. James 1:21.
29. 1 Sam 17:28.
30. Pavel Sudoplatov, "Atomic Secrets: Special Tasks," *Time*, April 25, 1994, p.64-72.
31. 1 Ki 6:3.
32. E.g., Gen 18:15; James 5:12.
33. O.E.D., s.v., "nay."
34. Gen 19:2; Rom 3:27.
35. NIV, NRSV, NASB: 1 Cor 12:22.
36. NRSV, NIV: 2 Ki 20:10.
37. NRSV, NIV: Gen 18:15.
38. NKJV: Rom 9:20.
39. NIV: 1 Cor 6:8.
40. Aaron Levin, "The Log-on Library," *Johns Hopkins Magazine*, Feb. 1992, p.12-19.
41. Is 3:3.
42. Lev 19:26; 2 Ki 17:17, 21:6; 2 Chr 33:6.
43. Ex 22:18.
44. Deut 18:11.
45. 1 Sam 15:23.
46. Patricia A. McKillip, "Once Upon a Time Too Often," *Writer*, Aug. 1992, p.18.
47. E.g., Ex 26:36; Ps 45:14.
48. Ex 26:36, 27:16, 28:39, 36:37, 38:18, 39:29.
49. Ex 26:36; Ps 45:14.
50. Ex 26:36, 39:29.

51. Ex 26:36.
52. Ex 38:18.
53. Jud 5:30.
54. Ps 45:14.
55. James D. Houston, "Crunched in California, *San Jose Mercury News*, Sept. 12, 1993, p.1C.
56. Is 51:8.
57. Job 18:19; Is 14:22.
58. Jud 12:14; 1 Tim 5:4.
59. Jud 12:14.
60. 1 Tim 5:4.
61. Is 14:22.
62. NIV, NRSV: Job 18:19.
63. Ex 19:17; Ezek 32:24.
64. 1 Ki 6:6.
65. Josh 15:19; Job 41:24.
66. NRSV, NIV: Ezek 31:18.
67. Ex 19:17.
68. Ezek 32:18.
69. Arthur Fisher, "Voyage to the Center of the Earth," *Popular Science*, Nov. 1988, p.76.
70. E.g., Gen 47:29; James 5:8.
71. NRSV: Heb 6:8.
72. NRSV: Num 8:19.
73. NRSV: Ps 85:9.
74. NIV: Ex 14:10, 32:19; NRSV: Num 18:4.
75. Gen 18:23.
76. Basil Wilson, "Fifty Years of Party Politics in Jamaica," *Everybody's*, July 1993, p.15-18.
77. Pro 25:20; Jer 2:22.
78. NASB, NIV, NKJV: Pro 25:20.
79. NRSV, NKJV, NASB: Jer 2:22.
80. Pro 25:20.
81. Larry Thompson, "Over-the-Counter Drugs: How Safe Are They?" *Washington Post Health*, Sept. 26, 1989, p.10-11.
82. Jos 6:27; Mk 2:1; Lk 1:65; Acts 2:6.
83. NRSV, NIV, NASB: Lk 1:65.
84. NRSV: Mk 2:1.
85. NKJV, NIV: Jos 6:27.
86. NKJV: Lk 1:65.
87. 1 Sam 14:19.
88. J. Page, "A Charged Particle Among the Force Fields of Her Times," *Smithsonian*, June 1991, p.122
89. Ps 91:3; Ezek 14:15,21; Rev 16:2.
90. Ibid.
91. Ibid.
92. Aaron Sachs, "Composting: Dirty Riches," *World Watch*, July/Aug.

1993, p.36-38.
93. Is 38:10.
94. Acts 22:6.
95. 2 Sam 4:5.
96. 2 Sam 19:7; Zech 14:7.
97. 2 Sam 2:29.
98. Bill Ott, "Literary Florida," *American Libraries,* June 1994, p.608.
99. E.g., Gen 29:15; Rev 18:17.
100. Is 8:10.
101. Is 40:23.
102. O.E.D., s.v., "nought."
103. Alex de Waal, "Politics Is the Cause and Cure of Famine," *Newsday,* May 2, 1993, p.40-41.
104. NRSV, NASB: Eph 6:4.
105. NIV, NKJV: Eph 6:4.
106. Lam 4:5.
107. Ps 144:12.
108. Acts 7:20,21.
109. Denise M. Topolnicki, "Why Private Schools Are Rarely Worth the Money," *Money,* Oct. 1994, p.98.

Chapter 15

1. Gen 37:7, 9, 43:28; Ex 18:7; 2 Sam 1:2, 14:4, 15:5; 1 Ki 1:16; 2 Chr 24:17.
2. Gen 37:9; Ex 18:7.
3. NKJV, NASB: 2 Sam 1:2, 14:4.
4. NASB: Gen 43:28; NKJV: 1 Ki 1:16; NIV: 2 Chr 24:17.
5. NIV: Gen 43:28; 2 Sam 1:2, 14:4.
6. 1 Ki 1:16.
7. Gen 37:7, 9; Ex 18:7.
8. E.g., Est 3:2; 1 Chr 21:21.
9. 1 Sam 24:8, 28:14; 2 Sam 9:8, 14:22; 1 Ki 1:23, 53; 1 Chr 21:21.
10. 2 Sam 9:8, 14:22; 1 Ki 1:23, 53; 1 Chr 21:21.
11. 1 Sam 24:8, 28:14.
12. David Brown, "Healing's Beside Revolution," *Washington Post,* Dec. 31, 1993, p.A1.
13. E.g., Lev 2:4; Is 44:30.
14. Lev 2:4; Num 31:50.
15. NRSV, NIV, NASB: 2 Chr 31:4; NKJV: Is 40:20; Ezek 44:30.
16. NKJV: Ezek 20:40, 44:30; NIV, NRSV: Dan 9:21.
17. NRSV: Is 40:20.
18. NRSV, NASB: Ezek 48:10; NASB: Ezek 48:9.
19. NKJV: Ezek 48:9, 10.
20. NRSV: Ezek 48:9; NIV: Ezek 48:10.
21. NIV: Ezek 48:9.

22. NIV, NASB, NRSV: Ezek 20:40.
23. NIV: Ezek 45:13, 16.
24. NRSV: Ezek 20:40; NASB: Ex 25:2.
25. 1 Ki 18:29,36.
26. William F. Buckley, "Burn the Flag? Well, No," *National Review,* July 10, 1995, p.75.
27. Ezek 27:9; Lk 19:13.
28. Ezek 27:7.
29. Ex 38:24; Jud 16:11; Ezek 27:16,19,21,22; Heb 13:9.
30. 1 Cor 14:16.
31. Ibid.
32. NIV: Ecc 10:6; NASB: Lk 14:19; NRSV: Neh 2:8.
33. NASB: Deut 2:3; NIV: Jos 1:15; NRSV: Deut 4:1.
34. Heb 13:9.
35. NKJV: Heb 13:9; NRSV: Ps 131:1.
36. NASB: Acts 18:5; NKJV: Ecc 3:10.
37. Jud 16:11; Ex 38:24.
38. Ibid.
39. Ezek 27:16,19,21,22.
40. Ibid.
41. Ezck 27:21,22.
42. Ezek 27:16,22.
43. Ezek 27:16,19,22.
44. Ezek 27:9; Lk 19:13.
45. Ibid.
46. Ezek 27:9.
47. Lk 19:13.
48. Ezek 27:7.
49. Ibid.
50. Gen 46:33, 47:3.
51. Acts 1:25; Lk 14:9.
52. Deut 7:1; Oba 1:19.
53. M.M. Werler, et al., "Periconceptional Folic Acid Exposure and Risk of Occurrent Neutral Tube Defects," *JAMA,* 1993, 269:1257-61.
54. L. Gordon Crovitz, "93: The Pacific Century: It's Beginning Ahead of Schedule," *Far Eastern Economic Review,* Dec. 30, 1993 & Jan. 6, 1994, p.28-32.
55. 1 Chr 19:6; Pro 30:23.
56. 1 Chr 19:6.
57. Gen 34:30; Ex 5:21; 1 Sam 13:4, 27:12; 2 Sam 10:6, 16:21; 1 Chr 19:6.
58. Gen 34:30; 1 Sam 13:4; 2 Sam 10:6, 16:21; 1 Chr 19:6.
59. Gen 34:30; 2 Sam 10:6.
60. 1 Chr 19:6.
61. 1 Sam 27:12.
62. 1 Sam 27:12; 1 Chr 19:6.
63. Susan Duerksen, "Single-payer Health Plan Qualifies for State Ballot," *San Diego-Union Tribune,* June 21, 1994, p.A1.

64. E.g., Ps 119:165; Matt 17:27.
65. E.g., Matt 26:31; Mk 14:27.
66. Matt 5:30, 18:6.
67. NKJV: Matt 11:6, 13:41, 57, 15:12, 17:27, 24:10; Mk 6:3; Lk 7:23, 17:2; Jn 6:61.
68. NRSV: Matt 26:31.
69. NRSV: Matt 18:6.
70. NASB: 1 Cor 8:13.
71. NIV: 2 Cor 11:29.
72. NRSV: Matt 11:6.
73. NASB: Matt 24:10.
74. NKJV: Matt 24:10.
75. NIV: Matt 24:10.
76. NASB: Matt 5:29.
77. NRSV: Matt 5:29.
78. Lam 3:45; 1 Cor 4:13.
79. Ibid.
80. Ibid.
81. Ezek 24:6.
82. Lam 3:45; 1 Cor 4:13.
83. 1 Cor 4:13.
84. Lam 3:45; 1 Cor 4:13.
85. Is 51:17; Ps 75:8.
86. 1 Cor 4:13.
87. 1 Ki 21:27.
88. E.g., Job 21:17; 1 Cor 11:25.
89. 1 Cor 11:25, 26.
90. Acts 24:26.
91. Ps 78:40; Matt 17:15.
92. NIV, NRSV: 2 Ki 4:8; NIV: 1 Cor 11:25.
93. NIV: 2 Cor 11:23.
94. NRSV: Heb 6:7.
95. NIV: Matt 18:21.
96. Matt 9:14.
97. Johnette Howard, "Neon Deion Born at the Prime Time," *Washington Post,* Nov. 6, 1994, p.D1.
98. Matt 17:15; Mk 9:22; Jn 18:12.
99. Job 33:29; Ecc 7:22; Lk 8:29; Rom 1:13; 2 Cor 8:22; Heb 10:11.
100. Cf. Mk 5:4 and Lk 8:29.
101. Job 33:29.
102. Matt 17:15; Mk 5:4; Matt 17:15; Rom 1:13.
103. 2 Tim 1:16; 2 Cor 8:22.
104. Heb 10:11.
105. Rom 1:13; Heb 9:26.
106. Acts 26:11.
107. 2 Cor 11:23; Heb 10:11.
108. Heb 10:11.

109. Heb 9:25, 26; 10:11.
110. Heb 6:7.
111. Stephen G. Pauker, "Some Familiar Trade-offs," *New England Journal of Medicine*, Dec. 1, 1994, p.1511.
112. Ex 29:23; Lev 8:26.
113. NASB, NIV, NKJV: Ex 29:23; NIV: Lev 8:26.
114. NASB: Ex 29:23; Lev 8:26.
115. Lev 8:26.
116. Michael Rogers, "The Nature of Muscles," *National Wildlife*, Aug./Sept. 1990, p.34-41.
117. Jeffrey Denny, "King of the Road," *Common Cause Magazine*, May/June 1991, p.18-24.
118. Luke 13:4.
119. Henry C. Thiessen, *Introductory Lectures in Systematic Theology*, (Grand Rapids: Wm. B. Eerdmans Publishing Co., 1949), p.126.
120. Maya Bell, "Some Exiles Fail to Rescue Relatives, Land in Cuban Jails," *Sun-Sentinel*, Jan. 30, 1994, sec. Local, p.1A.
121. Ps 28:5; Is 5:12; Col 2:12; 1 Cor 12:6.
122. Ps 28:5; Is 5:12.
123. Col 2:12; 1 Cor 12:6.
124. Ps 28:5; Is 5:12; Col 2:12; 1 Cor 12:6.
125. Ibid.
126. Ps 28:5; Is 5:12.
127. 1 Cor 12:6; Col 2:12.
128. Matt 26:10.
129. Mk 13:34.
130. Matt 9:6.
131. Frances Dinkelspiel, "Fed Ex Handles Tidal Wave of Packages," *San Jose Mercury News*, Dec. 22, 1994.
132. E.g., 2 Sam 6:23; 1 Ki 7:49.
133. Acts 7:38; Rom 3:2; Heb 5:11; 1 Pet 4:11.
134. 1 Ki 6:16, 23.
135. E.g., Num 23:7; Is 13:1.
136. E.g., Deut 18:11; 2 Chr 24:27.
137. 2 Sam 6:23.
138. Num 23:18.
139. Pro 31:1.
140. Is 13:1.
141. Hos 11:6.
142. E.g., Num 24:3; Is 14:28.
143. 2 Chr 24:27; Lam 2:14.
144. Pro 31:1.
145. Is 13:1.
146. Jer 50:36.
147. E.g., Jer 23:38; Mal 1:1.
148. Lam 2:14.
149. Pro 31:1.

150. Num 24:15.
151. Is 14:28.
152. E.g., Num 23:7; Jer 23:33.
153. 2 Chr 24:27.
154. 2 Sam 6:23.
155. Acts 7:38; Ro 3:2; Heb 5:11; 1 Pet 4:11.
156. Ibid.
157. 1 Pet 4:11.
158. Ibid.
159. Acts 7:38; Heb 5:12; 1 Pet 4:11.
160. Gerald Parshall, "The Feuding Fathers," *U.S. News & World Report,* Feb. 1, 1993, p.52-57.
161. Lloyd Grove, "Barry Goldwater's Left Turn," *Washington Post,* July 28, 1994, p.C1.
162. "Waldheim Honor Stirs Questions," *Associated Press News Service,* Aug. 6, 1994.
163. Lev 11:13; Deut 14:12.
164. Ibid.
165. Ibid.
166. Ibid.
167. Lev 11:18; Deut 14:17.
168. Boyce Rensberger, "Dinosaur Nest Discovery Challenges Assumptions," *Washington Post,* Nov. 4, 1994, p.A4.
169. Lev 11:13; Deut 14:12.
170. Ibid.
171. Lev 11:14.
172. Deut 14:13.
173. Lev 11:14; Deut 14:13.
174. Arther Spiegelman, "Famous Math Problem Solved by 600 People Around World," *Reuters,* April 26, 1994.
175. Ibid.
176. Ex 28:11,13,14,25, 39:6,13,16,18.
177. Ex 28:11,13,14,25, 39:6,16,18.
178. Ex 39:13.
179. Ex 28:14, 25.
180. Ex 28:11,13, 39:6,13,16,18.
181. Ex 28:14,25, 39:18.
182. Ex 28:11,13, 39:6, 13,16.
183. Ex 28:11,13,14,25, 39:6, 13,16,18.
184. Jos 17:9,18, 18:19, 19:14,22,29,33; Ps 65:8.
185. E.g., Jos 18:14; Num 34:12.
186. Jos 19:14, 33.
187. NIV: Jos 17:18.
188. NKJV: Jos 17:18.
189. NRSV, NKJV: 1 Sam 9:27.
190. NIV, NASB: 1 Sam 9:27.
191. NIV, NRSV: Jud 6:21.

192. NIV: Jos 18:16.
193. NRSV: Jos 18:16.
194. NASB: Jos 18:16.
195. Jos 15:5.
196. Conrad Brunner, "A Star Has Risen," *Indianapolis News,* Oct. 8, 1994, p.A1.
197. Ex 26:10; Num 34:3; Deu 30:4; Is 17:6.
198. NRSV, NASB, NKJV: Ex 26:10.
199. Ezek 17:4.
200. Jos 15:21.
201. Job 8:2.
202. Acts 4:16; Rom 13:8.
203. Ecc 10:11.
204. NRSV: Num 11:1; NIV: 1 Chr 5:16.
205. Pro 24:15.
206. Ps 79:10.
207. Jud 20:6.
208. 2 Chr 32:30.
209. NRSV, NKJV: Deut 24:8; NIV: 1 Sam 5:9; NASB: Lev 13:57.
210. Is 41:22; NKJV: Acts 5:24.
211. Jud 7:11.
212. Num 18:7; NIV: Col 4:5.
213. 1 Sam 14:2.
214. Pro 24:27; Is 44:13.
215. Song 8:1; Is 44:13.
216. Is 49:17.
217. Gen 19:13; Neh 5:1.
218. Lk 21:34.
219. Gen 33:13.
220. Jos 24:31.
221. 2 Cor 2:7.
222. Ecc 7:16, 17.
223. Jer 5:28.
224. Ps 57:1; Is 26:20.
225. Lev 25:27.
226. 2 Sam 18:23.
227. Nah 1:8.
228. Gen 9:19; Dan 9:27.
229. Deut 23:19; 2 Ki 7:17.
230. Gen 33:13.
231. Ex 23:29.
232. Jos 24:31.
233. Neill Herring, "No Joy in Mudville," *Southern Exposure,* Spring 1991, p.44-46.
234. Ps 57:1; Is 26:20.
235. NKJV: Zep 2:9; NIV, NRSV: Zech 9:8.
236. David Remnick, "At the End, Beleaguered, Broken and Bitter,"

Washington Post National Weekly Edition, Dec. 30, 1991-Jan. 5, 1992.
237. Job 15:29; Is 40:19.
238. Dan 3:22.
239. Ex 26:12.
240. 2 Chr 3:11; Pro 23:4.
241. Titus 1:7.
242. Ps 49:16.
243. Ecc 7:16.
244. Pro 8:29.
245. Ezek 41:25.
246. Matt 16:3.
247. Ezek 16:49.
248. Pro 21:24; Is 16:6; Jer 48:29.

Chapter 16

1. Joel 1:4,2:25; Amos 4:9.
2. Joel 1:4; NKJV, NIV, NRSV: Amos 4:9.
3. NASB: Amos 4:9.
4. NRSV: Joel 2:25.
5. Deut 28:42.
6. Is 51:8.
7. E.g., Matt 4:24; Acts 9:23.
8. Acts 8:7.
9. Matt 8:6.
10. Mk 2:5.
11. Ripley Hotch, "Computers Find Their Voice," *Nation's Business,* May 1992, p.49.
12. E.g., Is 13:8; Micah 4:9.
13. Ibid.
14. Is 13:8, 21:3, 26:17; Jer 22:23; Micah 4:9.
15. Jer 50:43.
16. Jer 48:41,49:22.
17. Is 21:3,Jer 22:23.
18. Is 13:8; Jer 48:41.
19. Jer 22:23.
20. Is 13:8.
21. Jer 48:41.
22. Micah 4:9.
23. Jer 13:21.
24. I Sam 25:31.
25. Ps 116:3.
26. Alexis Jetter, "Psychedelic Cure: Getting Off the Junkie Express," *Globe and Mail,* April 30, 1994, p.D5.
27. Ezek 23:21; Lk 11:27, 23:29; Rev 1:13.
28. Ezek 23:27; Lk 23:29.

29. Rev 1:13.
30. Ezra 4:19.
31. Ruth 4:5.
32. Ezek 23:20.
33. Ibid.
34. 2 Tim 1:7.
35. Elizabeth Coady, "Lovers Filing Suits Over Spread of Sexually Transmitted Diseases," *Atlanta Journal & Constitution,* Jan. 21, 1990, p.C1.
36. Ps 7:16.
37. Ibid.
38. Austin Murphy, "Back With a Vengeance," *Sports Illustrated,* Sept. 18, 1995.
39. Deut 18:8.
40. Acts 2:29,7:8,9; Heb 7:4.
41. Acts 2:29.
42. Jn 7:22; Rom 9:5,15:8.
43. Robert Cullen, "Rights and Foreign Policy: Collective Rights and Nationalism, *Current,* June 1993.
44. Ex 19:5; Deut 14:2, 26:18; Ps 135:4; Ecc 12:8, Titus 2:14; 1 Pet 2:9.
45. Ibid.
46. Titus 2:14.
47. Deut 26:18.
48. Ps 135:4.
49. Num 3:4.
50. E.g., Matt 20:2; Rev 6:6.
51. Matt 18:28; Mk 14:5; Lk 7:41, 10:35; Jn 12:5.
52. Mk 6:37; Jn 6:7.
53. Matt 22:19; Mk 12:15; Lk 20:24.
54. Matt 18:28; Lk 7:41.
55. Lk 10:35.
56. Mk 14:5; Jn 12:5.
57. Mk 6:37; Jn 6:7.
58. Jn 6:7.
59. Will Nixon, "Relief Disaster," *In These Times,* Aug. 22, 1994, p.29.
60. Pro 14:23; Lk 21:4.
61. Ibid.
62. Jud 6:6.
63. Mark Skousen, "Freedom for Everyone...Except the Immigrant," *The Freeman,* Sept. 1995, p.593.
64. E.g., Jn 17:12; Rev 17:11.
65. Ibid.
66. 2 Thes 2:3; 2 Pet 3:7.
67. Jn 17:12.
68. 1 Tim 6:9.
69. 2 Sam 22:5; Ps 18:4.
70. "United Nations Activities," *Bulletin on Ageing,* Winter 1993, p.1.
71. Ps 86:14.

72. Janet Fleischman, "Jauritania: Ethnic Cleansing," *Africa Report*, Jan./Feb. 1994, p.45.
73. Matt 23:5.
74. Ex 13:16.
75. Ezek 24:9.
76. Gen 30:37,38.
77. Ibid.
78. Jos 18:9.
79. Jer 2:23.
80. 1 Sam 10:5; Is 5:12, 30:29; 1 Cor 14:7.
81. I Ki 1:40; Jer 48:36; Ezek 28:13.
82. Rev 18:22.
83. 1 Ki 1:40; Matt 11:17; Lk 7:32; 1 Cor 14:7.
84. Is 5:12; Gen 48:36.
85. NKJV: Ezek 28:13; NASB: 1 Ki 1:40.
86. NRSV, NASB, NIV: 1Cor 14:7.
87. Lk 7:32.
88. 1 Cor 14:7.
89. Gen 4:21; Ps 150:4.
90. Dan 3:5,10,15.
91. Job 21:12, 30:31; Ps 150:4.
92. Dan 3:5,7,10,15.
93. Ibid.
94. Jessica Lipnack and Jeffrey Stamps, "Networking the World," *Futurist*, July/Aug. 1993, p.9.
95. Jn 19:2; Mk 15:17; Matt 27:29.
96. NASB: Matt 27:29; Mk 15:17; Jn 19:2; NRSV: Jn 19:2.
97. NKJV, NIV, NRSV: Matt 27:29.
98. NASB: Lev 22:5; NIV, NKJV: Ps 104:25.
99. Num 3:47; Ezek 44:20; Micah 1:16.
100. Num 1:2,18,20,22; 1 Chr 23:3,24.
101. 2 Sam 14:26.
102. NRSV, NKJV: Num 1:2,18,20,22.
103. NASB: Num 1:2,18,20,22.
104. NIV: Num 1:2,18,20,22.
105. NIV, NKJV: Num 3:47.
106. 2 Sam 14:26; NRSV, NASB, NKJV: Micah 1:16.
107. 2 Chr 4:12,13.
108. Ibid.
109. Ibid.
110. David Lamb, "On an Old Battleground, A New Peace," *Wichita Eagle*, Oct. 13, 1991, p.1D.
111. Job 9:25; Jer 51:31.
112. 2 Chr 30:6, 30:10; Es 3:13,15, 8:10,14.
113. Job 9:25.
114. NKJV, NRSV: Jer 51:31.
115. Est 3:13,15, 8:10,14.

116. 2 Chr 30:6,10.
117. Hab 2:1.
118. Ezek 40:14.
119. Art Kleiner, "The Ant, the Grasshopper, and the GNP," *Garbage,* Feb./March 1993, p.44.
120. E.g., Gen 25:29; Hag 2:12.
121. Gen 25:34; 2 Ki 4:40.
122. Hag 2:12.
123. Gen 25:30.
124. John Powers, "Feeling the Pinch," *Boston Globe,* Oct. 14, 1990, sec. Magazine, p.17.
125. E.g., 1 Ki 10:17; Jn 19:39.
126. Lk 19:13,16,18,24,25.
127. Lk 19:16,18.
128. Lk 19:16,18,20,24.
129. Lk 19:13,16,18,24.
130. 1 Ki 10:17; Ezra 2:69; Neh 7:71,72.
131. Ezek 45:12.
132. Flora Lewis, "A European Germany or a German Europe," *New Perspectives Quarterly,* Winter 1993, p.26.
133. Pro 10:8,10; 3 Jn 10.
134. Ibid.
135. NRSV, NASB: Pro 10:8.
136. NIV: Pro 10:10.
137. NRSV: 3 Jn 10.
138. NASB: 3 Jn 10.
139. NIV: 3 Jn 10.
140. Micah 2:6.
141. Micah 2:11.
142. E.g., Job 3:12; 1 Thes 4:15.
143. Ps 21:3.
144. E.g., 2 Sam 22:6; Matt 17:25.
145. 1 Thes 4:15.
146. Ps 18:5.
147. Ps 79:8.
148. Ps 119:147.
149. Job 3:12.
150. NASB: Ps 119:148; NKJV: Matt 17:25.
151. Is 20:3.
152. Eph 1:21; Col 2:10.
153. E.g., Jer 13:18; Titus 3:1.
154. Eph 1:21, 6:12.
155. Eph 3:10, Col 1:16.
156. Rom 8:38.
157. Rom 8:38.
158. Col 2:15.
159. Geoffrey Smith, "Must Royals Take a Back Seat?" *World Monitor,*

March 1993, p.36.
    160. Deut 23:1; 1 Ki 2:44; Ezek 21:44; Acts 5:2.
    161. E.g., Jud 9:31; 2 Pet 2:1.
    162. 1 Ki 2:44.
    163. Deut 23:1.
    164. Matt 2:7.
    165. NRSV: 1 Sam 24:4.
    166. NKJV: Jud 9:31.
    167. NRSV: Ps 31:4.
    168. NRSV: Pro 1:11.
    169. NIV: Matt 1:19.
    170. Job 4:12.
    171. 1 Sam 18:22.
    172. Ted Gup, "How the Federal Emergency Management Agency (FEMA) Learned," *Mother Jones,* Jan./Feb. 1994, p.28.
    173. Kathleen McAuliffe, "When Whales Had Feet," *Sea Frontiers,* Jan./Feb. 1994, p.20.
    174. Shervert H. Frazier, "Psychotrends," *Psychology Today,* Jan./Feb. 1994, p.32.
    175. 1 Chr 29:3; Acts 1:19; 1 Cor 7:7; Heb 11:23.
    176. NKJV, NASB: Zcts 1:19; NKJV, NIV, NASB: 1 Cor 7:7.
    177. 1 Cor 15:19.
    178. E.g., Gen 24:25; Is 30:24.
    179. Jud 19:19.
    180. NKJV, NASB: Gen 24:25.
    181. Is 30:24.
    182. Donald Culross Peattie, "The Web of Life," *American Horticulturist,* Oct. 1991, p.30.
    183. E.g., 1 Sam 10:5; Dan 3:15.
    184. E.g., 2 Sam 6:5; Neh 12:27.
    185. Dan 3:5,10,15.
    186. Dan 3:5,7,10,15.
    187. NASB, NIV, NRSV: Ps 51:8, 71:22.
    188. NIV: Ps 81:2.
    189. NRSV: Ps 150:3.
    190. Ps 57:8, 71:22, 108:2.
    191. NRSV, NASB: Gen 31:27; NIV: Ps 71:22.
    192. Dan 3:5,7,10,15.
    193. Matt 10:3, 18:17; Lk 5:27, 18:10,11,13.
    194. E.g., Matt 5:46; Lk 19:2.
    195. E.g., Matt 10:3; Lk 19:2.
    196. Ibid.
    197. Allen Abel, "Donnelly's Arm," *Sports Illustrated,* Feb. 20, 1995, p.164.
    198. 2 Sam 17:28; Dan 1:12,16.
    199. Dan 1:12,16.
    200. 2 Sam 17:28.

201. Job 13:12.
202. Lev 26:22.
203. William Murchison, "The Silver Foot Kicks Back," *National Review,* Nov. 7, 1994, p.26.
204. Num 11:4.
205. Ecc 10:1.
206. Gen 34:30.
207. Is 3:24.
208. Eric Ransdell, "To a Nation Dying Young," *U.S. News & World Report,* Aug. 8, 1994, p.39.

Chapter 17

1. E.g., Gen 19:4; Is 47:15.
2. E.g., Ex 13:7; Acts 9:32.
3. Deut 22:12; 1 Chr 9:24; Jer 49:36; Rev 20:8.
4. Jer 49:36.
5. Deut 22:12; Rev 20:8.
6. 2 Ki 22:4; 2 Chr 34:22; Neh 3:30; Zeph 1:10; Acts 28:30.
7. Gen 19:4.
8. 2 Ki 22:4; 2 Chr 34:22; Neh 3:30; Zeph 1:10; Acts 28:30.
9. Gen 19:4.
10. Mk 1:45.
11. Jer 50:26; Ezek 37:21.
12. Num 34:3; Josh 18:15.
13. Josh 15:5; Ezek 38:6.
14. Is 56:11; Mk 1:45; Acts 9:32, 16:3.
15. Ex 13:7; 2 Ki 22:4; 2 Chr 34:22; Est 2:3, 11, 13; Zeph 1:10.
16. Gen 19:4; Ex 13:7; Num 34:3; Deut 22:12; Josh 15:5; Is 47:15; Ezek 38:6; Mk 1:45; Acts 9:32, 16:3, 28:7.
17. 2 Sam 19:11; 2 Ki 23:7; Neh 3:30; Is 11:12; Zeph 1:10.
18. Jer 51:59.
19. Kevin Fedarko, "Deliverance," *Time,* Oct. 24, 1994, p.28-33.
20. Mk 12:42.
21. Matt 5:26.
22. Matt 22:19, 20:2,9,10,13; Mk 12:15; Lk 20:24; Rev 6:6.
23. Jn 18:28,33, 19:9; Acts 23:35.
24. E.g., Ps 55:15; Acts 10:42.
25. Ps 119:25; Rom 8:11.
26. Ps 119:50,93; 1 Cor 15:36; Eph 2:1,5; Col 2:13; 1 Pet 3:18.
27. Matt 27:27.
28. 1 Cor 15:45.
29. O.E.D., s.v. "quick."
30. Lev 13:10,24.
31. Lev 13:10.
32. Num 16:30; Ps 124:3.

33. Acts 10:42; Heb 4:12.
34. Ps 119:25,40.
35. Ibid.
36. 1 Cor 15:45.
37. Jn 5:21, 6:63; Rom 4:17; 1 Tim 6:13.
38. NASB: Ps 119:50, 93; 1 Cor 15:36; Eph 2:5; Col 2:13; 1 Pet 3:18.
39. NIV: Ps 119:50,93; 1 Cor 15:36; Eph 2:5; Col 2:13; 1 Pet 3:18.
40. NKJV: Eph 2:1,5; Col 2:13; 1 Pet 3:18.
41. NKJV, NRSV: Ps 119:50,93.
42. Acts 5:33, 7:54.
43. Acts 27:17.
44. *Steadman's Medical Dictionary*, s.v., "quick."
45. James Andrews, "Something Old, and New Finding Dollars and Sense in Historic Preservation," *Christian Science Monitor*, Nov. 2, 1994, sec. The U.S., p.4.
46. J. Madeleine Nash, "How did Life Begin?" *Time*, Oct. 11, 1993, p.68-74.
47. Ex 21:19, 21:28; Josh 2:20; 1 Sam 4:9; 1 Cor 16:13.
48. Ex 21:19, 21:28; Josh 2:20.
49. 1 Sam 4:9; 1 Cor 16:13.
50. NRSV, NIV, NASB: 1 Sam 4:9.
51. Ex 21:19, 21:28.
52. NRSV: Ex 21:19.
53. NASB: Ex 21:19, 21:28.
54. NIV: Ex 21:19, 21:28.
55. NIV, NRSV: Josh 2:20.
56. NASB, NKJV: Josh 2:20.
57. Jos 11:2.
58. Dan 2:21; Acts 1:7; 1 Thes 5:1.
59. Mk 1:26.
60. Ex 13:3.

Chapter 18

1. 1 Sam 25:14; Mk 15:29; Lk 23:29.
2. 1 Cor 5:11.
3. 1 Pet 3:9; 2 Pet 2:11; Jude 9.
4. 1 Tim 6:4.
5. NASB: Jude 9; NRSV: Num 16:1; NIV: Ps 102:8.
6. NKJV, NRSV, NASB: 1 Cor 5:11; NASB, NKJV: 2 Pet 2:11.
7. NASB, NIV: 1 Pet 3:9; NASB, NIV: 2 Chr 32:17.
8. NRSV, NIV: 2 Pet 2:11.
9. NRSV: Mk 15:29; Lk 23:39.
10. NKJV: Mk 15:29; Lk 23:39.
11. NKJV: 1 Sam 25:14; 2 Chr 32:17; 1 Cor 5:11; 1 Tim 6:4; 1 Pet 3:9; 2 Pet 2:11; Jude 9.

12. Ps 31:13.
13. 2 Ki 19:22.
14. Jn 9:28.
15. Mk 15:29; Lk 23:29.
16. Lk 16:14, 23:35.
17. Ann Leonard, "South Asia: The New Target of International Waste Traders," *Multinational Monitor,* Dec. 1993, p.21-24.
18. E.g., Gen 24:53; Rev 4:4.
19. Is 63:3.
20. Ex 12:35.
21. Num 31:20.
22. James 2:2.
23. NASB, NRSV, NIV: Ex 22:26.
24. NRSV: Deut 21:13.
25. NASB: 1 Tim 6:8.
26. NKJV, NRSV: Rev 4:4.
27. NRSV: Acts 22:20.
28. Roger Burns, "Of Miracles and Molecules: The Story of Nylon," *American History Illustrated,* Dec. 1988, p.25.
29. Lam 2:8; Nah 3:8.
30. Nah 3:8.
31. 2 Sam 20:15; Hab 2:1.
32. Ps 48:13; Is 26:1.
33. 2 Sam 20:15; Hab 2:1; Zec 9:3.
34. Ps 48:13; Nah 2:1; Lk 19:43.
35. Nah 3:8.
36. Ps 91:4.
37. Ps 48:13; Is 26:1; Hab 2:1.
38. 2 Sam 20:15; Hab 2:1.
39. Nah 2:5.
40. Lev 11:35; 2 Ki 11:8,15; 2 Chr 23:14.
41. Pro 28:15.
42. Lev 11:35.
43. 2 Ki 11:8,15; 2 Chr 23:14.
44. Ibid.
45. Pro 28:15.
46. NIV, NRSV, NASB: Zech 4:10.
47. Gen 41:5,7; Num 2:16,24; 1 Chr 12:33,38.
48. Gen 41:5,7.
49. Ibid.
50. Ps 81:2.
51. Ps 22:13; Ezek 22:15, 22:27; Matt 7:15; Lk 11:39.
52. Is 35:9, 46:11; Ezek 39:4.
53. Ps 22:13.
54. Matt 7:15.
55. Is 46:11; Ezek 39:4.
56. Gen 49:27; Pro 27:7.

57. Jer 2:30.
58. Gen 49:27.
59. Ps 22:13; Ezek 22:15, 22:27; Matt 7:15; Lk 11:39.
60. Matt 7:15.
61. Is 46:11; Ezek 39:4.
62. Ezek 22:15,27.
63. Matt 7:15.
64. Lk 11:39.
65. Is 35:9, 46:11; Ezek 39:4.
66. Gen 49:27; Ps 57:4.
67. Jer 2:30.
68. Martha Duffy and Helen Gibson, "Sorry, Wrong Number," *Time*, Sept. 5, 1994, p.79.
69. Gen 49:27; Nah 2:12.
70. Gen 49:27.
71. Is 35:9, 46:11; Ezek 39:4.
72. Les Line, "Terror of the Sky," *International Wildlife*, Sept./Oct. 1992, p.14-19.
73. Ex. 26:30; Lev 26:1; 2 Sam 24:18; Jn 2:20.
74. Lev 26:1.
75. NKJV, NRSV, NASB: 2 Sam 24:18.
76. NIV: Ex 26:30; Lev 26:1.
77. NIV: 2 Sam 24:18.
78. Jn 2:20.
79. NRSV: Zec 10:9; NIV: Hos 9:12.
80. Hos 9:12.
81. Ex 20:24; Is 8:2.
82. Ezra 6:2.
83. Neh 12:22.
84. Ezra 4:15; Est 6:1.
85. E.g., 2 Sam 8:16; Is 36:22.
86. Ibid.
87. Deut 31:28; Gal 4:15.
88. Ezra 6:2.
89. Is 16:11.
90. Ex 9:16.
91. 1 Sam 4:5.
92. 1 Chr 16:32.
93. Penelope Lemov, "Tough Times for TIF," *Governing*, Feb. 1994, p.18-19.
94. Ex 17:14; Jud 5:11.
95. 1 Sam 8:21, 17:31; Acts 11:4, 14:27.
96. NASB, NRSV: Ex 17:14.
97. NKJV: Ex 17:14; Jud 5:11.
98. 1 Sam 8:21.
99. Acts 11:4.
100. NASB, NIV, NKJV: Acts 14:27.

101. Carl Elliott, "Where Ethics Comes From and What to Do About It," *Hastings Center Report,* July/Aug. 1992, p.28-35.
102. E.g., Job 16:13; Rev 2:23.
103. NRSV, NASB, NIV: Job 16:13.
104. Job 19:27.
105. NIV, NRSV: Ps 7:9.
106. NASB, NKJV: Ps 7:9.
107. NASB: Ps 16:7.
108. NRSV: Pro 23:16.
109. NASB: Ps 73: 21.
110. NKJV, NASB, NRSV: Ps 139:13.
111. NIV, NASB, NKJV: Is 11:5.
112. NASB: Jer 11:20.
113. NRSV: Lam 3:13.
114. NKJV: Lam 3:13.
115. NIV: Ps 73:21.
116. NIV: Ps 139:13.
117. Jn 20:23.
118. E.g., Matt 26:28; Heb 10:18.
119. The exception is Rom 3:25.
120. Ibid.
121. Jn 20:23.
122. Deut 15:1,2,9, 31:10.
123. Lev 5:16.
124. E.g., Ex 39:23; Jn 19:24.
125. Ps 7:2.
126. Gen 37:29; Acts 16:2.
127. Jer 4:30.
128. Lev 10:6; Jn 19:24.
129. Gen 37:29.
130. Matt 27:51.
131. Mk 2:21.
132. Ps 7:2.
133. 1 Ki 19:11.
134. Is 64:1; Jer 36:24; Joel 2:13.
135. Is 64:1; Joel 2:13.
136. Joel 2:13.
137. James D. Houston, "Crunched in California," *San Jose Mercury News,* Sept.12, 1993, p.1C.
138. Joel Achenbach, "Guns & Kids," *Family Life,* Sept./Oct. 1994, p.67-73.
139. Jer 6:30; Rom 1:28; 2 Tim 3:8; Titus 1:16.
140. 2 Cor 13:5,6,7.
141. Jer 6:30.
142. NRSV, NIV: Rom 1:28.
143. NASB, NKJV: Rom 1:28.
144. NIV, NRSV: 2 Cor 13:7.

145. NKJV: 2 Tim 3:8.
146. NASB: 2 Cor 13:7.
147. NKJV: Titus 1:16.
148. NASB: Titus 1:16.
149. NRSV, NIV: Titus 1:16.
150. NRSV, NASB, NIV: 2 Cor 13:5,6.
151. Ps 15:4.
152. Neal Lawrence, "What's Happening to Our Children?" *Midwest Today*, Dec. 1993/Jan. 1994, p.6-14.
153. E.g., Gen 50:15; 1 Tim 5:4.
154. Jud 1:7; 1 Sam 15:21.
155. 2 Chr 6:33.
156. Ps 41:10; Jer 51:56.
157. NKJV: Deut 32:6.
158. NIV: 2 Sam 2:6.
159. NASB: 2 Sam 10:2.
160. NRSV: Is 59:18.
161. Ezra 9:13; Ezek 23:49.
162. Ps 28:4.
163. Beth Austin, "Floundering in Love," *Chicago Tribune*, March 5, 1989, sec. 6, p.1.
164. Num 10:25; Jos 6:9,13; 1 Sam 29:2; Is 52:12, 58:8.
165. Num 10:25; Jos 6:9,13; Is 52:12, 58:8.
166. Jer 18:22.
167. Job 12:6.
168. Ex 8:15; 1 Sam 11:3.
169. Ibid.
170. Ex 8:15.
171. Ps 94:13; Lam 2:18, 3:49.
172. Ps 94:13.
173. Job 20:20.
174. Bruce W. Nelan, "As the Plutonium Cools," *Time*, July 4, 1994, p.33-34.
175. Gal 5:21; 1 Pet 4:3.
176. Ibid.
177. Ibid.
178. Neh 9:25; Is 5:14, 24:8, 48:45; 2 Pet 2:13.
179. Rom 13:13; Gal 5:21; 1 Pet 4:3.
180. E.g., Ex 32:6; 2 Pet 2:13.
181. Ibid.
182. Is 22:13.
183. 1 Cor 10:7.
184. Gen 37:22; Ex 6:6; Lev 26:6; Ps 82:4, 144:7,11.
185. Lev 23:22; Zep 1:18.
186. NRSV, NASB, NIV: Ps 82:4.
187. NRSV, NASB, NIV: Gen 37:22.
188. NIV: Ex 6:6; NKJV: Ps 82:4.

189. Lev 26:6.
190. Ex 8:9; Lev 13:58.
191. Lev 23:22; Zep 1:18.
192. Zep 1:18.
193. Stephen G., "After Two Decades, His Ordeal Is Over," *Denver Post*, Sept. 23, 1990, sec. Magazine, p.8.
194. Kevin Fedarko, "Deliverance," *Time*, Oct. 24, 1994, p.28-33.
195. Titus 1:6; 1 Pet 4:4; 2 Pet 2:13.
196. Pro 23:20, 28:7; Lk 15:13; Rom 13:13.
197. Pro 23:20, 28:7; Lk 15:13; Rom 13:13; Titus 1:6; 1 Pet 4:4; 2 Pet 2:13.
198. NRSV: Titus 1:6.
199. NRSV, NASB: 2 Pet 2:13.
200. Pro 23:20, 28:7.
201. NRSV: Lk 15:13.
202. NASB: Lk 15:13.
203. NIV: Lk 15:13.
204. NKJV: Lk 15:13.
205. NASB: Rom 13:13.
206. NIV: Rom 13:13.
207. Rom 13:13.
208. Ezek 39:19.
209. Ps 73:7; Jer 48:45.
210. Ps 73:7; Jer 48:45.
211. Tim Walker, "The Vulture Who Preyed on Children," *European*, June 14-16, 1991, p.15.
212. Lev 13:2,10,19,28,43,56.
213. Ibid.
214. Lev 13:43.
215. Is 30:13.
216. O.E.D., s.v., "rising."
217. Ibid.
218. 2 Chr 13:7.
219. 2 Sam 2:18; Pro 5:19, 6:5; Song 2:9,17, 8:14, 13:14.
220. 1 Chr 12:8; Song 2:7, 3:5, 4:5, 7:3.
221. Deut 12:15,22, 14:5, 15:22.
222. 1 Ki 4:23.
223. Deut 15:22; Pro 6:5.
224. Pro 5:19.
225. Song 4:5, 7:3.
226. Deut 14:5; 1 Ki 4:23.
227. Ibid.
228. O.E.D., "roe."
229. Matt 2:1,7,16.
230. Col 2:8,20.
231. Ibid.
232. Daniel N. Nelson, "Ancient Enmities, Modern Guns," *Bulletin of the*

Atomic Scientists, Dec. 1993, p.21-27.
233. Job 8:11; Is 9:14, 19:15.
234. Is 35:7.
235. Ibid.
236. Is 9:14, 19:15.
237. NIV, NRSV: Ex 3:2; NRSV, NASB, NIV: Is 18:2.
238. NIV, NASB: Is 58:5.
239. NIV, NASB, NRSV: Jer 51:32.
240. NASB: Is 19:7.
241. Is 19:6.

Chapter 19

1. Dan 3:5,7,10,15.
2. Ibid.
3. OED., s.v., "sackbut."
4. Matt 24:15; Mk 13:14.
5. William Ecenbarger, "Passing the Torch," *Philadelphia Inquirer,* March 13, 1994, sec. Magazine, p.12.
6. Jer 31:14, 46:10.
7. Jer 31:25.Ezek 16:28.
8. Jer 31:14,25, 46:10; Ezek 16:28.
10. Jer 31:14,25, 46:10.
11. Ezek 16:28.
12. Jer 31:14.
13. Jer 46:10.
14. Jer 31:25.
15. Ezek 16:28.
16. 2 Pet 2:14.
17. Pro 1:31.
18. Paul Gray, "The Trouble with Columbus," *Time,* Oct. 7, 1991, p.52.
19. E.g., Gen 14:24; Rev 13:17.
20. Num 32:12; 1 Cor 2:2.
21. Ps 68:13.
22. E.g., Lev 13:30, 14:54.
23. Lev 13:32,34.
24. NRSV: Lev 13:2.
25. *Stedman's Medical Dictionary,* s.v., "scall."
26. Charles C. Mann, "How Many Is Too Many?" *Atlantic,* Feb. 1993, p.47.
27. 1 Sam 17:4; Lk 22:36.
28. 1 Sam 17:4.
29. Lk 10:4, 22:35,36.
30. Song 1:13.
31. Pro 19:10, 26:1.
32. Rom 1:27; 1 Cor 13:35.

33. 1 Cor 7:35, 12:24.
34. 1 Cor 12:23.
35. Ibid.
36. Pro 19:10, 26:1.
37. NASB:1 Cor 13:35.
38. NIV: 1 Cor 13:35.
39. NRSV: Rom 1:27.
40. NASB, NIV: Rom 1:27.
41. NKJV: Rom 1:27.
42. Ben Sherwood, "Wine and Poses," *Washington Monthly*, May 1993, p.22.
43. E.g., Ex 16:23; Zec 14:21.
44. 1 Sam 2:13; Job 41:20; Jer 1:13.
45. Gen 25:29; 2 Chr 35:13.
46. Ex 12:9; Lev 6:28; Num 6:19; 1 Sam 2:15; Lam 4:10.
47. Ezek 24:5.
48. 1 Sam 2:13; Job 41:20; Jer 1:13.
49. NRSV: 2 Ki 4:38.
50. NKJV, NIV: Zech 14:21.
51. NKJV: Ezek 24:5.
52. 2 Chr 35:13.
53. Gen 25:29.
54. Num 6:19; 1 Sam 2:15.
55. NIV: Ex 12:9; Lev 6:28.
56. Job 30:27.
57. Nancy Gibbs, "California: Aftershock," *Time*, Jan. 31, 1994, p.25.
58. E.g., Gen 7:13; 2 Cor 7:11.
59. NKJV, NRSV, NASB: Gen 7:13.
60. Lev 23:21.
61. NRSV, NIV, NASB: Ex 12:17.
62. Mort La Brecque, "Fractals in Chemistry: To Model the Otherwise Unmodelable," *Mosaic*, Summer 1992, p.12.
63. Ex 26:4, 36:11.
64. Ibid.
65. Ibid.
66. Amos 2:14.
67. E.g., Gen 23:6; Rom 3:13.
68. E.g., Gen 23:6; Lk 11:48.
69. Jud 8:32; 2 Sam 2:32.
70. NASB: 2 Sam 21:14.
71. NRSV, NASB: Deut 34:6.
72. Gen 23:6.
73. Steve Gushee, "The Holy Places," *Palm Beach Post*, Aug. 5, 1994, p.1D.
74. E.g., Lev 23:7; Num 29:35.
75. Ibid.
76. Ibid.

77. Javier Maria Iguiniz-Echeverria, "What Peru Needs Now," *World Monitor*, June 1992, p.10.
78. Suzanne Oliver, "Hairdressers, Anyone?" *Forbes*, May 22, 1995, p.122.
79. Ezek 43:14,17,20, 45:19.
80. Ezek 43:14.
81. Ezek 43:17,20, 45:19.
82. Lk 21:14; 1 Pet 5:10.
83. 1 Chr 6:54.
84. Ex 8:22, 9:4; Ezek 39:14, 13:49.
85. 2 Lev 20:26; Deut 4:41; Jud 4:11.
86. E.g., Num 28:13; Rev 21:21.
87. 1 Cor 12:11.
88. Ex 8:22.
89. NRSV, NIV, NASB: Ex 9:4.
90. NKJV, NASB: Matt 25:15.
91. NRSV, NIV, NASB: 2 Chr 26:21.
92. NKJV: 2 Chr 26:21.
93. NKJV: 2 Chr 28:28.
94. Zech 10:2.
95. NASB, NRSV: Is 1:25.
96. 2 Chr 32:21.
97. Ps 4:2.
98. R. Watson and D. Pedersen, "A Stunner for Major," *Newsweek*, April 20, 1992, p.38.
99. Is 2:4; Joel 3:10; Micah 4:3.
100. 1 Sam 13:20.
101. Is 2:4; Joel 3:10; Micah 4:3.
102. Ezek 23:34.
103. Job 2:8; Ps 22:15; Pro 26:23; Is 45:9.
104. Is 45:9.
105. Is 30:14; Ezek 23:34.
106. Job 2:8; Ps 22:15.
107. Ibid.
108. Ezek 23:34.
109. Ps 22:15; Is 45:9.
110. Is 30:14; Ezek 23:34.
111. Pro 26:23.
112. Job 41:30; Jer 19:2.
113. O.E.D., s.v. "shive."
114. 2 Chr 28:15; Ezek 16:10; Mk 6:9; Eph 6:15.
115. Jer 2:25; Is 11:15.
116. Is 11:15.
117. Jer 2:25.
118. Eph 6:15.
119. 2 Chr 28:15; Ezek 16:10; Mk 6:9; Eph 6:15.
120. Mark Clifford, "Pain in Pusan," *Far Eastern Economic Review*, Nov.

5, 1992, p.58.
- 121. 1 Sam 20:9.
- 122. Jn 10:12,13.
- 123. Jer 46:21.
- 124. Is 17:10.
- 125. Ex 28:35.
- 126. Matt 6:22; Lk 11:34.
- 127. Lev 27:2.
- 128. Acts 2:46; Eph 6:5; Cor 3:22.
- 129. Matt 6:22; Lk 11:34.
- 130. NIV, NKJV, NASB: Eph 6:5; Col 3:22.
- 131. Eph 6:5.
- 132. Hos 8:14.
- 133. 1 Chr 29:19.
- 134. 1 Ki 8:44.
- 135. Job 10:6.
- 136. Num 11:12.
- 137. 1 Sam 14:5; Ezek 27:3; Nah 3:8.
- 138. 2 Ki 2:19; Ps 48:2.
- 139. NASB: Neh 2:17; Dan 2:9; NIV: Gen 31:40; 1 Sam 13:6.
- 140. 2 Ki 2:19.
- 141. Nah 3:8.
- 142. Gen 47:11.
- 143. Bahgat Elnadi and Adel Rifaat, "Joseph Ki-Zerbo," *UNESCO Courier,* Feb. 1992, p.8.
- 144. Ecc 9:11; Dan 14,7, 9:22; Amos 5:16.
- 145. 1 Ki 5:6; 2 Chr 2:7,8, 34:12.
- 146. Ibid.
- 147. 2 Chr 2:7.
- 148. 2 Chr 2:8, 34:12.
- 149. 2 Chr 34:12.
- 150. Ecc 9:11; Dan 1:7, 9:22.
- 151. Anne H. Soukhanov, *Word Watch* (NY: Henry Holt and Co., 1995), p.136.
- 152. Jere Daniel, "Learning to Love (Gulp!) Growing Old," *Psychology Today,* Sept./Oct. 1994, p.61.
- 153. Gen 11:3; Ex 2:3.
- 154. Gen 14:10.
- 155. Gen 11:3; Ex 2:3; Gen 14:10.
- 156. Ibid.
- 157. Ibid.
- 158. Song 3:9.
- 159. E.g., Jud 18:9; Heb 6:12.
- 160. Pro 19:15; Ecc 10:18.
- 161. NASB: Pro 12:27; NKJV: Pro 18:9.
- 162. Matt 25:26.
- 163. NRSV: Jud 18:9.

164. NASB, NRSV: Pro 15:19.
165. NRSV, NIV, NASB: Pro 18:9.
166. NKJV: Rom 12:11.
167. NRSV, NASB: Heb 6:12.
168. Po 19:15.
169. Ecc. 10:18.
170. Pro 10:26.
171. Pro 6:6,9.
172. Ginia Bellafante, "Carousing Women," *Time,* June 12, 1995, p.79.
173. George H. Colt and Sasha Nyary, "The Frail Future of an Alligator Hole," *Life,* Sept. 1995, p.60.
174. 1 Sam 13:19; Is 44:12, 54:16.
175. 2 Ki 24:14, 24:16; Jer 24:1, 21:2.
176. Neh 3:8,32.
177. Is 40:19, 41:7, 46:6.
178. Acts 19:24.
179. 2 Tim 4:14.
180. 1 Sam 13:19; 2 Ki 24:14,16; Is 54:16; Jer 24:1, 29:2.
181. 2 Ki 24:14,16; Is 54:16; Jer 24:1, 29:2.
182. 2 Ki 24:14,16; Jer 24:1, 29:2.
183. Pro 25:4.
184. 2 Ki 24:14,16; Jer 24:1, 29:2.
185. 2 Tim 4:14.
186. Jer 14:6; Mal 1:13.
187. Jer 2:24.
188. Ibid.
189. NRSV, NASB, NIV: Jer 14:6.
190. NKJV: Mal 1:13.
191. Job 21:17.
192. E.g., Lev 15:9; Rom 3:19.
193. E.g., Gen 2:19; Rev 21:27.
194. E.g., Gen 4:15; Rev 22:17.
195. Gen 30:41; Mk 14:7; Rom 15:24.
196. E.g., Gen 31:32; 1 Cor 16:3.
197. Jud 19:20; 2 Sam 18:22,23; Zep 3:7.
198. E.g., Lev 13:12; Lk 17:37.
199. E.g., Jos 1:7; Rev 14:4.
200. 2 Cor 11:21.
201. David Ramsay Steele, "Why Stop at Term Limits?" *National Review,* Sept. 11, 1995, p.38.
202. Denis MacShane, "Ted's Europe," *History Today,* March 1995, p.49.
203. Anil Khosla, "Book Reviews: Far East," *Asian Affairs,* Feb. 1994, p.109.
204. Job 16:5.
205. Betsy Morris and Ruth M. Coxeter, "Executive Women Confront Midlife Crisis," *Fortune,* Sept. 18, 1995, p.60.
206. Is 2:6; Dan 2:27, 4:7, 5:7, 5:11; Micah 5:12.

207. Acts 16:16.
208. Jos 13:22; Is 2:6; Dan 2:27, 4:7, 5:7, 5:11; Micah 5:12.
209. Ibid.
210. Is 2:6; Micah 5:12.
211. Is 2:6.
212. NRSV, NIV, NASB: Dan 2:27, 4:7, 5:7,11.
213. Acts 16:16.
214. E.g., Lev 19:26; Jer 50:36.
215. Deut 18:10,14; 2 Ki 21:6, 2 Chr 33:6; Jer 27:9.
216. Lev 19:26; Jer 27:9.
217. Jud 9:37; Is 3:2.
218. Deut 18:10.
219. Peter Catalano, "Hurricane Alert!" *Popular Science,* Sept. 1995, p.65.
220. Jn 13:26,27,30.
221. Ibid.
222. Lina Lofaro, "What, Me Vote to Raise Taxes?" *Time,* Sept. 11, 1995, p.29.
223. E.g., Gen 34:25; Rev 16:2.
224. E.g., Gen 19:9; Acts 20:37.
225. Gen 49:23; Is 23:5.
226. Heb 10:29.
227. Deut 28:35; Job 2:7.
228. Rev 16:2.
229. NASB: Micah 2:10.
230. NRSV: Micah 2:10.
231. NIV, NKJV, NRSV: Gen 20:8.
232. Gen 41:57.
233. Jud 15:18.
234. NKJV, NASB: Mk 6:51.
235. Jer 14:17.
236. James Stolee, "In a Sunny Italian Palazzo, Amazing Human Transformations," Alberta Report, May 17, 1993, p.38.
237. Gen 24:12; 2 Jn 10,11.
238. Gen 24:12.
239. 2 Jn 10,11.
240. Dena Jones Jolma, "Why They Quit: Thoughts from Ex-Hunters," *Animals' Agenda,* July/Aug. 1992, p.38.
241. E.g., Ex 3:22, Col 2:8.
242. Ps 35:12; Is 22:4; Jer 48:3; Hab 1:3; Heb 10:34.
243. Ps 35:10; Is 21:2; Hos 7:1; Nah 3:16.
244. E.g., Gen 34:27; Col 2:15.
245. Is 33:1.
246. E.g., Is 16:4; Jer 51:56.
247. E.g., Jud 2:14; Jer 51:33.
248. Ex 3:22; 1 Sam 14:48.
249. 1 Pet 1:4.
250. Job 30:22.

251. Song 2:5.
252. Jer 12:12.
253. Is 16:4.
254. Is 54:16.
255. NRSV: Is 42:24; NASB: Jud 5:30.
256. Jer 18:4.
257. NRSV: 1 Sam 14:36; NKJV: Jud 2:14.
258. NIV: Jer 30:16; NASB, NRSV: Ps 17:9.
259. Cynthia McClintock, "Peru's Fujimori: A Caudillo Derails Democracy," *Current History*, March 1993, p.112.
260. Susan Dentzer, "The Rescue of Mexico," *U.S. News & World Report*, Jan. 23, 1995, p.48.
261. 2 Sam 22:19; Ps 18:18; Is 3:1, 19:13.
262. 1 Ki 10:19; 2 Chr 9:18.
263. E.g., Pro 28:17; Is 50:10.
264. Ex 17:12; 1 Ki 22:35; 2 Chr 18:34; Is 26:3; Lam 4:6.
265. Lev 13:5,37.
266. E.g., 1 Sam 15:16; Dan 4:35.
267. E.g., Ex 10:24; Lk 4:42.
268. Is 27:8.
269. NASB: Ps 18:18; NRSV: 2 Sam 22:19.
270. NKJV: Is 19:13; NRSV, NIV: Jer 49:35.
271. Is 45:7.
272. E.g., 1 Sam 9:13; James 1:24.
273. Acts 22:29; James 1:24.
274. NRSV: Acts 16:33.
275. NRSV, NIV, NASB: Acts 23:30.
276. NASB: Pro 7:22.
277. Leo R. Kass, "Am I My Brother's Keeper?" *Current*, Jan. 1995, p.4.
278. E.g., 1 Sam 13:6; Phil 1:23.
279. Job 20:22; Lam 1:3.
280. E.g., Gen 43:7; Acts 5:28.
281. Jer 19:9.
282. E.g., Job 18:7; 2 Cor 6:12.
283. Acts 26:5.
284. Job 12:23.
285. Deut 28:53,55,57; Job 36:16; Jer 19:9.
286. NASB, NRSV, NKJV: 1 Sam 14:28.
287. 2 Sam 24:14.
288. NRSV, NASB: Mk 1:43.
289. Lk 13:24.
290. NIV, NRSV: Pro 4:12.
291. 1 Sam 13:16.
292. Lam 1:3.
293. Deut 28:53,55,57.
294. Helen Vendler, "The Nothing That Is," *New Republic*, Aug. 7, 1995, p.42.

295. Gen 30:37; Lev 14:37.
296. Gen 30:35,39,40, 31:8,10,12.
297. NIV, NKJV: Gen 30:40, 31:12; NRSV: Gen 30:37.
298. NRSV, NASB: Gen 30:35, 31:12; NIV, NKJV, NASB: Gen 30:37.
299. Patrick Bedard, "The Plastic Surgeons," *Car & Driver,* March 1995, p.64.
300. Ex 32:20; Matt 21:8, 25:24, 25:26; Mk 11:8.
301. 2 Chr 34:4.
302. Ex 32:20; 2 Chr 34:4.
303. 1 Sam 17:52; 2 Ki 7:15.
304. Ezek 32:5; Ps 141:7.
305. Jud 6:17.
306. Jer 12:3.
307. Joel 3:10.
308. Ezek 28:24.
309. 2 Ki 19:6; Is 37:6.
310. Sharon Begley, "Postcards From the Edge," *Newsweek,* Dec. 19, 1994, p.54.
311. Paul Craig Roberts, "Guilty of Being Rich," *National Review,* Nov. 15, 1993, p.47.
312. 2 Sam 8:5, 18:3; Heb 2:18.
313. 2 Sam 21:17, 2 Cor 6:2.
314. Rom 16:2.
315. 2 Sam 8:5; 2 Cor 6:2.
316. Rom 10:2.
317. 2 Sam 18:3.
318. NKJV, NRSV: 2 Sam 21:17.
319. "Right to Punish China," *Economist,* Feb. 11, 1995, p.15.
320. Ezek 18:14; Mk 7:8,13; Gal 5:21.
321. Ibid.
322. Mk 7:8,13.
323. Ezek 18:14.
324. Gal 5:21; NRSV, NASB, NKJV: Ezek 18:14.
325. Allen Abel, "My Father, the Liberator," *Maclean's,* April 3, 1995, p.58.
326. Deut 32:25; 1 Sam 15:3; Jer 44:7.
327. 1 Sam 22:19; Ps 8:2; Lam 2:11; Matt 21:16.
328. Deut 32:25; Matt 21:16.
329. Deut 32:25.
330. Matt 21:16.
331. Lam 2:11.
332. 1 Sam 15:3.
333. Deut 32:25.
334. 1 Sam 22:19.
335. Jer 44:7.
336. Matt 21:16.
337. Ps 8:2.

338. Jer 44:7.
339. Deut 32:25.
340. 1 Sam 7:9.
341. Ps 78:71.
342. Deut 22:6.
343. Hopi Gesteland, "Gourmet or Garbage?" *Kiwanis Magazine,* Sept. 1991, p.40.
344. E.g., Ex 12:23; Rev 11:9.
345. E.g., Gen 20:6; Heb 7:23.
346. Ps 66:9,107:38; Acts 28:4; 1 Cor 13:4.
347. Acts 27:7; Rev 2:20.
348. NKJV, NIV, NRSV: 1 Tim 2:12.
349. NKJV, NRSV, NASB: Ex 12:23.
350. NRSV, NIV: 1 Cor 10:13.
351. 1 Ki 21:5.
352. Ps 46:9, 107:14,16; Is 27:9, 45:2; Nah 1:13; Lk 12:46.
353. Job 41:17.
354. E.g., Lev 5:8; Heb 4:12.
355. Ps 2:3.
356. NASB: Ps 107:16; NRSV: Ps 107:14.
357. Is 24:19.
358. Ps 136:13.
359. NIV, NRSV, NKJV: Num 16:31.
360. Heb 11:37.
361. Mk 10:9.
362. "The Siege of Somalia," *World Monitor,* June 1992, p.52-55.
363. NKJV, NASB: Ps 46:9.
364. NASB: Ps 107:14; NKJV: Nah 1:13.
365. NIV: Ps 107:14; Nah 1:13.
366. NIV, NRSV: Is 27:9.
367. NASB, NRSV, NKJV: Job 41:17.
368. Conrad Black, "Canadian Disintegration: American Integration?" *Current,* June 1995, p.19.
369. Michael Kinsley, "Generous Old Lady, or Reverse Racist?" *Time,* Aug. 28, 1995, p.76.
370. Hab 1:9; Lk 17:8; Rev 3:20.
371. 1 Cor 11:25.
372. Lk 17:8.
373. Rev 3:20.
374. 1 Cor 11:25.
375. Allan Leas, "Moody Responses," *Africa Events,* Oct./Nov. 1991, p.31.
376. Lev 21:18, 22:23; 2 Cor 9:1.
377. 2 Cor 9:1.
378. Thomas Fisher, "Gardenview," *Horticulture,* May 1994, p.42.
379. Robert A. Manning and James S. Przystup, "Virtual Policy," *National Review,* Sept. 11, 1995, p.48.

380. Kathryn Bowers and Patricia Thomas, "Handle With Care," *Harvard Health Letter,* Aug. 1995, p.6.
381. Diana Webb, "Saints and Cities in Medieval Italy," *History Today,* July 1993, p.15.
382. Ecc 5:12.
383. Fred Barnes, "Cheap Thrill," *New Republic,* June 19, 1995, p.46.
384. Acts 27:27.
385. 1 Tim 6:4.
386. Christopher Cullis, "Seeds of Revolution," *CWRU Magazine,* Nov. 1989, p.17.
387. Lk 2:7,12.
388. Lam 2:22; Ezek 16:4.
389. Job 38:9.
390. Job 38:9; Ezek 16:4; Lk 2:7,12.
391. Job 38:9.
392. Ezek 16:4.
393. Lk 2:7,12.
394. Gregory T. Pope, "Last Great Engineering Challenge: Alaska-Siberia Bridge," *Popular Mechanics,* April 1994, p.56.
395. Jer 12:5, 49:19, 50:44; 2 Pet 2:18; Jude 6.
396. 2 Cor 12:20.
397. Jer 12:5, 49:19, 50:44.
398. 2 Cor 12:20.
399. 2 Pet 2:18; Jude 6.
400. Ibid.

Chapter 20

1. Is 51:17.
2. Ex 35:22; Num 31:50; Is 3:20.
3. Ibid.
4. Ibid.
5. Ex 35:22; Num 31:50.
6. Ex 35:22.
7. Is 3:20.
8. Ex 35:22.
9. Gen 31:27; 1 Sam 10:25; Job 17:6; Is 5:12.
10. 1 Sam 18:6; Is 24:8, 30:2; Jer 31:4; Ezek 28:13.
11. 1 Sam 18:6; Is 5:12.
12. NKJV: Gen 31:27; NRSV: Is 24:8.
13. Ezek 28:13.
14. 1 Chr 13:8; NRSV: Ex 15:20.
15. Is 5:12; NASB, NRSV: Gen 31:27.
16. E.g., Ex 26:6, 39:33.
17. Ibid.
18. NASB: Ex 35:11; NRSV: Ex 39:33.

19. Is 27:9.
20. Ex 5:8,18; 1 Sam 18:27; 1 Chr 9:28.
21. NASB, NKJV: Ex 5:8; NASB, NIV, NKJV: Ex 5:18.
22. NRSV: Ex 5:18.
23. NIV, NASB, NRSV: 1 Sam 18:27.
24. 1 Chr 9:28.
25. Ps 90:9.
26. Ezek 22:9; Lk 24:11.
27. Lk 24:11.
28. Lev 19:16; Pro 11:13, 18:8, 20:19, 26:20,21.
29. Ibid.
30. NRSV, NIV, NASB: Lev 19:16.
31. NIV, NRSV: Pro 20:19.
32. NRSV, NASB: Pro 18:8.
33. Pro 11:13.
34. Jer 6:28.
35. Pro 16:28.
36. Neh 1:11.
37. Gen 40:1,9.
38. Jud 9:54; 1 Sam 31:16.
39. NIV, NRSV, NASB: 1 Sam 17:11; NKJV: 1 Sam 17:7.
40. Matt 13:25,26,27,29,30,36,37,40.
41. Ibid.
42. Ibid.
43. Deut 3:10.
44. 1 Sam 17:6; 1 Ki 10:16; 2 Chr 9:15.
45. 1 Ki 10:16; 2 Chr 9:15; 2 Chr 14:8.
46. 1 Ki 10:16; 2 Chr 9:15.
47. Ps 78:51.
48. Is 32:12; Ezek 23:3,21.
49. Is 32:12; Ezek 23:3.
50. Ezek 23:21.
51. Lorraine Copeland, "Back to the Sea: Defending the Aquatic Ape Theory," *Ocean Realm,* April 1993, p.35.
52. Hos 4:13.
53. Gen 35:8; Is 1:30.
54. Gen 21:33.
55. E.g., Gen 35:4; Is 1:30.
56. Is 6:13.
57. E.g., Jud 6:11; Ezek 6:13.
58. Is 6:13; Hos 4:13.
59. E.g., 2 Sam 8:14; 1 Ki 3:14.
60. Is 6:13; Hos 4:13.
61. 1 Chr 10:12.
62. 1 Ki 3:14; Ezek 6:13.
63. 1 Chr 10:12.
64. E.g., Gen 35:4; Is 1:30.

65. Is 16:8.
66. Ps 74:5.
67. Gen 15:5; Ps 22:17, 48:12.
68. 1 Ki 8:5; 2 Ki 12:10,11; 2 Chr 2:2, 5:6.
69. Gen 15:5; Ps 22:17, 48:12.
70. 2 Ki 12:10.
71. NRSV: 2 Ki 12:11.
72. NIV: 1 Ki 8:5.
73. NKJV: 2 Ki 12:11.
74. NIV: 2 Ki 12:11.
75. NRSV: 2 Chr 2:2.
76. NASB: 2 Chr 2:2.
77. NRSV: 2 Chr 5:6.
78. NASB, NRSV, NKJV: 2 Chr 9:1.
79. Ex 29:2, 30:5; 1 Cor 12:24.
80. Ezek 13:10,11,14,15,28.
81. Acts 24:25; Gal 5:23; 2 Pet 1:6.
82. 1 Cor 9:25; Titus 1:8, 2:2.
83. Ex 29:2.
84. Ex 30:5.
85. Ezek 46:14.
86. 1 Cor 12:24.
87. Ibid.
88. Ezek 13:10,11,14,15,28.
89. Ibid.
90. Gen 43:11.
91. Acts 24:25; Gal 5:23; 2 Pet 1:6.
92. NRSV, NASB: 1 Cor 9:25; Titus 1:8.
93. NRSV: Titus 2:2.
94. NASB: Titus 2:2.
95. NIV: Titus 1:8.
96. 1 Cor 9:25; Titus 2:2.
97. 1 Tim 3:2.
98. 1 Tim 3:11.
99. Titus 2:2.
100. Kenneth L. Woodward, "What Is Virtue?" *Newsweek*, June 13, 1994, p.38-39.
101. Tom McFeely, "Bon Voyage Quebec; Here's the Bill," *Alberta Report*, May 16, 1994, p.12-15.
102. Ex 26:17,19, 36:22,24.
103. Ibid.
104. Ibid.
105. Xiao Yuankai, "Progress Report: Renovating the Great Wall," *China Reconstructs*, March 1989, p.34.
106. Jud 17:5, 18:14,17,18,20; Hos 3:4.
107. Hos 3:4.
108. Jud 17:5, 18:14,17,18,20.

109. Jud 17:5, 18:14,17,18,20; Hos 3:4.
110. Ibid.
111. 2 Ki 23:24; Zech 10:2.
112. Jud 17:5, 18:14,17,18,20; Hos 3:4.
113. 2 Ki 23:24; Ezek 21:21; Zech 10:2.
114. Job 40:15.
115. Donald Goldsmith, "When Asteroids Strike the Earth," *Griffith Observer*, March 1994, p.2-10.
116. Matt 14:1; Lk 3:1,19, 9:7; Acts 13:1.
117. Lk 23:33.
118. Dan 6:7.
119. Ibid.
120. NIV, NASB, NRSV: Pro 11:13; NKJV: 1 Cor 7:25.
121. NRSV: Is 63:7; NKJV, NIV: Phil 4:8.
122. Rom 1:31.
123. Acts 4:16.
124. 1 Sam 19:4.
125. E.g., Gen 3:10; Rev 15:4.
126. William Ecenbarger, "Passing the Torch," *Philadelphia Inquirer*, March 13, 1994, sec. Magazine, p.12-18.
127. E.g., Gen 2:10; 2 Cor 2:13.
128. Lev 22:27; 2 Chr 32:33; Matt 5:17; Jn 19:12.
129. E.g., Gen 2:10; Acts 28:15.
130. E.g., Jer 38:11; Matt 11:1.
131. NRSV: 2 Chr 32:33.
132. NKJV: Lev 22:27.
133. NRSV, NIV, NKJV: Jn 19:12.
134. NASB: Matt 5:13.
135. NRSV: Matt 5:13.
136. Theo Sommer, et al., "Now Comes the Hard Part: 'Peace is Also a Struggle,'" *World Press Review*, Nov. 1993, p.8-14.
137. Jerry Mander, "Our Founding Mothers and Fathers, the Iroquois," *Earth Island Journal*, Fall 1991, p.30-32.
138. Ex 30:19.
139. Jos 23:6; 2 Ki 3:3, 13:2.
140. E.g., Gen 9:7; Rev 13:2.
141. Lk 21:21.
142. E.g., Gen 2:17; Rev 21:23.
143. E.g., Gen 35:14; Rev 21:12.
144. Lev 2:2; Jud 15:19.
145. E.g., Ex 25:24; Gal 3:15.
146. E.g., Ex 32:8; 1 Pet 3:9.
147. Ex 31:7; Ezek 16:16; Zep 2:7; 1 Cor 3:10,14.
148. E.g., Ex 22:6; 3 Jn 10.
149. Ps 24:1; Jer 50:3.
150. 1 Chr 15:15.
151. NASB: Matt 14:7; NRSV: Jer 31:26.

152. NASB: 1 Sam 10:17; 2 Chr 32:23; 2 Pet 2:6; NRSV: Num 8:15,22, 15:23; NKJV: Lev 22:27; 2 Chr 32:33; Ezek 43:27.
153. John Pike, "Ralpha: A New Space Station Is Born ... But Will It Fly?" *Ad Astra,* Jan./Feb. 1994, p.17-23.
154. Judith Goldhaber, "B Factory: The Curious Physics of CP Symmetry Violation," *LBL Research Review,* Summer 1991, p.18-21.
155. Hans Jonas, "The Burden and Blessing of Mortality," *Hastings Center Report,* Jan./Feb. 1992, p.34-40.
156. Russell Herman, "Solitary Waves," *American Scientist,* July/Aug. 1992, p.350-361.
157. Hans Jonas, "The Burden and Blessing of Mortality," *Hastings Center Report,* Jan./Feb. 1992, p.34-40.
158. J. Williamson, "Health Care for an Ageing Population," *Pharos,* Winter 1991, p.2-6.
159. Paula Span, "The On-Line Mystique," *Washington Post,* Feb. 27, 1994, sec. Magzine, p.10.
160. E.g., Ex 15:7; Heb 1:13.
161. Cathy McMullen, "Gay Teens," *Forum,* May 16, 1993, p.B1.
162. E.g., Gen 19:20; Acts 25:4.
163. Jud 18:15; Jer 50:5; Rom 15:24.
164. Gen 24:6; Ezek 40:3.
165. NRSV, NIV, NKJV: Jer 50:5.
166. NRSV: Jud 18:15.
167. NIV, NASB, NKJV: Rom 15:24.
168. David Burstein and Peter L. Manly, "Cosmic Tug of War," *Astronomy,* July 1993, p.40-45.
169. E.g., Gen 3:12; Rev 16:6.
170. Is 44:17.
171. Robert Brustein, "The Smashing of the Bell," *New Republic,* Aug. 14, 1995, p.26.
172. E.g., Ex 34:23; 2 Cor 12:8.
173. Ibid.
174. Ezek 21:14.
175. Peter Hellman, "Suffer the Little Children," *New York,* Feb. 21, 1994, p.26-32.
176. E.g., Gen 4:14; Rev 16:7.
177. Tom Bethell, "The Mother of All Rights," *Reason,* April 1994, p.40-47.
178. Is 40:20.
179. 1 Chr 27:26; Neh 10:37; Pro 13:23.
180. NRSV, NKJV, NASB: 1 Chr 27:26.
181. NIV: 1 Chr 27:26.
182. NRSV, NIV. Pro 13:23.
183. NASB, NKJV: Pro 13:23.
184. Gen 2:5,23.
185. Dennis T. Avery, "Feast or Famine?" *Far Eastern Economic Review,* Dec. 1, 1994, p.40.

186. Bob Drogin, "Trouble Down Under," *Los Angeles Times*, Sept. 19, 1993, sec. Magazine, p.16.
187. Ex 15:20; Job 21:12; Ps 81:2, 149:3, 150:4.
188. Ex 15:20; Jud 11:34; 2 Sam 6:5; 1 Chr 13:8; Ps 68:25.
189. E.g., Ex 15:20; Ps 150:4.
190. 2 Sam 6:5; 1 Chr 13:8; Job 21:12.
191. Jud 11:34.
192. E.g., Ex 15:20; Ps 150:4.
193. Ex 15:20; Job 21:12; Ps 81:2, 149:3, 150:4.
194. NASB, NKJV: Gen 31:27; NKJV: Ezek 28:13; NRSV: Is 24:8, 30:32.
195. Is 5:12; NASB, NRSV: Gen 31:27.
196. Is 3:18; Ezek 24:23.
197. 2 Ki 9:30.
198. Ezek 24:17.
199. Ezek 24:23.
200. Is 3:18.
201. Ibid.
202. 2 Ki 9:30.
203. Gen 49:14.
204. Matt 5:18; Lk 16:17.
205. 2 Ki 23:17.
206. Matt 5:18; Lk 16:17.
207. NASB: Matt 5:18.
208. NRSV: Matt 5:18; Lk 16:17.
209. NIV: Matt 5:18; Lk 16:17.
210. Andrew W. Singer, "The Whistle-Blower: Patroit or Bounty Hunter?" *Across The Board*, Nov. 1992, p.16-22.
211. Jud 16:9; Is 1:31, 43:17.
212. Is 43:17.
213. Is 1:31.
214. Jud 16:9.
215. Ps 76:4.
216. Gen 42:34; 1 Ki 10:15; Ezek 17:4, 28:5,18.
217. Is 23:8.
218. Gen 42:34; Ezek 28:5.
219. NASB, NIV: Ezek 17:4.
220. NRSV: 1 Ki 10:15.
221. NASB: 1 Ki 10:15.
222. NIV: 1 Ki 10:15.
223. NKJV: 1 Ki 10:15.
224. Is 47:15.
225. Daniel N. Nelson, "Ancient Enmities, Modern Guns," *Bulletin of the Atomic Scientists*, Dec. 1993, p.21-27.
226. 2 Sam 3:10.
227. Heb 11:5.
228. Col 1:13; Heb 11:5.
229. Jn 1:42.

230. 2 Sam 3:10.
231. Heb 11:5.
232. NIV: Heb 11:5.
233. NKJV: Heb 11:5.
234. David Zweig, "Clinton and China: Creating a Policy Agenda That Works," *Current History,* Sept. 1993, p.245-252.
235. E.g., Gen 38:27; 2 Thes 3:8.
236. Gen 35:16, 38:28; 1 Sam 4:19; Is 66:7,8.
237. Job 15:20; Ps 7:14; Is 13:8, 21:3; Jer 31:8; Micah 5:3; Rom 8:22.
238. Is 42:14; Hos 13:13; Rev 12:2.
239. Gal 4:27.
240. 1 Sam 4:19.
241. Is 21:3.
242. NRSV, NASB, NKJV: Job 15:20.
243. NRSV, NKJV: Ecc 2:23.
244. NRSV: Ecc 3:10.
245. NASB: Ecc 3:10.
246. NIV: Ecc 3:10.
247. NKJV, NRSV: Ecc 4:4.
248. NRSV, NASB: Is 53:11.
249. NIV: Is 53:11.
250. NASB, NIV: 1 Thes 2:9.
251. Ps 7:14; Is 23:4, 54:1, 66:7,8; Jn 16:21.
252. Robert Cullen, "The True Cost of Coal," *Atlantic Monthly,* Dec. 1993, p.38.
253. Ps 89:47.
254. Ps 39:4.
255. E.g., 1 Sam 18:21; Eph 2:15.
256. Is 6:2; Matt 27:51.
257. NASB: 2 Ki 4:33.
258. NKJV, NRSV, NASB: Ezek 21:19.
259. "Advice From a Caterpillar to Your Brain," *Economist,* Aug. 6, 1988, p.67.
260. E.g., Ex 26:1, 39:29.
261. Ibid.
262. Ibid.
263. Doug O'Harra, "Musk Ox on the Move," *Anchorage Daily News,* June 11, 1989, p.J-8.

Chapter 21

1. E.g., Gen 31:20; Jude 4.
2. Deut 4:42.
3. NKJV: Gen 31:26.
4. NKJV, NIV: Num 35:11.
5. NIV: Ps 35:8.

6. NKJV: Gal 2:4.
7. NKJV: Ps 35:8.
8. NKJV: Heb 13:2.
9. NASB: Jude 4.
10. Ps 35:8.
11. Gen 34:25.
12. Lev 26:33.
13. Matt 19:9.
14. Deut 27:6.
15. Jn 11:44.
16. Matt 9:16.
17. Is 10:1.
18. Lk 18:11.
19. Gen 49:4.
20. Elizabeth Razzi, "Scams That Add Insult to Injury," *Kiplinger's Personal Finance Magazine*, May 1994, p.86-90.
21. Steve Gushee, "The Holy Places," *Palm Beach Post*, Aug. 5, 1994, p.1D.
22. 1 Ki 7:30,34.
23. Ibid.
24. Jer 17:13.
25. Is 53:12; Acts 11:18.
26. Jn 11:14.
27. E.g., Ps 19:2; Matt 3:11.
28. Ross Terrill, "The Mao Legacy: 100 Years Young?" *San Francisco Examiner*, Nov. 14, 1993, sec. Magazine, p.10.
29. Winifred Gallagher, "How We Become What We Are," *Atlantic Monthly*, Sept. 1994, p.38.
30. Jud 8:15; Matt 11:20.
31. Mk 16:14; James 1:5.
32. NASB, NRSV, NIV: Jud 8:15.
33. NKJV: Jud 8:15.
34. NRSV, NASB: Matt 11:20.
35. NKJV: Matt 11:20.
36. NIV: Matt 11:20.
37. NIV: James 1:5.
38. Jud 8:15; Matt 11:20; James 1:5.
39. Mk 16:14.
40. Gen 31:36; Jud 8:1.
41. George E. Curry, "Jesse & Jews: Unity in the Community," *Emerge*, Sept. 1994, p.28-38.
42. E.g., Ex 22:25; Lk 19:23.
43. Neh 5:7,10; Pro 28:8.
44. E.g., Lev 25:36; Ezek 22:12.
45. Neh 5:7,10,11; Ps 15:5; Ezek 18:8,13,17, 22:12.
46. Neh 5:11.
47. Louis Crosier, "Home Equity Scams Foreclose on the American

Dream," *Public Citizen,* Summer 1994, p.10.
48. 1 Ki 20:42; Nah 1:8,9; Zech 14:11.
49. E.g., Ezek 40:31, 47:2.
50. E.g., Gen 49:26; Lk 11:31.
51. NASB, NKJV: Gen 49:26; NIV: 2 Ki 19:23; Is 14:13, 37:24.
52. E.g., Ex 26:4; Heb 7:25.
53. Acts 24:22.
54. Matt 5:26; 1 Thes 2:16.
55. Heb 7:25.
56. NASB, NRSV: Ex 26:4, 36:11.
57. NKJV: Ex 26:4, 36:11.
58. 1 Sam 14:2.
59. Ps 139:9; 1 Thes 2:16; Heb 7:25.
60. Ezek 32:23.
61. Song 7:5.

Chapter 22

1. Gen 4:12, 14; Acts 19:13.
2. Ps 109:10.
3. Gen 4:12, 14; Ps 109:10.
4. Ibid.
5. Pro 6:11.
6. William Drozdiak, "Jules Verne's Crystal Ball," *Washington Post,* Sept. 24, 1994, P.H1.
7. Gal 5:26.
8. Gal 5:26; Phil 2:3.
9. Pro 26:5,12,16, 28:11.
10. Pro 26:16, 28:11.
11. Pro 18:11.
12. Charles Trueheart, "Publish and Perish?" *Washington Post,* July 13, 1994, p.B1.
13. Gen 14:3, 8, 10, 37:14; Deut 1:7; Jos 10:40; 1 Ki 10:27; 2 Chr 1:15; Jer 33:13.
14. Gen 14:3, 8, 14:10, 37:14.
15. NKJV, NASB: Deut 1:7; NRSV, NIV, NKJV: Jos 10:40; NASB, NKJV: 1 Ki 10:27; 2 Chr 1:5; NASB, NKJV: Jer 33:13.
16. Deut 1:7; Jos 10:40; 1 Ki 10:27; 2 Chr 1:5; Jer 33:13.
17. 1 Ki 10:27; 2 Chr 1:5; Jer 33:13.
18. Jos 8:11; Jos 11:12, 16; 2 Chr 35:22.
19. Ps 60:6, 108:7.
20. Num 21:12; Deut 21:4, 6.
21. Num 32:9.
22. Deut 1:24.
23. Num 34:5; Jos 15:4, 47; 1 Ki 8:65; 2 Ki 24:7; 2 Chr 7:8; Ezek 47:19, 48:28.

24. Bob Drogin, "Trapped in a Vale of Tears," *Los Angeles Times,* Aug. 29, 1993, P.A1.
25. E.g., Jud 3:29; Neh 11:14.
26. Jos 20:46; 2 Chr 32:21.
27. 1 Sam 16:18; 2 Ki 24:16; 2 Chr 26:17.
28. 1 Sam 9:1, 16:8; 2 Ki 24:16; 1 Chr 7:2, 7:5, 12:8.
29. NASB: Jos 1:14; Jud 20:44.
30. NASB, NIV: Neh 11:6.
31. NASB, NIV: Is 33:7.
32. NIV, NASB, NKJV: 1 Chr 11:26.
33. NRSV: 1 Sam 16:18; NASB, NKJV: 1 Chr 7:5.
34. NIV: Ex 18:25; NASB: 1 Chr 9:13.
35. NASB: 2 Ki 24:16; 1 Chr 7:2, 5, 12:8.
36. Wilma L. Vaught, "In Defense of America: Women Who Serve," *USA Today Magazine,* March 1994, p.86-92.
37. Matt 5:13; Mk 9:50; Lk 14:34.
38. Gal 5:22.
39. Matt 7:23, 13:4, 23:28, 24:12.
40. Matt 24:12.
41. E.g., Matt 5:32, 19:9.
42. E.g., Mk 7:22; Gal: 5:19.
43. Jude 4.
44. Num 14:33; Rom 3:3.
45. NASB: Jer 3:22.
46. Matt 17:20.
47. Eph 4:21; Phil 2:3.
48. Lk 1:48.
49. Acts 17:11.
50. Lk 12:35; 2 Cor 8:12.
51. Matt 10:35; Gal 5:20.
52. Ibid.
53. 2 Cor 7:11.
54. Lam 5:3.
55. Ted Wendling and Dave Davis, "Lethal Doses: Radiation That Kills," *Plain Dealer,* Dec. 13, 1992, p.1A.
56. 1 Cor 13:4.
57. Jud 7:2.
58. Ps 94:4.
59. 1 Cor 13:4.
60. Is 10:15.
61. Job 15:25.
62. Job 19:5.
63. Edward G. Shirley, "Not Fanatics, and Not Friends," *Atlantic Monthly,* Dec. 1993, p.104.
64. Song 8:6; Jonah 4:8; 2 Cor 7:11.
65. Mk 14:31; Lk 6:48, 49, 11:53, 23:10.
66. Song 8:6; Jonah 4:8; Mk 14:31; Lk 6:48, 49, 11:53, 23:10; 2 Cor 7:11.

67. NRSV: Song 8:6; NRSV: Jonah 4:8; NASB: Jonah 4:8; NIV: Song 8:6.
68. Song 8:6.
69. NIV: Mk 14:31.
70. NASB: Ibid.
71. NIV: Lk 11:53.
72. Mk 14:31; Lk 23:10.
73. LK 23:10.
74. Ann Scott Tyson, "Prairie Preservation Moves Ahead," *Christian Science Monitor*, Nov. 4, 1994, sec. The U.S., p.1.
75. David Olinger, "On the Bear Track," *St. Petersburg Times*, Nov. 13, 1994, p.1B.
76. Brian Jaramillo, "Forgotten Prospects Get a Second Look," *Oregonian*, Nov. 15, 1994, p.DO1.
77. Tom Farrey, "Captain Mariner Firmly at Helm of Baseball Team," *Seattle Times*, Nov. 27, 1994, p.C1.
78. Peter Gorner, "Canadian Bares Emerald's Secret," *Montreal Gazette*, Aug. 4, 1994, p.A1.
79. Gen 25:28, 27:3, 5, 7, 19, 25, 31, 33.
80. NASB, NIV, NKJV: Ibid.; NIV: Gen 27:5, 7, 19, 25, 31, 33.
81. Gen 25:28, 27:3.
82. Gene Mueller, "Deer, Waterfowl, Turkeys Headline Hunting Parade," *Washington Times*, Sept. 23, 1994, p.G7.
83. 1 Ki 22:34; 2 Chr 18:33.
84. Deut 28:56; Acts 19:31.
85. Jud 9:17.
86. E.g., Gen 18:24; 2 Tim 2:25.
87. 1 Ki 22:34; 2 Chr 18:33.
88. Ibid.
89. Mk 12:34; Jn 21:12; Acts 7:32.
90. Ecc 5:14.
91. Gen 32:20; Ex 32:30.
92. Deut 28:56; Jud 9:17; Acts 19:31.
93. Michelle Trappen, "Picture Perfect," *Oregonian*, June 3, 1994, p.C01.
94. David L. Marcus, "Angola," *Dallas Morning News*, Aug. 7, 1994, p.1R.
95. Ecc 9:10.
96. NIV, NRSV: Ex 31:13; NRSV: 2 Chr 21:24.
97. Is 45:15.
98. NRSV: Gen 42:21.
99. Ps 58:11.
100. NKJV, NASB: Ps 66:19.
101. NASB: Jud 15:2.
102. NASB, NRSV: 2 Ki 4:14.
103. NASB: Job 19:13.
104. NRSV: Job 19:13.
105. NKJV: 2 Ki 4:14.
106. E.g., Matt 5:18; Lk 21:32.

107. E.g., Jn 5:24, 13:20.
108. 1 Cor 14:16; 2 Cor 1:20; Rev 3:14, 5:14, 7:12, 19:4.
109. NASB, NKJV: Acts 16:37.
110. NRSV: Acts 16:37.
111. NASB: Acts 26:9.
112. NIV: Acts 26:9.
113. NASB: 1 Cor 5:3.
114. NRSV: 1 Cor 5:3.
115. NRSV, NIV: 1 Cor 9:18.
116. NASB, NRSV, NIV: Gal 3:21.
117. NKJV: 1 Thes 3:4.
118. NRSV: Heb 2:16.
119. NIV: Heb 2:16.
120. NASB: Heb 2:16.
121. Neh 13:11.
122. Ps 111:7; 1 Tim 2:7.
123. Ibid.
124. Ps 111:17.
125. Ibid.
126. 1 Tim 2:7.
127. Ibid.
128. Lk 22:59.
129. Acts 4:27.
130. Lk 4:25.
131. Linda McCarty and Stan Hough, "Childhood Trauma: Cases of False Memory," *Winchester Star*, Oct. 28, 1992, p.1E.
132. Jer 22:14; Ezek 23:14.
133. Ibid.
134. Ibid.
135. Ex 25:5, 26:14, 35:7, 23, 36:19, 39:34.
136. Est 1:6.
137. Laurence Chollet, "Crime (Writer) of the Century," *Record*, June 26, 1994, p.E01.
138. Lk 24:4.
139. Ezra 3:1.
140. E.g., Ex 28:3, 39:41.
141. Diego Ribadeneira, "Utilizing Mystical Forces, Haitians Regard Voodoo as Vital to Their Defense," *Boston Globe*, July 13, 1994, sec. National/Foreign, p.1.
142. Zech 1:8.
143. 2 Ki 17:3.
144. Deut 22:12; Ps 22:18, 102:26; Matt 27:35; Jn 19:24; Heb 1:12; Rev 19:13, 16.
145. Deut 22:12; Ps 22:18; Heb 1:12; Rev 19:13.
146. Jud 4:18; 1 Sam 15:27.
147. Dan 7:9.
148. Deut 22:12; Ps 22:18; Rev 19:13.

149. Is 59:17.
150. Lk 6:29.
151. Ibid.
152. NIV: Deut 22:12; NKJV: Ps 102:26; Heb 1:12.
153. E.g, Lev 19:33; Is 11:13.
154. E.g., Num 20:15; 2 Pet 2:8.
155. E.g., Deut 28:20; Is 28:19.
156. 2 Chr 15:5.
157. Lev 18:18; Job 19:2; Ezek 32:9.
158. Acts 12:1; Is 7:6.
159. Ps 2:5.
160. Jud 16:16.
161. Ps 73:21.
162. Ps 78:41, 112:10.
163. 1 Ki 20:43, 21:4; Ps 112:10.
164. NASB, NIV, NKJV: Deut 28:20.
165. NRSV, NASB, NIV: Is 28:19.
166. Deut 28:20; Ecc 1:14, 2:22; Is 9:1, 28:19, 65:14.
167. Ibid.
168. 1 Sam 1:16; Job 5:2, 6:2, 10:17; Ecc 1:18, 2:23, 5:17.
169. Job 5:2; Pro 12:16.
170. Job 6:2.
171. Pro 12:16.
172. Ecc 5:17, 11:10.
173. Lynell George, "The Real West Side Story," *Los Angeles Times*, July 22, 1994, p.E1.
174. James L. Tyson, "Bumper Crop, Low Prices Bolster Farm Aid Programs," *Christian Science Monitor*, Nov. 10, 1994, sec. Economy, p.8.
175. 1 Sam 10:1; Rev 16:2, 3, 4, 8, 10, 12, 17.
176. Rev 16:2, 3, 4, 8, 10, 12, 17.
177. 1 Sam 10:1.
178. Jer 19:1, 10.
179. 2 Sam 16:1.
180. Jer 13:12.
181. Matt 26:7; Mk 14:3; Lk 7:37.
182. Hans Christian von Baeyer, "Atom Chasing," *Discover*, July 1992, p.42-49.
183. Ex 12:39; Jud 20:10; 1 Ki 4:27; 2 Chr 11:11, 23.
184. E.g., Gen 14:11; Lk 9:12.
185. E.g., 1 Ki 11:18; Matt 14:15.
186. E.g., Josh 9:11, 14.
187. NASB: Gen 14:11.
188. NKJV: Jud 17:10.
189. Neh 10:31.
190. NASB: Jud 17:10.
191. Jer 40:5; Lk 9:12.
192. Whistlin Dixie, s.v., "vittles."

193. James L. Tyson, "Farm Program Builds Ties Between Grower, Consumer," *Christian Science Monitor,* Sept. 19, 1994, sec. The U.S., P.1.
194. Is 32:6; Jer 29:23.
195. O.E.D., s.v., "villany."
196. Is 32:6.
197. Jer 29:3.
198. Is 32:6; Jer 29:3.
199. Acts 13:10, 18:14.
200. Pro 6:12.
201. Is 32:7.
202. Pro 6:12.
203. Edward G. Shirley, "Not Fanatics, and Not Friends," *Atlantic Monthly,* Dec. 1993, p.104.
204. Mk 5:30; Lk 6:19, 8:46; Phil 4:8; 2 Pet 1:3; 2 Pet 1:5.
205. Ruth 3:11; Pro 12:4, 31:10.
206. Pro 31:29.
207. Phil 4:8; 2 Pet 1:3.
208. NRSV, NIV: 2 Pet 1:3, 5.
209. Phil 4:8; NASB: 2 Pet 1:3, 5.
210. Mk 5:30; Lk 6:19, 8:46.
211. Matt 11:20.
212. 1 Cor 12:10.
213. Pro 11:16.
214. Ruth 3:11; Pro 12:4, 31:10, 29.
215. Ruth 3:11; Pro 12:4, 31:10.
216. Pro 31:29.
217. Ruth 3:11; Pro 31:10.
218. Ruth 3:11; Pro 12:4, 31:10, 29.
219. Michele Ingrassia, "Virgin Cool," *Newsweek,* Oct. 17, 1994, p.58.
220. Stephen Buckley and Debbi Wilgoren, "Young and Experienced," *Washington Post,* April 24, 1994, p.A1.
221. Is 5:12; Amos 6:5.
222. Is 14:4; Amos 5:23.
223. Amos 6:5; Is 5:12.
224. Ibid.
225. E.g., 2 Sam 6:5; Is 5:12.
226. Is 52:14; Lam 4:8; Dan 3:19.
227. Ibid.
228. Is 52:14; Lam 4:8.
229. Ibid.
230. Ibid.
231. NRSV, NKJV: Dan 3:19.
232. NASB: Ibid.
233. NIV: Ibid.
234. Bob Sylva, "Calling Kevin Starr," *Sacramento Bee,* Oct. 26, 1994, p.SC1.
235. E.g., Job 10:12; Jer 8:12.

236. Lk 19:44; 1 Pet 2:12.
237. Jer 8:12, 11:23, 23:12, 46:21, 48:44, 50:27; Hos 9:7.
238. Jer 10:15, 51:18.
239. 1 Pet 2:12.
240. Micah 7:4.
241. Elaine Appleton, "The War on Waste," *National Parks,* Sept./Oct. 1994, p.37-42.
242. Jud 13:12.
243. Deut 14:21.
244. Ibid.
245. John Geddes, "Chretien: 'Little Guy from Shawinigan' Leads Liberals Back to Power," *The Financial Post,* Dec. 25, 1993, p.6-7.

Chapter 23

1. E.g., Deut 28:48; Phil 4:11.
2. E.g., Deut 15:8; Song 7:2.
3. Jer 44:18; Jn 2:3; 2 Cor 11:9.
4. Jed 19:20; Phil 2:25.
5. E.g., 2 Ki 10.19; James 1:4.
6. Pro 10:21; Amos 4:6.
7. NKJV, NRSV, NASB: Mk 12:44.
8. 2 Cor 9:12.
9. Deut 15:8; Pro 28:16; Phil 2:25.
10. Job 30:3; Ps 23:1.
11. Is 3:16; 1 Tim 5:11; James 5:5.
12. Rom 13:13; 2 Pet 2:18.
13. Is 3:16, 1 Tim 5:11; James 5:5; Rom 13:13; 2 Pet 2:18.
14. Is 3:16; 1 Tim 5:11.
15. James 5:5.
16. Is 3:16.
17. NRSV: Rom 13:13.
18. NASB: Rom 13:13.
19. NIV: Rom 13:13.
20. NKJV: Rom 13:13.
21. NKJV: 2 Pet 2:18.
22. E.g., Jud 19:25; Ezek 23:44.
23. Is 47:8; Nah 3:4.
24. Ezek 23:44.
25. 1 Tim 5:6.
26. Jane Quinn, "The Big Tease," *Newsweek,* Aug. 7, 1995, p.64.
27. E.g., Gen 40:3; Acts 12:10.
28. 1 Chr 9:23,26:12; Neh 13:30.
29. Lev 24:12.
30. NKJV, NASB, NRSV: Gen 42:17.
31. NRSV, NIV, NASB: 2 Sam 20:3.

32. NASB: Gen 40:3.
33. NRSV, NASB, NIV: 1 Chr 26:16.
34. NIV, NRSV, NKJV: Is 21:8.
35. E.g., Lev 13:48,59.
36. Ibid.
37. E.g., Ex 22:24; Heb 1:11.
38. E.g., Gen 18:12; Rev 18:3.
39. E.g., Gen 19:13; Ezek 16:7.
40. Ps 6:7; Heb 8:13.
41. Phil 1:14.
42. Job 14:8; Matt 24:12.
43. Dan 8:9,10.
44. Lk 13:19; Heb 11:34.
45. Gen 19:13; Ps 6:7; Phil 1:14.
46. "Sun's Future Not So Bright," *Astronomy*, Oct. 1995, p.24.
47. Is 17:4.
48. Jud 19:17; 2 Sam 12:4; Is 33:8, 35:8; Jer 9:2, 14:8.
49. 2 Sam 12:4.
50. Jud 19:17; 2 Sam 12:4.
51. Jer 9:2.
52. Is 35:8; Jer 14:8.
53. Stanley Kauffmann, "Journeys to the Interior," *New Republic*, Dec. 20, 1993, p.36.
54. NRSV: Rev 18:17; NIV: Is 23:2.
55. Ps 102:23.
56. Is 30:17.
57. 1 Sam 15:12.
58. Pro 1:11.
59. Pro 7:11.
60. Pro 1:32.
61. 1 Sam 2:32; Ezra 9:12; Est 10:3; Job 21:13; 1 Cor 10:24.
62. NRSV, NASB, NIV: Job 21:13.
63. 1 Cor 10:24.
64. Est 10:3.
65. Jude 12.
66. *Steadman's Medical Dictionary*, s.v., "wen."
67. 2 Ki 20:7; Is 38:21.
68. Is 38:21.
69. Mary Redd, "Weather Talk," *Weatherwise*, Dec. 1991/Jan. 1992, p.36.
70. E.g., Gen 3:23; Rev 7:13.
71. Gen 29:4; Mk 6:2.
72. John Simon, "Fishman and Netwoman," *National Review*, Sept. 11, 1995, p.68.
73. Ps 121:1.
74. E.g., Gen 31:37; 2 Pet 2:11.
75. E.g., Gen 15:8; 1 Jn 2:18.
76. E.g., Gen 10:9; Rev 17:7.

77. E.g., Gen 1:30; Rev 18:19.
78. 2 Cor 11:21.
79. Lev 11:33; Num 14:24; Jn 6:22.
80. E.g., Gen 3:11; 1 Jn 4:3.
81. E.g., Gen 28:13; Jn 4:38.
82. Job 30:2; Is 55:11; Phil 3:16.
83. Num 36:3; 2 Pet 1:19.
84. E.g., Lev 11:35; Heb 9:18.
85. E.g., Gen 27:41; Heb 10:29.
86. Ps 119:9; Matt 6:31.
87. 2 Pet 2:11.
88. NASB: Jer 1:16; NKJV: Ps 68:9.
89. NASB: Ecc 8:9; NKJV: Job 6:24.
90. Jud 20:39.
91. Jn 17:26.
92. Num 21:14.
93. 2 Chr 28:5; Rom 13:5,7; 2 Cor 1:20, 2:8.
94. Russ Rymer, "The Life," *Health,* Nov./Dec. 1992, p.58.
95. Jane R. Hirschmann and Lela Zapiropoulos, "Teens, Food, and Body Image," *Mothering,* Spring 1994, p.57.
96. Hans Jonas, "The Burden and Blessing of Mortality," *Hastings Center Report,* Jan./Feb. 1992, p.34.
97. "Dam Good Business This, Chaps," *Economist,* Aug. 26, 1995, p.61.
98. Daniel Seligman, "Big Government Meets the Cleaning Lady," *Fortune,* Feb. 22, 1993, p.120.
99. Raj Chengappa, "Nuclear Dilemma," *India Today,* April 30, 1994, p.46.
100. Deut 32:41; Ps 7:12, 64:3; Ecc 10:10.
101. Ibid.
102. Deut 32:41.
103. NIV, NASB: Deut 32:41; Ps 7:12, 64:3; Ecc 10:10; NKJV: Ps 7:12, 64:3; Ecc 10:10.
104. Jer 46:4.
105. 1 Sam 13:21.
106. Adrian Karatnycky, "Bearish Outlook," *National Review,* May 29, 1995, p.42.
107. E.g., Matt 9:5; Acts 1:24.
108. Ibid.
109. Jer 50:44.
110. Jer 50:44.
111. Pro 8:26.
112. E.g., Jud 6:31; Heb 10:33.
113. E.g., Ezek 21:29; 2 Cor 9:13.
114. E.g., 1 Chr 4:10; Lam 1:21.
115. Ps 99:8; Is 12:1, 64:5; Rev 5:9, 11:17, 16:5.
116. E.g., Gen 15:2; Rev 6:10.
117. E.g., Gen 4:14; Rev 16:6.

118. Neh 9:17,33; Jonah 2:3.
119. Deut 13:16; 1 Sam 3:18; Jn 7:23, 13:10; 2 Cor 11:5.
120. NRSV: Jn 13:10.
121. NKJV, NASB: Jn 13:10.
122. NRSV, NIV, NASB: 2 Cor 11:5.
123. NKJV: 2 Cor 11:5.
124. John Steele Gordon, "Commerce Raider," *American Heritage,* Sept. 1995, p.20.
125. E.g., Gen 16:8; 1 Jn 2:11.
126. E.g., Josh 1:7; Rev 14:4.
127. Jn 8:22; Heb 11:18.
128. Jud 2:15; Est 8:17.
129. Lee Smith, "Mexico: Good, Bad, and Maybe Ugly," *Fortune,* may 1, 1995, p.22.
130. E.g., Gen 38:24; Hos 6:10.
131. E.g., Num 14:33; Nah 3:4.
132. E.g., Lev 19:29, Rev 19:2.
133. Ezek 16:33; Hos 4:14.
134. Eph 5:5.
135. 1 Tim 1:10; Heb 13:4; Rev 21:8, 22:15.
136. E.g., Ex 34:15; Hos 9:1.
137. Pro 6:26; Ezek 6:9, 16:30.
138. Lev 19:29; Is 57:3.
139. Gen 38:21.
140. Ezek 16:26.
141. John Elson, "Dirt From the Old Sod," *Time,* Aug. 30, 1993, p.64.
142. E.g., Gen 9:6; 1 Jn 3:17.
143. Pro 12:1; Matt 18:5.
144. NKJV, NIV, NASB: Matt 23:20.
145. Lk 23:9.
146. Num 25:18; Eph 6:11.
147. Jos 9:4.
148. Eph 6:11.
149. NRSV: Num 25:18.
150. NASB, NIV: Eph 6:11.
151. Jos 9:4.
152. Lk 20:23.
153. Pro 7:10.
154. Stephen Jay Gould, "Speaking of Snails and Scales," *Natural History,* May 1995, p.14.
155. D. Ansen, "Of Carnage and Comedy," *Newsweek,* June 8, 1992, p.59.
156. Matt 11:19; Lk 7:34.
157. Pro 23:20.
158. Pro 23:20; Matt 11:19; Lk 7:34.
159. Pro 23:20.
160. NRSV, NIV, NASB: Matt 11:19; Lk 7:34.

161. Song 5:1.
162. Stanley Kauffman, "Shades of Green," *New Republic,* Sept. 13, 1993, p.42.
163. E.g., Ex 22:23; Rev 21:27.
164. Jn 21:1.
165. NKJV, NIV, NRSV: 1 Sam 6:3.
166. Job 15:18.
167. E.g., Gen 24:21; 2 Cor 8:1.
168. E.g., Gen 21:26; Phil 1:22.
169. Gen 39:8.
170. Gen 39:8.
171. E.g., Ex 16:15; Acts 23:5.
172. NASB: Ex 2:4.
173. NIV, NRSV: Gen 24:21.
174. NRSV, NIV: Ex 2:4.
175. NKJV, NASB: Gen 24:21; 2 Cor 8:1.
176. NRSV, NKJV: 2 Cor 5:19.
177. NKJV: Josh 17:1; NASB: 2 Cor 5:19.
178. Gen 44:15; Mk 14:40.
179. John Wyatt, "Star Managers Set Her Course," *Fortune,* Sept. 18, 1995, p.243.
180. E.g., Ex 25:29; Phil 1:22.
181. Matt 6:31.
182. Samuel Cipman, "Piano Prodigy," *American Scholar,* Winter 1993, p.31.
183. Jud 16:7,8,9.
184. Ibid.
185. Dan 6:7.
186. E.g., Ex 21:29; Acts 16:13.
187. NKJV: Num 22:30.
188. NASB: Num 22:30.
189. NKJV, NASB: Dan 3:19.
190. NIV, NRSV, NASB: Mk 10:1.
191. Thomas Rosenstiel and Rich Thomas, "Pork Goes Republican," *Newsweek,* Aug. 14, 1995, p.34.
192. E.g., Lev 13:48,59.
193. Ibid.
194. E.g., Ex 28:14; 2 Ki 25:17.
195. NASB, NRSV: Ex 39:17.
196. NIV: Ex 39:17.
197. NASB, NIV NKJV: 2 Ki 25:17.
198. NRSV: 2 Ki 25:17.
199. NRSV, NKJV: Ex 28.14.
200. NASB: Ex 28:14.
201. Ex 28:14,22.
202. 2 Ki 16:17.
203. Ex 23:2,6; Deut 16:19; Ps 56:5; 2 Pet 3:16.

204. Gen 32:24.
205. Ex 23:2.
206. NRSV, NASB: Deut 16:19.
207. NIV, NKJV: Ps 56:5.
208. 2 Sam 23:1; 1 Chr 11:23.
209. Mk 5:4.
210. Keith B. Richburg, "Continental Divide," *Current*, Sept. 1995, p.23.
211. E.g., Gen 4:5; Rev 12:17.
212. Gen 4:6; Deut 3:26; Lam 5:22.
213. NASB, NIV, NRSV: Matt 22:7.
214. NKJV: Matt 22:7.
215. NRSV: Matt 2:16.
216. Gen 34:7.
217. Matt 21:15.
218. E.g., Gen 34:7; Rev 19:20.
219. Ruth 2:19.
220. Ps 139:15.
221. Num 31:51; Ps 31:19, 190:15; Jn 3:21.
222. NIV, NKJV, NRSV: Ex 36:4.
223. Num 22:23.
224. NIV, NRSV: Num 31:51.
225. Deut 21:3.
226. NRSV: 2 Sam 7:21; NASB: 1 Chr 17:19.
227. Ps 78:12.
228. Ps 46:8.
229. Ezek 27:19.
230. Rhoda Sherwood, "Natural Forces," *Earth*, Oct. 1995, p.70.

Chapter 24

1. O.E.D., s.v., "ye."
2. Ibid.
3. David Zizzo, "Ex-Politician Out to Help 'Info-Challenged' Voters," *Daily Oklahoman*, Aug. 14, 1994, sec. News, p.1.
4. Matt Crenson, "New Lab Will Try to Pin Tail on Anti-Matter," *Albuquerque Journal*, Jan. 30, 1994, p.H1.
5. E.g., Gen 20:6; Phil 1:18.
6. O.E.D., s.v., "yes."
7. Matt 17:25; Mk 7:27; Rom 3:29, 10:18.
8. Is 32:13.
9. Ps 19:10, 23:4, 137:1.
10. Penelope Lemov, "The Dilemma of Long-Term Care," *Governing*, June 1992, p.43-46.
11. Dianne Aprile, "Prozac," *Courier-Journal*, Feb. 18, 1990, p.1H.
12. Gen 19:3, 31:29, 42.
13. Ibid.

14. James E. Boothe, "America's Schools Confront Violence," *USA Today Magazine,* Jan. 1994, p.33-38.
15. Ezek 31:4.
16. NIV: Rom 16:21.
17. Ps 147:3.
18. Gen 22:5; Num 16:37, 23:15, 32:19; 2 Ki 4:25; Matt 17:20, 26:36.
19. NRSV, NIV: Gen 22:5; NRSV, NIV, NKJV: Num 23:15; Matt 26:36.
20. Num 32:19.
21. Matt 17:20.
22. NRSV: Num 16:37.
23. NIV: Num 16:37.
24. NRSV, NIV: 2 Ki 4:25.
25. Gen 22:5; Num 23:15; 2 Ki 4:25.
26. Num 16:37.
27. E.g., Gen 11:8; Ps 77:17; 1 Thes 1:8.
28. Ps 104:25.
29. Num 16:37, 23:15, 32:19; 2 Ki 4:25; Matt 17:20, 26:36.
30. 1 Sam 14:1.
31. Tracie Reddick, "Bravery Knows No Color," *Tampa Tribune,* sec. Baylife, p.1.
32. 2 Cor 1:12, 13:3; Eph 3:2.
33. Ps 40:5; Eph 1:19; 2 Pet 3:9.
34. Ex 18:19; 2 Cor 3:4; 1 Tim 1:8.
35. Ex 37:9.
36. 1 Sam 19:4.
37. Jud 18:15; Jer 50:5; Rom 15:24.
38. 1 Ki 7:8.
39. Pro 27:13.
40. Pro 15:24.
41. 2 Tim 3:5.
42. Phil 3:14.
43. Rev 8:13, 14:6, 19:17.
44. Bruce McCall, "An Impregnable—Yet Cozy—Casa Blanca," *Forbes FYI,* March 13, 1995, p.78.

Bibliography

Ayto, John. *Dictionary of Word Origins.* New York: Arcade Publishing, 1990.
The Barnhart Dictionary of Etymology, 1988 edition.
Bridges, Ronald F., and Weigle, Luther A. *The King James Bible Word Book.* Nashville: Thomas Nelson Publishers, 1994.
Carson, D.A. *The King James Version Debate.* Grand Rapids: Baker Book House, 1979.
Klein, Ernest. *A Comprehensive Etymological Dictionary of the English Language.* Amsterdam: Elsevier Publishing Co., 1966.
Lewis, Jack P. *The English Bible from KJV to NIV,* 2nd. ed. Grand Rapids: Baker Book House, 1991.
Opdycke, John P. *Harper's English Grammar,* rev. ed. New York: Harper & Row Publishers, 1965.
The Oxford English Dictionary, 1989 edition.
Partridge, Eric. *Origins: A Short Etymological Dictionary of Modern English.* New York: The Macmillan Co., 1966.
Pirkle, Estus W. *The 1611 King James Bible.* Southaven: The King's Press, 1994.
Random House Webster's College Dictionary, 1991 edition.
Skeat, Walter W., *An Etymological Dictionary of the English Language,* new and rev. ed. Oxford: Oxford University Press, 1909.
Skeat, Walter W., *The Concise Dictionary of English Etymology.* Hertfordshire: Wordsworth Editions, 1993.
Webster's Third New International Dictionary, 1986 edition.

Theological Works by Laurence M. Vance published by Vance Publications

The Other Side of Calvinism
475 pages   ISBN 0-9628898-0-6 $16.95

A definitive treatment of the subject, this book provides an intensive, detailed examination and analysis of the philosophical speculations and theological implications of Calvinism. Both an introductory and historical survey of Calvinism is furnished as well as a comprehensive doctrinal, theological, and exegetical investigation of the Five Points of Calvinism. The deductions and conclusions drawn are both interesting and informative, challenging and controversial. Extensively documented, this work includes upwards of 1700 quotations from over 250 Calvinistic authorities. This Bible-based critique also incorporates over 2000 Scripture citations. The book contains ten chapters, along with a preface, epilogue, three appendixes, and bibliography. It is further enhanced by subject, name, and Scripture indexes.

The Angel of the Lord
128 pages   ISBN 0-9628898-2-2 $5.95

An exhaustive analysis of the topic, this book explores the nature and identity of the angel of the Lord as well as his relationship to other angels and God himself. The authority for all assertions presented and conclusions drawn is the Holy Bible. Accordingly, the emphasis is on what the Bible veritably says. Although diverse sentiments are presented, the real concern is the exact, literal, precise, definite meaning of what the Bible specifically and unequivocally states. This entails both a meticulous and methodical approach to our understanding of the subject with the Bible forming an intrinsic part of the narrative. Considered theologically, this biblically-based examination of the angel of the Lord finds its background in Angelology and its fulfillment in Christology. From a practical standpoint, however, it seeks to assemble all the available biblical data concerning angels into one convenient source where the Bible is allowed to speak for itself and subsequently correct all errors, fallacies, and misconceptions of men. The book contains five chapters, along with a preface, footnotes, bibliography, and Scripture index.

Biblical Works by Laurence M. Vance published by Vance Publications

A Brief History of English Bible Translations
127 pages   ISBN 0-9628898-1-4 $5.95

A brief history that is as complete as it is concise, this book traces the origin and development of English Bible translations from before the invention of printing to the present day. A brief synopsis of all modern translations is provided as well as an extended treatment of all essential and significant versions found throughout history. An exhaustive appendix is included listing each translation by year and author. A survey of the formation and establishment of the printed editions of the Hebrew and Greek texts is also included since they are the primary foundation upon which all translations are based. The book contains five chapters, along with a preface, introduction, epilogue, appendix, and bibliography.

Archaic Words and the Authorized Version
589 pages   ISBN 0-9628898-4-9 $18.95

As suitable for reading as it is valuable for reference, this book provides an explicit and comprehensive examination of every word in the Authorized Version of the Bible that has been deemed archaic, obsolete, antiquated, or otherwise outmoded. The result is both a fascinating and encyclopedic study of words—their meaning, derivation, usage, and significance. The thesis of this seminal work is that the Authorized Version is no more archaic than daily newspapers, current magazines, and modern Bible versions. To further supplement the work and to substantiate the underlying thesis, reference is made not only to various newspapers and magazines, but to contemporary Bible versions like the New King James Version, the New International Version, the New American Standard Bible, and the New Revised Standard Version. This book is unique in that it seeks neither to criticize nor to correct the text of the Authorized Version. Extensively documented with over 5000 footnotes, the book contains twenty-four chapters and fourteen appendixes, with a preface, introduction, epilogue, and bibliography.